South African Family Practice Manual

SECOND EDITION

EDITORS

Bob Mash
Julia Blitz-Lindeque

Van Schaik
PUBLISHERS

Disclaimer

Although every effort has been made to ensure that the content of this publication is up to date and correct, the reader acknowledges and accepts that the publisher, editors and authors cannot verify all the details contained in this book. The reader therefore uses the recommendations, dosages, procedures, advice, facts, etc. herein at his or her own risk. The publisher, publisher's staff, editors and authors cannot be held responsible for any errors or omissions in the text, nor for any consequences (such as any loss, or direct, indirect, special, incidental, consequential or punitive damages) arising from such errors or omissions, or from using or applying the material in this book.

First edition 1995
Second edition 2006
Second impression 2007

ISBN 0 627 02615 X
13-digit ISBN 978 0 627 02615 7

Commissioning editor Rhodé Odendaal
Production coordinator Werner von Gruenewaldt
Editorial coordinator Daleen Venter
Copy editor Danya Ristić
Proofreader Wendy Priilaid
Illustrations by Marinda Pretorius
Cover design by Werner von Gruenewaldt
Cover photos courtesy of Merck Pharmaceuticals and Dr Saville Furman
Typeset in 9.5 on 11 pt Plantin by Pace-Setting & Graphics, Pretoria
Printed and bound by Paarl Print, Oosterland Street, Dal Josafat, Paarl, South Africa

Every effort has been made to obtain copyright permission for material used in this book. Please contact the publisher with any queries in this regard.

All references to the male gender are intended to denote the female gender as well.

PREFACE

This text is the long-awaited second edition of the *South African Family Practice Manual*. In many ways it is a new book and, as you will see from the list of authors, it constitutes a collaborative project involving people from various departments of Family Medicine in South Africa, and it represents a distillation of the practical experience of a wide spectrum of family physicians. The development of the *Manual* is a joint project of the South African Academy of Family Practice and Primary Care and the Family Medicine Education Consortium (FaMEC).

The *Manual* is a practical text that focuses on "How to do ..." that which is relevant to South African district health care. As such, some of the skills are appropriate only for rural or district hospitals while others are of more general applicability to primary care and general practice. The family physician in our context must be trained to function in *both* of these settings and our intention is to be inclusive of all possible tasks expected of him within the District Health System. In addition to practical clinical skills, the text includes a number of teaching, research and management skills. Note, however, that we have avoided providing clinical management guidelines – not only are there a number of initiatives in this area, but the constantly evolving evidence base and changing recommendations are also better suited to a more responsive electronic format such as a CD-ROM or the Internet.

This text should be invaluable to those of you specialising in Family Medicine via MMed or other training programmes, as it will guide and support your learning of the practical skills required to complete your programme. In particular, as South Africa moves towards more formal registrar posts as part of the HPCSA's training requirements, this *Manual* can be a cornerstone of the practical training component of their registrar programme. It will also be of great benefit as a reference book for interns, community service medical officers and practising family physicians, both within and outside South Africa. Furthermore, the *Manual* complements the *Handbook of Family Medicine* (Mash B. Handbook of family medicine. Cape Town: Oxford University Press; 2000), which outlines the theoretical principles and practice of Family Medicine in South Africa. In future the *Manual* may also be a valuable resource for the training of clinical associates within the district hospital.

We have taken great care to include the appropriate topics in the *Manual* and ensure that the information is not only up to date but also relevant to your context. However, you may wish that we had included other, or more, information. As this text is for you, we hope that you will feel free to contact us and give us your feedback.

Bob Mash rm@sun.ac.za
Julia Blitz-Lindeque julia.blitz-lindeque@up.ac.za

July 2006

FOREWORD

The knowledge which a man can use is the only real knowledge, the only knowledge which has life and growth in it and converts itself into practical power. The rest hangs like dust around the brain or dries like raindrops off stones.

Sir William Osler (1849–1919)

There are many excellent publications in the domain of family medicine filled with the theoretical and practical aspects of the discipline. However, the *South African Family Practice Manual*, with practical 'how to' texts, fills a unique and essential position in the family practice library. While the chapters are based on the best available evidence interpreted and tempered by experts of international standing, they are distinctively flavoured for practitioners in the developing world, especially for the family doctor working in community settings. These practitioners, faced with limited resources, must be competent to practise a wide variety of procedures, often performed only by specialists in the developed world, whilst also being adept at management, teaching, research and health service development. This *Manual* is a compendium of essential tools to achieve these tasks.

Patient safety is receiving increasing international attention. It is estimated that globally over ten per cent of those receiving health care have had their health affected by medical errors. The number of 'near misses' is even greater. A 1999 report revealed that one million people in the United States suffered from preventable medical injuries and 100 000 die from them every year. An unfortunate response of the profession is often 'defensive medical practice'. A positive aspect of defensive medicine could be closer adherence to guidelines and screening protocols, improved record keeping, and also more frequent consideration of patient consent. However, many practitioners prefer to avoid the responsibility of procedures and therapies, even if required and essential for their patients' health. Equally problematic are the calls for voluntary reporting by practitioners of mistakes and 'misses'. Surely the ideal response should be to increase the skills and competency levels of practitioners. Such elevated expertise could also possibly negate some of the adverse consequences of the drastically diminishing human health resources globally. This *Manual* will hopefully assist in raising the standard of safe health care for our communities.

I believe that Sir William Osler would have willingly endorsed the approach used in this *Manual*. The practical knowledge and expertise attained through utilisation of the guides in this publication could truly be *converted into practical power*.

Bruce LW Sparks
K.StJ. MBBCh (Witwatersrand), MFGP (SA), MRCGP, FCFP (SA), FRCGP, FRACGP
World President, WONCA (World Organisation of Family Doctors)
Professor and Head, Department of Family Medicine, University of the Witwatersrand, Johannesburg

The publication of this the second edition of the *South African Family Practice Manual* symbolises the seamless working relationship of the South African Academy of Family Practice/Primary Care and the Family Medicine Education Consortium (FaMEC). It is a partnership whose common vision is the development of the discipline of Family Medicine and it is in pursuit of this vision that we have developed a registrar training programme for future training of family physicians. Together we are embarking on developing a similar training programme for East Africa.

The publication of this *Manual* at this critical stage in our journey of development of the discipline of Family Medicine is very timely. We have here a practical tool that should form a companion for family physicians and primary care teams, not only in South Africa but also in the rest of our continent. As we roll out our unique brand of family physicians for the continent, we have a unique, practical textbook to assist them on their journey.

Shadrick Mazaza
National Chairman:
The SA Academy of
Family Practice/
Primary Care

SOUTH AFRICAN ACADEMY OF
FAMILY PRACTICE / PRIMARY CARE

The Family Medicine Education Consortium (FaMEC), as a network of the eight Family Medicine Departments and three Rural Health Units of South African Medical Schools, is committed to appropriate undergraduate and postgraduate education in Family Medicine and Primary Health Care in general. This commitment has led FaMEC to contribute as much as possible to the production of this second edition of the *South African Family Practice Manual*. The *Manual* is therefore aimed at providing undergraduate medical students, clinical associates, family medicine registrars, medical officers, and private and public family physicians with appropriate procedural skills that are needed at all primary health care settings including community level clinics, community health centres, non-governmental primary health care facilities, private practices and district hospitals. The *Manual* will also be useful beyond the borders of South Africa in the rest of Africa, especially now that FaMEC has a funded project in conjunction with East Africa for the development of Family Medicine. This textbook will indeed provide health care providers with ammunition to render quality health care with confidence at district level, and thus improve the quality of life of the majority of the people on the African continent.

The close working relationship and common vision between FaMEC and the South African Academy of Family Practice/Primary Care have made it possible for this *Manual* to be produced.

Khaya Mfenyana
Chairperson: Family
Medicine Education
Consortium

FaMEC

Family
Medicine
Education
Consortium

AUTHORS

Dr Shahieda Adams
Occupational and Environmental Health Research Unit
School of Public Health and Family Medicine
University of Cape Town

Prof. Julia Blitz-Lindeque
Department of Family Medicine
University of Pretoria

Prof. David Buso
Head, Department of Community Medicine
Walter Sisulu University

Dr Neil Cameron
Department of Community Health
Stellenbosch University

Prof. Ian Couper
Professor of Rural Health
University of the Witwatersrand

Prof. Marietjie de Villiers
Vice-dean (Education), Faculty of Health Sciences
Stellenbosch University

Dr Julie Dieterich
Department of Family Medicine
University of Pretoria

Dr Chris Ellis
Family Physician
KwaZulu-Natal

Dr Dries Engelbrecht
Department of Family Medicine
University of Pretoria

Dr Claudine Firmin
Department of Family Medicine
University of Pretoria

Dr Saville Furman
Family Physician, and part-time Lecturer in the Division of Family Medicine
University of Cape Town

Prof. Roland Peter Gräbe
Department of Orthopaedics
University of Pretoria

Prof. Derek Hellenberg
Division of Family Medicine
School of Public Health and Primary Health Care
University of Cape Town

Dr Paul Hill
Department of Family Medicine and Primary Care
Stellenbosch University

Dr Anriëtte Hoffeldt
Department of Family Medicine
University of Pretoria

Prof. Mohamed Jeebhay
Occupational and Environmental Health Research Unit, School of Public Health and Family Medicine
University of Cape Town

Dr Patrick Kenny
Department of Family Medicine
University of Pretoria

Prof. Bryan Kies
Department of Neurology
University of Cape Town

Dr Patrick Maduna
Department of Family Medicine and Primary Care
Medunsa Campus
University of Limpopo

Prof. Bob Mash
Department of Family Medicine and Primary Care
Stellenbosch University

Dr Sophie Mathijs
Department of Family Medicine
University of Pretoria

Prof. Keymanthri Moodley
Head, Bioethics Unit
Tygerberg Division
Stellenbosch University

Dr Silas Motsitsi
Department of Orthopaedics
University of Pretoria

Dr Menzeleleli Msauli
Department of Family Medicine
Walter Sisulu University

Dr Kat Mynhardt
Department of Family Medicine
University of Pretoria

Prof. Cyril Naidoo
Department of Family Medicine
Nelson R Mandela School of Medicine
University of KwaZulu-Natal

Dr Mosedi Namane
Division of Family Medicine
School of Public Health and Primary Health Care
University of Cape Town

Prof. Gboyega Ogunbanjo
Department of Family Medicine and Primary Care
Medunsa Campus
University of Limpopo

Dr Sarie Oosthuizen
Department of Family Medicine
University of Pretoria

Dr Richard Osinjolu
Department of Family Medicine
Walter Sisulu University

Dr Michael Pather
Department of Family Medicine and Primary Care
Stellenbosch University

Dr Isabel Pienaar
Department of Family Medicine
University of Pretoria

Dr Jonathan Pons
Family Physician
Swaziland

Prof. Steve Reid
Associate Professor of Rural Health and
Community-based Education
Nelson R Mandela School of Medicine
University of KwaZulu-Natal

Dr Andrew Ross
Department of Family Medicine
Nelson R Mandela School of Medicine
University of KwaZulu-Natal

Prof. Haroon Saloojee
Division of Community Paediatrics
Department of Paediatrics and Child Health
University of the Witwatersrand

Dr Helen Sammons
Centre for Rehabilitation Studies
Stellenbosch University

Prof. Bruce LW Sparks
Head, Department of Family Medicine
University of the Witwatersrand

Dr Hannes Steinberg
Department of Family Medicine
University of the Free State

Dr Annamarie Steyn
Department of Family Medicine
University of Pretoria

Dr Claire van Deventer
Department of Family Medicine
University of the Witwatersrand

Dr Dawie van Velden
Department of Family Medicine and Primary Care
Stellenbosch University

Dr Slade Vermaak
Department of Family Medicine
University of Pretoria

Dr Andries Visser
Department of Family Medicine
University of Pretoria

Dr Edwin Warambwa
Department of Family Medicine
University of Pretoria

Dr Jacobus Wessels
Department of Orthopaedics
University of Pretoria

Prof. Tuviah Zabow
Department of Psychiatry and Mental Health
University of Cape Town

Reviewers

In addition to the authors, the following people also acted as peer reviewers:

Prof. Pierre de Villiers
Head, Department of Family Medicine and Primary Care
Stellenbosch University

Prof. BG Lindeque
Department of Obstetrics and Gynaecology
University of Pretoria

Prof. James Loock
Department of Ear, Nose and Throat
Stellenbosch University

Prof. Campbell MacFarlane
Netcare Foundation Chair of Emergency Medicine
Department of Family Medicine
University of the Witwatersrand

Dr Shadrick Mazaza
Family Physician
Chairperson, South African Academy of Family Practice and Primary Care

Dr Zandy Rosochaki
Department of Family Medicine and Primary Care
Stellenbosch University

Dr Marietjie van Rooyen
Department of Family Medicine
University of Pretoria

Dr Dave Whitelaw
Department of Rheumatology
Stellenbosch University

Dr Malcolm Wright
General Practitioner
Organiser, Vocational Training Scheme Course
Hinchingbrooke Hospital
Huntingdon, United Kingdom

CONTENTS

Child health

1 How to do a developmental assessment

JACQUI COUPER, LORNA JACKLIN, IAN COUPER

Some principles

A mother's feelings are important. If the mother feels that there is a problem with her baby you should take her concern seriously and carry out a careful examination of the baby.

Milestones are useful guidelines for assessing developmental delay. A baby needs investigation if

- at 9 months he is not sitting, turning to sounds or making a variety of sounds
- at 12 months he is not crawling
- at 16 months he is not walking or saying a number of single words.

The quality of a baby's movement is also critical. He must have a variety of movements in limbs, hands and feet. Fisting of the hands or 'stereotype movements', for example both legs moving in exactly the same way, could indicate a problem.

What is a developmental assessment?

A developmental assessment is a systematic way of observing babies and children. You need to take all aspects of their growth and physical state into consideration. In the physical examination you should include the growth pattern, body proportions, physical features, general state of health and behaviour of the baby or child.

All practitioners dealing with babies and children should have a sound knowledge of developmental issues. Your early detection of a delay could lead to the diagnosis of underlying problems which, with intervention, would make a profound difference to the baby's or child's future.

Child developmental skills can be divided into six areas:

1. Gross motor
2. Fine motor
3. Visual perception
4. Language (speech and hearing)
5. Social
6. Other cognitive skills

There is interaction between all the areas of development. For example, a child who is clumsy could present as being socially delayed because he is unable to dress himself or use eating utensils. The critical task is for you to recognise that there is a problem, which you can then investigate further.

It is essential that you assess vision and hearing as part of the developmental screening – difficulties in these areas could cause delays whereas detection can lead to immediate intervention. You can do this through observation and by questioning of the caregiver. Ask them, for example: Does the child respond to sounds, such as a passing car or plane? Does he follow people around a room with his eyes?

Indications of a developmental problem

Note that early indications of a developmental problem in a baby are as follows:

- Sucking problems
- Excessive drooling
- Extremely floppy head
- Poor quality of movement, such as fisted hands, stereotype movements
- Poor eye contact and lack of focus on objects
- No response to sounds
- Poor interaction with people, such as not responding to family or strangers
- Excessive crying
- Sensory defensiveness, such as sensitivity to noise, a dislike of being handled by others, fear of movement, and a dislike of textured food

It is difficult to make a definitive diagnosis in children under two years. However, children should be able to do the following and, if not, this may be an indication of a developmental problem:

- Gross motor – runs (two years), balances on one leg (three years), hops on each leg (five years)
- Fine motor – holds a pencil in fist (two years), between finger and thumb (three years) and can control it (five years)

- Visual perception – makes towers (six blocks at two years) or builds puzzles (two pieces from three years)
- Language – follows two-step commands (two years), gives name and age (four years)
- Social – takes off clothes (two years), does buttons (four years), dresses alone (five years)
- Other cognitive – points to four body parts (two years), identifies body parts (four years)

For a full assessment, you should consult the standard developmental charts that are provided in most paediatric and child health textbooks. Take note of tone (posture, sitting position) and coordination (running, hopping), which are often subtle pointers to a problem.

Pitfalls

Try to avoid the following pitfalls of developmental assessments:

- Giving the child a label, for example "slow", "floppy", "ADD"
- Making conclusions about a child based only on developmental milestones
- Failing to take context and cultural issues into account

If you are in doubt, refer the child to a developmental paediatrician or occupational therapist for further assessment. Describe your findings in terms of all aspects of the child's development.

Table 1.1 Developmental milestones

Milestones – The first year			
Age	**Average milestones**	**He might be able to**	**He should be able to**
6 weeks	• Holds head up briefly • Turns briefly to sources of light or sound • Communicates by crying	• Follow objects with his eyes • Smile voluntarily • Lift and turn his head when lying on his back	• React to sudden movement or loud sound • Suck strongly
6 months	• Reaches out and grasps objects • Puts objects into his mouth • Bounces when held in a standing position	• Sit unaided • Imitate the sound of other voices • Make double-syllable sounds like "goo-goo" • Look for dropped toys	• Roll over and back again • Use both hands • Have control over limb and hand movement • Babble and coo
12 months	• Walks while his hands are held • Walks while holding on to furniture • Stands unsupported for a few seconds • Says at least five words • Understands simple instructions • Responds to own name • Points to objects	• Take a few steps unaided • Roll and catch a large ball	• Say "mama" or "dada" • Crawl or creep with legs extended • Put food in his mouth
Milestones – The second year			
This year sees extensive muscle and nerve development, which allows the child to become more mobile, as well as enabling the development of language, fine muscular coordination and improved social skills			
Age	**Average milestones**	**He might be able to**	**He should be able to**
18 months	• Walks unaided • Can walk backwards • Throws a ball without falling • Makes two-word sentences • Understands most instructions • Can point to body parts • Can scribble using a crayon	• Successfully feed himself with a spoon • Turn the pages of a book • Identify pictures in a book	• Make an effort to walk
24 months	• Runs • Kicks a ball • Climbs up and down stairs • Builds a tower of six blocks • Can draw horizontal and vertical lines • Says short phrases • Refers to himself by name	• Undress himself • Walk on tiptoe • Repeat nursery rhymes and songs • Jump on both feet	• Walk unaided • Use at least two-word sentences • Understand simple commands

Source: http://www.bodyandmind.co.za

2 How to assess growth and classify malnutrition in children

HAROON SALOOJEE AND IAN COUPER

Measurements

The most common physical measurements for evaluating growth are weight, recumbent length (birth to two years) or standing height (children older than two years who are able to stand straight), and head circumference (until two years).

Assessment of weight alone (that is weight-for-age) is not useful because it cannot distinguish a tall, thin child from one who is short but well proportioned. However, it is used in the Road to Health (RTH) card and is therefore the most frequently available measure of growth in South African children (see Figure 2.1). Its usefulness lies in comparison with previous measurements (that is of the child at a younger age) and observing trends over time rather than absolute values. Weight-for-length, or -height, is the preferred measurement as it is better associated with body composition and nutritional status than weight alone.

You need to make serial measurements of weight, recumbent length and head circumference part of scheduled well-baby health visits. Current recommendations are that the visits follow the immunisation schedule (that is at six, ten and fourteen weeks after birth, at nine and eighteen months and at five years). More frequent monthly monitoring is indicated when there is concern, or any risk factors are present, or you are monitoring the child's response to nutritional therapy. Also perform the measurements at the time of illness visits.

To yield accurate measurements, you should obtain weights and measures using calibrated, well-maintained equipment and standardised measurement techniques.

Growth charts

It is recommended that the new WHO (World Health Organization) Child Growth Standards be used for assessing and monitoring the growth of South African infants and children (Figures 2.2 to 2.11). These standards are based on healthy children living under conditions favouring achievement of their full genetic growth potential in a diverse set of countries, namely Brazil, Ghana, India, Norway, Oman and the United States. Further, the mothers of these children engaged in fundamental health-promoting practices, namely breastfeeding and not smoking. For the sake of completeness, the WHO's international norms for achievement of motor milestones in children are also included. (See Figure 2.12 and Chapter 1 in this regard.)

The following are important points for you to consider when interpreting patterns of growth on a growth chart:

- The centile positions of weight, length/height and head circumference should be similar to each other in a normal child. A gross deviation in one indicates a potential problem.

- The 50th centile is not the ideal for each child.

- Children above the 50th centile are not necessarily overweight.

- Children plotted below the 3rd or above the 97th centile may still be normal.

- The growth curve obtained from serial measurements is more important than the current actual centile.

- In most children, height and weight measurements consistently follow along a "channel" (that is on or between the same centile/s). However, normal children may shift centiles for both length and weight in the first two to three years of life and during puberty.

- Crossing of two or more centiles downwards from a previously established growth curve reflects growth failure or failure-to-thrive.

- Breastfed infants grow differently from formula-fed infants during the first year of life; they tend to become leaner after 3–4 months of life.

- Preterm infants may take 24–36 months to catch up to their genetic potential.

Malnutrition

The WHO and the National Center for Health Statistics (NCHS) use a cut-off point of below two negative standard deviations (SDs) to classify low weight-for-age (underweight), low height-for-age or stature-for-age (stunting) and low weight-for-height (wasting) as moderate undernutrition; and below three negative SDs to define severe undernutrition. Table 2.1 illustrates this system of measurement.

Table 2.1 Definitions of commonly used anthropological measurements

Term	Description
Underweight	Weight-for-age < −2 SDs of NCHS/WHO reference values, or < 80% of median weight-for-age
Stunting	Height-for-age < −2 SDs of NCHS/WHO reference values, or < 90% of median height-for-age
Wasting	Weight-for-height < −2 SDs of NCHS/WHO reference values, or < 80% of median weight-for-height
Severe undernutrition	Severe wasting < −3 SDs of reference (< 70% weight-for-height), or severe stunting < −3 SDs of reference (< 85% height-for-age), or the presence of oedema of both feet, or clinically visible severe wasting

Note: These definitions should be interpreted in conjunction with the WHO Child Growth Standards (see Figures 2.2 to 2.11). Two standard deviations above and below the mean is the area between the 3rd and 97th centiles. In each case < −2 SDs means less than the 3rd centile on the respective chart.

The cut-off points for different malnutrition classification systems are listed in Table 2.2. The classifications of "mild", "moderate" and "severe" differ in each of the classification systems. The South African RTH system uses weight-for-age (see Figure 2.1).

The most widely used system is the WHO classification in which Z-scores can be equated with standard deviations. It is recommended that you use this method for analysis and presentation of data. The RTH system is typically seen in clinic-based growth monitoring systems.

The Wellcome classification is also commonly used. It is based on weight-for-age, as is illustrated in Table 2.3. While it differentiates the clinical forms

Table 2.2 Cut-offs used in two malnutrition classification systems

System	Cut-off	Malnutrition classification
WHO	< −1 to > −2 Z-score	Mild
	< −2 Z-score to > −3 Z-score	Moderate
	< −3 Z-score	Severe
RTH	> 80% of median	Normal
	60% − < 80% of median	Mild-to-moderate
	< 60% of median	Severe

Table 2.3 Wellcome classification of infantile nutrition

Condition	60–80% of standard* weight	Less than 60% of standard* weight
No oedema	Underweight	Marasmus
Oedema	Kwashiorkor	Marasmic kwashiorkor

* "Standard" refers to the 50th percentile (median); the term is used in preference to "expected" weight.

of severe malnutrition, it fails to differentiate the underweight category.

Obesity

Globally, obesity has replaced undernutrition as the biggest public health concern in children. It is most useful for you to use body mass index (BMI)-for-age to screen children from two years onwards so that you can identify those who may be at risk for conditions and illnesses related to excess body fat.

The BMI is an anthropometric index of weight and height, defined as body weight in kilograms divided by height in metres squared, that is:

$$BMI = \frac{weight\ (kg)}{height\ (m^2)}$$

Because adiposity varies with age and gender during childhood and adolescence, BMI is age- and gender-specific. Consequently, BMI is plotted according to age, using gender-specific charts.

New BMI cut-off points for paediatric overweight and obesity are now linked to the widely accepted adult obesity cut-off points: BMI > 25 kg/m^2 for overweight and > 30 kg/m^2 for obesity.

BMI normally rises steeply in infancy, falls during the preschool years to a minimum around 4–6 years, and rises again in adolescence.

IMMUNISATIONS

Vaccine	Site	Date given day / month / year	Signature
BCG	Right arm	/ /	
Polio 0	Oral	/ /	
Polio 1	Oral	/ /	
DTP 1	Left thigh	/ /	
Hib 1	Left thigh	/ /	
Hep B 1	Right thigh	/ /	
Polio 2	Oral	/ /	
DTP 2	Left thigh	/ /	
Hib 2	Left thigh	/ /	
Hep B 2	Right thigh	/ /	
Polio 3	Oral	/ /	
DTP 3	Left thigh	/ /	
Hib 3	Left thigh	/ /	
Measles 1	Right thigh	/ /	
Polio 4	Oral	/ /	
DTP 4	Left arm	/ /	
Measles 2	Right arm	/ /	
Polio 5	Oral	/ /	
DT 1	Left arm	/ /	
BCG Repeat	Right arm	/ /	
Other ( )		/ /	
Other ( )		/ /	

PRIMARY SCHEDULE / BOOSTERS

Vitamin A

Date given	Signature	Date given	Signature
/ /		/ /	

In need of special care (mark with X)

Was the baby less than 2,5kg at birth — yes / no
Are any brothers or sisters **underweight**? — yes / no
Is the baby a twin? — yes / no
Is the baby **bottle fed**? — yes / no
TB contact? — yes / no
Does the mother need more **family support**? — yes / no
Are there any reasons for **taking extra care**? — yes / no
(for example: single parent etc.)

Road to Health Chart

Department of Health

GW 8/123

IMPORTANT: always bring this card when you visit any health clinic, doctor or hospital and present the card on school entry

boy / girl

Child's name

Child's ID number

Date of birth — day / month / year

Place of birth

Birth weight

Birth length

Birth head circumference

Problems during pregnancy / birth / neonatally

APGAR 1 min. / 10 min.

Gestational age (wks)

Mother's Serology

Antenatal:
Delivery:

Mother's file numbers -

Card given and mother taught by:

Mother's name:

Father's name:

Who does the child live with?

How many children has the mother had?

Number born

Number alive now

Date information given: day / month / year

Vision screening (3-5 years)

Date: day / month / year

Result: L: R:

Hearing screening (7-9 months)

Manchester Rattle used? yes / no

Date: day / month / year

Result: L: R:

Address of Clinic 1 visited:

Address of Clinic 2 visited:

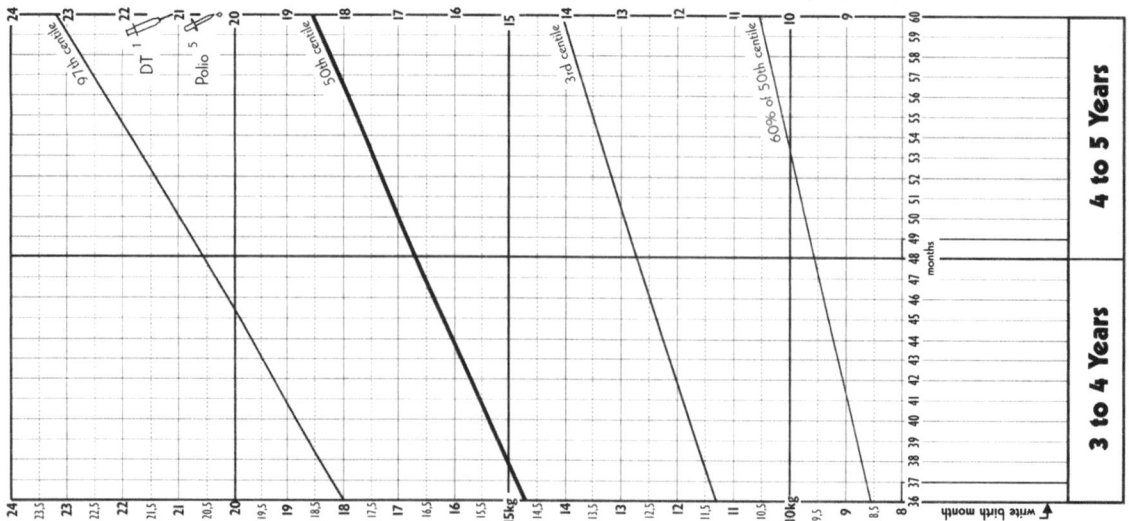

Figure 2.1 Road to Health card

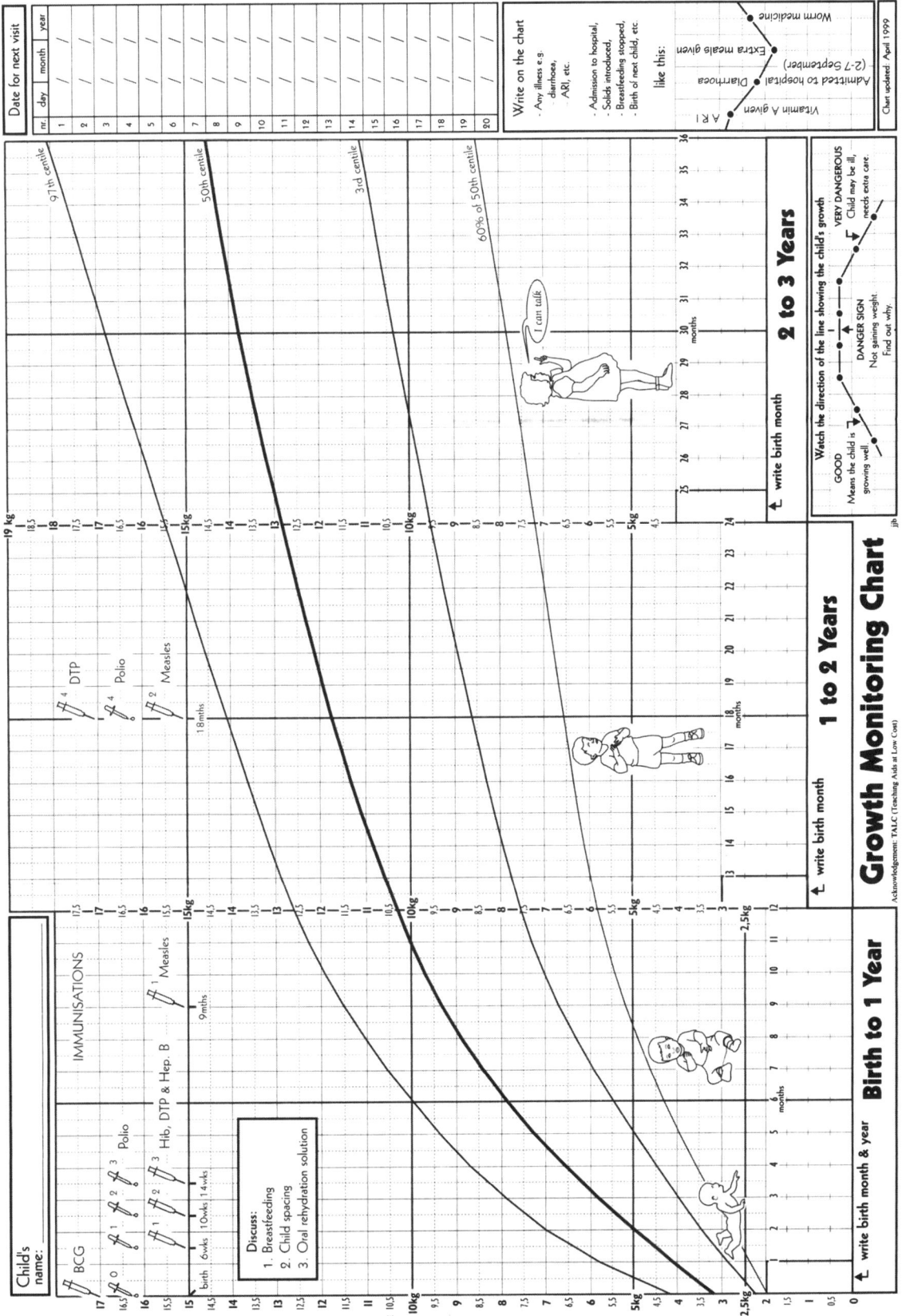

Figure 2.1 Road to Health card (continued)

Weight-for-length BOYS

Birth to 2 years (percentiles)

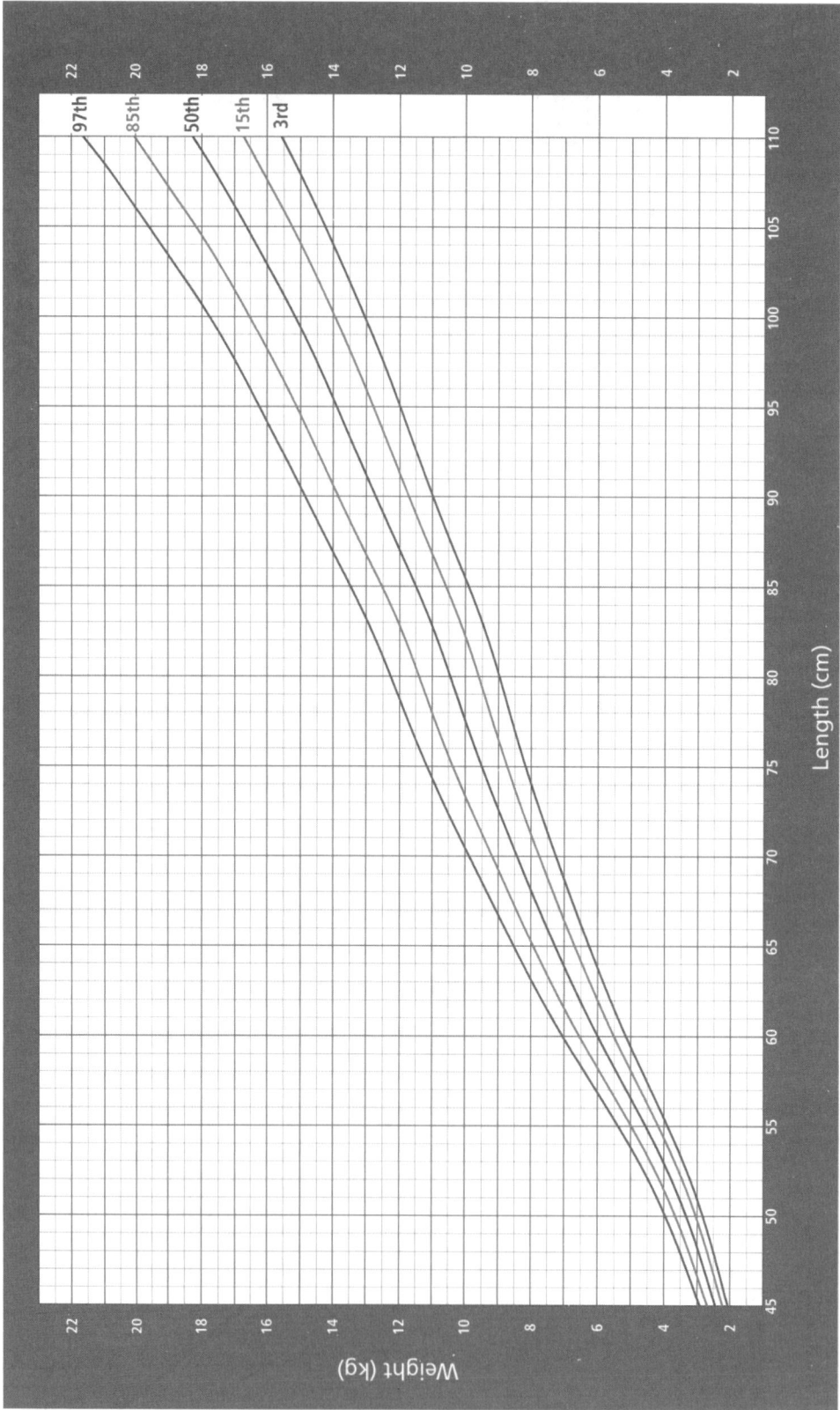

World Health Organization

WHO Child Growth Standards

Figure 2.2 Weight-for-length percentiles: Boys, birth to 2 years

Weight-for-length GIRLS

Birth to 2 years (percentiles)

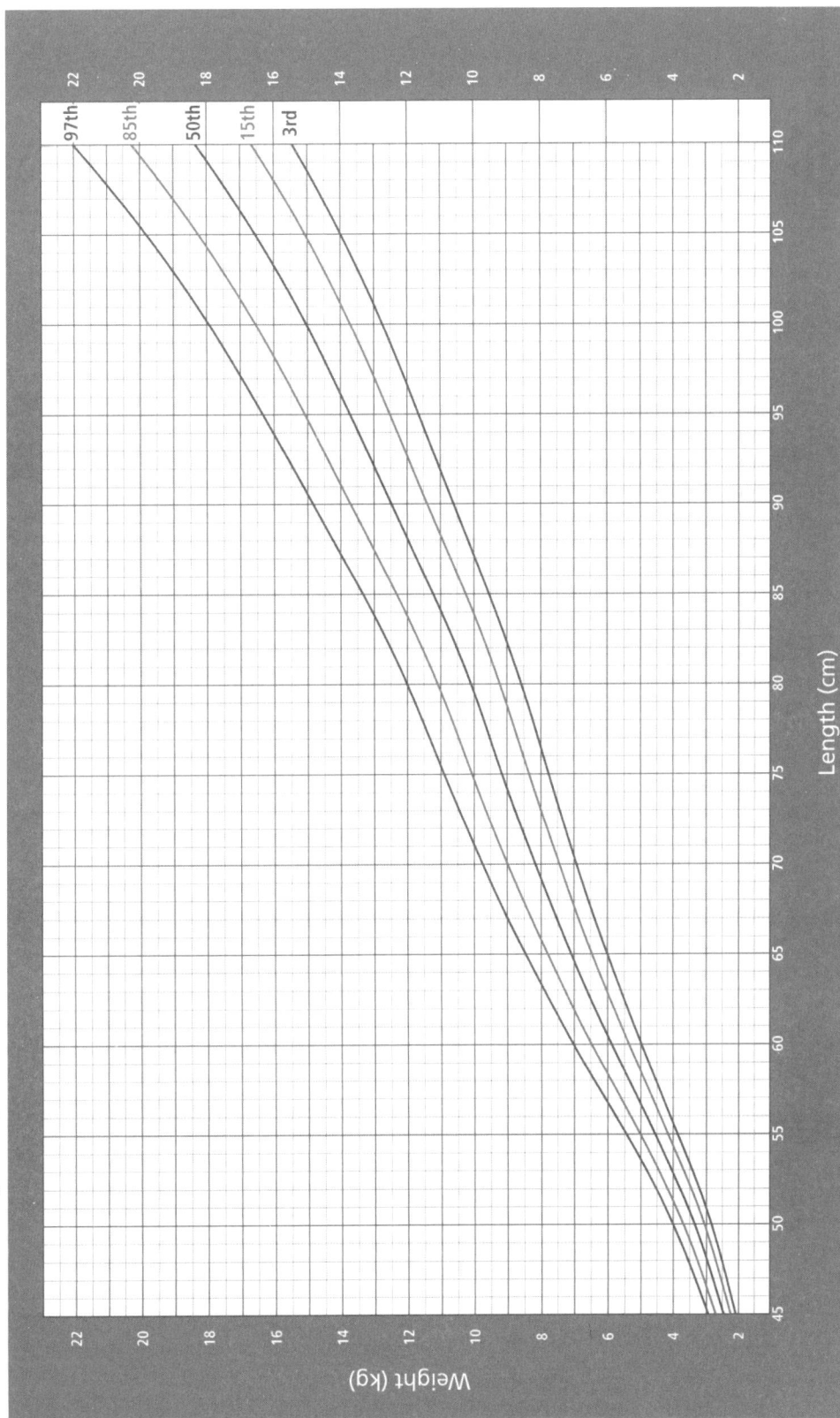

World Health Organization

WHO Child Growth Standards

97th
85th
50th
15th
3rd

Weight (kg)

Length (cm)

Figure 2.3 Weight-for-length percentiles: Girls, birth to 2 years

Weight-for-height BOYS

2 to 5 years (percentiles)

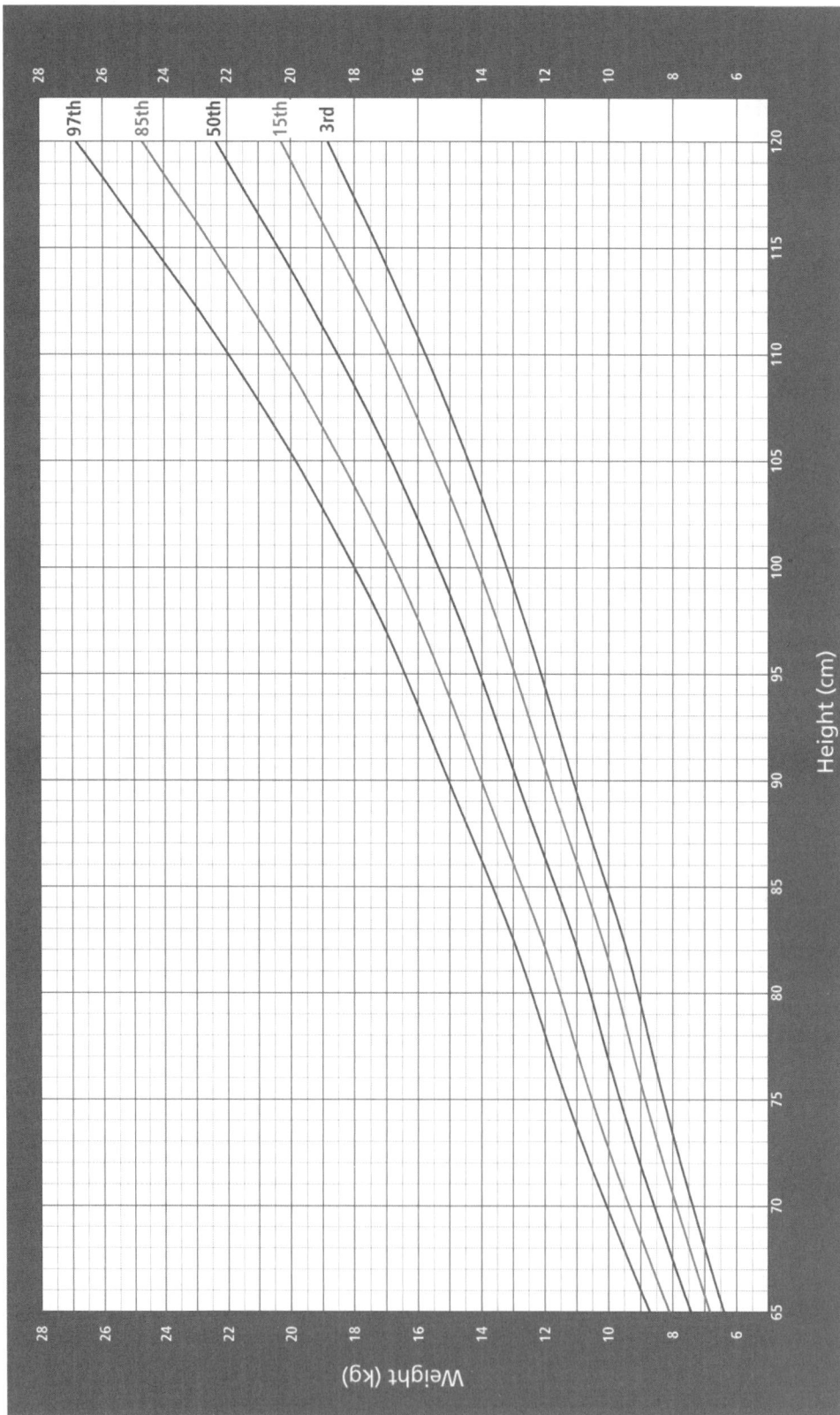

WHO Child Growth Standards

Figure 2.4 Weight-for-height percentiles: Boys, 2–5 years

Weight-for-height GIRLS

2 to 5 years (percentiles)

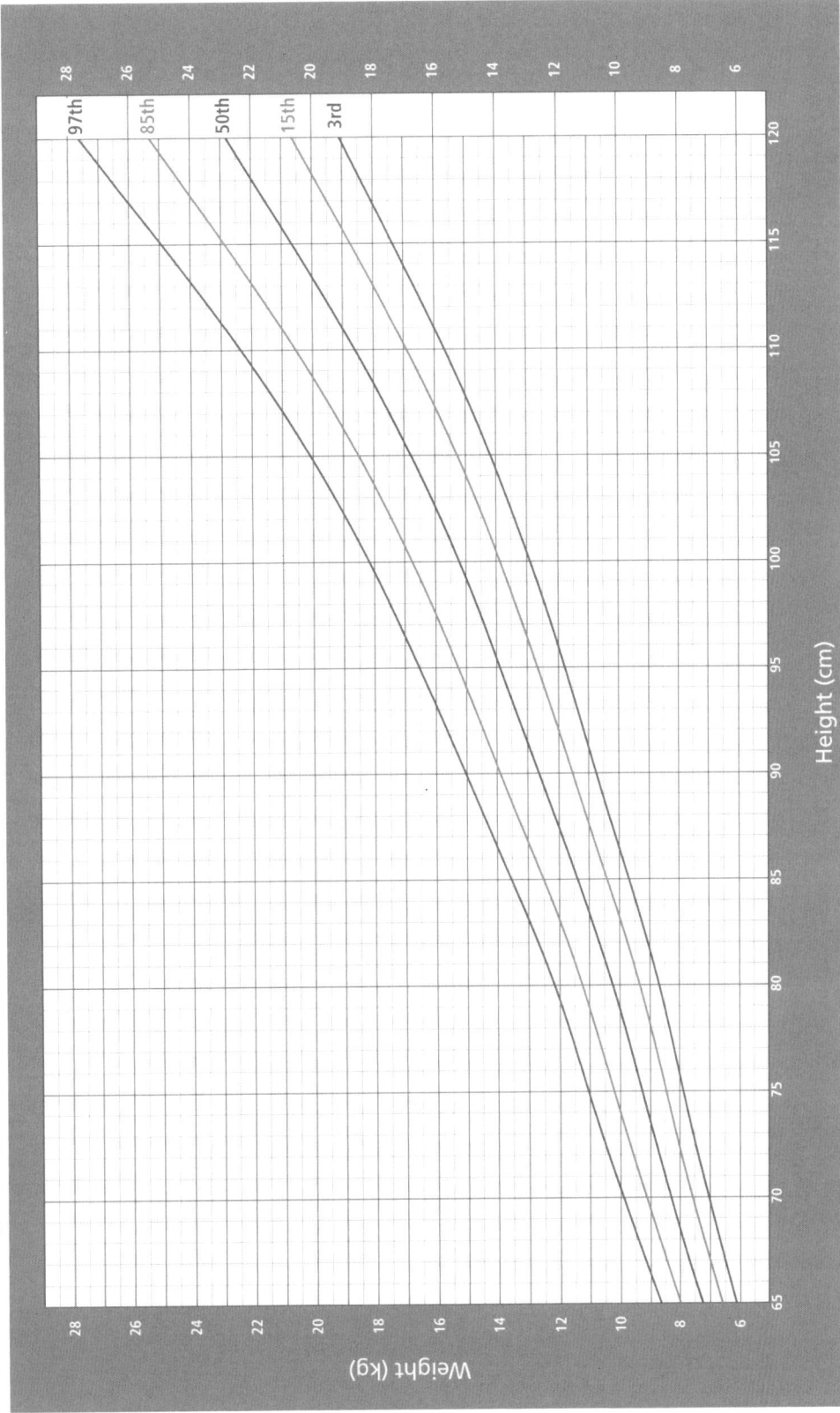

Figure 2.5 Weight-for-height percentiles: Girls, 2–5 years

WHO Child Growth Standards

Weight-for-age BOYS

Birth to 5 years (percentiles)

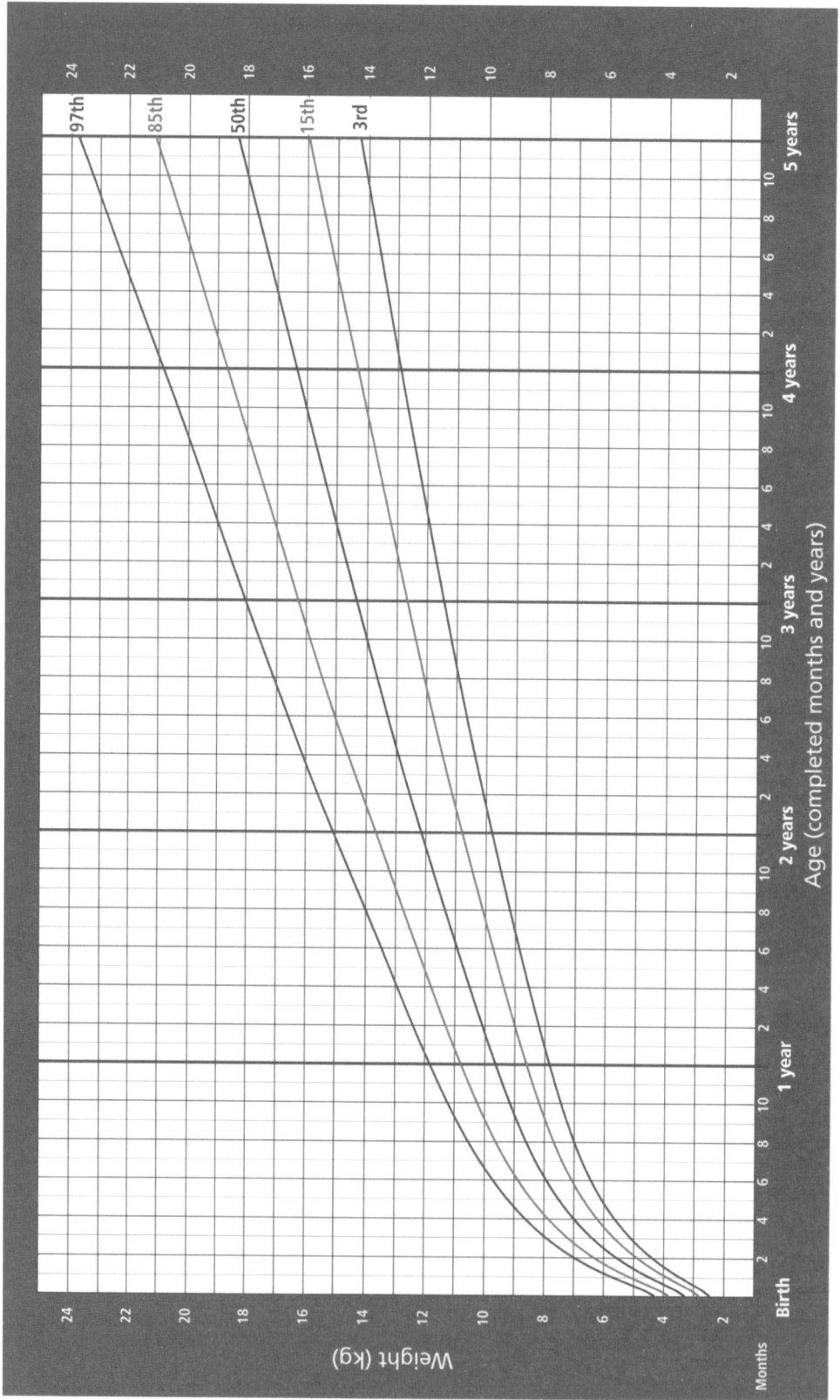

World Health Organization

Figure 2.6 Weight-for-age percentiles: Boys, birth to 5 years

WHO Child Growth Standards

Weight-for-age GIRLS
Birth to 5 years (percentiles)

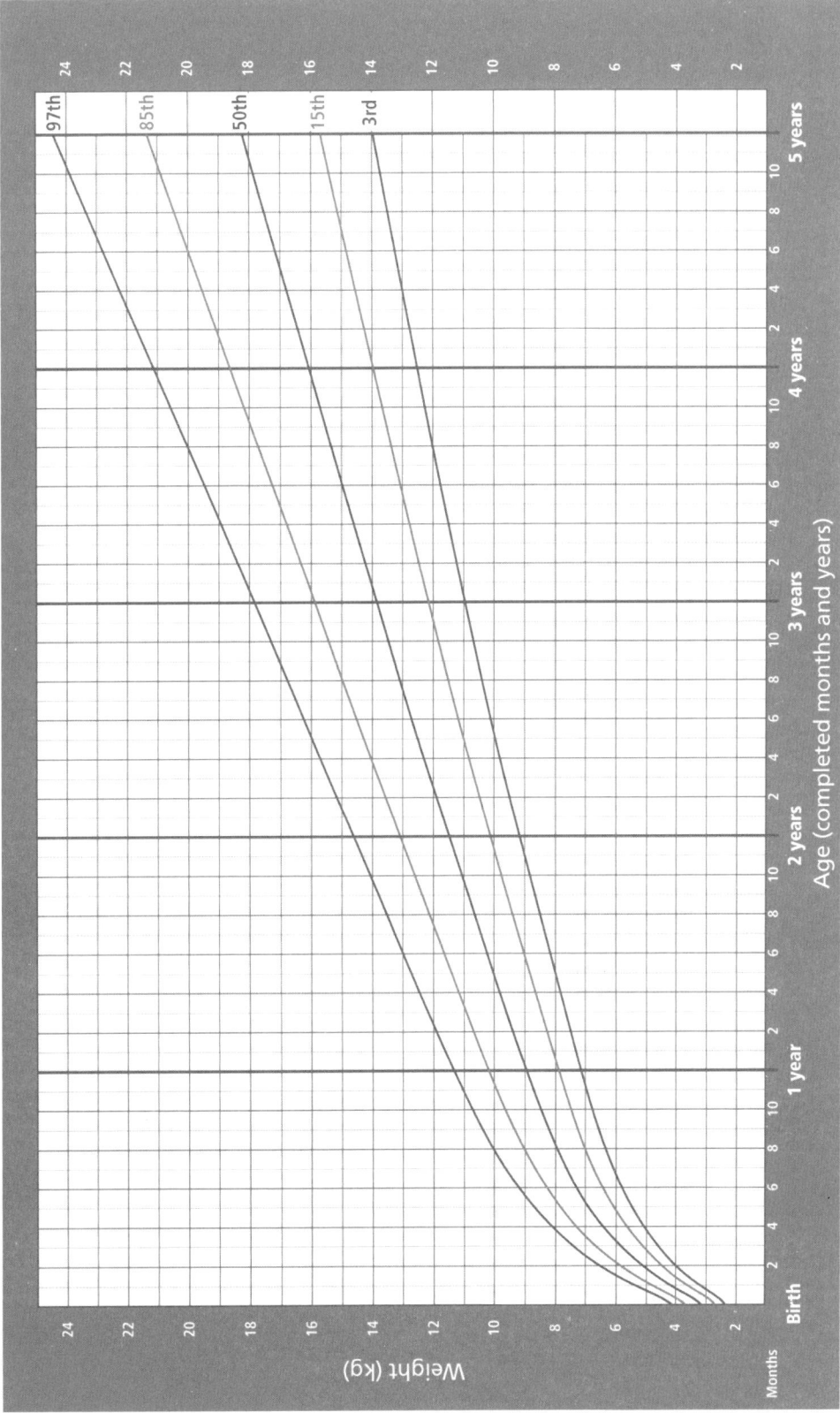

World Health Organization

WHO Child Growth Standards

Figure 2.7 Weight-for-age percentiles: Girls, birth to 5 years

Length/height-for-age BOYS

Birth to 5 years (percentiles)

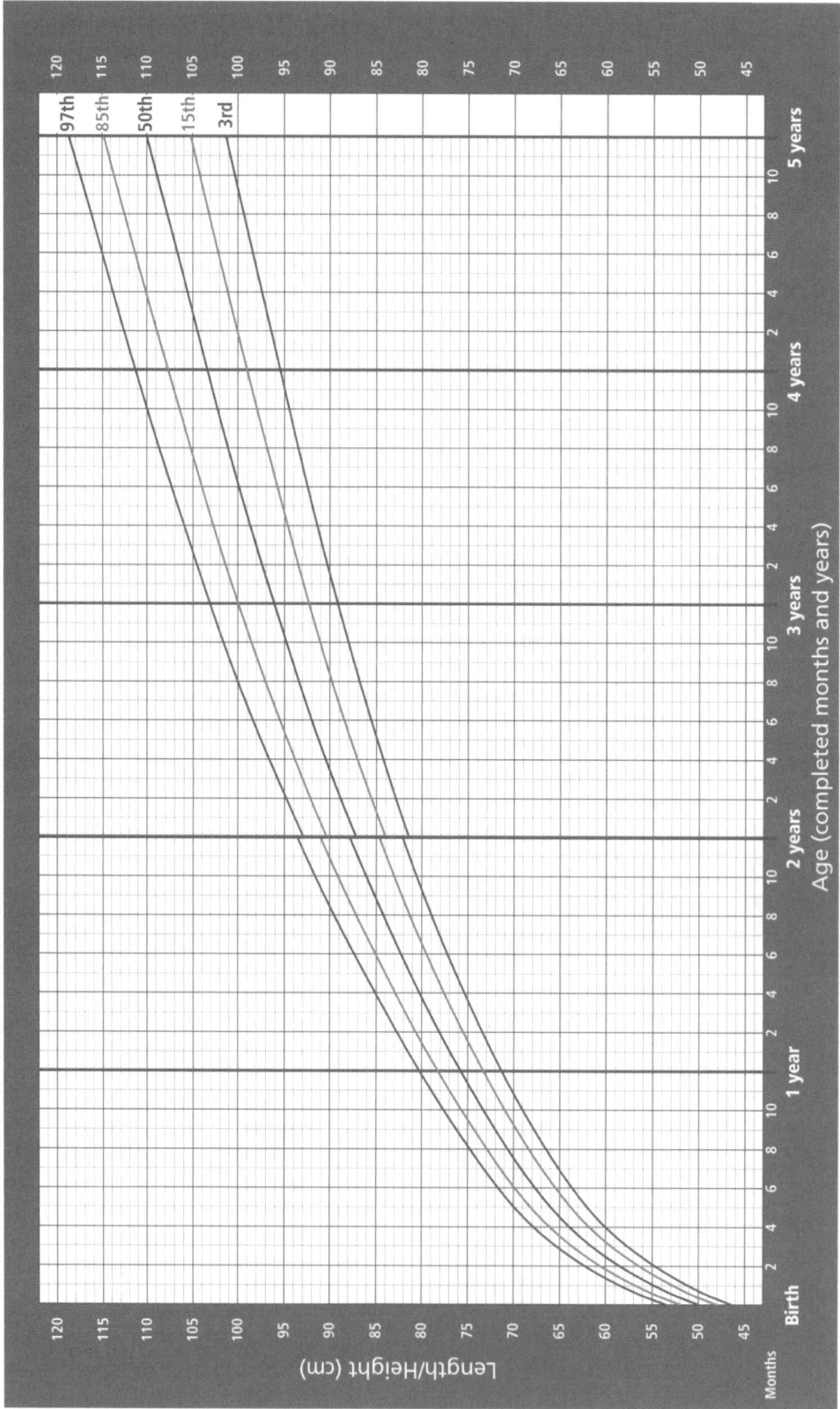

World Health Organization

WHO Child Growth Standards

Figure 2.8 Length/height-for-age percentiles: Boys, birth to 5 years

Length/height-for-age GIRLS

Birth to 5 years (percentiles)

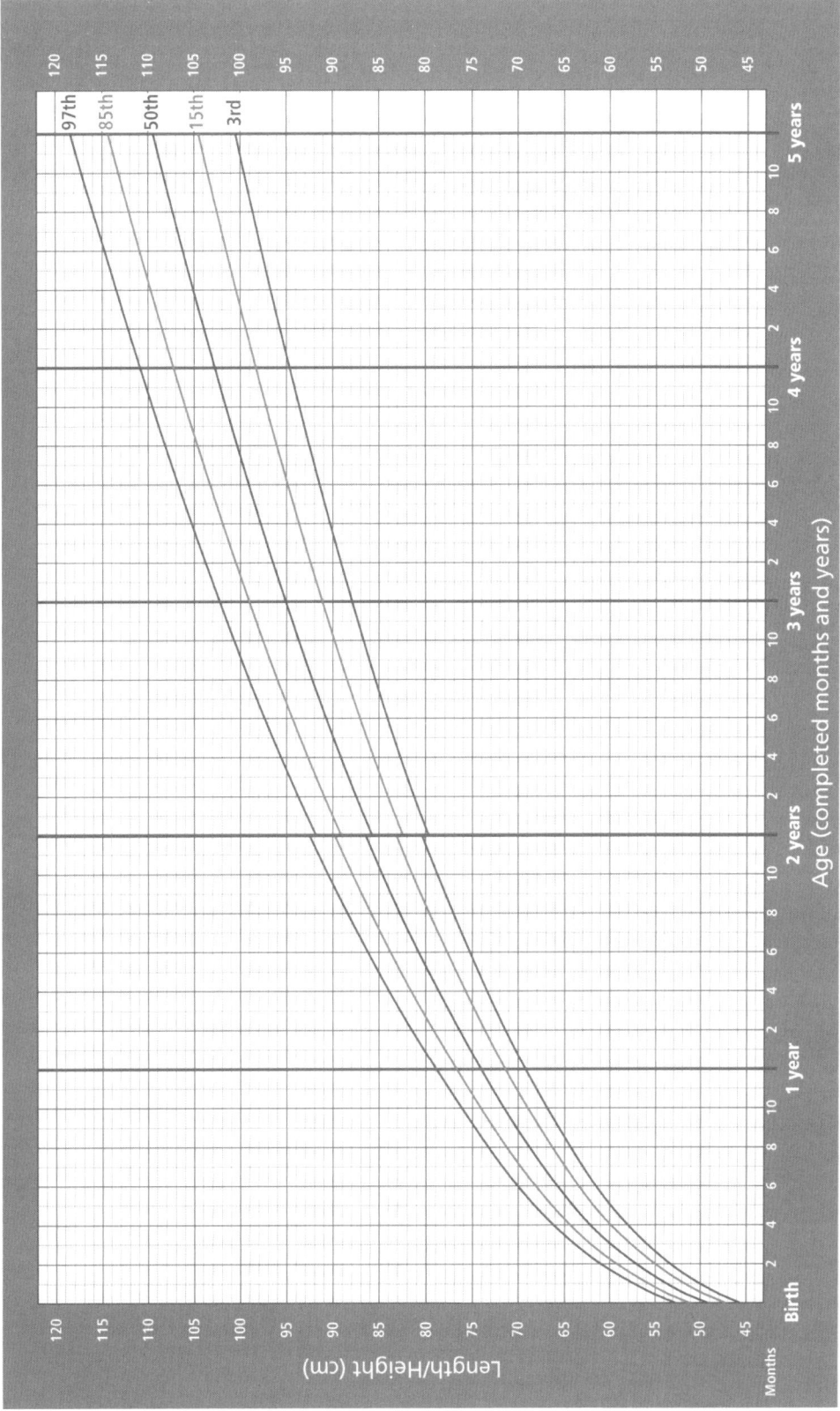

World Health Organization

WHO Child Growth Standards

Figure 2.9 Length/height-for-age percentiles: Girls, birth to 5 years

BMI-for-age BOYS

Birth to 5 years (percentiles)

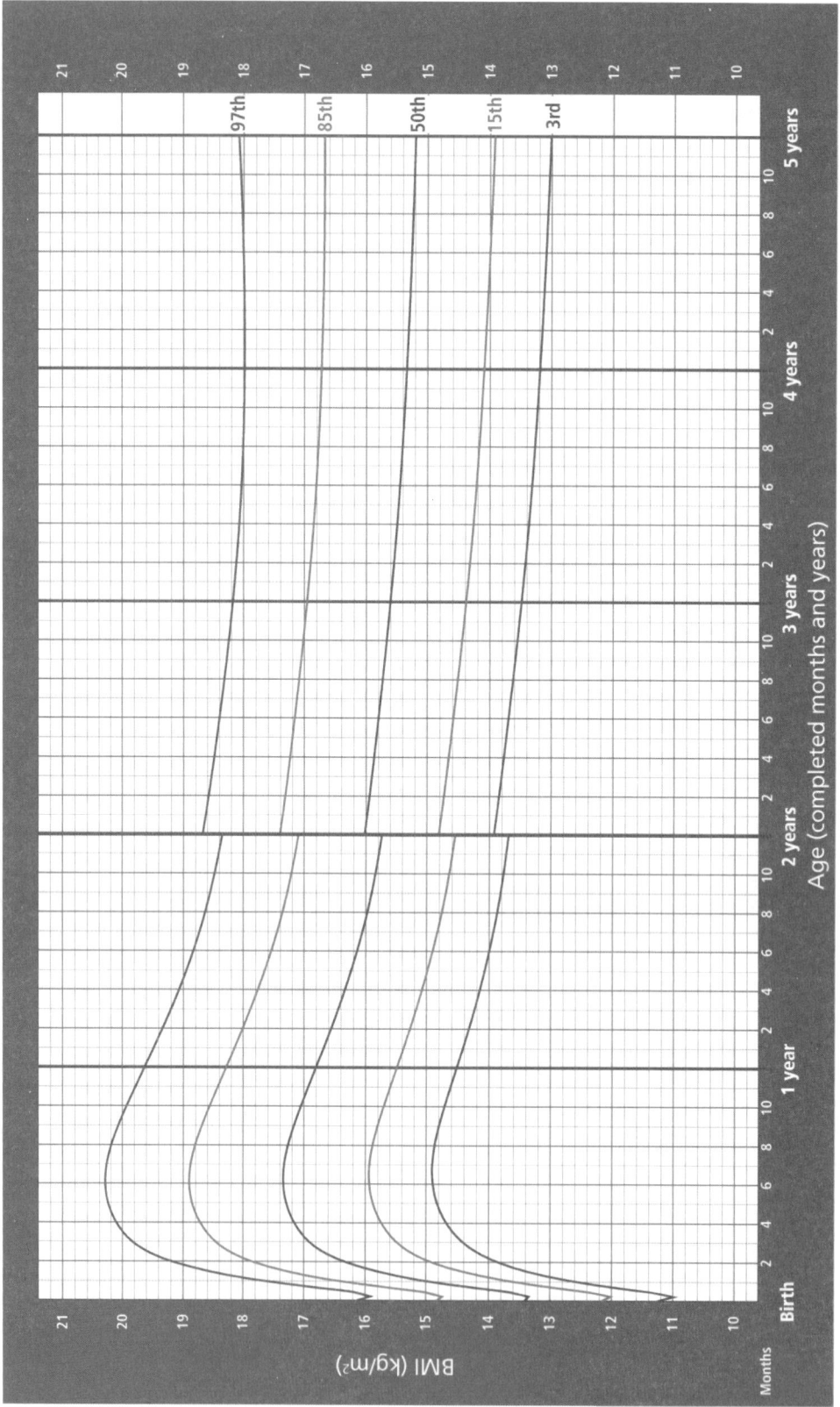

Figure 2.10 BMI-for-age percentiles: Boys, birth to 5 years

© Van Schaik Publishers

BMI-for-age GIRLS

Birth to 5 years (percentiles)

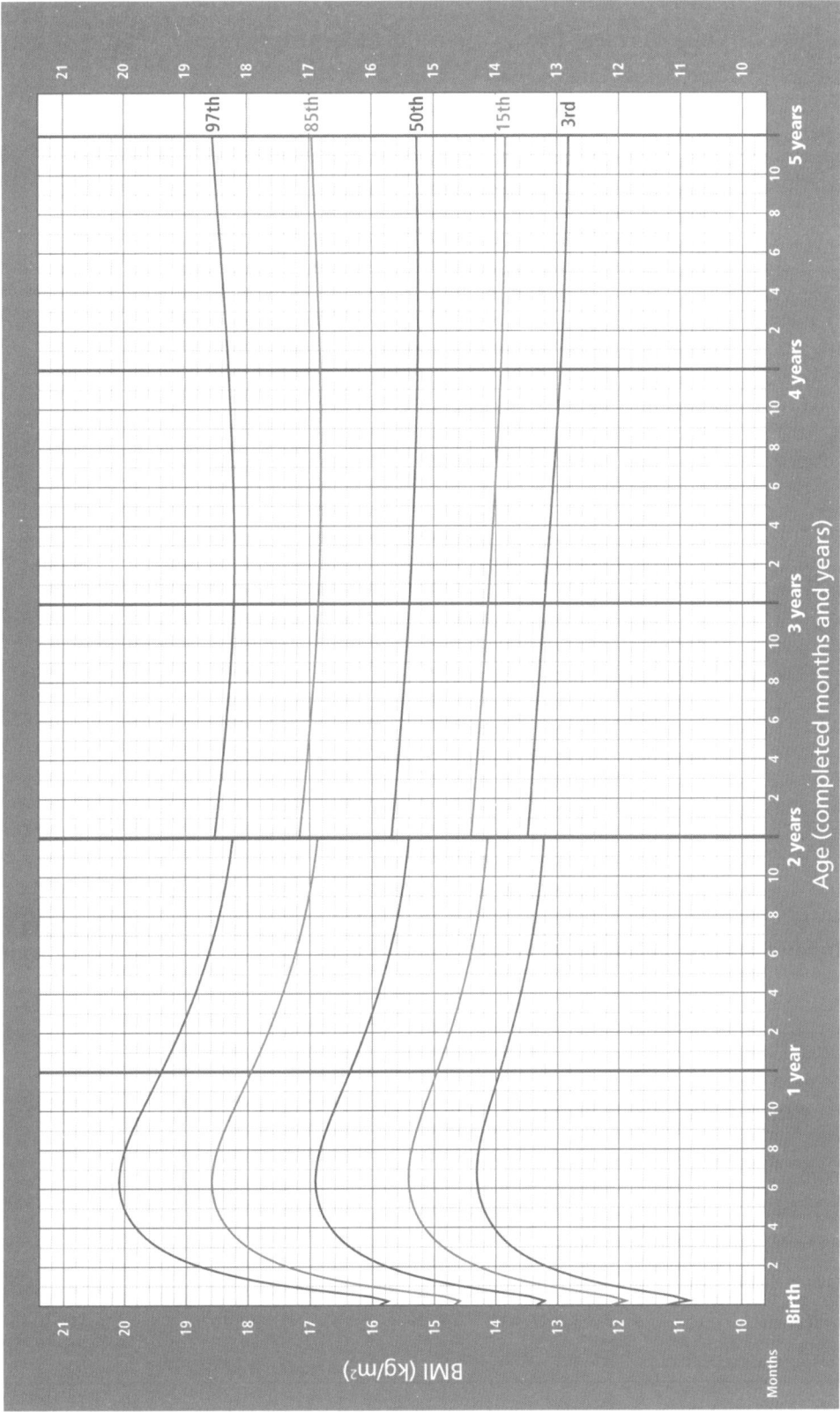

World Health Organization

WHO Child Growth Standards

Figure 2.11 BMI-for-age percentiles: Girls, birth to 5 years

Windows of achievement for six gross motor milestones

World Health Organization

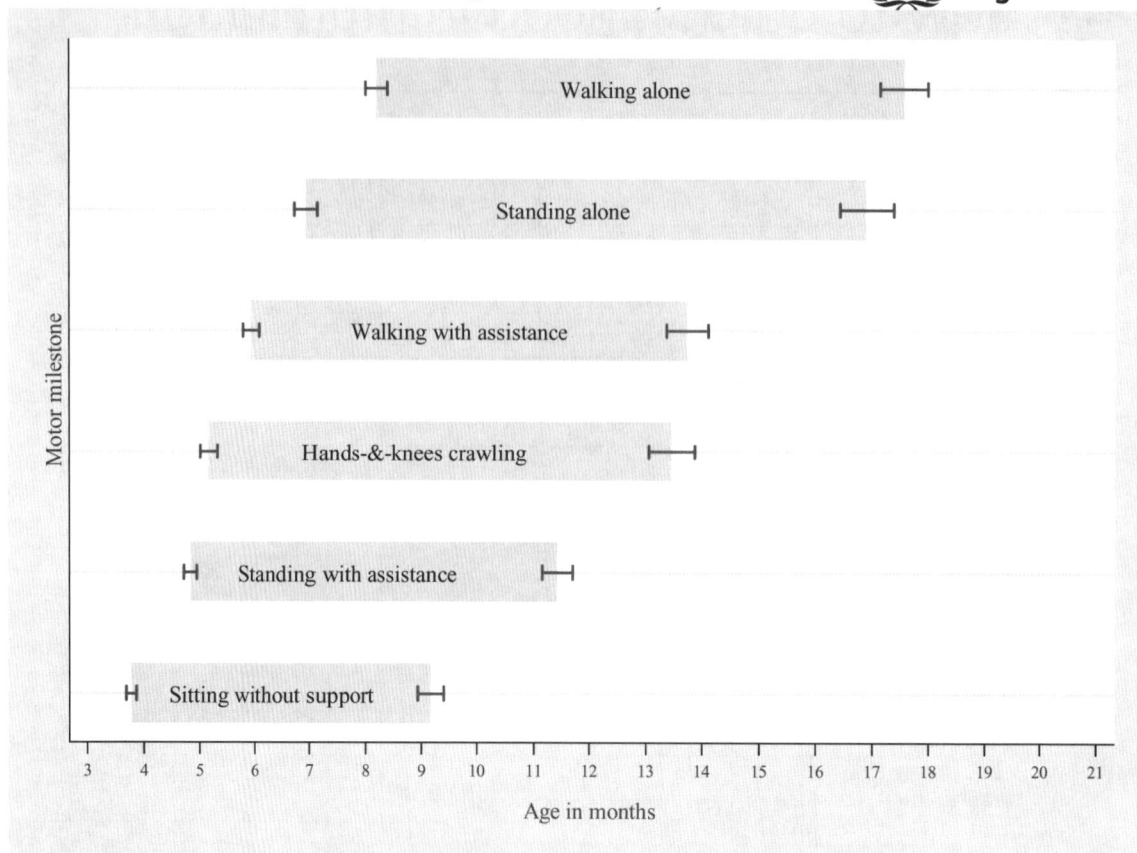

Reference: WHO Multicentre Growth Reference Study Group. WHO Motor Development Study: Windows of achievement for six gross motor development milestones. Acta Paediatrica Supplement 2006;450:86-95.

Windows of achievement for six gross motor milestones

World Health Organization

| Motor milestone | Left-bound | Box boundary (age in months) | | Right-bound | 95% C.I. | |
| | | 95% C.I. | | | | |
		Lower	Upper		Lower	Upper
Sitting without support	3.8	3.7	3.9	9.2	8.9	9.4
Standing with assistance	4.8	4.7	5.0	11.4	11.2	11.7
Hands-&-knees crawling	5.2	5.0	5.3	13.5	13.1	13.9
Walking with assistance	6.0	5.8	6.1	13.7	13.4	14.1
Standing alone	6.9	6.8	7.1	16.9	16.4	17.4
Walking alone	8.2	8.0	8.4	17.6	17.1	18.0

Reference: WHO Multicentre Growth Reference Study Group. WHO Motor Development Study: Windows of achievement for six gross motor development milestones. Acta Paediatrica Supplement 2006;450:86-95.

Figure 2.12 Windows of achievement for six gross motor milestones

3 How to do childhood immunisation

HAROON SALOOJEE AND IAN COUPER

The Expanded Program on Immunization (EPI) of the WHO began in 1974. The South African Department of Health adopted it in 1995 and called it the EPI (SA).

Why immunise?

Immunisation not only protects the individual but also curbs the spread of disease within the community. For disease to be kept under control, a certain percentage of individuals within a community need to be immunised. It is important that we maintain a high level of immunisation coverage even when the condition is becoming rare so that we can prevent outbreaks prior to final eradication. Furthermore, the Department of Health estimates that every R10 spent on vaccines saves R70 in medical costs and R250 in overall costs.

Table 3.1 summarises the vaccines that are part of the EPI (SA) Immunisation Schedule.

Table 3.1 Recommended South African childhood vaccination schedule

Birth	TOPV 0	BCG	
6 weeks	TOPV 1	DPT-Hib 1	HBV 1
10 weeks	TOPV 2	DPT-Hib 2	HBV 2
14 weeks	TOPV 3	DPT-Hib 3	HBV 3
9 months			Measles 1
18 months	TOPV 4	DPT 4	Measles 2
5 years	TOPV 5	DT	

BCG = Bacillus Calmette-Guérin
TOPV = trivalent oral polio vaccine
DPT = diphtheria, pertussis and tetanus vaccine
HBV = hepatitis B vaccine
Hib = *Haemophilus influenzae* B
DT = diphtheria and tetanus vaccine

The recommended sites for administering these vaccines are as follows:

- **BCG:** The right upper arm at the insertion of the deltoid muscle
- **DPT, Measles, HBV and Hib:** The lateral aspect of the thigh in infants under one year. The deltoid muscle is the preferred site in children older than one year. Hib is usually diluted into the DPT and they are given together, while the HBV should be given on the opposite side of the body. You should use a 25–30 mm-long 23-gauge needle for deep intramuscular (IM) injection.

Remember to record on the Road to Health (RTH) card at which site you injected the vaccine, for example (R) thigh or (L) thigh or (R) arm.

The vaccines

BCG

BCG vaccine is a live, attenuated strain of *Mycobacterium bovis*. In 1998, the Department of Health changed the method of BCG administration from the subcutaneous route to the intradermal route. This provides a more consistent dose delivery and is a more accurate method of administration. BCG is only moderately protective against primary TB, with an efficacy of 50%. However, the vaccine is more than 80% effective against childhood TB, especially against the severe forms of the disease, that is miliary TB and TB meningitis.

Polio

Originally, the WHO set 2000 as the target year to eradicate polio world-wide. By the end of 2005, polio was still reported in 21 countries. The last reported case of wild-type polio in South Africa was in 1989. However, this country has not yet been certified as polio free, owing to inadequate surveillance measures. Oral polio vaccine causes paralytic poliomyelitis in about one in one million recipients and their contacts.

DPT

Diphtheria and tetanus toxoids are protein antigens. Acellular pertussis vaccine (DTaP) is now preferred to whole-cell pertussis vaccine in the USA. It is more effective – 85% versus 48% – and has fewer adverse effects.

Hepatitis B

In Africa, the predominant route of spread or transmission of hepatitis B is horizontal, particularly between siblings. In South Africa, a plasma-derived vaccine is used. Recombinant DNA vaccines are preferred internationally. No differences have been observed between the two types of vaccines with regard to safety, efficacy and immunogenicity. Infants born to HbsAg-positive mothers should receive both 0.5 ml of hepatitis B immune globulin within 12 hours of birth and hepatitis B vaccine. Give the second dose of vaccine at 1–2 months, and the third at 6 months.

Hib conjugate

Immunity to infection by *H influenzae* type b is acquired through the formation of antibodies to the capsular polyribosephosphate (PRP) moiety. Hib vaccine has PRP coupled to a protein carrier. This improves vaccine efficacy and provides immunogenicity in younger infants, who are at highest risk for invasive disease.

Since the introduction of Hib conjugate vaccines in 1988 in developed countries, the incidence of invasive *H influenzae* infection has declined by at least 95% in infants and children. A similar trend is being observed in South Africa.

Measles

Infants in developing countries are susceptible to measles at a younger age. Up to a third of measles cases can occur in infants under nine months of age. Thus, you should usually give the vaccine at 6–9 months of age and repeat it at 18 months.

Mass catch-up immunisation campaigns have been conducted in South Africa since 1996. The aim was to interrupt measles transmission and to increase immunisation coverage rapidly. The campaigns have been spectacularly successful in southern Africa. Measles was targeted for eradication in South Africa by 2003. However, in 2004, a countrywide epidemic with over 760 cases (including deaths) resulted in a revision of the eradication target.

Other vaccines available in South Africa

There are other vaccines which do not form part of the EPI (SA), but you can provide them on an individual basis at the parents' cost. These vaccines are effective, but high costs limit their widespread use. If the child's parents can afford them, they are all indicated.

Measles, mumps, rubella (MMR) vaccine

You usually administer this when the child is 15 months of age, and you should repeat it when the child is 11–12 years.

Varicella vaccine (Var)

The live, attenuated varicella vaccine (Var) is now recommended in the USA immunisation schedule. Uninfected children may receive Var during any visit after their first birthday – usually between 12 and 18 months. Uninfected children younger than 13 years should receive two doses at least one month apart.

The efficacy of a single dose of Var is about 90% in healthy children, 85% in leukaemic children and 70% in healthy adults. Immunity has been shown to persist for more than 20 years. The vaccine is available in South Africa, and in future it is likely to be marketed in combination with MMR.

Influenza vaccine

There is evidence to recommend the routine administration of this vaccine to every child. At present, it is recommended for high-risk infants, for example those with a chronic chest condition.

Children with special circumstances

Children with HIV

Children with HIV should receive all childhood vaccines at the intervals recommended for children. You can administer live vaccines, including oral polio. BCG is contraindicated in symptomatic HIV-infected children. Antibody responses to Hib and hepatitis vaccines have been shown to be poorer in HIV-infected infants. Nevertheless, you should administer both.

Children with delayed or unknown immunisation

You should give the required vaccines at the same time, taking care to use different sites. You can give the primary doses six to eight weeks apart. In children five years old or less, at least three doses of DPT are required. For children older than five years, you should administer DT (that is no pertussis) instead. In children older than 18 months, a single dose of measles vaccine is needed. After two years of age Hib conjugate vaccine is not given.

Children at risk because of cardiac or respiratory disease

Children of six months or older with chronic cardiac or respiratory conditions should receive annual influenza vaccinations.

Common side-effects

You need to give parents advice on what to do about common reactions to immunisation. The following are frequent, but not serious, side-effects and *do not* contraindicate further vaccination:

- Pertussis-containing vaccines, including DPT, frequently cause mild to moderate systemic and local effects. About 50% of children who are given DPT vaccine develop some swelling and redness at the injection site, 30% become moderately febrile and 60% become tearful or irritable. DT has fewer side-effects than DPT.
- A dose of paracetamol (15 mg/kg) 30 minutes before the vaccination and 3–4 hourly thereafter for the next 24 hours can significantly reduce symptoms.
- Hib vaccine causes transient swelling and redness at the injection site in about 5% of infants, but this resolves within 24 hours.
- MMR vaccine may be followed about 7–10 days later by a fever lasting two or three days, malaise and/or rash, but the recipients of the vaccine are not infectious.

Contraindications

False contraindications

The following conditions are *not* contraindications to immunisation with any of the vaccines on the standard EPI (SA) schedule:

- Family history of any adverse reactions following vaccination
- Family history of convulsions
- Previous pertussis-like illness, measles, rubella or mumps infection
- Prematurity (vaccination should not be postponed)
- Stable neurological conditions such as cerebral palsy and Down syndrome
- Contact with an infectious disease
- Asthma, eczema, hay fever or "sniffles"
- A history of allergy
- Treatment with antibiotics
- Treatment with locally acting steroids (inhaled or low-dose topical)
- Child's mother being pregnant
- Child being breastfed
- History of jaundice after birth
- Below weight in an otherwise healthy child
- Over the age recommended in vaccination schedule
- Recent or imminent surgery
- Replacement corticosteroids
- Adherence to homeopathic practices

Valid contraindications

Do not re-administer in the case of a serious reaction to a previous dose or a constituent of any vaccine.

Do not administer live vaccines to a pregnant woman or to children undergoing immunosuppression, including those with malignant disease or those receiving chemotherapy treatment.

In the case of pertussis, do not give further doses if an evolving neurological problem such as encephalopathy occurs within seven days of the administration of a dose.

Use *every contact* that you have with a child to check his immunisation status.

---

4 How to administer an intramuscular injection to a child

H A R O O N   S A L O O J E E   A N D   I A N   C O U P E R

General principles

The **sites** for the administration of intramuscular (IM) injections include the following:

- **Quadriceps** muscle group of the upper, outer side of the thigh (just above the midpoint between the knee and hip). This site is preferred because of the small risk of giving the injection intravenously, hitting the femur with the needle or injuring the sciatic nerve.
- **Gluteus** muscle group in the buttock. This muscle group is difficult to use for IM injection because of variable amounts of fat and subcutaneous tissue and the danger of injury to the sciatic nerve and major blood vessels in the region. If you are using this site, use only the upper, outer quadrant of the muscle, and always aspirate before injecting.
- **Deltoid** muscle group. You can use this site for giving immunisations in a child *older than one year* but not for other injections.

You can help to minimise pain during administration of the injection by

- using a sharp needle of the smallest diameter that will allow fluid to flow freely, for example 22- to 24-gauge
- ensuring that no fluid for injection is in the needle at the time of insertion into the skin
- using a minimal volume for injection, for example 2 ml or less at any single injection site
- avoiding rapid injection of material
- using alternative injection sites for subsequent injections.

Complications

Potential complications of IM injections include

- inadvertent intra-arterial or intravenous injection
- infection from contaminated injection material
- neural injury – typically the sciatic nerve after injections in the buttock
- local tissue damage due to injection of irritants.

Equipment

To administer an injection, you need the following:

- A sterile needle of the smallest size that will allow fluid to flow freely, for example 22- to 24-gauge
- A sterile syringe of the smallest size available that has adequate markings for the proper dose, for example 1–3 ml
- Dry cotton wool ball
- Antiseptic solution

Procedure

To administer an injection, follow this procedure:

- Wash your hands.
- Explain the injection procedure to the caregiver and ask her to reassure the child.
- Ensure that the caregiver is close to the child and able to restrain the child gently, if necessary.
- Select the site for injection.
- Draw the material for injection into the syringe and expel air from syringe.
- Ensure that the drug and dose are correct.
- Grasp the centre of the target muscle between your thumb and forefinger, if possible.
- Insert the needle at a 45-degree angle in the thigh, and a 90-degree angle at any other site, through the skin with a single quick motion. This is illustrated in Figure 4.1.
- Withdraw the plunger of the syringe slightly to ensure that the tip of the needle is not in a vein.
- If the needle is in the muscle, no blood will enter the needle. Then you should slowly inject the material with steady pressure for three to five seconds.

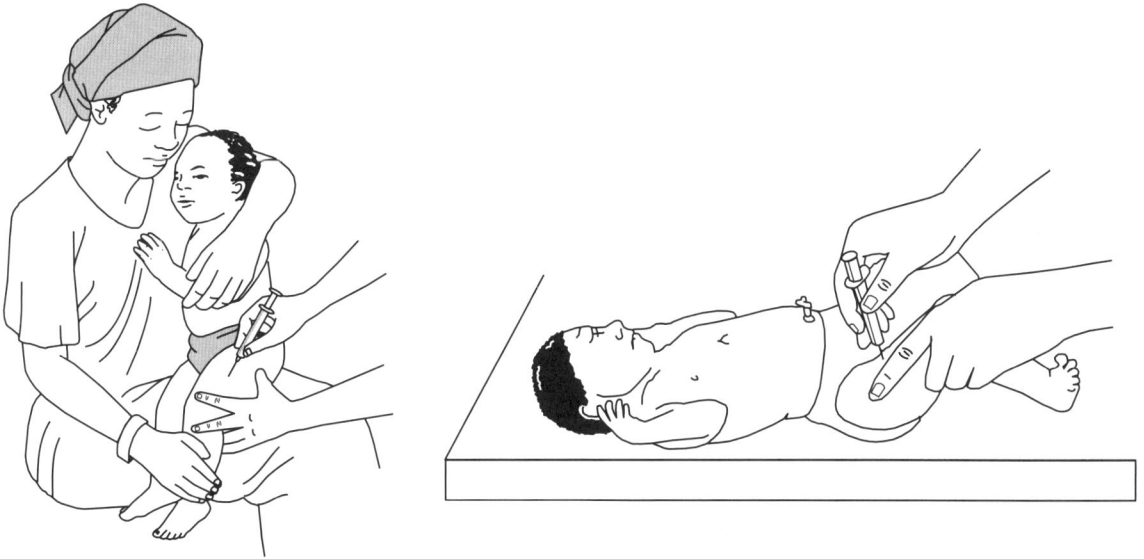

Figure 4.1 Administering an intramuscular injection into the thigh

- If the needle is in a vein, blood will pass through the needle into the syringe. In this case
  - withdraw the needle without injecting the material
  - apply gentle pressure to the site with a dry cotton wool ball to prevent bruising
  - place a new, sterile needle on the syringe
  - choose a new site for injection
  - repeat the procedure described above.
- Upon completion of the injection, withdraw the needle and apply gentle pressure with a dry cotton wool ball.
- Record the site of the injection, and rotate the site of subsequent injections.

5 How to do a suprapubic bladder aspiration in an infant

HAROON SALOOJEE AND IAN COUPER

It is not recommended that you insert a urinary catheter in an infant to collect a specimen – rather aspirate the urine with a needle. This is the most reliable way of collecting a non-contaminated sample of urine in infants.

You can do an aspiration when

- an infant is ill and urgently requires a urine culture
- you have obtained an equivocal result from a urine bag sample.

Do not take a suprapubic sample when

- the infant has an empty bladder, which is evident if his napkin is wet
- the infant's abdomen is markedly distended
- the infant has a haemorrhagic disorder
- the infant has any genitourinary anomalies.

Procedure

You need to follow this procedure in order to take a suprapubic urine sample from an infant:

- Check that the infant has not voided during the past hour. Do this by checking for a dry napkin or by applying a urine collection bag for at least 30 minutes prior to aspiration.
- Place the infant on a table or firm examining couch.
- Have an assistant help you to immobilise the infant in a supine position with the legs held down gently. This is illustrated in Figure 5.1.
- Clean the suprapubic area with antiseptic.
- Perform the aspiration using a sterile 10-ml syringe with a sterile 21-gauge needle.
- Puncture the skin 1.0–1.5 cm above the symphysis pubis in the midline.
- Insert the needle at a 10–20-degree angle to the vertical, pointing slightly toward the fundus of the bladder in a cephalad position, to a depth of 1–2

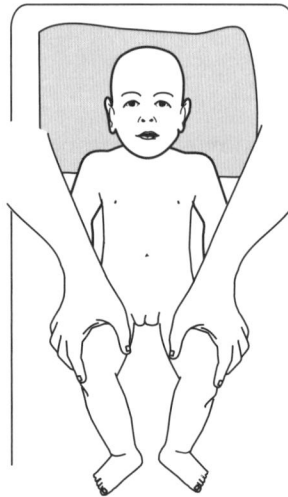

Figure 5.1
Positioning of the infant

cm, with slight traction on the plunger of the syringe. This is shown in Figure 5.2.

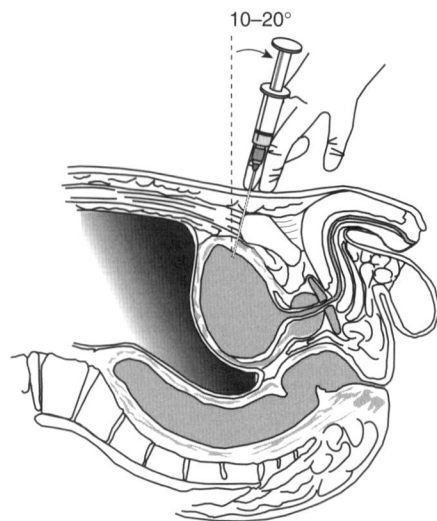

10–20°

Figure 5.2 Fingers identifying symphysis pubis to guide placement of the needle

- Aspirate the urine, withdraw the needle and remove the syringe.
- Apply gentle pressure over the puncture site until any bleeding stops.
- Transfer the urine into a sterile sample bottle.

It is essential for you to note the following:

- If you do not obtain any urine, you should withdraw the needle. Do not aimlessly probe and do not make repeated attempts.
- Occasionally, the infant will void spontaneously during the procedure. Be ready to catch some of the stream.

6 How to get intravenous access in a child

HAROON SALOOJEE AND IAN COUPER

You can use various sites to establish an intravenous (IV) line. Common sites that you can use for a child are as follows:

- Veins on the back of the hand or top of the foot. These are the most commonly used and preferred sites.
- Veins on the forearm, the front of the elbow, or around the ankle or knee. However, you should minimise use of the veins around the knee because there is a greater risk of the needle coming in contact with bone.
- Scalp veins in the midline of the forehead, the temporal area, or above or behind the ear. This is shown in Figure 6.1.

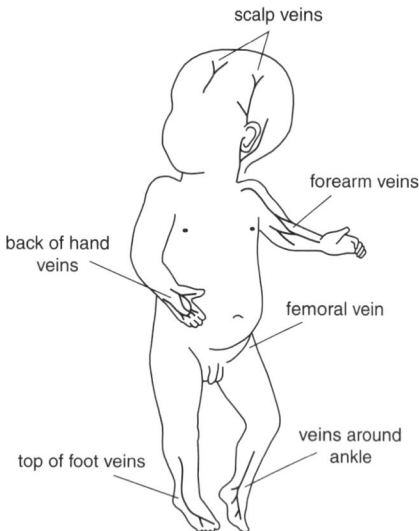

Figure 6.1 Common sites for IV access in infants and young children

If, in an emergency situation, you cannot establish a peripheral IV line, use an umbilical vein catheter in a neonate (see Chapter 79), a central vein such as the external jugular vein or an intraosseous line (see Chapter 7).

Equipment

To insert a peripheral IV line, you need the following:

- Clean examination gloves
- An alcohol swab or cotton wool ball soaked in antiseptic solution
- Sterile infusion set with IV fluid. Use a micro-dropper with 60 drops per minute flow rate, if one is available.
- A sterile butterfly set or cannula of 23- to 25-gauge. If the IV line is required for a blood transfusion, ensure that the cannula is large enough, that is 22-gauge, so that the blood does not clot in the cannula during the transfusion.
- Adhesive strapping
- A rubber band and razor blade – for shaving hair – if you are using a scalp vein
- An arm board or splint

Procedure

You should follow this procedure when establishing an IV line:

- Prepare the solution to be infused, ensuring that the entire infusion set is filled with fluid and does not contain any air. If you are using a butterfly set, ensure that it is filled with IV fluid. Air embolism can occur easily in babies, therefore it is essential that you ensure that there are no air bubbles in the set before beginning the infusion.
- Wash your hands and put on clean examination gloves.
- Ensure that there is an *effective* light source – you must be able to see properly what you are doing.
- Prepare the skin over the vein using the swab or cotton wool, and allow to dry.
- Have an assistant press on the skin near the vein to act as a tourniquet. If you are using
  - a vein on the hand, foot, arm or leg, have the assistant gently encircle the limb with their

forefinger and thumb above the chosen site of insertion

- a vein on the scalp, have the assistant press over the vein below the chosen site of insertion, or place a rubber band as a tourniquet around the baby's head. Figure 6.2 shows this alternative.

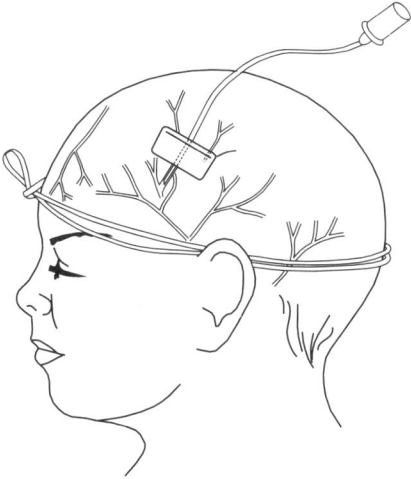

Figure 6.2 A rubber band acting as a tourniquet for a scalp vein

- Insert the needle at a 15-degree angle through the skin, with the bevel of the needle facing upward. If you are using
  - a butterfly set, a small amount of blood will flush back into the tubing when the vein is punctured; do not push in the needle any further

- a cannula, once blood fills the hub of the cannula, withdraw the needle partially while continuing to push the cannula in. When the hub of the cannula reaches the skin at the puncture site, withdraw the needle completely. Dispose of the needle according to recommended infection prevention procedures (see http://www. who.int/hiv/topics/precautions/universal/en/).

- Have the assistant remove their finger and thumb from around the baby's limb, or remove or cut the rubber band if a scalp vein was used.

- Connect the infusion set to the cannula or butterfly set:
  - Infuse the fluid into the vein for a few seconds to make sure that the vein has been successfully cannulated. The fluid should run freely and there should be no swelling around the site of the cannula.
  - If swelling develops around the site of infusion, withdraw the needle from the vein and repeat the procedure using a different vein.
  - Cannulation of a scalp artery will result in a pulsatile spurting of blood. Withdraw the needle and apply pressure until the bleeding stops.

- If using a vein in the hand, arm, foot or leg, immobilise the limb (e.g. using an arm board or splint, and adhesive strapping or thin paper tape) to minimise movement (see Figure 6.3).

- Secure the cannula or butterfly set in position using strips of adhesive strapping, as shown in Figure 6.4.

- Inspect the infusion site every hour. Look for redness and swelling around the insertion site of the cannula, which indicate that the cannula is not in the vein and that fluid is leaking into the subcuta-

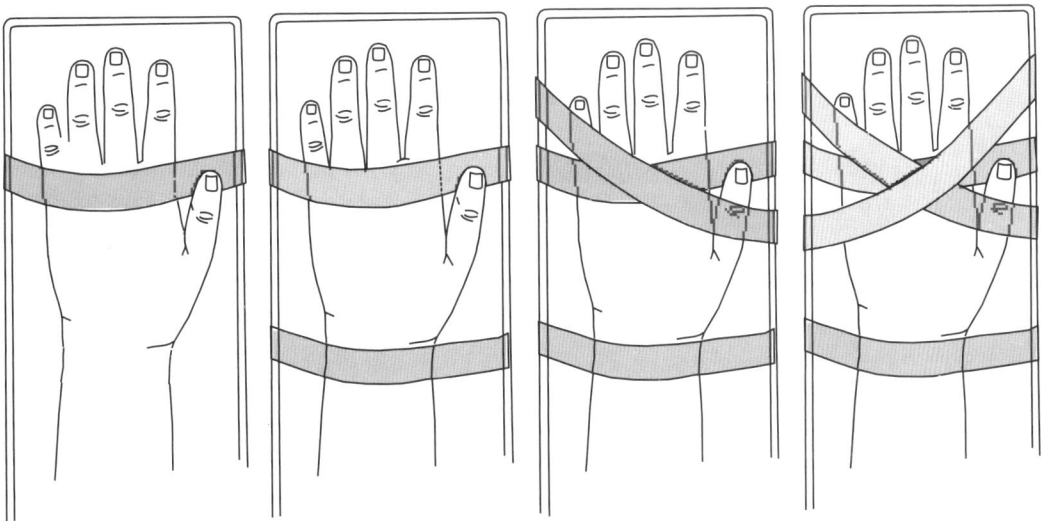

Figure 6.3 Immobilising the hand

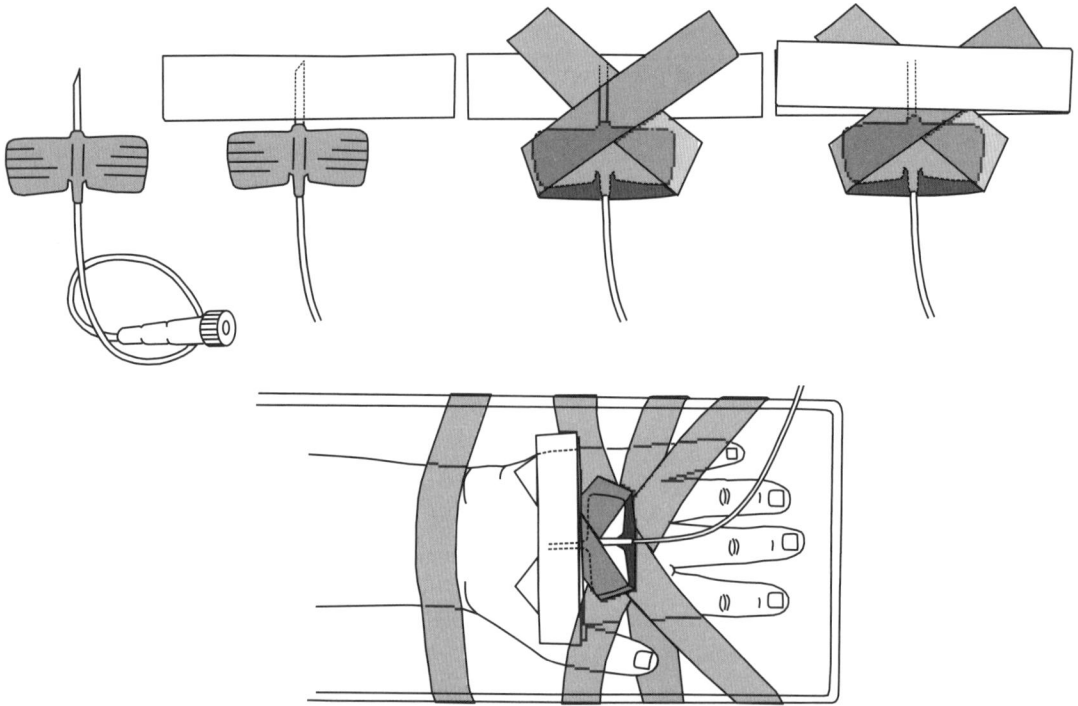

Figure 6.4 Securing the butterfly set in place

neous tissue. If redness or swelling is seen at any time, you need to stop the infusion, remove the needle and establish a new IV line in a different vein.

- Check the volume of fluid infused and compare it to the volume you prescribed.
- Record all your findings.
- Change the infusion set and fluid bag every 48 hours, even if the bag still contains IV fluid, as it can be a major source of infection.

"IV locks" are used to provide convenient intravenous (IV) access in children who require intermittent IV administration of medications (such as antibiotics) without a continuous infusion of IV fluids. A frequently encountered problem with an IV lock is the loss of patency because of clot formation within the catheter. To prevent clot formation, catheters are commonly flushed with saline after each administration of IV medication or every 12 hours when the device is not in use – usually 0.5 to 1 ml is needed.

7 How to establish an intraosseous infusion in a child

HAROON SALOOJEE AND IAN COUPER

When carried out by a well-trained and experienced health worker, intraosseous infusion is a safe, simple and reliable method of giving fluid and drugs *in an emergency*. You can give almost all parenteral fluids and drugs required in an emergency using this route. Depending on your expertise, you can establish intraosseous access rapidly – even in 1–2 minutes.

You should remove the intraosseous line as soon as other IV access is established – within eight hours, if possible – and you should not place an intraosseous line if there is infection at the intended insertion site or if the bone is fractured.

The procedure is painful, but no anaesthetic is required because the procedure is performed only in an emergency.

Equipment

To perform an intraosseous infusion, you need the following:

- Clean examination gloves
- An alcohol swab or cotton wool ball soaked in antiseptic solution
- A sterile intraosseous needle, a bone marrow needle, a spinal needle with a stylet or a 22-gauge needle. The latter is suitable only for neonates when the bony cortex is still relatively soft, or if there is no alternative.
- A sterile infusion set with IV fluid. Use a micro-dropper if one is available.
- Adhesive strapping
- A sterile 5-ml syringe
- Elastic bandage
- A padded splint

Procedure

You should follow this procedure when establishing an intraosseous infusion:

- Prepare the infusion solution, ensuring that the entire infusion set is filled with fluid and does not contain any air.

- If you are using a regular hypodermic needle, attach a 5-ml syringe filled with 3 ml of IV fluid and flush the fluid through the needle.
- Identify the insertion site:
  - The preferred site is the proximal end of the tibia, and the rest of the description below applies to this site. The site is 1 cm below and 1 cm medial to the tibial tuberosity. Palpate the tibial tuberosity then locate the site one finger's breadth below and medial to the tuberosity.
  - You could also use the site at the distal end of the femur, which is 2 cm above the lateral condyle.
- Wash your hands and put on sterile gloves.
- Prepare the skin over the insertion site using the swab or cotton wool and allow to dry.
- Position the child's leg with the knee bent at about 30 degrees to the straight position and the heel resting on the table.
- Stabilise the leg by grasping the thigh and knee above and lateral to the cannulation site, with the fingers and thumb of your left hand (which is no longer sterile) wrapped around the knee, taking care that your fingers are not directly behind the insertion site.
- Hold the needle – with the attached syringe if you are using a hypodermic needle – in your other hand at a 90-degree angle to the selected insertion site, with the bevel pointing towards the feet.
- Advance the needle using a twisting or drilling motion and moderate, controlled force. Stop immediately when there is a sudden decrease in resistance to the needle, as this indicates that the needle has entered the marrow cavity. The needle should be fixed in the bone.
- If you are using a bone marrow or intraosseous needle, remove the stylet and attach the syringe.
- Aspirate 1 ml of the marrow contents using the 5-ml syringe to confirm that the needle is correctly positioned. The aspirate should look like blood. If you fail to aspirate marrow content it does not

necessarily mean that you have placed the needle incorrectly. Continue with the next step.

- Slowly inject 3 ml of normal saline to check for proper placement of the needle. Look for swelling, which indicates leakage of fluid under the skin, at the front of the leg or in the calf muscle at the back of the leg.
  - If there is swelling, remove the needle and try again.
  - If there is no swelling but you found it difficult to infuse the fluid, the needle may have entered the posterior bone cortex. Withdraw the needle approximately 0.5 cm and cautiously inject IV fluid again.
- If you do not detect any problems, attach the infusion set to the needle, as shown in Figure 7.1.
- Secure the needle in place using tape, and place a back slab on the leg as for a fractured femur, ensuring that the elastic bandage does not interfere with the needle or the infusion set.
- Inspect the infusion site every hour. Look for redness and swelling around the insertion site of the cannula and in the child's calf muscle, which indicate that the cannula is not in the vein and that fluid is leaking into the subcutaneous tissue. If redness or swelling is seen at any time, you need to stop the infusion, remove the needle and attempt to establish a peripheral IV line or a new intraosseous line at a different site.

- Check the volume of fluid infused and compare it to the volume you prescribed. Flow rates may alter dramatically with changes in the position of the leg.
- Record all your findings.
- Remove the intraosseous needle as soon as alternative IV access is available – within eight hours, if possible.

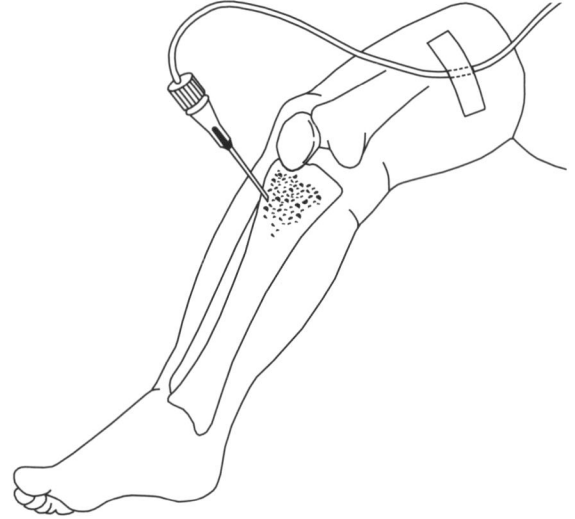

Figure 7.1 Intraosseous infusion

8 How to perform a lumbar puncture in a child

HAROON SALOOJEE AND IAN COUPER

A lumbar puncture (LP) is an important part of the complete work-up of an infant or child suspected of sepsis. Moreover, an LP is essential to confirm the diagnosis of suspected meningitis or encephalitis.

Indications

You need to perform an LP on any infant or child who has symptoms that are suggestive of meningitis, for example seizures or intractable vomiting, or an unexplained fever, or the purpuric rash of meningococcal disease. You may also find an LP useful in the evaluation of an infant with a suspected intracranial bleed, in which you would need to assess the presence of blood in the cerebrospinal fluid (CSF).

Contraindications

You should not perform an LP in the following instances:

- An extremely ill infant or child – the procedure may exacerbate his condition
- Infection at the site of the LP
- Congenital anomalies of the lower spine, for example meningomyelocele
- Bleeding diathesis, for example disseminated intravascular coagulation and haemophilia
- Signs of raised intracranial pressure – unequal pupils, irregular breathing, rigid posture or paralysis of limb or trunk

Before proceeding with the LP, you need to bear in mind that respiratory arrest, or apnoea, may result from excessive flexion of the neck as this compromises the airway, and that you should use an aseptic technique to prevent infection.

Preparation

To ensure that the LP is successful, you need to make these preparations:

- Be ready to resuscitate the child if necessary. Ensure that drugs and equipment for resuscitation are readily available.
- Avoid respiratory compromise by correct positioning.
- Collect a blood glucose sample for comparison with CSF glucose (see below).
- Avoid hypothermia in a newborn by limiting exposure to the procedure area.
- If an intravenous line is needed as part of treatment, insert it before proceeding with the LP.
- Get an assistant to help you during the procedure.
- Proper positioning and restraint of the child is crucial for the LP to succeed. Place the child facing the assistant and nearest to the side of table or couch from which you will work. The preferred position is for the child to be sitting. His legs are straightened and the back is curved forward, as shown in Figure 8.1. Alternatively, the child could lie on his side with the back at right angles to the bed.
- In order to keep the spine in a flexed position, hold the child with one hand behind his neck and shoulders – not the head – and your other hand behind the thighs. This is illustrated in Figure 8.2. Maintain the neck in partial extension, not flexed toward the chest.

Procedure

You need to follow this procedure when performing an LP:

- Set aside a grey-top test tube and two red-top test tubes for the CSF investigations.
- Wash your hands and put on sterile gloves. Ensure that the technique is aseptic at all times.
- Prepare the skin of the lumbar area with an antiseptic. First clean the area of the puncture, and then the remainder of the back in a concentrically

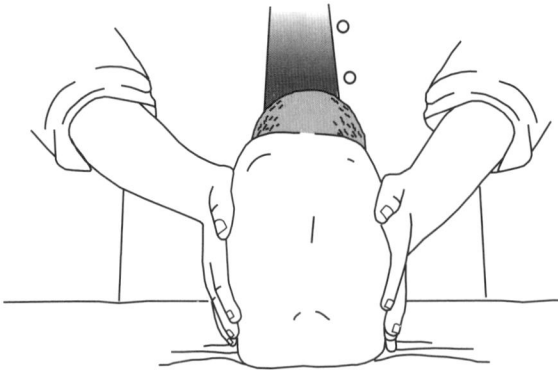

Figure 8.1 Sitting position during a lumbar puncture

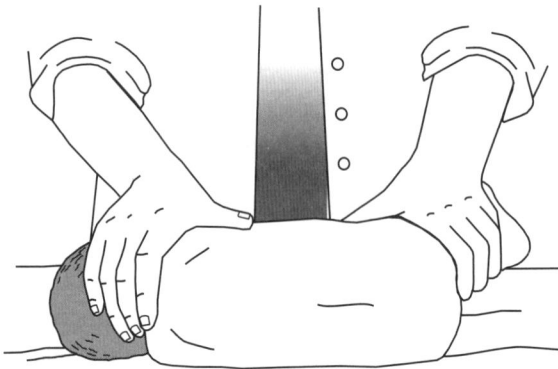

Figure 8.2 Lying position during a lumbar puncture

enlarging circular pattern. Cover the surrounding area with sterile towels.

- Carry out the puncture between the fourth and fifth lumbar processes. This point is located by the level of iliac crests – a line joining the highest points of the two iliac crests passes just above the fourth lumbar spine.

- Insert the bevelled needle of 22- to 24-gauge in the midline. The needle should be parallel to the bed and angled towards the child's umbilicus. Gradually advance it by 1 cm. You might feel a slight "pop" as the needle enters the subarach-

noid space. If CSF does not come out, rotate the needle slightly.

- Allow the CSF to drip into three test tubes. Each tube should contain about 0.5–1 ml of fluid. Send them for testing. The grey tube is for glucose; the red tubes are for biochemistry and microscopy (that is cell count and gram stain). You can compare the CSF glucose to the blood glucose sample that you took earlier.

- If you encounter bone you cannot redirect the needle in place. Pull the needle back to just beneath the skin and then redirect it. If this fails, that is the tap is "dry", try another space between the third and fourth lumbar processes.

- If you over-advance the needle you will traverse the spinal canal and encounter bone. Bleeding from the anterior venous plexus almost always occurs, resulting in bloody CSF. This is known as a "traumatic tap". However, the tap may partially clear in some instances. If the bleeding does not clear, you can
  - send the fluid that you obtained for culture testing, if the indication for the LP was suspected meningitis
  - immediately repeat the procedure at one higher lumbar space (do not go higher than L3–4)
  - repeat the procedure in 24 hours.

- Remove the needle once you have collected the CSF. Apply direct pressure to the puncture site with a sterile cotton wool swab until bleeding or leakage of the fluid stops.

- Apply a sterile dressing and an adhesive bandage over the needle puncture site.

It is essential for you to remember the following:

- Always inspect the CSF that you obtained for turbidity and colour.

- In many neonates the CSF may be mildly xanthochromic (that is yellow), but it should always be clear.

- If it is indicated, you could identify meningitis sooner than it will take for the microscopy results to come back from the lab by utilising a urine dipstick test to identify the presence of white blood cells in the CSF. However, this crude test does not negate the need for microscopy.

Van Schaik Publishers

9 How to assess a child's chest radiograph

HAROON SALOOJEE

The radiographs of sick children offer a challenge owing to differences in appearance that can be attributed to age-related growth and development. This chapter does not offer guidance on the general interpretation of the chest radiograph (CXR). See also Chapter 31. Instead, it highlights issues particular to infants and children that you must consider when interpreting a CXR in this age group.

Anatomical differences

In children of *six years and older*:

- The appearance of internal structures of the chest is similar to that of adults.

- The left hilum is normally higher than the right because of the position of the heart. When the heart is in a normal position, two thirds of it lies to the left of midline, and one third lies to the right.

- The left hemidiaphragm is usually 2 cm lower than the right because of the position of the heart.

- In adolescent girls, the mammary gland shadows are often asymmetrical, giving the false appearance of a faint, fluid-like density that is more prominent on one side of the film than on the other side. A lateral view will clearly show that the densities are external to the chest cavity.

In children *younger than six*:

- The hilar regions are normally apparent as white streaks fanning out from the centre. Overvascularity, seen as unusual whiteness, in the hilar regions is associated with congestive heart failure and congenital heart malformations such as left-to-right shunts. Undervascularity on a properly exposed film, or darkness in the hilar regions, indicates right-to-left shunting.

- Bronchovascular markings radiate and taper outward from the roots of each lung such that the markings become invisible in the peripheral halves of the lungs. The bronchovascular markings are normally more conspicuous on the right side.

- The presence of the thymus makes the evaluation of CXRs of infants and children difficult. The thymus normally appears as a smoothly outlined mediastinal mass that merges imperceptibly with the superior part of the heart shadow. Sometimes you can see an angulated notch on the inferior aspect of the right lobe of the thymus as it rests above the heart. This is known as the "sail sign" and it is normal. The thymus usually becomes inconspicuous by the age of five. The appearance of the thymus can vary. It can occupy the entire anterior part of the thorax, extending down to the diaphragm and out to the lateral wall of the thorax. When a child is stressed, the thymus shrinks, and when it is indented by the ribs, the thymus has a wavy border.

The cardiothoracic ratio is the ratio of the greatest cardiac transverse diameter to the greatest internal thoracic transverse diameter. Figure 9.1 shows the method of calculating it. Determination of this ratio is the most widely used method for estimating the size of the heart. In order to minimise magnification of the heart, you should preferably use the posteroanterior (PA) view on a film that you have obtained during adequate inspiration.

The ratio is most sensitive for detecting left ventricular enlargement in older children, because the left ventricle enlarges toward the left side of the chest wall. If you find that the ratio is larger than normal on a frontal view, you need to obtain a lateral chest film to confirm the presence of cardiac enlargement.

Adequacy of the CXR

There are four important aspects to evaluating the adequacy of a CXR in a child. We will explore each of them in turn.

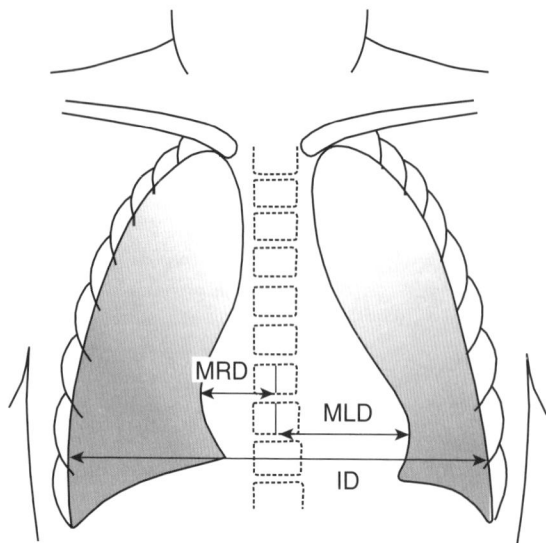

$$\text{Cardiothoracic index (ratio)} = \frac{(MRD + MLD)}{ID}$$

MRD = greatest perpendicular diameter from midline to right heart border

MLD = greatest perpendicular diameter from midline to left heart border

ID = internal diameter of chest at level of right hemidiaphragm

The ratio of the heart to the thorax in a baby should be 65% or less from birth to one year, about 50% during the second year of life and less than 50% as the child grows older. The ratio is larger during the first year of life because the heart is in a more transverse position in the chest.

Figure 9.1 Calculating the cardiothoracic index

Projection and position

For a CXR of a child that is able to stand, the X-ray tube is aimed so that the X-rays pass through the patient from the posterior to the anterior, yielding the PA view. This is the preferred view because the scapulae are moved out of the lung fields and because the heart, which is an anterior structure, is positioned close to the film plate and therefore is not magnified. In the case of sick children who cannot be transported to the radiology department of a hospital or clinic, a portable machine is used to obtain either an antero-posterior (AP) or a supine view.

Penetration of film

On a properly exposed radiograph, the vertebral column is barely visible through the heart shadow. If you are able to see the bronchovascular markings then the exposure is correct. You can also check for correct exposure by looking at the soft tissues around the neck and arms. If these and skin edges are very light or white, the radiograph is underexposed. If the edge of the skin line is difficult to find, the radiograph is overexposed.

Inspiration

In children *older than three years*:

• You can determine the adequacy of inspiration by counting the number of ribs that are visible above the diaphragm.

• During good inspiration, you should be able to see six to seven anterior ribs above the diaphragm. During poor inspiration, you can see five or fewer anterior ribs above the diaphragm.

Alternatively, count 10 posterior ribs. Although it is possible to do so on either side, it is better for you to count the ribs on the left side of the chest.

• You can use two methods to identify the anterior parts of ribs:
  – They appear to curve downward, whereas the posterior parts that attach to the spinal column are relatively horizontal.
  – Because they are connected to the sternum by cartilage, and cartilage is radiolucent, the anterior ribs seem to end at about the midclavicular line on a CXR.

In children of *one to three years old*:

• You can determine adequacy of inspiration by noting the following:
  – Less than one third of the heart should be projected below the apices of the hemidiaphragms.
  – Both hemidiaphragms should be rounded and the sixth or seventh anterior rib should intersect the diaphragm.
  – The lungs should be filled with air and thus are radiolucent, appearing black.

In children *less than one year old*, it is not useful for you to count the number of ribs visible above the diaphragm because while the radiograph shows lung volume in only two dimensions, the lungs inflate in all directions. Moreover, the thoracic cage is pliable and flexible, and diaphragmatic excursion is far less than in adults. Therefore, your evaluation of the degree of inspiration in infants is more a matter of your practical experience than your scientific knowledge.

Rotation

In children *three years and older*, the easiest way in which you can detect rotation is to locate the medial ends of the clavicles. If no rotation is present, the medial ends of the clavicles are equidistant from the sternum and they look symmetrical. If you can see more of the medial end of the right clavicle, the child was rotated to the right for the radiograph, and vice versa.

In children younger than *three years*:

- It is more challenging for you to determine rotation because the medial ends of the clavicles are difficult to see.

- The easiest way is to look first at the cardiac shadow. Note that the side of the chest that has the greater than usual amount of cardiac shadow may be the direction toward which the child was rotated.
- Also look for longer segments of the anterior ribs. The side that has the longest anterior rib segments is the side opposite to the direction of rotation.
- A third way is to compare hyperlucency of one lung with the other. The lung that appears most radiolucent is the direction toward which the child was rotated. Rotation of the chest to one side or the other is the most common cause of apparent hyperlucency of one lung.

10 How to do a skin test for tuberculosis in a child

HAROON SALOOJEE AND IAN COUPER

Tuberculoprotein, or tuberculin, in the form of purified protein derivative (PPD) is an antigen used to aid the diagnosis of tuberculosis (TB) infection. There are several kinds of tuberculin skin tests, the most reliable of which is the Mantoux method.

Indications in children *younger than six years* are as follows:

- Symptoms or signs suggestive of TB
- A positive contact history
- Any child in whom TB is suspected, including those with pneumonia and loss of weight

Positive results are difficult to interpret in children *older than six years*.

You need to note that children who have had a reactive TB skin test in the past will probably always show a positive result to a test in the future – do not use the test again in attempting to diagnose TB.

Equipment and procedure for a Mantoux test

To perform a Mantoux test, you need the following:

- An alcohol swab
- A syringe, preferably 1 ml, such as a tuberculin or insulin syringe
- A 25-gauge needle with a short bevel, or the smallest size available

You should follow this procedure to perform the TB test:

- The test is usually done on the anterior aspect of the forearm, about half way between the wrist and the elbow. The left arm is preferred. Request the parent or nurse to support the forearm gently but firmly.
- Clean the skin on the arm at the injection site either with an alcohol swab or with soap and water. Allow the skin to dry before administering the injection.

- Into the most superficial layer under the skin (that is intradermally), inject 0.1 ml of PPD (RT23 2 tuberculin units or PPD-S 5 tuberculin units) with the bevel of the needle facing upwards.
- You have reached the correct depth if a small bump, or weal, forms as the tuberculin is injected. If a weal does not appear, you have injected the tuberculin too deeply and you need to repeat the injection.
- Instruct the parent and/or the child to keep the site uncovered and not to scratch or rub the area.
- Instruct the parent that should severe swelling, itching or pain occur, they must contact you or the clinic immediately.
- Record the date and time that you did the test on the child's clinic record or Road to Health card.

Measurement of results of a Mantoux test

To measure the results of the test, you need to do the following:

- Read the test 48–72 hours after administering the injection. It is better to read the test closer to 72 hours as the reaction is greatest then, thereby reducing the chances of a false negative reading.
- Measure the horizontal induration or hard swelling that is palpable, not just visible, at about 90 degrees to the long axis of the forearm. Use the "ball-point technique" for doing this accurately. Holding a pen perpendicular to the skin, draw a transverse line starting about 1 cm from the margin of the reaction, and move towards the reaction. The pen usually stops where it encounters the induration. Repeat on the opposite side of the reaction. The distance between the two pen marks is the width of induration.
- Use a tape measure or ruler to measure the induration. Record the result in millimetres (no induration = 0 mm).

36 Van Schaik Publishers

Interpretation of results

There are different cut-off points for the test results (that is width of induration) for children of different ages, children with HIV and other risk groups. The following provides some guidelines.

When the induration resulting from the PPD test is *less than 5 mm* then you can conclude that the test is negative. You can interpret a negative test result to mean that the child has not been infected with the tuberculosis bacteria, or that he has been infected recently and insufficient time has elapsed for the body to react to the skin test. An apparently "negative reaction" may also be due to an inability to mount a response due to severe immunosuppression, including severe TB. Significantly, a negative skin test does not exclude TB, especially in a child that is ill.

If the child's immune system is suppressed – in the case, for example, of HIV infection, severe malnourishment or prednisone therapy – and if he has had household contact with an adult with active TB and his clinical condition is suggestive of TB, then an induration *equal to or greater than 5 mm* can be considered positive.

If the child's clinical condition is suggestive of TB then an induration *equal to or greater than 10 mm or more* can be considered positive.

When the induration is *equal to or greater than 15 mm* then you can conclude that the test is positive in any person tested.

False positive and negative results

False positives can result from a previous natural infection with *M tuberculosis*, from infection with a variety of non-tuberculosis mycobacteria (that is a cross-reaction), or from a TB vaccination with a live but weakened (attenuated) mycobacterial strain, such as Bacillus Calmette-Guérin (BCG). There is no reliable way for you to ascertain whether a positive TB skin test is due to a previous vaccination against TB. However, it is uncommon for reactions due to BCG to be equal to or greater than 5 mm, especially more than two years after the vaccination was administered.

Up to 20% of people infected with TB may not have a reactive skin test. **False negatives** may result from

- immunosuppression, such as AIDS, severe malnutrition, acute infection, cancer and recent chemotherapy
- live vaccinations, for example measles and polio, within the last four weeks
- recent or current viral infections
- poor administration technique.

Response to the result

Your response to the test result should depend on the clinical condition of the child. In general following a **negative** test result, you should observe the child. However, start TB prophylaxis using the standard regimen in children under five years who are direct household contacts of adults with active TB. If you strongly suspect TB, for example in cases of weight loss and history of exposure to a smear-positive contact, start the child empirically on TB treatment, investigate him for microbiological evidence of TB and repeat the skin test after one month.

A **positive** test result does not necessarily mean that the child has active TB. You need to do further testing. Obtain a chest X-ray and examine it for disseminated disease. Also obtain gastric washings if the child is younger than about five years, or sputum, and test for acid-fast bacilli. Start TB prophylaxis if the child tests positive and you have excluded active TB disease, that is the child does not have any clinical, microbiological or radiographic evidence of TB.

The tine test

Another method of TB skin testing is the multiple puncture test. It is also called the "tine test" because the small test instrument has several tiny tines that lightly prick the skin. The tines are either coated with dried tuberculin or used to puncture through a film of liquid tuberculin.

You can read the test by measuring the size of the largest papule. Because it is impossible for you to precisely control the amount of tuberculin used in this test, the Mantoux test should rather be done, as the dose is more accurate. Positive reactions to tine tests should always be confirmed with a Mantoux test, unless there is a blister over the site of the injections (grade 3) or ulceration over the site of the injections (grade 4).

Adult health

11 How to perform a brief, appropriate neurological examination

BRYAN KIES

When you perform a neurological assessment the history that you obtain from the patient will guide the focus and extent of the examination. Common neurological symptoms are headache, seizures, weakness and sensory disturbance. You should direct the examination to detect signs of raised intracranial pressure and structural pathology in the cerebral hemispheres, brain stem, cerebellum, spinal cord, spinal roots or the peripheral nervous system.

Examination of higher mental function

The examination of cognitive functioning is described in Chapter 64 on the mini-mental state examination. The presence of a receptive or expressive dysphasia localises to the dominant cerebral hemisphere. Impaired memory and orientation indicate cerebral cortical dysfunction, as is found in dementia. Sensory inattention and astereognosis are signs of cortical sensory disturbance.

Examination of the cranial nerves

A visual field defect, such as hemianopia, quadrantanopia or scotoma, may indicate a lesion in the optic nerve, optic chiasm, optic tract, optic radiation or visual cortex. Papilloedema is usually a sign of raised intracranial pressure, but you can also find it in malignant hypertension. If diplopia is present, determine whether it is caused by a 3rd, 4th or 6th cranial nerve palsy. In a 3rd cranial nerve palsy, if the pupil is dilated, the likely cause is compression, and if the pupil is spared then an intrinsic lesion like nerve ischaemia is the likely cause.

Weakness of the lower face, with sparing of the forehead, is seen in upper motor neurone 7th nerve facial palsy, for example internal capsule or cortical lesion. Weakness of the upper *and* lower face indicates that the lesion is lower motor neurone, located in the pons or periphery, as is seen in Bell's palsy.

The combination of deafness and reduced facial sensation points to a lesion in the cerebellar pontine angle, such as an acoustic neuroma.

In a bulbar palsy, there are signs of lower motor neurone dysfunction, where dysarthria and dysphagia are accompanied by a wasted fasciculating tongue. In a pseudobulbar palsy, the signs are of upper motor neurone pathology, such as bilateral strokes, motor neurone disease or multiple sclerosis, and the tongue is spastic and the jaw jerk is brisk.

Table 11.1 summarises the tests of the cranial nerves.

Examination of the motor abilities

An abnormal gait will often characterise the patient's type of motor dysfunction. Tone, power, tendon and superficial reflexes should be symmetrical – any asymmetry points to the pathological side. Weakness, wasting and fasciculations indicate lower motor neurone pathology, which may be in the distribution of a specific peripheral nerve, such as femoral or radial, or nerve root, for example C5 or S1.

In established upper motor neurone lesions such as stroke or cerebral mass lesion, you can expect increased tone, brisk tendon reflexes, an extensor plantar response, and the upper motor neurone pattern of weakness where the weakness is maximal in the extensor muscles of the patient's arm and the flexor muscles of the leg.

You can expect upper motor neurone signs below the level of the lesion, sphincter symptoms and a sensory level in an established spinal cord lesion. In peripheral polyneuropathy the weakness is maximal in the patient's distal muscles, and his tendon reflexes are reduced or absent. In myopathy and myasthenia gravis the weakness is maximal proximally, with normal tendon reflexes and sensory examination.

Tables 11.2 and 11.3 show the reflex tests and motor system power grading.

Examination of the sensory abilities

The patient's history can guide you to focus on the regions where abnormal sensation may be demon-

Table 11.1 Tests of the cranial nerves

Cranial nerve	Function	Test
1 Olfactory	Smell	Use substances such as coffee or soap, and test one nostril at a time
2 Optic	Vision	Test visual acuity, visual fields, optic disc and pupillary response
3 Oculomotor	Eye movement	Test eye movements (test nerves 3, 4 and 6 together)
4 Trochlear	Eye movement	Test ability to look down and inward. Note possible compensatory tilt of the head or diplopia while walking down stairs
5 Trigeminal	Masseter muscle Sensory	Test ability to clench the teeth Test ability to feel sensation on both cheeks, and the corneal reflex
6 Abducens	Eye movement	Test abduction of the eye
7 Facial	Facial movement	Test the ability to raise eyebrows, wrinkle forehead, blow out cheeks, show the teeth or smile
8 Auditory	Hearing	Test hearing of whispering. Use the Rinne and Weber tests
9 Glossopharyngeal	Gag	Test the soft palate on both sides
10 Vagus	Gag	Test the soft palate on both sides
11 Accessory	Shoulders	Test the ability to lift up or shrug the shoulders using the trapezius muscle. Test turning of head with sternomastoid muscle
12 Hypoglossal	Tongue	Test the ability to stick out the tongue

Table 11.2 Reflex tests

Reflexes	Nerve roots
Biceps and brachioradialis	C5 and 6
Triceps	C7 and 8
Knee	L2, 3 and 4
Ankle	S1 and 2

Table 11.3 Grading of motor system power

Power grading	Result
0	You cannot detect active contraction
1	You can feel a flicker of muscle contraction by palpation, but no movement
2	You note that contraction is weak, but movement is possible if the limb is positioned without gravity
3	You note that contraction is weak, but movement is possible against gravity
4	You note that power is reduced, but movement is possible against gravity and resistance
5	You note normal power

strated. Encourage the patient to compare an area of normal sensation with areas of altered sensation. Remember to delineate the borders of the abnormal sensory area.

Your screening sensory examination should determine if there is

- a hemisensory disturbance, as seen in a lesion in the brain stem or internal capsule
- a sensory level, as seen in spinal cord lesion
- a "glove and stocking" peripheral reduction, as seen in peripheral polyneuropathy
- a disturbance in a dermatome, as seen in root lesions
- a disturbance in the distribution of a peripheral nerve, as seen in a mononeuropathy.

The examination may test sharp and light touch sensation. Impaired joint position sense is indicative of a large fibre neuropathy or spinal posterior column pathology.

In your notes, include reference to the dermatomes. Figure 11.1 shows the anterior and posterior views of the dermatomes.

Examination of coordination

In cerebellar hemisphere lesions the signs include nystagmus, intention tremor and heel-shin ataxia. In central cerebellar lesions gait ataxia is prominent.

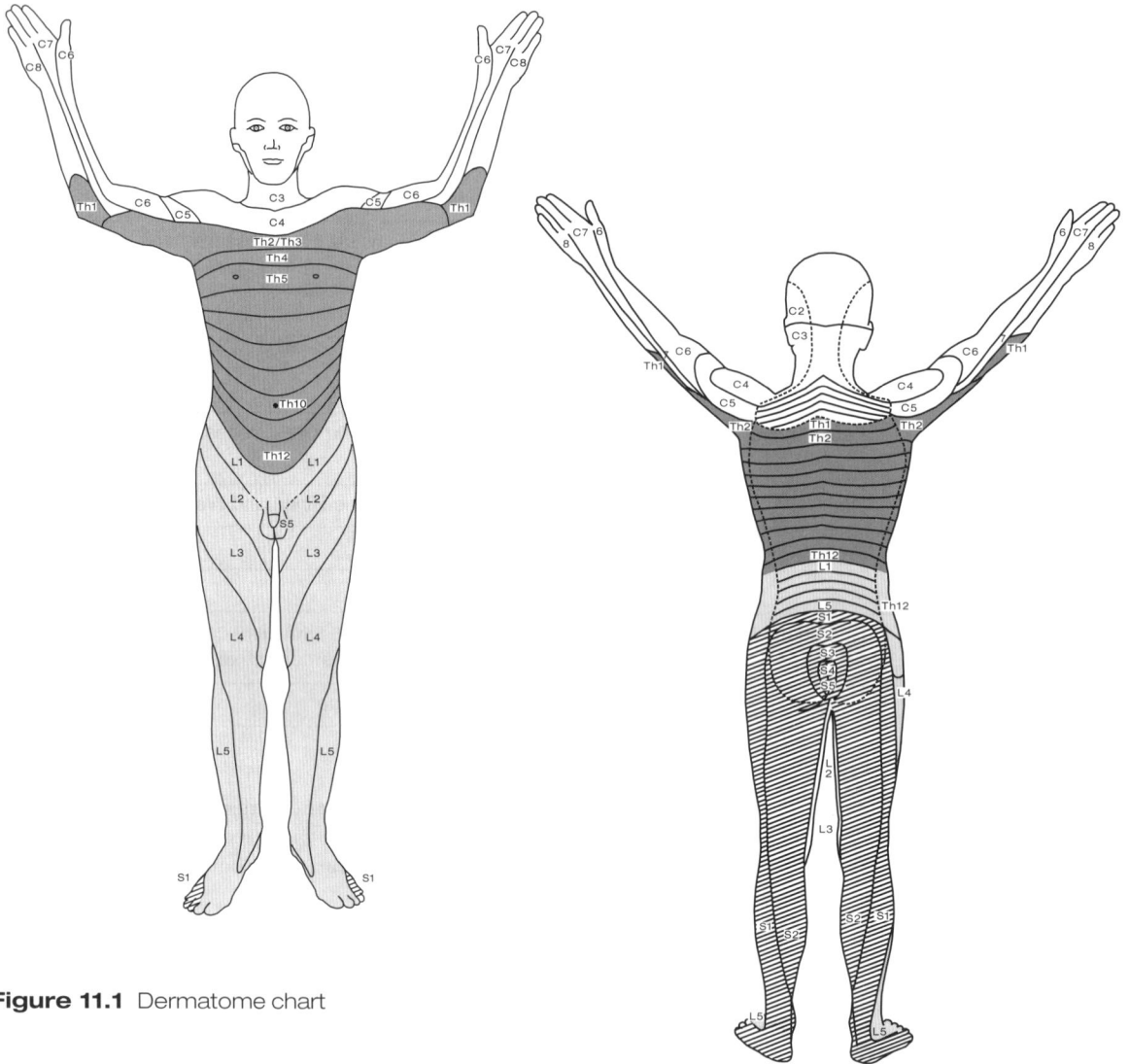

Figure 11.1 Dermatome chart

Here is an example of an abbreviated neurological examination that looks for focal neurological signs or raised intracranial pressure (Burch & Keeton 2000: 52).

For the exam, ask the patient to remove his socks and shoes.

During the exam, note whether the patient

- can walk heel-to-toe towards the examination couch
- can lift himself up on his toes and then on heels
- is able to open his mouth and move the tongue from side to side.

To guide the exam, you can

- perform the Romberg test
- palpate the patient's scalp for scars, old fractures and surgical lesions
- perform fundoscopy
- test the patient's eye movements, facial expressions and hearing ability.

Upper limbs	Power	shoulder abduction and wrist extension
	Reflexes	biceps and triceps reflex
	Coordination	finger-nose test, alternating movements test both hands
Lower limbs	Power	hip flexion
	Reflexes	knee and ankle reflexes, plantar response
	Coordination	heel-shin test
Whole body	Sensation	light touch and pinprick on face, arm and leg (proximally and distally)

Van Schaik Publishers

12 How to perform a lumbar puncture in an adult

CYRIL NAIDOO AND ANDREW ROSS

Indications

You can carry out a lumbar puncture (LP) for diagnostic purposes, therapeutic purposes – such as when you need to inject a cytotoxic agent – or when performing a myelogram. You should consider the need for an LP in any patient with

- neck stiffness
- unexplained fever
- altered level of consciousness
- an unexplained fit
- a high index of suspicion for meningitis and signs of meningism, that is neck stiffness, Kernig's sign

(passive extension of the knee while the hip is flexed causes pain) or Brudzinski's sign (which is flexion of the neck producing reflex flexion of the hips and knees). This is shown in Figures 12.1 and 12.2.

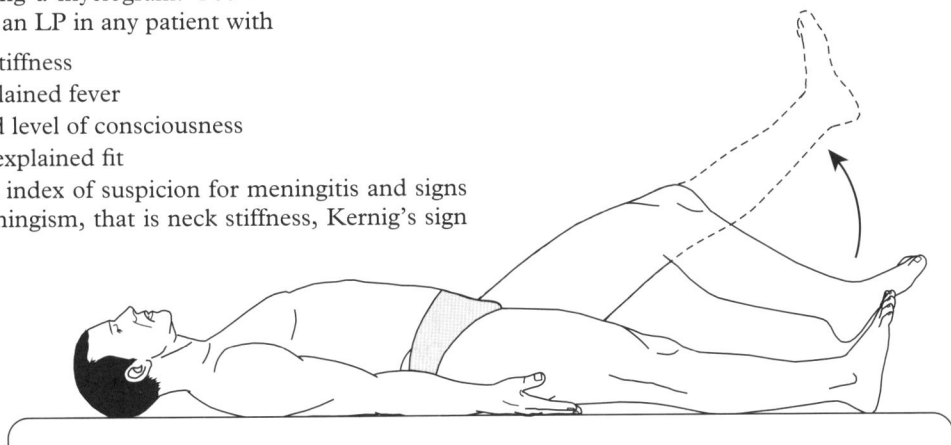

Figure 12.1 Passive extension of the knee while the hip is flexed causes pain, which indicates Kernig's sign

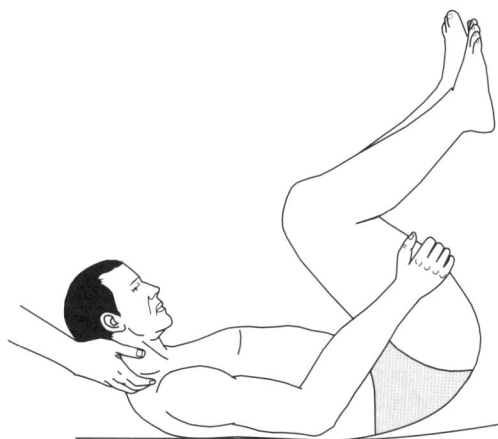

Figure 12.2 Flexion of the neck produces reflex flexion of the hips and knees, which indicates Brudzinski's sign

Contraindications

You must not perform an LP if there is

- infection at the LP site
- suspected raised intracranial pressure
- severe thrombocytopaenia
- suspected cord compression.

Procedure

Before you begin the procedure, explain to the patient what you are going to do, so that he knows what to expect. Discuss the indications and the possible complications, and obtain the patient's consent.

Place the patient on the edge of the bed in the knee-to-chest, or foetal, position with the neck flexed. If the LP is not possible in this position, attempt the procedure while the patient is in a sitting position.

Using a sterile technique, prepare the trolley with the necessary equipment and open all the appropriate supplementary packs. Also, take blood from the patient so that you can compare the blood glucose level to the CSF glucose level.

You need to follow this procedure when performing an LP:

- Scrub your hands and forearms, and put on sterile gloves.
- Clean and drape the area.
- Identify the site. The L 3/4 space lies level with the iliac crest – you can use this space or anywhere below it. The site is illustrated in Figure 12.3.

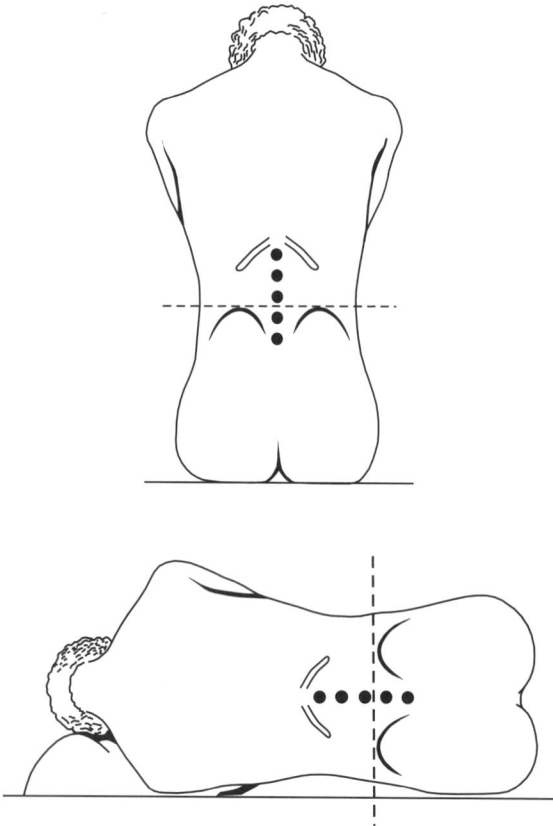

Figure 12.3 Surface anatomy of the L 3/4 space

- Using a 20- to 22-gauge spinal needle, insert the bevel, with the stylet attached, perpendicular to the long axis of the spine or slightly angulated towards the umbilicus.
- You may feel a slight resistance as the needle passes through the ligamentum flavum, the dura and the arachnoid layers. This is often 4–5 cm deep.
- Push the needle slightly beyond the resistance. The procedure is shown in Figure 12.4.

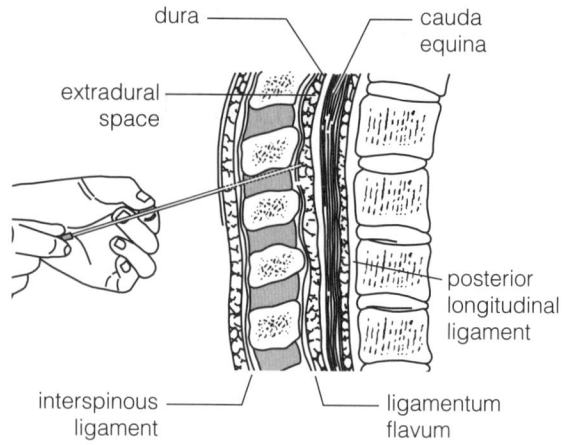

Figure 12.4 Inserting the LP needle

- Withdraw the stylet and collect the flow of cerebrospinal fluid (CSF). If you are going to do manometric studies, put the manometer in place and allow the CSF to run up the column. Read off the height. Normal CSF pressure is 100–150 mm CSF.
- If you encounter bone, withdraw the needle and re-insert it at a different angle. If the position appears correct but CSF does not appear, rotate the needle to free any obstructing nerve roots.
- Having collected sufficient fluid, that is about 3–5 ml per specimen bottle, remove the needle.
- Dress the site with a clean gauze swab and a dressing.
- Once the procedure is complete, the patient should lie on his back for a few hours to decrease the incidence of post-LP headache.
- Make notes in the patient's record of the time of the procedure, the number of attempts, and the clarity and colour of the CSF.
- Compare the CSF glucose level with the glucose level of the blood that you took earlier. The CSF glucose level should be two thirds of the patient's blood glucose.
- Label the specimen bottles correctly and have them taken to the laboratory. Commonly, you could ask the laboratory to test for the following:
  - Microscopy, culture and sensitivity
  - Total protein, globulin, chloride and glucose
  - If you suspect cryptococcal infection, ask for an Indian ink stain. Antigen testing can be performed if the stain test result is negative.
  - If you suspect TB, ask for a Ziehl-Nielsen stain for acid- and alcohol-fast bacilli (AFBs) and culture.

13 How to do a rapid musculoskeletal screening examination

BOB MASH

When a patient complains of generalised body pains, painful joints or stiffness, it is helpful for you to have a rapid method of screening for musculoskeletal problems before you embark on a more detailed examination. You can then focus on any abnormalities that you picked up during the screening.

For the screening, have the patient sitting on a chair with his shoes and socks removed.

Table 13.1 summarises the steps you need to take to perform the screening.

Table 13.1 Screening for musculoskeletal problems

Focus on	Ask the patient	Observe and evaluate
Temporo-mandibular joint (TMJ)	Open and close your mouth Jut your lower jaw forward	Range of motion of TMJ
Cervical spine	Turn your head to the left side then to the right. Tilt your head to the left then to the right, towards the shoulders	Cervical rotation and lateral flexion
Shoulders (both at the same time)	Place your hands behind your head, elbows to the side Lower your arms Move your hands behind you to the small of your back	Glenohumeral, sternoclavicular and acromioclavicular movement
Elbows (both at the same time)	Bring your arms forward, straight in front of you Bend then straighten both elbows	Flexion and extension
Wrists (both at the same time)	Hold your hands out in front of you with the palms down Bend hands down Bend hands up Turn your hands over, palms up	Swelling or deformity Flexion, extension and supination
Hands/fingers (both at the same time)	Make a fist Extend and stretch the fingers out Touch each fingertip to the thumb of the same hand Gently squeeze across the patient's metacarpo-phalangeal joints	Flexion and extension Fine precision/dexterity Tenderness
Hips (first one side then the other)	Raise your foot 15 cm off the floor keeping the knee bent Move your knee out and then in over the midline Repeat this with the other leg	Flexion, abduction and adduction

Table 13.1 Screening for musculoskeletal problems (continued)

Focus on	Ask the patient	Observe and evaluate
Knees (first one side then the other)	Bend your knee Straighten your knee Repeat this with the other leg	Swelling or deformity Flexion and extension
Ankles/feet (first one side then the other)	Lift your foot off the floor and bend the foot up Straighten and stretch your ankle Turn the sole of your foot inwards and then outwards Repeat this with the other foot	Swelling Dorsiflexion and plantar flexion Inversion Eversion
Spine	Stand up Bend forwards and attempt to touch the floor without bending the knees	Ability to rise out of the chair (spine, hips, knees and ankles) Lumbar spine and hip flexion
Gait	Walk the distance of the room then return	Symmetry, smooth rhythmic flow The knee should be extended at heel strike and flexed at all other phases of the swing Ability to turn quickly

Source: Doherty, Dacre, Dieppe, Snaith 1992, as adapted by the Pharmacia Patient Partners 2000

14 How to examine for and inject a painful shoulder

MOSEDI NAMANE

Screening for shoulder problems

To screen for a shoulder problem, ask the patient

- to fully raise his arm, that is full abduction
- to place his hand behind his head, that is external rotation at 90-degree abduction in which his hand is placed behind the head with the elbow pulled fully back
- to place his hand behind his back to touch his shoulder blade on the other side, that is internal rotation in extension where the hand should be able to touch the opposite scapula.

If your patient is able to do this without experiencing pain then there is no shoulder disease and the pain is referred – most commonly from the neck, rarely but possibly from the diaphragm.

Inspection

Ask the patient where he feels the pain. If he points to the insertion of deltoid in the upper arm the pain is typical of a rotator cuff syndrome. If he points to the lower neck region unilaterally then you need to inspect his neck as the source of pain. Bilateral pain in the lower neck region is often stress-related or part of a fibromyalgia syndrome. Pain may also be localised to the acromioclavicular joint or experienced diffusely over the shoulder from the glenohumeral joint. Look for asymmetry between the shoulders, for previous trauma and for muscle wasting.

Movements

In order to examine the patient's shoulder movements, you need to check his range of flexion, extension, internal and external rotation, and abduction. The screening test above tests most of these active movements, but you can also test passive range of movement. To check the rotation, ask the patient to keep the flexed elbow close to his side and test for internal and external rotation. The forearm acts as a pointer of range of rotation. Limitation of movement in all directions is typical of a "frozen shoulder", which results from adhesive capsulitis or glenohumeral joint disease.

We will now explore the methods for testing certain aspects of the patient's movement.

Painful arc

Ask the patient to abduct his arm and to tell you when he experiences pain. Difficulty or weakness initiating abduction may indicate a tear of the rotator cuff. Pain in the region of 70–120 degrees suggests impingement of the rotator cuff, and pain on full abduction suggests pain from the acromioclavicular joint. This could be the result of osteoarthritis, for example when the joint may be tender and may produce crepitus as well.

Impingement sign

Press on and just below the acromion and abduct the patient's arm passively. If this causes him pain then the rotator cuff may be impinging in the subacromial space with inflammation.

Resisted abduction

Ask the patient to keep his internally rotated arm, that is with his thumb pointing downwards, abducted at 70 degrees while you push downwards. Inflammation or impingement of the rotator cuff will cause pain and the patient may not be able to resist your pressure. Note that this differentiates rotator cuff from joint pain, as in this procedure the joint is not moving and therefore is unlikely to be the source of the pain.

Apprehension test

Stand behind the patient and abduct his shoulder to 90 degrees. Slowly externally rotate his shoulder while pushing forward on the humeral head with the thumb of your other hand. The patient's experience of apprehension, fear or refusal may indicate chronic anterior instability.

Draw test

Draw one of the patient's hands across his chest towards and even beyond the other shoulder. This places stress on the acromioclavicular joint and will elicit pain in the joint when it is diseased.

Once you have established the cause and site of the patient's shoulder pain, you can consider the need for an injection. Advise your patient to rest the joint for 24–48 hours after any steroid injection.

Injection of a subacromial bursa – the lateral approach

You can inject the subacromial bursa to treat inflammation of the rotator cuff or the glenohumeral joint, as the two structures communicate.

To use the lateral approach for the injection, you need to follow this procedure (see Figure 14.1):

- Prepare the injection with 40–80 mg methyl prednisolone acetate (Depo-Medrol), or 6 mg betamethasone (Celestone Soluspan) with 1 ml 2% lignocaine.
- Feel along the inferior aspect spine of the scapula to where it turns sharply at the site of the acromion.
- Palpate the depression between the acromion and the head of the humerus.
- Follow an aseptic technique. Insert the blue 23G or black 22G needle below the acromion to a depth of 1.5 cm and at an upwards angle beneath the acromion of about 10 degrees below the horizontal.

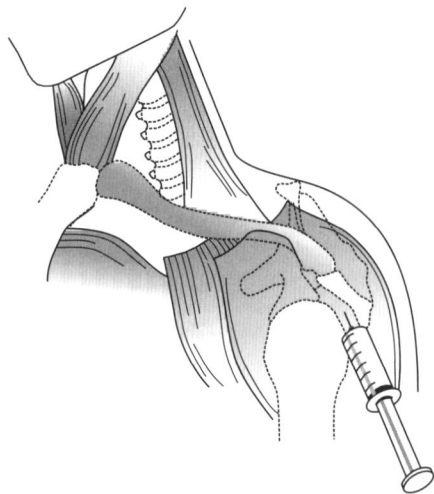

Figure 14.1 Injection of the subacromial bursa – a lateral approach

The injection should be easy and neither meet with resistance nor cause pain.

If your diagnosis is correct the lignocaine will quickly relieve the pain.

The posterior approach

This approach is easier than the lateral in a well-built or obese patient. To use the posterior approach for the injection, you need to follow this procedure (see Figure 14.2):

- Prepare the injection with 40–80 mg methyl prednisolone acetate (Depo-Medrol), or 6 mg betamethasone (Celestone Soluspan) with 1 ml 2% lignocaine.
- Feel along the inferior aspect spine of the scapula to where it turns sharply at the site of the acromion.
- Insert the blue 23G needle about 1 cm below and 1 cm medial to this point and aim upwards about 45 degrees to the horizontal and towards the sternoclavicular joint.

The injection should be easy and neither meet with resistance nor cause pain.

If your diagnosis is correct the lignocaine will quickly relieve the pain.

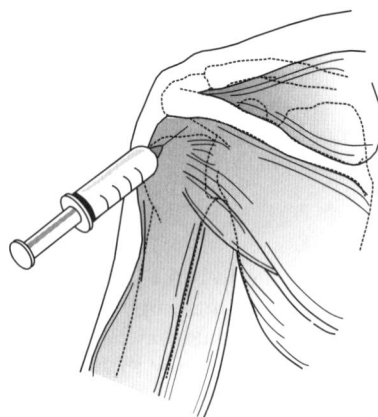

Figure 14.2 Injection of the subacromial bursa – a posterior approach

Injection of the glenohumeral joint – the anterior approach

To use the anterior approach for this injection, you need to follow this procedure:

- Prepare the injection with 40–80 mg methyl prednisolone acetate (Depo-Medrol), or 6 mg betamethasone (Celestone Soluspan) with 1 ml 2% lignocaine.
- Palpate anteriorly for the coracoid process and the head of the humerus.

- Identify the depression between them just lateral to the coracoid.
- Approach from in front in the sagittal plane and, with a blue 23G needle, enter the glenohumeral joint.

Injection of the acromioclavicular joint

To administer this injection, follow this procedure:

- Prepare the injection with 4–10 mg methyl pred-nisolone acetate (Depo-Medrol) with 0.5 ml 2% lignocaine.
- Palpate along the clavicle to feel the site of the acromioclavicular joint at the distal end.
- Identify the bony outlines and mark the site between the distal end of the clavicle and the acromion.
- Clean the skin and, with an aseptic technique, inject from above into the joint space using an orange 25G or brown 26G needle.

15 How to examine for and inject tennis elbow and golfer's elbow

MOSEDI NAMANE

Lateral epicondylitis, or tennis elbow

The condition is an enthesitis of the common extensor origin at the lateral humeral epicondyle. The inflammation is usually caused by strain or trauma. The patient complains of elbow pain that is aggravated, for example, when he opens a door, wrings out washing, drives a car or does gardening. On examination you find tenderness over the lateral epicondyle. Pain can also be produced at this site by resisted dorsiflexion of the wrist.

Medial epicondylitis, or golfer's elbow

The lesion is similar to the tennis elbow but occurs at the medial humeral epicondyle, which is the site of the common flexor origin. Here, the symptoms are exacerbated by resisted volarflexion of the wrist.

Management

For a mild condition you can prescribe non-steroidal anti-inflammatory drugs (NSAIDs) and refer your patient for physiotherapy.

In the case of failed conservative therapy or a severe condition, it is advisable that you administer a steroid injection. Follow this procedure:

- Prepare a mixture of 3–6 mg betamethasone (Celestone Soluspan) and 0.5 ml 2% lignocaine in a small syringe.
- Use a 23- or 25-gauge needle for the patient's comfort, and a sterile technique.
- At the site of maximal tenderness, insert the needle at right angles to the skin and gently advance it until the point rests on the bone.
- Inject the steroid mixture fanning out over the area.
- Advise your patient to rest the joint for 24–48 hours post-injection for maximum benefit.

Figures 15.1 and 15.2 illustrate the method of administering injections for the two abovementioned conditions.

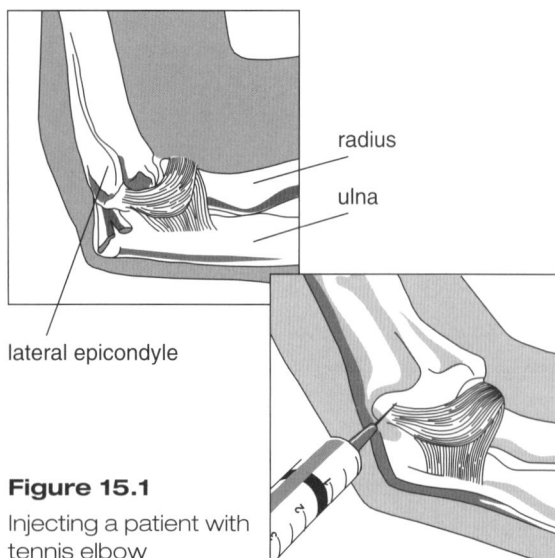

radius

ulna

lateral epicondyle

Figure 15.1

Injecting a patient with tennis elbow

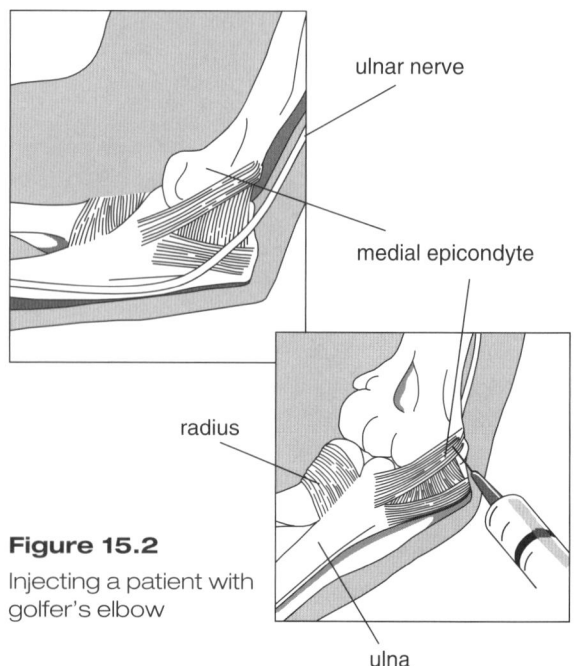

ulnar nerve

medial epicondyte

radius

Figure 15.2

Injecting a patient with golfer's elbow

ulna

How to examine for and inject De Quervain's tenosynovitis

MOSEDI NAMANE

De Quervain's tenosynovitis is inflammation of the tendons of the abductor pollicis longus and extensor pollicis brevis muscles. These two tendons form the radial border of the anatomical "snuff-box" at the base of the thumb. With overuse, resulting from repetitive cutting of material with scissors, for example, inflammation of these tendons may develop at the point where the tendons cross the radial styloid process.

The patient complains of wrist pain and pain on extension with abduction of the thumb. On examination you may see swelling and/or redness. Palpation is painful and there may be warmth at the site of pain. When the thumb is moved you may feel crepitus as the inflamed tendon slides through its sheath. At times, pain is poorly localised – you can elicit pain in the tendon by stretching it. This manoeuvre is called the "Finkelstein test" and it is shown in Figure 16.1.

If the symptoms disable the patient or persist after you use conservative measures, such as oral non-steroidal anti-inflammatory drugs (NSAIDs), resting the wrist joint with a splint or physiotherapy, you should inject a steroid into the tendon sheath. You need to follow this procedure:

- Prepare the injection with 3 mg betamethasone (Celestone Soluspan) and 0.5 ml 2% lignocaine.
- Identify the most tender area and mark the skin at the site.
- Clean the site with an antiseptic solution.
- Using a sterile technique, fit a 25-gauge needle to the syringe.
- Insert the needle obliquely along the line of the tendon just below your marking. Figure 16.2 shows this.
- Advance the needle while slowly injecting the steroid solution.
- When the needle enters the sheath a bleb or weal will form because the mixture enlarges the sheath. You can either see or palpate this.
- Inject the rest of the solution slowly.
- Once you have removed the needle, occlude the injection site with a plastic spray or small dressing.
- Advise the patient to rest the joint for 24–48 hours post-injection.

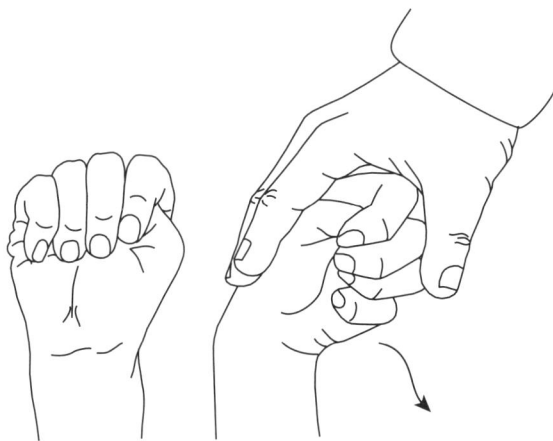

Figure 16.1 Finkelstein test

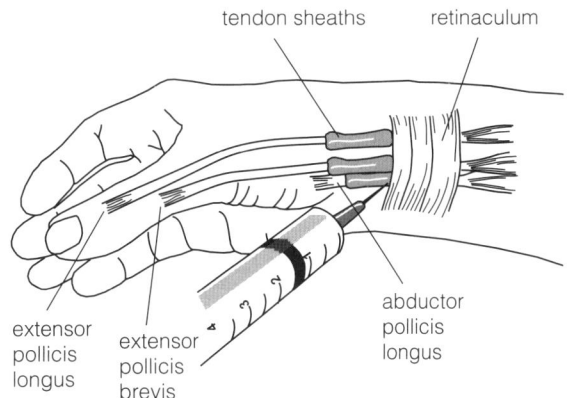

Figure 16.2 Injecting the tendon sheath in De Quervain's tenosynovitis

17 How to examine and inject for carpal tunnel syndrome

MOSEDI NAMANE

Carpal tunnel syndrome (CTS) results from median nerve compression in the carpal tunnel at the wrist, which causes pain, numbness and paraesthesia in the radial three-and-a-half fingers. The symptoms are usually worse at night, and pain can be referred up the arm. Wasting of the thenar eminence can occur when CTS has been present for a long time.

The two diagnostic signs that are employed for CTS are Phalen's sign and Tinel's sign.

Phalen's sign

This sign elicits symptoms of CTS when the patient's wrist is flexed to its maximum and held for at least one minute, as is shown in Figure 17.1.

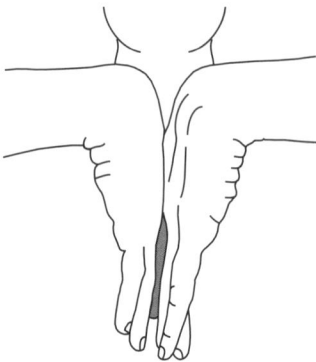

Figure 17.1 Phalen's sign test

Tinel's sign

This sign elicits symptoms of CTS when you cause pain over the distribution of the median nerve by tapping over the middle of the volar aspect of the hyper-extended wrist, as is illustrated in Figure 17.2.

Management

The underlying cause informs your method of management. For example, you should correct metabolic causes related to hypothyroidism pharmacologically.

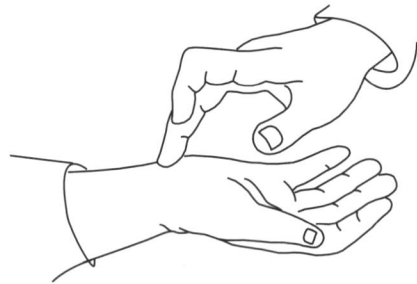

Figure 17.2 Tinel's sign test

When CTS is related to oedema of pregnancy or trauma, you can apply a wrist splint in a neutral position, particularly at night. When CTS is due to inflammation, you can also administer a steroid injection into the carpal tunnel to relieve symptoms by reducing the swelling. Figure 17.3 shows the process of administering the injection. In persistent cases, refer patients for surgical decompression of the nerve.

To administer the injection, you need to follow this procedure:

- Observe strict sterile measures.
- Identify the palmaris longus tendon by flexing the wrist against resistance.
- Prepare the injection with a mixture of 0.5 ml 2% lignocaine either 20 mg methyl prednisolone acetate (Depo-Medrol) or 3 mg betamethasone (Celestone Soluspan).
- Use a small needle – preferably a 23-gauge.
- Insert the needle at an angle of about 30 degrees to the forearm at the level of the middle or distal crease on the ulnar side of the palmaris longus tendon and for a distance of about 5–10 mm.
- Avoid piercing visible blood vessels.
- The injection should be painless and should not meet with resistance.
- Advise the patient to rest the wrist for 24–48 hours post-injection.

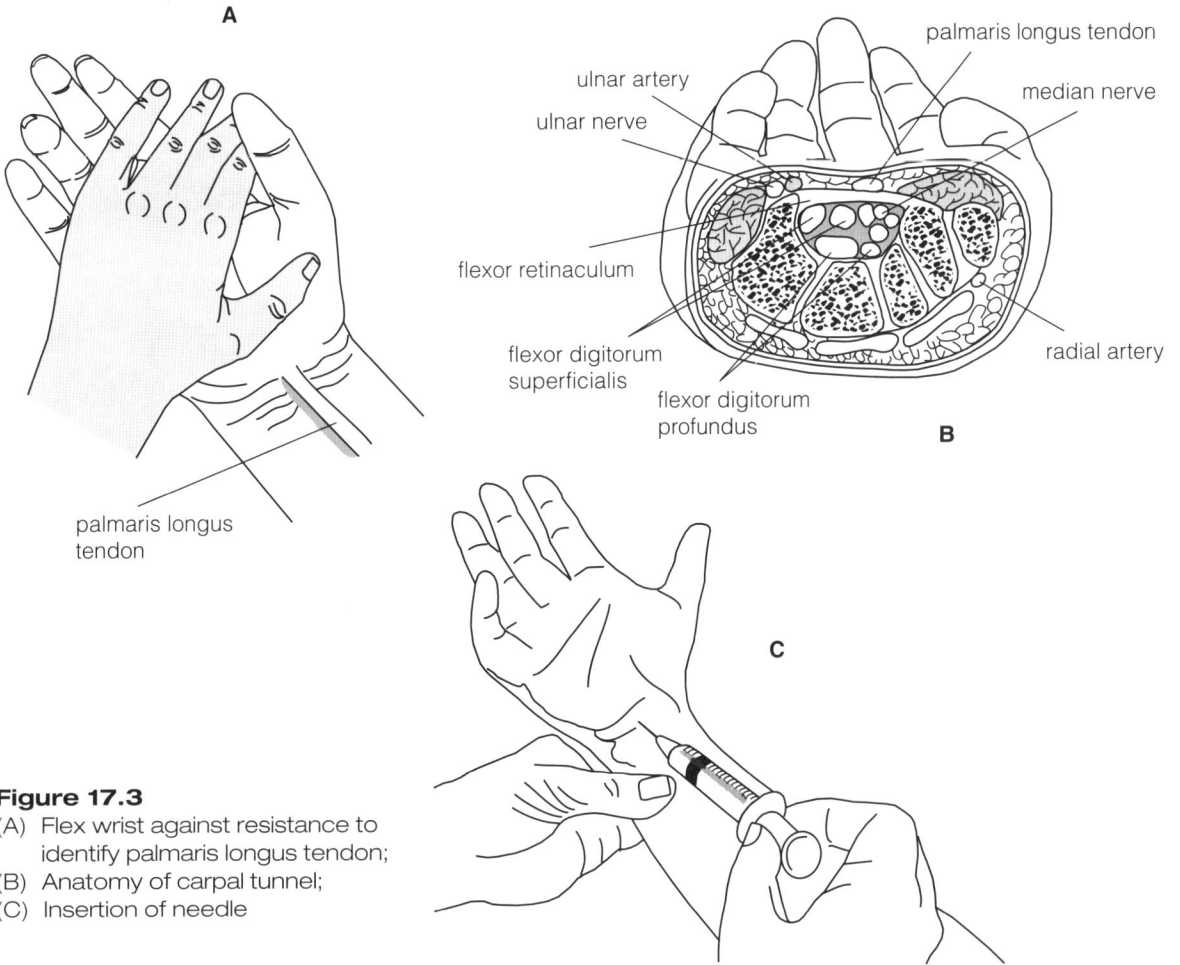

Figure 17.3

(A) Flex wrist against resistance to identify palmaris longus tendon;
(B) Anatomy of carpal tunnel;
(C) Insertion of needle

18 How to examine and assess low back pain

BOB MASH

Low back pain is common in family practice and is usually self-limiting and uncomplicated. As a family physician, you may develop a false sense of security and miss serious pathology or waste time and resources in over-assessing the majority of patients.

You can triage patients into three groups:

1. Simple low back pain. These patients may become chronic or recurrent.
2. Nerve root irritation, where the pain radiates down the leg to the foot.
3. Possible serious spinal pathology.

Look out for these signs that indicate the possibility of serious spinal pathology (Royal College of General Practitioners (RCGP) 1999):

- The patient is HIV positive (especially those in Stages 3 and 4).
- The patient has systemic upset, such as weight loss, night sweats and high temperature.
- The patient is younger than 18 years or older than 55.
- There is a history of significant trauma, with possible fractures.
- There is a history of cancer, with possible metastases.
- There is a history of chronic corticosteroid use, with possible osteoporosis.
- There are associated neurological problems, for example bladder dysfunction, bowel dysfunction, saddle anaesthesia and weakness of the lower limbs.
- The pain is thoracic.
- The pain is more inflammatory in nature – the patient suffers early morning stiffness and feels worse with rest.
- The pain is progressive and chronic.

Remember that low back pain may originate from intra-abdominal pathology. The extent of your assessment depends on how you have triaged the patient.

Assessment

We will now explore methods of assessing simple low back pain.

Stance

The patient is examined standing and sitting. A simian stance, which includes flexion of the spine, hips and knees, is suggestive of spinal stenosis. You need to look for

- any associated surface signs, such as café au lait spots, neurofibromas (indicating neurofibromatosis), hairy naevus (indicating possible spina bifida) or surgical scars
- the lumbar lordosis, or curvature, and note if it is absent (indicating possible pelvic infection, osteoarthritis or vertebral infections)
- any scoliosis, which is often protective due to pain, or due to leg shortening; note if it is fixed or mobile with posture.

Movement

The patient is standing. Ask him to touch his toes and record how far from the floor he can reach. This combines flexion of lumbar spine, thoracic spine and hips and therefore is not a discriminating test. However, it does give you some indication of the degree of loss of function.

Ask the patient to slide his hand down the outside of his leg and record how far lateral flexion is possible on each side.

Palpation

While your patient sits on the edge of the examination couch, you should palpate the following areas:

- Between the lumbar vertebral spines. Note any deformity or abnormal prominence of vertebrae which needs further investigation.
- The paraspinal muscles. These are often tender in simple low back pain.
- The sacroiliac joints. These are often tender in simple low back pain.

- The renal angles. You should further investigate any tenderness here.

Abdominal examination

The patient is supine. Exclude any evidence of intra-abdominal pathology, such as pelvic inflammatory disease, tumours or aneurysms. Consider the need to perform a vaginal or rectal examination.

The majority of your patients do not need any special investigation. In chronic simple low back pain consider the association with depression, psychosocial problems, occupational factors and occasionally secondary gain due to the expectation of financial or other compensation because of the back pain. In these cases a holistic assessment is clearly required.

Nerve root irritation

In addition to all of the above procedures, also perform the following tests.

Hip examination

Examine the hip with the patient supine, as you could confuse pain in the buttocks, groin and hip regions with nerve root irritation. Refer also to Chapter 20.

Straight leg raising

The patient is supine. Raise his straight leg from the examination couch, as is shown in Figure 18.1A. Ask him where he feels pain or paraesthesia. Pain in the leg may imply a lateral disc prolapse, and sciatic nerve roots L4, L5, S1, S2 and S3 should cause pain radiating below the knee. Pain elicited in the back may imply a central disc prolapse.

Be careful not to interpret tightness in the hamstring muscles as nerve root irritation. You can demonstrate true nerve root irritation by aggravating it with dorsiflexion of the foot (Figure 18.1B) or applying firm pressure in the popliteal fossa with your thumb and having the patient's knee slightly flexed. This is known as the "bowstring test" (Figure 18.1C).

If you doubt the genuineness of the response, ask the patient to sit up on the couch for some other reason or to straighten his legs while sitting on the edge of the couch. Genuine nerve root irritation will make both of these actions difficult.

Neurological examination

The patient is supine. Check his power, sensation (using a pinprick test) and reflexes of the lower limbs while focusing on the most likely nerve roots. See also Chapter 11.

Reverse Lasegue test

The patient is prone. Flex his knee, as shown in Figure 18.2. This puts tension on the femoral nerve

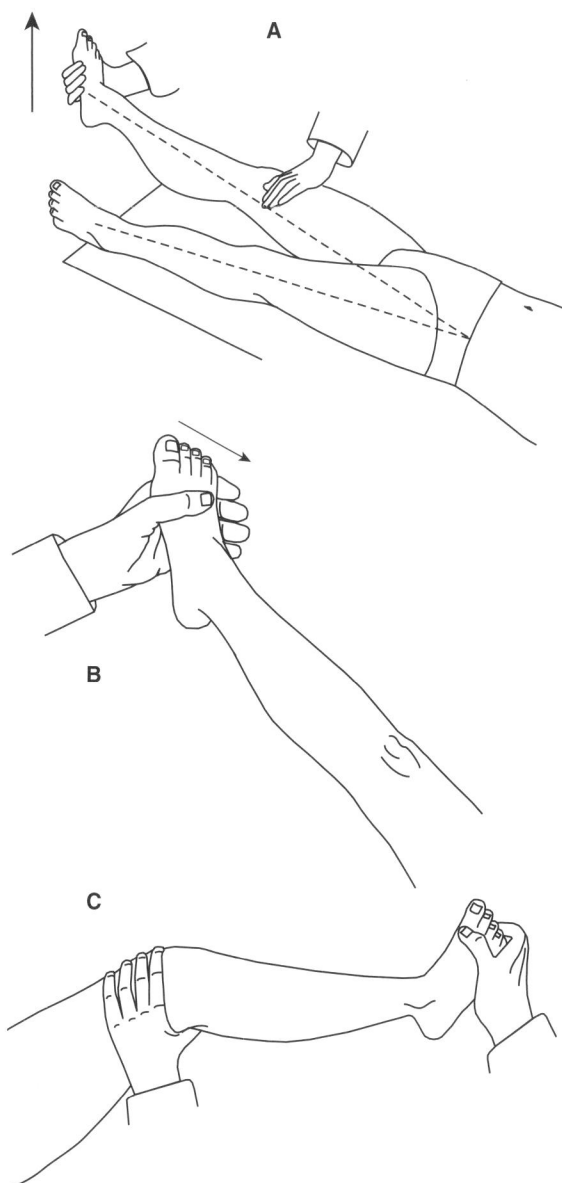

Figure 18.1 Straight leg raising test: (A) Straight leg raising; (B) Additional dorsiflexion; (C) Bowstring test

roots (L2, 3 and 4) and causes pain in its distribution. You could aggravate the irritation by extending the hip at the same time.

You should consider special investigation and referral in patients who do not improve with conservative management.

Possible spinal pathology

In addition to the procedures described above, you can also consider the following tests or measurements, when they are relevant:

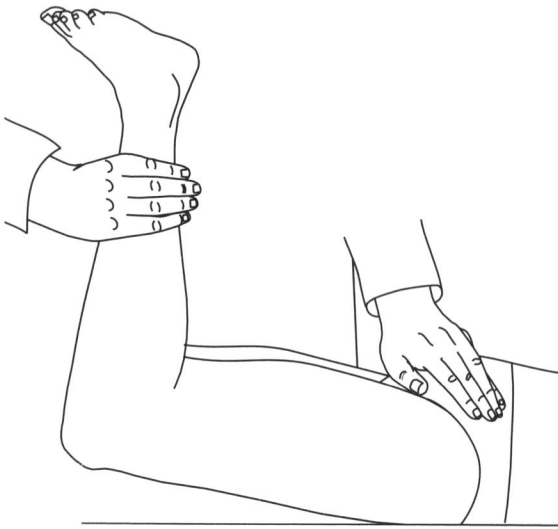

Figure 18.2 Reverse Lasegue test

- Measure the movement in your patient's lumbar spine. This is a modified version of Schober's method, and it is illustrated in Figure 18.3. Position a tape measure with the 10-cm mark level with the dimples of Venus, or the posterior superior iliac spines, while he is standing up straight. Mark the skin at 0 and 15 cm. Ask the patient to fully flex while you anchor the upper end of the tape measure. Compare the 15-cm mark on his skin with the tape measure and note the increase in distance. A normal measurement is 5 cm or more. This should be reduced in ankylosing spondylitis.

- Measure the patient's chest expansion at the level of the 4th intercostal space for ankylosing spondylitis. A normal measurement is 6 cm or more.

- A number of tests are recognised for examining the sacroiliac joints as a source of pain. All the following procedures have been suggested:
  - Flex the hip and knee while the patient is supine and forcefully adduct his hip.
  - Press down hard on the sacrum and upper natal cleft while he is prone.
  - Distract the pelvis by compressing the anterior superior iliac spines while he is supine.
  - Press firmly on the greater trochanter while he is lying on his side.

Consider all patients with possible spinal pathology for further investigation and referral.

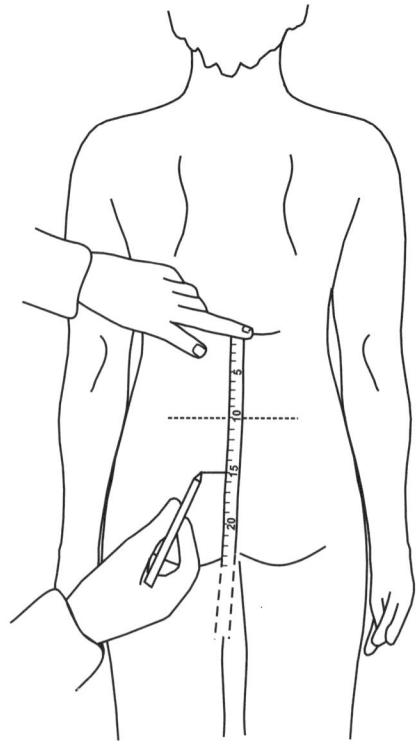

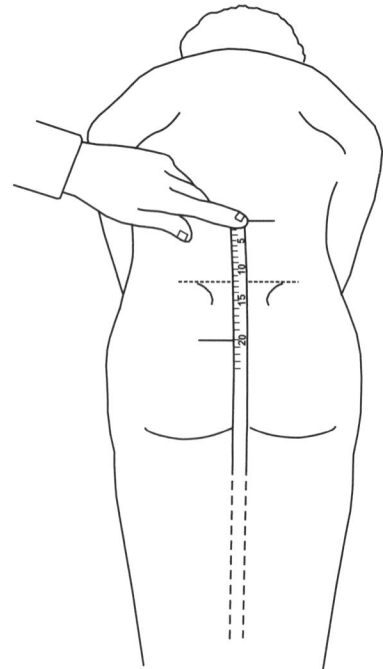

Figure 18.3 Modified Schober's method of testing for spinal pathology

Van Schaik Publishers

19 How to measure shortening of the legs

MOSEDI NAMANE

Genuine shortening of the lower limb may result in compensatory mechanisms such as pelvic tilting and lumbar scoliosis, low back pain, plantar flexion of the foot or knee flexion on the opposite side. The shortening may be caused by pathology affecting the femur or tibia, for example polio, fractures, slipped upper femoral epiphysis and Perthes' disease.

You can measure true leg length from the anterior superior iliac spine to the medial malleolus. Run a tape measure from just under the distal border of the anterior iliac spine to the inferior border of the medial malleolus while your patient is lying on the examination couch in a supine position. Figure 19.1 shows this procedure.

You can also measure apparent shortening as the distance from the xiphisternum to the medial malleolus.

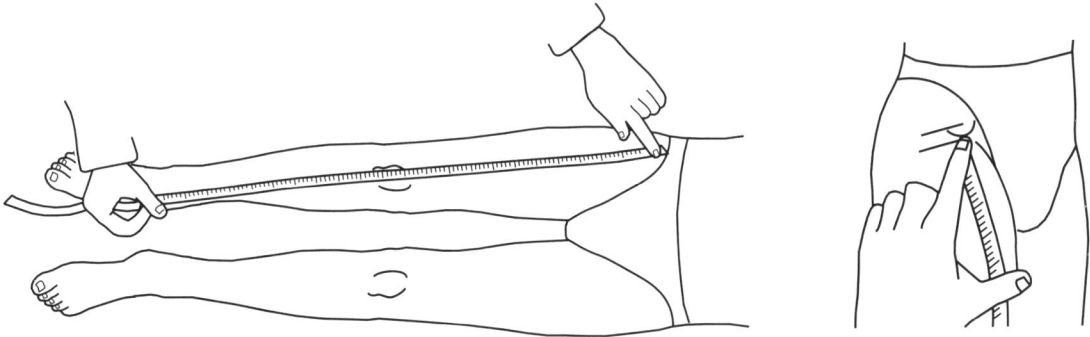

Figure 19.1 Measuring leg shortening

20 How to diagnose and inject trochanteric bursitis

MOSEDI NAMANE

Trochanteric bursitis is a common cause of soft-tissue rheumatism around a hip joint. Your patient complains of pain over the lateral aspect of the hip extending down the thigh. Be careful not to diagnose this as osteoarthritis of the hip – rather, it is inflammation of one or more of several bursae at the greater trochanter and may include tendinitis of the insertion of gluteus medius. On palpation, the inflamed bursa is tender. It is important for you to exclude hip joint pathology by examining the hip joint and making sure that there is no limitation in joint's movement.

To treat mild bursitis, prescribe analgesics and refer the patient to a physiotherapist for local application of ultrasound and shortwave diathermy. Your patient could benefit from using heat therapy over the painful site at home, such as a hot-water bottle or a warmed beanbag.

If the bursitis is severe and disabling, you should inject the site with a steroid. Follow this procedure, which is illustrated in Figure 20.1:

- Identify the palpably tender point.
- Employ strict sterile measures.
- Prepare the injection with a mixture of 6 mg betamethasone (Celestone Soluspan) or 40 mg methyl prednisolone acetate (Depo-Medrol) with 1 ml 2% lignocaine.

- Use a long 19- to 21-gauge needle that will reach the bursa, which lies over the femoral bone. In plump patients, you may need to use a spinal needle.
- Insert the needle at right angles to the skin and advance it until it touches the bone before giving the injection.
- Advise the patient to rest the leg for 24–48 hours post-injection.

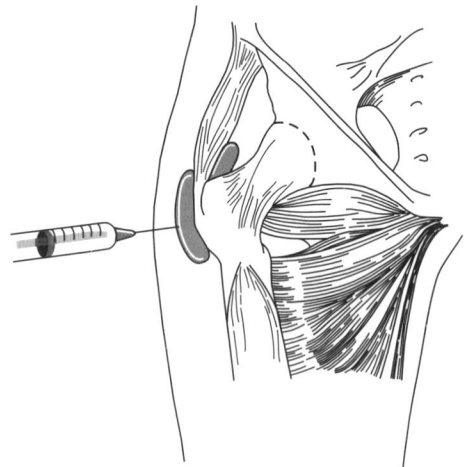

Figure 20.1 Injecting a trochanteric bursitis

21 How to examine, aspirate and inject an inflamed knee

MOSEDI NAMANE

Look for signs of inflammation such as tenderness, especially along the joint line, swelling, redness and/or warmth. You can also demonstrate fluid in the joint by doing a patella-tap or by milking fluid from one side of the joint to the other.

Patella-tap

First squeeze the synovial fluid from the suprapatella pouch downwards into the knee joint and then tap the patella against the femoral condyles, keeping your squeezing hand in position. The fluid will bounce the patella back.

Milking technique

Place the patient's knee in extension and milk the fluid into the knee joint from the suprapatella pouch. Then force the fluid to the lateral/medial side of the joint by pushing on the opposite side with your hand. The fluid that you have pushed appears as a bulge on the opposite site.

Knee arthrocentesis, or aspiration and injection of the joint

To perform a knee arthrocentesis, you need to follow this procedure:

- As always, observe a sterile technique.
- Have the patient lying supine on the examination couch with his leg extended.
- Prepare the injection with a mixture of either 40 mg methyl prednisolone acetate (Depo-Medrol) or 6 mg betamethasone (Celestone Soluspan) with 1 ml 2% lignocaine.
- The site of entry is just below the medial midpoint of the patella, that is between the medial midpoint of the patella and the medial femoral condyle. You could use a lateral approach but this is slightly more difficult. The site is between the lateral midpoint and lateral femoral condyle.

- Use either a 19- or a 21-gauge needle.
- Attach the needle to an empty syringe and insert it at right angles to the skin. This is shown in Figure 21.1.

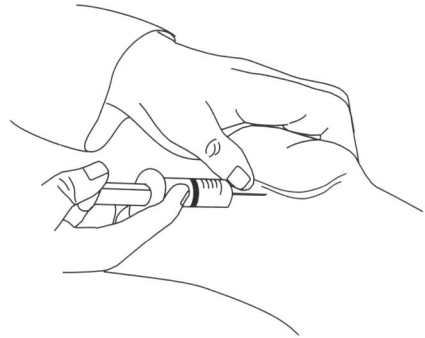

Figure 21.1 Aspirating the joint

- Once you have aspirated the synovial fluid into the syringe, remove the syringe and leave the needle *in situ*.
- Check the aspirate for blood or presence of pus. In either case, refer the patient rather than giving him the steroid injection.
- If the aspirate is neither bloody nor septic, attach the prepared syringe and inject the steroid mixture through the same needle.
- Advise the patient to rest the leg for 24–48 hours post-injection.

You can send the aspirate to the laboratory for appropriate investigations such as

- microscopy and culture
- cell count
- presence of crystals on microscopy, or polarising light, if available.

Occasionally, you may need to perform the aspiration to determine the presence of intra-articular haemorrhage following trauma.

22 How to assess an injured ankle

DAWIE VAN VELDEN

Ligament injuries of the ankle are the most common of all sports injuries that we see in general practice. They occur in most jumping sports and ball sports, such as soccer and rugby. About 85% of tears involve the lateral ligaments with only 15% involving the medial, or deltoid, ligament. Figures 22.1 and 22.2 illustrate the anatomy. The rehabilitation of these injuries is often inadequate and has serious consequences for the active sportsperson.

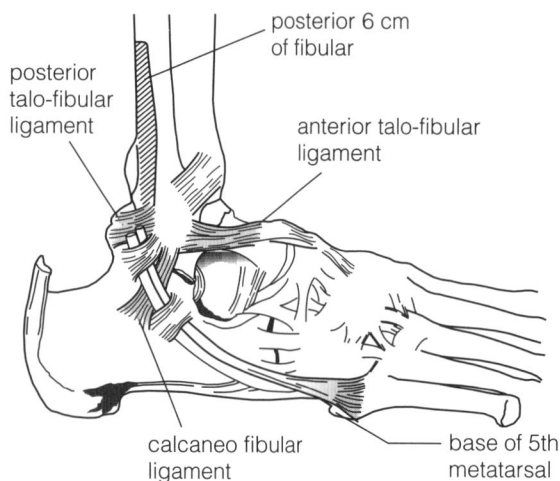

Figure 22.1 Lateral ligament anatomy

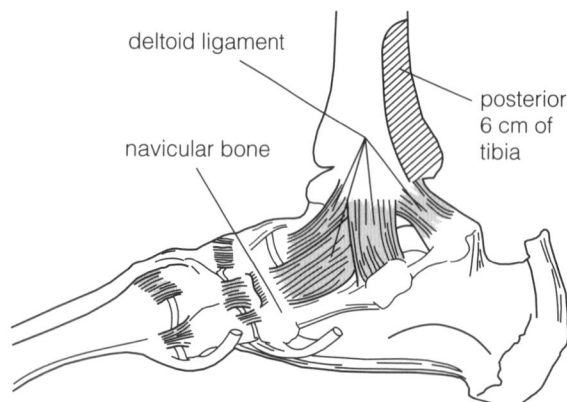

Figure 22.2 Medial, or deltoid, ligament anatomy

Mechanism of the injury

The injury is usually a supination-inward rotation or forced inversion sprain of the foot. Tears occur when the patient has exceeded the range of movement of the ankle joint. The most common injury usually involves simply an inversion force that tears the anterior talo-fibular ligament on the lateral side of the joint. With additional force, supination or adduction, tearing of the calcaneo-fibular ligament occurs. The posterior talo-fibular ligament is usually torn only in severe injuries and almost never in sports injuries.

Diagnosis

You should classify ligament injuries as Grade I, which is a sprain; Grade II, which is a partial tear; or Grade III, which is a total tear. The degree of swelling and pain is not necessarily an indication of the severity of the injury. Grade II injuries may present with minimal swelling or bruising, whereas Grade I injuries may show marked swelling and bruising.

The most important aspects of your decision concerning treatment are the stability of your patient's ankle and the likelihood of a fracture. Clinical stress testing may be done at the place where the injury occurred, before the secondary spasm has taken place. Radiological stress testing is usually done later, as X-ray facilities are frequently unavailable.

Tears of the anterior talo-fibular ligament give rise to antero-posterior laxity, which you can detect both clinically and radiologically as a positive "anterior drawer" test, that is pulling the foot forwards in relation to the tibia. If the calcaneo-fibular ligament is also torn then lateral instability will be present. These tests may be significant in athletes and patients under 40 years of age.

Ottawa rules for radiograph necessity

If you suspect a fracture, you may order a radiograph. According to the evidence-based Ottawa rules, which are applicable to patients between 18 and 55 years of age, one can safely reduce the number of radiographs taken by up to 33%. (Stiell, McKnight, Greenberg et al. 1994; Stiell, Wells & Laupacis et al. 1995). Many of the patients showing positive tests will not have a fracture, but the chance of a fracture being missed is remote and considerable cost may be saved through the application of the rules. While applying the rules, you must continue to consider other severe ligament injuries, diastasis injuries and other foot fractures.

The indications for radiography of ankle and midfoot injuries are as follows:

- The patient is unable to bear weight on his ankle or foot immediately after the injury, and cannot walk four consecutive steps in the consulting room, that is bearing weight twice on each foot.
- There is tenderness over the posterior edge of either the distal 6 cm of the fibula or tibia (which includes the malleoli – see Figures 22.1 and 22.2).
- There is tenderness over the proximal head of the 5th metatarsal, which suggests an avulsion fracture of the peroneal tendon (see Figure 22.1).
- There is tenderness over the navicular bone (see Figure 22.2).
- The patient is older than 55 years of age or younger than 18.

The Ottawa rules do not apply if he or she

- is intoxicated
- has suffered multiple painful injuries
- is pregnant
- has a head injury
- has diminished sensation due to neurological deficit.

In addition if there is tenderness over the proximal fibula neck, this suggests a fracture and associated rupture of the syndesmosis at the ankle.

Management

An ankle ligament injury that is inadequately rehabilitated may present with persistent pain and loss of function. Common associated problems are a loss of range of motion (ROM) in the ankle joint, especially dorsiflexion, weakness of the peroneal muscles and impaired proprioception. An untreated ligament injury can result in stretching of the ligament, which in turn can result in permanent instability, with recurrent sprains.

You should subject all ankle injuries in the acute phase to the routine treatment of rest, ice (that is application of an ice pack), compression and elevation (RICE) for the first 48 hours. You do not neces-sarily have to prescribe non-steroidal anti-inflammatory drugs.

Grade I and II injuries

In sprain and partial tear injuries, it is essential that you prescribe early mobilisation – you can suggest crutches, if necessary. Management involves restoration of full dorsiflexion by active and passive mobilisation of the ankle joint, a programme of strengthening exercises for the peroneal muscles as well as proprioceptive exercises. This includes extension and flexion of the ankle joint starting with ROM exercises within the range of comfort and followed by gradual resistance exercises. Ideally, a physiotherapist should supervise the patient's exercises, which you must introduce early in the rehabilitation phase.

When the ligaments are damaged, proprioceptive fibres are torn and the normal reflex that prevents the ankle from "going over" may be lost. You can encourage the patient to rehabilitate through using a "wobble board", balancing on one leg or walking on a sandy beach (an uneven surface forcing you to rehabilitate your proprioception, and at the same time offering a soft landing should you fall over!).

Grade III

In the case of a total tear, the patient's ankle may well be unstable. You need to apply plaster immobilisation at 90-degree dorsiflexion which the patient must wear for four weeks. He can use crutches initially, although partial weight bearing is allowed. Later on encourage the patient to put his full weight on the ankle whilst still in plaster, provided that this does not cause severe pain.

After removal of the plaster, rehabilitation must commence as for the partial tear, and the patient should continue the programme until he regains full movement and strength. You can support the ankle joint with adhesive strapping – preferably with a reusable external ankle brace – for three to six weeks. This provides some mechanical support by protecting the ligament from further over-stretching; it also helps to restore proprioceptive sensation in the ankle joint.

Surgical treatment

Surgery is rarely indicated. In some recorded studies the results were worse in operated cases than in non-operated cases. In the few cases that continue to show recurrent attacks of ankle instability, you may need to perform surgical reconstruction of the ankle ligaments.

Final rehabilitation

Once the patient has achieved full range and strength in the ankle, he can start functional exercises. These consist of straight-line running and sudden stopping, as well as figure-of-eight and zigzag running. The sportsman should support his ankle with an external ankle brace, such as an Aircast ankle support, throughout the rest of the season. The assistance of a bio-kinethesist is of great value in this regard as it aims at the patient's successful re-integration into competitive sport. Nevertheless, it usually takes about six to eight weeks before the patient can return to sport, even in the best hands.

Prevention

You can suggest that the patient use prophylactic strapping to support his or her ankle, although this may be expensive. The use of re-usable ankle braces is becoming more popular. Preventive bracing or strapping is advisable in patients with gross ligamentous laxity because of their heightened vulnerability to ankle injury.

23 How to examine the feet of diabetics

BOB MASH

Annually, you need to examine the feet of all Type II diabetics and of patients who have had Type I diabetes for more than five years.

Inspection

Assess the following:

- Look inside the patient's shoes for foreign bodies and inspect the soles for uneven wear.
- Check the patient's skin for callosities, corns, fungal or bacterial infection, macerated areas between the toes, trophic nail changes, atrophy or decreased sweating.
- Inspect the patient's feet for clawing of toes, hallux valgus, Charcot deformity, wasting from motor neuropathy, and surgical scars or other effects.

Palpation

On palpating the patient's feet, check the following:

- Warm feet may be due to infection, increased blood flow from sympathetic denervation or acute Charcot foot.
- Cold feet may be due to ischaemia.
- Oedema could be caused by neuropathy, infection, heavy proteinuria, heart failure or calcium antagonists.
- Weakness in the feet may be the result of motor neuropathy.
- Absent pulses could be the result of peripheral vascular disease.

Percussion

The patient's ankle reflexes may be absent, present with reinforcement or present without reinforcement.

Sensation

To check for sensation in the patient's feet, apply the following (Mollentze 2003):

- Pressure with a standardised 5.07 (10 g force) nylon monofilament. If the patient does not detect the filament at any one of the six sites shown in Figure 23.1 when applied with enough pressure to buckle the filament then there is risk of subsequent ulceration (sensitivity is more than 90% to predict ulceration).
- A pinprick test to the dorsum of the big toe. Ask the patient whether or not this is painful.
- A tuning fork (128 Hz) to the bony prominence of the dorsum of the big toe just proximal to the nail bed or medial malleolus to test the patient's ability to sense vibration.

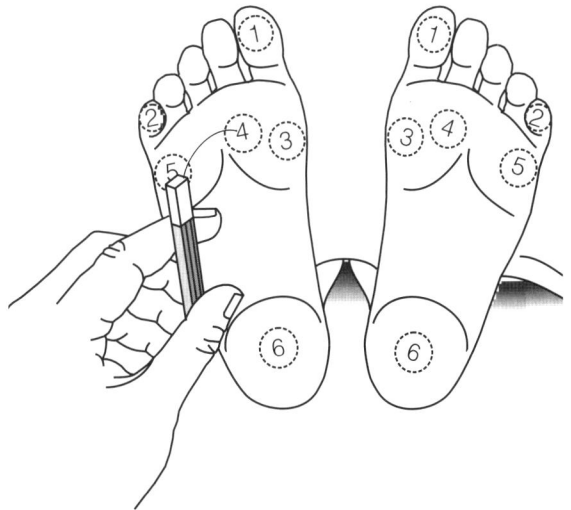

Figure 23.1 Six sites for pressure testing on the feet of a diabetic

Van Schaik Publishers 63

24 How to interpret radiographs of arthritic joints

BOB MASH

With regard to patients with joint pains you will often have a radiograph taken so that you can look for signs of arthritis. If you find signs, the radiograph can also help you to differentiate between different types of arthritis.

Osteoarthritis, or degenerative disease

Typical radiographic features of osteoarthritis (illustrated in Figure 24.1) include the following (Scarisbrick 2002):

- Localised narrowing of the joint space – due to loss of cartilage – that is most marked on the weight-bearing surfaces
- Osteophytes. These may break off the bone to form loose bodies
- Subchondral sclerosis, especially adjacent to the joint space narrowing
- Subchondral cysts

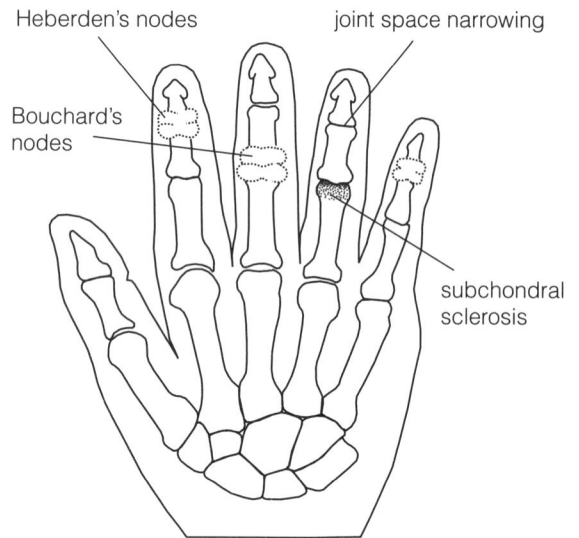

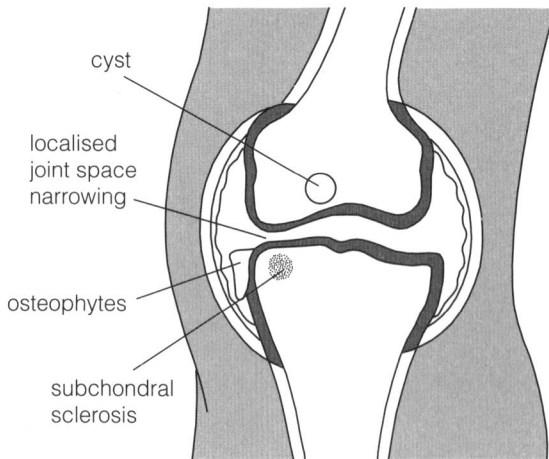

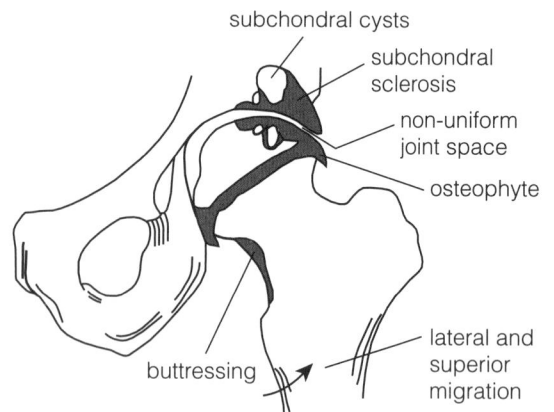

Figure 24.1 Features of osteoarthritis in small and large joints

Inflammatory arthritis

Typical radiographic features of inflammatory arthritis, illustrated in Figure 24.2, include the following (Scarisbrick 2002):

- Narrowing of the joint space that is diffuse as opposed to localised
- Central or marginal erosions
- Lack of osteophytes
- Minimal subchondral sclerosis
- Peri-articular osteoporosis. This is often the first sign
- Peri-articular soft-tissue swelling
- Cystic lesions
- Deformities, subluxations and dislocations

Other forms of arthritis

Table 24.1 summarises the features of other arthritic conditions.

Table 24.1 Features of other arthritic conditions

Type of arthritis	Features
Rheumatoid	Bilateral, symmetrical, found especially in the small joints of the hand as shown in Figure 24.2
Ankylosing spondylitis	Bilateral, symmetrical, reactive sclerosis and bony ankylosis affecting the sacro-iliac joints, pelvis and spine
Psoriatic	Asymmetrical, found in the distal joints of the hand, erosions with tapered bone ends and fluffy periostitis (this is called the "mouse ear" appearance)
Reiter's syndrome	Asymmetrical, found in the lower limbs
SLE	Bilateral, symmetrical, found especially in the hands, with reversible deformities, normal joint space, soft-tissue atrophy and osteonecrosis in major joints
Gout	Asymmetrical, lack of osteoporosis and normal joint space, soft-tissue swelling and tophi that may be calcified, erosions which have a "punched out" appearance, usually separate from the articular surface

Source: Scarisbrick 2002

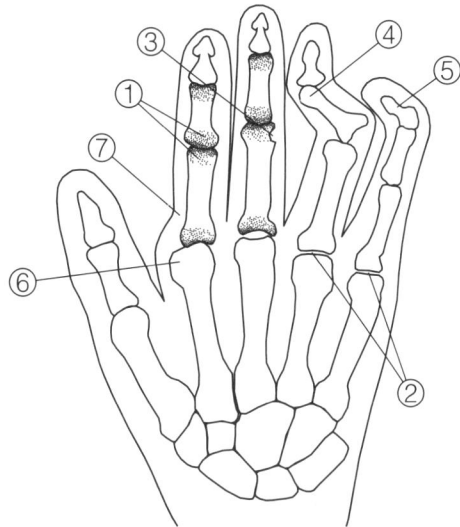

1 – periarticular osteoporosis
2 – diffuse joint space narrowing
3 – marginal erosions
4 – Boutonnière deformity
5 – swan-neck deformity
6 – subluxations and dislocations
7 – symmetrical soft-tissue swelling

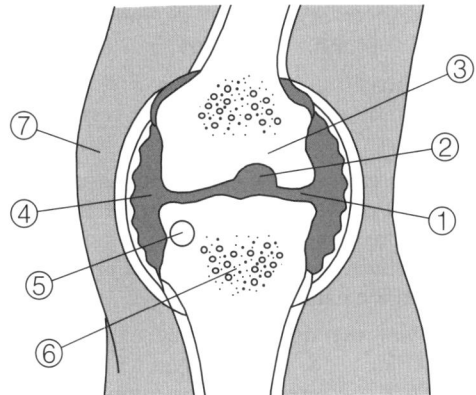

1 – diffuse joint space narrowing
2 – marginal or central erosions
3 – absent or minimal subchondral sclerosis
4 – lack of osteophytes
5 – cystic lesions
6 – osteoporosis
7 – periarticular soft-tissue swelling

Figure 24.2 Features of inflammatory arthritis in small and large joints

25 How to record an electrocardiogram

PAUL HILL

You need to record an electrocardiogram (ECG) meticulously as an incorrect recording can lead to incorrect diagnosis, assessment and management.

Procedure

You need to follow this procedure to record an ECG:

- Ensure that your patient is relaxed, comfortable and warm. In this way, you minimise the potential artefacts of muscle tremor.
- Avoid sources of electrical interference, such as mains power and other electrical instruments.
- Before attaching the electrodes, prepare the skin with a spirit wipe and remove excessive hair to ensure good electrical contact.
- Place the electrodes carefully to ensure normal shape and quality of the ECG wave form. Table 25.1 summarises, and Figure 25.1 illustrates, the ideal positions in which you should place the electrodes on the patient's body.
- When you use non-disposable electrodes, keep them clean, and through regular maintenance ensure that they are free of corrosion.

- Set the ECG paper speed at 25 mm per second.
- Set the calibration, or standardisation, to ensure that 10 mm equals 1 mV so that you can convert wave height into a meaningful voltage (see Figure 26.1). When the pressure of the writing stylus on the graph paper is correct, the standardisation signal will display perfect right angles.

Table 25.1 Ideal limb and chest positions for electrode placement

Lead	Position
RL	Right leg, inside calf between knee and ankle
LL	Left leg, as above
RA	Right arm, just above the wrist
LA	Left arm, as above
V1	Fourth intercostal space, right sternal edge
V2	Fourth intercostal space, left sternal edge
V3	Midway between V2 and V4
V4	Fifth intercostal space, midclavicular line
V5	Same level as V4, anterior axillary line
V6	Same level as V4, midaxillary line
V6R	Fourth intercostal space, right midclavicular line

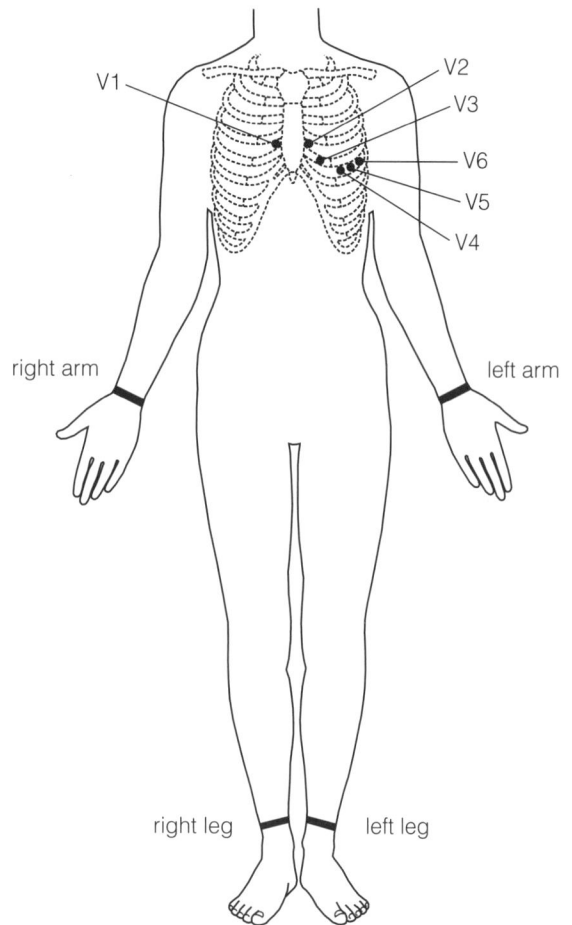

Figure 25.1 Ideal limb and chest positions for electrode placement

Van Schaik Publishers

ECG artefacts

Artefacts are *avoidable*. This fact cannot be over-emphasised. When present, the following artefacts can cause you to struggle to interpret an ECG (see Figure 25.2):

• **Baseline irregularity**, caused by mains interference or muscle tremor, may hinder your assessment of P wave morphology and rhythm.

• **Insufficient ink** or **stylus malfunction** can lead to indistinct tracings.

• **Wandering baselines** may make the ST segment, PR interval and iso-electrical line impossible to determine.

• **Intermittent tracing** may give you the impression of arrhythmias, extra beats or non-existent pauses. You may find that rhythm is thus difficult to determine.

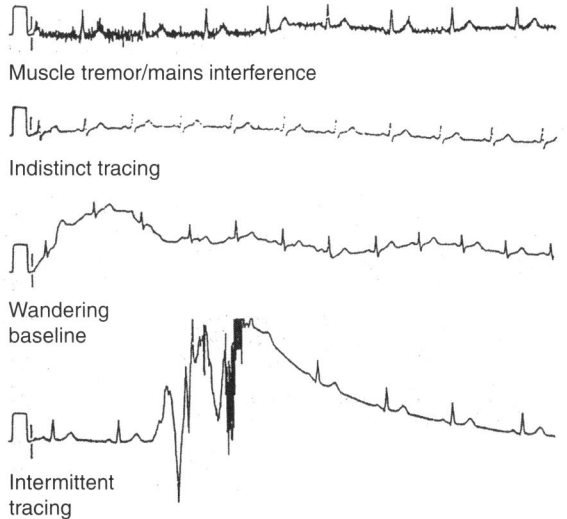

Muscle tremor/mains interference

Indistinct tracing

Wandering baseline

Intermittent tracing

Figure 25.2 Various ECG artefacts

26 How to interpret an ECG

PAUL HILL

An ECG can provide the following information:

- Rhythm abnormalities, that is arrhythmias
- Conduction disorders
- Ischaemia and myocardial infarction
- Structural abnormalities, such as chamber hypertrophy, dextrocardia and cardiomyopathy
- Electrolyte imbalance
- Inflammation, for example pericarditis and myocarditis
- Hypothermia, thyroid disease, malignancy, drugs, e.g. digoxin

Systematic approach to ECG interpretation

When you assess a standard 12-lead ECG, you need to provide documentation, record the quality of the ECG and interpret the ECG. We will now explore these three steps in more detail.

Documentation

You must record your patient's name, the date and time of the recording of the ECG.

Recording quality

As mentioned in the previous chapter, if baseline drift is present, you will find it difficult to interpret the ST segments. Skeletal muscle or mains interference can similarly affect your evaluation of the ST segment. You need to check the calibration signal before you attempt quantitative analysis. The standard calibration is 1 mV equals 10 mm, and therefore half-standard calibration is 1 mV equals 5 mm. This is essential for measuring voltage criteria in your diagnosis of chamber hypertrophy. This is illustrated in Figure 26.1. The normal paper speed is 25 mm per second, which implies that 1 mm (little square) equals 40 milliseconds (0.04 secs) and 5 mm (big square) equals 200 milliseconds (0.2 secs).

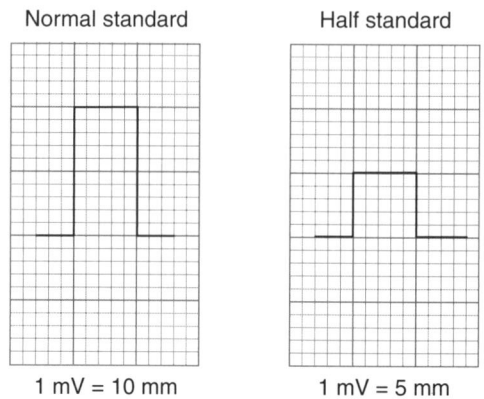

Figure 26.1 ECG showing standard and half-standard calibrations

Interpretation

You can conduct your analysis methodically using the following sequence:

- Rhythm
- Rate
- Electrical axis
- P waves
- PR interval
- QRS complex
- ST segments
- T waves
- QT interval
- U wave

We will now explore each of these aspects in more detail.

■ RHYTHM

Rhythm represents the frequency and time relationships of atrial and ventricular depolarisation. The P waves and QRS complexes are used to determine normal rhythm as well as its disturbances. Check whether the QRS complexes are occurring at regular intervals. If not, assess whether there is any pattern to the irregularity.

The criteria for sinus rhythm are as follows:

- P waves must be present and regular.
- The P wave form should be consistent.
- The frequency of P waves should be between 60 and 100 per minute.
- Each P wave should be followed by a QRS complex. The PR interval should be within normal range and constant.

■ RATE

Three hundred of the 5 mm blocks (0.2s) make up the duration of one minute. Figure 26.2 illustrates this. If the rhythm is regular, one way in which you can calculate the rate is to count the number of large blocks between the RR interval and to divide this into 300. Note that this rule does *not* apply to rhythms other than sinus rhythm.

Another method would be for you to count the RR or PP intervals over a six-second period (that is 30×5 mm blocks) and to multiply this figure by 10 to calculate rate per minute. This is useful for irregular rhythms, and is shown in Figure 26.3.

■ THE ELECTRICAL AXIS

In your analysis of the morphology of the QRS complexes in the limb leads, an important piece of information that you can gain is the position of the electrical axis. The dominant direction of all the QRS vectors is known as the "mean QRS axis". This is measured in the frontal plane. The limb leads of the standard ECG lie in the frontal plane, viz. standard leads I, II and III, and leads aVR, aVL and aVF.

By analysing the direction and magnitude of the QRS deflections of these leads, you can determine

5 large squares

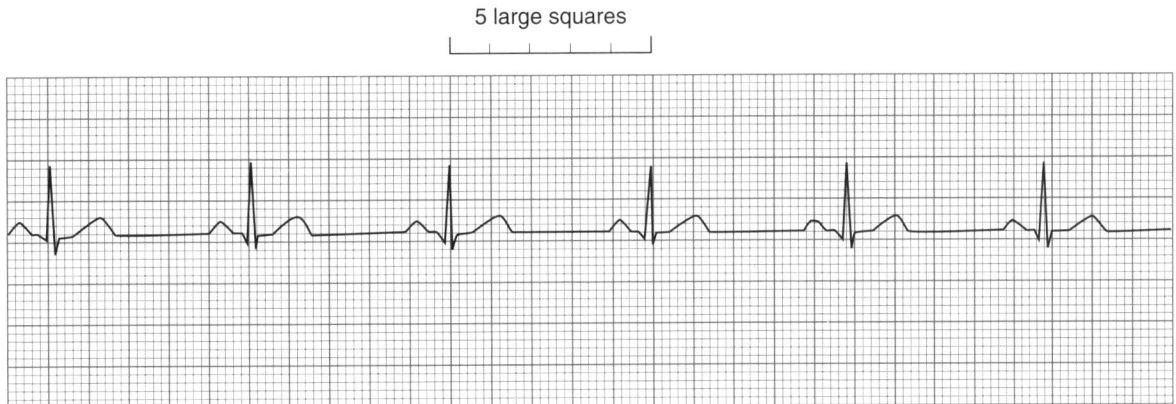

Figure 26.2 Calculating the heart rate when the rhythm is regular

Key points: • 1 QRS complex every 5 large squares
• 300 large squares correspond to 1 min
• Rate = 300/5 = 60 beats/min

Source: Houghton & Gray 2003. p. 20. Reproduced by permission of Edward Arnold

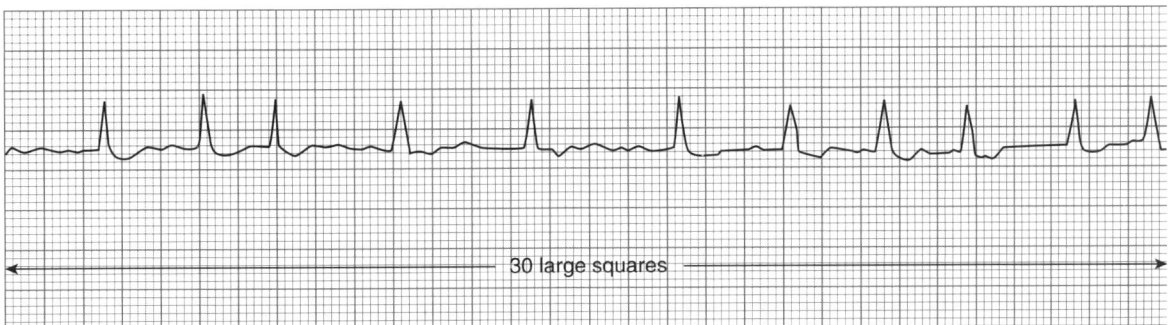

Figure 26.3 Calculating the heart rate when the rhythm is irregular

Key points: • 30 large squares contain 11 QRS complexes
• 30 large squares correspond to 6 s
• Rate = 11×10 = 110 beats/min

Source: Houghton & Gray 2003. p. 20. Reproduced by permission of Edward Arnold

the mean electrical axis. To understand this concept more clearly, consider that the heart lies in the centre of an equilateral triangle, the apices of which are the shoulders and the groin. This is shown in Figure 26.4.

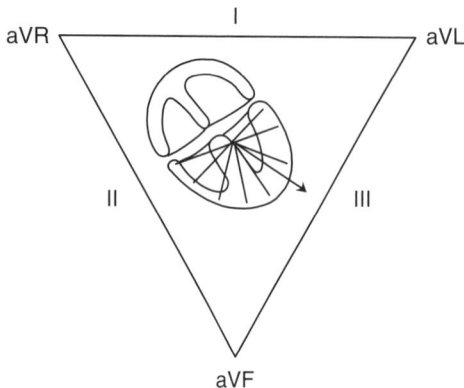

Figure 26.4 Equilateral triangle surrounding the heart

Leads aVR, aVL and aVF record from the right, left and inferior apices respectively, and the standard lead axes lie along the sides of this triangle. A hexaxial reference system, illustrated in Figure 26.5, has been derived with each adjacent lead axis separated by an angle of 30 degrees. By convention, angles measured in a clockwise direction from the positive pole of lead I are said to be positive, and angles measured in an anticlockwise direction are seen as negative.

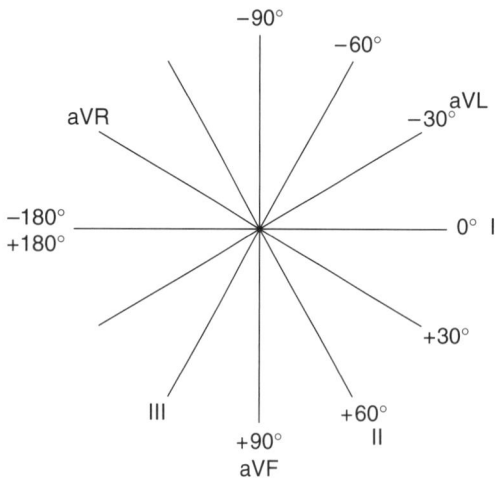

Figure 26.5 Hexaxial reference system

Normally, the electrical axis lies between 0 and +90 degrees. Deviation of the axis between +90 and +180 is said to be **right axis deviation**; **left axis deviation** exists between – 30 and –180 degrees.

To determine the **frontal plane axis**, measure the axis with reference to the hexaxial reference sys-

tem. The simplest method of calculating the electrical axis is as follows:

- Determine which is the smallest and most equiphasic QRS complex.
- Note that the axis lies at right angles to the equiphasic QRS complex.
- If the lead at right angles to the equiphasic complex is positive, the axis points in the direction of this lead. If negative, it points away from this lead.

You can also use the following method to work out the cardiac axis:

- A predominantly positive QRS complex in both leads I and II means that the axis is *normal.*
- A predominantly positive QRS complex in lead I and a predominantly negative QRS complex in lead II means that there is *left axis deviation.*
- A predominantly negative QRS complex in lead I and a predominantly positive QRS complex in lead II means that there is *right axis deviation.*

Calculation of the electrical axis helps you firstly to detect the abnormal, and secondly to facilitate the understanding of ECG variations in normal people. Left axis deviation of less than – 30 degrees is sometimes seen in people with normal hearts. A stocky build, obesity or sometimes ascites can result in horizontal left heart position, which will give rise to this ECG appearance. Left axis deviation of greater than – 30 degrees is always abnormal.

■ **THE P WAVE**

We are unsure of the reason for Einthoven using the letters P, Q, R, S and T for the major deflections on the ECG, but you must adhere to this convention and use these labels consistently. (This is illustrated in Figure 26.6.) You can only call a negative deflection beginning a QRS complex a Q wave.

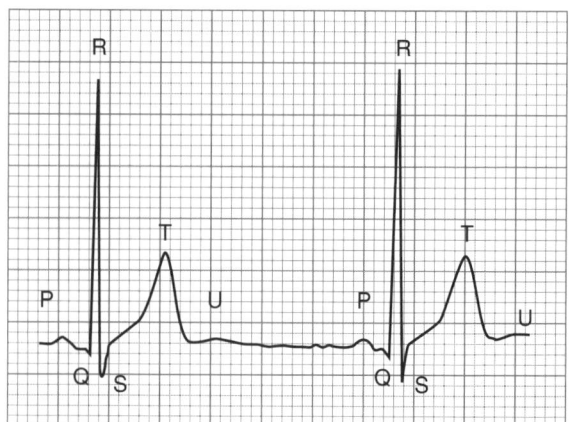

Figure 26.6 Einthoven conventions for labelling ECG deflections

The P wave represents the depolarisation of both left and right atria. You will not see sinus node discharge on the ECG. You must deduce sinus origin of atrial depolarisation from the P wave axis and rate. The normal P wave axis lies between +30 and +70 degrees. The normal P wave will thus be relatively flat in lead aVL and will always be upright (positive) in standard lead II. If the P wave is flat or negative in II, it is unlikely to be as a result of sinus node discharge.

Tall peaked waves indicate right atrial enlargement. This is referred to as "P pulmonale" because right atrial enlargement is often secondary to pulmonary disorders. P waves that are abnormally wide – more than 0.08 secs or two small squares – could indicate left atrial enlargement due to mitral valve stenosis and thus are known as "P mitrale".

■ THE PR INTERVAL

The PR interval represents the electrical impulse spreading from the SA node to the aV node, down the bundle of His, and then down the right and left bundle branches. You can measure the PR interval from the start of the P wave to the start of the R wave. The normal range is from 120 to 200 milliseconds, which is represented as 3–5 small squares on the ECG paper at 25 mm per second.

■ THE QRS COMPLEX

The QRS complex represents the depolarisation of both ventricles. If the initial deflection following the P wave is downward it is called a Q wave. An initial upward defection is termed an R wave. The S wave denotes terminal ventricular depolarisation. Upper and lower casing is used to denote the relative sizes of QRS deflections.

The *normal* depolarisation of the interventricular septum from left to right causes a small "septal" **Q wave** in any of leads II, aVL or V5–6. **Pathological Q waves** are more than 25% of the height of the following R wave and wider than 1 mm (40 ms). This is shown in Figure 26.7.

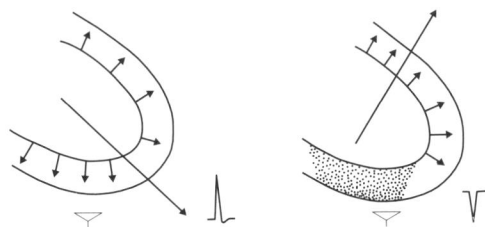

Figure 26.7

Pathological Q waves. The left panel shows the net vector force. Therefore, an electrode placed over the left ventricle will reflect a positive R wave. The shaded area in the right panel represents an infarct involving the anterior wall. The resultant net vector force is directed posteriorly away from the infarct zone, resulting in Q waves.

In **left bundle branch block** (LBBB), the interventricular septum has to depolarise from right to left – a reversal of the normal pattern. This causes a small Q wave in lead V1 and a small R wave in V6. The right ventricle is normally depolarised via the right bundle branch, causing an R wave in lead V1 and an S wave in lead V6. Then the left ventricle is depolarised by the right, causing an S wave in lead V1 and another R wave in lead V6. This is shown in Figure 26.8.

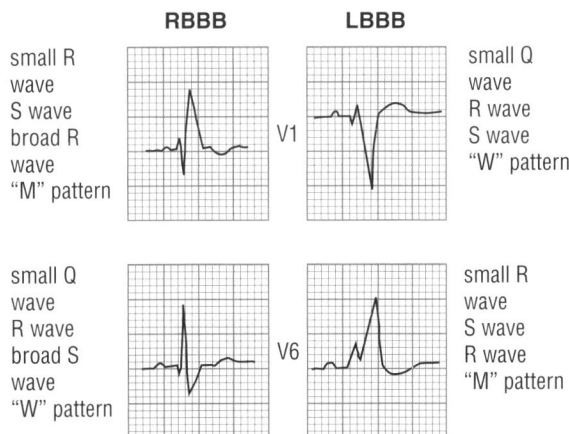

Figure 26.8 Depolarisation between left and right bundle branch blocks

In **right bundle branch block** (RBBB), the interventricular septum depolarises normally from left to right, causing a tiny R wave in lead V1 and a small septal Q wave in lead V6. The left ventricle is normally depolarised via the left bundle branch, causing an S wave in lead V1 and an R wave in lead V6. Then the right ventricle is depolarised by the left, causing another R wave in V1 and an S wave in V6.

The **normal QRS** width is 1–3 small squares, or 40–120 milliseconds. If the QRS is wide, there is left bundle branch block, right bundle branch block, pre-excitation or a ventricular rhythm.

Normally, V1 shows an rS pattern and V6 a qR pattern. The R wave progressively increases in size from V1 to V6, although it may fall off slightly between leads V5 and V6, or V4 and V5, as is shown in Figure 26.9.

The S wave in V2 may be deeper than in V1. From V2 onwards, however, the S wave depth decreases. In the right precordial leads, the initial deflection is positive. In the progression from V1 to V6 a point is reached where the initial deflection is no longer positive but becomes negative. When this occurs, the transition zone has been crossed. When the transition zone is in the region of V3/V4, the heart is in the intermediate position. If the transition zone occurs between V2/V3 or V1/V2, you can refer

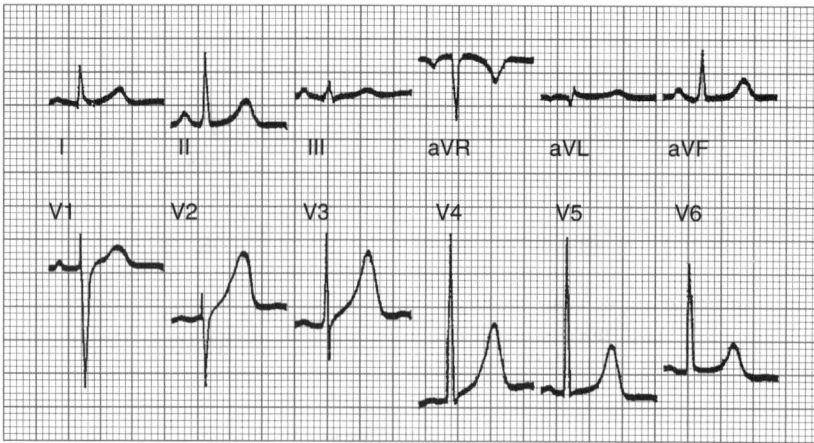

Figure 26.9 Normal ECG showing normal morphology and mean frontal QRS axis of +60 degrees

to the presence of counter-clockwise rotation. When the transition zone is between V4/V5 and V5/V6, clockwise rotation is present.

As far as dimensions are concerned, at least one R wave in the precordial leads must exceed 8 mm, the tallest R wave must not exceed 25 mm and the deepest S wave should not exceed 25 mm. The sum of the tallest R wave in the left precordial leads and the deepest S wave in the right leads should not exceed 35 mm.

The QRS complexes differ in their morphology in each lead and give different information depending on whether they are limb leads or precordial leads. The **precordial** leads reflect information regarding

- the right ventricle and posterior portion of the left ventricle – V1 and V2
- the anteroseptal left ventricle – V1 to V4
- the left lateral ventricle – V5 and V6.

The **limb** leads reflect information regarding

- the inferior wall of the left ventricle – standard leads II, III and aVF
- the high left lateral ventricle – standard leads I and aVL.

Note that no lead – either limb or precordial – is orientated directly to the posterior portion of the heart.

■ THE ST SEGMENT

This segment represents early repolarisation. Normally, the segment is iso-electric, that is it lies at the same level as the ECG's baseline, which is the horizontal line between the end of the T wave and the start of the P wave. ST segments do not deviate above or below the iso-electric line by more than 1 mm. They can be elevated, depressed, up-sloping, down-sloping or distorted by the P wave.

■ T WAVES

These waves are usually concordant with the QRS complexes, and they represent the second part of ventricular repolarisation. Because the repolarisation phenomenon is accelerated during phase three of the transmembrane action potential, the upstroke of the T wave is slower than the downstroke on the ECG. The T wave morphology is usually negative in V1, sometimes in V2 and lead III, and always in aVR. T waves can be inverted, peaked, biphasic, notched or flat.

■ THE QT INTERVAL

You can measure this interval from the beginning of the QRS complex to the end of the T wave. It represents the total duration of ventricular depolarisation and repolarisation. The beginning of the QRS is best determined in leads with an initial Q wave, viz. standard leads I or II, or leads aVL, V5 and V6. If a prominent U wave is present, the midpoint between the T and U waves is taken as the end of the T wave. The QT interval changes with tachycardia and bradycardia. It also shortens with a decrease in the RR interval. For this reason, you need to use Bazett's formula to measure the corrected QT interval or QTc. Bazett's formula, shown in Figure 26.10, is calculated as follows:

$$QTc = \frac{QT}{\sqrt{RR}}$$

Note that at a heart rate of 60 beats per minute with an RR interval of 1 sec, the measured QT intervals are the same as the RR intervals. At a normal heart rate of 60–100 beats per minute, the QT interval should not exceed half of the RR interval. A normal QTc is 0.35–0.43 sec long.

■ THE U WAVE

The U wave follows the T wave, usually in the same

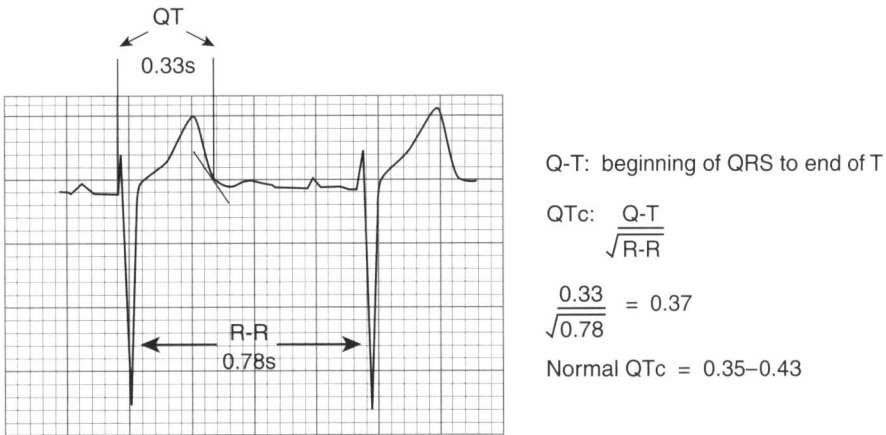

Figure 26.10 Bazett's formula

Q-T: beginning of QRS to end of T

QTc: $\dfrac{Q\text{-}T}{\sqrt{R\text{-}R}}$

$\dfrac{0.33}{\sqrt{0.78}} = 0.37$

Normal QTc = 0.35–0.43

direction as the T wave. This wave is best observed in leads V2–V4, and its genesis is uncertain and controversial.

Normal variants in an ECG

There are a number of variants of the ECG complex. We will now discuss certain of the more common variants.

Non-specific T wave variation and inversion may occur in the following circumstances:

- As an orthostatic response, that is resulting from a change from lying to standing positions
- Post-prandially
- With hyperventilation
- As a response to anxiety
- In mitral valve prolapse

An important variant in electrocardiography is the **early repolarisation syndrome**, as found in vagotonia or "athlete's heart". This is characterised by concave, mildly upward ST segments, relatively tall R waves, occasionally inverted T waves, narrow but prominent Q waves, rapid transition and tall R waves in the left precordial leads. Figure 26.11 illustrates this.

Another variant that we commonly note in clinical practice is *prolongation* of the PR interval with age. A PR interval of more than 0.20 seconds is accepted as normal in a patient who is over the age of 70.

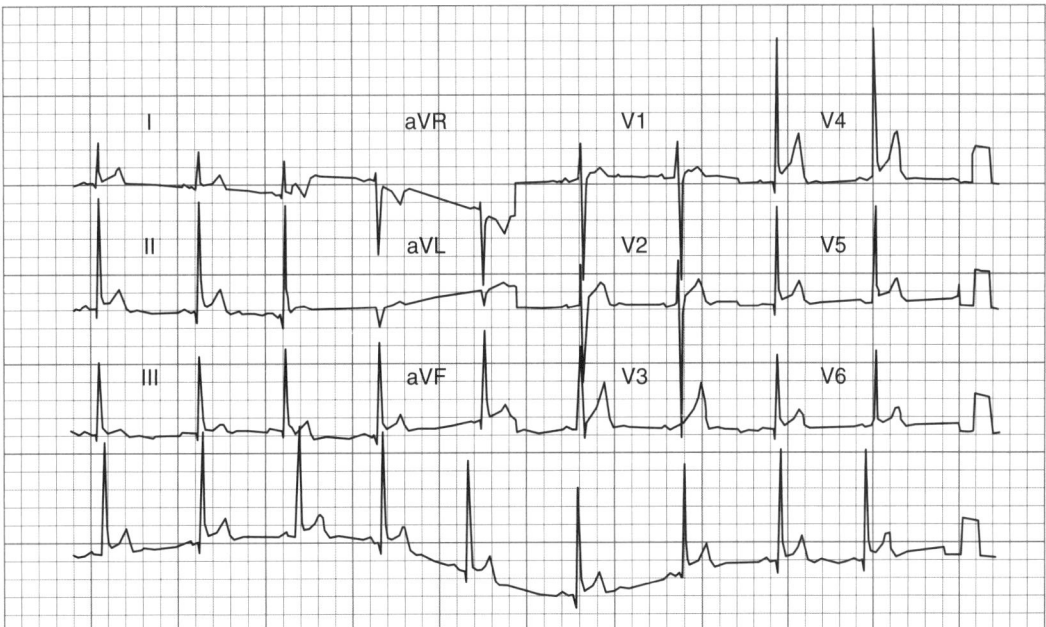

Figure 26.11 ECG of early repolarisation syndrome

Myocardial infarction patterns

We call acute prolonged chest pain when the patient is at rest, or makes minimal effort, "acute coronary syndrome" (ACS). The ECG patterns that can be encountered in ACS consist of

- acute ST segment elevation myocardial infarction (STEMI)
- acute non-ST segment elevation myocardial infarction (NSTEMI)
- T wave inversion
- normal ECG.

The sequence of ECG changes which occur in myocardial infarction are

- hyperacute peaked T waves
- ST segment elevation
- pathological Q waves.

Elevation of cardiac markers such as CK-MB and troponins provide you with further information. Another way in which you can classify ACS is as follows:

- Unstable angina with or without ECG changes and negative Troponin T
- NSTEMI with or without ECG changes and a positive Troponin T
- STEMI and a positive Troponin T

In ischaemia of the **ventricles**, an additional current of injury is generated. If ischaemia is **endocardial,** the current of injury will be directed from outside the heart towards the cavity. An ECG electrode will reflect this as a negative current which will depress the ST segment, because the current is moving away from the electrode.

If the ischaemia of the ventricle is on the **epicardial** side of the myocardium or if it traverses the thickness of the muscle, the current of injury generated will be directed from inside the heart towards the outside. An electrode placed over the ischaemic area will thus register ST segment elevation. Figures 26.12 and 26.13 show these currents of injury.

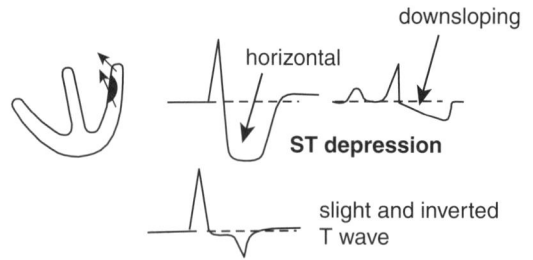

Figure 26.12 Current of injury in endocardial ischaemia

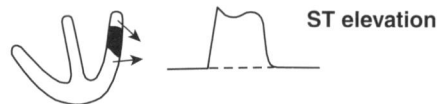

Figure 26.13 Current of injury in epicardial and full thickness ischaemia

Anterior wall infarction

Figure 26.14 shows this type of infarction.

Inferior wall infarction

Figure 26.15 shows this type of infarction.

Posterior wall infarction

Figure 26.16 shows this type of infarction.

Myocardial ischaemia

You can see the ECG abnormalities in myocardial ischaemia only while your patient experiences pain. ST segment depression is the most common abnormality and is usually horizontal. There may also be T wave flattening or inversion. Figure 26.17 shows this type of ischaemia.

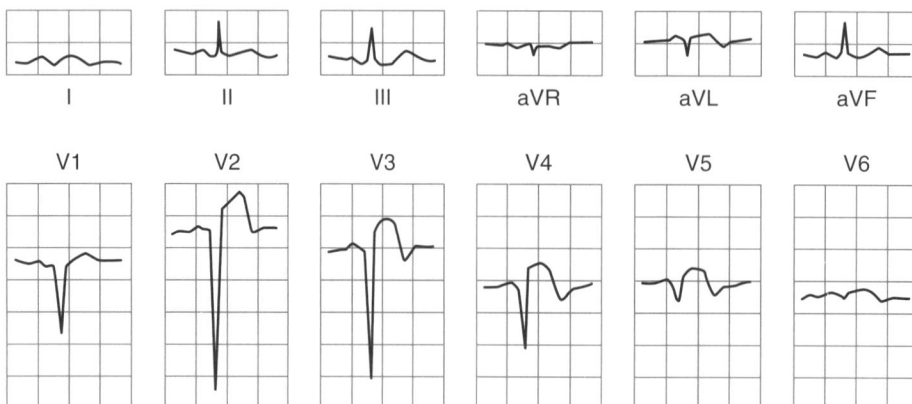

Extensive anterior infarction reflected by: QS complexes with coved and elevated S-T segments, and inverted T waves in leads V1 to V6, AVL and standard lead I.

Figure 26.14 Infarction of the anterior wall

Hyperacute phase

Tall R waves with slope-elevation of the S-T segments, and tall widened T waves in: standard leads II and III and lead aVF

Fully evolved phase

Pathological Q waves in standard lead II

Coved and elevated S-T segments with inverted T waves in standard leads II and III and lead aVF

Apical extension is suggested by the diminished R wave and flat T wave in lead V6

Chronic stabilised phase

Pathological Q waves in standard lead II and lead aVF

QS complex in standard lead III

No S-T segment or T wave changes of injury or ischaemia

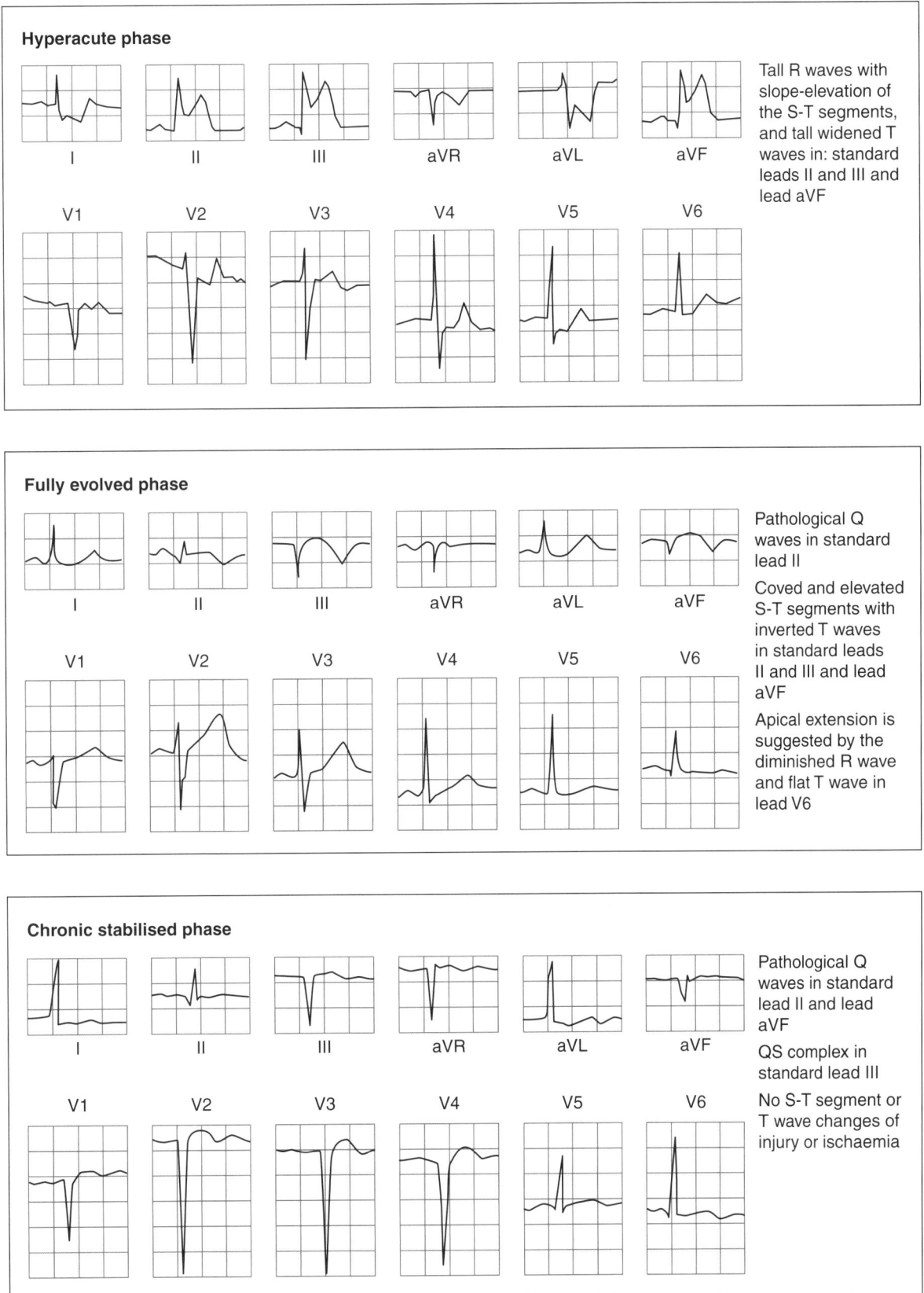

Figure 26.15 Infarction of the inferior wall

Mirror image or inverse image of the fully evolved presentation

Mirror image of QS complex = Tall and wide R wave

Mirror image of elevated S-T segment = Depressed S-T segment (rare)

Mirror image of inverted T wave = Tall wide T wave

Posterior wall infarction:

Tall R and upright T waves in leads V1 to V3, with ST depression.

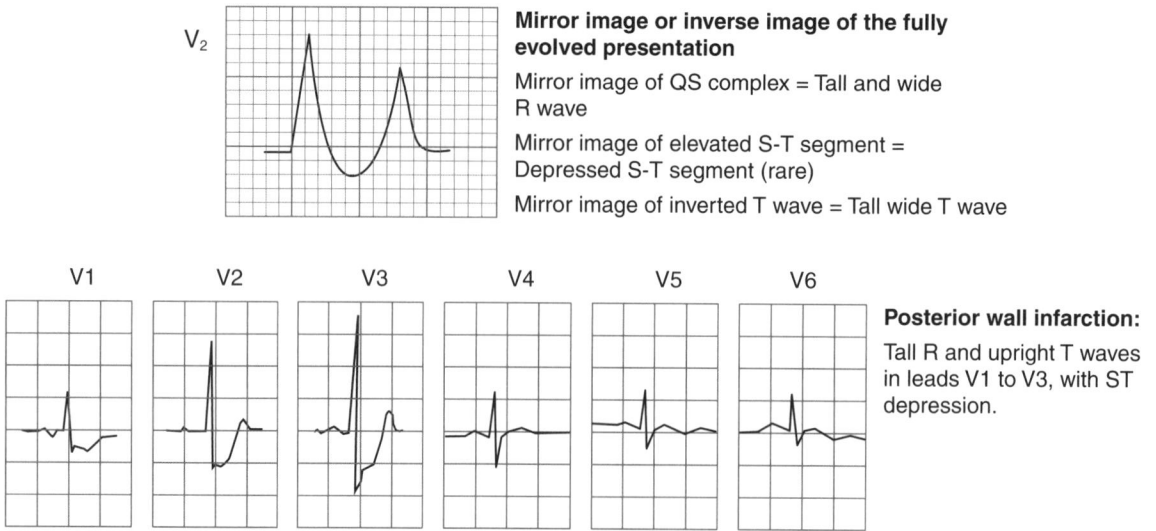

Figure 26.16 Infarction of the posterior wall

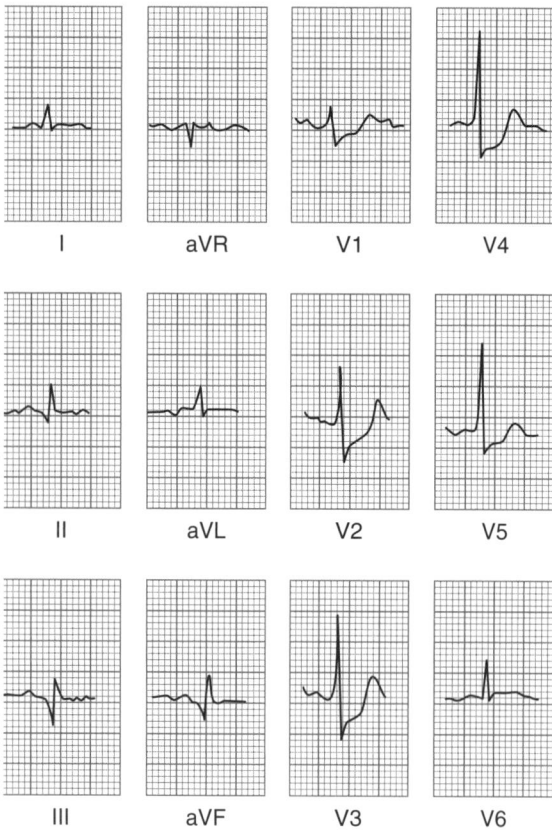

Figure 26.17 Myocardial ischaemia

Key point: • Anterior ST segment depression with angina

Source: Houghton & Gray 2003. p. 171. Reproduced by permission of Edward Arnold

Pericarditis

The ST segment elevation of pericarditis, shown in Figure 26.18, has four characteristics that may help you to distinguish it from myocardial infarction:

1. The ST segment elevation is typically widespread, affecting all those leads that look at the inflamed myocardium. Leads aVR and V1 usually show reciprocal ST segment depression.
2. The ST segment elevation is characteristically concave upwards.
3. T wave inversion occurs only after the ST segments have returned to baseline.
4. Q waves do not develop.

Arrhythmia patterns

Cardiac arrhythmias are common presentations to medical practitioners and in emergency departments. The ECG is the key to accurate diagnosis and further management. Important points that you need to remember are as follows:

• The ECG on a monitor screen is insufficient unless the patient is pulseless.
• The ECG must be documented on paper, not only for the patient's records but also to facilitate careful analysis of arrhythmias that you may misinterpret on a monitor screen.
• You need to obtain a good quality 12-lead ECG that allows analysis of P and QRS morphology, axis and duration – this is not possible from a single rhythm strip.

We will now explore certain arrhythmic patterns.

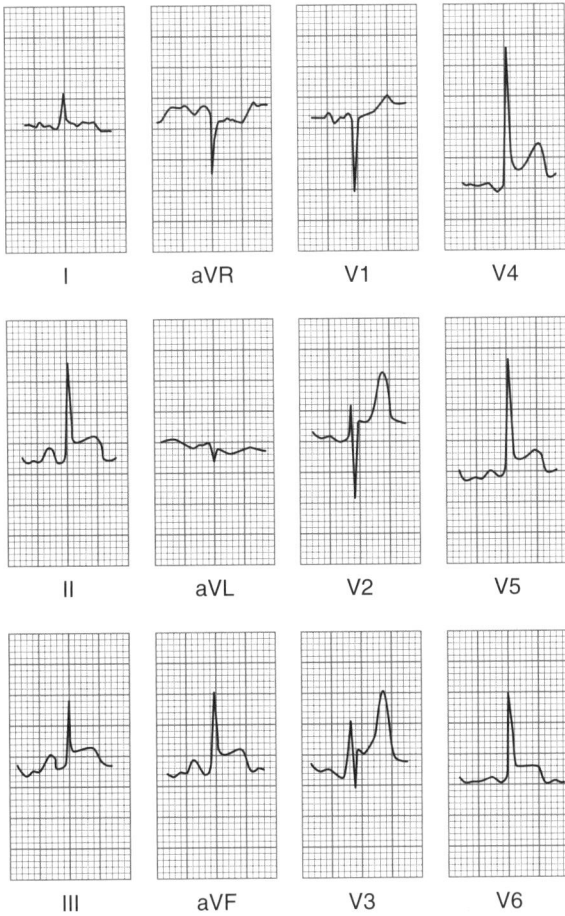

Figure 26.18 Pericarditis

Key point: • Widespread "saddle-shaped" ST segment elevation

Source: Houghton & Gray 2003. p. 168. Reproduced by permission of Edward Arnold

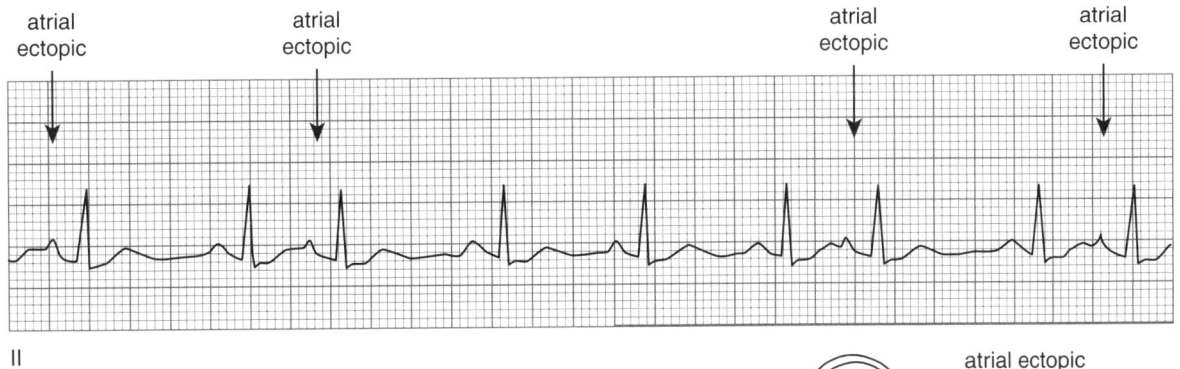

Ectopic beats

Ectopic beats are those that occur earlier than expected. They are classified into atrial, aV junctional and ventricular ectopics. They can also be called "extrasystoles" or premature beats.

You can identify **atrial ectopics** by noting a P wave that appears earlier than expected and has an abnormal shape, as is shown in Figure 26.19.

Ventricular ectopics give rise to broad ventricular complexes. If retrograde conduction does not occur, there will usually be a full compensatory pause before the next normal beat because the SA node will not have been reset. Ventricular ectopics can occur at the same time as the preceding T wave and such "R on T" ectopics can trigger ventricular arrhythmias. The term "bigeminy" is used to describe the case of one ectopic following a normal beat, as is shown in Figure 26.20.

Tachyarrhythmias

Tachycardia refers to a heart rate of more than 100 beats per minute. Mechanisms of the arrhythmias may involve

• enhanced or abnormal automaticity
• triggered activity
• re-entry.

The tachycardias can be divided into two main groups:

1. Origin *above* the level of the ventricles:
   (a) Sinus tachycardia
   (b) Atrial fibrillation
   (c) Atrial flutter
   (d) Atrial tachycardia
   (e) Atrioventricular junctional re-entry tachycardias

Figure 26.19 Atrial ectopic beats

Key points: • P waves earlier than expected
• P wave abnormally shaped

Source: Houghton & Gray 2003. p. 60. Reproduced by permission of Edward Arnold

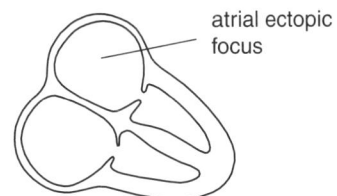

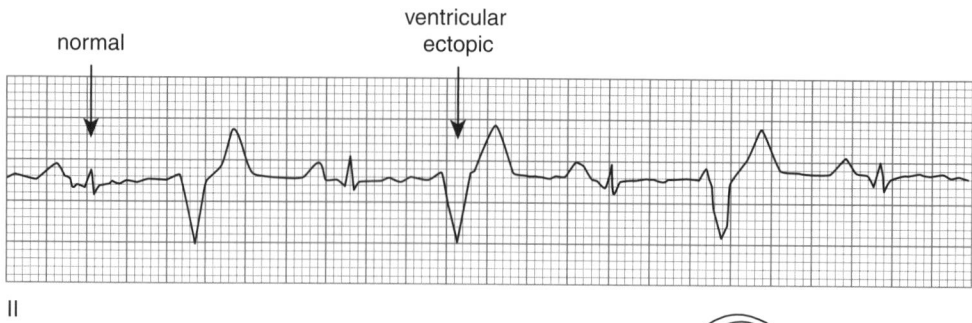

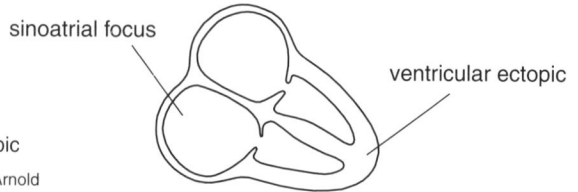

Figure 26.20 Bigeminy

Key point: • Each normal beat is followed by a ventricular ectopic

Source: Houghton & Gray 2003. p. 62. Reproduced by permission of Edward Arnold

2. Origin *from* the ventricles:
   (a) Ventricular fibrillation
   (b) Monomorphic and polymorphic ventricular tachycardia
   (c) Ventricular ectopics

Moreover, we can categorise tachycardia as either narrow complex tachycardia, in which QRS duration is shorter than 120 milliseconds, or wide complex tachycardia, in which QRS complex is longer than 120 milliseconds.

You need a good quality ECG in order to be able to make the two basic observations. This should be a 12-lead ECG where the *widest* QRS should be measured rather than a single lead monitor strip, which may give misleading results. The basic observations could be one of the following four combinations:

1. Wide and regular
2. Narrow and regular
3. Wide and irregular
4. Narrow and irregular

■ SINUS TACHYCARDIA

In this instance, the rate is 100–120 beats per minute, as is shown in Figure 26.21. Beware of diagnosing sinus rhythm at rates of over 120 per minute. There is a P wave before each QRS complex. Note that atrial flutter with a 2:1 block and a rate of 150 beats per minute can be mistaken for a sinus tachycardia.

■ ATRIAL FIBRILLATION

Here the rhythm is irregularly irregular, as is shown in Figure 26.22. Rate varies and may be slow, normal or fast. Sometimes it is extremely fast. There are no P waves and the atrial tracing varies from extremely fine to fairly coarse. The QRS complexes are narrow (shorter than 0.12 sec); they occur irregularly and are often rapid.

Any irregular rhythm or tachycardia is by default atrial fibrillation. Occasionally, other rhythms may be irregular, that is atrial flutter with irregular block, multifocal atrial tachycardia, second-degree heart block, atrial or ventricular ectopic beats and some ventricular arrhythmias like polymorphic ventricular tachycardia.

■ ATRIAL FLUTTER

In this case there are usually flutter waves in a saw-tooth pattern with a rate of 300–450 per minute, as is illustrated in Figure 26.23. The ventricular rate depends on the degree of aV block, which can be

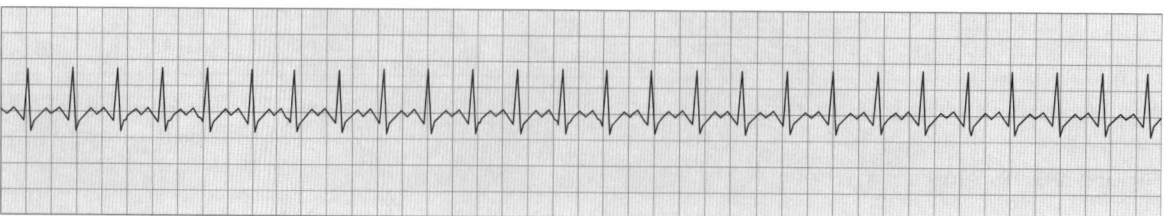

Figure 26.21 Sinus tachycardia – heart rate is 150–180 beats/min, P waves upright and followed by QRS complexes

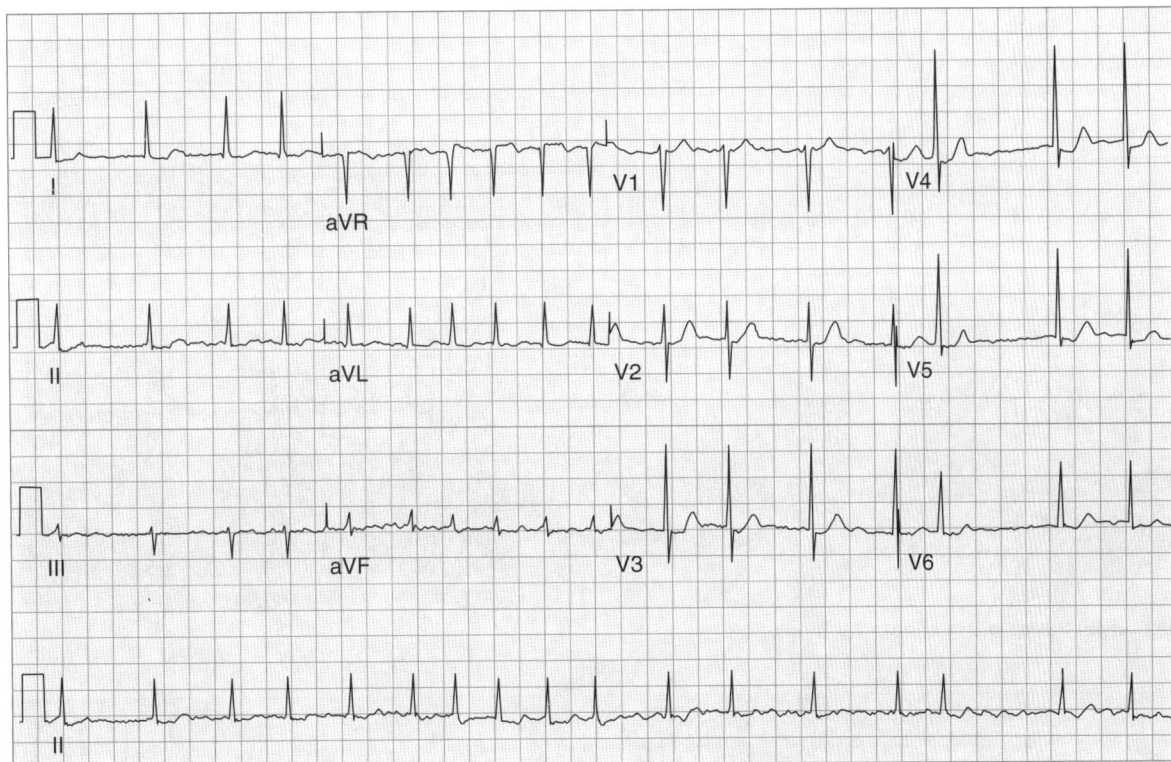

Figure 26.22 Atrial fibrillation – narrow QRS complex tachycardia with irregular RR intervals, fibrillating baseline and absent P waves

variable, even in the same patient. There is frequently atrial flutter with a 2:1 block and a ventricular rate of 150 per minute. The QRS is narrow (shorter than 0.12 sec).

■ ATRIAL TACHYCARDIA

Illustrated in Figure 26.24, this type of tachycardia is not common. Clues include the presence of P waves, frequently with abnormal morphology or axis and varying AV block. P waves may be focal, arising from an ectopic pacemaker site, or occasionally scar related. Impulses are generated by an ectopic focus somewhere within the atrial myocardium rather than the sinus node.

■ ATRIOVENTRICULAR JUNCTIONAL RE-ENTRY TACHYCARDIAS

Also known as AVJRT, and illustrated in Figure 26.25, these tachycardias are either aV nodal re-entry tachycardia (AVNRT) or aV re-entry tachycardia (AVRT). Both are aV node dependable, and they may be indistinguishable. The age of presentation may be different. AVRT peaks bimodally in infancy and later adolescence while AVNRT tends to occur later in adulthood. Clues may be sudden onset of supraventricular tachycardia (SVT), P

waves that could be hidden or at the end of the QRS, and otherwise normal hearts.

AVNRT occurs because there are two pathways in the normal aV node: one fast and one slow. Less commonly, SVTs can arise from a circuit involving an accessory conduction pathway, such as in Wolf-Parkinson-White syndrome. During these tachycardias, if conduction is antegrade down the aV node and retrograde up the accessory pathway, the QRS complexes are narrow. If the conduction is antegrade down the accessory pathway and retrograde up the aV node, the QRS complexes are widened. P wave are sometimes visible as retrogradcly conducted waves after the QRS complex.

■ VENTRICULAR TACHYCARDIA

Also known as VT, this is a broad complex tachycardia – QRS is longer than 0.12 sec – which is essentially regular and at a rate greater than 100 per min. Occasionally, you may doubt whether a patient with a broad complex tachycardia has VT or SVT with aberrant conduction, that is an SVT in the setting of an aberrant pathway or bundle branch block.

This type of tachycardia may be monomorphic or polymorphic. **Polymorphic** either degenerates into ventricular fibrillation or self-terminates. However,

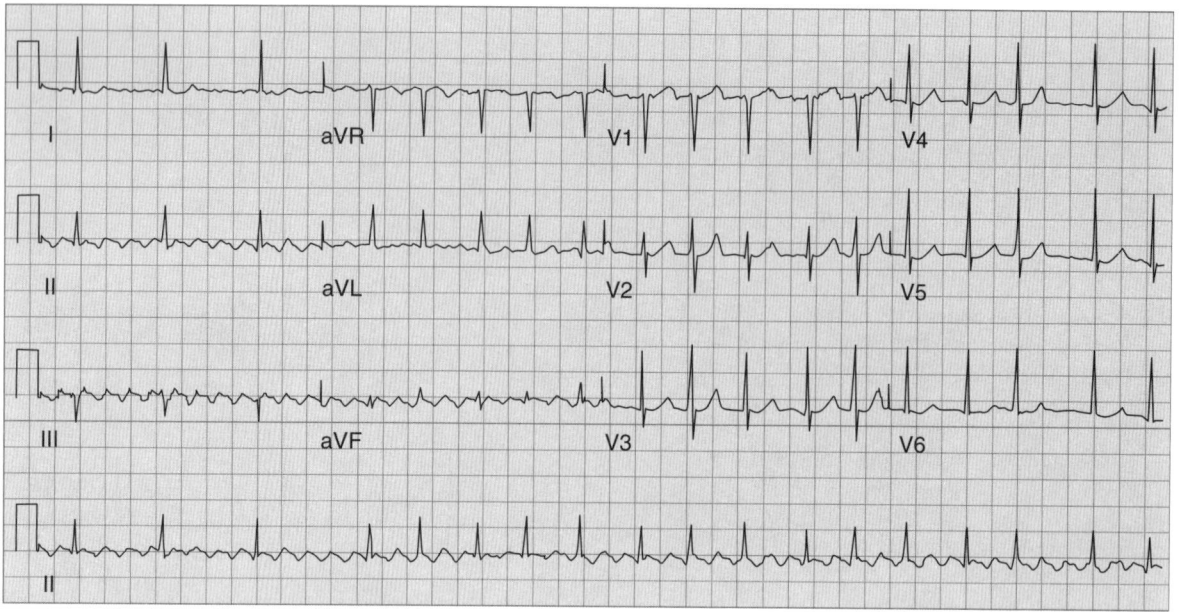

(A) Atrial flutter with variable AV block

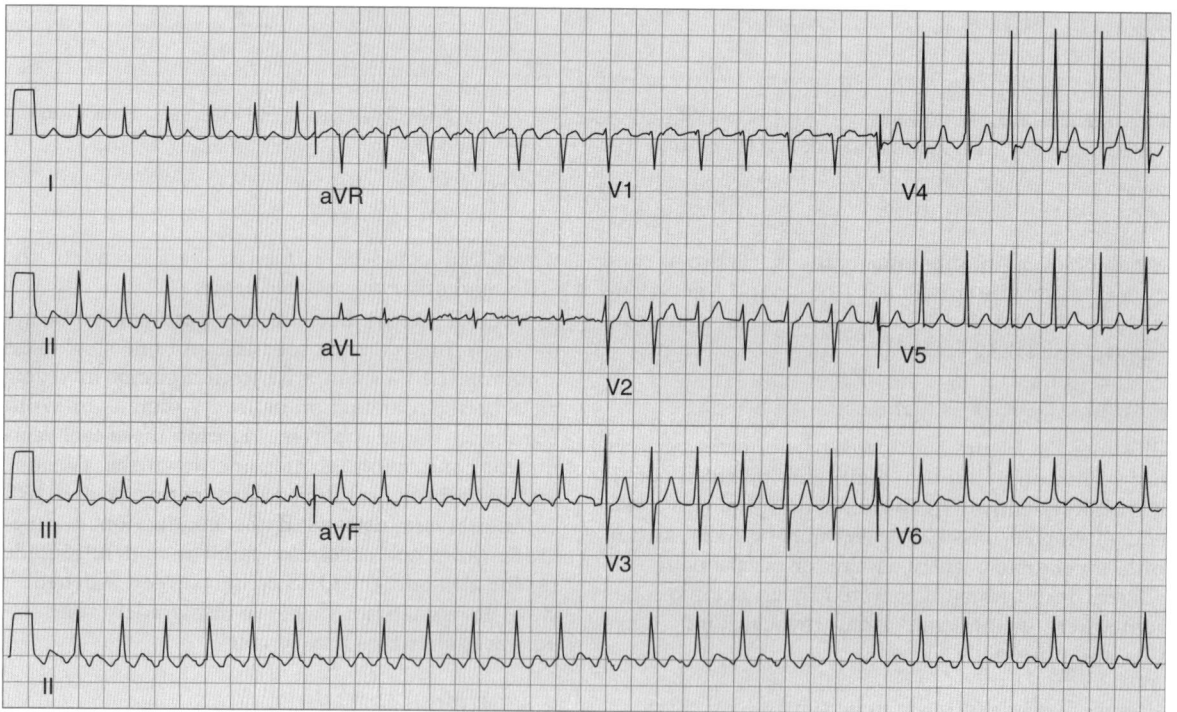

(B) Atrial flutter with 2:1 AV block

Figure 26.23 Atrial flutter

it is frequently recurrent and often associated with the long QT syndrome. All the QRS complexes are broad and the configuration varies from beat to beat.

Illustrated in Figure 26.26, ECG features typical of VT are as follows:

- QRS width is longer than 0.14 sec.
- There is concordance across chest leads, that is QRS complexes V1–V6 are predominantly all upright or all downward.
- There is evidence of aV dissociation. Half of all patients with VT will have a 1:1 retrograde con-

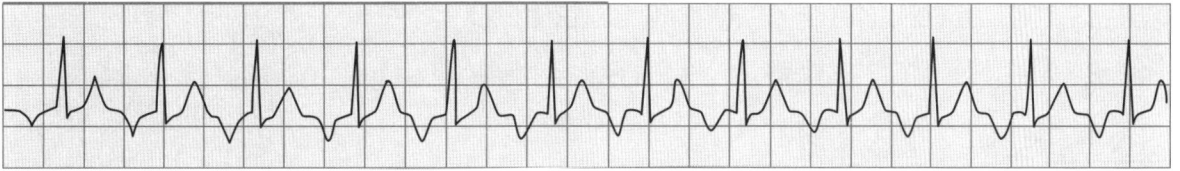

Figure 26.24 Atrial tachycardia

Key points: • Heart rate is 125 beats/min
• Abnormally shaped P waves

Source: Houghton & Gray 2003. p. 39. Reproduced by permission of Edward Arnold

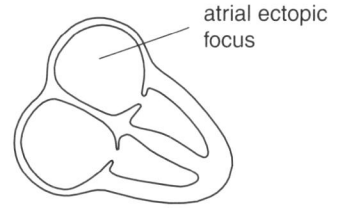

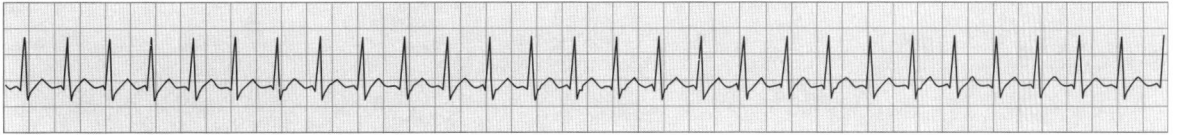

Figure 26.25 Atrioventricular junctional re-entry tachycardias – narrow QRS complexes with hidden P waves

duction of impulses to atria. The other half will show evidence of aV dissociation which is highly specific for VT. ECG manifestations of aV dissociation are the presence of **fusion beats**, which are hybrids of a normally conducted impulse and the impulse originating from the ventricle, and **capture**, which is a normally conducted impulse. These two occur only when the VT is relatively slow.

A variant of polymorphic VT, **torsades de pointes** is associated with a long QT interval. Note the undulating pattern on the ECG with a variation in the direction of the QRS complexes. Prolongation of the QT interval and torsades de pointes can occur with certain anti-arrhythmic drugs, hypocalcaemia, myocarditis, and hereditary syndromes.

■ VENTRICULAR FIBRILLATION

As shown in Figure 26.27, this type of fibrillation is characterised by a chaotic zigzag pattern on the ECG. There are no P waves or QRS complexes. There is no effective cardiac output with this rhythm.

■ ASYSTOLE

Asystole implies no spontaneous electrical activity, and thus the ECG shows no QRS complexes. This is illustrated in Figure 26.28.

■ PULSELESS ELECTRICAL ACTIVITY

This activity is also known as PEA and "electro-

mechanical dissociation". The heart continues to work electrically but fails to provide circulation. Figure 26.29 shows this type of activity, causes for which include hypoxia, hypovolaemia, hypothermia, cardiac tamponade, tension pneumothorax and thromboembolism. PEA can exist in conjunction with any of the cardiac rhythms that would normally sustain a rhythm.

Bradyarrhythmias

In adults, bradycardias refer to a heart rate of below 60 beats per minute. There are two major mechanisms of bradyarrhythmias. The first is impulse generation failure due to a sinus node problem, secondary to sick sinus syndrome, hypothyroidism, hypothermia, hypoxia, hypercarbia, head injury, hyperkalaemia, drugs or infiltration. Figure 26.30 shows this type of mechanism.

The second mechanism of bradyarrhythmia concerns conduction abnormalities, that is heart blocks, due to aV node or ventricular conduction system problems. These can be caused by ischaemia, infarction, degeneration, drugs, inflammation, fibrosis, infiltration or congenital abnormalities.

■ SECOND-DEGREE aV BLOCK

There are two types of such blocks:

1. **Mobitz Type 1 (Wenckebach):** PR interval increases until a QRS complex is dropped. This is a benign rhythm. It can repeat in a cyclical fashion. Figure 26.31 shows this type of block.

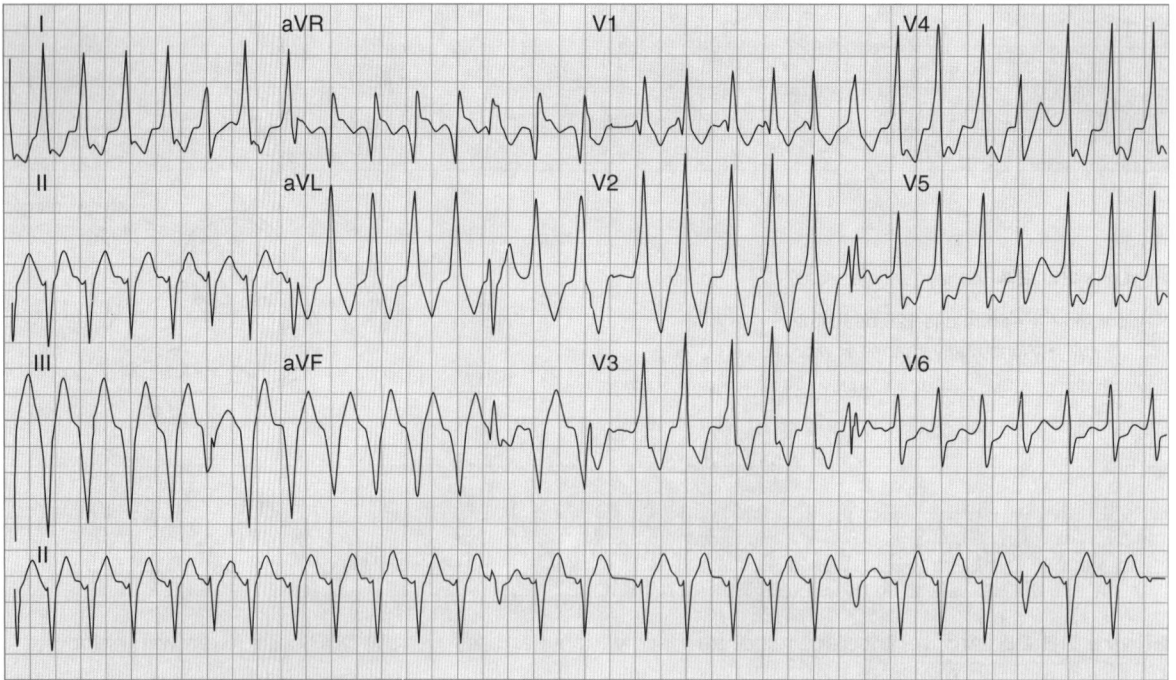

Figure 26.26 Ventricular tachycardia – a broad complex tachycardia showing concordance across the chest leads, capture and fusion beats

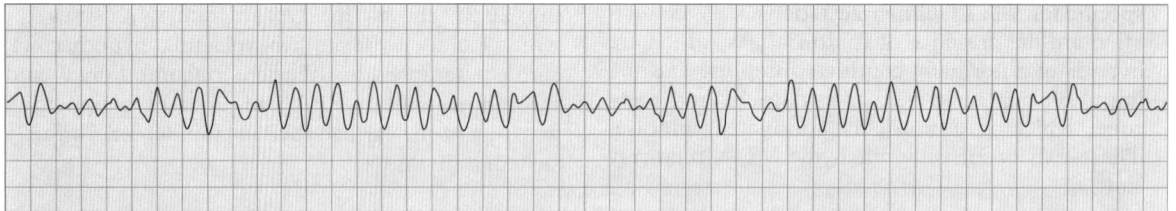

Figure 26.27 Ventricular fibrillation – chaotic ventricular activity

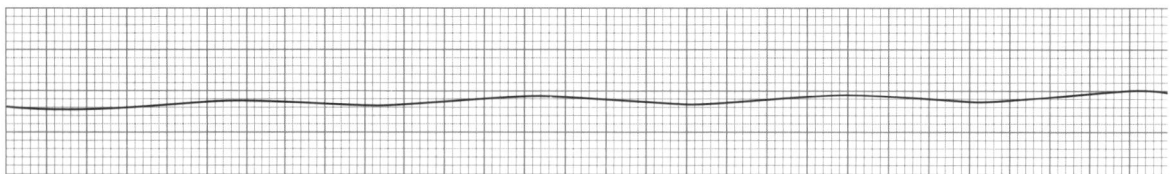

II

Figure 26.28 Asystole

Key point: • No spontaneous electrical activity

Source: Houghton & Gray 2003. p. 251. Reproduced by permission of Edward Arnold

2. **Mobitz Type 2:** There is incomplete conduction of atrial depolarisations to the ventricles. Some impulses are conducted, others are not. This rhythm can degenerate into third-degree heart block. The conducted beats have a normal PR interval. Figure 26.32 shows this type of block.

■ **THIRD-DEGREE HEART BLOCK**

This is a bradycardia, usually with no regular relationship between P waves and QRS complexes. The width of the QRS complex depends on how far down the conducting system the block occurs. An alternative pacemaker takes over the pacing function from the SA node, and the lower the block, the

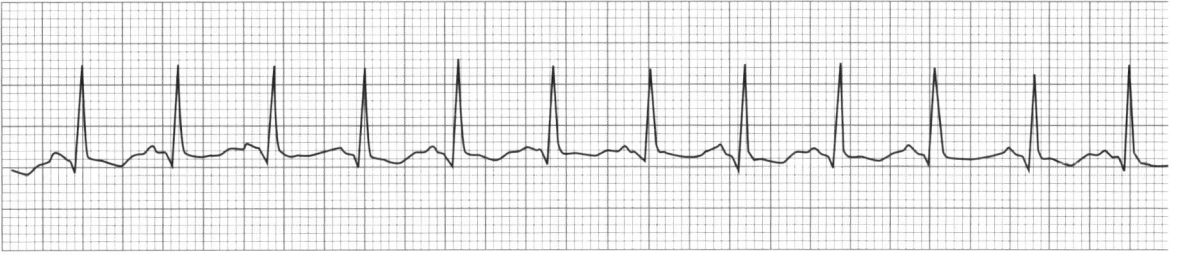

II

Figure 26.29 Pulseless electrical activity

Key point: • QRS complexes (in the absence of a cardiac output)

Source: Houghton & Gray 2003. p. 252. Reproduced by permission of Edward Arnold

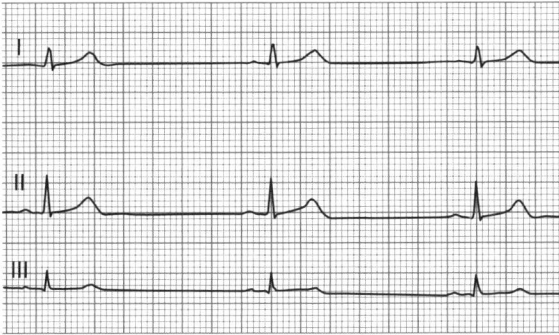

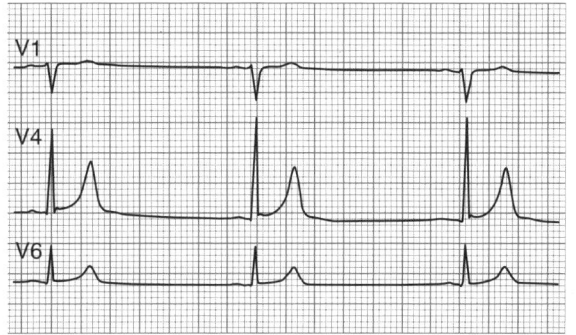

Figure 26.30 Sinus bradycardia

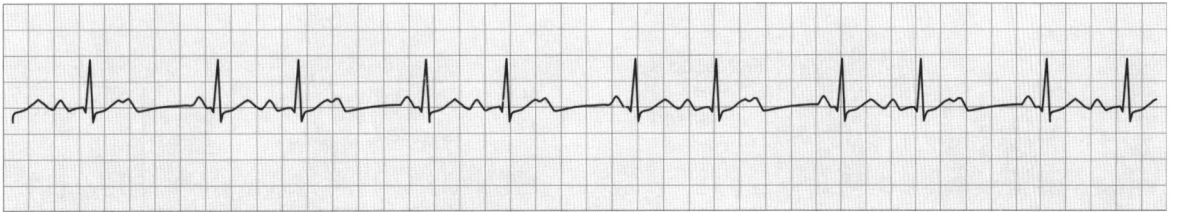

Figure 26.31 Mobitz Type 1 block – progressive lengthening of PR intervals with subsequent failure of P wave to be conducted to the ventricles

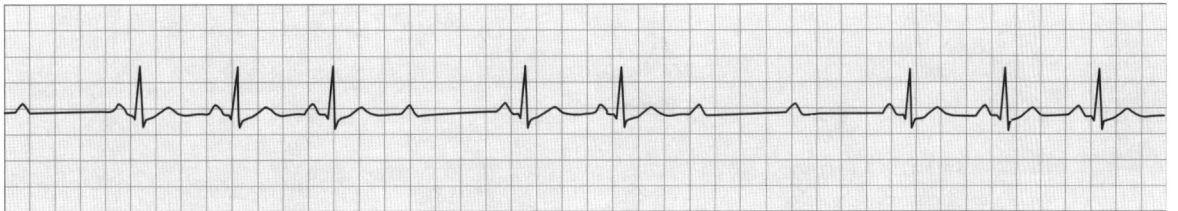

Figure 26.32 Mobitz Type 2 block – PR interval is normal and constant, but occasional P waves fail to be conducted to the ventricles

wider the QRS complexes and the slower the ventricular rate. Figure 26.33 shows this type of block.

Electrolyte disturbances on an ECG

We will now discuss the various types of electrolytic disturbances.

Hyperkalaemia

If ECG abnormalities are present and the patient's serum potassium level is above 6.5 mmol per litre, you need to be aware of the risk of fatal cardiac arrhythmias. As shown in Figure 26.34, the following ECG findings may be present in hyperkalaemia:

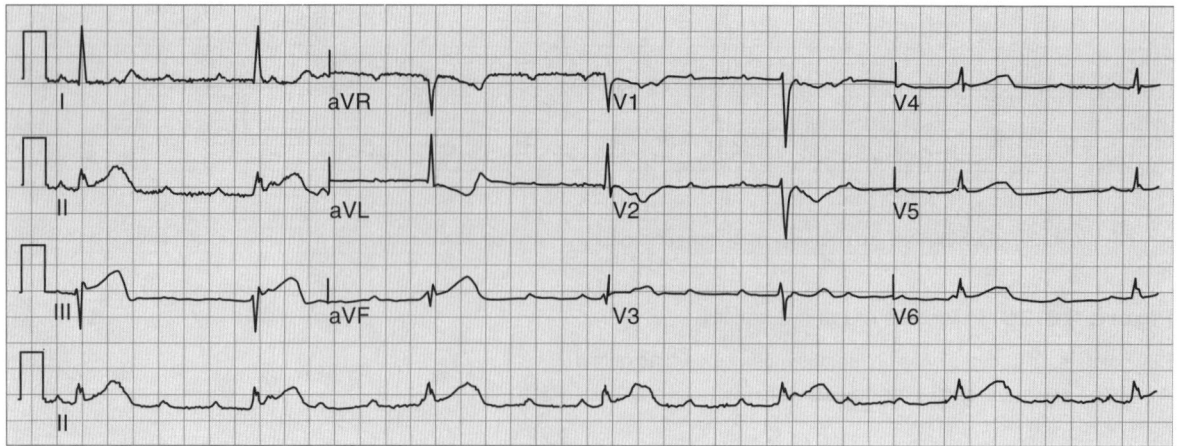

Figure 26.33 Third-degree heart block – ventricular rate 42 beats/min with no relationship between P waves and QRS complexes

- Tall "tented" T waves
- Widening of the T waves
- Flattening and occasional loss of the P wave
- Lengthening of the PR interval
- Widening of the QRS interval
- Arrhythmias

Hypokalaemia

Hypokalaemia is most commonly caused by diuretics, such as loop and thiazide. The following ECG changes, shown in Figure 26.35, may be present:

- First-degree heart block
- Depression of the ST segment
- Prominent U waves

Hypercalcaemia

The shortened QT interval in hypercalcaemia results from abnormally rapid ventricular repolarisation. This condition is shown in Figure 26.36.

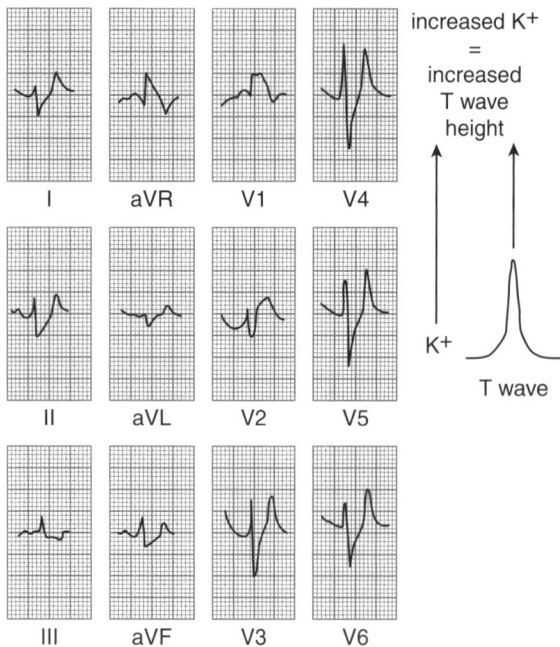

Figure 26.34 Hyperkalaemia

Key point: • Tall "tented" T waves

Source: Houghton & Gray 2003. p. 179. Reproduced by permission of Edward Arnold

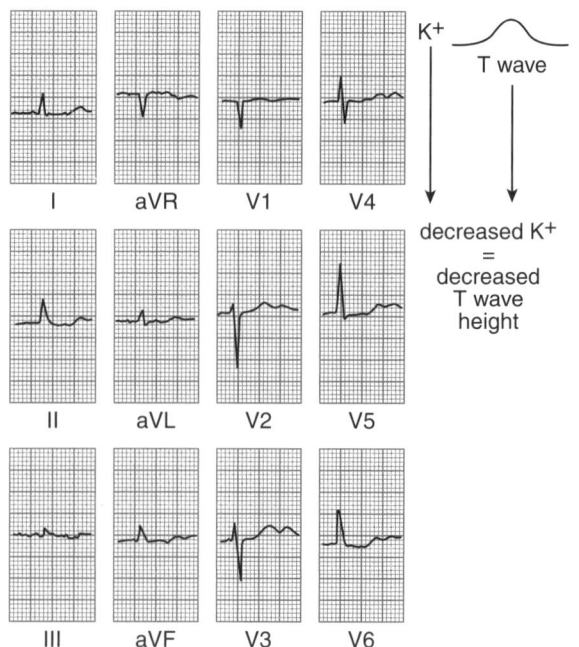

Figure 26.35 Hypokalaemia

Key points: • Small T waves • Prominent U waves

Source: Houghton & Gray 2003. p. 182. Reproduced by permission of Edward Arnold

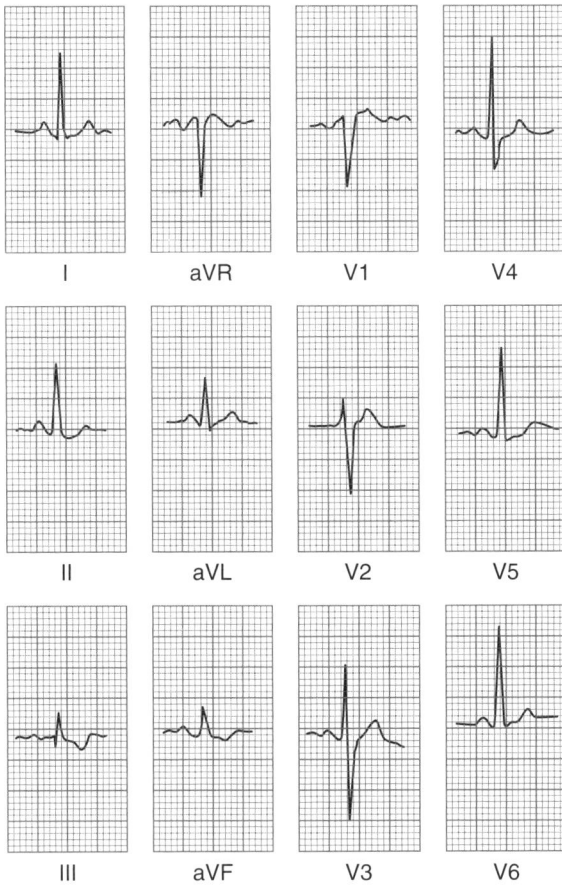

Figure 26.36 Short QT interval in hypercalcaemia

Key points: • QT interval is 0.26 s
• Heart rate is 100 beats/min, QT_C interval is 0.34 s

Source: Houghton & Gray 2003. p. 196. Reproduced by permission of Edward Arnold

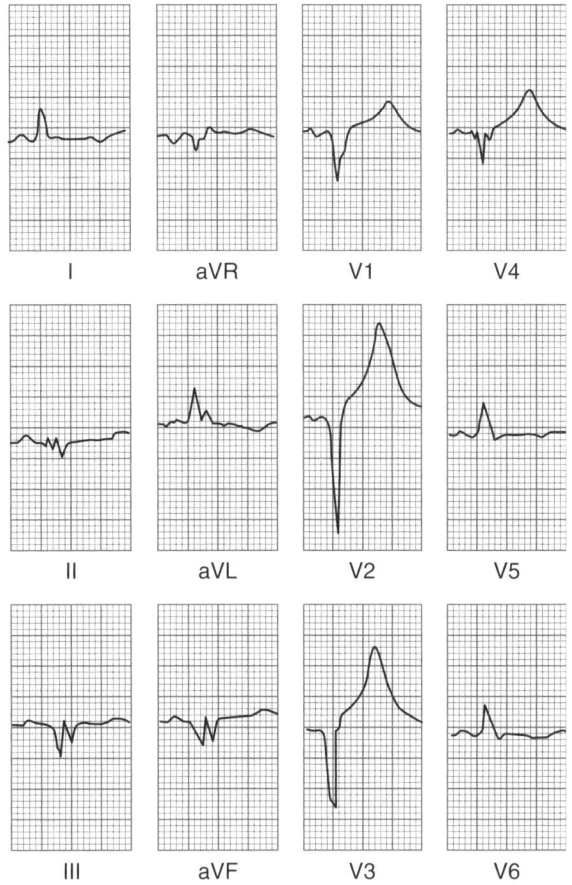

Figure 26.37 Long QT interval in hypocalcaemia

Key points: • QT interval is 0.57 s
• Heart rate is 51 beats/min, QT_C interval is 0.52 s

Source: Houghton & Gray 2003. p. 199. Reproduced by permission of Edward Arnold

Hypocalcaemia

Hypocalcaemia is associated with prolongation of the QT interval. Figure 26.37 illustrates this condition.

Effects of digoxin on an ECG

Digoxin effect

As shown in Figure 26.38, the ECG changes may be present in therapeutic dosages, and may include the following:

• ST segment depression, that is like a "reverse tick"
• Reduction in T wave size
• Shortening of the QT interval

Digoxin toxicity

There may be clinical symptoms associated with digoxin toxicity, which is shown in Figure 26.39, for example anorexia, nausea, vomiting, abdominal pain and visual disturbance. Arrhythmias are more likely if the patient is hypokalaemic. The following ECG changes may be seen:

• T wave inversion
• Almost any arrhythmias, for example sinus bradycardia, paroxysmal atrial tachycardia with block, atrioventricular block, ventricular ectopics, ventricular bigeminy and ventricular tachycardia

Structural abnormalities of the heart on an ECG

We will now explore certain of such abnormalities.

Left ventricular hypertrophy

Hypertrophy of the left ventricle causes tall R waves in the leads that look at the left ventricle, that is I, aVL, V5 and V6, and the reciprocal changes of deep

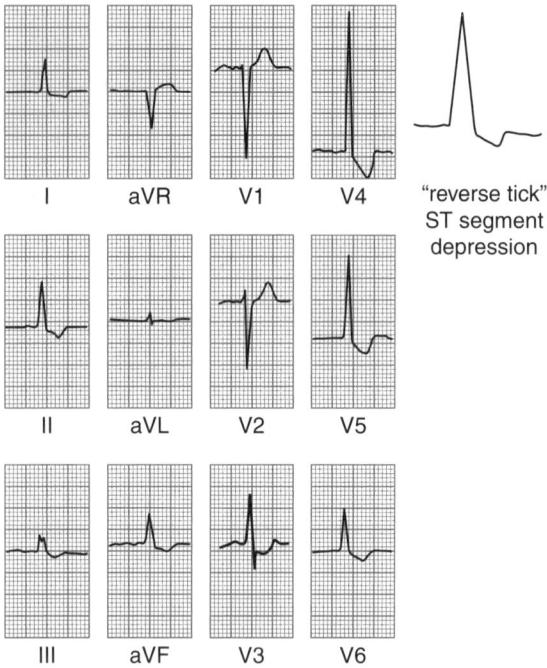

Figure 26.38 Digoxin effect

Key point: • "Reverse tick" ST segment depression

Source: Houghton & Gray 2003. p. 174. Reproduced by permission of Edward Arnold

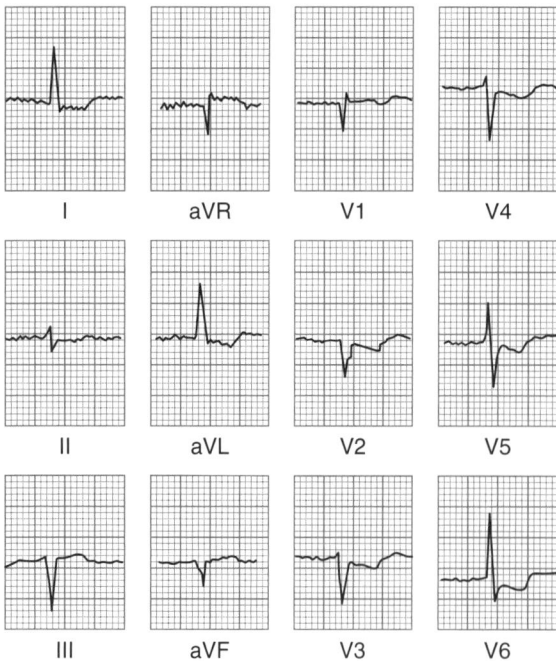

Figure 26.39 Digoxin toxicity

Key points: • T wave inversion in leads V2–V6
• Patient on digoxin for atrial fibrillation

Source: Houghton & Gray 2003. p. 190. Reproduced by permission of Edward Arnold

S waves in leads that look at the right ventricle, that is V1 and V2.

The following ECG changes may be seen in left ventricular hypertrophy, which is illustrated in Figure 26.40:

• The R wave in V5 or V6 exceeds 25 mm.
• The S wave in V1 or V2 exceeds 25 mm.
• The total of the R wave in V5 or V6 plus the S wave in V1 or V2 exceeds 35 mm.

However, these findings may also be present in young, thin, healthy people as a normal variation.

ST segment depression and T wave inversion provide evidence of **left ventricular strain** which should be present in true left ventricular hypertrophy.

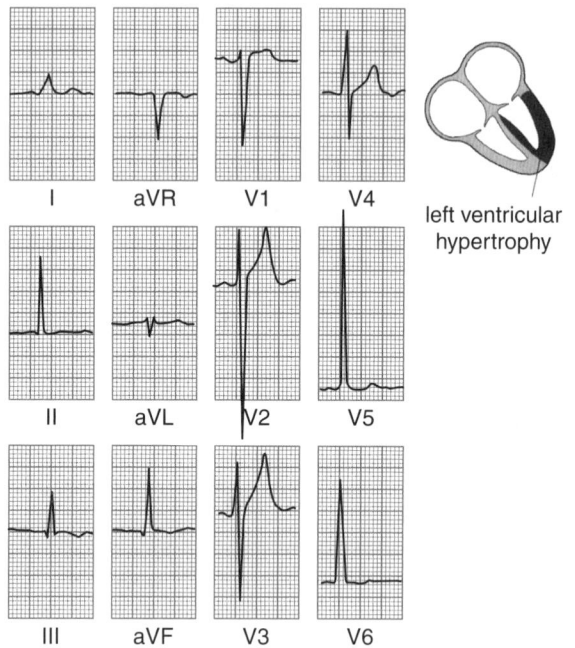

Figure 26.40 Left ventricular hypertrophy

Key points: • 41-mm R wave in lead V5
• 35-mm S wave in lead V2

Source: Houghton & Gray 2003. p. 136. Reproduced by permission of Edward Arnold

Right ventricular hypertrophy

Right ventricular hypertrophy, illustrated in Figure 26.41, causes a dominant tall R wave in the leads that look at the right ventricle, particularly V1. Other ECG changes include:

• Right axis deviation.
• Deep S waves in V5 and V6.
• Right bundle branch block.

ST segment depression in leads V1–V3 and T wave inversion in V1–V3 provide signs of **right ventricular strain**, which is also illustrated in Figure 26.41.

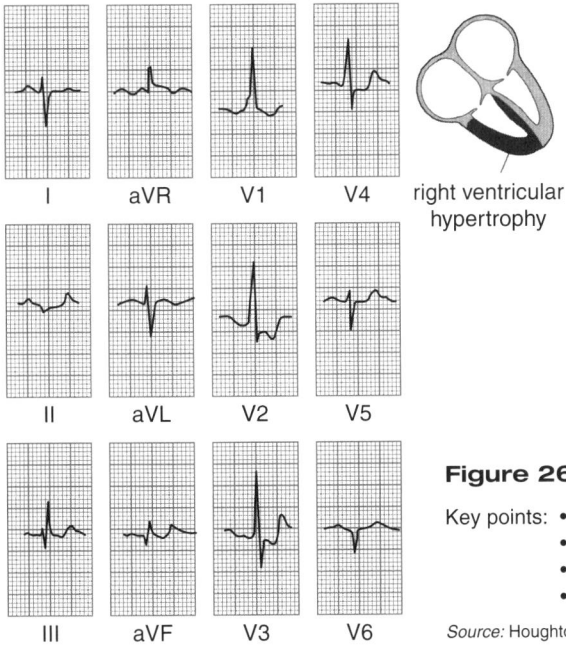

Figure 26.41 Right ventricular hypertrophy with "strain"

Key points:
- Dominant R waves in leads V1–V4
- Deep S waves in leads V5 and V6
- Right axis deviation
- ST segment depression/T wave inversion in leads V1–V3

Source: Houghton & Gray 2003. p. 137. Reproduced by permission of Edward Arnold

27 How to do an exercise ECG test

PAUL HILL

We use exercise electrocardiography for the assessment of patients with ischaemic heart disease and exercise-related arrhythmias. You can also find it useful for assessing effort tolerance and prognosis.

Indications

You can perform an exercise ECG in the following instances:

- Diagnosis of chest pain
- Risk stratification in stable angina
- Risk stratification after myocardial infarction
- Assessment of exercise-induced arrhythmias
- Assessment of the need for a permanent pacemaker
- Assessment of exercise tolerance
- Assessment of the patient's response to treatment

Risks and contraindications

Note that there are risks to performing exercise ECGs, such as a morbidity of 2.4 per 10 000 and a mortality of 1 in 10 000. Therefore, you must take the patient's history and perform a careful clinical examination before embarking on the procedure.

Absolute contraindications to an exercise ECG are as follows:

- Myocardial infarction within the previous seven days
- Unstable angina – rest pain within the previous 48 hours
- Severe aortic stenosis or hypertrophic obstructive cardiomyopathy
- Acute myocarditis
- Acute pericarditis
- Uncontrolled hypertension – systolic more than 250 mmHg, diastolic more than 120 mmHg
- Uncontrolled heart failure
- A recent thromboembolic episode
- Acute febrile illness

Technique

You need to perform the procedure under the strict supervision of people who are trained in CPR, and with all the necessary drugs and equipment available.

The two most common protocols used are the **Bruce protocol** and the **modified Bruce protocol**. Figure 27.1 shows these protocols. The latter begins with a lighter workload than the former and is particularly suitable for frail patients or those being assessed after a recent myocardial infarction. Monitor the patient's symptoms and ECG throughout the procedure, and check the blood pressure every three minutes.

When to stop

A good prognosis is the patient's ability to achieve the target heart rate with no symptoms or significant ECG changes. The target heart rate is 220 minus the patient's age in years. You must stop the test if

- the patient asks for it to be stopped
- the systolic blood pressure falls by more than 20 mmHg
- the heart rate falls by more than 10 beats per minute
- sustained ventricular or supraventricular arrhythmias occur
- there is greater than 2 mm ST depression and chest pain
- there is greater than 3 mm asymptomatic ST segment depression
- there is conduction disturbance and chest pain
- there is non-sustained ventricular tachycardia
- the patient experiences dizziness
- the patient experiences marked breathlessness
- the patient suffers severe fatigue or exhaustion.

Interpretation

Figure 27.2 illustrates the results of an exercise test of a patient with coronary artery disease. The most common indicator of such disease is the development of ST segment depression with exercise – the

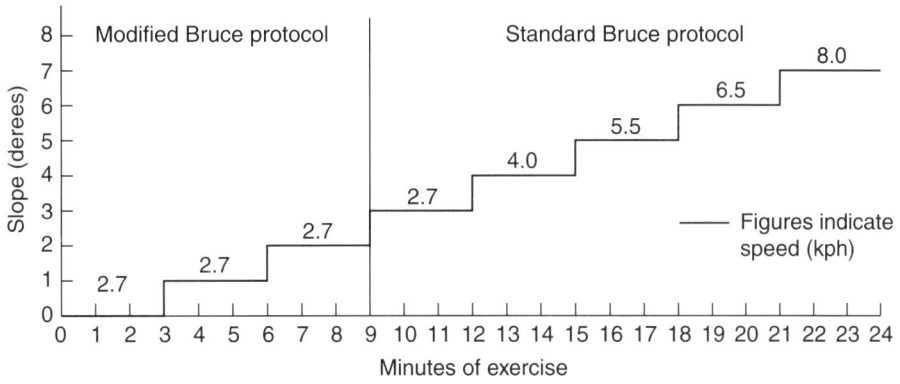

Protocol	Modified Bruce			Standard Bruce				
Stage	01	02	03	1	2	3	4	5
Speed (kph)	2.7	2.7	2.7	2.7	4.0	5.5	6.8	8.0
Slopes (degrees)	0	1.3	2.6	4.3	5.4	6.3	7.2	8.1

Figure 27.1 Bruce protocol and modified Bruce protocol

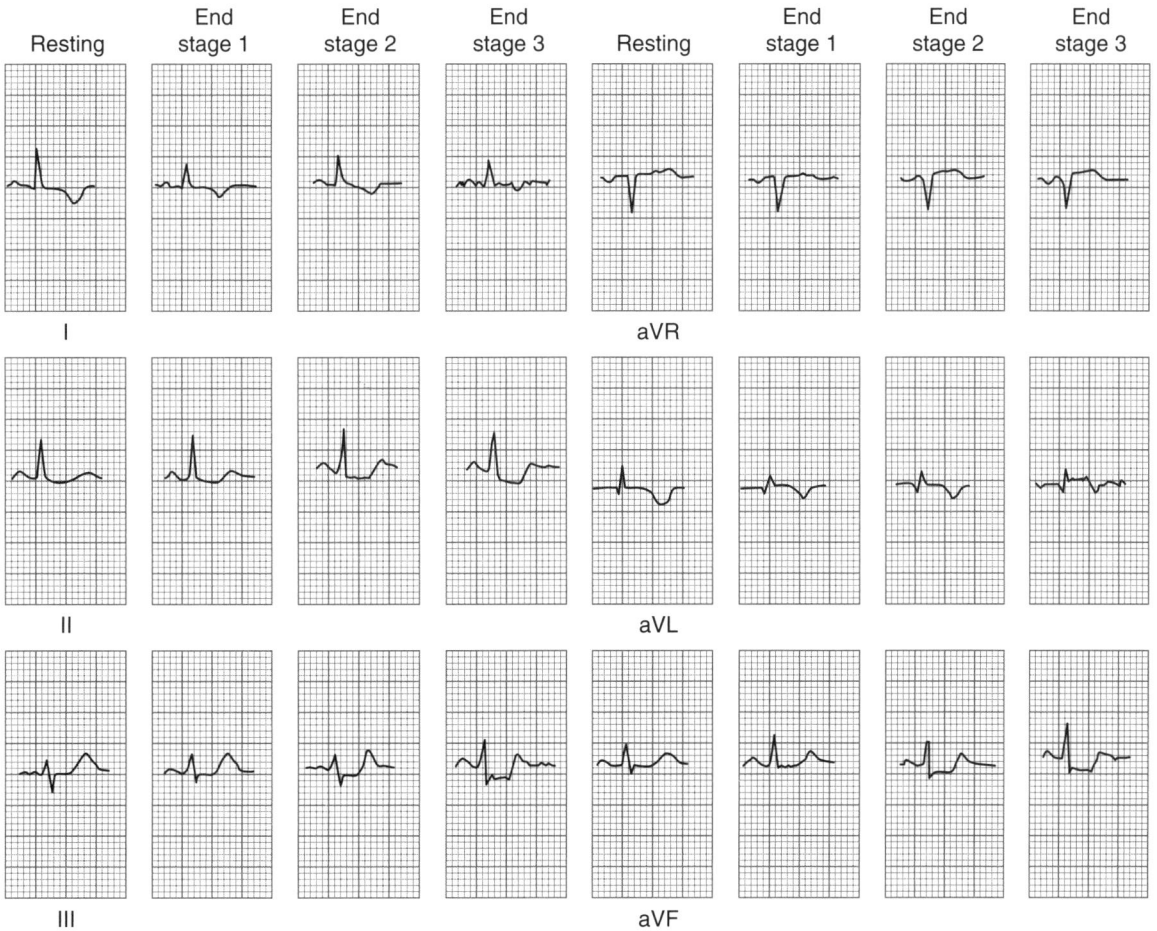

Figure 27.2 Exercise text of a patient with coronary artery disease

Key point: • Inferolateral ST segment depression during exercise

Source: Houghton & Gray 2003. p. 239–40. Reproduced by permission of Edward Arnold

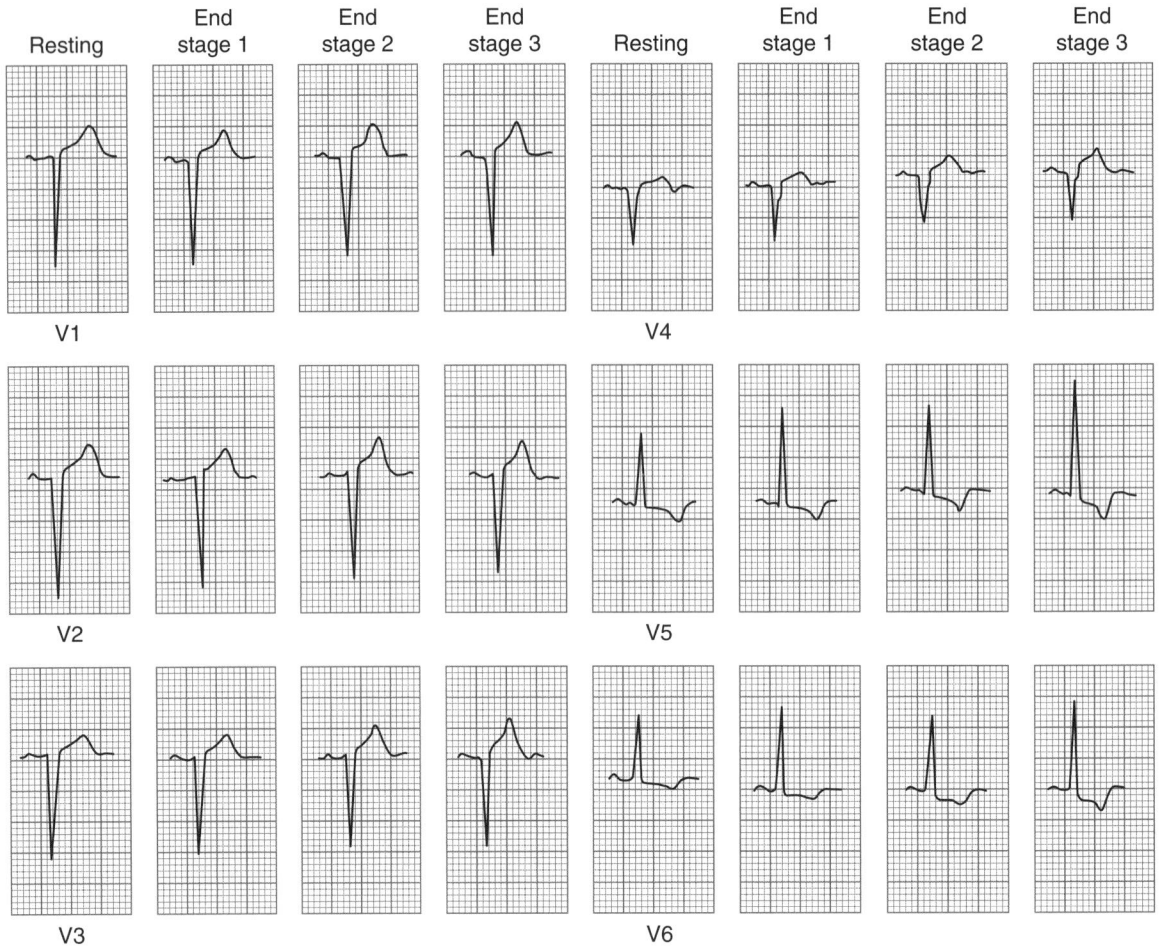

Figure 27.2 (continued)

greater the depression the higher the probability of the disease. Take care when measuring ST segment depression while the patient is exercising, as depression of the J point is normal, which means the junction of the S wave and the ST segment. The ST segment slopes up sharply after the J point and returns to the baseline within 60 ms or 1.5 small squares. Thus you must measure ST segment depression 80 ms, or two small squares, beyond the J point. Figure 27.3 illustrates this point.

Note that ST depression may not be the only significant result, as T wave inversion can also develop during exercise. Bundle branch block may develop too, although not necessarily with significant coronary artery disease. A fall in systolic blood pressure often indicates significant coronary disease.

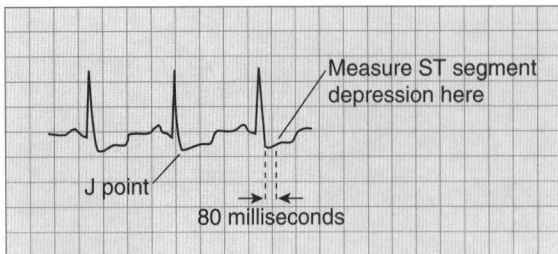

Figure 27.3 The J point

Source: Houghton & Gray 2003. p. 238. Reproduced by permission of Edward Arnold

Key points: • The J point is the junction of the S wave and ST segment
• Measure ST segment depression 80 ms after the J point

28 How to use inhalers and spacers

BOB MASH

To manage asthma and chronic obstructive pulmonary disease (COPD), the patient must adequately adhere to your prescribed dose of medication as well as successfully deliver the medication to his lungs. Inhaler technique, therefore, is an important part of patient education and clinical follow-up. As a family physician you need to have examples of the inhalers available and placebo devices to demonstrate the technique. You should be able to use correctly all the devices that you prescribe.

There is a wide variety of devices ranging from the classic metered dose inhaler (MDI) to powder-based diskhalers and breath-activated devices. The pharmaceutical insert usually provides instructions with each device. As is illustrated in Figure 28.1, advise your patient to follow these steps when using a typical MDI:

1. Shake the inhaler to mix the medication and propellant.
2. Remove the cap and check that there are no foreign bodies inside the inhaler.
3. Hold the inhaler in an upright position.
4. Exhale fully.
5. Place the lips closely around the mouthpiece.
6. Activate the inhaler by pressing down on the canister and at the same time taking in a slow, deep breath. Take only one puff at a time.
7. After breathing in the medication, hold your breath for up to 10 seconds.
8. Wait for a minute and then repeat if a second puff is required.
9. Wash your mouth after inhalation of corticosteroids.

Figure 28.1

Using an inhaler

Spacers help to reduce the amount of coordination required and increase deposition of medication in the lungs. Therefore, advise that spacers are used in the following instances (Motala, Kling, Gie, Potter et al. 2000):

- **Children under three years of age:** The delivery system of choice is an MDI with a spacer. The spacer should be fitted with a facemask. Nebulisers are an alternative, but you should prescribe them only if the child is not able to use an MDI and a spacer. Do not advise the patient to use dry powder devices and breath-activated MDIs.

- **Children between three and five:** The delivery system of choice is an MDI with a small volume spacer (250–300 ml). The spacer should be used with a mouthpiece. Should the child be unable to manage a mouthpiece, he may use a facemask. Breath-activated systems are not indicated. Dry powder devices are generally not indicated, but some have been used successfully in children as young as three years. You need to evaluate this on an individual basis. Nebulisers are seldom indicated for this age group and should be used only if children refuse to use spacers.

- **Children older than five:** The delivery system of choice is an MDI with a large volume spacer (greater than 500 ml). The spacer should be used with a mouthpiece. Dry powder devices and breath-activated devices can be used successfully. Nebulisers should only be used in this age group in exceptional circumstances, that is if they refuse to, or really cannot use the devices above!

- **Adults who are unable to use an MDI correctly.**

- **Adults and children who are on inhaled corticosteroids** to maximise the benefit, and reduce systemic absorption and local side-effects such as dysphonia and candidiasis.

While facilitating the patient's use of an MDI, spacers still require a certain amount of technique, and the patient can also use them incorrectly. Some spacers have a valve that allows inspiration only from the chamber. The patient should breathe in one puff at a time only, as the percentage of medication delivered to the lungs from multiple simultaneous activations actually decreases.

After activating the device and filling the spacer chamber with medication, the patient should use the spacer immediately by taking a number of slow, deep breaths through the mouthpiece. Static electricity diminishes the amount of drug delivered but it can be minimised in a stainless steel spacer or a low static spacer, or by priming a plastic spacer with multiple activations from an MDI. Advise the patient to clean the spacer once a week with liquid detergent without rinsing, and allow it to air-dry – this avoids the build-up of static electricity.

Although plastic cups do not make efficient spacers, patients can make a spacer at home from a 500-ml plastic cold-drink bottle. He should cut a hole that fits the MDI mouthpiece in the base of the bottle. This can be done by heating a metal rod that is bent to the same size as the inhaler's mouthpiece and using it to melt through the plastic to make a hole of the correct size.

29 How to do office spirometry

SAVILLE FURMAN

The peak-flow meter is a useful office tool in the assessment of respiratory disease. The patient can also use it effectively at home. However, spirometry is essential for a complete respiratory evaluation, not only for curative purposes, but also for screening, early detection and surveillance programmes. The basic spirometric procedure involves the measurement of gas volume and rate of airflow during a maximal, forced expiration. It measures the forced expiratory volume in one second (FEV1) as well as the forced vital capacity (FVC). FEV1 and FVC are related to height, age and gender.

Indications

The most frequent clinical indications for spirometry in family practice are as follows:

- **To confirm a diagnosis:** Results could reveal that there is
  - no lung disease (FEV1/FVC > = 75%)
  - obstructive airways disease, such as COPD, asthma or a lung tumour (FEV1 to FVC ratio is reduced)
  - restrictive lung disease, that is lung fibrosis, chest wall problems, pleural effusion or pulmonary oedema (FEV1 and FVC are both reduced so the ratio of FEV1 to FVC is normal or even raised)
- **To grade respiratory impairment:** At the start of treatment, in medico-legal cases or prior to surgery.
- **To monitor changes in lung function:** In patients with chronic respiratory diseases you would use spirometry to evaluate their responses to treatment and to document disease progression.
- **To screen for lung disease:** You can consider screening in the following patients:
  - Long-term smokers
  - Patients who are exposed at work to potentially

harmful substances known to cause respiratory disease – you need to determine their pre-employment baseline lung function.
- Patients with significant exposure to substances known to cause respiratory diseases

Contraindications to spirometry include cost, absence of good technique and time constraints.

We will now discuss the two kinds of spirometers.

Volume-type spirometers

These spirometers determine volume directly and have the advantages of being inexpensive and easy to operate. However, data processing and storage capacity may be limited unless the spirometer contains a microprocessor.

Flow-type spirometers

These spirometers make use of a flow-sensor, or pneumotach, to derive volumes. They are computerised, provide quick reference values, produce flow-volume loops enabling instant pattern recognition and can usually store large data sets. However, they require greater expertise to operate, calibrate and maintain.

To operate this kind of spirometer you need to understand the principles underlying the measurements. Moreover, you must be able to ensure optimum patient cooperation, provide acceptable, reproducible results and recognise common abnormalities.

Make the patient feel comfortable by loosening any tight clothing. Have him sit upright on a firm chair with his chin slightly elevated and neck slightly extended. He must maintain this posture during the forced expiration. It is recommended that you use a nose clip, as shown in Figure 29.1, to prevent air from escaping through his nostrils. Before beginning the procedure, explain and demonstrate the use of the nose clip and mouthpiece to the patient.

Figure 29.1 Using a nose clip in a spirometry test

Methods

There are two main test manoeuvres:

1. **Expiratory-only method:** This is recommended for mass screening.
2. **Inspiratory-expiratory method:** You can use this method to record inspiration and expiration in order to generate a flow volume curve on a flow-type spirometer. Figures 29.2 and 29.3 show these curves. Once the patient has inserted the mouthpiece, he must breathe quietly for several moments and then make a complete expiration. This should be followed by a rapid and forceful inspiration and, finally, a rapid, forceful and complete expiration. Some programmes prompt for an expiratory manoeuvre followed by an inspiratory manoeuvre.

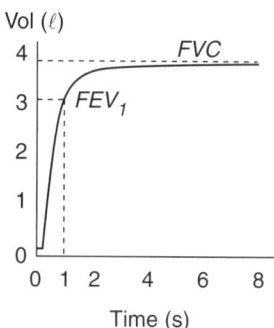

Figure 29.2

Volume–time curve

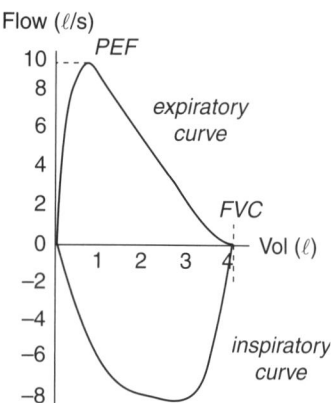

Figure 29.3

Flow–volume curve

Results

Probably the most useful test for which you can use the spirometer is the response to a bronchodilator. With it, you can determine whether the patient's airway obstruction is reversible with inhaled beta-2 agonists. This process is illustrated in Figures 29.4 and 29.5.

You can standardise a bronchodilator test as follows:

- Obtain two reproducible FEV1 readings from the patient.
- Administer two puffs (400 µg) of salbutamol or equivalent.

Age: 59   Height: 154 cm   Sex: Female

	PREDICTED	MEASURED	%
VC	2.36	–	–
FVC	2.40	1.62	68
FEV1	2.01	0.99	49
FEV1 %	78	61	−17
PEF	335	198	59

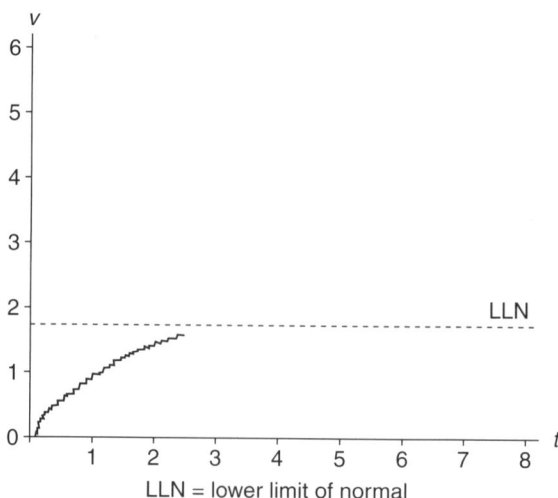

LLN = lower limit of normal

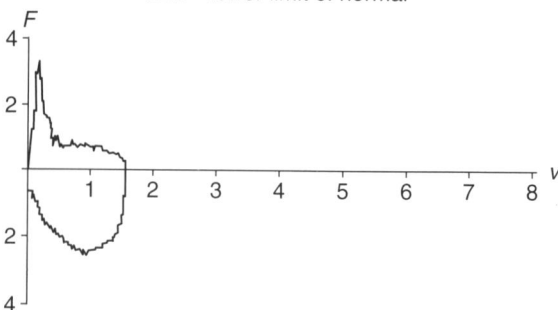

A 59-year-old female came for an evaluation to see if she fitted the criteria to partake in an asthma study. This was the baseline reading. She had not had any beta-2 agonists for at least 6 hours.

Figure 29.4 Airway obstruction before the patient inhaled beta-2-agonists

- Wait for at least 10 minutes, ideally 20–30 minutes.
- Obtain two more reproducible FEV1 readings.
- Evaluate the best post-bronchodilator FEV1 for a significant improvement of at least 200 ml *and* 12% from the pre-bronchodilator FEV1.

Using the above criteria, reversibility testing to corticosteroids is also possible. In patients who use a bronchodilator more than once a day you should test the FEV1 before and after a two-week course of 30 mg prednisolone per day or 500 µg inhaled beclomethasone per day.

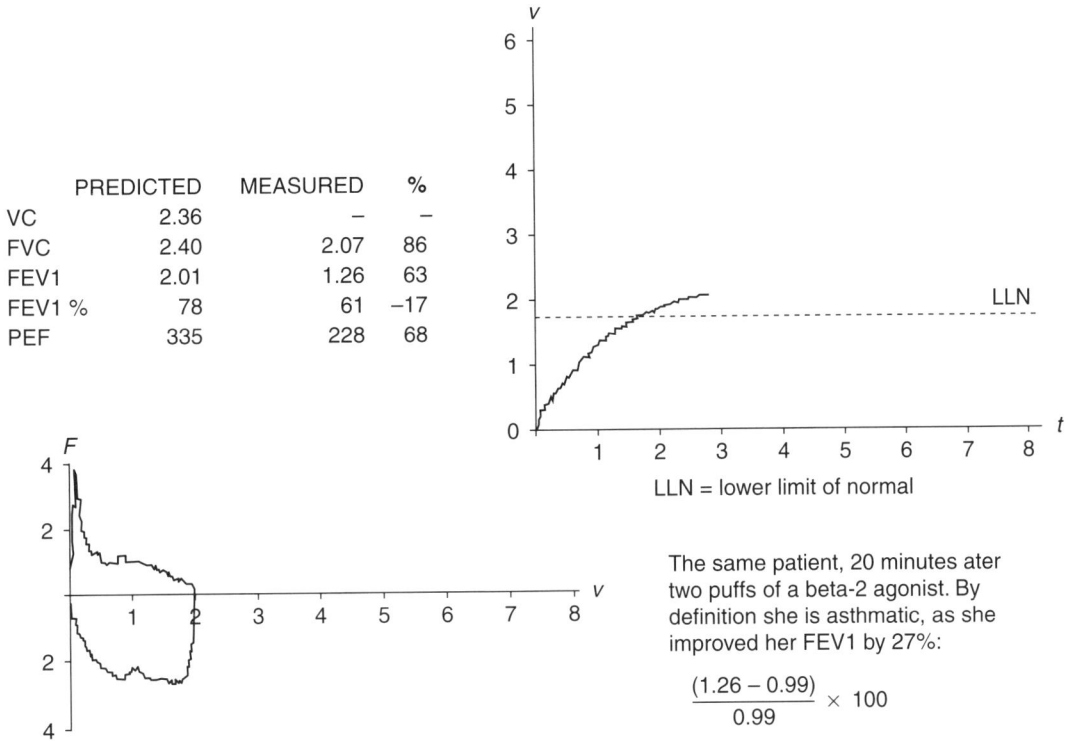

	PREDICTED	MEASURED	%
VC	2.36	–	–
FVC	2.40	2.07	86
FEV1	2.01	1.26	63
FEV1 %	78	61	–17
PEF	335	228	68

LLN = lower limit of normal

The same patient, 20 minutes ater two puffs of a beta-2 agonist. By definition she is asthmatic, as she improved her FEV1 by 27%:

$$\frac{(1.26 - 0.99)}{0.99} \times 100$$

Figure 29.5 Airway obstruction slightly relieved after the patient inhaled beta-2-agonists

30 How to use a peak expiratory flow meter

BOB MASH

The peak expiratory flow (PEF) meter is an essential tool in your diagnosis and assessment of asthmatic patients.

Indications for using the PEF meter are for the assessment of

- severity and response to treatment in an acute asthmatic attack
- severity and monitoring of control in chronic persistent asthma
- reversibility of lower airway obstruction and differentiation of asthma from chronic obstructive airways disease
- home monitoring of symptoms and control of asthma.

The variety of PEF meters available all work on the same principles. Once you have made sure that the marker is on zero, ask the patient to

- stand up, in order to give maximum expiratory effort
- take in a big breath
- hold the meter, place the mouthpiece in his mouth, and make a good seal with his lips
- exhale through the meter as forcefully as possible, giving his peak expiratory flow.

Take the reading three times, encouraging the patient to achieve his peak expiratory flow rate. Low readings may be due to a poor effort or technique on the part of the patient, and you should record it as such in his file. Record the highest reading.

You can determine the predicted PEF from Figures 30.1 and 30.2, which require you to know the patient's gender, age and height. These figures give a predicted mean for the patient – individual scores may be higher or lower than the mean. Once you have discovered the patient's best PEF rate then you can use it as a better benchmark than the PEF predicted in the graphs. (See Figures 30.1 and 30.2.)

Ideally, the patient should have a PEF meter and should keep an asthma diary to record peak flow readings. He must bring these along to check-ups and casualty visits. You and he should have a written management plan in place that describes what he needs to do if the PEF is below 60%, or if he experiences warning symptoms of an imminent attack.

Table 30.1 summarises the assessment of severity in acute asthma.

Table 30.2 summarises the assessment of severity in chronic asthma.

Table 30.3 summarises the assessment of reversibility and differentiation of asthma from COPD.

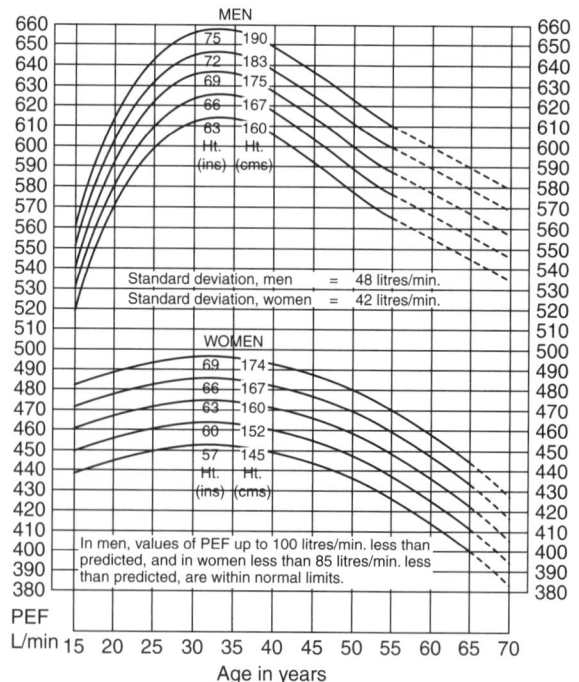

Figure 30.1 PEF in normal adult subjects

Source: Gregg I, Nunn AJ. Peak expiratory flow in normal subjects. BMJ, 1973;3: **282**

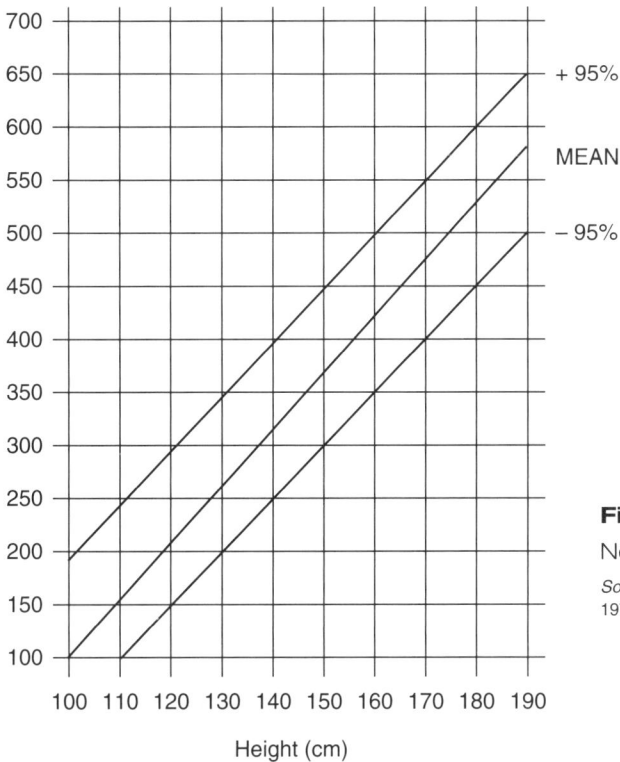

Figure 30.2

Nomogram for children

Source: Godfrey et al. Nomogram. Br J Dis Chest, 1970; 64: 15

Table 30.1 Assessment of severity in acute asthma

Observation	Moderate	Severe	Imminent respiratory arrest
PEF after initial bronchodilator	50–75% of best or predicted	< 50% of best or predicted	< 100 ℓ per min
Breathless **Posture**	When talking Prefers to sit	At rest Hunched forward	Exhaustion
Talks in	Phrases	Words	
Alertness	Agitated	Agitated	Drowsy or confused
Respiratory rate	Increased	Often > 30 per min	
Accessory muscles	+	++	Paradoxical thoraco-abdominal movements
Wheeze	Loud	Usually loud	Absent – so called "silent chest"
Pulse	100–120 per min	> 120 per min	Bradycardia
PaO$_2$ on air (partial pressure of oxygen in arterial blood)	> 8 kPa	< 8 kPa May be cyanosed	Cyanosis
SaO$_2$ on air (oxygen saturation)	91–95%	< 90%	

Source: SA Pulmonology Society. Guidelines for the management of asthma in adults in South Africa. Part II. Acute asthma. S Afr Med J. 1994 Jun;84(6): 332–8

Table 30.2 Assessment of severity in chronic asthma

	Intermittent	Persistent		
		Mild	**Moderate**	**Severe**
Frequency of daytime symptoms	< = 1 per week	2–4 per week	> 4 per week	Continuous
Frequency of night-time symptoms	< = 1 per month	2–4 per month	> 4 per month	Frequent
PEF	> = 80%	> = 80%	60–80%	< 60%

Source: Lalloo UG, Bateman ED, Feldman C, Bardin PG et al. Guidelines for the management of chronic asthma in adults – 2000 update. SAMJ, 2000 May, 90(5): 540–52

Table 30.3 Assessment of reversibility and differentiation of asthma from COPD

Criteria	COPD	Asthma
Age of onset	Often in middle-age adult life	Often from childhood
Smoker or ex-smoker	Usually a history of >10 pack years	Non-smoker or short history of smoking
Atopic history	Unusual	History of atopy such as eczema, allergic rhinitis and urticaria
Pattern of breathlessness	Persistent and consistent	Episodic and variable. May be able to document a diurnal variation in PEF at home or see a wide variation in PEF readings in the medical record
Reversibility in obstruction	Little reversibility	Reversibility, such as increase in PEF > 15% after beta-2-agonist inhalation or after a two-week course of corticosteroids

Source: Lalloo UG, Bateman ED, Feldman C, Bardin PG et al. Guidelines for the management of chronic asthma in adults – 2000 update. SAMJ, 2000 May, 90(5): 540–52

31 How to read a chest radiograph

CYRIL NAIDOO AND ANDREW ROSS

In order for you to be able to interpret a chest X-ray (CXR) and detect any abnormalities, you need to understand the anatomy of the chest. This is illustrated in Figure 31.1. Figure 31.2 shows the posterio-anterior (PA) view and Figure 31.3 shows the lateral view of the anatomy of the chest on CXRs.

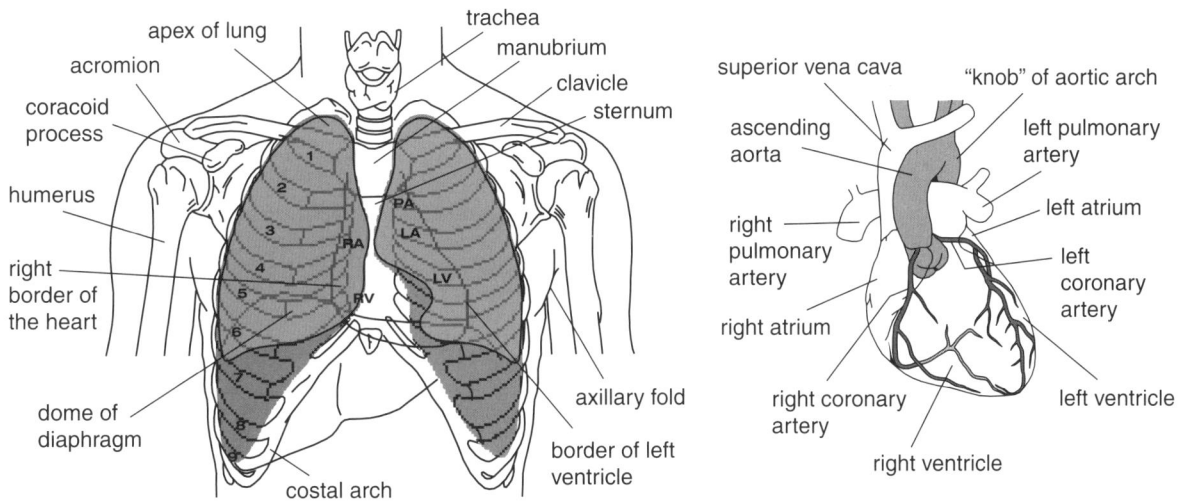

Figure 31.1 Anatomy of the adult chest

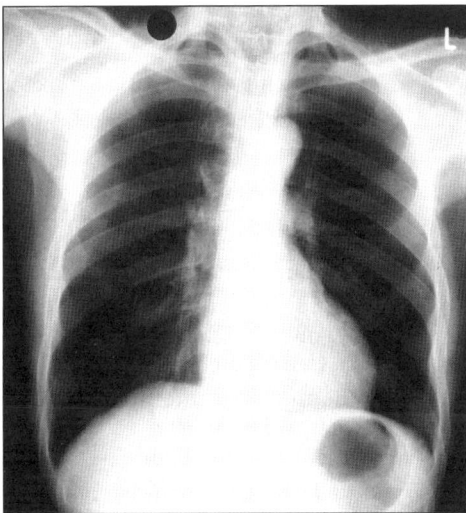

Figure 31.2 PA radiograph view of the anatomy of the chest

Radiographic factors

These factors are important in obtaining an adequate radiograph:

- **Exposure factors:** Greater than 120 Kilovolts, taking into consideration the patient's physique and size.
- **Good inspiration:** You should be able to see at least 11 ribs posteriorly above the diaphragm.
- **Good position:** The patient should stand erect, his anterior chest wall should be flat against the cassette and his hands must be on his hips. The tube should be more than 1 m from the cassette at level of T3.

Reading a CXR

It is important that you understand the clinical context and reason for requesting the CXR so that you can interpret it accurately. Be systematic and consis-

Figure 31.3 thyroid gland — apex of lung — trachea — scapula — right pulmonary arteries and vein — left atrial boundary — oblique fissure (right) — border of left ventricle — right hemidiaphragm — left hemidiaphragm — pleural reflection — gastric air bubble — horizontal fissure, right lung — AO — PT — LA — RV — LV — apex — liver

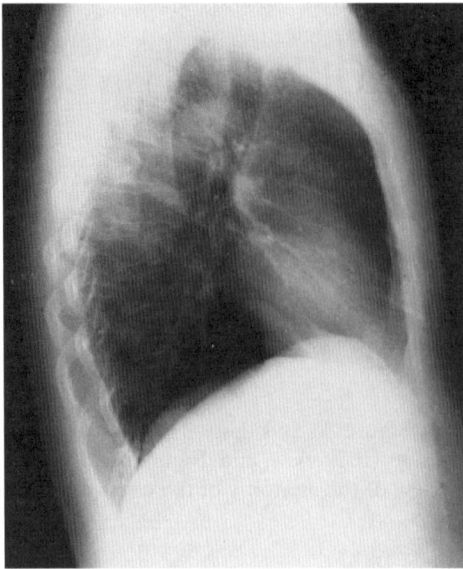

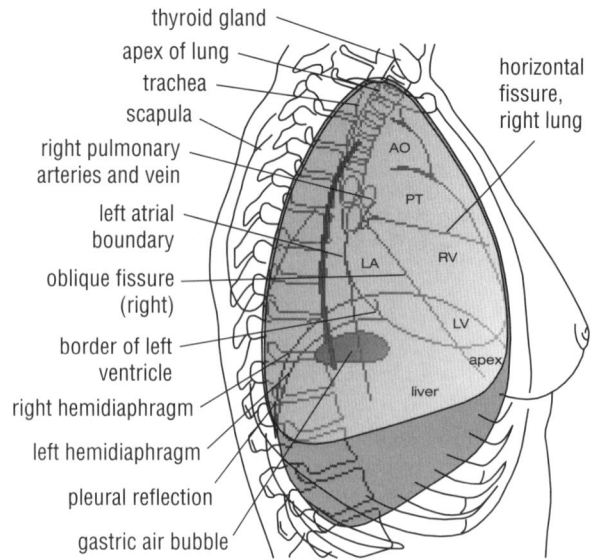

Figure 31.3 Lateral radiograph view of the anatomy of the chest

tent in the manner in which you assess all CXR films:

• Identify the patient and film. Record the patient's name, and the date and time of the CXR.

• Check the type of radiograph. Are all the requested views included? Is the entire anatomical area included? Note the projection, that is anterio-posterior (AP), PA or lateral.

• Check the patient's position. Is it central or rotated? Are the medial edges of the clavicle equidistant from the spine?

• Check the CXR penetration. Is it over- or underexposed? You should just be able to see vertebral bodies through the heart.

• Check the patient's inspiration. You should be able to see 11 ribs posteriorly and seven ribs anteriorly.

• Start assessing the CXR peripherally and then read towards the centre.

When reading a CXR, you need to look for the following:

• **Soft tissues:** Look for artefacts due to jewellery or clothing. In females check that both breast shadows are present. Look for soft-tissue calcification, subcutaneous gas (see Figure 31.4) and axillary and clavicular shadows. *Compare both sides.*

• **Skeleton:** Count all the ribs. Check for focal lesions such as lytic or sclerotic metastases (see Figure 31.5), and fractures or skeletal deformities. Check both clavicles and both shoulders, and the cervical and thoracic spine. Look for evidence of osteoporosis.

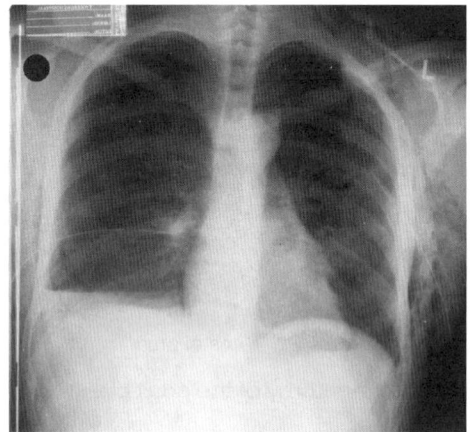

Figure 31.4 Right haemopneumothorax and surgical emphysema seen clearly in the soft tissues of the left axilla. Intercostal drains seen bilaterally

• **Pleura:** These are normally not visible. Check whether the costophrenic angles are sharp or blunt. Look for pneumothorax. See Figure 31.4.

• **Airways:** Check whether the trachea is central or shifted (see Figure 31.5). Look for endotracheal or other tubes (see Figure 31.4).

• **Lungs:** Divide the lungs into upper, middle and lower zones and *compare both sides.* Look at the pulmonary vascularity (see Figure 31.6).

• **Diaphragm:** The right hemi-diaphragm is 2–3 cm higher than the left. Compare the shape and position. Look for free air under the diaphragm in an erect CXR (see Figure 43.7).

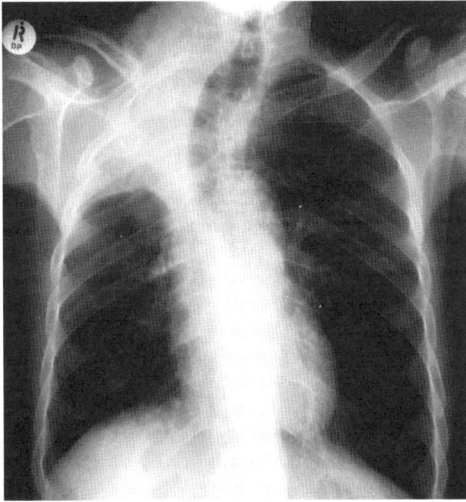

Figure 31.5 Carcinoma of right upper lobe bronchus, causing collapse. Airway displaced to the right. Metastases seen in right clavicle and soft-tissue swelling in neck due to lymphadenopathy

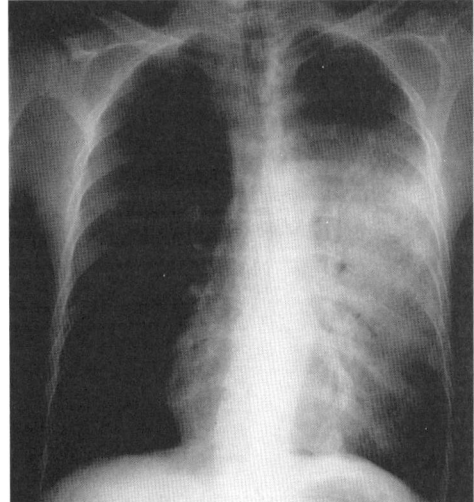

Figure 31.6 Left upper lobar pneumonia showing consolidation and air bronchograms

- **Hilar regions:** The left is 2 cm superior to the right. Check the position, contour and density. Look for hilar masses or lymphadenopathy. See Figure 31.7.
- **Mediastinum:** Check the position with two thirds of the transverse diameter of the heart to the left of the spine, and one third to the right. In the superior mediastinum the trachea should be central and anterior to the thoracic spine.
- **Heart:** Check the heart size; the cardio-thoracic ratio is normally less than 50%. Also check the position and shape. Look for enlargement of the ventricles and straightening of the left heart border. See Figure 31.8.

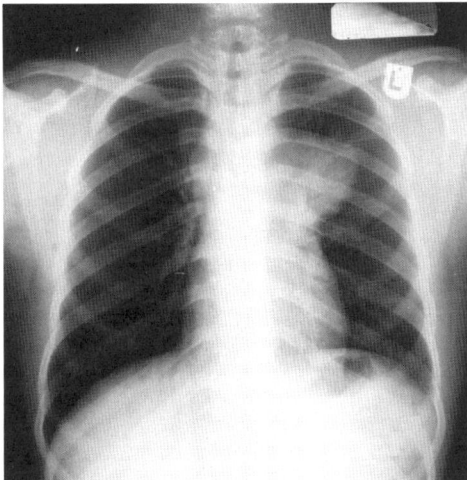

Figure 31.7 Bilateral parahilar mediastinal masses (due to Hodgkin's disease)

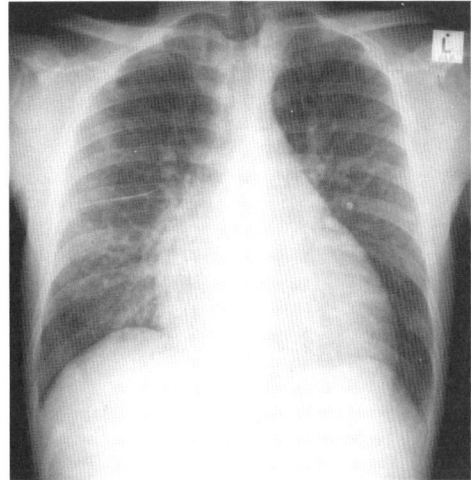

Figure 31.8 Congestive cardiac failure with cardiomegaly and pulmonary congestion

32 How to do a pleural tap

CYRIL NAIDOO AND ANDREW ROSS

Indications

You would perform a pleural tap to obtain pleural fluid for diagnostic purposes, and occasionally to relieve the patient's symptoms.

Materials

You need the following:

- Jelco of 18–20 gauge
- A 10-ml syringe
- Cleaning materials

Procedure

You need to follow this procedure to perform a pleural tap:

- Explain the procedure to the patient and obtain his consent.
- Ask the patient to be seated and to bend forward with his hands on his knees.
- Percuss the area of dullness.

- Identify and mark the rib. Do not go below the ninth rib, and avoid the cardiac region and the section above the axillary crease. Frequently, the best place is in the eighth intercostal space postero-laterally.
- Clean the area thoroughly.
- Insert the needle just above the superior rim of the lower rib.
- Gently advance the needle perpendicular to the surface, while aspirating with the syringe, until fluid is collected. If the puncture fails, remove the needle, aspirating all the time, and start again in an adjacent space.
- If you plan to remove fluid for symptomatic relief, conduct the drainage slowly and do not collect more than 800 ml per episode. Though rare, pulmonary oedema and syncope could occur if you remove the pleural fluid too quickly. Use a larger, 50-ml syringe to remove fluid for symptomatic relief.
- Request a post-procedure chest radiograph to exclude a pneumothorax.

33 How to do a pleural biopsy

ANDREW ROSS AND CYRIL NAIDOO

Indications

You would perform a pleural biopsy to obtain pleural tissue for a definitive tissue diagnosis.

Materials

You need the following:

- An Abrams pleural biopsy needle, as is shown in Figure 33.1. This consists of an outer needle that has a cutting groove into which tissue either prolapses or is aspirated. The cutting trocar is then advanced, cutting the biopsy. The needle is removed and reopened, and the specimen is taken out.
- Local anaesthetic with 1% lignocaine

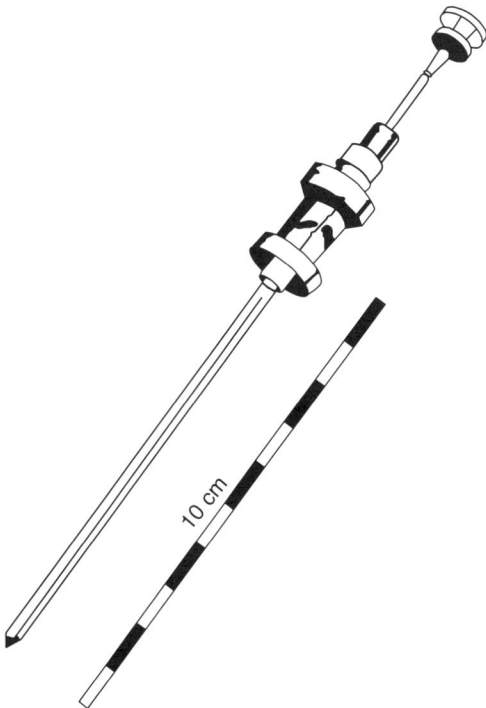

Figure 33.1 A pleural biopsy needle

Procedure

As illustrated in Figure 33.2, you need to follow this procedure when performing a pleural biopsy:

- Explain the procedure to the patient and obtain his consent.
- Ask the patient to be seated, and to bend forward with his hands on his knees.
- Clean the area thoroughly.
- Identify and mark the rib. Do not go below the ninth rib, and avoid the cardiac region and the section above the axillary crease. Frequently, the best place is in the eighth intercostal space postero-laterally.
- Inject a small amount of local anaesthetic at the site of biopsy and anaesthetise down to the pleura.
- Make a 2-cm incision through the skin parallel with the ribs.
- Insert the needle at right angles to the ribs. In order to avoid damaging the neurovascular bundle, the needle must penetrate the pleura just above the lower rib of the intercostal space you have chosen. Use a rotary motion to advance the needle into the chest. Initially aim for the centre of the rib. Once you have made contact with the rib, inch your way up the rib to its upper margin and enter the pleural space. A sudden "give" will indicate that you have entered the pleural space through an intercostal space into the pleural cavity.
- Rotate the cutting trocar to open the needle. If you can aspirate the pleural fluid then the needle is within the pleural cavity and it is safe for you to biopsy the pleura.
- Angle the needle either inferiorly or horizontally within the intercostal space, placing the cutting groove up against the pleura. *Never* angle the needle superiorly, as this could damage the neurovascular bundle above.
- Rotate the cutting trocar to the closed position, cutting the biopsy.

- If you are able to take multiple tissue fragments through the same incision, this improves the diagnostic yield of the procedure.
- Send the tissue in formalin to the laboratory for histology.
- Request a post-procedure chest radiograph to exclude a pneumothorax.

Complications

While performing the biopsy, you could experience these complications:

- A pneumothorax could result if you puncture the lung parenchyma.
- If you pierce the inferior rather than the superior border of the rib, you could puncture the vascular or nerve bundles.

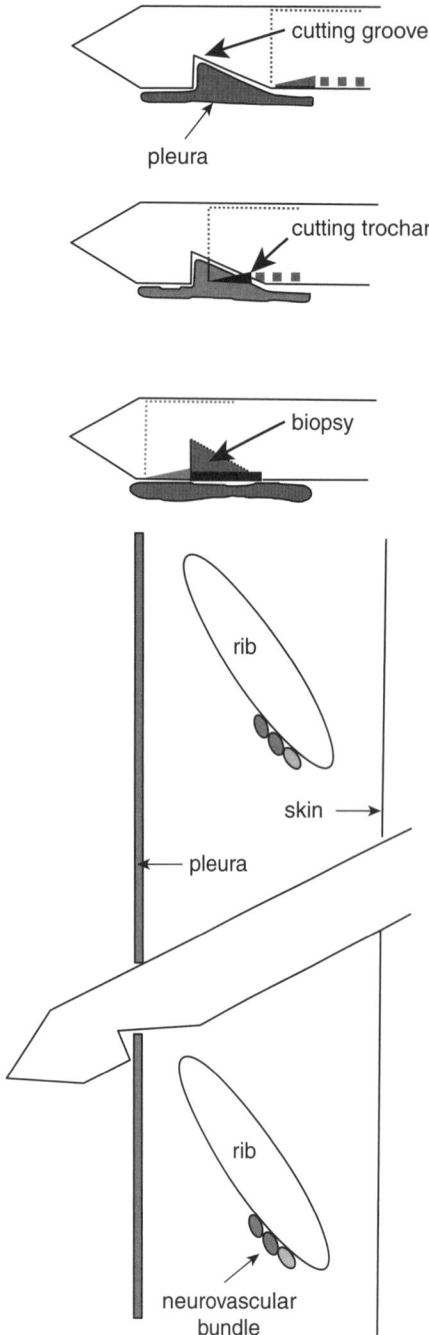

Figure 33.2

Performing a pleural biopsy

34 How to insert an intercostal chest drain

CYRIL NAIDOO AND ANDREW ROSS

Indications

You can use an intercostal chest drain (ICD) in the following clinical scenarios:

- Pneumothorax
- Haemothorax
- Haemopneumothorax
- Acute empyema

Equipment

You need the following:

- Sponge forceps
- Chest drain tubes of varying size
- Sterile tubing with a connector
- A calibrated chest drain bottle with the appropriate fittings, containing sterile water
- Large, curved artery forceps
- A scalpel handle with blade
- A needle holder and suture 2/0 thread on a curved cutting needle
- A 10-ml syringe with needle and 1% lignocaine.
- Antiseptic solution, gauze swabs and sterile gloves

Procedure

As is shown in Figure 34.1, you need to follow this procedure when inserting an ICD:

- Explain the procedure to the patient and obtain his consent.
- Ask the patient to lie supine with his hand and arm raised above his head to give you access to his chest.
- Prepare the skin with a suitable antiseptic solution.
- Remove the trocar from the chest drain – it is not used at all in this procedure.
- Infiltrate the skin, muscle and pleura with 1% lignocaine at the fifth or sixth intercostal space, just anterior to the mid-axillary line.

- If it is present, aspirate fluid from the chest cavity to confirm your diagnosis.
- Make a small transverse incision just above the rib to avoid damaging the vessels under the lower part of the rib.
- Use the artery forceps to bluntly dissect through the muscle, penetrate the pleura and enlarge the opening. The opening should be large enough to allow your gloved finger of roughly the same diameter as the tube to enter the chest cavity. With your finger, you can also clear any adhesions.
- Clamp the proximal end of the tube and then employ the same forceps to grasp the tube at its distal tip and introduce it into the chest. Never use the trocar to force the tube into the chest cavity. Connect the tube to the underwater drainage system and unclamp. Mark the initial level of the fluid in the drainage bottle.
- Close the incision with interrupted skin sutures, using one stitch to anchor the tube to the skin by wrapping the ends around the tube several times and tying off. Use a size 2/0 suture on a curved needle.
- Leave another purse string suture untied around the wound and tube to close the wound when you remove the tube.
- Apply a gauze dressing.

After-care

Once you have performed the procedure:

- Note whether the drainage system is patent. It is if the fluid level swings freely with changes in the intrapleural pressure.
- Encourage the patient to cough vigorously immediately after you have inserted the drain. This helps to remove fluid and/or blood from the pleural space.
- Request a chest radiograph immediately to check whether the procedure has been performed cor-

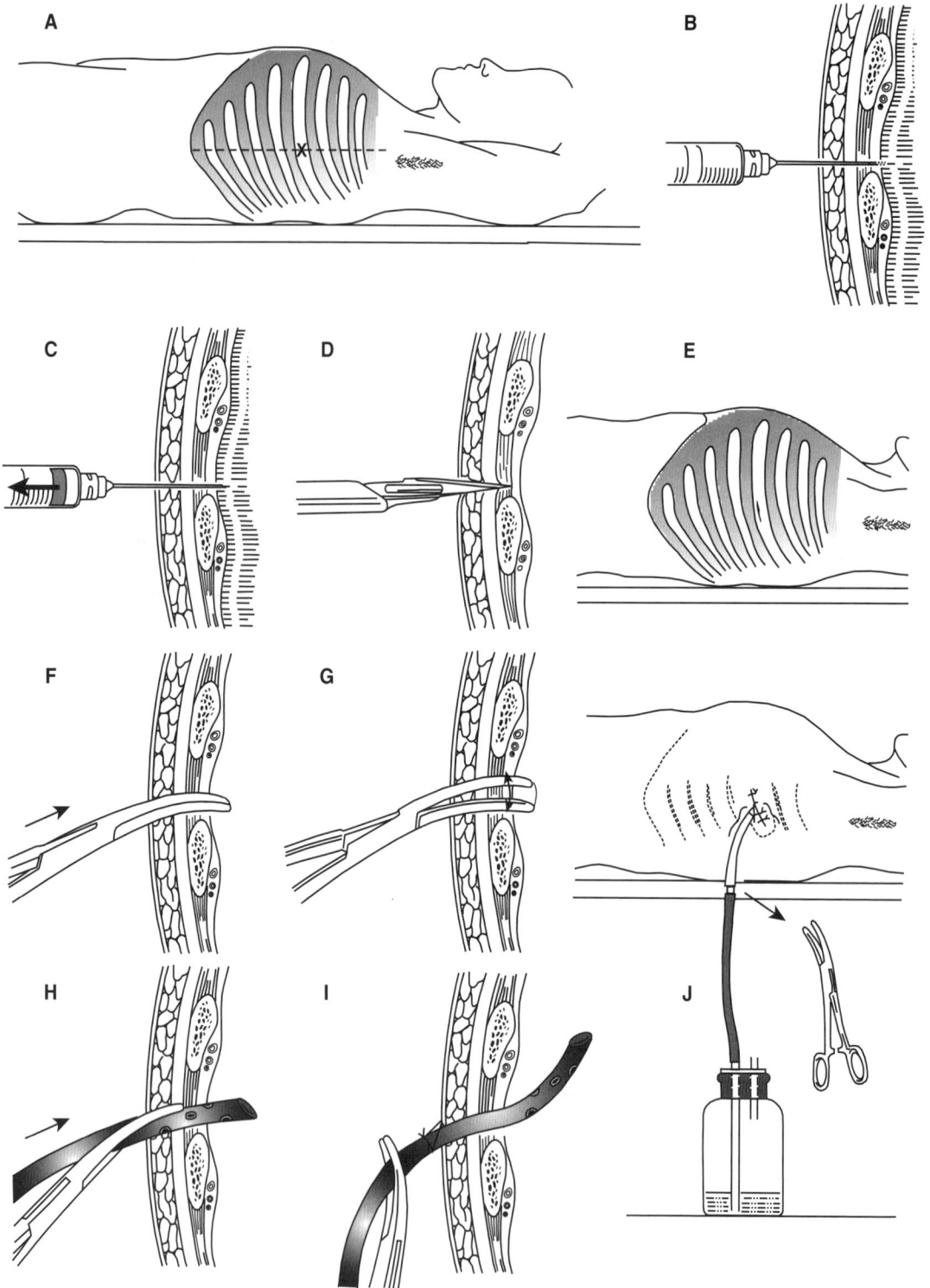

Figure 34.1 Underwater-seal chest drainage: (A) Site for insertion of the tube; (B) Infiltrating all layers of the chest wall at the proposed site with local anaesthetic; (C) Aspirating fluid from the pleural cavity; (D and E) Making a small incision; (F and G) Enlarging the incision and penetrating the pleural space with forceps; (H and I) Introducing and fixing the tube; (J) Connecting the underwater-seal drainage bottle (note the untied purse-string suture)

rectly. Change the bottle at least once every 48 hours, replacing with sterile equivalents.

- Note that persistent bubbling over several days suggests a bronchopleural fistula. In this case, refer your patient for a specialist opinion.

Dos and don'ts of ICDs

Do:

- Remove trocar from the chest drain before beginning the procedure.
- Clamp the drain only when you change the bottle.
- If the drain becomes disconnected, reconnect it and ask patient to cough.
- If there is a persistent air leak, consider low pressure suction.
- Observe the patient for post-expansion pulmonary oedema.
- If you note that no drainage has occurred for 12 hours and the drain is no longer swinging or bubbling, clamp the tube for six hours and do a chest radiograph. If, on the chest radiograph, you see that the lung is satisfactorily expanded and/or the fluid in the pleural cavity has drained adequately, you can remove the clamped tube.

Don't

- clamp the drain (unless you are changing the bottle), as this can result in a tension pneumothorax
- allow the drain to be lifted above the patient's chest level, as this can cause the contents to siphon back into the chest.

Removal of the drain

You need to remove the drain as soon as it has served its purpose. For a simple pneumothorax, you can often remove it within 24 hours. To remove the drain, ask the patient to perform a Valsalva manoeuvre – that is a forced exhalation against a closed mouth and pinched nose – while you rapidly remove the drain and close the wound with the purse string suture that you left for this purpose. Cover the wound with a gauze dressing, and request a post-procedure chest radiograph to exclude a pneumothorax.

35 How to nebulise a patient

CYRIL NAIDOO AND ANDREW ROSS

There is now good evidence that inhaled medication delivered via a spacer can be as effective as a nebuliser (Cates, Bara, Crilly, Rowe 2004).

Indications

You can advise the use of a nebuliser in the following cases:

- Patients who are unable to use inhaler devices, such as young children, the elderly and those with disabilities
- Acute severe asthma attack
- Previous life threatening acute severe asthma
- Uncontrolled severe asthmatic on maximum medication
- Your discretion, for example a post-operative patient or a patient with respiratory infection and lower airways obstruction

Home-based nebulisers

Generally, nebulisers are over-prescribed. It is not necessary for all asthmatics to have their own portable nebuliser. You and your patient should decide whether he needs to purchase one.

You should apply these guidelines in your decision to prescribe a home nebuliser (Lalloo, Bateman, Feldman, Bardin et al. 2000):

- **Pre-prescription:**
  - Optimise other steps in asthma management. A nebuliser is not a substitute for adequate preventer and controller medication.
  - Stabilise the patient's asthma with a short course of oral prednisone.
  - Refer him to a pulmonologist for review.
- **Supervision:**
  - Give verbal and written instructions on how the patient must use the nebuliser, on the frequency of use and on what action he must take in the event of worsening asthma.
  - Emphasise the need for him to attend follow-up visits.
- **Follow-up:**
  - Review the case within two weeks.
  - Try to avoid regular nebuliser use.
  - If the patient needs nebulisation more than three times a day, refer him to a pulmonologist or admit him to hospital for stabilisation.

Procedure

You should follow this procedure when nebulising a patient:

- Confirm the indication and explain the procedure to your patient.
- If supplemental oxygen is available, give it until the nebuliser is ready.
- Perform and record a peak expiratory flow (PEF) meter rate reading prior to nebulisation, and record other key signs such as pulse rate and respiratory rate.
- Select the correct size facemask or mouthpiece.
- Ensure that all parts of the nebuliser are working and that the nebuliser fitting is compatible with the oxygen device.
- Select the appropriate nebuliser solutions and consider contraindications to the medications. Note that pre-mixed nebuliser solutions and combinations are available in single-dose vials.
  - Salbutamol 5 mg in 2.5 ml
  - Fenoterol 0.5 mg in 2 ml
  - Ipratroprium bromide 0.5 mg in 2 ml
  - Fenoterol 1.25 mg with ipratropium bromide 0.5 mg in 4 ml
- Check the drug concentrations and expiry dates on the containers.
- Draw up the solution and inject it into the nebuliser chamber, or squeeze the plastic vial contents into the chamber.

Van Schaik Publishers

- Connect the nebuliser to the facemask or mouthpiece.
- If you are using a portable compressor, place it on a hard surface and ensure that the filter is clean and the compressor is connected to an electrical socket.
- Attach the nebuliser to the compressor tubing and turn on the power.
- Ensure that the nebuliser is held in an upright position and that the patient is sitting upright.
- Position the mouthpiece or facemask on the patient and ask him to breath in and out slowly until all the medication is finished. This usually takes about 10 minutes.
- If the mixture is not being nebulised then gently shake the nebuliser.

- Assess the patient's response to the nebulisation by remeasuring the PEF rate and other key signs such as pulse and respiratory rate.

Post-procedure

Follow these steps once the nebulisation has finished:

- Soak the nebuliser, mouthpiece and measuring devices in warm water with a mild detergent.
- Wipe the facemask clean with a paper towel dabbed with the detergent.
- Rinse each piece thoroughly in warm running water.
- Do not share uncleaned tubings and mouthpieces or facemasks.

36 How to reduce a paraphimosis

ANDREW ROSS AND CYRIL NAIDOO

Paraphimosis is a urological emergency occurring in uncircumcised males, in which the foreskin becomes trapped behind the corona and forms a tight band of constricting tissue. The patient's penile foreskin is retracted, swollen and painful. The glans of the penis is visible, surrounded by an oedematous ring with a proximal constricting band.

This condition is usually caused by self-retraction of the foreskin, sometimes during sexual intercourse. It should be distinguished from balanitis, which is an inflammation of the foreskin.

Pathophysiology and clinical presentation

When the foreskin becomes trapped behind the corona for a prolonged time, it may form a tight, constricting band of tissue. This circumferential ring of tissue can impair the blood and lymphatic flow to and from the glans and foreskin. As a result of penile ischaemia and vascular engorgement, the glans and foreskin may become swollen and oedematous. If left untreated, penile gangrene and autoamputation may follow in days or weeks.

A patient with paraphimosis often presents with penile pain, but pain may not always be present. The glans appears enlarged and congested, with a collar of swollen foreskin around the coronal sulcus. A tight, constricting band of tissue appears immediately behind the head of the penis. The remainder of the penile shaft is flaccid and unremarkable.

Procedure

Treatment involves reduction of the foreskin, which should be followed by a circumcision six weeks later.

As illustrated in Figure 36.1, you should follow this procedure when reducing a paraphimosis:

- Prepare the skin of the genitalia with a bland antiseptic.

- Prepare an injection of local anaesthetic. *Never* use adrenaline.

- Isolate the penis with a perforated towel and inject the anaesthetic in a ring around the base of the penis. See Chapter 37 on penile ring block.

- Once local analgesia is achieved, take hold of the glans in the fist of one hand and squeeze firmly. You may need a gauze swab to attain a firm grip.

- Exert continuous pressure for 3–5 minutes, changing hands if necessary, until the oedema passes proximally under the constricting band to the shaft of the penis.

- After the swelling of the glans has subsided, you can usually pull the foreskin over the glans. To reduce the foreskin, place the thumbs of both hands on the glans and wrap your fingers behind the foreskin. Apply a gentle but steady and forceful pressure to the glans with your thumbs, and exert counter-traction to the foreskin with your fingers as you pull down the foreskin. When you perform the procedure properly, the constricting band of tissue should come down distal to the glans with the foreskin.

- The essence of getting the glans back through the foreskin is not to stretch the foreskin, but to compress the glans. By gently squeezing the glans and pushing it with your thumbs, the blood will move back down the penis and make the glans smaller. You can then push it back through the narrowest part of the foreskin. A drop or two of cooking oil or K-Y jelly on the glans may help.

- If this manoeuvre fails, you can make numerous small punctures in the foreskin. Called the "puncture" technique, this allows the oedematous fluid to escape from the foreskin. Then you can usually pull the foreskin back over the glans.

- If a severely constricting band of tissue precludes all forms of conservative therapy, you can make an emergency dorsal slit in the foreskin – the urethra is situated on the ventral surface. Then attempt to pull the foreskin over the glans.

- Perform a circumcision six weeks after reducing the paraphimosis to prevent recurrence.

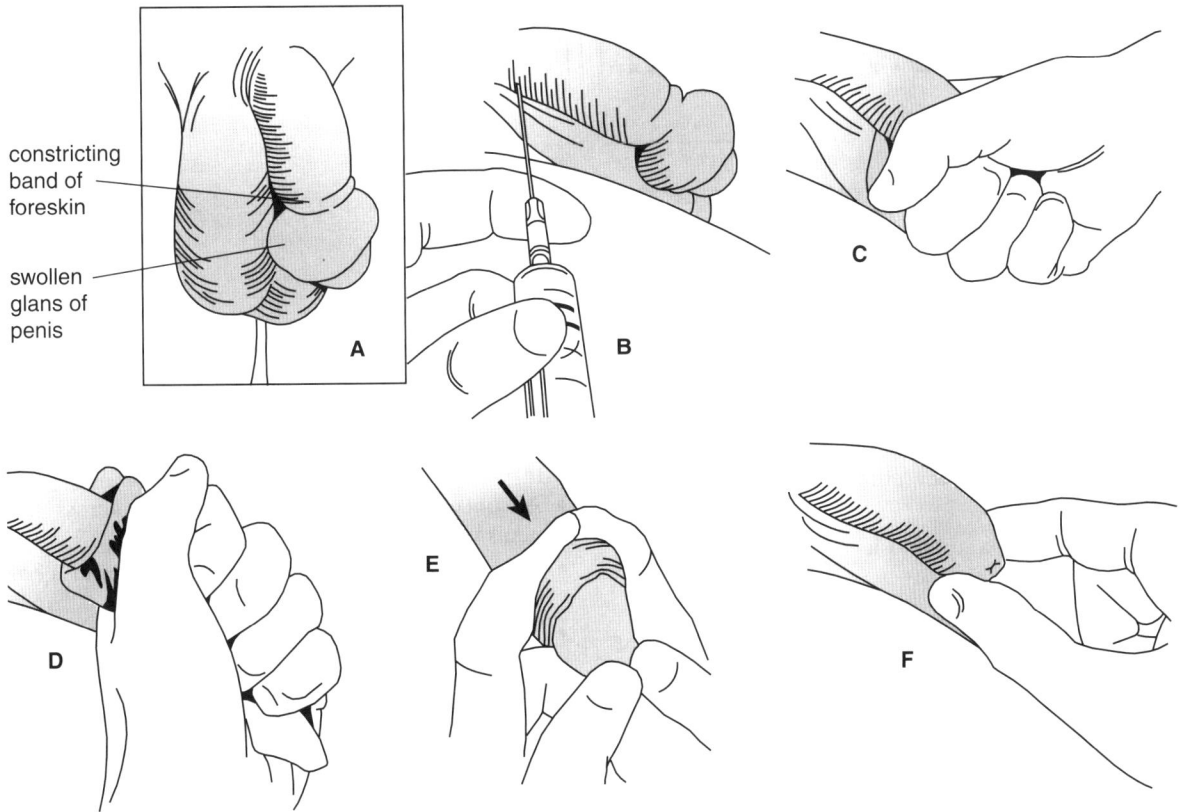

constricting
band of
foreskin

swollen
glans of
penis

A

B

C

D

E

F

Figure 36.1 Reducing a paraphimosis: (A) The affected penis; (B) Injecting local anaesthetic in a ring around the base; (C and D) Squeezing the oedematous part of the penis; (E and F) Pulling the foreskin over the glans

37 How to give a ring block of the penis

ANDREW ROSS

Indications

You would perform the procedure in the following cases:

- Reduction of paraphimosis
- Circumcision
- Cutaneous biopsy
- Cautery of warts on the foreskin or on the glans of the penis

The foreskin of the penis is innervated by two dorsal cutaneous nerves which traverse the penis in the 1 o'clock and 11 o'clock positions. Infiltration of these nerves at the base of the penis usually leads to complete anaesthesia. To ensure that the nerves are adequately blocked, you need to make a ring block completely around the base of the penis.

Procedure

You need to follow this procedure to ring block the penis:

- Prepare an injection with 3–5 ml bupivacaine or lignocaine. *Never* add adrenaline – this could cause the penis to become gangrenous.

- Raise a subcutaneous skin weal at the 10 o'clock position.
- Advance the needle subcutaneously across the penis towards the 2 o'clock position.
- Aspirate to ensure that the corposa cavernosa has not been entered.
- Inject the anaesthetic at the 1 o'clock and 11 o'clock positions.
- Pull the needle back to the 10 o'clock position and advance the needle subcutaneously towards the 8 o'clock position. Inject local anaesthetic as you pull the needle back from the 8 o'clock towards the 10 o'clock position.
- Remove the needle and repeat the procedure on the other side. Start at the 4 o'clock position and advance towards the 2 o'clock position, injecting local anaesthetic as you withdraw the needle. Then advance the needle towards the 8 o'clock position and inject local anaesthetic as you withdraw the needle to ensure that all four quadrants are anaesthetised.

Figure 37.1 illustrates this procedure.

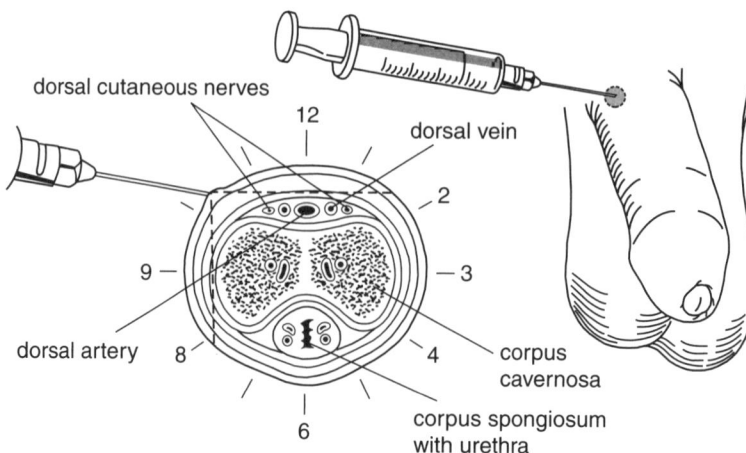

Figure 37.1 Ring blocking the penis

38 How to do a vasectomy

ANDREW ROSS

Vasectomy is a method of contraception. The patient should receive counselling and should give informed consent (see Chapter 140) before the procedure takes place. He must understand the following:

- The procedure is irreversible and permanent. Do not mention the possibility of re-anastomosis to him.
- The operation is almost always successful, but sterility cannot be *guaranteed* since there is a small chance of failure.
- Sterility will not be immediate. It can take up to eight weeks for the patient to become completely sterile.

Procedure

Vasectomy is usually carried out under local anaesthesia, but you can administer general anaesthesia if the patient is nervous or has undergone previous inguino-scrotal surgery.

As illustrated in Figure 38.1, you need to follow this procedure to perform a vasectomy:

- Place the patient in a supine position.
- Cleanse and shave the pubis and external genitalia.
- If you are using local anaesthesia, inject a weal of 1% lignocaine and make an incision of 2–3 cm in the scrotal raphe.
- Infiltrate the deeper tissues, picking up each layer in turn to inject anaesthetic.
- At each stage, allow a few minutes for the local anaesthetic to take effect.

- Hold up the vas from one side with a pair of tissue forceps and infiltrate its connective tissue sheath with lignocaine.
- Open the sheath, isolate the vas with two artery forceps at least 1 cm apart. Excise the section of vas between the forceps. The cut ends will be characteristically conical, with the outer fibro-muscular tissues retracting from the lumen.
- Ligate the testicular end and replace it within the connective tissue sheath.
- Turn the proximal end back on itself and ligate it so that it lies outside the sheath.
- Repeat the procedure on the other vas.
- Close the scrotal wound with 2/0 catgut stitches, making sure to include the dartos layer.

An alternative method is as follows:

- Identify the vas by pinching it between your thumb and finger at the lateral side of the neck of the scrotum.
- Incise the skin directly above it.
- Catch the vas with a pair of tissue forceps before it slips away.

This procedure is best done while the patient is under general anaesthesia.

After-care

Advise that your patient wears a scrotal support for 48 hours after the operation. You can perform semen analysis 6–8 weeks later to confirm sterility.

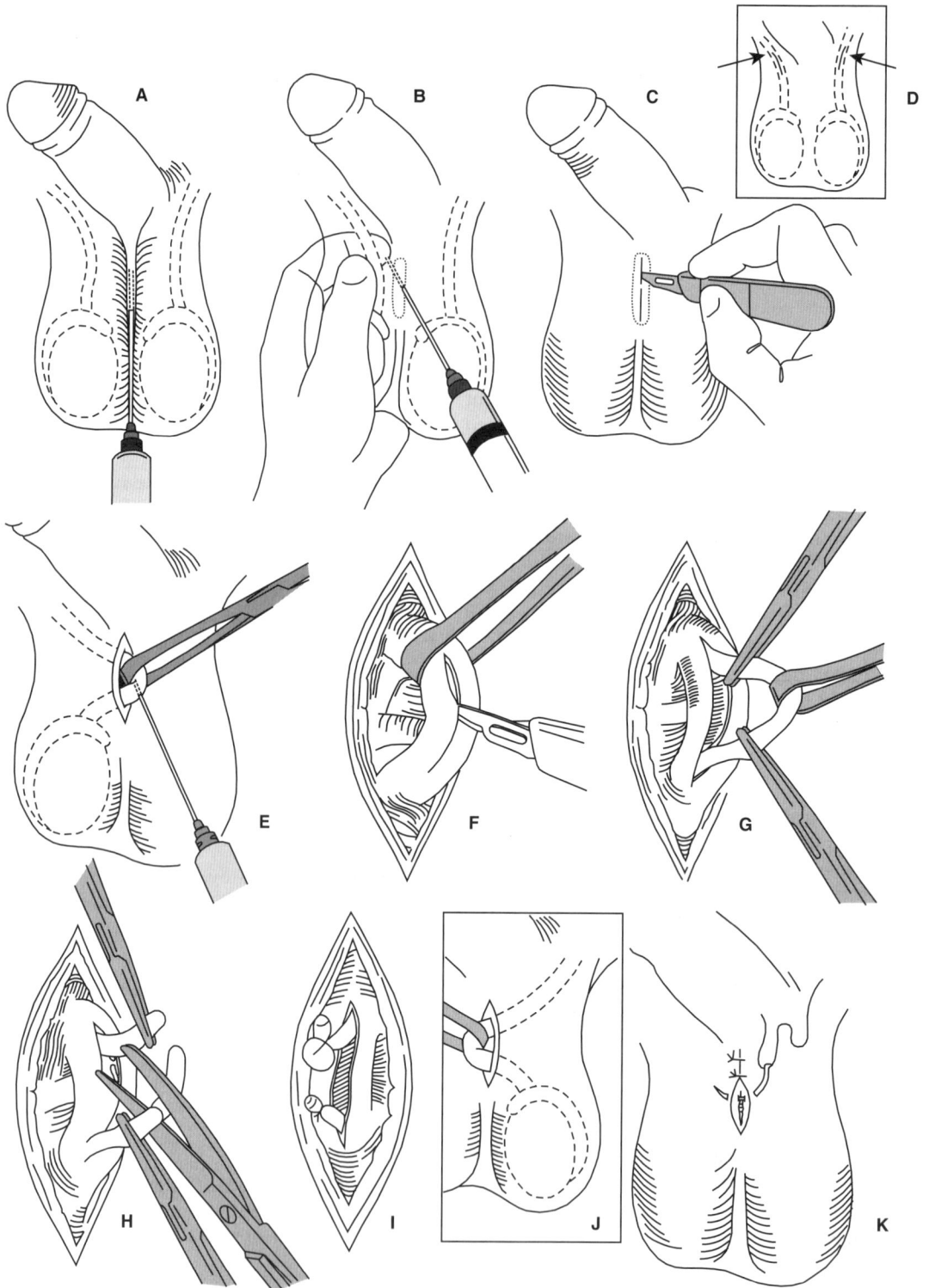

Figure 38.1 Performing a vasectomy: (A and B) Injecting local anaesthetic; (C) Making the incision; (D) Alternative sites for infiltration and incision; (E) Infiltrating the tissue around the vas with local anaesthetic; (F and G) Opening the sheath and isolating the vas between artery forceps; (H) Excising a segment; (I) Ligating the cut ends of the vas; (J) Dealing with the other vas; (K) Closing the wound

39 How to do a circumcision

ANDREW ROSS AND CYRIL NAIDOO

Circumcision is the surgical resection of the foreskin at the level of the corona of the glans, allowing the glans to be fully exposed while preserving enough frenulum to permit erection.

Indications

You would perform a circumcision in the following instances:

- Phimosis
- Paraphimosis (six weeks after reduction)
- Recurrent balanitis
- Injury to the foreskin
- Elective, that is at the patient's request

Equipment

You need the following:

- Four sponge forceps
- Tissue forceps
- A scalpel handle and blade
- Small dissecting scissors
- Stitch scissors
- Sutures – 2/0, 3/0 and 4/0 chromic catgut, ties and atraumatic needles
- Sutures – 2/0 and 3/0 with cutting needles
- Three small, curved artery forceps
- Three small, straight artery forceps
- One large, curved artery forceps
- A needle holder
- A 10-ml syringe with needle, prepared with 1% lignocaine
- Sterile gloves

Procedure

As illustrated in Figure 39.1 A to H, you need to follow this procedure to perform a circumcision:

- Do a penile ring block (see Chapter 37) or administer general anaesthetic.
- Prepare all external genitalia with a bland antiseptic. If the foreskin can be retracted, carefully clean the glans and the preputial furrow; if not, clean as best you can.

- Isolate the penis with a sterile perforated towel.
- If a phimosis is present you may need to stretch the opening of the foreskin (A).
- Take hold of the foreskin dorsally in the midline with two pairs of forceps (B and C).
- Cut down between the forcep blades almost to the corona. Leave a 2 mm fringe at the patient's corona (D and E).
- Excise the foreskin by extending the dorsal slit obliquely around either side to the frenulum (F).
- Trim the inner preputial layer of foreskin, leaving at least 2 mm of mucosa (G).
- Catch the cut edges of the frenulum and the bleeding arteries of the frenulum with a catgut suture, leaving the suture long as a traction stitch to steady the penis (H).
- Insert a similar traction stitch to unite the edges of the prepuce dorsally.
- Catch and tie any bleeding vessels on either side of the raw area. Cauterise as required.
- Unite the edges of the prepuce with interrupted absorbable catgut sutures – 2/0–3/0 – and cut the stitches short.

Take care not to cut the glans and not to use diathermy on the actual glans. *Never* use adrenaline in the local anaesthetic.

After-care

Once you have performed the procedure, dress the penis in loose layers of Vaseline gauze covered with dry gauze. Ask the patient to retain this dressing for 24 hours. Thereafter, provide only protection from rubbing against the clothes until the healing is complete. The stitches will separate in 10–15 days.

Complications

If you fail to secure the artery of the frenulum sufficiently, you could cause a haematoma. An early-morning erection could cause dehiscence of the stitches.

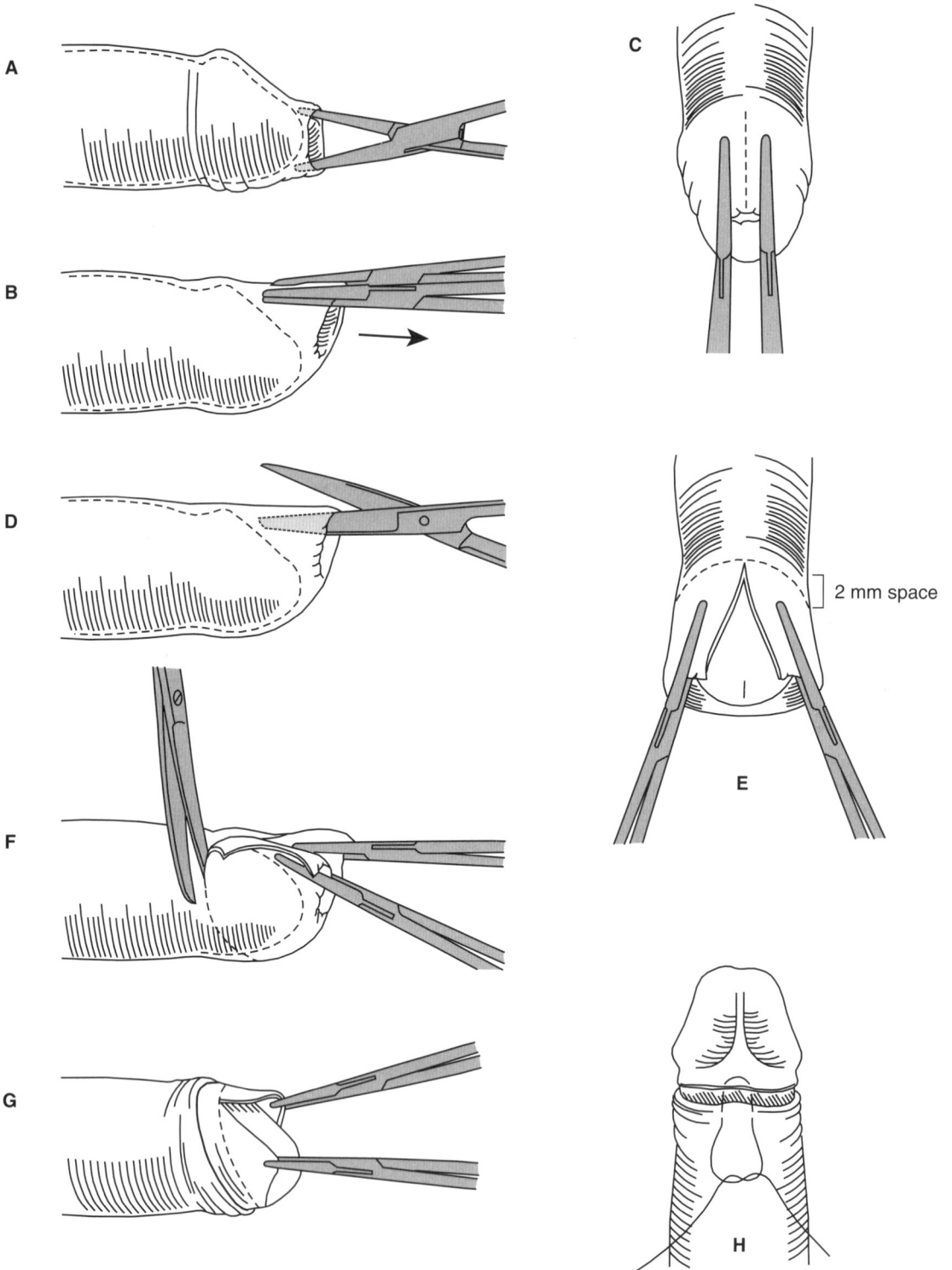

Figure 39.1 Performing a circumcision: (A) Stretching the opening of the foreskin; (B and C) Holding the foreskin with two pairs of forceps; (D and E) Cutting down the midline dorsally; (F) Excising the foreskin; (G) Trimming the inner layer of foreskin (dotted line); (H) Ligating the artery of the frenulum

40 How to insert a urinary catheter

ANDREW ROSS AND CYRIL NAIDOO

You need to be sure of the reasons for inserting a urinary catheter as the type of catheter you choose will depend upon the following:

- If used only to empty the bladder at present, or for a few days, use a Foley's catheter.
- If longer-term permanent bladder drainage is required, use a silicon catheter.

Indications

You would use a urinary catheter in these circumstances:

- Acute retention of urine. Common causes include urethral strictures, prostatic disorders and paraplegia.
- Chronic retention. You would catheterise to
  - measure the volume of residual urine
  - treat renal failure associated with urinary retention
  - empty the bladder intermittently following spinal cord injury.
- Prior to surgery
- Prevention of skin breakdown in an incontinent patient
- Monitoring of urine output in a seriously ill patient

Contraindications

A fractured pelvis with disruption of the urethra is a contraindication for the insertion of a urethral catheter – such an injury requires the insertion of a suprapubic catheter. Any bleeding from the urethra after trauma may be a sign of urethral disruption.

Equipment

You need the following:

- The appropriate sizes of catheter: females 10–14, males 16–18. If there is stricture you may need a smaller one; if the prostate is enlarged you may need a 20.

- A sterile pack with towels, gallipot for disinfectant (Savlon solution), cotton wool swabs and a container for the urine
- A sterile syringe – the volume is according to the size of the bulb of the catheter.
- A needle
- K-Y jelly
- A good light source

Procedure

Explain to the patient what you are going to do. Clarify that although he will feel some discomfort his cooperation will help to speed up the procedure.

You need to follow this procedure to insert a urinary catheter:

- Position the patient in a supine position with his hips and knees flexed and separated.
- Prepare the tray.
- "Pour" the catheter from its outer covering onto the sterile tray. It must still be in its inner plastic covering.
- Put on sterile gloves and clean the genitalia.
- Drape the patient appropriately.
- Draw up the required amount of water into the syringe in readiness to fill the bulb of the catheter – according to the catheter specifications.
- Tear off the plastic covering over the tip of the catheter and do not handle the catheter itself.
- Dip the tip of the catheter into the K-Y jelly.
- Insert the lubricant or anaesthetic jelly into the urethra.
- Hold the penis with your left hand and take the catheter with your right hand.
- Put the catheter into the urethral meatus and advance the catheter slowly. In men it is helpful for you to hold the shaft of the penis with your left hand and to move the penis upwards and towards the abdomen as you are advancing the catheter.

- Continue to advance the catheter until urine starts to fill its plastic cover.
- Sometimes there is muscular resistance from the sphincter just before the catheter goes into the bladder. Continue to maintain firm but gentle pressure. After 15–30 seconds the sphincter will relax and you will find it easy to insert the catheter.
- You may experience difficulties owing to an enlarged prostate or a urethral stricture.
- Once urine starts to flow, push the catheter in by another 5–10 cm and inflate the balloon with the sterile fluid in the syringe.
- Once the balloon has been inflated partially withdraw the catheter until the balloon abuts on the bladder neck.
- Connect the urine bag to the catheter.
- Strap the catheter to the patient's thigh, being careful to leave sufficient length to prevent the catheter from pulling on the urethra.

Do not force the catheter – this could create a false passage, cause urethral bleeding and intolerable pain, and increase the risk of infection.

After-care

Once you have performed the procedure

- always decompress a distended bladder slowly
- change the catheter if it becomes blocked or infected (remember that silicon catheters need to be changed monthly)
- encourage good fluid intake to help prevent infections and calculi formation.

Complications

These complications could occur:

- Infection
- Obstruction
- Calculi formation
- Urethral stricture
- The catheter falls out

Inserting a suprapubic catheter

Indications and contraindications

You would insert this type of catheter in the following circumstances:

- Acute retention following fractured pelvis and disruption of the urethra
- Acute retention and failure to pass a urethral catheter
- Urethral trauma

- People who require long-term catheterisation and are sexually active
- Following certain gynaecological operations, such as colposuspension for stress incontinence
- Some wheelchair-bound people find this method simpler
- People who cannot perform self-catheterisation
- Long-term catheterisation for incontinence. Although such catheterisation is not recommended, at times you might feel it is appropriate to avoid skin problems or other medical complications.

Equipment

You need the following:

- A suprapubic catheter with trocar and cannula
- A 10-ml syringe and 20-gauge needle
- 20 ml 1% lidocaine
- A sterile pack with towels, gallipot for disinfectant (Savlon solution), cotton wool swabs and container for the urine
- A sterile syringe – the volume is according to the size of the bulb of the catheter
- K-Y jelly
- A good light source

Procedure

Explain to the patient what you are going to do.

You need to follow this procedure when inserting a suprapubic catheter:

- Position the patient in the supine position.
- Determine the bladder limits by palpation or percussion – ensure that the patient has a full bladder.
- Prepare the tray and open the suprapubic catheter onto the tray.
- Put on sterile gloves and clean between the umbilicus and pubis.
- Drape the patient appropriately.
- Keep in the midline and make sure that you can palpate or percuss the bladder. Raise a weal with local anaesthetic in the midline over the bladder. Once the skin infiltration is completed, continue with deep infiltration. Continue down to the bladder and aspirate urine with the needle you used to infiltrate the anaesthetic.
- Where you have infiltrated with local anaesthetic, make an incision with the point of the scalpel.
- Introduce the trocar and cannula and advance them vertically, with care.
- After meeting with some resistance they will pass easily into the cavity of the bladder, as confirmed by the flow of urine when you withdraw the trocar from the cannula.

- Remove the trocar from the sheath.
- Insert the catheter down the sheath, well into the bladder.
- Once the catheter is in the bladder, inflate the balloon with 10 ml of sterile water.
- Following balloon inflation slide the sheath back along the catheter shaft until it is external to the abdomen. Pull the tear-down strip and remove the sheath from the catheter.
- Fix the catheter to the patient's skin with a stitch.
- Connect the catheter to the urine bag.

Figure 40.1 shows how the procedure is carried out.

Removal

To remove the catheter remove the anchoring suture, deflate the balloon completely and withdraw. If catheterisation is to be discontinued, apply a dry dressing to puncture site. If re-catheterisation is necessary, it may be possible for you to reinsert a normal catheter through the tract that you have already created.

Complications

There could be mechanical complications such as catheter dislodgement or obstruction, and failed introduction. There could also be infection and urine leaking around the catheter – this is normal around a new catheter site.

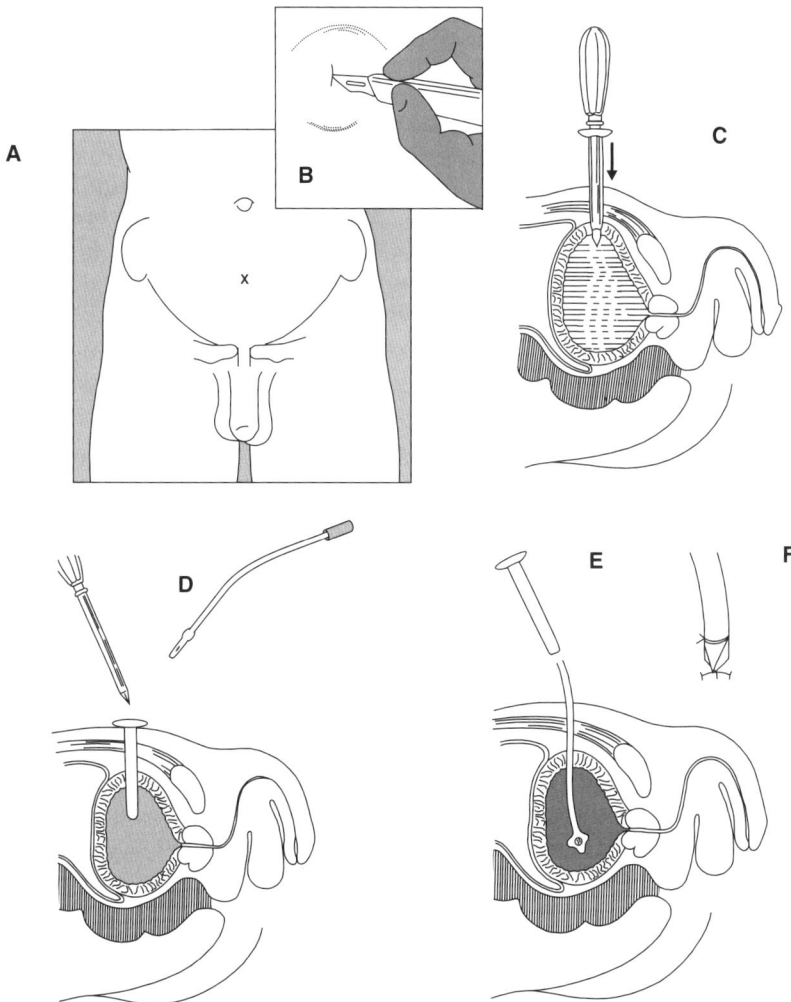

Figure 40.1 Inserting a suprapubic catheter: (A) Site of puncture; (B) Making a small incision after injecting local anaesthetic; (C) Introducing the trocar and cannula through the abdominal wall into the bladder; (D) Withdrawing the trocar and inserting the catheter; (E) Withdrawing the cannula (sometimes these split open to facilitate their removal); (F) Fixing the catheter to the skin

41 How to do proctoscopy and sigmoidoscopy

ANDREW ROSS AND CYRIL NAIDOO

Indications

You can perform a proctoscopy under these circumstances:

- Any disturbance in bowel motion, such as diarrhoea, constipation and tenesmus
- History of passing blood, melaena or mucus per rectum
- Discomfort or pain on defecation
- Anal swelling or feeling of incomplete defecation
- Part of a full medical check-up
- Urinary symptoms
- Tissue biopsy of anal lesion or prostate

Usually, you should follow a digital rectal examination with an examination using a proctoscope. The advantage of proctoscopy is that it enables you to view the whole of the anal canal and biopsy any lesions that you felt during the rectal examination.

Procedure

You must explain to the patient the purpose and nature of the examination, and clarify that the procedure usually does not hurt.

To perform a proctoscopy, you need to follow this procedure:

- Position the patient on a couch or bed in the left lateral position, with his hips fully flexed and both knees drawn up towards his chest. His buttocks should project just beyond the edge of the bed.
- Talk to your patient throughout the examination. Be gentle and do not hurry. Use warm instruments.
- Put on sterile gloves and part the buttocks to inspect the perianal region, natal cleft and the anal margin.
- Warm and lubricate the proctoscope. Hold the handle of the proctoscope with your fingers and press your thumb firmly on the head of the obturator. This grip will keep the two parts of the

instrument assembled. The handle should point posteriorly.

- Introduce the proctoscope. When you touch the rectal sphincter it will contract. Wait a few seconds for it to relax and then press firmly and gently in the axis of the anal canal. Keep pressing until you feel the proctoscope slip easily into the anus.
- Introduce the scope to its full length, and instruct the patient to take deep breaths with his mouth open.
- Remove the obturator and direct the light into the scope.
- Remove any faecal material, mucus or blood.
- Align the scope so that you can clearly see the lumen of the gut.
- Slowly withdraw the instrument while maintaining its alignment in the gut so that you can view any mucosal lesions, including piles or polyps. Note the appearance of the mucosa and assess its integrity. Take a biopsy sample from any obviously or possibly abnormal area under direct vision, using special biopsy forceps.
- Remove the tissue sample through the proctoscope. Warn the patient that the biopsy may cause some discomfort. If you are removing tissue from below the dentate line, it is essential to inject an anaesthetic with adrenalin around the biopsy site prior to removing any tissue, as the epithelium lining the anal canal is extremely sensitive and the biopsy can cause severe pain.

How to do rigid sigmoidoscopy

This examination normally follows a rectal examination and a proctoscopy. It allows you to inspect at least 25 cm of the patient's sigmoid colon.

Indications

You can perform this exam in these situations:

- Symptomatic colorectal disease, where proctoscopy has proved inconclusive or has not revealed any abnormalities
- When abnormalities have been detected at proctoscopy, but when additional lesions are suspected, for example in patients with polyposis
- To monitor the patient's response to treatment, for example in amoebic colitis
- To facilitate the introduction of a flatus tube to decompress and reduce a sigmoid volvulus

Procedure

You need to explain to the patient the purpose and nature of the examination, and clarify that the procedure usually does not hurt.

To perform a rigid sigmoidoscopy, you must follow this procedure, as illustrated in Figure 41.1:

- Administer a preliminary enema or perform bowel washout. If the patient has constipation, administer a mild laxative one or two days before the examination.
- Check the equipment, particularly the light-head, the eyepiece fitting (window) and the inflation pump (bellows) to ensure that they fit together and that enough light reaches the end of the scope.
- Warm and generously lubricate the sigmoidoscope. Ask the patient to breath in and out regularly while you gently insert it with the obturator in position. Hold the obturator firmly to prevent it from being dislodged backwards.
- Here, the examination is similar to a proctoscopy – while introducing the sigmoidoscope, point it towards the umbilicus and when it is through the anal sphincter, swing it backwards.
- Advance the sigmoidoscope backwards and upwards. If you meet with any obstruction, remove the obturator at this point. If you can advance the sigmoidoscope by 10 cm, remove the obturator at the end of the 10 cm.
- Attach the eyepiece, which usually carries the light source and pump connections.
- To view the gut wall and the bowel lumen, introduce a little air and align the scope.
- Introduce air at intervals to open up the bowel lumen gradually beyond the scope.
- Gently advance the instrument, keeping it accurately within the lumen of the bowel.
- Should your view be obscured at any time by rectal contents, remove the eyepiece and evacuate the material using a dental cotton wool roll held firmly with biopsy forceps.
- If you find too much stool, send the patient to the toilet. If this is unsuccessful, give him an enema and re-attempt the procedure after the enema has worked.
- If your view is not obstructed, follow the lumen at all times. Progressively change the direction of the scope to keep within the lumen.
- Do *not* advance the sigmoidoscope if you cannot see the lumen in front of it.
- *Never* force the scope. If there is a blind area in the way, withdraw the scope and then advance it again.
- The recto-sigmoid junction may be difficult to pass through. Do not rush the procedure – the junction may relax if the difficulty is due to spasm. If it does not relax, make no further attempts to advance the scope.
- Do most of the examination as you withdraw the scope. Rotate the sigmoidoscope as you withdraw it so that you inspect every part of the mucosa.
- Never use force when using forceps to take a biopsy specimen from the wall of the bowel.
- If the patient experiences discomfort during the examination, check for proper alignment of the sigmoidoscope. Release air by removing the eyepiece or by disconnecting the pump tubing; then reassemble the instrument and continue the examination.
- If necessary, you can remove and reintroduce the scope and repeat the examination.
- At the end of the examination, let out the air from the gut before withdrawing the scope.
- Remember to remove some stool to test for occult blood.

Complications

The principal risks of this examination are perforation of the colon or bleeding. Although perforation generally requires surgery, certain cases may be treated with antibiotics and intravenous fluids. Bleeding may occur at the site of either a biopsy or polyp removal. Typically minor in degree, such bleeding may stop by itself or be controlled by cauterisation. Occasionally, surgery is necessary.

Fortunately, both perforation of the colon and bleeding are quite rare. Because bleeding may sometimes occur up to three weeks after a colon polyp has been removed, you should tell your patient not to plan to travel to any remote areas without medical access during this period of healing.

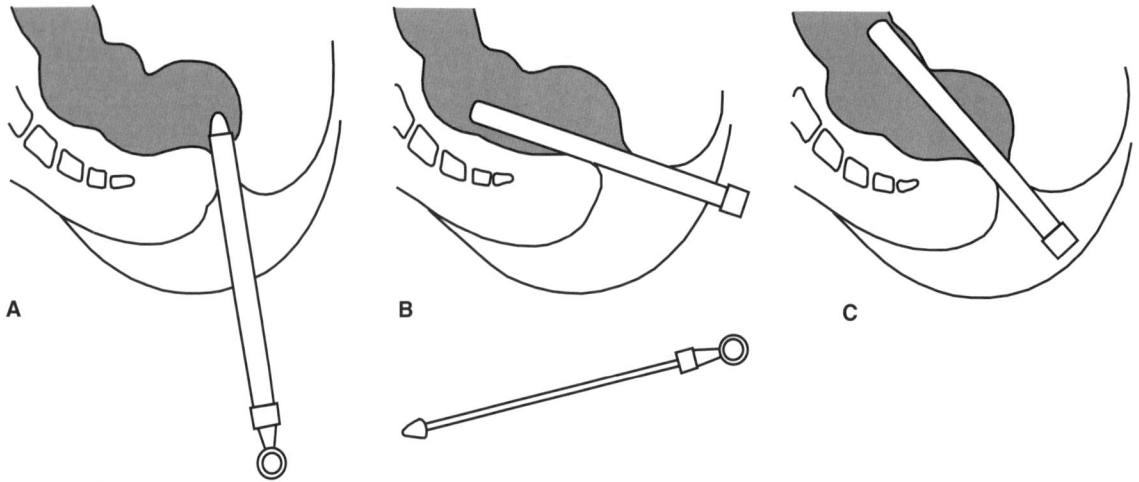

Figure 41.1 Performing a sigmoidoscopy: (A) Pointing the scope towards the umbilicus; (B) Swinging the scope backwards once it is through the anal sphincter, and advancing it backwards and upwards; removing the obturator at about 10 cm; (C) Advancing the scope, keeping it accurately within the lumen of the bowel

42 How to manage haemorrhoids

ANDREW ROSS AND CYRIL NAIDOO

Often referred to as "piles", haemorrhoids are classified as follows:

- **Perianal haematomas.** These are less common than internal haemorrhoids. A small lump develops on the outside edge of the anus. It can be extremely painful at first, but it frequently settles and shrinks to a small skin tag.
- **Internal haemorrhoids.** As illustrated in Figure 42.1, these arise above the dentate line and are graded as follows:
  - **First-degree** haemorrhoids are small swellings on the inside lining of the anus. They cannot be seen or felt from outside the anus.
  - **Second-degree** haemorrhoids are larger and may prolapse from the anus, but reduce spontaneously.
  - **Third-degree** haemorrhoids are prolapsed from the anus, but can be reduced with a finger.
  - **Fourth-degree** haemorrhoids are permanently prolapsed and cannot be reduced.

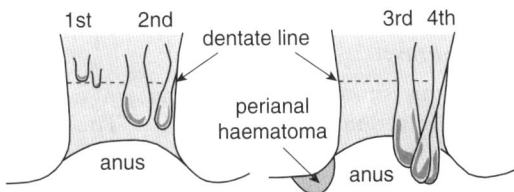

Figure 42.1 Different grades of haemorrhoids

You can confirm your diagnosis of haemorrhoids by performing a rectal examination with proctoscopy. Moreover, you may need to perform a sigmoidoscopy to exclude any associated rectal conditions, for example carcinoma of the rectum.

Prevention and lifestyle management

Haemorrhoids are common. Useful aspects of prevention are for the patient to

- avoid becoming overweight, and to lose weight if he is overweight
- keep stools soft so that they pass easily, thus decreasing pressure and straining
- eat a high-fibre diet, which helps to reduce constipation and straining
- exercise regularly.

The treatment of haemorrhoids depends on the severity of the patient's symptoms. In addition to the measures listed above, the following measures may be all that the patient needs to take to allow small haemorrhoids to settle:

- Avoiding dehydration by drinking plenty of water and fruit juice
- Avoiding causes of constipation, such as painkillers that contain codeine

Treatment

Symptomatic treatment

You can prescribe pain-relieving creams and ointments that contain an anaesthetic. These can help to ease the discomfort and allow bowel motion. The patient may need cold packs and strong analgesia if the haemorrhoids become thrombosed.

Definitive treatment

You may need to perform injection sclerotherapy, rubber banding or haemorrhoidectomy to treat persistent or highly painful piles. Table 42.1 summarises the factors involved.

We will now discuss each of these treatments in more detail.

Injection sclerotherapy

Injection sclerotherapy using phenol-in-oil is a quick, safe, one-person outpatient technique. However, repeated treatments may be necessary to attain lasting effects.

Table 42.1 Treatment modalities for haemorrhoids

Treatment modality	Suggested patient group
Dietary modification/ fibre supplementation and local pain-relieving creams	Unlikely to curb symptomatic haemorrhoids. May be useful in the subgroup of patients with constipation and/or symptoms of straining
Injection sclerotherapy	First and second degree haemorrhoids. Safe in pregnancy. Repeat treatment often required
Rubber banding	Recommended treatment for first- and second-degree haemorrhoids
Surgical haemorrhoid-ectomy	Definitive treatment for failure of non-operative modalities and as primary therapy for third- and fourth-degree haemorrhoids

Indications

You would need to perform this procedure in the case of symptomatic first- and second-degree haemorrhoids in which conservative management has failed, and in second-degree haemorrhoids in those patients who cannot tolerate rubber band ligation.

Contraindications

Sclerotherapy is contraindicated in the management of external haemorrhoids, and thrombosed or ulcerated internal hemorrhoids, as well as in the presence of inflammatory or gangrenous piles.

Procedure

Injection of sclerosing agents causes fibrosis of the vascular cushions, which obliterates the haemorrhoids.

To perform sclerotherapy, you need to follow this procedure:

- Insert a proctoscope into the anal canal. As you slowly withdraw the proctoscope, the piles will bulge over the proctoscope's rim.
- Clean the base of the pile with antiseptic solution.
- Inject 3 ml 5% phenol-in-oil into the submucosa around the pedicles of each of the primary haemorrhoidal sites just above the dentate line.

Figure 42.2 illustrates this procedure.

You can assure the patient that the injections should not be painful. However, he may experience discomfort for two or three days after the procedure.

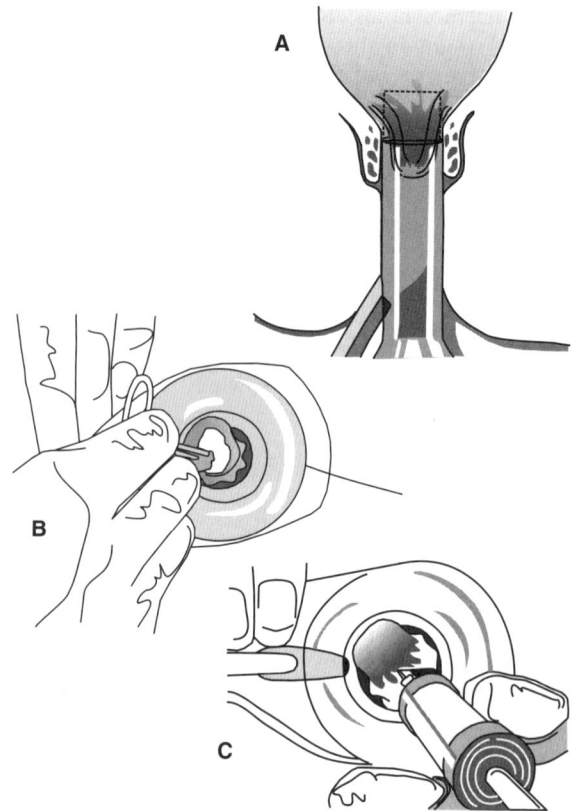

Figure 42.2 Performing injection sclerotherapy: (A) Slowly withdraw the proctoscope until the piles prolapse into the lumen; (B) Clean the base of the pile; (C) Inject into the base of the pile – above the dentate line

This usually resolves, and the patient can note some benefit after 6–10 days. You may need to repeat the treatment, often up to three times with an interval of up to six weeks between injections.

Complications

Although this is rare, it is possible that you may misplace the injection into the prostate. This causes haematuria and fever, but it usually settles without treatment.

Sclerotherapy has the advantages of being inexpensive and easy to carry out in the outpatient setting. However, its effect is not as permanent as other treatment modalities and treatment may need to be repeated.

Rubber banding

Rubber band ligation is recommended as the initial mode of therapy for first- and second-degree haemorrhoids (Shanmugam et al. 2005). It is a simple, inexpensive, office-based procedure that can be applied to most patients with bleeding and/or prolapsing haemorrhoids. Rubber band ligation offers excellent results in the treatment of internal haemorrhoids. Patient satisfaction has been well documented with 79% being cured with a single treatment (Nisar & Scholefield 2003).

The treatment involves removal of excess tissue and healing by secondary intention with resulting fibrosis and fixation. The technique requires two people to perform.

Equipment

You need the following:

- A banding instrument, as shown in Figure 42.3
- A proctoscope
- Lubricant
- Grasping forceps
- Rubber bands
- A loading cone
- Forceps and cotton wool to wipe away faeces
- A good light source

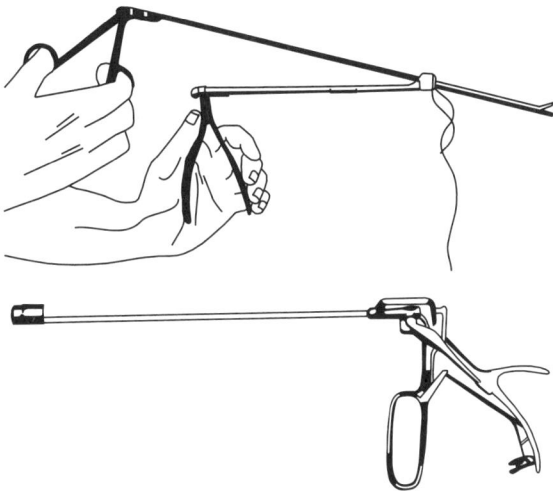

Figure 42.3 Full view of the banding instrument with grasping forceps threaded through the drum (note that the thread is attached to the rubber band to withdraw the band, if necessary)

Procedure

Explain to the patient that it is not necessary for you to use a local anaesthetic, although he should take an analgesic before the procedure begins and again afterwards.

As illustrated in Figure 42.4, to perform rubber banding, you need to follow this procedure:

- Administer a cleansing enema.
- Load one or two rubber bands onto the drum of the banding instrument, using the loading cone.

Then remove the loading cone. You will find that having a thread attached to the bands is useful if you must remove the bands from the anal canal, for example if the banding is painful.

- Insert the lubricated proctoscope into the anus and guide it into position with the relevant pile prolapsing over the rim.
- Grasp the haemorrhoid through the proctoscope. *Take care* to avoid application to the dentate line, as immediate, severe pain results. Grasp the haemorrhoid at least 7 mm above the dentate line. See Fig 42.1 for the anatomy.
- While using your other hand to grip the ligator, pass its drums over the haemorrhoid, ensuring that the dentate line is at least 2 mm below the drum. See Fig 42.4A.
- Compress the trigger mechanism to release the tight rubber band around the neck of the haemorrhoidal stalk. See Fig 42.4B.
- Remove the proctoscope and cut the thread short.

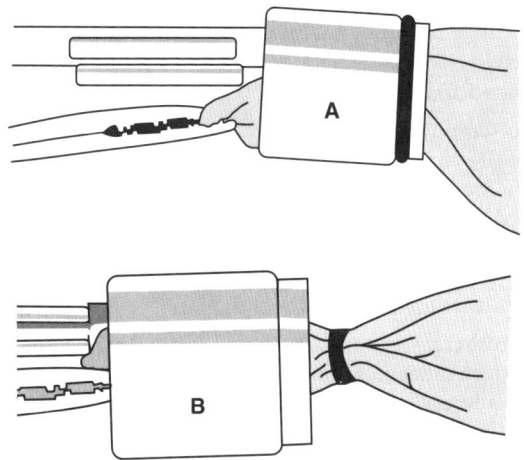

Figure 42.4 Performing rubber banding

When the pile separates, you will see it with the band as well as slight bleeding within the toilet pan. The ulcer that results will heal slowly. Inform your patient that he needs to return to hospital immediately if large bleeding occurs – it is probably due to secondary haemorrhage.

Follow-up

Advise your patient to take analgesia before and afterwards, and to keep the stools soft with a high-fibre diet, bulking agents and stool softeners.

Complications

Rubber band ligation is associated with a low complication rate – less than 2%. Complications include

- a vaso-vagal response to proctoscopy and the placement of the bands
- secondary haemorrhage 7–10 days post-procedure when the banded bundle sloughs off
- anal pain
- pelvic sepsis (though this is rare).

If the haemorrhoidal symptoms persist after two or more banding sessions, you should consider surgical haemorrhoidectomy.

Incising a perianal haematoma

A perianal haematoma is a purple swelling at the anal margin caused by rupture of a perianal vein following straining during defecation or some other effort involving a Valsalva manoeuvre. The inflamed area is tense, tender and easily visible upon inspection of the anal verge as a swelling about the size of a pea. It is usually associated with considerable pain.

Management consists mainly of relieving the pain by local and oral administration of analgesics, and by helping the patient to avoid constipation. If he presents within 24 hours, aspirate the haematoma using a 19-gauge needle while the blood is still fluid, without local anaesthetic.

If the patient presents from 24 hours to 5 days, when the blood has clotted, make a simple incision under local anaesthetic over the haematoma. Removal of the clot will relieve the pain and discomfort.

If the patient presents after six days, it is best to leave the haematoma alone unless it is extremely painful or infected, though the latter is rare. Resolution is shown in the appearances of wrinkles on the previously stretched skin.

43 How to read an abdominal radiograph

ANDREW ROSS AND CYRIL NAIDOO

The radiographic views that you can have of the abdomen are the supine, erect, lateral and lateral decubitus views. Acute films include supine and erect abdominal radiographs (AXRs) as well as erect chest radiographs (CXRs). Plain radiographs are useful in detecting

- free intraperitoneal air
- retroperitoneal and intramural gas
- small and large bowel obstruction
- radiopaque calculi
- soft-tissue masses and free fluid.

In order for you to be able to interpret an AXR and detect any abnormalities, you need to understand the anatomy of the abdomen as well as the radiographic anatomy. Figure 43.1 illustrates the anatomy of the abdomen and Figures 43.2 to 43.8 illustrate various radiographic views of the abdomen.

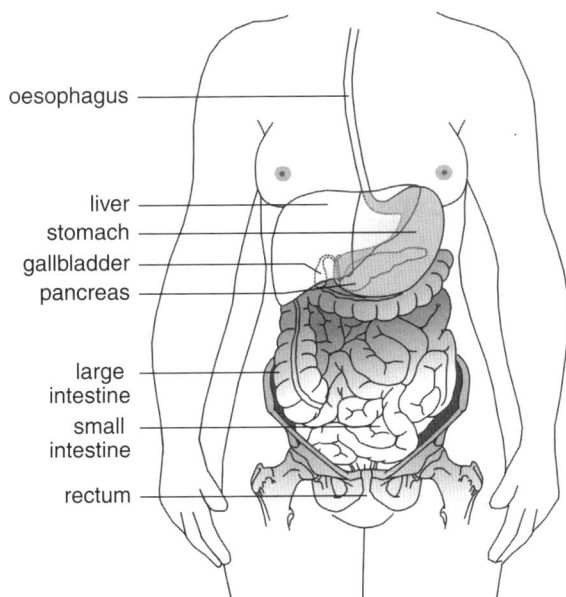

Figure 43.2 Sigmoid volvulus

Normal findings on an AXR are intraluminal air in the stomach and colon, and air fluid levels in the stomach and occasionally in the proximal duodenum.

When requesting an AXR your requirements must be clear and specific, as follows:

- Erect CXR for air under the diaphragm
- Erect AXR or left side down decubitus view when looking for air fluid levels

Reading an AXR

You need to interpret the AXR in the context of the patient's illness, that is his presenting symptoms, the physical findings and the reasons for your request of

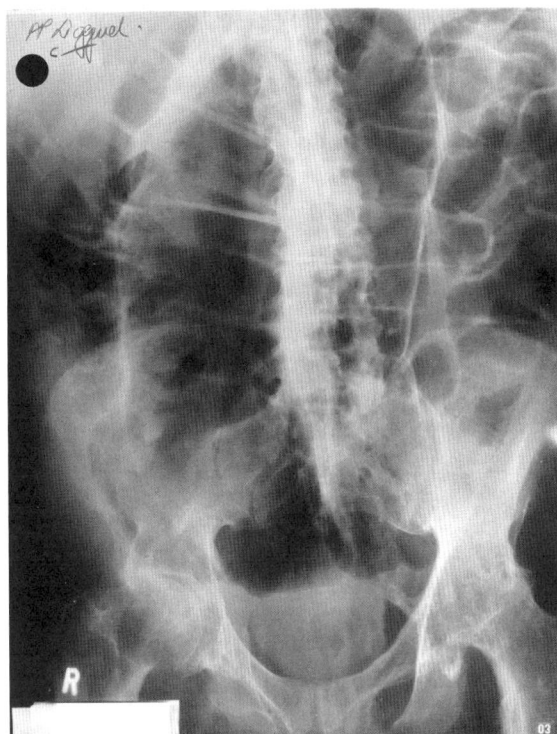

Figure 43.1 Anatomy of the adult abdomen

127

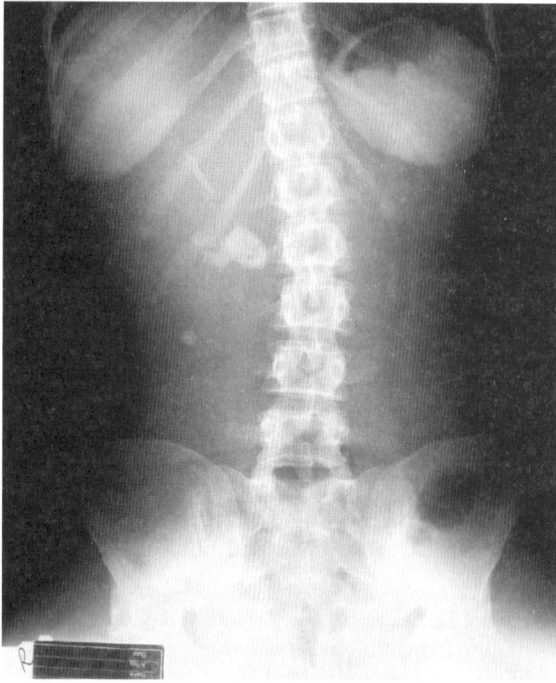

Figure 43.3 Calcification in the right kidney

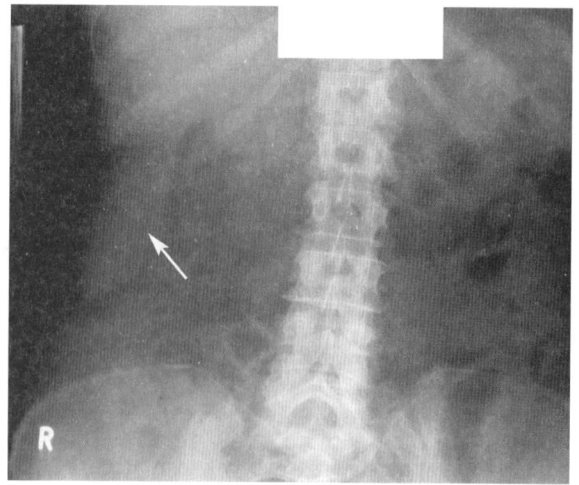

Figure 43.5 A normal variant – an extension of the right lobe of the liver, the edges of which can be seen (and which should not be confused with hepatomegaly)

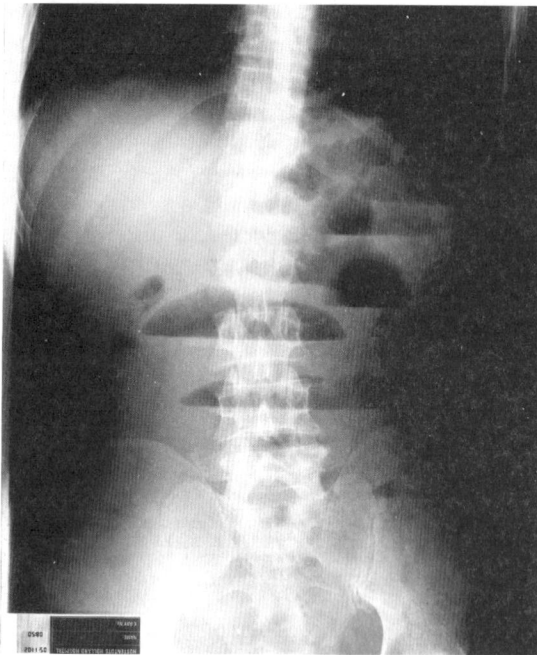

Figure 43.4 Air–fluid levels can be seen on the erect film due to paralytic ileus or obstruction

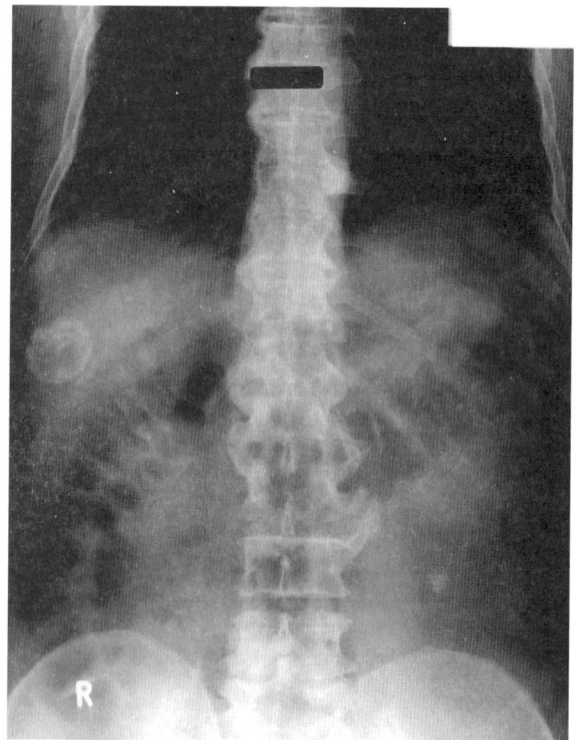

Figure 43.6 Calcified hydatid cyst. Note also severe degenerative changes in lumbar spine

the AXR. Be systematic – examine all parts of the film in an orderly, consistent manner, as follows:

• Record the patient's name, and the date and time of the AXR.

• Check the quality of the AXR. Are all the requested views included? Is the entire anatomical area included? Note the projection – AP, PA or lateral. Is the film over- or under-exposed? Check the anatomical markers showing right or left side. '

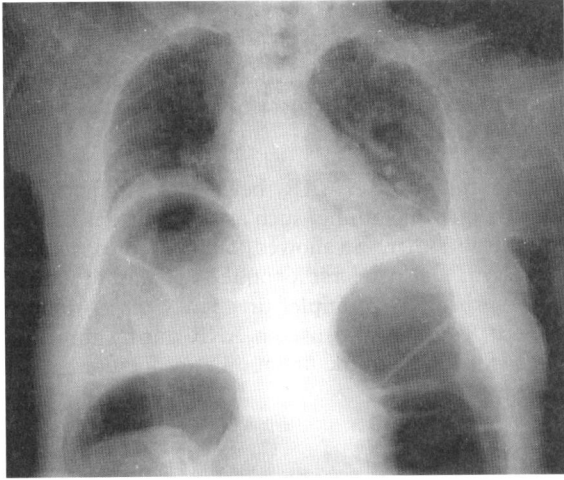

Figure 43.7 Chest X-ray, which is the best view to detect free air under the diaphragm

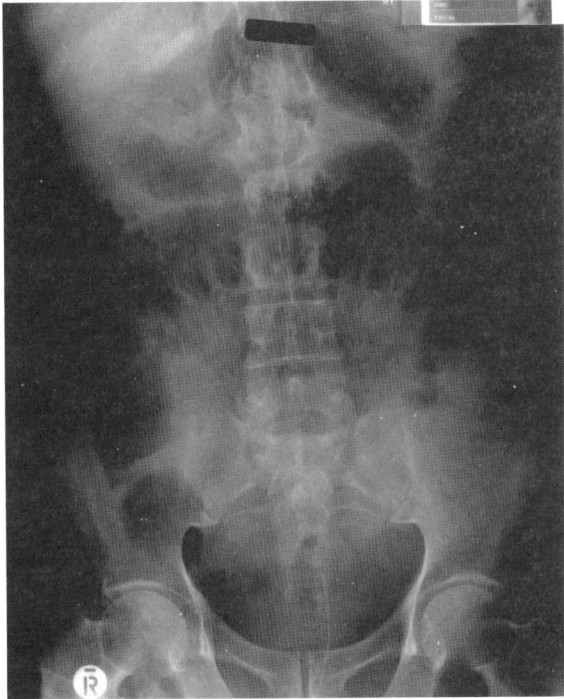

Figure 43.8 Small bowel obstruction

Source: Prof. Steenkamp, Hottentots Holland Hospital, Western Cape

- Look at the bony skeleton.
- Look at the bowel gas pattern. The stomach should be in the left upper quadrant. The colon should frame the edge of the abdomen in the erect film and is fixated at the hepatic and splenic flexures. Usually there is no air in the small bowel, but in obstruction you may see air–fluid levels with valvulae coniventes extending across

the lumen. If there is gas in the small-bowel or if you suspect a small bowel obstruction, you should request a decubitus or erect film of the abdomen.

- Look for abnormal dilatation of the bowel:
  - Jejunum > 3.5 cm diameter
  - Mid small bowel > 3 cm. Dilated jejunum has valvulae coniventes or folds transversely across the diameter of jejunum.
  - Ileum > 2.5 cm
  - Colon > 5.5 cm or caecal diameter > 8cm at the base. Haustra interdigitate (then do not cross the full diameter of the colon), unlike valvulae coniventes in the jejunum.

- Look for faecal loading or impaction.
- Check the psoas outline bilaterally – it should be symmetrical with the lateral border slightly concave.
- Check the renal outlines. The left kidney is normally slightly higher than the right kidney. The kidneys are usually 10–12 cm long or the length of 3–4 vertebral bodies. The upper poles are more medial and lie parallel to the psoas muscle. The difference in size should be less than 1 cm.
- Check the outline of the liver and spleen. Note whether the inferior border of liver is well defined, especially laterally.
- Look for free air or collections of free fluid. Free fluid will displace the pre-peritoneal fat line laterally. In the supine view, if you see both sides of the bowel wall then you can suspect free air. Another sign is the appearance of the falciform ligament in the right upper quadrant, which becomes outlined by air. Remember that 20% of perforations do not initially show free air. If you suspect a perforation, lie the patient on his left side to limit leakage of the gastric contents while waiting for the AXR. A duodenal perforation in the part behind the peritoneum can allow gas to collect around the kidneys.
- Look for radiopaque calculi and calcification in the region of the following:
  - The liver
  - The gall bladder – only 15% of gallstones calcify.
  - The kidneys – only 15% of ureteric and renal stones do *not* calcify.
  - The ureters, along the transverse processes of the lumbar vertebrae. Phleboliths may be present in the pelvic veins, which you should not confuse with calculi. Phleboliths are oval, smooth and internally lucent; calculi are dense, with irregular margins.

- The prostate

- The bladder wall. The bladder may be visible if radiolucent fat or blood surrounds it – this is known as a "tear drop" bladder. Calcification in the full bladder wall may be due to TB or bilharzia. TB leads to a small rigid bladder. In bilharzia the bladder wall is not rigid and collapses when the bladder is emptied.

- The pancreas – stippled calcification and crosses the midline

- The uterus. It will be visible if radiolucent fat surrounds it. Fibroids may calcify, as may an ovarian fibroma (though this is rare). Dermoid cysts may show calcification.

- The aorta. Calcification could be seen in aneurysms, atherosclerosis, diabetes and Takayasu's disease.

When studying the AXR, beware of artefacts that may be due to clothing, such as shirt buttons overlying the abdomen. Swallowed foreign bodies, such as coins, may also be radiopaque. Remember that if you suspect a multiple pregnancy in a female patient, you can also use an AXR during the third trimester to determine the number of foetuses.

How to perform a liver biopsy

CYRIL NAIDOO AND ANDREW ROSS

Indications

You would perform a liver biopsy in these situations:

- Evaluation of chronically elevated aspartate aminotransferase (AST) and alanine aminotransferase (ALT) levels of uncertain cause
- Confirmation of specific diagnosis in chronic liver or neoplastic disease
- Grading and staging of chronic hepatitis
- Evaluation of the patient's response to treatment, such as in autoimmune hepatitis
- Evaluation of the cause of acute hepatitis
- Investigation of a pyrexia of unknown origin

Contraindications

You would not perform the procedure in these cases:

- An uncooperative patient
- Impaired coagulation: PT (Prothrombin time) greater than or equal to four seconds over control, INR (International Normalised Ratio) greater than or equal to 1.5, bleeding time longer than or equal to 10 minutes or platelets less than 70 000 × $10^9/\ell$
- Vascular tumours, such as haemangioma
- High-grade biliary obstruction
- Tense ascites

Relative contraindications include ascites, severe chronic lung disease, infection of the right pleural cavity or below the diaphragm, amyloidosis, myeloproliferative disease and hereditary haemorrhagic telangiectasia.

Procedure

Before you begin the procedure, you need to

- obtain the patient's written, informed consent (Chapter 140)

- check that the platelets are more than 70 000 × $10^9/\ell$ – if they are low, transfuse with platelets
- check INR < 1.5 – if it is more than 1.5 give fresh frozen plasma
- ensure that the patient has *not* taken anti-coagulants for five days
- ensure that he has not taken NSAIDs for one day
- ensure that he has not eaten for eight hours.

To perform the percutaneous technique, you need to follow this procedure:

- Use a 40–130 mm, 14- to 18-gauge, cutting or spring-loaded needle (Figure 44.1)
- Establish an IV line.
- Ask the patient to lie on his back or slightly turned towards his left side with his right hand above his head.
- Mark the outline of the liver with a surgical pen.
- If you cannot palpate the liver abdominally, percuss the outline of liver during inspiration and expiration. The upper border frequently corresponds to a point along the midaxillary line at the second or third intercostal space above the costal margin. Mark this location with a surgical pen.
- The needle can be inserted below the costal margin in an area of dullness over the liver or through an intercostal space anterior to the mid-axillary line, just below the area of maximal dullness on expiration. Once you have identified a suitable site, prepare the area with Betadine solution and place sterile drapes around the intended site of insertion of the biopsy needle.
- Inject local anaesthetic around the intended insertion site down to the capsule of the liver. Make a small incision with a surgical blade through the skin where you injected the local anaesthetic.
- Ask your patient to hold his breath for 5–10 seconds while you take the biopsy.
- Insert the biopsy needle – with the obturator fully retracted or extended (depending on make) to cover the specimen notch – through the skin and

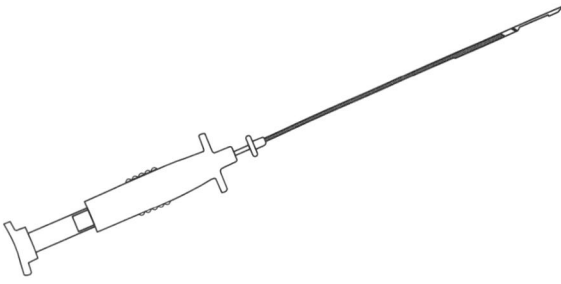

Figure 44.1 The liver biopsy needle

into the liver, ensuring that the specimen notch is within the liver.

- Depending on the make of the biopsy needle, move either the obturator or cannula to expose the specimen notch.
- Cut the tissue that has prolapsed into the specimen notch by reversing the preceding action.
- Perform two biopsies to ensure an adequate tissue sample.

If you are unsure of a suitable site, you can perform the biopsy under ultrasound guidance. The whole procedure should take less than 20 minutes.

Once you have performed the procedure

- monitor your patient carefully
- observe his vital signs and any symptoms for at least two hours
- discharge him if he is well after six hours of observation and bed rest
- admit him if there is evidence of bleeding, bile leak, pneumothorax or pain that requires more than one analgesic dose.

Complications

The following complications can occur:

- About 20–30% of patients experience pleuritic, peritoneal or diaphragmatic pain that responds well to simple analgesia.
- Vasovagal reaction, that is fainting
- Fewer than 1% of patients suffer severe complications.
- Haemorrhage – in the peritoneal cavity, within the liver, in the subcapsular space, within the biliary tree or another organ such as the gallbladder, lung, kidney or colon
- Bile peritonitis
- Infection
- Haemothorax
- Arteriovenous fistula
- Reaction to anaesthetic
- A low percentage – 0.03% – of patients die.

Eyes, ENT and skin

45 How to examine the eye

JONATHAN PONS

Of the various tests and methods of eye examination, the measurement of visual acuity, pupillary reflexes and ophthalmoscopy are the most important. We will now discuss each of these in detail.

Visual acuity

Follow these steps to test your patient's distance vision:

- Make sure that the examination room is well lit.
- Use a Snellen chart, or "E" chart for illiterate patients.
- Ask the patient to stand 6 m from the chart.
- Ask the patient to occlude one eye with the palm of his hand.
- Check that he is not peeping nor exerting undue pressure on his occluded eye.
- He should state aloud each letter that he can read, or with his fingers mimic the direction of the "E" on the chart.
- He should read successively smaller letters until he can no longer distinguish each letter.
- You can record visual acuity (VA) using this convention: VA equals the distance tested over the lowest line read. For example, a VA tested at six metres where the last line read was the 24 metre line is recorded as 6/24.
- Test the other eye.
- If the patient wears glasses then test with them on.
- When vision is less than 6/12, improvement with a pinhole denotes a refractive error.
- If he cannot read the top line at 6 m, make him step 1 m closer until he can read the top line, and record his vision accordingly (for example 3/60 means he read the top line at 3 m).
- If he cannot read the letters at all, test finger counting and record "CF" if he counts fingers.
- If he cannot count fingers, test hand movements and record "HM" if movement of your hand is detected.

- If he cannot distinguish hand movement, test for light perception with a bright torch and record "LP" if it is detected.
- If he cannot perceive light, conclude that the patient has no perception of light, and record "NPL".

Visual acuity in infants and small children

Follow this procedure:

- Have the infant seated on an adult's lap.
- Hold a toy 30–50 cm from the infant's face.
- Watch the eyes for fixation and following movements; occlude one eye at a time without touching the face.
- If there is no response, use a torch.
- If the child can pick out individual small items, such as beads or "hundreds and thousands" cake decorations, his visual acuity is better than 6/24.
- Determine if a red reflex is present and equal.

Once you are comfortable with conducting this test, train a clinic assistant to perform it as this will save your own time. The test should take about five minutes and must precede further eye examination.

Visual fields: Confrontation testing

In this test, the principle is to compare the patient's visual field with your own. Follow these steps:

- Sit 1 m from and directly opposite your patient.
- Ask him to occlude one eye with the palm of his hand.
- Close your eye that is directly opposite his occluded eye.
- Ask him to fixate his open eye on your open eye.
- Bring your hand half-way between yourself and the patient in four different quadrants.
- Show one, two or five fingers and ask him to count them.
- Repeat the test for the other eye.

- Record the results on a grid, as shown in Figure 45.1.

You can conduct a similar test by asking the patient to compare the hue or intensity of identical coloured objects, for example the red top on a bottle of eye drops, that you hold in separate quadrants. If there is a field defect the top may appear faded or colourless.

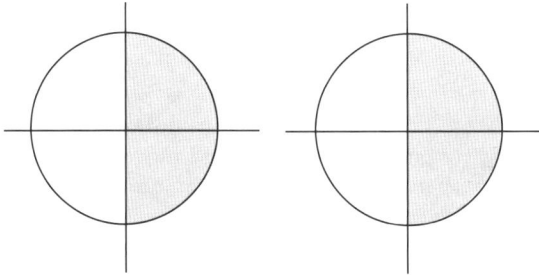

Figure 45.1 Results of a confrontation test as viewed by the patient with a right homonymous hemianopia

Pupillary reflexes

The most important signs to detect are

1. afferent defect (optic nerve or retinal abnormality)
2. efferent defect (3rd cranial nerve or iris muscle abnormality).

Detecting an afferent defect

Ensure a darkened room, ask the patient to fixate on the distance (Figure 45.2A), and use the brightest available torch.
   Swinging flashlight test:
- Illuminate one pupil for three seconds and then rapidly swing the light to illuminate the other pupil, then back to the first eye, etc.
- Watch how the pupils respond during the test (Figure 45.2B).
- An afferent defect is seen if the pupil paradoxically dilates on being illuminated (Figure 45.2C), then as you swing to the other normal eye, the normal eye briskly constricts. The vision is worse in the eye with the afferent defect.

Detecting an efferent defect

Shine the light into each eye several times as above and observe the following:

- Light shone into the affected eye will elicit poor constriction in that eye, whilst the normal eye will constrict normally.
- Light shone into the normal eye elicits good constriction, whilst the abnormal eye will not constrict normally.

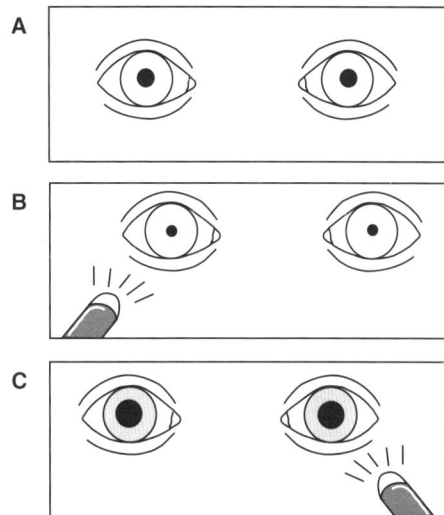

Figure 45.2 Swinging flashlight test: (A and B) = normal pupil reflexes; (C) left afferent defect

Red reflex

This simple test should be part of the routine examination of the eyes. Here, the principle is to test for any opacities in the media, or clear parts of the eye, using the following steps:

- Set the ophthalmoscope at zero, and stand 40 cm or an arm's length away from the patient.
- Whilst looking through the ophthalmoscope, shine the light into each pupil. The vessels and colour of the choroid should elicit a red reflection.
- A poor red reflex could be caused by any ocular pathology that prevents light reaching the retina and being reflected back to the observer.
- Look out for a black spot or "spider-web" appearance in the red reflex, which may be the result of an early cataract.

Eyelid eversion

The principle of this examination is to exclude a foreign body from under the upper eyelid tarsal plate and any other pathology such as the cobblestone appearance of the mucosa in allergic conjunctivitis. Follow this procedure, as illustrated in Figure 45.3:

- It is essential that the patient looks downwards.
- Place a cotton wool bud or a match or an orange stick horizontally on the upper eyelid above the tarsal plate.
- Hold his eyelashes and lower part of the upper eyelid with your thumb and index finger, and pull the eyelid downwards.
- Carefully turn the eyelid inside out over the cotton wool bud.

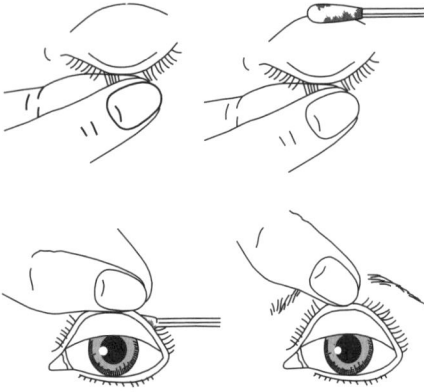

Figure 45.3 Performing an eyelid eversion

Cornea

The principle of this examination is to detect opacities and size. Follow this procedure:

- Shine a torch from different angles across the patient's cornea.
- Look for haziness, which suggests corneal oedema, or whiteness, which suggests scarring or ulceration.
- The corneal diameter in babies is ≤ 12.5 mm. If it is much greater this could be the result of congenital glaucoma. Measure with a ruler.
- Test the sensation with a wisp of cotton wool.

Fluorescein staining

The naked eye may not detect corneal defects due to ulceration or abrasions. Perform this test after trauma or foreign body sensation. Follow this procedure:

- Use fluorescein-impregnated strips.
- Moisten the strips with a drop of saline or artificial tears.
- Touch the strip to the inside of your patient's lower lid.
- Illuminate the cornea with an ophthalmoscope that has a cobalt blue filter.
- Look for epithelial defects, which stain bright green.
- If you do not have a blue light, you could use a strong white light, which may reveal areas of staining.

Anterior chamber: Eclipse sign

In this test, the principle is to quickly determine the depth of the anterior chamber, especially before instilling dilating drops. If the anterior chamber is deep, the iris is slightly convex. If shallow, the iris is extremely convex.

Shine a light from the temporal side on the cornea while facing your patient. In a normal anterior chamber, the entire iris is lit up evenly (Figure 45.4A). In a shallow anterior chamber, the iris protrudes more and half the iris is in shadow (Figure 45.4B). *This eye should not be dilated* – it may precipitate an attack of angle closure glaucoma.

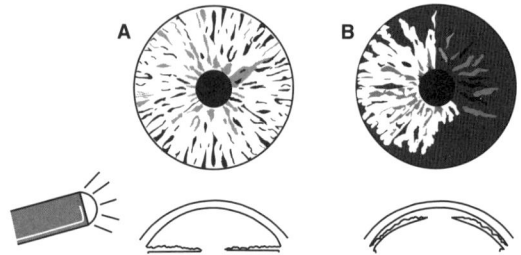

Figure 45.4 Anterior chamber depth test

Dilating the pupil

The principle here is to enable more effective ophthalmoscopy by dilating the pupil. However, you should not dilate a pupil in the following circumstances:

- Shallow anterior chamber (detected by the eclipse sign)
- Anterior chamber intra-ocular lens after cataract surgery
- A comatose patient, as this could confuse the clinical signs
- A patient who has to drive home, as accommodation is lost for a few hours

Follow this procedure:

- Use a short-acting mydriatic such as tropicamide (Mydriacyl) or cyclopentolate (Cyclogyl). Do not use atropine as it will cause a prolonged mydriasis.
- Put one drop in the patient's eye and repeat this every five minutes for two further applications.
- Note that a dark iris is more difficult to dilate – you may need more drops.

Ophthalmoscopy

The principle of this test is to systematically examine the internal anatomical structures of the eye from the cornea to the retina.

After testing for the red reflex, follow this procedure:

- With your right eye, look into your patient's right eye and he should look into the distance.
- Place your left hand on his forehead to steady yourself and use your thumb to elevate his upper eyelid.

- Look at the structures from front to back using the following ophthalmoscope settings:
  - Cornea +20
  - Iris +15
  - Lens +12 to +8
  - Vitreous +8 to +4
  - Fundus 0 (rotate the dial of the ophthalmoscope until the vessels or the optic nerve is clearly seen).

- With regard to the optic nerve head, look at the normal pink colour, the ratio of the optic cup to the optic disc (normal ≤ 0.4), the edges, the shape and the vessels coming from the disc.

- To examine the macula, ask the patient to look at your ophthalmoscope light and note the white foveal reflex in the middle of the macula.

- Follow the retinal vessels out from disc to periphery. Look for haemorrhages, exudates and abnormal vessels.

Schiotz tonometry

The principle of this test is to measure the intraocular pressure with this commonly available and simple device. Follow this procedure:

- Check for proper calibration by placing the tonometer footplate with weighted plunger in place on the testing plate in the case. The tonometer should register 0. Figure 45.5 shows this instrument.

- Start with the 5.5 g weight on the tonometer.

- Ask the patient to focus his vision on the ceiling, either lying flat or seated with his head tilted back.

- Place a drop of topical anaesthetic into each eye.

- Spread the eyelids with your non-dominant hand, without applying pressure to the globe.

- Hold the instrument with the thumb and index finger of your dominant hand with the scale facing you. See Figure 45.5.

- Keeping the instrument vertical, lower it onto the cornea until the footplate is resting on the cornea.

- Read the scale.

- Using the calibration table in the case, determine the intraocular pressure. Note that the lower the scale reading, the higher the pressure. Normal intraocular pressure is less than 21 mmHg.

- If the scale reading is less than 5, add the 7.5 g weight and repeat the measurement, determining the intraocular pressure from the corresponding table.

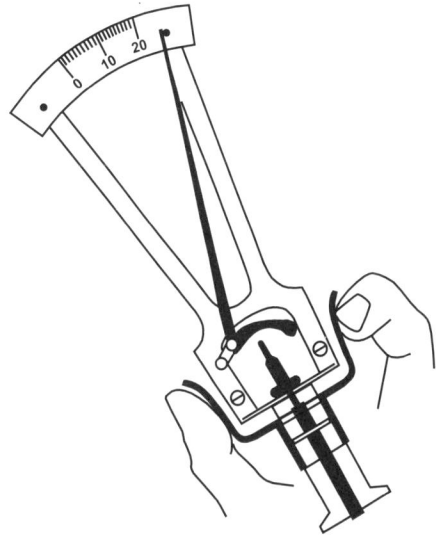

Figure 45.5 The Schiotz tonometer

To then clean the Shiotz tonometer

- remove the plunger from the cylinder by removing the weight and unscrewing the bolt around the plunger

- wipe the footplate and plunger with alcohol; use the pipe cleaner from the case to clean the plunger bore.

After cleaning, rinse the footplate and plunger with water and wipe them dry, without touching them with your fingers. Avoid using the tonometer on patients with conjunctivitis as this could spread the infection.

Schirmer's test

You can use this test to measure tear flow when you suspect dry eye syndrome. Follow this procedure:

- To exclude keratoconjunctivitis sicca, or dry eye syndrome, use standard Schirmer tear test strips – 0.5 x 3.5 cm.

- Instil local anaesthetic drops.

- Bend the terminal end of the paper strip at the indentation and hang it into the inferior conjunctival fornix laterally.

- Ask the patient to keep his eyes open.

- Remove the strip after five minutes and measure the distance between the indentation and furthest extent of moisture or wetting. Record the distance in millimetres and compare the height of moisture with the picture on the packet. Normal is 12 mm.

46 How to treat the eye

JONATHAN PONS

A basic knowledge of the following simple procedures will be invaluable.

Instillation of eye drops

The principle of this approach is to maximise the penetration of the drops. Follow this procedure:

- Ask the patient to look up.
- Retract his lower lid with your finger.
- Instil the eye drops or 1 cm ointment into the inferior fornix.
- To encourage corneal absorption, ask him to occlude his nasolacrimal duct by pressing 1 cm medial to and below the medial canthus.

Irrigation of the eye

Eye irrigation is essential to remove particulate material from the eye, or to treat an acid or alkali chemical injury or splash from plant sap. Follow this procedure:

- Ask the patient to lie supine.
- Instil two drops of local anaesthetic, such as Novescein.
- Keep the eyelids open manually or with the help of swabs under your fingers.
- Remove particulate material by rolling a moistened cotton wool bud across the conjunctiva. Remove larger particles with forceps.
- Irrigate with normal saline or other isotonic solution using drip tubing or a squeeze bottle. Do this for at least 15 minutes with at least 1 ℓ of fluid.
- If the patient has a chemical injury, check the pH of the conjunctival sac with urinary pH sticks and continue irrigating until the pH level is neutral, that is 7.4.

Removal of a foreign body from the cornea

Follow this procedure:

- Position the patient lying down. Stand at his head and shine a good light, preferably held by an assistant, onto his eye.
- Instil local anaesthetic drops, such as Novescein.
- Hold the patient's upper and lower lids apart with your thumb and index finger.
- If the foreign body is not embedded, wipe it off the corneal surface with a cotton wool bud moistened with saline or Novescein.
- If the foreign body is embedded, use the bevel of a needle mounted on a syringe to remove it. Approach from the lateral side whilst taking care that the needle is held parallel to the cornea.
- If there is a ring of rust, either curette it with the needle or use a burr. In many cases, the ring will be easier to remove a few days later. It is better to leave a small rust ring than to risk creating a corneal scar.
- Instil antibiotic ointment and pad the eye for 24 hours.

Patching the eye

A comfortable eye pad brings considerable relief for corneal abrasions or injury. Follow this procedure:

- Clean the patient's forehead and cheek with alcohol to remove skin oils.
- Ask him to close his injured eye.
- Apply either a sterile eye pad or folded gauze swab.
- Tape it across from the forehead to the zygoma.
- For pressure patching, first place a folded eye pad or gauze folded into quarters. Then patch as above.

Take care not to patch a child for longer than a day as this may impair visual development.

Incision and drainage of a chalazion or Meibomian cyst

A chalazion (or Meibomian cyst) is a mostly noninfective, non-tender nodule that appears on the tarsal plate. This is easily drained in the procedure room. To treat it, follow this procedure:

- Instil local anaesthetic drops.
- Inject lignocaine around the cyst through the skin.
- Evert the patient's eyelid with the Meibomian clamp, ensuring that the opening is over the swelling.
- Using an 11 or 15 blade, make a vertical incision over the chalazion mass perpendicular to the lid margin.
- Curette out the contents.
- Instil antibiotic eye ointment and a pad.

Sub-conjunctival injection

This is an effective means of delivering medication to the eye, especially in inflammatory conditions:

- Draw up the drugs in an insulin or 2.5-ml syringe.
- Use either an insulin or a 25G needle.
- Instil a drop of Novescein (topical anaesthetic) into the inferior fornix.
- With the thumb of one hand to pull down the lower lid, approach the eye from the lateral aspect.
- Insert the needle superficially under the conjunctiva of the inferior fornix, entering laterally and aiming medially and posteriorly for about 3 to 5 mm.
- Inject slowly and as you do so, the inferior fornix should fill with the medication.

Repair of eyelid laceration

In this procedure, it is important that you ensure excellent lid apposition before completing the rest of the repair, as this prevents long-term corneal complications. Follow this procedure:

- Make a thorough examination to exclude visual loss or lacrimal duct injury or scleral rupture. These will require referral.
- Instil local anaesthetic drops.
- Inject 2% lignocaine, which may be with adrenaline, into the wound.
- Using 6.0 vicryl with a spatulated needle, approximate the eyelid at the grey line. This is the area just posterior to the lashes, at or just before the conjunctiva begins. A mattress suture with a buried knot will approximate the lid margin accurately. There are four bites (Figure 46.1):

  - Starting in the wound, make a deep bite that comes out 3 mm from the wound at the grey line.
  - Then make a shallow bite into the grey line on the same side (1 mm from the wound).
  - Follow this by a shallow bite on the other side, starting in the wound and coming out in the grey line (1 mm).
  - Finally, make a deep bite, starting at the grey line (3 mm from the wound) and ending deep in the wound, where you tie it.

- Suture the tarsal plate with 6.0 vicryl, taking care that the sutures do not penetrate to the palpebral conjunctiva, otherwise the cornea would be scratched. Begin the suture from the outside rather than the conjunctival side. One suture, or perhaps two, should suffice.
- You should *not* need to suture the conjunctiva.
- Suture the skin using 6.0 nylon or similar. Leave the suture ends long and tape them together onto the skin. This will prevent the ends from traumatising the cornea and help with removal four or five days later.
- Apply chloramphenicol eye ointment in the conjunctival sac and to the wound.
- Remember to give your patient tetanus toxoid prophylaxis.

Figure 46.1 illustrates this procedure.

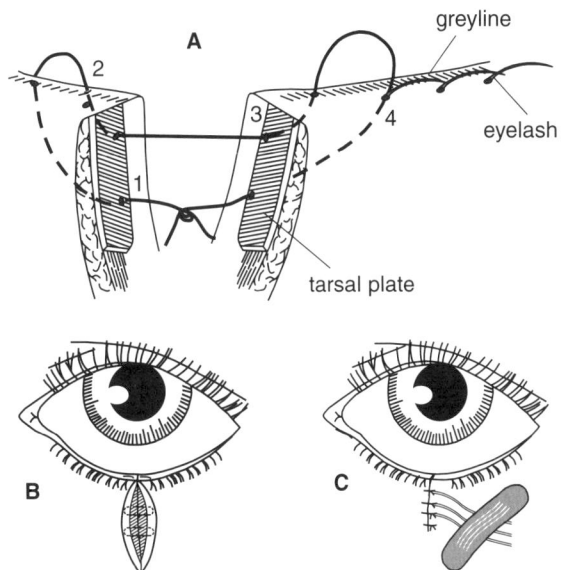

Figure 46.1 Repairing an eyelid laceration: (A) Eyelid margin repair; (B) Tarsal plate repair; (C) Skin closure

47 How to remove a foreign body from the nose

PATRICK KENNY

Children tend to insert things into their noses. The foreign bodies (FBs) may become infected, producing a purulent discharge that is unilateral or aspirated into the bronchi. When you attempt to remove the FB, be careful not to push it in deeper or cause aspiration. Note that the child may cooperate only for the first attempt, especially if it is painful, and therefore it is important for you to maximise the likelihood of success.

Make sure that you conduct the examination with a good source of light – a head lamp is ideal – and preferably with a nasal speculum. If necessary, you can wrap the child in a blanket and ask the mother or caregiver to hold him securely on her lap.

There are various techniques for removing foreign bodies from the nose, as follows:

- The easiest technique is to close the patient's mouth and the other nostril, and tell him to blow his nose or sneeze out the FB.

- You can also try a "kiss and blow" technique, in which you cover the child's mouth with your lips and blow inside until you feel a little resistance – caused by the closed glottis. Blow again forcefully, so that the FB is pushed out through the nostril.

- Alternatively, try to remove the object with a paper clip or hairpin bent to form a "spoon", as shown in Figure 47.1. You can also use a bent Jobson-Horne probe.

- Pass the probe behind the FB, then snare the FB and roll it forward.

- You can also try to remove the FB with Tilley's or "crocodile" forceps, as shown in Figure 47.2. This is a good option for soft FBs such as paper, foam or cotton wool, but not for hard FBs such as beans and beads.

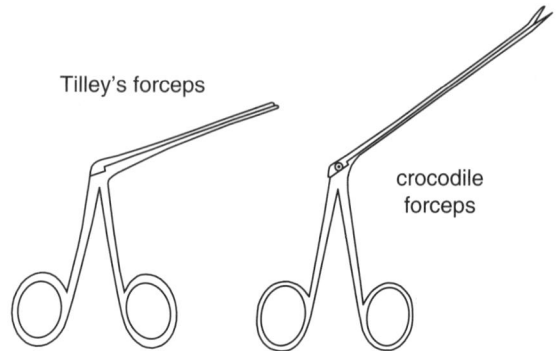

Tilley's forceps

crocodile forceps

Figure 47.2 Tilley's and crocodile forceps

- Lastly, you can connect a piece of rubber tubing to gentle wall suction and try to suck out the object. Use a large rubber catheter cut at right angles at the tip and smear K-Y jelly on the end. To prevent the hissing noise from possibly frightening the child, pinch the catheter closed until the tip is next to the FB. Alternatively, you could attach the bulb from a pneumatic otoscope or sphygmomanometer to give suction, as shown in relation to the ear in Figure 47.3.

If you do not succeed in removing the FB with any of these methods then you should consider removal under general anaesthetic.

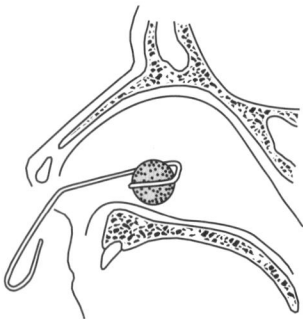

Figure 47.1
Paper clip or hairpin probe

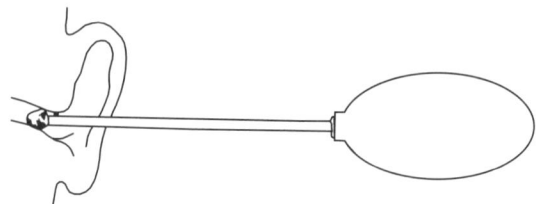

Figure 47.3 Pneumatic otoscope bulb

48 How to remove a foreign body from the ear canal

PATRICK KENNY

Children tend to insert foreign bodies (FBs) into their ears.

As with removing FBs from the nose, you must have a good light source – ideally a head lamp. You need to take care not to damage the eardrum. If the FB is a live insect first kill it by inserting water or plant/baby oil into the ear.

As has been described in detail in Chapter 47, you can use a number of techniques for the removal:

- Syringe the ear with lukewarm water. This may succeed in dislodging the object. Note, however, that vegetable matter such as beans may swell up with water. (See Figure 49.2 illustrating the syringing of an ear in Chapter 49.)

- Use crocodile or Tilley's forceps (see Figure 47.2 in Chapter 47) if the FB, such as cotton wool or paper, is clearly visible and soft. For soft FBs that are deeper in the ear, you can try a dental broach with a slight hook on the end to snare some threads.

- Alternatively, try to remove the object with a bent paper clip or hairpin (see Figure 47.1 for the nose), or a Jobson-Horne probe (Figure 48.1).

- Lastly, you can try to use gentle wall suction or a pneumatic otoscope bulb with a short piece of rubber tubing connected to it, as shown in Figure 48.2.

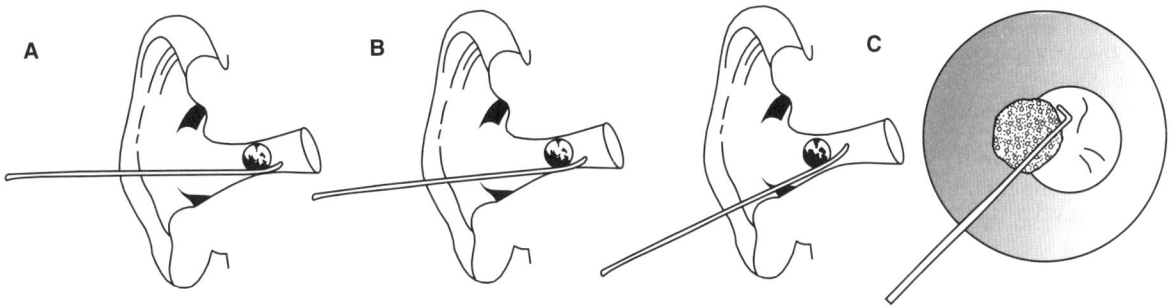

Figure 48.1 Use of a Jobson-Horne probe to remove FB from ear: (A) Probe inserted under FB; (B) Tip is lifted gently by depressing outer end of probe; (C) Gently lever or roll the FB out

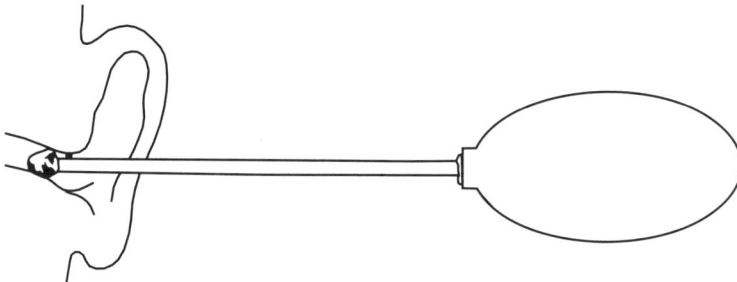

Figure 48.2 Gentle suction with a pneumatic otoscope bulb

49 How to examine and treat an ear

PATRICK KENNY

We will first discuss the examination of the ear.

External ear

When examining the external ear, you need to observe the size, shape and position of the pinna. Moreover, you should note the presence of surgical scars around the ear and look for congenital abnormalities, such as accessory auricles, skin tags and pre-auricular sinuses.

Otoscopy

In preparation for performing an otoscopy, straighten the patient's ear canal by gently lifting the pinna upwards and backwards. Select the largest speculum that will comfortably fit into his ear canal, since this will give you the best view and admit the most light. Then gently insert the otoscope along the line of the ear canal and check

- for wax or foreign bodies (FBs) in the ear canal
- for inflammation or discharge in the ear canal
- the eardrum, the light reflex, the pars tensa with the handle and lateral process of the malleus, and the tympanic membrane. These are illustrated in Figure 49.1.

Some otoscopes have an attachable pneumatic bulb that you can use to assess the mobility of the eardrum.

Assessment of hearing

In an adult, a basic voice test can assess hearing as either normal, moderate loss or severe deafness. Explain that you want the patient to repeat back to you what you say. Stand behind the patient and occlude the ear that is not being tested by pressing the tragus back over the canal. Gently rub the tragus to prevent this ear from hearing what you say. Then stand as far away as possible from the other ear and whisper a combination of numbers and letters such

as 7B8 or 3S9. If the patient cannot hear this, repeat in a normal voice and finally in a loud voice. You can repeat the test in the other ear.

Classify the patient's hearing as follows:

- **Heard whispered voice:** normal hearing
- **Heard normal voice, but not whispered voice:** moderate hearing loss
- **Heard only loud voice:** severe hearing loss

Tuning fork test

Using Weber's test, you would place a vibrating tuning fork in the centre of your patient's forehead and ask him where he hears it loudest. He has normal hearing if he hears it loudest in the middle of his head; he has abnormal hearing if he hears it loudest in one ear. In the latter case, there is either a conductive loss in the ear and the sound is being transmitted better through the bone or there is a sensori-neural loss in the other ear.

Using Rinne's test, you would place the vibrating tuning fork on the mastoid for 2–3 seconds then move it close to the external auditory meatus. Ask the patient to determine which is louder. This compares air with bone conduction. In a conductive hearing loss the bone conduction makes the sound louder, while in a sensori-neural loss the sound made by the fork in both positions is diminished.

We will now explore the methods of treating ear problems.

Syringing

Indications for syringing include impacted wax, removal of foreign bodies, and removal of discharge and inflammatory debris from the ear canal. **Contraindications** to syringing include previous surgery to the ear and the presence of a dry perforation. **Complications** include trauma to the ear canal and subsequent otitis externa, and inadvertent syringing of a dry perforation which leads to activation of a chronic otitis media.

 © Van Schaik Publishers

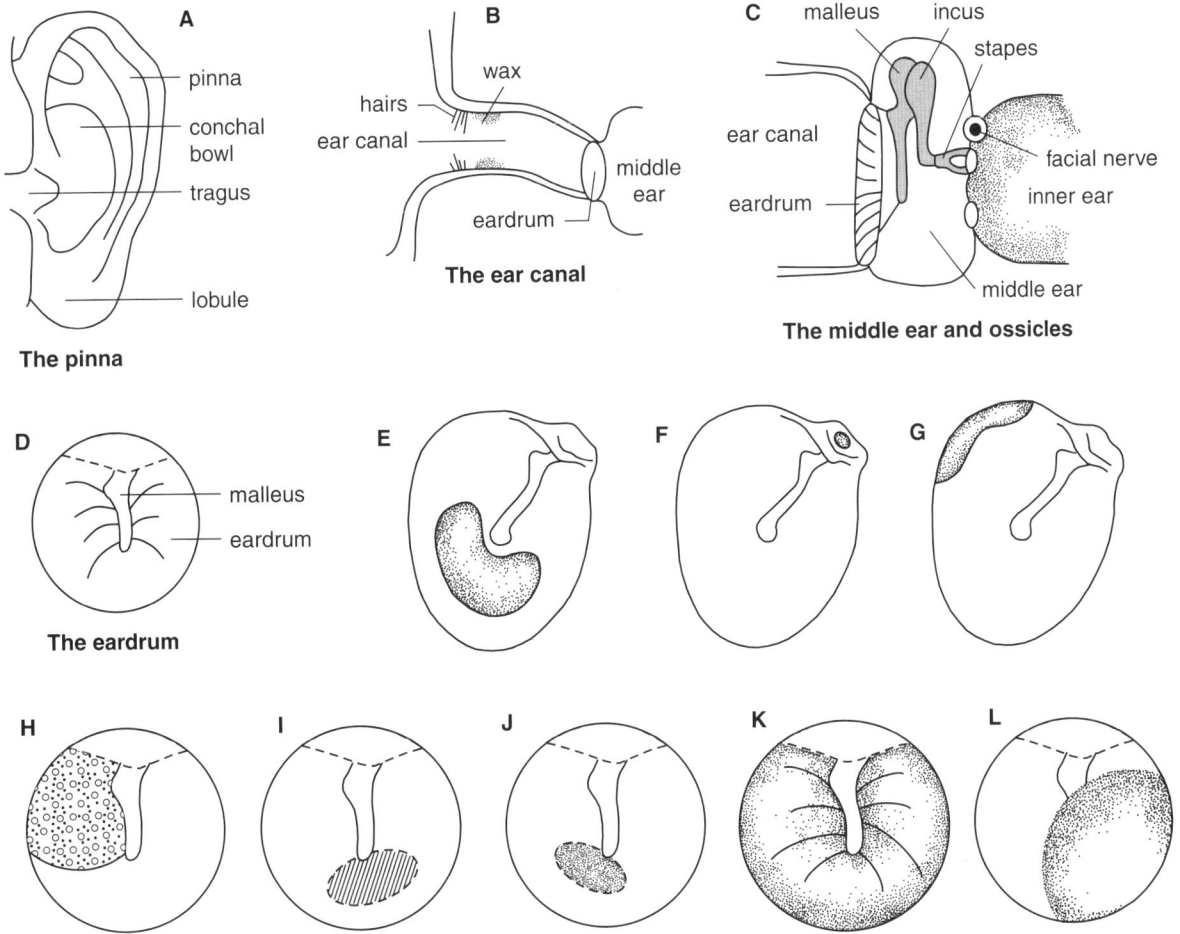

Figure 49.1 Multiple panels showing the anatomy of the ear and variations in appearance of the eardrum in schematic form: (A) External ear; (B) Ear canal; (C) Middle ear; (D) Normal eardrum; (E) Central perforation; (F) Attic perforation; (G) Marginal perforation; (H) Cholesteatoma; (I) Thin membranous scar; (J) Tympanosclerosis; (K) Bulging red inflamed drum; (L) Inflammatory swelling obscures drum

Dried impacted wax dissolves in water – you do not need to use sophisticated wax drops. Ask the patient to lie down with his ear uppermost and fill the canal with water. Using the tragus, pump the ear intermittently for 10 minutes, refilling the canal if necessary. This may be sufficient to soften the wax. If not, ask the patient to continue with the pumping a few times during the day, then try the syringing again later.

Procedure

Explain the procedure to the patient and ask him to tell you if he feels dizzy or pain, or if the water enters his throat. Seat him on a chair and stand at his side. Children should be seated on the parent's lap with their head and body gently but firmly held.

To syringe the ear, you need to follow this procedure:

- Prepare a 20-ml syringe with either a suction catheter cut short or a wide-bore IV plastic cannula.

- Fill a jug, bowl or kidney dish with tap water at body temperature. Check this with your finger. The patient will feel dizzy if it is too hot or too cold.

- Draw up the water into the syringe and make sure that the plunger can move freely inside the barrel.

- Drape a towel or other waterproofing over the patient's shoulder and neck.

- Ask him to hold another kidney dish or styrofoam cup under his ear to catch the water. A styrofoam cup with a bite taken out of the rim can fit easily under the ear.

- Using a good light to see clearly, advance the nozzle into the patient's external auditory meatus and simultaneously apply traction to the pinna in an upward and backward direction to straighten the canal.

- Advance the plunger to fill the ear canal with water and then more forcefully discharge the jet of water towards the roof of the ear canal, again in a posterior-superior direction.

- When the syringe is empty, examine the canal for the persistence of the FB, wax or other damage. If there *is* any damage stop syringing and prescribe drops to prevent infection and advise the patient about possible symptoms of otitis externa as a complication.

- Record your findings.

- Repeat this process until you have removed the FB or wax.

- Ensure that the patient is dry and clean.

Figure 49.2 shows how to syringe the ear.

Cleaning or dry mopping

This is indicated to dry a discharging ear. Wind a thin twist of cotton wool on the end of an orange stick so that the twist extends beyond the wooden tip to form a fluffy end. Ensure that the twist is of smaller diameter than the ear canal itself. It might help you to break the orange stick in half and use the broken end to hold the twist. A Jobson-Horne probe can also be used if available.

The adult patient should sit sideways on a chair, and the child should either lie down or sit on his mother's lap, with his head and body held firmly. It is important that you have a good light source to help you conduct the procedure.

Follow this procedure:

- Gently pull the pinna backwards to open and straighten the canal.

- Gently introduce the cotton wool twist into the meatus and rotate it to remove pus or particles of desquamated skin. The fluffy tip of the twist prevents the stick from damaging the eardrum. Do not push too hard.

- Withdraw the twist and examine it for pus, wax or bloody material. Discard the twist immediately – to prevent cross infection.

- Continue the dry mopping with a new cotton wool twist if it is not painful for the patient.

- It is essential that you repeatedly inspect with an otoscope during the procedure.

You can teach patients suffering from chronic active otitis media to dry mop at home before inserting their ear drops.

If dry mopping is not successful then you can consider gentle syringing. Gentle suction with a feeding tube connected to a suction tip may also be helpful in the removal of pus or debris from the ear canal.

Suturing the pinna or ear lobe

Lacerated ear cartilage itself does not need suturing, but the skin on both sides of the ear may need it. Insert subcuticular sutures to prevent scarring.

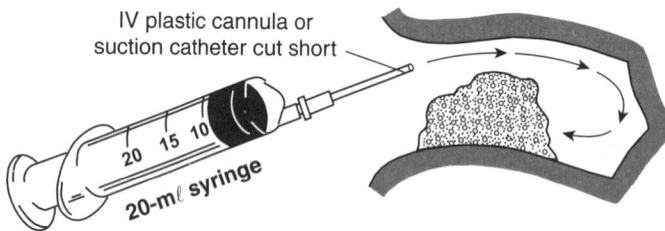

Figure 49.2

Syringing wax or a foreign body from an ear

50 How to examine the mouth and throat

PATRICK KENNY

We will first explore the manner in which you should examine your patient's mouth and throat.

Ask your patient to remove any dentures, as these may hide important pathology. To view the whole oral cavity, you need a good light – preferably a head lamp – and one or two tongue depressors.

The tongue

When examining your patient's tongue, look at

- the upper surface
- the edges
- the under surface.

Carefully examine the side of the tongue right at the back as carcinomas may easily be missed in this region.

The mouth

Follow this process when examining your patient's mouth:

- Look at the floor of his mouth, his lower teeth and the gum line, both on its inner and outer surfaces.
- Use a tongue depressor to lift his cheek away from his upper teeth, and look at the parotid duct opening, which is opposite the upper second molar.
- Examine his upper teeth and gums, then look at the hard and soft palates.
- Note the presence or absence of tonsillar tissue, and look at the surface of the posterior pharyngeal wall.
- Test his ability to move his tongue, and then test his ability to move his palate by asking him to say "aah".
- Finally, place a gloved finger into his mouth and palpate the base of his tongue and the floor of his mouth. By placing your other hand under his jaw, you can palpate his submandibular glands.

The neck

As pathology in the oral cavity may drain to the cervical lymph nodes, it is important that you also palpate for lymphadenopathy.

We will now discuss the method for taking a throat swab.

Taking a throat swab

Follow this procedure to take a throat swab:

- Focus a bright light – preferably a head lamp – into your patient's open oral cavity.
- Ask him to open his mouth widely. Depress his tongue gently with a tongue blade.
- Ask him to say a long "aah" – this lifts the uvula and aids in reducing the gag reflex.
- Guide the swab over his tongue into the posterior pharynx.
- Swab the mucosa behind the uvula and between the tonsillar pillars with a gentle sweeping motion. Figure 50.1 shows how you can do this. *Take care not to touch the lateral walls of the buccal cavity.*
- Immediately place the swab into a sterile container for transport to the laboratory.

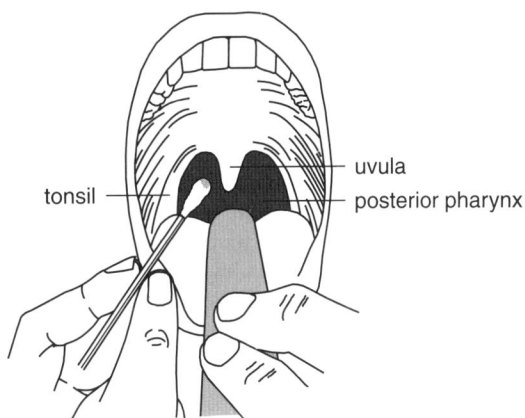

Figure 50.1 Taking a throat swab

Performing indirect laryngoscopy

You should perform indirect laryngoscopy in order to view the hypopharynx, larynx and vocal cords, which are not visible on direct examination of the oral cavity, as described above.

Explain to your patient that you are going to use an angled mirror placed up against his soft palate to look down on his vocal cords.

You need to follow this procedure to perform the indirect laryngoscopy:

- Sit close to and directly in front of the patient, facing him.

- Ensure that you are positioned so that ambient light falls on him and that you are not looking into it.

- Use a head lamp and an angled laryngeal mirror.

- Although the procedure does not require local anaesthetic, some patients have a strong gag reflex. You can significantly reduce it by spraying the soft palate and the oropharynx with local anaesthetic.

- Ensure that the mirror is warm to prevent it from misting up. Either heat it gently over a flame, or briefly hold it in hot water. Against the back of your hand, test that it is not too hot before putting it in your patient's mouth.

- Ask him to lean forward slightly, to open his mouth and to put out his tongue.

- With a small square gauze swab in one hand, hold the tip of his tongue between your middle finger and thumb, gently pulling it towards his chin. With your index finger, gently lift his upper lip.

- Ask him to relax his tongue entirely, to allow you to pull on it, and to breathe gently in and out. This tends to make the tongue drop to the floor of the mouth, out of your line of vision, and it also assists in reducing the patient's gag reflex.

- Hold the laryngeal mirror in your other hand and place it steadily against his soft palate, pushing the soft palate upwards and backwards. An image of the vocal cords appears in the mirror. The shaft of light from the head lamp should shine directly onto the laryngeal mirror in order to light up the vocal cords. If you are not used to using a head lamp you need to consciously move your head, rather than just your eyes, in order to ensure that the beam of light from the lamp falls on the mirror. This is illustrated in Figure 50.2.

- Systematically examine the tongue base; the valleculae; the hypopharynx, including the pyriform fossae and the postcricoid area; and the larynx itself, as shown in Figure 50.3.

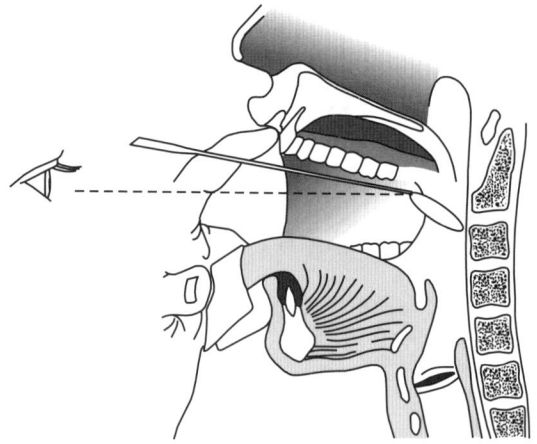

Figure 50.2 Indirect laryngoscopy

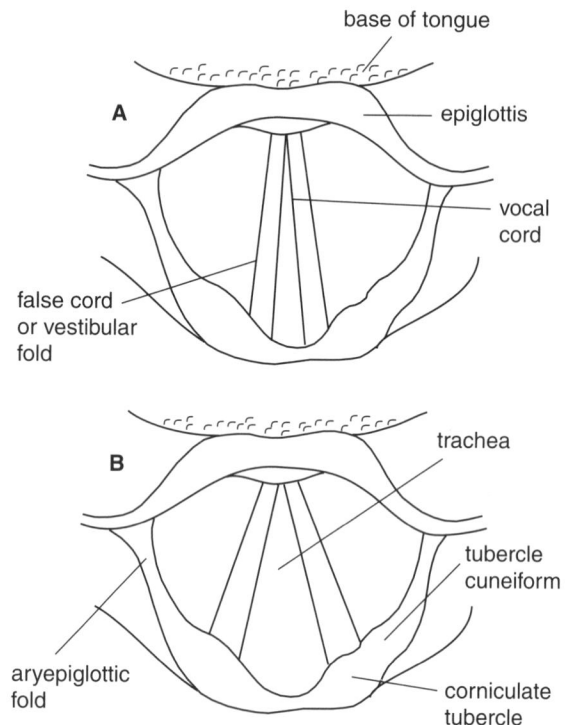

Figure 50.3 Anatomy of area viewed during indirect laryngoscopy with (A) closed and (B) open vocal cords

- Carefully exclude any tumours, irregular lesions or ulcerations of the mucosa.

- Also exclude pooling of saliva in the postcricoid area, which is suggestive of obstruction of the oesophagus.

- It is essential that you check that your patient's vocal cord movement is not impaired. Ask him to sing a high "eeh" note, and check that there is full adduction of the cords, confirming recurrent laryngeal nerve function.

51 How to do a tonsillectomy

PATRICK KENNY

Tonsillectomy is performed under general anaesthetic. Adults are usually intubated with a nasotracheal tube, and children with an orotracheal tube.

Today, blunt dissection remains the method of choice, as this is the best method of removing all lymphoid tissue.

To perform a tonsillectomy, you need to follow this procedure:

- Ensure that your patient's tongue is in the midline and that the blade of the gag is long enough for you to gain access to the base of his tongue bilaterally. The tonsil is grasped and pulled medially, as shown in Figure 51.1.

- Incise the mucosa of the anterior pillar over the lateral border of the tonsil using dissecting scissors. Extend the incision from between the uvula and the upper pole of the tonsil down to the base of the tongue. Remember to dissect the mucosa of the anterior and posterior pillars carefully in order to preserve as much as possible (Figure 51.2).

- The plane of dissection is the alveolar tissue between the capsule of the tonsil and the superior constrictor of the pharynx. You find this plane by exerting sufficient tension on the tonsil, pulling it medially and then pushing the closed scissors tip through the incised mucosa and opening the tip. The peritonsillar fossa will thus be opened.

- Insert one blade of the tonsil-holding forceps into the fossa and grasp the tonsil. As in all surgery, dissection of tissue under tension is the easiest and least traumatic. Firmly pull the tonsil medially and dissect it out using a dissecting instrument (Figure 51.3). Dissect as close as possible to the tonsil – do not damage blood vessels and tissue lateral to the tonsil. If you make the dissection too deep, you could damage the muscle and cause further bleeding. But if you make the dissection too shallow, lymphoid tissue will remain behind. Note, too, that some fibres of the superior constrictor implants onto the capsule – you must dissect them carefully.

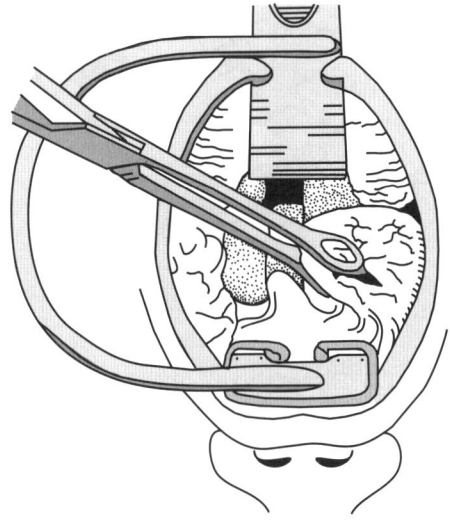

Figure 51.1 Pulling the tonsil medially

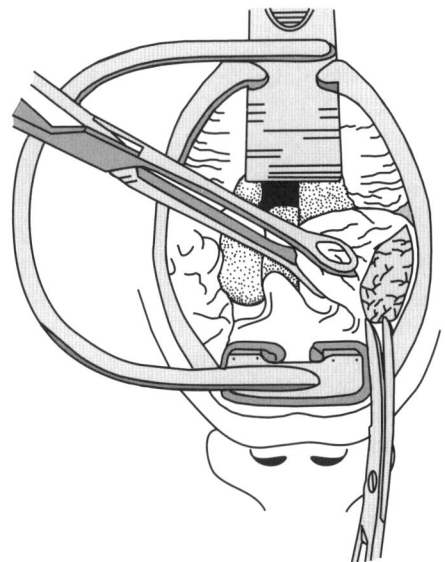

Figure 51.2 Dissecting the mucosa

- Continue the dissection just onto the base of the tongue (Figure 51.4). Use a snare to cut the final attachment.

- The operation is not over until you have all the bleeding under control. You must achieve absolute haemostasis, using either ligatures or diathermy. Always cauterise superficially. You could pack a gauze swab soaked in POR 8 (Ornipressin) or 50% dextrose in the fossae to control the bleeding. Ensure that the fossae are dry before you reverse the anaesthetic.

Once the operation is over, aspirate the blood clot in the nasopharynx.

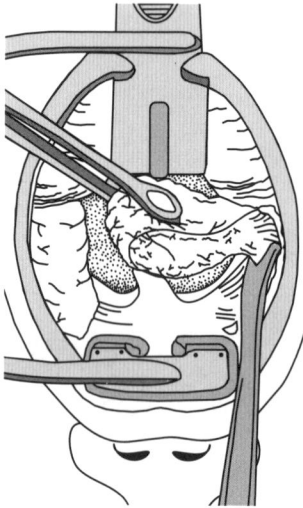

Figure 51.3 Dissecting the tonsil out using a dissecting instrument

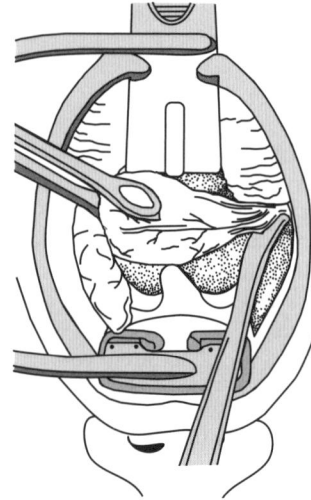

Figure 51.4 Dissection onto the base of the tongue

52 How to drain a peritonsillar abscess or quinsy

PATRICK KENNY

You can drain a peritonsillar abscess in primary care, but you should refer the following patients to hospital:

- Children
- Patients who are severely ill
- Those with breathing difficulty
- Those with bilateral abscesses
- Those with a large abscess that obstructs the pharynx or may extend posteriorly
- Those in whom drainage in primary care has been unsuccessful

Some patients may require IV fluids for hydration and/or analgesia prior to the procedure.

Equipment

To perform the procedure, you need

- a head lamp
- 10% topical lignocaine spray
- 1% lignocaine-adrenaline for local anaesthesia
- a 25-gauge needle and 2-ml syringe for local anaesthesia
- a tongue depressor
- wall suction
- IV line and fluids if necessary
- 16-gauge IV needle and 10–20-ml syringe for aspiration
- a no. 11 scalpel blade and angulated forceps for incision.

Procedures

There are two procedures for draining a peritonsillar abscess, which we will now explore.

Aspiration procedure

Follow this procedure:

- Ask the patient to sit with his head resting against a headrest and to open his mouth.

- Depress his tongue with a tongue depressor.
- Spray the mucosa over the abscess with topical anaesthetic.
- Inject the local anaesthetic into the palatoglossal arch at the location of the abscess – first intra-epithelially and then deeper. Draw back on the syringe to ensure that you are not injecting into a vein. Applying some suction on the syringe will cause blood to be sucked back if you are in a vein. You may need to anaesthetise at the superior, middle and lower regions.

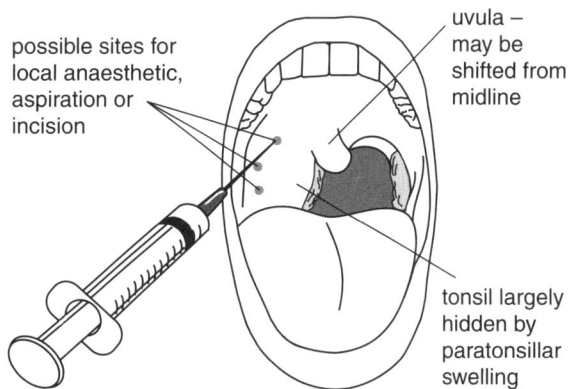

Figure 52.1 Aspiration of peritonsillar abscess

- Insert a large needle into the abscess where the pus is localised and aspirate the pus, as shown in Figure 52.1.
- Review the patient the next day. If necessary, repeat the aspiration.

Incision procedure

Follow this procedure:

- Anaesthetise your patient as described above.
- Make a 1–1.5 cm incision with a guarded scalpel where the abscess is bulging parallel to the palatal arch, as shown in Figure 52.2.

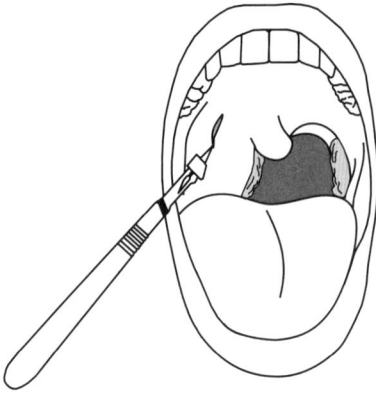

Figure 52.2 Right peritonsillar abscess, and a guarded blade to drain it

- Use angulated forceps to open up the abscess cavity. Direct the instrument straight backwards to avoid damaging the carotid artery.
- Suction out all the pus.
- Wait until the bleeding stops.
- Ask the patient to rinse out his mouth with a mouthwash.
- Review him the next day.

Prescribe penicillin and analgesia for the patient – start with procaine or benzathine benzylpenicillin 1.2 million IM for an adult, and review him the next day. In the case of penicillin allergy, use erythromycin.

53 How to take a nasal swab

PATRICK KENNY

To take a nasal swab, follow this procedure:

- With the thumb of one hand, gently elevate the tip of your patient's nose.
- Moisten the tip of a small nasopharyngeal swab with sterile water or saline and gently insert it into one of the nares.
- Guide the swab backward and upward along the nasal septum until you feel a distinct "give", which indicates that you have reached the posterior pharynx.

- Gently remove the swab.
- Repeat the procedure through the other nares.

The swab can be spread on a slide and fixed for cytology. Different cause of rhinitis can be identified:

- Neutrophils suggest infection.
- Eosinophils suggest allergy or vasomotor rhinitis.
- Columnar cells suggest normal mucosa.
- Metaplastic or squamous cells suggest atrophy.

54 How to manage epistaxis, or a nose bleed

PATRICK KENNY

Administration of first aid

We do not necessarily need to seek professional medical help in order to administer first aid to a person suffering from epistaxis (even if it is ourselves). We can follow this procedure:

- Sit leaning forwards and keep calm.
- Press the nose closed with thumb and forefinger over Little's area continuously for 5–10 minutes.
- Applying an ice pack on the forehead and back of the neck causes reflex vasoconstriction and also helps to control the bleeding.
- If necessary, place a piece of cotton wool in the nostril and compress again.
- If the bleeding continues, we should seek professional medical help.

Figure 54.1 shows this simple procedure.

Professional medical treatment

To treat epistaxis professionally, you need to follow this procedure:

- Identify the site of bleeding, ideally with a head lamp and nasal speculum or with an otoscope. Is the bleeding coming from the septum (Little's area) superiorly or posteriorly?
- Ask the patient to blow his nose to remove clots. Alternatively, gently suction out the clots.
- Constrict the mucous membrane with a lignocaine-adrenaline mixture. Apply this for about three minutes either with cotton wool to the bleeding site or by inserting a tampon soaked in the mixture.
- If the bleeding point is visible as a small clot, carefully cauterise an area of no more than 4 mm with a silver nitrate stick (Figure 54.2). Then irrigate the surrounding mucosa with normal saline in cotton wool. After irrigation, dry the nose.
- If the bleeding point cannot be seen and treated, and the bleeding continues, consider packing the nose, that is applying an anterior tamponade, as follows:
  - Pack the nose with a long piece of ribbon gauze soaked in BIPP (bismuth iodoform paraffin paste).
  - Starting deep, pack from the floor upwards and forwards with an angulated Tilley's forceps until you have filled the nose. Leave a piece of

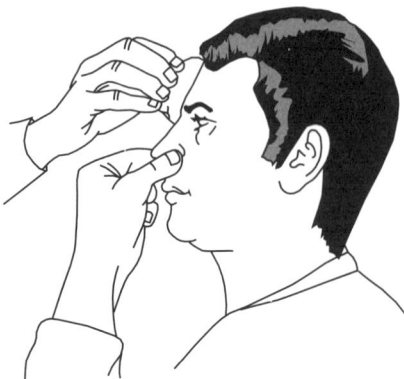

Figure 54.1 First aid for a bleeding nose

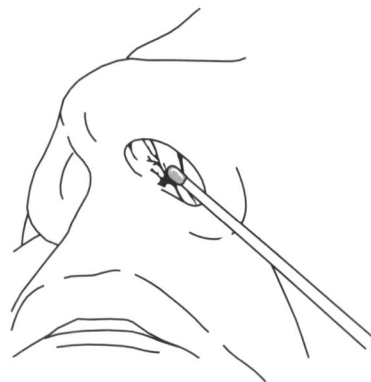

Figure 54.2 Cauterisation with a silver nitrate stick

Van Schaik Publishers

tape outside the nostril so that you can remove the pack later. Pack the anterior part of the nose last.

– Leave the pack in place for at least a day but no more than three days.

• If the bleeding is not controlled with the anterior tamponade, proceed to a posterior tamponade, as follows:

– Remove the pack that you used for the anterior tamponade. Place a 14F Foley catheter with a 30-ml balloon in the bleeding nostril and push it in gently until the tip is visible in the naso-pharynx. The tip of the catheter may be cut off to prevent it irritating the back of the patient's throat. *Take care* not to damage the balloon.

– Inflate the balloon with 10 ml saline or water – not air, as air leaks out. This is illustrated in Figure 54.3.

– Pull back the catheter until it feels "locked" and then inflate it further, if necessary, until it feels well secured.

– Fasten the catheter correctly onto the patient's cheek to prevent pressure on the nostril as it could cause necrosis.

– Pack his nose as described above.

– Admit him for about 24 hours for observation and treatment.

– Deflate the catheter within 12 hours, and re-assess.

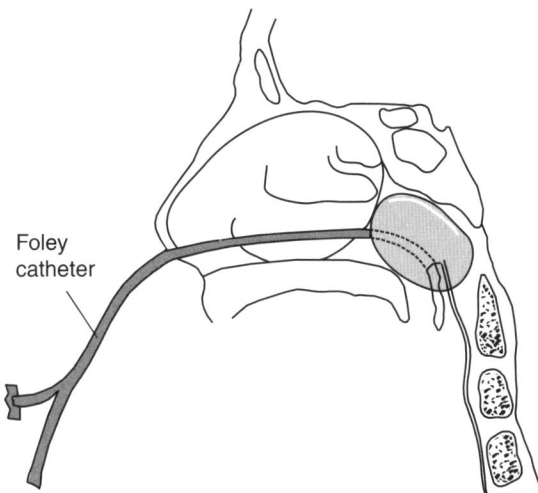

Figure 54.3 Semi-inflated Foley catheter in nasopharynx and posterior nasal cavity

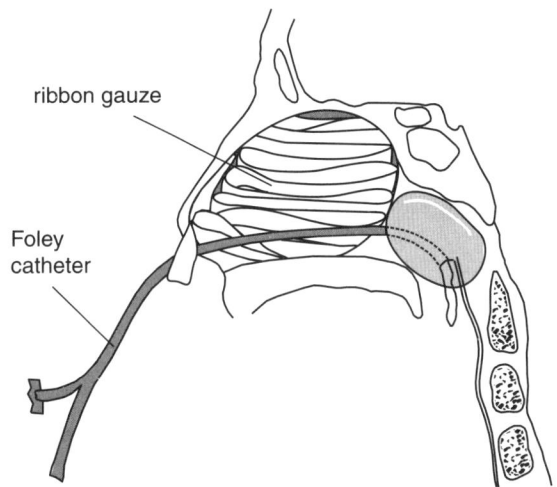

Figure 54.4 Foley catheter and anterior nasal pack in position

55 How to evaluate nasal trauma

PATRICK KENNY

Anatomy

The external nose

The skeleton of the nose is made of bone and cartilage. The upper one third consists of the nasal bones, which are attached to the frontal bone and the maxilla. The lower two thirds of the nasal skeleton is cartilaginous, the main components of which are the septal, lateral nasal and major alar cartilages.

The skeleton is covered with skin, which is thin over the nasal bridge and thicker with more sebaceous glands over the nasal tip.

The nasal septum

This is the midline division between each nasal cavity. It is made of thin, flat, bony sheets posteriorly and cartilage anteriorly. The lower end of the septum sits in a groove in the crest of the maxilla. The maxillary bone makes up the majority of the floor of the nasal cavity. The septum is often slightly deviated into one or other nasal cavities and can cause nasal obstruction if this is a pronounced feature.

The septum is rich in blood supply, especially anteriorly, where four arteries anastomose. This is

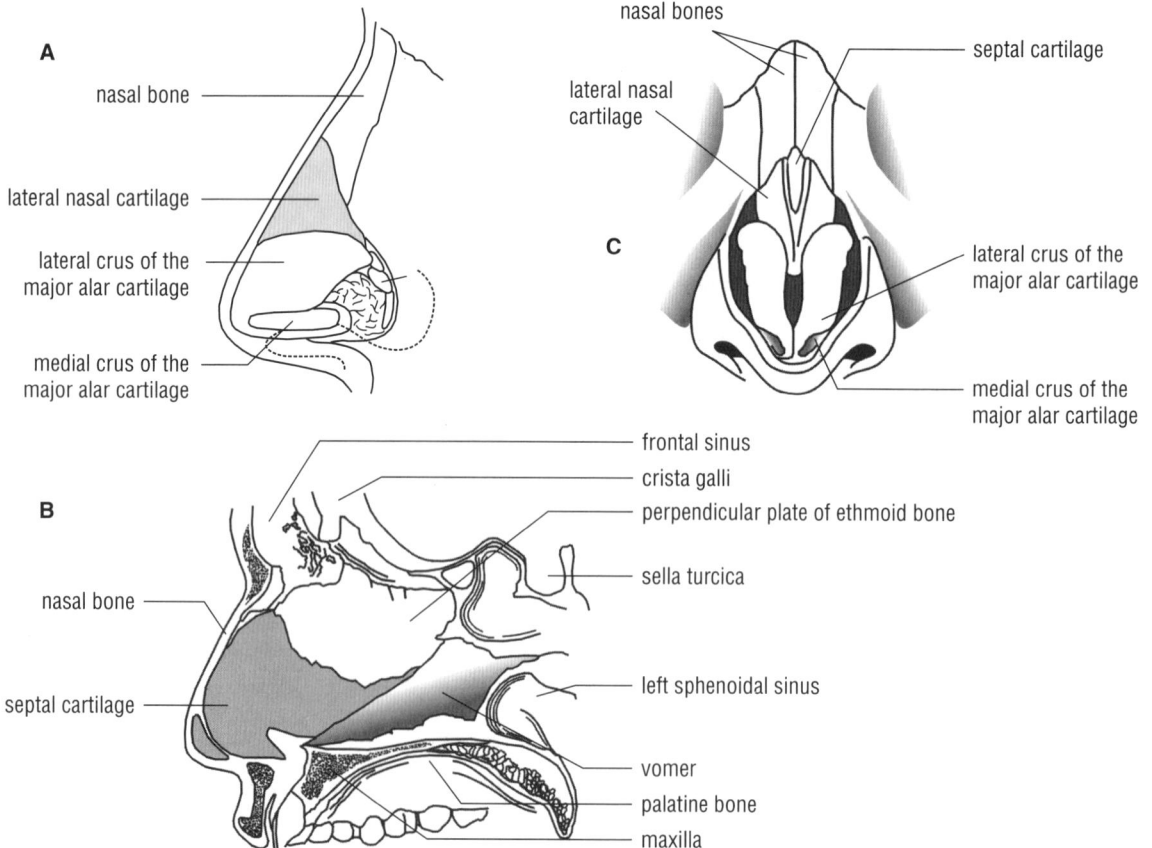

Figure 55.1 The bone and cartilages of the nose: (A) Lateral view; (B) Nasal septum; (C) Frontal view

known as "Little's area" and it is the most common site for nose bleeds. The blood supply of Little's area and the nasal septum is from the anterior ethmoidal artery, the sphenopalatine artery, the greater palatine artery and the septal branch of the superior labial artery.

Examination

To begin your assessment of a patient's nose trauma, ask him these questions:

- When did the injury occur?
- What was the mechanism that caused the injury?
- Did he experience epistaxis?
- Has the appearance of his nose changed?
- Is he experiencing any new onset of nasal obstruction?

Then follow this procedure:

- Evaluate the nose internally and externally, using proper lighting – ideally a head lamp – and suction.
- Check the septum for deviation, perforation, haematoma, mucosal tears and fracture.
- Examine the external nose for nasal deviation, and palpate the nasal bones for instability, crepitus or motion.
- Examine the surrounding structures, such as the eyes, sinuses, teeth, oral cavity and cervical spine.

You can confirm the diagnosis that you make as a result of this examination, and you can assess the extent of the damage, by requesting and interpreting a radiograph.

Management

You need to reduce a nasal fracture in the first few hours following the injury, or 3–14 days after the oedema has resolved. You should reduce nasal fractures in **adults** under local anaesthesia. Sedate the patient 30–45 minutes before the reduction procedure, and give two sprays of topical lignocaine spray into each nostril a few minutes prior to the reduction. Give additional anaesthetic for the external nose by injecting about 2.5 ml 2% lignocaine near the infratrochlear and infraorbital nerves on each side of his nose. **Children** require general anaesthesia in order for nasal fractures to be reduced.

To perform the reduction, follow this procedure:

- Manipulate the fracture into a good position by internal and external traction.
- Place a blunt elevator, such as the Ash-Walsham, under the depressed nasal bone.
- Lift the bone anteriorly and laterally while applying pressure to the other side of the patient's nose to bring the nasal dorsum to the midline.
- You can stabilise the position of the nose by packing internally with cotton wool strips soaked in BIPP and splinting externally.
- Remove the splint after 10–14 days.

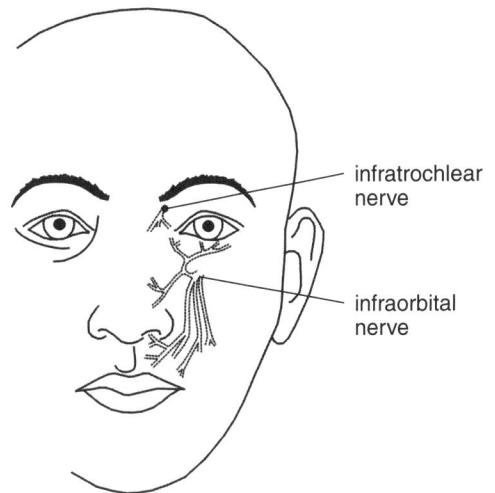

Figure 55.2 Sites for injecting local anaesthetic

56 How to conduct skin prick testing

DEREK HELLENBERG

Skin prick testing (SPT) is an inexpensive, quick and accurate way of identifying the causative allergens in the atopic patient (Toerien et al. 1994). The test depends on the introduction of allergen extract into the dermis resulting in an immunoglobulin-E (IgE) mediated response, which is characterised by an immediate weal and flare reaction.

Although SPT is safe, you need to ensure that the following are available when you perform the test:

- Injectable adrenaline – 1:1 000
- Oxygen
- Oral and injectable promethazine
- Hydrocortisone injection
- Inhaled bronchodilator

Factors which influence SPT are as follows:

- All medicines containing antihistamine need to be stopped prior to testing.
- The very young and the very old have suppressed skin reactivity.
- Incorrect technique
- Loss of potency of allergen solutions owing to incorrect or prolonged storage

SPT can be used to

- identify new allergens, and in selected cases also to facilitate your diagnosis of food, drug or insect allergy
- identify patients for specific allergen immunotherapy and to monitor the efficacy of that therapy at regular intervals
- monitor changes in patients' allergen sensitivity over a period of time or at re-emergence of symptoms.

Common allergens that the Red Cross Children's Hospital (Cape Town), for example, use in SPT are as follows:

- Acacia
- Alternaria
- Aspergillus
- Banana
- Bermuda grass
- Botrytis
- Cats
- Chenopodium
- Chocolate
- Cladosporium
- Compositae
- Dandelion
- Dogs
- Egg white
- Epicoccum
- Feathers
- Fish
- Grasses
- Histamine
- House-dust
- Maize
- Milk
- Mite F
- Mite P
- Nettle
- Oak
- Oranges
- Peanuts
- Pepper tree
- Pine tree
- Plane tree
- Plantain
- Syringa tree
- Tomato
- Wheat

Procedure

An SPT is best performed on the volar or inner aspects of forearms, avoiding flexures and wrist areas. In children under three years of age, the test may be more easily performed on the child's back. In each case, explain the procedure to the patient.

To perform an SPT, you need to follow this procedure:

- Ensure that the patient's skin is clean and free of active eczema. With a pen, mark a grid at 2 cm intervals and place a drop of the relevant allergen on the arm at the end of each line.
- The order follows a standard list of allergens used for easy identification.
- Prick the skin through the drop with a lancet with a 1-mm point.
- Between each prick, wipe the lancet with dry gauze.

- Blot the solutions off the test site.
- Watch for the reactions – they should occur within 10–15 minutes.
- Assess the results. In some patients a delayed skin reaction occurs about 3–5 hours after the skin test has been performed. It is important that you remind all patients to look out for these.

Include a positive and negative control in each series of tests. You can use the diluent that you used to preserve the allergen extract as the negative control. The positive control of 1 mg/ml histamine HCL solution can help you to detect if there is suppression of the response by medication, or you can use it as a comparison to other positive skin reactions.

You can regard a reaction of 3 mm greater than the negative control as positive. Table 56.1 summarises the grading.

Table 56.1 Grading of an SPT reaction

Grade	Indications
+	No weal, 3 mm flare
++	2–3 mm weal with flare
+++	3–5 mm weal with flare
++++	More than 5 mm weal, may have pseudopodia

* *Note:* This chapter is based on Appendix ix in The ALLSA handbook of practical allergy (Toerien, Potter & Buys 1994).

57 How to do a wide-needle aspiration biopsy of a lymph node

BOB MASH

Otherwise known as a "WNAB", this procedure is particularly useful in patients who are HIV positive and in whom you suspect TB lymphadenitis, as you can perform it in the office without the need for a full excision biopsy of the node. Generalised lymphadenopathy is common in Stages 1 and 2 HIV-infection and does not require biopsy. However, you should biopsy asymmetrical, significantly enlarged (greater than 1 cm) or chronically inflamed nodes using a WNAB. Apart from TB, consider other, less common causes such as lymphoma or disseminated Kaposi's sarcoma.

Procedure

To perform a WNAB, you need to follow this procedure:

- Clean the patient's skin with Betadine or alcohol.
- Anaesthetise his skin using 1 ml 2% lignocaine with an insulin syringe, or ethyl chloride spray.
- Draw a small amount of normal saline through a 16- or 18-gauge needle into a 5-ml syringe, then discard the saline.
- Insert the needle into the node and draw back the plunger to create a vacuum.
- Partially withdraw and reinsert the needle at different angles.

- Do not withdraw the needle completely, and maintain a continuous vacuum throughout.
- Release the vacuum pressure before withdrawing the needle.
- Remove the syringe from the needle and pull 2–3 ml air into the syringe, reattach the needle and gently spray the contents over a glass slide.
- Distribute the material using the edge of another slide.
- Allow the material to air-dry and send the slide unfixed to the laboratory for auramine or Ziehl-Nielsen stain.
- Send a second, fixed slide for cytology. If it is bloodstained, repeat aspiration with a smaller needle.
- You can send larger amounts of aspirated purulent or caseous material in a specimen jar for myco/bacterial microscopy and culture.

Contraindications

Aspiration biopsy should be avoided if squamous cell carcinoma is a possibility to avoid dissemination of the cancer along the needle track. While a WNAB may collect more diagnostic material than a fine-needle aspiration biopsy (See Chapter 103) the potential of creating a fistula is higher and the procedure requires local anaesthetic as it is more painful.

58 How to do a skin biopsy, cryotherapy and electrotherapy

DEREK HELLENBERG

Skin biopsy

You would do a skin biopsy to

- make a diagnosis
- confirm a diagnosis that you made from the patient's medical history and physical examination
- check the edges of tissue that was removed with a tumour to make certain that all the diseased tissue was removed.

A skin biopsy can also serve a therapeutic purpose, that is when a lesion is removed completely during the biopsy procedure.

You need to obtain a sample of tissue that best represents the lesion. Choose the relevant biopsy technique and location for the procedure. If you perform an excisional biopsy, you remove the lesion completely. In an incisional biopsy, you remove a portion of the lesion.

Procedures

There are various procedures that you can use to perform the biopsy, as follows:

- **Shave biopsy:** Use a scalpel or razorblade to shave off a thin layer of a raised and suspicious lesion parallel to the skin.
- **Scalpel biopsy:** For large or deep lesions, use a scalpel to make a standard surgical incision or excision to remove tissue. You should close the wound with stitches.
- **Punch biopsy:** Screw a small cylindrical punch into the lesion through the full thickness of the skin and remove a plug of tissue. You may need to place one or two stitches to close the wound.
- **Scissors biopsy:** Use scissors to cut off surface skin growths and lesions that grow from a stalk of tissue.
- **Skin scrapings:** Use a scalpel blade to scrape the skin off a lesion.

To prepare for the procedure, you need to

- clean the site of biopsy with alcohol or a disinfectant
- inject a local anaesthetic into the skin around the lesion
- always use sterile gloves and surgical instruments to reduce the risk of infection.

Once you have completed the procedure and removed the biopsy tissue, you can control bleeding by applying pressure or by cauterising the immediate area with electricity or chemicals. You can place stitches in the wound, or bandage it and allow it to heal on its own. Prevent drying and structural damage to the tissue sample by placing it immediately in an appropriate preservative, such as formaldehyde.

We will now explore the procedures themselves in further detail.

■ SHAVE BIOPSY

Follow this procedure:

- Inject local anaesthetic into the area.
- Use a double-edged razorblade.
- For protruding lesions, hold the blade flush with the surrounding skin and shave off the lesion.
- Smooth out the edges with electrocautery at a low setting.
- Apply a dressing if necessary.

■ SCALPEL BIOPSY

It is best to completely excise a lesion which you suspect to be a squamous cell carcinoma. Thus you would use the scalpel biopsy procedure in this case.

Follow this procedure:

- Measure the size of the lesion and determine the 3:1 ratio for the area to be excised, as shown in Figure 58.1.
- Orient the ellipse with the appropriate skin lines – either Langer's lines or the patient's own particu-

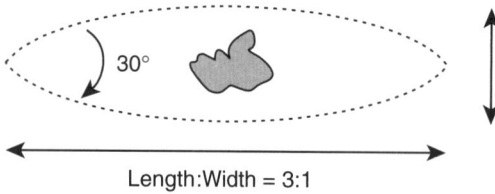

Length:Width = 3:1

Figure 58.1 Measurements for the incision in a scalpel biopsy

lar skin tension line pattern. If necessary, mark the ellipse using a surgical marking pen.

• Prepare the area with Betadine solution and drape.

• Anaesthetise the area by injecting anaesthetic just beneath the lesion, to either side, to the far end of the ellipse, and to the near end as you remove the needle. This allows only one puncture site, which will be removed with the excised tissue.

• Using a size 15 scalpel blade, cut from one corner of the ellipse to the other, keeping the blade perpendicular to the skin. Alternatively, cut from the corners of the ellipse to the middle on either side. Carry the incision through the full skin thickness.

• Grasp the tissue to be removed and undermine just below the dermis.

• Re-approximate the skin edges to determine if further undermining is necessary for closure.

• If necessary grasp the wound edges with a skin hook, and undermine with blunt dissection to free the dermis from the subcutaneous tissue. You must perform 3 cm of undermining to allow 1 cm of closure.

• Re-approximate the skin, trying to evert the edges, and close the wound with interrupted sutures.

• You may remove the sutures as follows:
  – From the face – 3–5 days
  – From the scalp and trunk – 7 days
  – From the feet and hands, and areas of high tension – 10–14 days

■ PUNCH BIOPSY

You would perform a punch biopsy in the following circumstances:

• It is a useful adjunct to clinical differential diagnosis in managing inflammatory dermatoses and suspected malignancies.

• It allows sampling of a full-thickness skin plug and thus is useful in appropriately identifying disease processes that affect the deeper dermis.

• When the lesion is too large for simple excision or when complete removal would result in substantial disfigurement of the patient.

• You may use it when you think that the lesion is benign but you wish for histological confirmation.

To perform a punch biopsy, you need to follow this procedure:

• Identify the area to be sampled:
  – When there are several areas to choose from, select an early lesion or one that is well advanced. Sample larger lesions near the edge of an advancing border.
  – Biopsy of a suspected skin cancer requires special consideration. If a lesion appears to be a basal cell carcinoma, you can take samples throughout since most sections will yield representative tissue.
  – You should include the most clinically suspicious area, that is the most raised or darkly pigmented.

• Wipe the area with alcohol and allow it to dry.

• Using your thumb and index finger, stretch the skin perpendicular to the lines of lesser tension – Langer's lines. This allows for formation of an elliptical defect parallel to those lines.

• Using the appropriate size punch trephine – usually 2–4 mm – place the end over the area to be biopsied and twist in a back-and-forth motion to at least the level of the dermal-subcutaneous interface. Figure 58.2 shows this motion.

• If you encounter pigmented tissue at the base of the specimen, you need to continue the depth of the punch well into the subcutaneous fat. It is

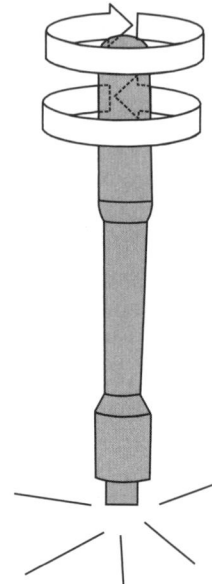

Figure 58.2 Twisting motion of the punch trephine

essential that you extend the biopsy to the entire depth of the lesion, since depth in millimetres is the major prognostic feature of Stage I and II melanoma.

- Lift the specimen out of the skin punch hole with a needle, as shown in Figure 58.3. Use a scalpel to cut through and separate it at the base.

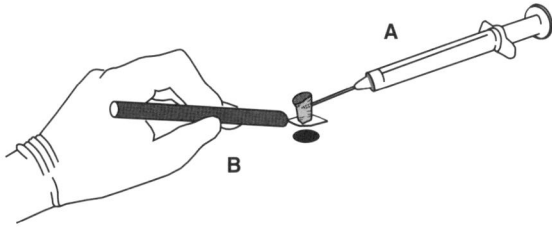

Figure 58.3 Removing the punch biopsy specimen: (A) Lift up with a needle; (B) Separate specimen through the base with a scalpel

■ SCISSORS BIOPSY

This is intended for skin tags and small lesions with a pedunculated base. Usually no local anaesthetic is required and the lesion is stretched with forceps and then cut flush with the skin. Control bleeding by applying pressure or if on a hidden area a silver nitrate stick may be used to cauterise the bleeding point.

■ SKIN SCRAPINGS

Collection and processing of skin scrapings

Skin scrapings are typically taken to confirm the diagnosis of fungal infections and to distinguish them from other pathology, such as eczema. Follow this procedure:

- Thoroughly sponge the infected area with 70% ethanol to remove surface contaminants. If you suspect a yeast infection, replace the ethanol with sterile saline solution or distilled water.
- Take the scrapings from the active border areas of lesions using a sterile scalpel.
- Place the scrapings in sterile Petri dishes, between two clean microscopic slides or in clean envelopes, and send them to the laboratory for mycological microscopy and culture.
- While you collect skin specimens it is important for you to note whether there is any moist exudate present on the lesions – if so, collect and examine this too. Exudative lesions are usually erythematous and painful, and are generally caused by candida.
- If feasible, you can also examine for the presence of fungal elements in your own practice.

- Place several scrapings in a drop of 10% potassium hydroxide solution (KOH) and cover with cover slip.
- Pass the mount several times over a flame to warm it gently.
- Examine the preparation under a bright field microscope to detect fungal elements.
- If the slide is negative, do not discard it immediately. Retain it in a moist chamber and re-examine it after few hours or a day as the fungus may become more evident.

Collection and processing of hair

Follow this procedure:

- Note that the technique for collecting the specimen depends on the fungus involved:
  - In the case of piedra, you can clip off the nodule-bearing hairs with scissors.
  - Dermatophytes first attack the roots of hair, causing hair to break just above the roots. It is thus necessary for you to scrape the lesion with a sterile scalpel, as well as pull out the stubs of broken hair with tweezers.

- Other details regarding collection and transportation are the same as for skin scrapings, described above.

Collection and processing of nails

Follow this procedure:

- Clean the patient's nails with 70% ethanol.
- Collect nail shavings by scraping with a scalpel blade from the proximal to the distal end of the nail or take clippings from the end with scissors. Discard the first 4–5 scrapings as these may not contain active fungal elements.
- Send the specimens to the laboratory and process them in the same way as for skin scrapings, as described above. If you are going to examine them yourself, use 40% KOH instead of 10% KOH.

Table 58.1 summarises the features that you can see using a microscope (this applies to skin scrapings looked at with KOH for fungal elements).

Cryosurgery

This is the rapid application of cold to the tissue to produce a controlled destruction of benign and pre-malignant epithelial lesions.

The lateral spread of the ice formation is approximately 1.3 times that of depth, as illustrated in Figure 58.4. The average spread of the lateral ice rim beyond the lesion should extend 2–3 mm. This usually correlates to 20–40 seconds of freeze for skin

Table 58.1 Features seen on direct microscopic examination (it refers to skin scrapings looked at with KOH for fungal elements)

Features	Presumptive diagnosis
Small hyphae (2–3 μ), regular, some branching, sometimes with rectangular arthrospores found only in skin, nail scrapings and hair	Dermatophyte group
Hyphae, pseudohyphae (distinct points of constriction) with budding yeast forms	*Candida spp.*
Hyphae, usually small (3–6 μ) and regular in size, dichotomously branching at 45 degrees with distinct cross septa	*Aspergillus spp.*
Hyphae, irregular in size, ranging from 6–50 μ, ribbon-like and devoid of septa	Phycomycetes (rhizopus, mucor, absidia)
White or black soft or hard granules seen in exudate	Suggestive of actinomycosis

lesions. You can accomplish the greatest amount of destruction of abnormal tissue by using the freeze-thaw-refreeze procedure.

You do not need to administer anaesthesia as freezing the tissue in itself provides anaesthesia. Moreover, areas treated with cryotherapy usually heal with minimal or no scar formation. Assure your patient that you can minimise any scarring and pigmentary changes by applying an appropriate depth of freeze.

To perform cryosurgery with liquid nitrogen, you need to follow this procedure:

- **Using a cotton-tip applicator:**
  - Place the desired amount of liquid nitrogen in a vacuum container and loosely secure the opening.

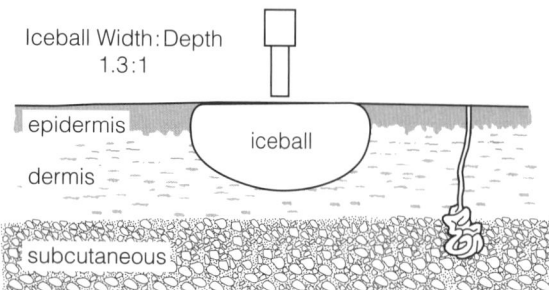

Figure 58.4 Lateral spread of the ice formation

- Dip the applicator into the liquid nitrogen and place it on the lesion. Since liquid nitrogen evaporates quickly, you will probably need to repeat this several times to obtain adequate freeze.
- Create a freeze zone extending 2–4 mm around the lesion. It should require about 30 seconds of thaw time.
- Repeat the freeze-thaw cycle once for smaller lesions and twice for larger or deeper lesions.
- Cotton-tip applicators with propellant are also commercially available.

Electrosurgery

Do not confuse electrosurgery with electrocautery. The latter involves destruction of tissue by heat application. Electrosurgery refers to the use of a high-frequency electrical apparatus which transfers a current into the tissue via a cold-tipped electrode. It is in the tissue that the electrical energy is converted to heat energy.

Altering the delivery characteristics of the electrical current allows you to fulgurate, desiccate or incise the lesion.

Electrosection

This is comparable to scalpel incision, except that it causes a small amount of heat-induced tissue damage. You can use electrosection when you need to excise and preserve the tissue for pathological interpretation. Indications for this procedure include naevi, basal cell carcinomas, keratoacanthomas and fibromas.

Electrodesiccation and electrocoagulation

These are performed when the treatment electrode comes into contact with the tissue, resulting in dehydration and coagulation.

When you use minimal power settings, most of the damage is epidermal and the risk of scarring is reduced. This is referred to as **electrodesiccation** and is shown in Figure 58.5. By increasing the power settings, you can bring about coagulation of the deeper tissues and thus increase the potential for subsequent scarring. This is referred to as **electrocoagulation**.

Note that electrofulgaration (see below) and electrodesiccation usually occur simultaneously as the electrode passing over the surface of the lesion is not in constant contact, thus desiccation and fulgaration are combined.

You can use electrodesiccation for actinic keratoses, common warts, condylomas, seborrhoeic keratoses and basal cell carcinomas (following shave biopsy). Indications for electrocoagulation include telangiectasias and hemangiomas.

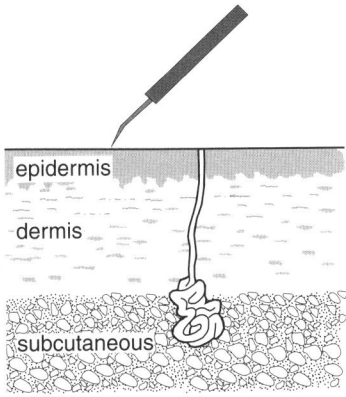

Figure 58.5 Electrodesiccation

Electrofulguration

This does not involve contact with the tissue. The term refers to the use of extremely high voltage, low amperage, high frequency electrical energy that is capable of creating a spark gap between the electrode and the protruding lesion. Cutaneous lesions treated by this method usually heal rapidly, since there is minimal dermal damage, with good cosmetic results.

Figure 58.6 illustrates this method of treatment.

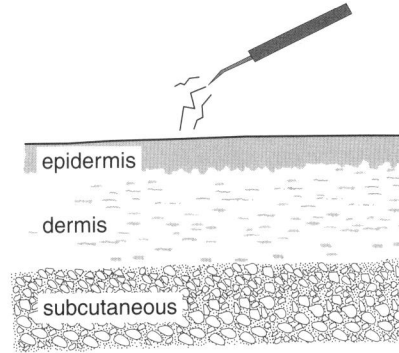

Figure 58.6 Electrofulgaration

59 How to excise a sebaceous cyst

Sebaceous cysts are caused by blockage of a sebaceous gland and collection of sebum. They are connected by the blocked duct to the skin, and this punctum is often visible. They should otherwise be freely mobile and not attached to deeper structures. Common sites are the scalp, face, back, neck and scrotum.

You should perform the excision under local anaesthetic as follows:

- Shave away any hair to expose the cyst and surroundings for at least 1 cm.
- Clean the skin.
- Infiltrate local anaesthetic around the cyst using a field block, as shown in Figure 59.1.

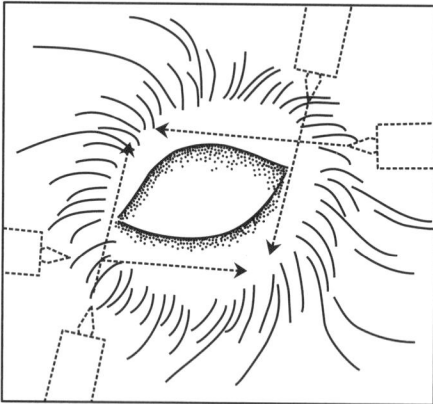

Figure 59.2 Incising the cyst area

- With curved mosquito forceps using blunt dissection, free the cyst from the surrounding tissue, as shown in Figure 59.3.

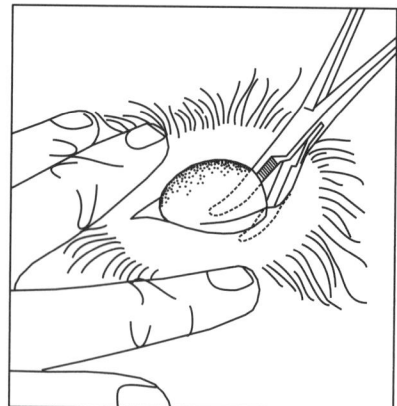

Figure 59.1 Anaesthetising the cyst area

- With a number 15 scalpel blade, make a vertical incision over the lesion extending 0.5 cm beyond the margin on either side, as shown in Figure 59.2.
- If you can see the punctum, make elliptical incisions on either side of it.
- Try to avoid incising or puncturing the cyst capsule. If you do so, the "cheesy" contents will start to spill out.

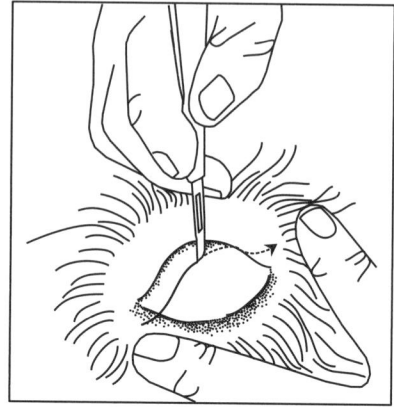

Figure 59.3 Freeing the cyst from surrounding tissue

- Using toothed forceps, lift the cyst out of the wound and free it from the underlying tissue with curved Mayo scissors or the scalpel, as shown in Figure 59.4.

164 © Van Schaik Publishers

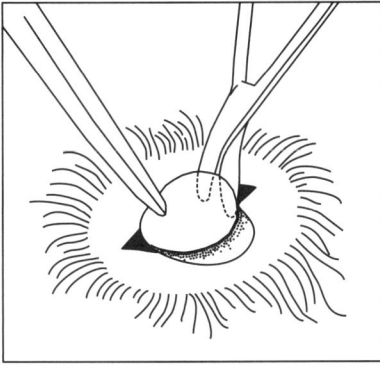

Figure 59.4 Freeing the cyst from the underlying tissue

- Remove the cyst and control any bleeding.
- Suture the wound edges together with 3/0 silk or Ethilon® using a curved needle.
- Apply a dry dressing.
- Usually, you can remove the sutures after one week.

60 How to apply a compression bandage for chronic venous ulcers

BOB MASH

Chronic venous ulcers usually occur on the patient's lower leg above the ankle. They are associated with signs of stasis eczema, hyperpigmentation and sclerotic skin (Saxe, Jessop & Todd 1997). Underlying venous insufficiency may be related to varicose veins, obesity, previous deep vein thrombosis, reduced ankle movement and a sedentary lifestyle. The pathophysiology is failure of the calf muscle pump owing to venous incompetence, paralysis or immobility. High venous and capillary pressure increases vascular permeability with tissue oedema and perivascular deposition of fibrin. This creates a barrier to diffusion around the capillaries and leads to skin necrosis (Blair, Wright, Backhouse et al. 1988).

It follows, therefore, that reversal of this process requires compression to improve venous circulation (Kousa 2003).

To generally manage the condition you need to

- correct anaemia
- treat diabetes
- treat cardiac failure
- treat active cellulitis
- treat any arterial disease.

Try to avoid the common mistake of applying different types of dressings without providing adequate compression to enable healing. The type of dressing that you choose depends on the state of the ulcer.

Note, for example, whether there is necrotic slough, secondary infection or clean granulation tissue.

Contraindications to compression include significant arterial disease with poor peripheral pulses and, on Doppler assessment, a low ankle–brachial arterial pressure ratio of less than 0.8, as this would worsen peripheral vascular disease.

Four-layer compression bandaging can sustain adequate compression for up to a week and achieve better healing rates than do traditional single-layer bandages. The compression bandages can be applied with the same degree of stretch from the patient's ankle to the knee, as the amount of compression varies with the diameter of the leg but will always be higher at the ankle than at the knee.

The four layers include

1. dressing of ulcer, that is gauze impregnated with zinc or a hydrocolloid
2. inner layer of orthopaedic wool to absorb exudates and redistribute pressure around the bony points of the ankle
3. standard crêpe bandage applied at mid-stretch, with overlap
4. elasticated cohesive bandage at mid-stretch, with overlap.

Advise your patient that following healing, it is important to prevent relapse by using high-compression elastic stockings.

61 How to remove an ingrowing toenail

BOB MASH

If conservative methods such as bathing the toe in antiseptic solutions and changing to more spacious footwear fail to relieve the problem then minor surgery is indicated to remove the ingrowing toenail (IGTN). Simple nail avulsion combined with phenolisation is the most effective method (Cates, Barra, Crilly, Rowe 2004) – it can be performed even if the IGTN is infected.

To perform the surgery, follow this procedure:

- Inject 2% lignocaine without adrenaline as a ring block (see Chapter 37).
- Apply a tourniquet made of rubber tubing, or a glove, around the base of the toe to reduce bleeding. Secure the tourniquet with forceps.
- Clean the toe with Betadine solution.
- Remove any debris from the lateral nail fold and loosen the nail.
- Using straight scissors, cut a 3–5 mm-wide slice of the toenail and extend the cut below the proximal nail fold to include the root of the nail. See Figure 61.1.

Figure 61.1 Cutting the toenail

- Remove the slice by rotating it with forceps, ensuring that you also remove the root. See Figure 61.2.

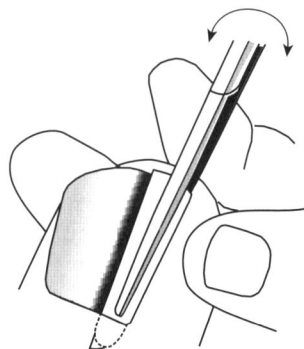

Figure 61.2 Removing the slice of toenail

- Dry the hole that results, and insert a cotton wool bud dipped in 80% phenol into the hole.
- Rotate the bud for 45 seconds, and repeat two or three times. *Take care* not to allow phenol to touch the normal skin. See Figure 61.3.
- Clean the area and remove any remaining phenol with a cotton wool bud soaked in normal saline.
- Remove the tourniquet.
- Cover the wound with Jelonet and a dressing.
- Advise your patient that from the next day, he should shower twice a day for 10–15 minutes and clean the wound until there is no more discharge.
- If there was active infection before the procedure, follow up carefully within 24–72 hours for signs of ongoing infection.

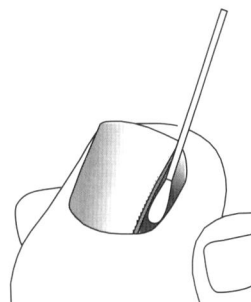

Figure 61.3 Phenolisation of the nail bed

62 How to treat warts

DEREK HELLENBERG

If the patient's warts are asymptomatic, there is no treatment necessary other than for cosmetic reasons. The exception is genital warts, which may be oncogenic.

Advise your patient not to pick at or bite the warts, as this may encourage them to spread.

In general, you can suggest to your patient that to keep wart tissue soft and flat he should use keratolytics such as wart paint, which consists of 20% salicylic acid, 20% lactic acid in collodion or a 40% salicylic acid plaster. He should apply it daily to soften and reduce the keratin. Occlusion with non-porous tape enhances the effect.

Paring or filing the keratin can also help to reduce the bulk of the lesion.

We will now explore the various more specific methods of treatment for the particular areas that can be affected with warts (Saxe 1997).

Curative/destructive measures

To apply each of these methods, you need to follow these procedures:

- **Cryotherapy** is the treatment of choice as it is usually over 50% effective in most areas:
  - It is easy to perform.
  - It is only mildly painful – with the exception of plantar and periungual warts.
  - It leaves little scarring.
  - You need to use liquid nitrogen on a cotton applicator for 15–45 seconds, or a cryospray.
  - You need to see the patient again only after three weeks, as inflammation and the scab may mask the site.
  - You should treat any residual warts again, and warn your patient that warts may recur at the site of treatment for up to six months.
- **Electrodesiccation** and **curettage** require local anaesthesia:
  - Once the anaesthesia has taken effect, insert the treatment electrode into the wart and apply the current until the wart tissue whitens, swells and softens – usually 5–10 seconds.
  - Curette lightly.
  - Your skilful use leaves little or no scarring, and is effective. However, excessive electrodesiccation causes scarring.
- You can apply **Canthandrin** to the wart in your office:
  - Cover the wart with non-porous tape for 4–24 hours, and for a shorter time for children and thin skin areas.
  - The relapse rate is high if you do not curette the wart under local anaesthetic within two or three days.
  - The painless application makes this easy to use on children, but it often forms a painful blister 6–24 hours later.

Facial warts in the beard area

The patient can develop immunity after 6–24 months, which leads to spontaneous clearing of the warts. Advise him to allow his beard to grow during this time.

You can destroy individual lesions with liquid nitrogen or electrodesiccation when he comes to see you every two or three weeks.

To treat the warts topically:

- Apply 5-fluorouracil cream or lotion twice daily to the entire beard area. It is postulated to work by killing the growing cells, but it usually provokes inflammation, which may encourage involution. Advise your patient to use the cream for at least three weeks.

Or:

- Advise your patient to use Whitfield's ointment or 5% salicylic acid cream twice daily.

Or:

- Alternatively, he can use 5–10% benzoyl peroxide twice daily.

You may need to prescribe a mild corticosteroid to relieve discomfort.

Genital warts

You can detect subtle or latent lesions by soaking the affected area for 3–5 minutes with 5% acetic acid solution, which causes white patches to appear. White vinegar diluted half and half with water also makes an acceptable solution. Furthermore, you can compress the areas with moistened gauze.

In the case of this kind of wart, you also need to check for other sexually transmitted infections – conduct a serologic test for syphilis and HIV infection.

To treat the warts **cytotoxically**:

- Apply 20–25% podophyllin in benzoin to the warts with a cotton swab. Dispense this only to trustworthy patients in a 1–2-ml bottle. If not used correctly by the patient at home it can cause severe inflammation or ulceration of the skin, therefore application by the doctor is preferred.

- Protect the surrounding skin with zinc oxide or petrolatum.

- Rinse the area with soap and water – after 30 minutes on the vulva and up to four hours later on the shaft of the penis.

- Applications should be repeated at weekly intervals, with the time of application until rinsing increasing, if tolerable. The lesions will shrink if they are responsive. Three to four applications are often required for complete disappearance of the warts.

- You may need to use light cryotherapy and podophyllin in resistant cases.

- Severe local irritation can result from excessive, prolonged or large area application.

- Systemic absorption and cytotoxicity can occur if a large area is painted. The foetus of a pregnant woman is particularly at risk, therefore you should not use more than a tiny amount in this case.

- If the warts are numerous or large, treat only part of the lesions on each visit.

If podophyllin fails or the patient cannot return weekly, there are the following other methods of destruction of wart tissue:

- **Liquid nitrogen cryotherapy:**
  - This is mildly to severely painful.
  - It is effective.
  - The patient should return for follow-up in two weeks so that you can check for regrowth or new lesions.

- **Electrocautery:**
  - This is painful – you must administer local anaesthesia.
  - It often leaves a mild scar.
  - Sometimes this is the therapy of last resort in huge perianal warts.
  - The patient must return for follow-up soon after treatment and undergo repeated treatments.

- **Laser destruction:**
  - The cure rate is higher, though also more expensive, than with cautery.
  - It is a bloodless procedure.
  - The vapour plume may contain a viable wart virus, which is of uncertain danger to you and your staff.

- **Interferon alfa-2b immunological therapy:**
  - You need to inject this into the base of the wart three times a week for three weeks.
  - You can treat only five lesions per course.
  - Note that the technique of injection is delicate.
  - As a result of the treatment, the patient may suffer flu-like symptoms – fever and chills occur in at least 50% of patients, and you must monitor his white cell count and liver functions.
  - This is extremely expensive.
  - The cure rate is 40–60% in recalcitrant warts.
  - You should reserve this treatment for the most recalcitrant of warts and administer it only if you have the necessary experience.

Periungual warts

You do not need to treat these warts if they are not painful. Advise your patient to stop biting his nails and cuticles.

To treat these warts palliatively:

- Apply keratolytic agents – 20% salicylic acid and 20% lactic acid in collodion – twice daily to reduce bulk and keep the wart soft.

- The treatment is more effective if you occlude the warts with non-porous tape.

- Periungual warts under the distal nail edge and those on the distal portion of the lateral nail folds usually have projections which extend deeply under the nail. Destruction of the visible, superficial portion almost always results in regrowth of the wart. To be curative, destructive therapies must be deep, thus they are painful and may cause slight deformity of the periungual tissue. Even then, cure rates are less than 50% after one treatment.

- You must treat such warts on the proximal nail fold gently to avoid permanent injury to the underlying nail matrix – this would result in permanent nail deformity.

Plantar warts

To treat these warts:

- Apply Vaseline to protect the healthy surrounding skin, then apply wart paint (salicylic acid/lactic acid liquid preparations) to the wart.
- Cover with a plaster.

- Advise the patient to soak his foot in hot water daily and to carefully remove the softened, loose keratin with a scraper or brush.

Molluscum contagiosum

To treat these warts, advise your patient to choose from the following options:

- Apply benzoyl peroxide cream daily.
- Curette out the contents.
- Apply wart paint daily.
- Apply liquid nitrogen twice a week.

Mental health

63 How to certify a patient under the Mental Health Care Act 17 of 2002

TUVIAH ZABOW

Introduction

Mentally ill, intellectually disabled or other psychologically impaired persons behave in ways that may be detrimental to their own health and/or the safety of other people. This is characterised by their relative lack of insight into these behaviours and the need for intervention and treatment. The law aims to provide for their control and treatment – it is for their own protection as well as for the protection of the community.

You may take the necessary actions by formal or informal procedures, depending on the severity of the disturbed state, the amount of insight that the patient retains and the need for management. The emphasis is intended to be more on treatment and protection than on detention of the patient. Legal decisions affecting a patient requiring attention include hospitalisation without consent and administration of his property.

Managing the mentally ill in terms of the Act

The abovementioned legislation repeals the Mental Health Act 18 of 1973, which is widely considered to be outdated. The "new" Act is directed primarily at aspects of care provision and is thus termed the "Mental Health Care Act" as opposed to the previously named "Mental Health and Mental Disorders Act". The Mental Health Care Act sets out criteria considered essential in defining the nature and severity of mental disturbance to be addressed in relation to the provision of treatment, the facilities, and the personal and property rights of the individual patient. The qualification to provide the necessary evidence is defined according to the different professionals concerned.

Aims

The Act aims to provide for the appropriate care, treatment and rehabilitation of people who are mentally ill, as well as to protect members of the public and their property from these people. The different procedures that you need to follow to admit your patient to a treatment facility are set out with the provision of Review Boards to supervise and monitor every mental health establishment and to address appeals.

The Act has further provided for the care and administration of the property of the mentally ill person. In particular, the statutes safeguard the human rights of the mentally ill so as to protect them against potential exploitation and abuse. Overall, the legislation provides for and coordinates mental health services within the general health services and the communities in which the mentally ill person resides.

Definitions

The Act defines each term or concept utilised in the law. Some of the more important definitions in this Act are as follows (Mental Health Care Act, 2002 (Act No. 17 of 2002) also accessed online 26/8/05 at http://www.acts.co.za):

(i) **Assisted care, treatment and rehabilitation** means the provision of health interventions to people incapable of making informed decisions due to their mental health status and who do not refuse the health interventions;

(ii) **Associate** means a person with a substantial or material interest in the well-being of a mental health care user or a person who is in substantial contact with the user;

(iii) **Health establishment** means institutions, facilities, buildings or places where persons receive care, treatment, rehabilitative assistance, diagnostic or therapeutic interventions or other health services and includes facilities such as community health and rehabilitation centres, clinics, hospitals and psychiatric hospitals. The head of a health establishment may be medically qualified or not and may not be a mental health care practitioner;

(iv) **Involuntary care, treatment and rehabilitation** means the provision of health
interventions to people incapable of making
informed decisions due to their mental
health status and who refuse health intervention but require such services for their
own protection or for the protection of others;

(v) **Mental health care practitioner** means a
psychiatrist or registered medical practitioner or a nurse, occupational therapist, psychologist or social worker who has been
trained to provide prescribed mental health
care, treatment and rehabilitation services;

(vi) **Mental health care user** means a person
receiving care, treatment and rehabilitation
services or using a health service at a health
establishment;

(vii) **Mental illness** means a positive diagnosis
of a mental health-related illness in terms of
accepted diagnostic criteria;

(viii) **Voluntary care, treatment and rehabilitation** means the provision of health interventions to a person who gives consent to
such interventions.

Human rights

It is worth reiterating that the Mental Health Care
Act aims to protect the rights of mentally ill people.
These rights include

• the right to dignified and humane treatment
• freedom from discrimination in terms of access to
all forms of treatment
• the right to privacy and confidentiality
• the right to protection from physical or psychological abuse
• the right to adequate information about their clinical status.

Moreover, mentally ill people have the right to be
treated under the same professional and ethical
standards as other ill people. This must include
efforts on your part to promote the greatest degree of
self-determination and personal responsibility in
your patient. Admission and treatment should
always be carried out in the patient's best interest
and in the least restrictive environment. Chapter III
of the Act covers the rights and duties relating to
mental health care users. These rights and duties are
in addition to any rights and duties that they may
have in terms of any other law.

It is important to note that the reporting of inci-
dents of exploitation and abuse is a significant
requirement addressed in the Act. Any person witnessing any form of abuse against a mental health
care user, that is the patient, must report this fact to

the Mental Health Review Board concerned or may
lay a charge with the South African Police Service.

Mental Health Review Boards

Chapter IV of the Act makes provision for the establishment of Review Boards specifically to ensure the
protection of the rights of people who are committed
into care, treatment and rehabilitation without their
consent, as well as other related responsibilities.
Such a Board must be set up in respect of every
health establishment that provides mental health
care, treatment and rehabilitation services. The
Review Board may be set up for a single, a cluster or
all health establishments in a province.

The Board may consult or obtain representations
from any person, including a person or body with
specific expertise, and may summon any person to
appear before it as a witness. The Board should
consist of no fewer than three and no more than five
members, who must be South African citizens.
Membership must consist of at least a mental health
care practitioner, a magistrate, an attorney or an
advocate, and a member of the community.

Admission to hospital for care and assessment

Chapter V of the Act deals with voluntary, assisted
and involuntary mental health care. This chapter
regulates the procedure authorising the provision of
care, treatment and rehabilitation.

The procedure followed depends on the severity
of the patient's illness. The principle of choosing the
least restrictive environment must be followed. The
least restrictive and preferred situation is one in
which the person has the ability to agree to admission, that is a voluntary patient. He is required to
understand the circumstances and the implications
of the admission, and agree to be admitted and
treated. Even in the presence of severe mental illness, a person may have the ability to understand
and agree.

The procedure followed is indicated by the needs
of the specific patient and the nature of his disorder.
No person who suffers or is alleged to suffer from
mental illness shall by reason of such illness be
detained at any place other than in accordance with
the provisions of the Act. Patients who are mentally
ill can be admitted to hospital under various categories. Evaluation of these patients should take
place as soon as possible and with particular attention to predictability and prevention of violence to
themselves – as a suicide risk, for example – and to
others. Such patients include voluntary and assisted
patients, which provides for the majority of admissions. These patients either agree to being admitted
or do not object.

If the person is severely mentally ill, is placing
himself or others at risk as a result of that illness,
and is refusing the admission for treatment which he

needs, he requires involuntary hospitalisation. You need to make this decision in the context of his longitudinal history, present mental state, the need to intervene in the early stages of relapse and the need to protect him or others from harm. The guiding principle should be the best interests of the patient. You should not admit patients involuntarily for convenience or any other reason.

Advise the patient of his status, of the avenues of appeal and of the manner of discharge open to him. Medical certificates in support of the application and affidavits provided, preferably by a close relative, are necessary for his admission. The rights of appeal against admission are available to him, his relatives or other interested persons, and may be made to the Mental Health Review Board of the area.

Patients are admitted under three categories ranging in level of restriction, namely voluntary, assisted or involuntary.

■ VOLUNTARY CARE

Voluntary patients are reviewed and treated in the same manner as people with other health problems. A mental health care user who submits voluntarily to a health establishment for care, treatment and rehabilitation services is entitled to appropriate mental health care or to be referred to a more suitable health establishment.

■ EMERGENCY CARE PATIENTS INCAPABLE OF MAKING AN INFORMED DECISION

Any person or health establishment that provides care, treatment and rehabilitation services to a mental health care user, or admits the user in circumstances in which he could not make an informed decision, must report this fact in writing in the prescribed manner to the relevant Review Board within 24 hours. Further procedures in terms of the appropriate category must then be followed.

If the patient is considered to be incapable of making an informed decision he may be admitted either as an "assisted" or as an "involuntary" mental health care user, depending on whether or not he objects to admission. The procedure includes submission of applications, your examination of the person, and a review and confirmation by a Review Board.

■ ASSISTED CARE

Figure 63.1 illustrates the process that we will now explore.

An application in writing must be made to the head of the health establishment concerned. This is granted if, at the time of the application, there is

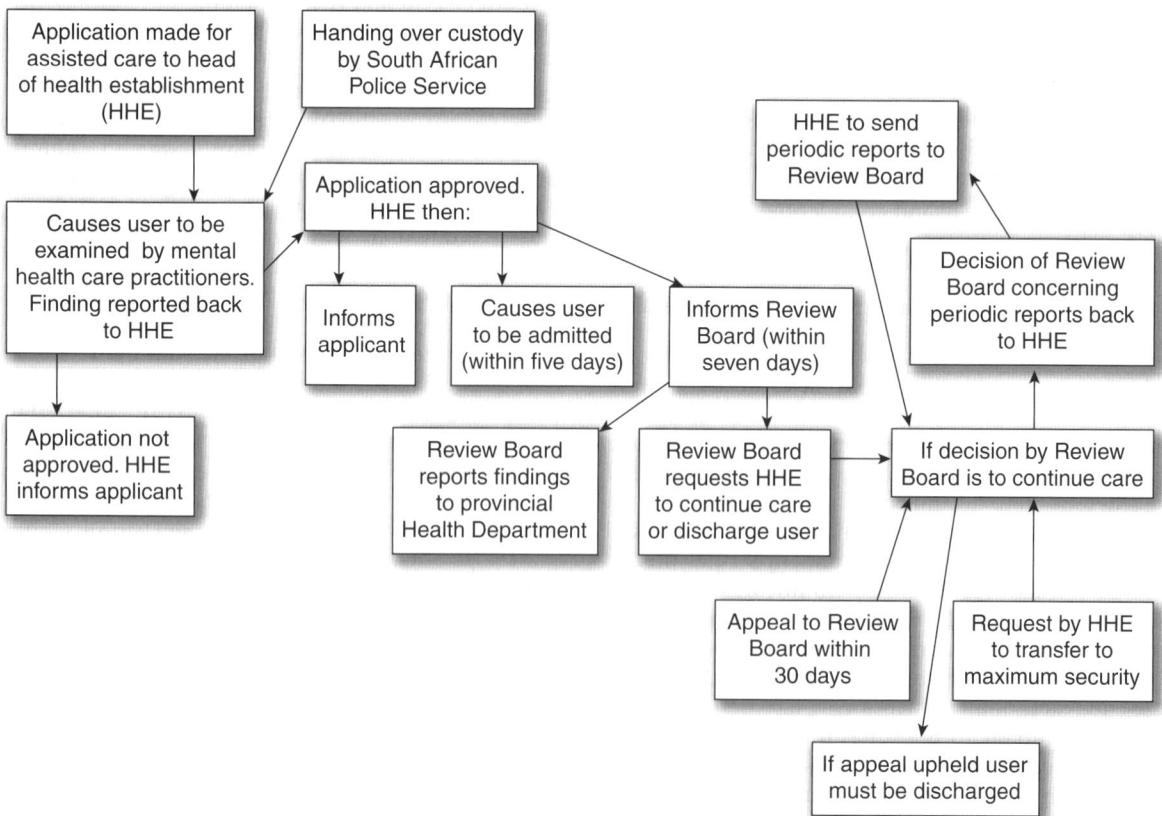

Figure 63.1 Admission, care and treatment of an assisted mental health care user

reason to believe that the mental health care user has a mental illness of such a nature that

- he is likely to inflict serious harm on himself or on others
- or his care, treatment and rehabilitation is necessary for the protection of his financial interests or reputation.

The admission procedures for assisted patients, or patients not opposing the application, are of a less formal or compulsory nature, and can be termed a "third party voluntary procedure".

The application may be made by the spouse, next of kin, partner, associate, parent or guardian of a mental health care user. However, if the user is below the age of 18 years, the application must be made by his parent or guardian. If any of the listed persons is unwilling, incapable or not available to make such an application, you may make it.

The applicant must have seen the patient within seven days prior to making the application and set out the grounds on which he or she believes that care, treatment and rehabilitation services are required. The application form is available at all health establishments where there are at least two mental health care practitioners who are able to examine such a person in terms of the Act. The head of the health establishment concerned must cause the mental health care user to be examined by two such practitioners. At least one of them must also be a medical practitioner. The head must be satisfied of their opinion that the restrictions and intrusions on the rights of the mental health care user to movement, privacy and dignity are proportionate to the care, treatment and rehabilitation services he requires.

Copies of the reports are sent to the applicant and to the Mental Health Review Board. The Board reports on its findings and makes a recommendation for the further hospitalisation or discharge of the patient.

■ INVOLUNTARY (COMPULSORY) INPATIENT CARE

Figure 63.2 illustrates the process that we will now discuss.

At the time of the application, the mental health care user is incapable of making an informed decision on his need for care, treatment and rehabilitation services, and is unwilling to accept or opposes those services.

In this situation, the Act provides the state with the power to commit the patient, if the degree of his mental illness or suspected mental illness is of such a severity as to fit the definition in the Act, and his condition presents a danger to himself or others. This procedure emphasises the need for your assessment of the patient prior to a final order for hospitalisation being made. Similar processes to those applicable to "assisted" or non-opposing patients are set out. In addition, provisions are made for a 72-hour assessment period which may enable a user to recover from an illness before being committed to a psychiatric hospital. Finally, the decision of the Review Board in these cases is sent to a judge for further consideration.

An application is made in the same way as for assisted users, and must also be made in writing using the particular form. As pointed out above, the application form is available at all health establishments where there are at least two mental health care practitioners who are able to examine the patient. Also, the application form and the practitioners' findings must be submitted to the head of the health establishment concerned. The form is also available online at www.info.gov.za/notices/2004/27117/27117c.pdf

The establishment that does not provide the services must refer the applicant to an establishment in the closest proximity that does provide them. Where an applicant is unable, for whatever reason, to fill in the written application, he or she shall be assisted by a staff member at the health establishment concerned.

A 72-hour assessment period is instituted once the head of the health establishment grants application for involuntary care. The two mental health care practitioners assess the user during this time. As the medical practitioner conducting the assessment, you determine the treatment programme and the place in the establishment where the patient is to be kept at this time to ensure his safety and that of others.

Within 12 hours of the end of the assessment period, you submit a written report to the head of the health establishment, indicating your recommendations on the physical and mental health status of the patient. Note that the head may discharge or transfer the patient to voluntary status *during* the assessment period.

If the head believes that the mental health status of the user warrants further involuntary care, treatment and rehabilitation services on an *inpatient* basis, he or she must request the Review Board to approve such services. The Review Board, within 30 days of receipt of the documents, must send a decision on further services on an inpatient basis with reasons to the applicant and the head of the health establishment.

If, following the assessment period, the user is to be cared for, treated and rehabilitated on an inpatient basis, and if he has been admitted to a health establishment which is not a psychiatric hospital, he must be transferred to a psychiatric hospital for the services until the Review Board concerned makes a decision.

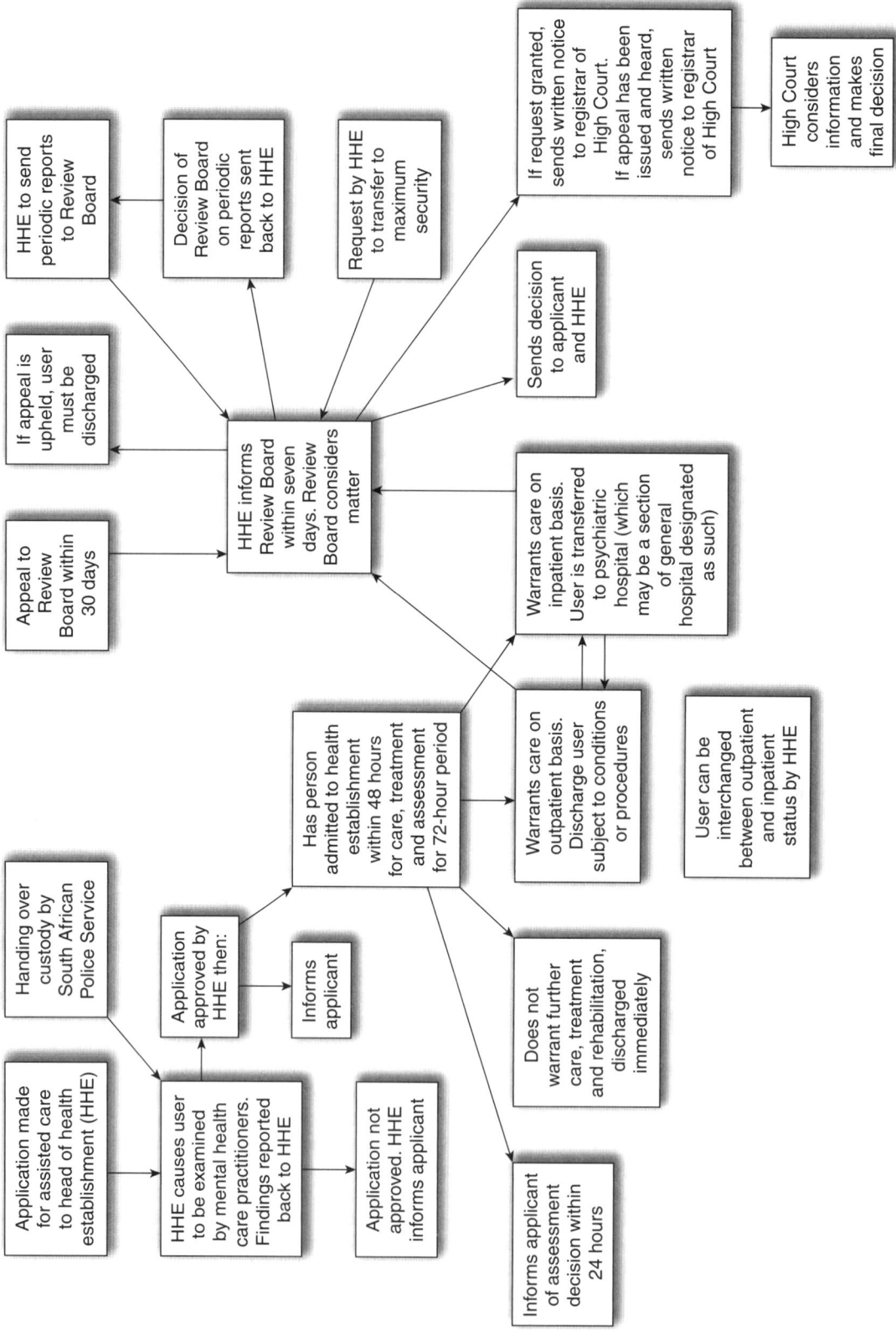

Figure 63.2 Admission, care and treatment of an involuntary mental health care user

The relevant chapter of the Act also deals with maximum security facilities, which at times are required for mentally ill people for further detention by permission of the Review Board.

■ INVOLUNTARY OUTPATIENT CARE

If a mental health care user's mental health care status warrants further involuntary care, treatment and rehabilitation services on an outpatient basis, the head of the health establishment concerned must provide the patient and his custodian with a schedule of conditions relating to such care.

Review

We will now examine the various reviews which mental health care users in each category must undergo.

■ JUDICIAL REVIEW

In the involuntary group, a judicial review on the need for further involuntary care, treatment and rehabilitation services must take place within 30 days of receipt of the documents submitted by the Review Board for involuntary users. After review and investigation, the High Court may order further hospitalisation of the patient and, if necessary, for his financial affairs to be managed and administered according to the provisions of Chapter VIII of the Act. Alternatively, the Court may order the immediate discharge of the patient.

■ PERIODIC REVIEW REPORTS

You need to do these reviews and make the reports six months after the commencement of care, treatment and rehabilitation services in all assisted and involuntary users. Thereafter, you can do them every 12 months.

■ LEAVE OF ABSENCE REVIEW

The head of the health establishment concerned may grant leave of absence to an assisted or involuntary mental health care user for a period not exceeding two months at a time.

■ REVIEW TO GIVE CONSENT TO TREATMENT AND OPERATIONS FOR ILLNESS OTHER THAN MENTAL ILLNESS

An involuntary mental health care user, and an assisted user who is capable of consenting to treatment or an operation, may decide whether or not to have treatment or an operation. Where you deem a user to be incapable of consenting to such treatment, owing to mental illness or intellectual disability, a court-appointed curator, a spouse, next of kin, a parent or guardian, a child over the age of 18, a sibling, a partner or an associate may give consent.

The head of the health establishment where the user resides may grant consent only if

- none of the above persons is available, and attempts have been made to locate them
- this has been confirmed in writing
- he or she has been informed of the relevant alternative treatments
- he or she is satisfied that the most appropriate intervention is to be performed
- you have recommended the treatment or will perform the operation.

This information and action must be documented in the user's clinical record before such treatment or operation can take place.

■ REVIEW TO DISCHARGE ON RECOVERY

When the mental health care user is capable of making an informed decision, the head of the establishment must enquire as to whether he is willing to continue with mental health care treatment. If the assisted or involuntary user consents to further treatment then he should be admitted as an assisted or voluntary patient. If he no longer has a mental illness, as defined in the Act, the head of the establishment shall arrange for his discharge according to accepted clinical practices.

Administration of property

Chapter VIII of the Act provides for the care and administration of property of the mental health care user. It states that an administrator is to be appointed to administer and manage the property when the need arises. Any person over the age of 18 may apply to a Master of a High Court for the appointment of an administrator for a mentally ill person or person with severe or profound intellectual disability. After considering the application, the Master either appoints or declines to appoint an administrator.

The Act also sets out the procedures to appeal the decision as well as the powers and functions of the administrator.

Intervention by members of the South African Police Service

A member of the South African Police Service (SAPS) may have reason to believe, with the aid of personal observation or information obtained from you, that owing to his mental illness or severe or profound intellectual disability a person is likely to inflict serious harm on himself or others. The member must apprehend the person and cause him to be taken for assessment to an appropriate health establishment administered under the auspices of the state. The patient is handed into the custody of the head of the health establishment, or a person designated by the head to receive such a person.

If, according to the assessment, the patient is deemed likely to inflict serious harm on himself or others, he must be admitted to the health establishment for a period not exceeding 24 hours so that an application can be made for involuntary admission. Failing this application, the patient must be discharged immediately. If he seems unlikely to cause harm, he must be released immediately.

If an assisted or involuntary mental health care user has absconded, the head of the health establishment may request assistance from the SAPS to return him to the establishment. The SAPS must comply with the request, and must take note of the estimated level of threat that the user poses.

Only in exceptional circumstances, and upon your recommendation, may the head of the establishment request this type of assistance from the SAPS. The mental health care user who must be transferred back to the establishment may be held in custody at a police station for a period of not more than 24 hours so that the transfer can be effected. You would need to accompany the patient during the transfer.

Appeals

A mental health care user, spouse, next of kin, partner, associate, parent or guardian may, within 30 days, appeal against the head's decisions to the Review Board.

Mentally ill prisoners and state patients

The Mental Health Care Act and the Criminal Procedure Act provide in detail for the criminal responsibility of the mentally ill offender, the management of prisoners and the procedures that need to be followed.

Authorisation and licensing

An application for a licence to operate a hospital that provides mental health services must be made in accordance with the applicable general health legislation. The hospital must meet specific criteria suitable for admission of assisted and involuntary users.

The licensing of community facilities or services not directly run under the auspices of an organ of the state, and which are not designated hospitals but which provide residential or day-care facilities for five or more people with mental disorders, shall in terms of the Act obtain a licence to operate from the provincial department concerned.

We will now explore some scenarios which illustrate the manner in which the Act can be applied.

Scenario 1

■ SCENE

A 70-year-old woman has features suggestive of hypomania. She lives in a home for the aged but the facility cannot manage her symptoms. She refuses admission to hospital. None of her relatives is contactable. She is in danger of self-harm.

■ ACTION

The woman cannot be admitted as a voluntary or an assisted user, but procedures to admit her as an involuntary user must be initiated. The action to be undertaken in terms of the Act is for an application to be made by a person in charge of the home, or a social worker. Certificates are then issued by two mental health care practitioners, such as a psychiatric sister and the medical practitioner. The woman is admitted to a health facility, on the list designated by the Minister of Health, for the 72-hour assessment period. If she settles and is manageable, she may be returned to the home or remain in the facility as an assisted or voluntary user. If her condition persists in severity, she requires transfer to an appropriate facility for further treatment.

Scenario 2

■ SCENE

A 25-year-old woman has been managed as an outpatient for depressive symptoms. She is markedly anxious, has intermittent suicidal ideation and is agreeable to being admitted to an inpatient programme.

■ ACTION

The woman needs to be evaluated as competent to be a voluntary patient. As such, she can be admitted. If she is not competent, she could be admitted as an assisted patient with the application made by a family member or, failing that, a professional together with two mental health care practitioners' certificates.

Scenario 3

■ SCENE

A 20-year-old man is found wandering on the streets in a deteriorated physical state and showing features of mental illness. The SAPS brings him to the local hospital emergency room where he is examined by the medical practitioner.

■ ACTION

In terms of the Act, the man is admitted as an assisted or involuntary user, depending on whether he is assessed as opposing admission or agreeing to it. He is transferred immediately to a designated psychiatric facility if he cannot be managed in the hospital to which he was admitted for the 72-hour assessment period.

64 How to do a mini mental-state examination

BOB MASH

This examination is intended to assess a patient's cognitive functioning, which consists of these attributes:

- Orientation
- Attention
- Concentration
- Memory
- Abstracting ability
- Intelligence
- Insight
- Judgement
- Use of language

You can use the examination to detect impairment in your patient's cognitive functioning and to monitor the progress of a disease or the effect of treatment. Remember that this is a screening test – it does not lead to a specific diagnosis. The patient's score may be impaired in a variety of illnesses such as dementia, delirium, mental retardation, schizophrenia and depression.

The examination's main clinical use, however, is to detect the possible presence of dementia. A moderately demented patient will usually score less than 24 out of 30. In addition, the expected score may vary depending on a patient's age and education level. One study, conducted in a group of American people, defined expected median and percentile scores for different ages and educational levels. Table 64.1 shows the adapted examination structure.

You may also have to modify the examination depending on the language spoken by your patient. Table 64.2 shows this type of adapted examination.

Table 64.1 A mini-examination adapted for the patients' ages and levels of education

Education level	Age in years													
	18–24	25–29	30–34	35–39	40–44	45–49	50–54	55–59	60–64	65–69	70–74	75–79	80–84	≥ 85
0–4 years														
Lower quartile	21	23	23	20	20	20	20	20	19	19	19	18	16	15
Median	23	25	26	24	23	23	22	22	22	22	21	21	19	20
Upper quartile	25	27	28	27	27	26	25	26	26	25	24	24	23	23
5–8 years														
Lower quartile	24	25	24	23	25	24	25	25	25	24	24	22	22	21
Median	28	27	26	27	27	27	27	27	27	27	26	26	25	24
Upper quartile	29	29	28	29	29	29	29	29	29	29	28	28	27	27
9–12 years														
Lower quartile	28	28	28	28	28	27	27	27	27	27	26	25	23	23
Median	29	29	29	29	29	29	29	29	28	28	28	27	26	26
Upper quartile	30	30	30	30	30	30	30	30	30	29	29	29	28	28
Higher degree														
Lower quartile	29	29	29	29	29	29	28	28	28	28	27	27	26	25
Median	30	30	30	30	30	30	30	29	29	29	29	28	28	28
Upper quartile	30	30	30	30	30	30	30	30	30	30	29	29	29	29

Source: Crum, Anthony, Bassett, Folstein 1993. p. 2386–91.

Table 64.2 A mini mental-state examination adapted for language spoken by the patient

Test	Score	Point
Orientation		
1. What is the		
(a) year?	_____	1
(b) season?	_____	1
(c) date?	_____	1
(d) day?	_____	1
(e) month?	_____	1
2. Where are we?		
(a) Country	_____	1
(b) Province	_____	1
(c) Town or city	_____	1
(d) Floor of building	_____	1
(e) Address/name of building	_____	1
Registration		
3. Name three objects, taking one second to say each. Then ask the patient to repeat all three after you have said them. Give one point for each correct answer. Rehearse the answers until the patient learns all three.	_____	3
Attention and calculation		
4. Serial sevens (100–7, and so on). Give one point for each correct answer. Stop after five answers. Alternatively, spell "world" backwards, or "herfs" (for Afrikaans-speaking patients).	_____	5
Recall		
5. Ask for the names of the three objects learned in question 3 above. Give one point for each correct answer.	_____	3
Language		
6. Point to a pencil and a watch. Have the patient name them as you point.	_____	2
7. Have the patient follow a three-stage command: "Take this paper in your right hand. Fold the paper in half with both hands. Put the paper on the floor."	_____	3
8. Have the patient repeat "No ifs, ands or buts" (or "Nog vis, nog vlees, nog voël" if Afrikaans speaking).	_____	1
9. Have the patient read and obey the following written instruction: "Close your eyes" (use large letters).	_____	1
10. Have the patient write a sentence of his choice. (The sentence should contain a subject and an object, and should make sense. Ignore spelling errors when scoring.)	_____	1
11. Have the patient copy the design below. (Give one point if all the sides and angles are preserved and if the intersecting sides form a diamond shape.)	_____	1
Total score Date _____	_____	30

Source: Robertson, Allwood & Gagiano 2001. p. 338–9.

65 How to screen for mental problems

BOB MASH

Up to one in four of all patients attending primary care clinics have a mental problem that meets formal diagnostic criteria, but in most settings less than half of these are detected (Ustun & Sartorius 1995). There are many reasons for this, which relate to yourself, your patient and the prevailing health system. For example, patients frequently present with somatic symptoms such as headache, chest pain, dizziness, back pain, dyspepsia and palpitations. It is a challenge for you to consider physical as well as psychological causes – often there is a predisposition to pursue and exclude physical disease. However, because these conditions are so common it is important for you to frequently consider and screen for them as part of the consultation.

The commonest conditions in primary care, and the ones that most often enter the differential diagnosis with physical conditions, are as follows:

- Depression
- Anxiety disorders, that is generalised anxiety, social phobia, agoraphobia, panic disorder and post-traumatic stress disorder
- Alcohol use disorders
- Unexplained somatic complaints
- Chronic tiredness
- Sleep problems

The presentations of these conditions commonly overlap. For example, sleep problems may be a feature of depression, alcohol or anxiety disorders. Depression or anxiety may accompany alcohol use disorders, and depression and anxiety frequently coexist. It makes sense, therefore, for you initially to test one hypothesis of "mental problem" that covers all these possibilities and then to pursue in more diagnostic detail the avenue that seems most relevant.

You can thus use the set of questions provided in Figures 65.1 or 65.2 to test the hypothesis of "mental problem" in the consultation, alongside questions that test for other physical possibilities (Mash 2002). You can adapt these generic questions, based on those developed by the World Health Organisation (WHO), to make sense in other languages or practice populations, as the example for Khayelitsha shows (see Figure 65.2).

If the patient's main complaint is one of unexplained somatic complaints, chronic tiredness or sleep problems, assess them further as shown in Figure 65.3. If the patient responds positively to the hypothesis of "mental problem", you can then consider the possibility of a more specific disorder, such as post-traumatic stress (Figure 65.4), anxiety (Figure 65.5), depression (Figure 65.6) or alcohol abuse (Figure 65.7 and Chapter 66).

These questions can be used to test the hypothesis of whether your patient suffers "mental problems". The questions are taken directly from the ICD-10 Classification.

1. Low mood or sadness? . . . . ❏
2. Loss of interest or pleasure? . . . . ❏
3. Decreased energy and/or increased fatigue? . . . . ❏
4. Have you had any problems with sleep? . . . . ❏
5. Feeling tense or anxious? . . . . ❏
6. Worrying a lot about things? . . . . ❏
7. (a) Number of standard drinks in a typical day when drinking?
   (b) Number of days per week having alcoholic drinks?

If positive to **any one** of these questions, further assessment may be required.
   Positive to *1, 2, 3* or *4*, consider **depression.**
   Positive to *5* or *6*, consider **anxiety disorders.**
   If *7(b)* is 21 per week or more for men, or 14 per week or more for women, consider **alcohol use disorders.**

Figure 65.1 Generic mental problems checklist

These questions can be used to test the hypothesis of whether your patient has "mental problems". The questions were developed in the context of Khayelitsha – a Xhosa-speaking township.

1. Are you thinking too much? . . . . ❏
2. How are you sleeping at the moment? . . . . ❏
3. Do you feel exhausted or tired even when you are not working hard? . . . . ❏
4. Do you feel sad or like crying for no reason? . . . . ❏
5. As a person there are things that you enjoy doing – do you find that you no longer enjoy these things?
   For example, listening to music or going out with friends. . . . . ❏
6. Do you sometimes have the feeling as though you are going to hear bad news? . . . . ❏
7. *(a) Have you ever felt you should cut down on your drinking? . . . . ❏
   *(b) Have people annoyed you by criticising your drinking? . . . . ❏
   *(c) Have you ever felt bad or guilty about your drinking? . . . . ❏
   *(d) Have you ever had an "eye-opener" first thing in the morning to steady your nerves or to get rid of
      a hangover? . . . . ❏
8. Have you experienced traumatic events that made you feel extremely threatened or endangered?
   Or witnessed someone else in this situation? . . . . ❏

If positive to **any one,** further assessment may be required.

   If positive to *2, 4, 5*, consider **depression**.
   If positive to *1, 2, 6*, consider **anxiety disorders**.
   If positive to more than one of the subsections of *7*, consider **alcohol use disorders**.
   If positive to *8*, consider **post-traumatic stress disorder**.

* Question 7 consists of the four CAGE questions referred to in Figure 65.7 and Chapter 66.

Figure 65.2 Mental problems checklist adapted for the Khayelitsha context

Sleep problems

Difficulty falling asleep, frequent or long periods of being awake, early morning wakening, restless or unrefreshing sleep

Is there a medical problem or pain that interferes with sleep? ⬜
- Asthma, heart failure, arthritis, indigestion, backache

Are there any medications that might affect sleep? ⬜
- Theophylline, steroids, decongestants, some anti-depressants

Are there lifestyle issues that may affect sleep? ⬜
- Drinking alcohol, coffee, tea or eating before sleep
- Taking day time naps
- Changes in routine – i.e. shift work
- Disruptive noises at night
- Overcrowding

Consider a more specific mental disorder ⬜
- Depression, anxiety, PTSD, alcohol disorder

Consider a more specific sleep disorder ⬜
- Has anyone told you that your snoring is loud and disruptive? **Consider sleep apnoea**
- Do you get sudden uncontrollable sleep attacks during the day? **Consider narcolepsy**

Chronic tiredness

Tired all the time, tires easily, tired despite rest

Is there a medical problem that may cause tiredness? ⬜
- Anaemia, infectious hepatitis, glandular fever, influenza, heart failure, diabetes ...

Are there any medications that might cause tiredness? ⬜
- Hypnotics, sedating anti-depressants, anti-histamines, steroids

Are there lifestyle issues? ⬜
- Doing too much at home or work
- Doing too little

Consider a more specific mental disorder ⬜
- Depression, anxiety, PTSD, alcohol disorder

Consider chronic fatigue syndrome ⬜
- Severe disabling fatigue of at least 6 months' duration, present for at least 50% of the time and affecting both physical and mental functioning. Other symptoms such as myalgia, and sleep and mood disturbance may be present.

Somatic complaints

Nausea, vomiting, abdominal pains, headaches, chest pains, difficulty breathing, skin rashes ...

Is there a medical problem that may explain them? ⬜
- Arthritis, peptic ulcer, asthma, angina ...

Are there any medications that might cause them? ⬜

Are there lifestyle issues? ⬜
- Occupational factors, i.e. musculoskeletal problems

Consider a more specific mental disorder ⬜
- Depression, anxiety, PTSD, alcohol use disorder

Consider a somatoform disorder if there are ⬜
- many physical symptoms without a physical explanation
- frequent medical visits in spite of negative investigations (often to more than one doctor, specialists and emergency departments)
- no other specific mental disorders.

Figure 65.3 Sleep problems, chronic tiredness and somatic complaints algorithms

CHECKLIST

I. Have you seen or experienced a traumatic event that made you feel very afraid, helpless or shocked? That is, rape, domestic violence, or any event that was experienced as a trauma for the individual person . ☐

If YES to the above, continue below:

1. Do you re-experience the event in any of the following ways?

Recurring memories of the event in thoughts or pictures . . . . ☐
Recurring and distressing dreams of the event ☐
Acting or feeling as if you are back in the event . . . . ☐
Becoming distressed when something reminds you of the event . . . . ☐

2. Do you avoid certain things that remind you of the event?

People, places or activities associated with the event . . . . ☐
Feelings associated with the event . . . . ☐
Thoughts associated with the event . . . . ☐
Unable to remember important parts of the event . . ☐

3. Is your mood affected in any of the following ways?

As a person there are things that you enjoy doing – do you find that you no longer enjoy these things, that is listening to music or going out with friends? . . . . ☐
Feeling detached or separate from other people . . . . ☐
Having a reduced or restricted range of emotions and feelings, for example, being unable to have loving feelings . . . . ☐
Difficulty thinking about or planning your future, for example do not expect career, marriage, children, normal life span . . . . ☐

4. Do you

have sleep problems? . . . . ☐
feel more angry or irritable than usual? . . . . ☐
find that recently you forget things easily or have difficulty getting your mind to work? . . . . . ☐
Often have the feeling as though you are going to hear bad news? . . . . ☐
Startle or "get a fright" very easily? . . . . ☐
Feel more anxious or worried than usual? . . . . ☐

Summing up:

Consider PTSD if one or more symptoms in all four categories and symptoms have been present for more than one month.

PTSD is often accompanied by significant distress in relationships, work or family functioning.

FLOWCHART

If the patient has symptoms of PTSD:

Consider whether other medical conditions could be causing the symptoms
e.g. thyrotoxicosis

➡

Consider whether the symptoms could be related to medication
e.g. theophyllline, beta-agonists

➡

Consider whether the person has depression

➡

Consider whether the person has an alcohol use disorder

➡

Consider whether the person has another specific anxiety disorder
* *Panic disorder*
* *Agoraphobia*
* *Social phobia*

➡

Post-traumatic stress disorder
In PTSD, co-morbidity of panic attacks, phobic avoidance and depression is common.

Figure 65.4 Post-traumatic stress disorder assessment guide

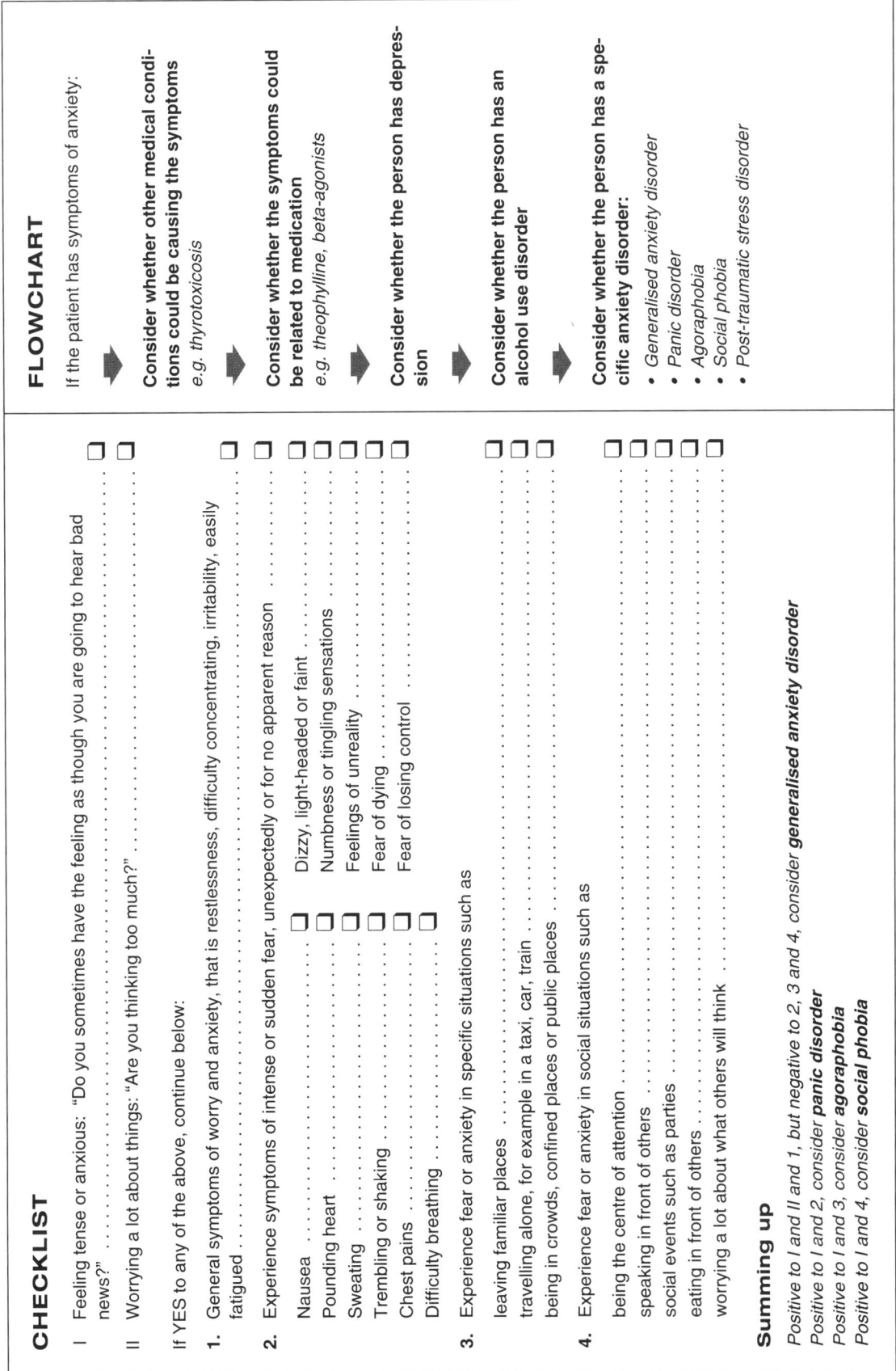

CHECKLIST

I   Feeling tense or anxious: "Do you sometimes have the feeling as though you are going to hear bad news?" .... ☐ ☐

II Worrying a lot about things: "Are you thinking too much?" ....

If YES to any of the above, continue below:

1. General symptoms of worry and anxiety, that is restlessness, difficulty concentrating, irritability, easily fatigued .... ☐ ☐

2. Experience symptoms of intense or sudden fear, unexpectedly or for no apparent reason .... ☐ ☐ ☐ ☐ ☐

    Nausea .... ☐
    Dizzy, light-headed or faint .... ☐
    Pounding heart .... ☐
    Numbness or tingling sensations .... ☐
    Sweating .... ☐
    Feelings of unreality .... ☐
    Trembling or shaking .... ☐
    Fear of dying .... ☐
    Chest pains .... ☐
    Fear of losing control .... ☐
    Difficulty breathing ....

3. Experience fear or anxiety in specific situations such as .... ☐ ☐ ☐

    leaving familiar places ....
    travelling alone, for example in a taxi, car, train ....
    being in crowds, confined places or public places ....

4. Experience fear or anxiety in social situations such as .... ☐ ☐ ☐ ☐ ☐

    being the centre of attention ....
    speaking in front of others ....
    social events such as parties ....
    eating in front of others ....
    worrying a lot about what others will think ....

Summing up

*Positive to I and II and 1, but negative to 2, 3 and 4, consider **generalised anxiety disorder***
*Positive to I and 1 and 2, consider **panic disorder***
*Positive to I and 1 and 3, consider **agoraphobia***
*Positive to I and 1 and 4, consider **social phobia***

FLOWCHART

If the patient has symptoms of anxiety:

Consider whether other medical conditions could be causing the symptoms
e.g. thyrotoxicosis

→

Consider whether the symptoms could be related to medication
e.g. theophylline, beta-agonists

→

Consider whether the person has depression

→

Consider whether the person has an alcohol use disorder

→

Consider whether the person has a specific anxiety disorder:

• *Generalised anxiety disorder*
• *Panic disorder*
• *Agoraphobia*
• *Social phobia*
• *Post-traumatic stress disorder*

Figure 65.5 Anxiety assessment guide

CHECKLIST

I. Low mood/sadness: "Do you feel sad or like crying for no reason?" ☐

II. Loss of interest or pleasure: "As a person there are things that you enjoy doing, such as listening to music or going out with friends. Do you find that you no longer enjoy these things?" ☐

III. Decreased energy and/or increased fatigue: "Do you feel exhausted or tired even when you are not working hard?" ☐

If YES to any of the above, continue below:

1. Sleep disturbance: "How are you sleeping at the moment?" ☐

2. Appetite loss/increase: "How are you eating at the moment? Have you lost interest in food?" ☐

3. Concentration difficulty: "Does your mind have difficulty working? Do you find that recently you forget things easily?" ☐

4. Psychomotor retardation or agitation: "Do you feel that you are slowed down and take longer to do things?" ☐

5. Decreased libido: "Have you lost interest in sex?" ☐

6. Loss of self-confidence or self-esteem: "Do you feel less worthy than or beneath other people?" ☐

7. Thoughts of death or suicide: "Have you had thoughts about ending your life?" ☐

8. Feelings of guilt: "How are other people feeling about you? Responding to you? What do you feel about this? Is it your fault?" ☐

Summing up

Positive to I, II or III and at least five positive from 1 to 8. All occurring most of the time for two weeks or more is an indication of **depression**.

FLOWCHART

If the patient fulfils the diagnostic criteria for depression:

➡

Consider whether other medical conditions could be causing the symptoms:
Neoplasms, arthritis, thyroid disorders, chronic infectious diseases, chronic medical conditions, for example heart problem, diabetes

➡

Consider whether the symptoms could be related to medication:
Beta blockers, antihypertensives (for example reserpine, methyldopa), contraceptives, corticosteroids

➡

Consider whether the person has an anxiety disorder or post-traumatic stress disorder

➡

Consider whether the person has an alcohol use disorder

➡

Treat for depression

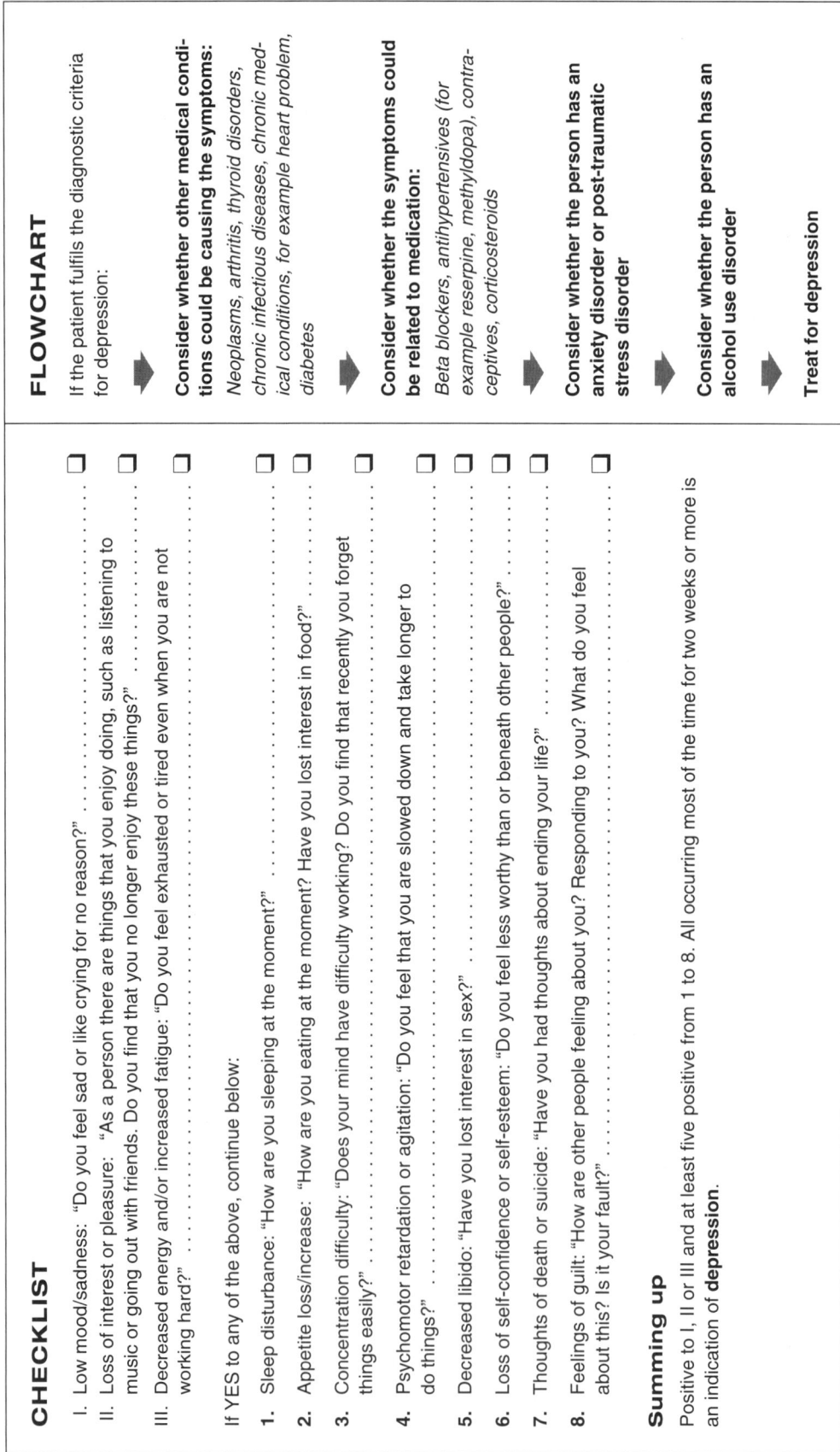

Figure 65.6 Depression assessment guide

CHECKLIST

I. How many days in a week do you have a drink?

II. How many drinks do you or your friends have in a day? If you are a group of six friends, how many beers do you normally drink?

If I and II suggest the amount is above the safe limit or if there is a regular/hazardous pattern of drinking then continue with the CAGE questions below:

1. Have you ever felt you should **C**ut down on your drinking? .... ☐
2. Have people **A**nnoyed you by criticising your drinking? .... ☐
3. Have you ever felt bad or **G**uilty about your drinking? .... ☐
4. Have you ever had an **E**ye-opener first thing in the morning to steady your nerves or to get rid of a hangover? .... ☐

Summing up

Scoring two or three positive answers to the CAGE is highly suggestive of harmful alcohol use and four positive answers is suggestive of alcohol dependence.

Safe limits for standard drinks are: Men > = 21/wk and Women > = 14/wk.

A standard drink refers to: 1 bottle or glass of beer (285 ml)/1 measure or tot of spirit (30 ml)/1 glass of wine (120 ml)

FLOWCHART

Make a full assessment and decide if the patient has a diagnosis of "**harmful alcohol use**" or "**alcohol dependence**":

1. Harmful alcohol use
- *Physical, psychological and social problems suggest harmful alcohol use.*

2. Alcohol dependence
- *Loss of control, strong desire, tolerance and withdrawal symptoms suggest alcohol dependence.*

Clinical: Explore symptoms and examine for physical signs:

1. Have you been unable to stop, reduce or control your drinking? .... ☐
2. Have you ever felt such a strong desire or urge to drink that you could not resist it? .... ☐
3. In the days after you stop drinking have you ever had one of the following problems?

   Being unable to sleep ☐ Headaches ☐
   Feeling nervous or restless ☐ Fits ☐
   Sweating ☐ *Klontjies or horries* ☐
   Heart beating fast ☐ Taking an eye-opener ☐
   Your cup trembles when you hold it in your hand ☐

4. Have you ever continued to drink when you knew you had a sickness that might be made worse by drinking, that is liver disease, high blood pressure? .... ☐

5. Physical problems include:

   Hangovers/blackouts ☐ Poor coordination ☐
   Injuries past and present ☐ Liver disease ☐
   Sexual problems ☐ Brain damage – organic brain ☐
   Abdominal problems. ☐ disorders
   Hypertension ☐

Consider blood tests (mean corpuscular volume and gamma glutamyl transferase)

Individual: Explore psychological problems:
Consider whether the person has depression, anxiety disorder or post-traumatic stress disorder.

Context: Explore family and social effects of drinking:
- *Use genogram*
- *Difficulties and arguments with family/friends*
- *Difficulties at work: absenteeism, warnings, dismissal*
- *Financial problems: spending income on drink*
- *Legal problems: trouble with police, courts, driving, community structures (that is street committee)*
- *Leisure time: How do you enjoy yourself at the weekends? Does this involve drinking?*

Figure 65.7 Alcohol use disorders assessment guide

66 How to screen for an alcohol drinking problem

BOB MASH

Screening for alcohol problems in the consultation is an important preventative activity that tends to be avoided or omitted. Problem drinking has profound medical and social consequences, such as hypertension, cardiomyopathy, homicide, unsafe sex, domestic violence and foetal alcohol syndrome. However, screening methods vary in specificity and sensitivity, with examination findings and laboratory tests being particularly unreliable. Problem drinking can be conceptualised as "harmful alcohol use" when the person is not dependent on alcohol but experiences harmful consequences of drinking. "Alcohol dependence" indicates a situation where in addition the person is physically addicted and experiences withdrawal reactions.

Therefore, interviewing your patient is often the most useful method. Most approaches question the consequences and not just the amount and frequency of drinking, as heavy drinkers tend to deny or minimalise the amount that they drink.

Your interviewing methods, however, must also be brief enough to be easily incorporated into a normal-length consultation.

Brief interventions in primary care can be effective in reducing problem drinking, but you should refer patients with alcohol dependence for more intensive intervention. It is particularly important that you screen pregnant women.

In general, the safe limits for standard drinking are as follows:

- Men less than or equal to 21 units per week
- Women less than or equal to 14 units per week

A standard drink or unit refers to

- one bottle or glass of beer (285 ml)
- one measure or tot of spirit (30 ml)
- or one glass of wine (120 ml).

The CAGE Questionnaire uses only four questions (CAGE refers to the keywords Cut down, Annoyed, Guilty and Eye-opener in the four questions) and has good sensitivity (74–89%) and specificity (79–95%) for alcohol dependence, but is less sensitive for harmful alcohol use or problem drinking. Furthermore, the questions give little information on the amount or pattern of drinking and on whether the problem is current (US Preventative Services Taskforce 2002 p. 567–82).

The questions are as follows:

1. Have you ever felt you should **cut down** on your drinking?
2. Have people **annoyed** you by criticising your drinking?
3. Have you ever felt bad or **guilty** about your drinking?
4. Have you ever had an **eye-opener** first thing in the morning to steady your nerves or to get rid of a hangover?

If your patient replies in the affirmative to two or three of these questions he is likely to be using alcohol harmfully, and if he replies in the affirmative to all four questions, he may well be alcohol dependent.

An alternative to the CAGE Questionnaire is the 10-item Alcohol Use Disorders Identification Test (AUDIT) Questionnaire that may have higher sensitivity (92%) and specificity (94%) for harmful alcohol use or problem drinking (US Preventative Services Taskforce 2002 p. 567–82). Table 66.1 shows this questionnaire.

Following screening, you may need to perform a longer interview to assess your patient further. You can make a three-stage assessment (Mash 2002), as is shown in Table 66.2.

Table 66.1 The AUDIT Questionnaire

Question	Score				
	0	**1**	**2**	**3**	**4**
How often do you have a drink containing alcohol?	Never	Monthly or less	2–4 times/month	2–3 times/week	4 or more times/week
How many drinks do you have on a typical day when you are drinking?	None	1 or 2	3 or 4	5 or 6	7–9*
How often do you have six or more drinks on one occasion?	Never	Less than monthly	Monthly	Weekly	Daily or almost daily
How often during the last year have you found that you were unable to stop drinking once you had started?	Never	Less than monthly	Monthly	Weekly	Daily or almost daily
How often during the last year have you failed to do what was normally expected of you because of drinking?	Never	Less than monthly	Monthly	Weekly	Daily or almost daily
How often during the last year have you needed a first drink in the morning to get yourself going after a heavy drinking session?	Never	Less than monthly	Monthly	Weekly	Daily or almost daily
How often during the last year have you had a feeling of guilt or remorse after drinking?	Never	Less than monthly	Monthly	Weekly	Daily or almost daily
How often during the last year have you been unable to remember what happened the night before because you had been drinking?	Never	Less than monthly	Monthly	Weekly	Daily or almost daily
Have you or someone else been injured as a result of your drinking?	Never	Yes, but not in last year (2 points)	Yes, during the last year (4 points)		
Has a relative, doctor or other health worker been concerned about your drinking or suggested that you cut down?	Never	Yes, but not in last year (2 points)	Yes, during the last year (4 points)		

*Five points if the response is 10 or more drinks on a typical day

A score of greater than 8 out of 41 is suggestive of problem drinking and indicates a need for more in-depth assessment. A cut-off of 10 points has been recommended to provide greater specificity.

Table 66.2 Three-stage assessment

Clinical: Explore symptoms and examine for physical signs.

1. Have you been unable to stop, reduce or control your drinking? . . . . ❑

2. Have you ever felt such a strong desire or urge to drink that you could not resist it? . . . . ❑

3. In the days after you stop drinking have you ever had one of the following problems?

Being unable to sleep . . . . ❑		Headaches . . . . ❑
Feeling nervous or restless . . . . ❑		Fits . . . . ❑
Sweating . . . . ❑		*Klontjies* or *horries* . . . . ❑
Heart beating fast . . . . ❑		Taking an eye-opener . . . . ❑
Your cup trembles when you hold it in your hand . . . . . ❑		

4. Have you ever continued to drink when you knew you had a sickness that might be made worse by drinking, that is, liver disease, high blood pressure? . . . . ❑

5. Physical problems include:

Hangovers/blackouts . . . . ❑	Hypertension . . . . ❑
Injuries past and present . . . . ❑	Poor coordination . . . . ❑
Sexual problems . . . . ❑	Liver disease . . . . ❑
Abdominal problems . . . . ❑	Brain damage – organic brain disorders . . . ❑

Consider blood tests (mean corpuscular volume and gamma glutamyl transferase) . . . . ❑

Individual: Explore psychological problems:

* *Consider whether the person has depression, anxiety disorder or post-traumatic stress disorder.*

Context: Explore family and social effects of drinking:

* *Use genogram*
* *Difficulties and arguments with family/friends*
* *Difficulties at work: absenteeism, warnings, dismissal*
* *Financial problems: spending income on drink*
* *Legal problems: trouble with police, courts, driving and community structures (that is, street committee)*
* *Leisure time: How do you enjoy yourself on the weekends? Does this involve drinking?*

Forensics

67 How to take care of a sexually assaulted woman

SARIE OOSTHUIZEN

Your main functions in this situation are to serve the patient and the judicial process.

Triage and resuscitation

Measure the patient's vital signs and assess her for medical emergencies to ensure prompt treatment. Preserve the forensic evidence as follows:

- Take oral swabs before she may be given something to eat or drink.
- Take swabs before she uses the toilet. If this is absolutely impossible, she must not wipe herself afterwards.
- Take swabs from any wounds before dressing or covering them.
- Do not clean or remove debris or foreign matter from the patient.

Acute stress incident debriefing

Reassure the patient about safety and confidentiality. Look after her physical needs, as described above, while consulting in a quiet, private environment. Give emotional support and time for her to relate the incident.

Avoid secondary victimisation as follows:

- Do not conduct an unsympathetic or rushed debriefing.
- Do not show disbelief.
- Do not question the patient rudely or make insensitive remarks.

Give information and allow time for questions by the patient regarding

- medical examination and evidence collection
- post-exposure prophylaxis (PEP) and risk of HIV
- treatment options
- follow-up
- support systems and disclosure.

Clinical medical examination

Liaise with the police investigator for background information on the case. Check whether the patient, or her guardian, has signed the consent form SAP 308. By doing so, the patient consents to being subjected to examination by a medical officer and to the recording of the findings for criminal proceedings. She also consents to the taking of all necessary specimens for laboratory tests and for the taking of appropriate photographs of injuries related to the reason for this examination.

Victims who are as yet undecided about reporting a sexual assault to the police, or those choosing not to report it, must sign the consent form (similar to a "consent to operation" form) of the hospital or health care facility to consent to examination and documentation. (Reporting to the police gives tacit consent, otherwise the health care worker must obtain explicit consent from the victim.)

To perform the examination, you need to follow this procedure:

- Document the full history in the patient's file.
- Do the clinical examination with empathy and preserve her dignity by introducing yourself and allowing time for her to pose questions before you proceed with taking forensic evidence (see below).
- Have a professional nurse, or third person of the patient's choice, present during the examination.
- Ensure that her body is exposed as little as possible during the examination, and proceed to each following step only with her consent.
- Record the consultation in a register with the name of the police station, case number, file number, date of consultation and the name of the police investigator.

Collecting forensic evidence

To collect forensic evidence, you need to follow this procedure:

G.P.S 01/02

J 88 (81/805259)

| REPORT BY AUTHORISED MEDICAL PRACTITIONER ON THE COMPLETION OF A MEDICO-LEGAL EXAMINATION *To be completed in legible handwriting and signed on every page* | 1 |

A. Demographic Information

| 1. Police Station: | 2. CAS No.: | 3. Investigating officer: Name and number: | 4. Time ⬚⬚ : ⬚⬚   Day Month Year ⬚⬚⬚⬚⬚⬚ |

5. Name of medical practitioner:

6. Registered qualifications:

7. Phone number:

8. Fax number:

9. Place of examination

10. Physical practice address or stamp:

11. Full names of person examined: 12. Sex: M ⬚ F ⬚   13. Date of birth/apparent age:

Figure 67.1 Demographic information

- In order to meticulously collect evidence, use the Sexual Assault Evidence Collection Kit (SAECK) if the victim arrives within 72 hours of the assault.
- You can take forensic swabs of the posterior fornix and cervical os up to five days after the assault.
- Maintain the integrity of the chain of evidence by
  - never leaving the kit unattended
  - always having the nurse present as a witness.

Completing the documentation

Once you have been presented with the signed SAP 308 form, you need to complete the J88 form. The relevant sections of this form are illustrated below.

To fill in the form, you should follow these guidelines:

- Do not allow the police to write on the form, and complete the whole report in your own handwriting.
- Sign every page.
- Do not use abbreviations.
- Avoid using technical terms.

- Use the 24-hour notation for time, for example 19:30 (which stands for half-past seven in the evening).
- Provide the following demographic information (see Figure 67.1):
  - Your own name, qualifications and contact details
  - The patient's full name as it appears on her identity document or birth certificate. Put her nickname (if any) in brackets
  - The patient's gender
  - Her date of birth. This is especially important in the case of children whose exact age could be of legal importance. Use the day, month, year format, for example 13 01 1955.
- Identify the source of the information – give the name of any third party providing information.
- Provide the following general history information (see Figure 67.2):
  - Document the patient's previous injuries or admissions to hospital in an effort to establish whether there is a pattern of abuse.

B. General History

1. Relevant medical history and medication:

Figure 67.2 General history information

C. General Examination			
1. Condition of clothing:			
2. Height (cm):	3. Mass:		4. General body build:
5. Clinical findings: In every case the nature, position and extent of the abrasion, wound or other injury must be described and noted together with its probable date and manner of causation. The position of all injuries and wounds must also be noted on the sketches.			

Figure 67.3 General examination information

– Include any medication that the patient may be taking that could cause or aggravate bruising or bleeding, influence her mental awareness or affect her decision making.

- Provide the following information that you gather while conducting the general examination (see Figure 67.3):

– Give a one-sentence history to remind yourself about the circumstances of the case when you get to court. For example: "Ms A said that she was sexually assaulted last night by a man known to her." Never give the actual name of the alleged perpetrator.

– Document your clinical findings systematically, making use of the sketches on page four of the form. Number each injury so as not to omit any injuries, and so as to document the anatomical positions of the injuries correctly. Pay particular attention to left and right sides on the sketches.

– In the conclusion of this section (see Figure 67.4), you must state whether the external injuries that you found are compatible with the reported circumstances and time of the assault.

– If the injuries appear to have been inflicted with an object, describe them in terms such as "sharp force injuries" or "blunt force injuries" rather than trying to guess what the object was.

- Provide the following information when conducting a gynaecological examination of a female patient (see Figures 67.5 to 67.8):

– Use the acronym TEARS, which stands for **T**ears, **E**cchymosis, **A**brasions, **R**edness and **S**welling, so as not to miss any injuries.

– Use the clock notation illustrated in Figure 67.9 to describe the position of the injuries, for example, "posterior fourchette tear at six o'clock".

– Document the hymen configuration as annular, crescentic, fimbriated, cribriform, cuff-like or carunculae myrtiformes.

– Do not use the terms "rape", "hymen intact" or "alleged rape" in the conclusion of this section, as this could inadvertently help the defence team.

– Conclude that the absence of injuries does not exclude penetration of the vulva or vagina, or that the injuries you found are compatible with forcible dry penetration past the labia minora or into the vagina.

– State whether the injuries or healing areas are compatible with the stated time of assault.

8. Conclusions
....
....
....
.... *Signature of medical practitioner*
....
....

Figure 67.4 Conclusion of the general examination

E. Gynaecological Examination (State clinical findings)		
1. Breast development: Tanner stage 1–5 ☐	2. Pubic hair: Tanner stage 1–5 ☐	3. Mons pubis:
4. Clitoris:	5. Frenulum of clitoris:	
6. Urethral orifice:	7. Para-urethral folds:	
8. Labia majora:	9. Labia minora:	
10. Posterior fourchette: scarring: tears:	bleeding: increased friability:	
11. Fossa navicularis:		
12. Hymen: configuration:	13. Opening diameter (mm): Transverse ☐☐ Vertical ☐☐	
14. Swelling:	15. Bumps:	16. Clefts:
17. Fresh tears (position):	18. Synechiae:	19. Bruising:
20. Vagina: Number of fingers admitted:	bleeding: discharge:	tears:
21. Cervix:	erosion: bleeding:	discharge: other:
22. Perineum:		

Figure 67.5 Gynaecological information

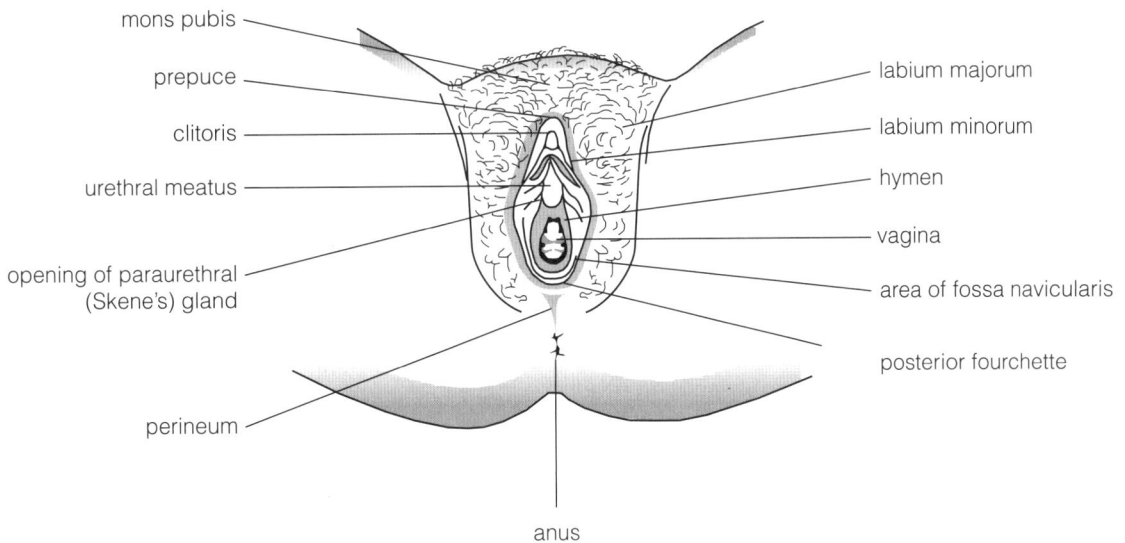

Figure 67.6 Female genitalia

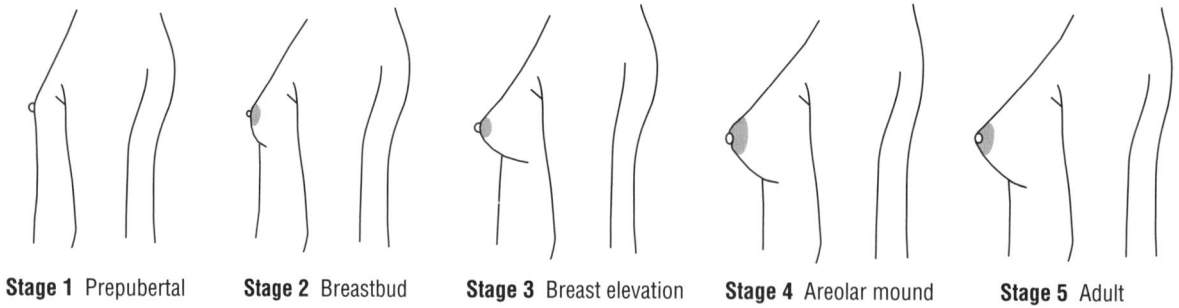

Stage 1 Prepubertal   **Stage 2** Breastbud   **Stage 3** Breast elevation   **Stage 4** Areolar mound   **Stage 5** Adult

Figure 67.7 Tanner stages of breast development

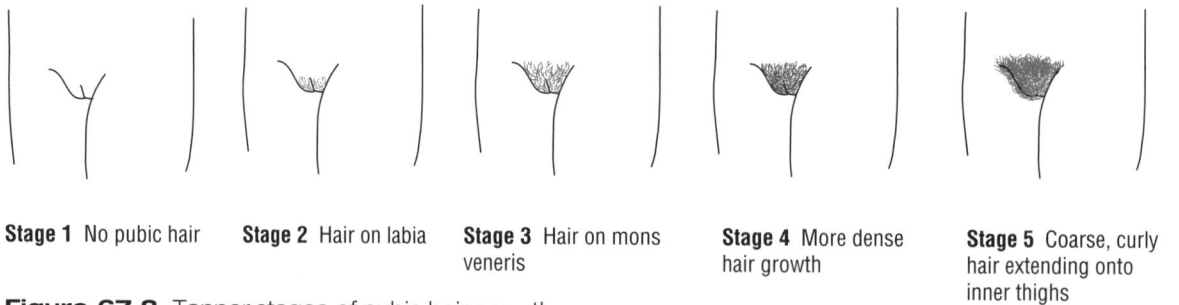

Stage 1 No pubic hair   **Stage 2** Hair on labia   **Stage 3** Hair on mons veneris   **Stage 4** More dense hair growth   **Stage 5** Coarse, curly hair extending onto inner thighs

Figure 67.8 Tanner stages of pubic hair growth

Figure 67.9 Clock notation

- Provide the following information concerning the samples you have taken for investigation (see Figure 67.10):
  - In the case of a female victim, take a urine sample to test for pregnancy.
  - State the name, rank and force number of the police investigator to whom you hand any samples. Ensure that the officer signs the form.
  - State your final conclusions.

If you submit a J88 form that is as complete, legible and comprehensible as you can possibly make it, it is unlikely that you will receive a subpoena to testify to the case in court.

While not part of the J88 form itself, when applicable you can do photo documentation, having gained the consent of the patient in writing. Keep this documentation securely in your possession until it may be required by court. Moreover, you need to keep your own clinical notes in your filing system so that you can do proper follow-up consultations.

Treatment

You must treat any external injuries and provide pain relief such as paracetamol and/or non-steroidal anti-inflammatory drugs (NSAIDs).

Having checked the patient for allergies, and drug interactions if she is on chronic medicine, give the following preventative treatment:

- Follow the post-exposure prophylaxis (PEP) protocol. When the patient qualifies, give her counselling on
  - the risk of transmission of HIV
  - the side-effects of the drugs
  - the efficacy of the drugs
  - the importance of adherence
  - the importance of follow-up visits
  - having safe sex during the treatment and monitoring period.
- Follow the sexually transmitted infections (STI) protocol.
- Give pregnancy post-coital prophylaxis, if necessary.
- Give tetanus toxoid 0.5 ml sc stat.
- Start immunoglobulin and hepatitis B vaccination if the victim has had no previous vaccination.
- Perform baseline blood investigations – full blood

F. Samples taken for investigation		
1. Forensic specimens taken: Urine sample for pregnancy test: Positive ☐ Negative ☐		Seal number of Evidence Collection Kit:
2. Specimens handed to: Name: Signature:	Rank and Force number:	
8. Conclusions		*Signature of medical practitioner*

Figure 67.10 Information concerning samples taken for investigation, and final conclusion

count, HIV ELISA and hepatitis B virus antibody status.

Furthermore, you need to evaluate the immediate risk of suicide and promptly refer the patient to a psychiatrist, if necessary.

Statistics

You need to keep detailed demographic statistics of the age and gender and the residential addresses of all the sexual assault victims that you examine and treat. Also keep outcome statistics of the follow-up rate, adherence, and the rate of contracting infections in order to comply with the guidelines of the Health Professions Council of South Africa (HPCSA).

Police investigator briefing

Ensure that the police investigator signs the J88 form in order to document the receiving of the SAECK. The police investigator must also sign the clinic/ practice register in which you record the police station, case number, file number and date of consultation. File a duplicate of the J88 in the patient's file.

Once again liaise with the police investigator to discuss the relevance of injuries and findings that you documented. Allow the patient to disclose any new and relevant information mentioned during the medical examination to the police investigator.

Follow-up and support systems

You need to establish a patient-friendly environment for the patient, especially in the case of attachment trauma (trauma where the perpetrator is a family member, spouse, boyfriend or girlfriend).

The environment needs to provide accessible, comprehensive care and support.

Involve a social worker in all child cases and in victims of attachment trauma. Discuss disclosure and family support with the patient and her family.

Make appointments for follow-up visits to comply with the PEP protocol.

Look out for signs of post-traumatic stress disorder presenting one month after the assault and significantly affecting important areas of the patient's life, such as family and work. Symptoms include

- recurrent and intrusive recollections of the trauma, including images, thoughts or perceptions
- persistent avoidance of stimuli such as activities, places or people associated with the trauma
- persistent symptoms of increased arousal with difficulty in falling asleep or staying asleep, irritability and inability to concentrate.

Involve the psychologist and psychiatrist in these cases – the psychologist in particular can help with relaxation techniques.

Provide ongoing counselling, which includes

- ensuring confidentiality
- re-establishing a sense of safety
- reducing the impact of the traumatic event
- recovering the patient's self-esteem, while managing cognitive, emotional and psychological symptoms
- breaking the cycle of self-blame and guilt
- helping the patient to contact support organisations which might include a "place of safety"
- involving the family in counselling
- providing guidance in relationships.

68 How to notify a death

PATRICK MADUNA

You need to use the death notification form BI 1663 to notify a death.

Definitions

In the form, certain terms are defined as follows:

- **Immediate cause of death:** This is the final disease or condition resulting in death.
- **Stillborn:** If a baby is stillborn, it has had at least 26 weeks of intrauterine existence but showed no sign of life after complete birth.
- **Underlying cause of death:** This is either
  - the disease or injury which initiated the train of morbid events leading directly to death
  - or the circumstances of the accident or violence which produced the fatal injury.

Structure of the form

The aim of the form is to collect information in the event of death or stillbirth. The form consists of two pages:

- **Page 1:** Registration of death or stillbirth. Figure 68.1 is a sample of this page.
- **Page 2:** Notification of death and demographic information for statistical purposes. Figure 68.2 is a sample of this page.

You need to complete the form in duplicate by using carbon paper between the original and duplicate pages. For record and control purposes, you must preserve the duplicates for at least five years.

You must fill in the following sections of the form:

- Page 1:
  - Section A: Particulars of deceased individual/stillborn child
  - Section D: Certificate of attending medical practitioner/professional nurse
- Page 2:
  - Section F: Demographic details
  - Section G: Medical certificate of cause of death

Completing the form

You should complete the form properly and promptly so that the family can obtain a burial order. Once a death occurs, you, a forensic pathologist or a health professional appointed to register the death must view the body as accurately as possible and fill in the required sections. If the exact name and/or ID number of the deceased individual is not known, you need to make every effort to positively identify him and obtain his identity details from his family.

Each form has a unique serial number, which appears at the top of pages 1 and 2. It is used to ensure effective control of stock and to curb fraudulent use of forms. Also at the top of each page is space for a file number and date, which you or an appointed health professional must complete if the death occurred in a health facility. This file number will be the hospital or clinic file number of the deceased. The date refers to the date of completion of the form.

Note that you need to complete the form in black ink, ticking the blocks where applicable. When filling in the deceased's surname and forename(s), write only one letter per block. Once you have completed the form, place page 2 in a sealed envelope and attach it to page 1. Hand the form to the informant or the person in charge of the funeral.

Section A: Particulars of the deceased individual/stillborn child

If the deceased's personal information is not available, Home Affairs officials or funeral undertakers are responsible for filling in these details, for example ID number, marital status, place of birth and citizenship.

Follow this procedure with regard to the specific personal details of the deceased:

- If you do not know any of the particulars, leave the relevant space on the form blank.

- The **ID number** must be copied into Section F of page 2. This number is not required in the case of a stillborn child.
- Record the **age** of the deceased in completed years or, if he was under one year, in completed months. If the birth date is unknown, use the age of the deceased to estimate the year of birth. Use the year, month, day format, for example 1970 03 23.
- The "**surname**" refers to the deceased's surname, and in the case of a married woman, the "**maiden name**" is the surname of the deceased before she was married.
- Record all **given names** and **forenames** of the deceased.
- Write out the deceased's **gender** in full.
- For neonatal deaths, state the **number of hours** that the baby was alive after birth.
- Select the appropriate **marital status** of the deceased.
- Record the deceased's **place of birth**. Record either the municipal district or the country of origin if the deceased was born abroad.
- Write out in full the **place of death**, namely the city, town or village where the death occurred.
- Write out in full the deceased's **citizenship**.
- The "**place of registration of death**" refers to the name of the city, town or village where the registration of death takes place.
- If possible, affix the **left thumb print** of deceased persons of 16 years and older in the space provided. This is for identification purposes and is particularly important if the deceased's ID number is unknown or his identity is uncertain. This is not applicable for stillborn babies and children.

Section D: Certificate of attending medical practitioner/professional nurse

You, or an appointed health professional, are required to certify whether or not the deceased named in Section A died solely and exclusively owing to natural causes. If the answer is "yes" then tick the first block. You or the health professional must also complete Section G.

If you, or the health professional, feel that you are not in a position to certify that the deceased died exclusively owing to natural causes then tick the second block. In this case, you, or the health professional, are then required to contact a police officer, who will open a docket and arrange for transport of the body to the government mortuary.

Once you have ticked the appropriate block, you, or the health professional, are required to

- fill in your **postal address** and **postal code**

- provide your Health Profession Council of South Africa (HPCSA)/South African Nursing Council (SANC) **registration number**
- write out your **full name**
- **sign** the form
- state the **date** of the certification of the death in the full year, month, day format.

Section F: Demographic details

You need to complete this section in consultation with the informant. If the informant is not available at the time of certification, then you should seek the aid of a Home Affairs registrar or the funeral undertaker.

You need to follow this procedure when filling in this section of the form:

- Ensure that the deceased's **ID number** is correctly printed on *both* pages in case the two pages get separated.
- Select the **place of death**.
- Fill in the **name of the facility or institution** where death occurred. If death occurred at home, record the deceased's **street address**.
- Ensure that the **residential address** of the deceased includes the street name and number; the name of the suburb; census enumerator area; magisterial district; city, town or village; province; country and postal code. If the address is not urban, record the name of the plot/farm, and the nearest town or village, magisterial district, postal code, name of the province and country. This allows analysis of the data by health regions.
- Tick the **highest educational class** that the deceased achieved. Do not fill in the block labelled "code" – it is for official use only.
- Record the **occupation** of the deceased. This refers to the type of work he did for most of his working life.
- Write out in full the **type of business or industry** in which the deceased worked. For example, the business in which an accountant worked could be a construction, chemical, manufacturing or food company.
- Tick the appropriate box to state the **smoking status** of the deceased if he started smoking less than five years ago, answer "no". If he smoked more than five years ago, but for less than six months, answer "no".

Section G: Medical certificate of cause of death

Only you or an appointed health professional should fill in this section. In some instances, the district surgeon or forensic pathologist can also do it. This section replaces the former medical death certificate. To the best of your knowledge, complete the cause of death.

To fill in this section, you need to follow this procedure:

- In Part 1 you need to list the **diseases, injuries or complications** that caused the death. First state the immediate cause of death, that is the final disease or condition that resulted in death. Then list the conditions leading to the immediate cause of death sequentially, and enter the underlying cause of death last. Do not enter the mode of dying, for example cardio-respiratory failure. Rather enter a specific, full, medical disease term. Note that you should list only one cause per line. It is important that you provide the approximate time interval between the disease or conditions and the onset of disease and death to clarify the actual order of events.

- In Part 2 you need to state the **other significant conditions** that contributed to death but did not result in the underlying cause of death given in Part 1.

- Note that the nosological coding of the cause of death (ICD-10) is for official use only.

See Table 68.1 for examples.

At the bottom of the certificate, you need to provide the following additional information:

- If the death notification is for a stillbirth or perinatal death, give the baby's **birth weight** in grams.
- If the deceased is female, indicate whether or not she was **pregnant** 42 days prior to death.
- Indicate the **race** of the deceased.
- Select the **method of ascertainment** of the cause of death.

Table 68.1 Examples of completion of Section G

Example 1

Part 1

A   *Pneumocystis carinii* pneumonia
B   Acquired immunodeficiency syndrome
C

Part 2

Kaposi's sarcoma

Example 2

Part 1

A   Bronchopneumonia
B   Measles
C

Part 2

Malnutrition

Example 3

Part 1

A   Ventricular fibrillation
B   Inhalation of toxic chemicals
C   Accidental chemical burns

Part 2

REPUBLIC OF SOUTH AFRICA
DEPARTMENT OF HOME AFFAIRS

83/BI – 1663
Page 1

NOTIFICATION / REGISTER OF DEATH / STILLBIRTH

in terms of the Births and Deaths Registration Act,
1992 (Act No. 51 of 1992)

Space for Bar Code

SERIAL No: A0 4415936

9 9 9 9

• *Must be completed in black ink (please tick ✓ where applicable)*
• *Please refer to instructions*

FILE No: DATE:

A PARTICULARS OF DECEASED INDIVIDUAL   / STILLBORN CHILD

Identity number of deceased

Date of death   Y Y Y Y   M M   D D

Date of birth   Y Y Y Y   M M   D D

Surname

Maiden Name (If female)

Forenames

Age at last birthday   years

Sex

If death occurred within 24 hours after birth number of hours alive

MARITAL STATUS OF DECEASED   Single ☐   Civil Marriage ☐   Living as married ☐   Widowed ☐

Religious Law Marriage ☐   Divorced ☐   Customary Marriage ☐

PLACE OF BIRTH (Municipal district or country if abroad)..

PLACE OF DEATH (City / Town / Village)..

PLACE REGISTRATION OF DEATH ....

CITIZENSHIP OF DECEASED ....

Left thumb print of deceased

B PARTICULARS OF INFORMANT

Identity number

Initials and Surname

Relationship to deceased   Parent ☐   Spouse ☐   Child ☐   Other kin ☐   Other (specify) ☐

Postal address

Postal Code

Left thumb print of informant

Diallin g

Was the next of kin of the deceased a smoker* during the past five years?   Yes ☐   No ☐   Refuse to answer ☐

Date   Y Y Y Y   M M   D D   Signature..........................

Telephone No.

C PARTICULARS OF FUNERAL UNDERTAKER

Initials and Surname

Designation No.   Place of burial / cremation...

Date   Y Y Y Y   M M   D D   Signature..........................

Office Stamp of Funeral Undertaker

D CERTIFICATE BY ATTENDING MEDICAL PRACTITIONER / PROFESSIONAL NURSE

I, the undersigned, hereby certify that the deceased named in **Section A,** to the best of my knowledge and belief, died solely and exclusively due to NATURAL CAUSES, as specified in **Section G.** ☐

I, the undersigned, am not in the position to certify that the deceased died exclusively due to natural causes. ☐

Initials and Surname

Date Signed   Y Y Y Y   M M   D D   Signature..........................

Postal address

Postal Code

SAMDC / SANC Reg. No.

E CERTIFICATE BY DISTRICT SURGEON / FORENSIC PATHOLOGIST

I, the undersigned, hereby certify that a medicolegal post-mortem examination has been conducted on the body of the person whose particulars are given in **Section A** and that the body is no longer required for the purpose of the Inquest Act, 1959 (Act No. 58 of 1959) and that the cause of death is:

Natural (Cause of Death as indicated in **Section G**) ☐   Unnatural ☐   Under investigation ☐

Initials and Surname

Place of post-mortem..................................   Date   Y Y Y Y   M M   D D

Mortuary reference ....   Date signed   Y Y Y Y   M M   D D   Signature.................

Postal address

Postal Code

SAMDC Reg. No.

F FOR OFFICIAL USE ONLY   Initials and Surname or Registrar

Registration of Death approved and Burial Order issued

Postal address

Postal Code   Date   Y Y Y Y   M M   D D

Force No./ Designation No.

Persal No.

Signature...

Office Stamp

* Someone who smokes tobacco on most days

Supplied by **LITHOTECH SP** Tel.: (012) 327-3239

Figure 68.1 Page 1 of the notification/register of death/stillbirth

NOTIFICATION / REGISTER OF DEATH / STILLBIRTH
INFORMATION FOR MEDICAL AND HEALTH USE ONLY
*(After completion **seal** to ensure <u>confidentiality</u>)*

83/BI – 1663
Page 2

Space for Bar Code

- *Must be completed in black ink (please tick [✓] where applicable)*
- *Please refer to instructions*

FILE No: DATE:

SERIAL No: AO 4415936

F DEMOGRAPHIC DETAILS

Initials and Surname of deceased

Identity number

PLACE OF DEATH
1. Hospital: (Inpatient [ ]   ER / Outpatient [ ]   DOA [ ])   2. Nursing Home [ ]   3. Home [ ]
4. Other (Specify) [ ]

FACILITY NAME:
(If not an institution, give street name and number) ....

USUAL RESIDENTIAL ADDRESS OF DECEASED (Where someone lived on most days)

Street name and number
Name of Plot, Farm, etc.
Suburb / Village
Town / City
Province / Country
Postal Code

Magisterial district
Census enumerator area

DECEASED'S EDUCATION (Specify [✓] only highest class completed / achieved)

None	Gr1	Gr2	Gr3	Gr4	Gr5	Gr6	Gr7	Gr8 Form 1	Gr9 Form 2	Gr10 Form 3 NTC1	Gr11 Form 4 NTC2	Gr12 Form 5 NTC3	Univ Tech	CODE

USUAL OCCUPATION OF DECEASED
(give type of work done during most of working life. *Do not use "retired".*

TYPE OF BUSINESS / INDUSTRY (e.g. Mining, Farming etc.)
Refer to instructions.

....

Was the deceased a smoker* five years ago?   ([✓])   Yes [ ]   No [ ]   Do not know [ ]   Not applicable (minor) [ ]

G MEDICAL CERTIFICATE OF CAUSE OF DEATH

PART 1 Enter the disease, injuries or complications that caused the death. Do not enter the mode of dying, such as cardiac or respiratory arrest, shock or heart failure. **List only one cause on each line.**

Approximate interval between onset and Death (Days / Months / Years)

FOR OFFICE USE ONLY
ICD-10

IMMEDIATE CAUSE (Final disease or condition resulting in death)
(a)..................................
Due to (or a consequence of)

Sequentially list conditions, if any, leading to immediate cause.
(b)..................................
Due to (or a consequence of)

Enter UNDERLYING CAUSE last (Disease or injury that initiated events resulting in death)
(c)..................................
Due to (or a consequence of)

(d)..................................
Due to (or a consequence of)

PART 2 Other significant conditions contributing to death but not resulting in the underlying cause given in **Part 1** ....

If a **female**, was she pregnant 42 days prior to death? ([✓])   Yes [ ]   No [ ]

If **stillborn**, please write mass in grams [ ][ ][ ][ ]

Do you consider the deceased to be: African [ ]   White [ ]   Indian [ ]   Coloured [ ]   Other [ ] (Specify) ....

Method of ascertainment of cause of death:

1. Autopsy [ ]   2. Opinion of attending medical practitioner [ ]   2. Opinion of attending medical practitioner on duty [ ]

4. Opinion of registered professional nurse [ ]   5. Interview of family member [ ]

6. Other [ ] (Specify) ....

* Someone who smokes tobacco on most days

Supplied by LITHOTECH SP Tel.: (012) 327-3239

Figure 68.2 Page 2 of the notification/register of death/stillbirth

69 How to appear in court as a state witness

SARIE OOSTHUIZEN

In order for you to give evidence in court in an honest and confident manner, you need to follow this procedure:

- Prepare in advance. Study all the relevant records and any forms that you have completed, particularly the J88, which will be submitted as evidence.
- Do research and obtain the necessary knowledge of the anatomy, the injuries or the diseases in the case.
- Follow the correct dress code for appearing in court. If uncertain, err on the side of formality.
- Give honest testimony – do not guess.
- Ensure that the tone of your voice and your body language are confident, professional, polite and impartial.
- Speak slowly and give time for court translation and documentation during your testimony.
- Ask for the question to be rephrased if you are unsure of what was asked.
- Ask for a recess to obtain an expert's opinion, if necessary.
- Leave the court after your testimony, and do not liaise with the defence or the prosecution.

Administration

70 How to fill in a sick leave certificate

JULIE DIETERICH

A sick leave certificate is an important document and it should always be factually correct. For example, if you are giving your patient a certificate without having examined him, mention this specifically in the certificate by writing "as reported to me" or "according to information given to me". You can use reasonable medical grounds as the basis for determining the period of sick leave, that is the illness, the patient's overall condition and the type of work he does (Teichler 1995).

If your patient takes time, or a single day, off work to visit you, give him a **certificate of attendance** for that day only. You would give him a **sick leave certificate** to *recommend* that he take a longer period off work in order to recover sufficiently from illness. However, the company or institution for which the patient works usually determines the period he may take as sick leave. It is the employer's right to grant or withhold sick leave, based on the Basic Conditions of Employment Act (BCEA) of 1997.

The certificate

We will now discuss the various parts of the certificate.

Particulars of the doctor

Your name, address and qualifications should be written legibly or printed on the certificate, and you should sign it (HPCSA 2004).

Particulars of the patient

Your patient's name and some means of identification, such as his employee number or medical file number, must appear on the certificate (HPCSA 2004).

Diagnosis and confidentiality

Do not disclose the nature of your patient's problem without informing and obtaining consent from him. If he does not give consent then you should use terminology such as "illness" or "follow-up visit".

If the employer wishes to confirm the necessity and duration of the sick leave, he may ask the in-house doctor, if one is available, to contact you. Maintain confidentiality as to the nature of your patient's illness or injury between yourself and that doctor, and give *only* the need for the sick leave to the employer. Alternatively, the employer may seek a second opinion from another doctor, in which case confidentiality is again maintained and the employer is responsible for paying the other doctor.

Further comment

According to the HPCSA (2004), you must

- delete and initial any unnecessary or irrelevant information on a printed form
- initial all corrections
- give the date and time of the examination
- give the date of writing the certificate – occasionally you may need to complete the certificate some time after having seen the patient, on request of your patient or his employer
- state the exact period of recommended sick leave, but beware of filling in the back-to-work date according to the patient's work/shift/leave programme when he does not need that much sick leave
- indicate whether the patient is totally indisposed for work or whether he can perform light duties, if available
- provide a sick leave certificate if the patient is absent more than two consecutive days, or more than twice in an eight-week period
- prevent fraud by keeping certificate pads or books safely
- *take care* when noting the date; writing the day after the month makes it more difficult to fraudulently change the date (this is however not an HPCSA requirement)
- report anyone that you suspect of fraud to the police or other relevant authorities
- note that should an employer suspect you of fraud, he should contact you, and may contact the HPCSA or the South African Medical Association.

71 How to assess a patient requesting a disability grant

HELEN SAMMONS

Introduction

Today, people with all degrees of impairment are finding it increasingly difficult to compete in the open labour market despite the Employment Equity Act 55 of 1998, and the Government Gazette Numbers 23702 and 23718. In this chapter, we explore why certain information is required in order for you to make a decision regarding your patient's work potential with regard to the completion of the application form. You can also apply this process to the completion of any other medical form pertaining to work potential.

Administrative requirements

When a patient applies for a disability grant, the following administrative criteria need to be met. The applicant must

- be a South African citizen
- be resident in South Africa
- be 18 years old or older (Social Assistance Act 1992)
- reside in the area where he is applying for the grant
- comply with the means test – should he qualify for the grant, the amount payable is according to a sliding scale of income that he or his partner receives from another source
- submit a recent, that is less than one month old, medical report that was completed by a medical officer who is in the service of the state
- submit the following supporting documentation:
  - his or his partner's ID
  - marriage certificate, divorce order or affidavit of estrangement
  - the salary slip of the partner, proof of fixed deposits, bank statements for the last three months, and proof of financial assistance
  - his unemployment card or affidavit of unemployment

  - proof of accommodation, rent or municipal valuation certificate.

Medical evaluation and completion of the disability grant form

Consider the form as a motivational letter. Those involved in processing the form do not see the patient, thus you need to clearly and legibly state on the form the classification and the reasoning towards the decision.

The following actions and information are required for you to make a decision regarding your patient's work potential:

- As the patient grows **older**, his employment opportunities and ability to be trained for alternative occupations generally decline. A **young** patient with aptitude can be considered for completion of school studies or further training.

- A patient with a **qualification** below Grade 9, who is unsuitable for a clerical-type occupation, is assessed for work as a manual labourer. Someone who has suffered a cortical insult may not function on a level equivalent to pre-morbid functioning.

- An **occupational history** reveals the nature of the patient's work experience, skills acquired, and the quality and quantity of his past work record. Reasons for the termination of service may reflect his motivation to work and work habits. Work may have been the precipitator of the illness or injury, and can lead to psychological and/or financial implications on future work placement. Returning to work post-injury can highlight the impact of the impairment on his participation in the work environment.

- Once the patient has indicated the reasons why he cannot participate in the open labour market, his further history – **present complaints and disablements** – supports these complaints and symptom complexes:

– In order to be able to work he must be functionally independent and complete self-care in a reasonable time period. He must have adequate mobility in order to make use of his own or public transport, safely and timeously in peak traffic conditions. Whether he has sedentary or manual work, he must be able to manoeuvre himself in the work environment, for example visit various departments, attend to basic hygiene needs and deal with barriers that may be found in the workplace such as stairs, uneven terrain and obstacles.

– His ability to participate in domestic, gardening and community activities such as shopping gives an indication of his endurance in physical tasks and cognitive ability.

– Chronic illness and financial consequences following a disabling condition can depress the patient, limit his optimal functioning and influence his behaviour when presenting for a disability assessment. If a patient who is still in employment seeks boarding and presents you with a disability grant form, do not immediately comply with his request, as the financial benefits for him can be disappointing. First consider all the treatment and alternative funding options – for example sick and ordinary leave, chronic leave benefits, unemployment insurance, insurance funds, etc. – and communicate with his employer until his condition is stabilised or you can determine a realistic prognosis.

• You need to consider all **diagnoses**, indicating the length, severity and impact of the combination of impairments.

• Your consistent findings on examination, that is the **details of disablement**, objectively verify what has been reported in history taking. As the patient may be seeking secondary gain, such as financial benefits, your casual observation, for example observing the patient in the waiting room, on entering the examination area, while undressing and dressing, adds value to the examination. Functional information may be more valuable than rigid examination. For example, observe the range of movement of his joints or level of dyspnoea during dressing and undressing, as well as his ability to walk heel-to-toe, turn and crouch. Side-room and special investigations, such as intelligence questionnaires, mini mental-state examination, peak flow, blood levels, etc., are required only if this will change the outcome and management of the patient.

• The patient's **treatment and adherence** needs to be optimal. Ascertain if adherence is possible. Subnormal intellectual or cognitive functioning, poor support infrastructure, side-effects from medication, insulin resistance in attempting to lose weight may well be justifiable reasons for suboptimal adherence.

• The patient will not receive a grant if he is practising **substance abuse**. This is not tolerated, but it needs investigation and referral as appropriate.

• Note any **lack of motivation** to work or comply with treatment if there is no underlying pathological cause.

• A **temporary disability** could be granted until the patient's rehabilitation is complete and the final outcome is evident. Longstanding impairments may need re-prescription, or reconsideration of orthoses and devices that were discarded during the adult patient's growth spurts and teenage years.

• Younger patients who have had **limited access** to the open labour market owing to medical reasons may benefit from work rehabilitation.

• If the patient is unfit for open labour, you need to indicate if productive activity would be of benefit, such as a protected workshop, an activity group, home activity, community involvement or structured domestic environment. An occupational therapist, community sister or the family can organise this. If he is capable of limited/protected work in the open labour market, he may receive remuneration for this and a disability grant *as well*, according to the means test. This is encouraged, especially in areas where there are no protected workshops.

• Under the Social Assistance Act of 1992, the patient can receive assistance if he is unable to participate in employment and thus is unable to provide adequately for his maintenance.

To compete in the open labour market, the person needs to meet the following requirements:

• The person needs to have the endurance and cardiovascular stamina to perform for a minimum of eight hours per day and five days a week, and with at least 80% productivity. There is an inverse relationship between the ability to sustain a repetitive task and the percentage of maximum strength demanded. Because the relationship is exponential, the total work that can be performed is greater at lower levels of power (Demeter, Anderson & Smith 1996). Manual employment requires physical strength, good balance (static and dynamic), the ability to lift and carry, push or pull weights, to climb and to have a range of flexibility. A work assessment unit can test all this.

• The person needs good bilateral hand function to do manual labour and to achieve adequate productivity in clerical tasks.

- He must be able to utilise public or private transport.

- He must be able to tolerate the stress of a normal working environment.

- Light duty is not a component of the open labour market. Occasionally, a person who becomes ill or injured while in employment may be accommodated back into the workforce in a protected capacity, as stated in the Employment Equity Act of 1998.

- In order to run a viable home industry, he must be able to obtain raw materials, manufacture a sellable product, market the product, access the selling market and have business skills – a minimum of Grade 10 is required.

- The medical and work prognosis may differ, for example:

  - A traumatic amputation has a good medical prognosis if the skin graft over the stump has healed, but it may have a poor work prognosis as the graft is over the weight-bearing area of the prosthesis and will continuously break down if the patient has to wear the prosthesis for a normal working day, even in sedentary work.

  - An above-knee amputee is almost never capable of performing labour work. This patient may also be unsuitable for clerical work owing to experience, educational level and age limiting training opportunities.

In light of all the above information, you need to decide and clearly indicate whether the patient

- qualifies for a disability grant

- does not qualify owing to lack of functional limitation. If this is your decision, complete the form stating this so that your opinion is recorded in the patient's file and can be compared to subsequent forms submitted to the Department of Social Services.

- qualifies for a temporary period grant, such as six or twelve months, or a permanent period grant. A permanent disability will be medically reviewed after five years.

- requires further investigation, such as work evaluation, or referral, for example to gain a specialist's opinion, in order for you to reach a decision. You can refer a patient who presents with justifiable symptoms but lacks sufficient evidence to an occupational therapist, preferably at a work assessment unit. Do not refer a patient for work evaluation if you require collateral information such as frequency of epilepsy or angina episodes. The patient must be fully medically and surgically

treated and rehabilitated before being referred for work evaluation. You can evaluate concomitant factors such as intellectual or cognitive function. If a work evaluation report is available, refer to this and include a copy of it with your completed form. A disability grant may be recommended in the interim if the patient suffers sufficient functional limitation, or withheld, with a review date, once the specialist's opinion has been received.

Once you have made your decision, you need to follow this procedure to adequately complete the form:

- Your patient must be present at the time you complete the form and should be identified by means of an ID document. Record your patient's **name** and **ID number** as they stand on the ID document.

- The **address** confirms that he resides in the catchment area.

- Note the **file number** of the patient at your facility. Together with a copy of the completed form in the patient's file, this hastens completion of subsequent forms and reports.

- Indicate if the grant should be administered by someone else in the case, for example, of intellectual impairment, recent substance rehabilitation or psychiatric illness. Be attentive to the beneficiary of an administered grant who is not deriving the benefit.

- Against the list of diagnoses, complete the following relevant information:

  - An **epileptic** patient is considered unfit for work in the open labour market if he has more than three seizures per month, considering all the above information. He and you need to consider transport to work, the nature of work to be performed, infrastructure at work, intellectual functioning, role of substance use, therapeutic levels of medication, and therapeutic combinations and options.

  - An **effort tolerance level** equal to or worse than grade 2b denies the patient the ability to work in the open labour market. (This means the patient is unable to walk at a normal pace on level ground for more than 500 m, although he can walk 100 m.) The patient should attempt to cease smoking, but this or the addition of medication will not necessarily improve function if there is structural damage present.

  - A patient with **pulmonary tuberculosis (PTB)** may receive a grant for six months if he is functionally limited.

  - An **HIV-positive** patient can be considered for a grant when he shows signs of complications and limitation of functional endurance, usually in stages III and IV.

- Being variable, **asthma** in a patient requires a history of functional ability, number and severity of acute episodes/admissions, and steroid dependency.

- A patient with **chronic cardiovascular disease** may appear well controlled on examination but lack the endurance required for employment in the open labour market.

- A patient who has recovered good muscle strength following a **cerebrovascular accident** (including head injuries) may have limited impairment of cognition, tone, sensation, coordination or balance on examination, but severe limitation of function.

- If you are unsure of the prognosis, you should obtain help in completing the form from the patient's specialist if he has **malignancies** or a **psychiatric condition**.

- Evaluate whether a **visually impaired** patient can deliver a satisfactory quality of work. Correct refractive errors. A patient awaiting cataract surgery can receive a grant until the surgery is performed. A patient with partial or total blindness with no education or skill competencies should be considered for a permanent grant.

- If a patient lacks effective **communication skills** with people other than family members, consideration is given for a grant. Consider communication skills and a hearing aid. Look at the "whole patient" – language barriers are not a reason for disability.

- A patient with an **IQ below 70** qualifies for disability. This is equivalent to 10 years of age and younger. Consider the highest grade that the patient has passed, as well as his ability to interact socially and communicate; tendency to get lost; ability to do errands, work with money, remember a grocery list; quality of self-care and domestic tasks; quality of history; and his ability to function without supervision.

- A **unilateral amputee** with a well-fitting prosthesis is able to do manual labour provided that there are no systemic, stump or prosthetic complications. An **above-knee amputee** generally cannot compete as a labourer, but he can do clerical work if good prosthetic fit allows him to wear the prosthesis for a full working day, including travelling time.

• Indicate if the patient is receiving any **treatment** – medical, physical or other – that may influence the outcome. Note his response to the treatment as well as the work prognosis.

• Indicate whether the patient is practising **substance abuse or use**.

It might seem time consuming to complete the disability grant form, especially if this is the only reason that the patient came to you and has minimal medical problems. But the process often reveals a host of unresolved problems. If you remain objective in the assessment of your patient and at the same time contribute to his well-being through holistic management, the presentation of the disability grant form can achieve a satisfactory outcome for your patient and yourself.

72 How to notify a medical condition

NEIL CAMERON

Duty of notification

As a health professional who is certified competent to diagnose disease, you are required by law to report certain conditions to the local health department. Do not hesitate to notify – it is better to over-notify than to under-notify.

Notification is important, even if the system is not perfect. It helps the health department to identify certain conditions of public health importance for these reasons:

- Individuals or groups affected by the condition can be followed up and treated.
- An early warning of an outbreak can help to control the spread.
- Patterns and trends by person, time and place can be monitored to
  - inform planning and resource allocation
  - identify possible risk factors.

You should not wait for laboratory confirmation, if this means unduly delaying the necessary action. For example, you should bring to the attention of those responsible to take action profuse watery stools and severe dehydration or someone with fever and a bleeding tendency or a farmer with a severe headache, fever and a tick bite. Remember, too, that there is a margin of error in any laboratory result. For example, response to a major cholera epidemic may be delayed because the laboratory reagents have expired and give incorrect results.

Procedure

You need to find out the identity of the person responsible in the province for outbreak response. If you maintain periodic, informal, friendly contact with that person it will be easier for you to reach him or her in an emergency. Keep the contact details up to date.

There is a form that you need to fill in to notify a medical condition, namely the GW17/5 form. Fig-ure 72.1 is an example of this form. You can obtain books of the form from your local health department. Make sure that you have them available in your consulting area. Your support staff can help you by completing the non-diagnostic details. You can find more useful information about this form at the Department of Health's website: www.doh.gov.za (search for the document "The notification system in a nutshell").

Notifiable conditions in South Africa

Listed alphabetically, the following are the notifiable conditions in this country. The conditions listed in bold usually require rapid action from the local health authority – you should urgently notify them telephonically.

- **Acute flaccid paralysis (AFP)**
- Acute rheumatic fever
- **Anthrax**
- Brucellosis
- **Cholera**
- Congenital syphilis
- Diphtheria
- **Food poisoning** (involving four or more people)
- Haemophilus influenza type b (Hib)
- **Haemorrhagic fevers of Africa**, namely Congo fever, dengue fever, Ebola fever, Lassa fever, Marburg fever, Rift Valley fever
- Lead poisoning
- **Legionellosis**
- Leprosy
- Malaria
- **Measles**
- **Meningococcal infections**
- Paratyphoid fever
- Plague
- Poisoning from any agricultural or stock remedies
- Poliomyelitis
- Rabies (specify as human case or contact)

G.P.-S. 02/02

GW 17/5 (81/336007)

Notification of medical condition

[Sections 32, 47 (i) (a) and 47 (i) (b) of Act No. 63 1977]
Department of Health

Please print ● Where appropriate, mark the correct box with a tick (✓) ● Complete in duplicate. Original to be sent to local authority where patient was diagnosed: copy to remain in book.

Aanmelding van mediese toestand

[Artikels 32, 47 (i) (a) en 47 (i) (b) van Wet No. 63 van 1977]
Departement van Gesondheid

Gebruik asseblief drukskrif ● Waar toepaslik, merk die korrekte blok (✓) ● Voltooi in duplikaat. Die oorspronklike word gestuur aan die plaaslike owerheid waar die pasiënt gediagnoseer is: die afskrif bly in die boek.

DETAILS OF PATIENT·							BESONDERHEDE VAN PASIËNT
Surname				Van	First names		Voornaam
Age	Ouderdom	Gender	Male ☐ Manlik / Female ☐ Vroulik	Geslag	Ethnic group	Asian ☐ Asiër / Coloured ☐ Kleurling / Black ☐ Swart / White ☐ Blank	Etniese groep

Residential address .... Woonadres

If resident on a farm, state farmer's name as well as name and number of farm. In other rural areas, give name of chief, induna, village, nearest hill or river, nearest school or clinic .... Indien woonagtig op 'n plaas, noem die boer se naam sowel as die naam en nommer van die plaas. In ander landelike gebiede, gee die naam van die stamkaptein, induna, dorp, naaste heuwel of rivier, naaste skool of kliniek

District .... Distrik

Tel. No. .... Tel. No.

Name and address of employer, school, crèche or other institution where patient spends much of the day .... Naam en adres van werkgewer, skool, crèche of ander instelling waar die pasiënt 'n groot gedeelte van die dag is

Tel. No. .... Tel. No.

DETAILS OF MEDICAL CONDITION		BESONDERHEDE VAN MEDIESE TOESTAND
Medical condition		Mediese toestand
Date of onset	Aanvangsdatum Date of death (if applicable)	Sterftedatum (indien van toepassing)
Possible place of infection		Moontlike plek van infeksie
Diagnosis was based on	Clinical history and examination only ☐ Net kliniese geskiedenis en ondersoek / Clinical and other investigations ☐ Kliniese en ander ondersoeke	Diagnose is gebaseer op

RESULTS OF INVESTIGATIONS				ONDERSOEKRESULTATE
Investigation (excluding TB sputum) ↓	Ondersoek (TB sputum uitgesluit)	Results	↓	Resultate
				Awaiting results ☐ Wag vir resultate
				Awaiting results ☐ Wag vir resultate
				Awaiting results ☐ Wag vir resultate
If TB, give sputum results →	Microscopy	Positive ☐ Positief / Negative ☐ Negatief / Awaiting results ☐ Wag vir resultate	Mikroskopie Culture	Positive ☐ Positief / Negative ☐ Negatief / Awaiting results ☐ Wag vir resultate Kultuur ← Indien TB, gee sputum resultate

REFERRED TO			VERWYS NA
Name of hospital or clinic			Naam van hospitaal of kliniek
Patient Registration No.	Pasiënt Registrasie No.	Date of administration	Datum van opname

NOTIFIED BY			AANGEMELD DEUR
Name			Naam
Address	Adres	Profession	Medical practitioner ☐ Geneesheer / Nurse ☐ Verpleegster / Other ☐ Ander	Beroep
		Signature	Handtekening
Tel. No. .... Tel. No.		Date	Datum

Local authority: If a copy of this notification is to be sent to another local authority, please confirm whether you will include this notification in your weekly summaries (GW 17/3 or 17/4).

Yes ☐ Ja
No. ☐ Nee

Plaaslike owerheid: Indien 'n afskrif van hierdie aanmelding aan 'n ander plaaslike owerheid gestuur word, bevestig asseblief of hierdie aanmelding by weeklikse opsomming (GW 17/3 of 17/4) ingesluit gaan word.

REPLY BY LOCAL AUTHORITY			ANTWOORD DEUR PLAASLIKE OWERHEID
Reply to referring doctor/nurse with brief report of further findings and management.			Antwoord aan verwysende dokter/verpleegster oor verdere bevindinge en hantering.
Signature	Handtekening Date	Datum Tel. No.	Tel. No.

Figure 72.1 The notification of a medical condition form

- **Smallpox** and any smallpox-like disease, excluding chickenpox
- Tetanus
- Tetanus neonatorum
- Trachoma
- Tuberculosis:
  - pulmonary and other forms, except cases diagnosed solely on the basis of clinical signs and symptoms
  - in the case of any child younger than five years with a significant reaction following tuberculin testing
- Typhoid fever
- Typhus fever, namely epidemic louse-borne typhus fever, endemic flea-borne typhus fever
- Viral hepatitis A, B, non-A, non-B and undifferentiated
- Whooping cough
- **Yellow fever**

Also notify any other possible condition, which could have serious public heath consequences (**such as SARS or any case with unusual features**, which could suggest accidental or deliberate release of a harmful biological or other agent).

In order for the situation to be monitored, you should then fill in the GW17/5 form and send it to the local health department. Make sure that your contact details are correct.

Acute flaccid paralysis (AFP) and suspected measles

Globally, mass immunisation campaigns are periodically undertaken to eradicate polio and, eventually, measles. It is extremely important that you actively monitor any suspected outbreaks of these diseases. In such a situation, Department of Health staff should fill in specific forms to notify.

■ AFP

A case of AFP is defined as a child under 15 years with sudden, floppy weakness of a limb that is not due to trauma, but includes Guillain-Barré syndrome. In South Africa, in order for us to achieve the international polio eradication surveillance targets, we need to identify – and certify as not due to polio – 300 such cases each year.

All cases of AFP *must* be reported, preferably telephonically. Two stool specimens 24 hours apart should be sent for virus isolation, refrigerated or on ice to prevent bacterial overgrowth, to the National Institute for Communicable Diseases (NICD) via the National Health Laboratory Services (NHLS). This is to ensure that the wild virus is eradicated and that the southern Africa region as a whole can be declared polio free.

■ MEASLES

A suspected case of measles is defined in any person with a maculopapular rash, fever and one of the three "Cs", namely conjunctivitis, coryza or cough. As a result of the success of mass immunisation campaigns, most cases of suspected measles are now actually due to other viral infections such as rubella. The cases of measles that *do* occur tend to be in adults or infants who as yet have not been immunised.

You should take blood from any patient with suspected measles, and a urine sample for viral isolation in a sterile container; keep it in the fridge and send it to the local NHLS within 48 hours.

All laboratory investigations for measles and polio are done in the NICD laboratory in Johannesburg. It is accredited by the WHO to confirm any cases.

If you do not know whom to contact, contact the hospital infection control nurse, the provincial Immunisation and Communicable Disease Control person or the local NHLS for details of the specimens and procedures. It is important that you get to know the people involved in the process before there is a crisis.

Filling in of the notification form may be a problem. The form might not be available, you may feel you do not have the time, you may be frustrated with the lack of feedback that you experienced and/or you may feel that your action may make no difference.

Persevere. Even in a busy practice, with little extra effort you can make sure that the GW17/5 is available in your consulting room or clinic, you can ensure that the relevant patient's demographic details are filled in accurately and you can enter the diagnosis made on proper clinical grounds or with laboratory confirmation. This *will* make a difference.

Notification is about establishing communication. Taking an interest in the notifiable conditions in your area will help you identify infectious diseases earlier and encourage those who compile information to see it as more than simply a bureaucratic exercise. Moreover, in a possible epidemic situation, your ability to initiate effective action will be greatly increased.

Use these telephone numbers in the case of an outbreak:

- National Institute for Communicable Diseases: (011) 386 6000 or the 24-hour hotline: 082 883 9920

Go to these websites for information on global communicable disease outbreaks:

- www.who.int/csr/don/en/
- www.cdc.gov
- www.promedmail.org

HIV and AIDS

Unfortunately, it is unlikely that mandatory notification can prevent the spread of HIV or help people suffering from AIDS. You should suggest that your patients undergo voluntary counselling and testing, as well as think about voluntary partner notification. In a social climate that encourages care and support for people living with AIDS, this type of action is far more likely to control the spread than is mandatory notification, which comes with the risk of increasing the fear and the stigma that those suffering from the disease experience.

There are large, well-conducted HIV surveys funded by the Department of Health and the Human Sciences Research Council (HSRC), which give more than adequate estimates of the burden of HIV disease in South Africa.

It is important that you note that there are certain occupational health conditions that should also be notified (see Chapter 75).

73 How to refer a patient

DEREK HELLENBERG

In South Africa, especially in the public sector, the quality of communication between levels of health care is poor for many reasons. As a family physician, you have a "gatekeeper" role to play in terms of referring a patient appropriately to higher levels of care and with adequate information to guide the receiving doctor.

Referral in an emergency

Where at all possible, try to speak to the receiving medical officer (MO) when you refer a patient who requires emergency intervention. This may

- help your patient to avoid long waiting times in a busy emergency unit
- assist in directing him to the appropriate specialty in secondary and tertiary hospitals.

To the MO, you need to give the following information telephonically:

- Your patient's name, age and gender
- Your working diagnosis and the reason for your belief that this patient needs to be seen urgently
- The emergency treatment that you have given thus far

Ask the MO if there is anything else he or she would like you to do before dispatching the patient. Tell your patient the name of the receiving MO and where to locate him or her.

In addition to the information that you provide telephonically, you need to submit a referral letter. The letter should contain the following information:

- Demographic data of the patient and the time at which you assessed him
- The name of the doctor you spoke to at the receiving hospital, the time at which the conversation took place, and the location at which you arranged for the patient to be seen
- The primary problem or working diagnosis, and your reason for referral

- Your subjective and objective clinical findings, and results of any side-room tests or special investigations that were done
- Any background information available regarding the patient's past medical history, medications and allergies. In some cases, information regarding the patient's family and work context may also be relevant.
- The treatment you have given up to the point of transfer
- Your instructions to the ambulance personnel
- Your description to the patient about what to expect when he is in hospital in terms of additional tests and treatment
- The contact details of a close relative of the patient, if he is unconscious

It is important that you sign the referral letter and put it in an envelope. Address the envelope clearly and legibly to the receiving MO. Include the following, which you can print in capital letters: **Urgent – for attention Doctor (insert name) as discussed telephonically**.

Referral to an outpatient department

In this situation, you should include the following information in your referral letter:

- The date of the appointment, and the names of the outpatient department and hospital
- Your patient's name, gender and age
- The primary problem or working diagnosis, and your reason for referral. Your expectations of the outpatient department should be clear, as follows:
  - Assess the patient and refer him back for further management. (This would be one option out of the four given here where essentially you ask for a second opinion but are willing to continue managing the problem, as opposed to a referral where you expect to have no further

involvement in the management of the problem.)

- Perform a special investigation, such as a gastroscopy.
- Admit and investigate him.
- Take over all further management.

• The presenting complaints, your examination findings, results of any side-room tests and special investigations that were done, as well as the treatment you have provided to date

• Background information regarding previous medical history, medications and allergies, and any other relevant individual and contextual factors

• Your description to the patient about what to expect when he is in hospital in terms of additional tests and treatment

• Your name and qualifications, and all details of your practice

Sign the letter and put it in an envelope. Clearly and legibly address the envelope to the outpatient department and hospital. Also indicate the time and date of the patient's appointment there.

Occupational
medicine

74 How to assess fitness for driving at work

SHAHIEDA ADAMS

Health standards for drivers are important because they impact on public health. In a country like South Africa, where road accidents account for a large percentage of overall mortality, it is necessary to ensure that as a family practitioner involved in examining vehicle drivers you are aware of the standards for certifying vehicle driver fitness, and that you comply with such standards.

Legal requirements

Various statutes are relevant to work fitness and disability in South Africa. The most important of these is the Road Traffic Act (RTA) 93 of 1996, which specifically outlines the broad categories of health conditions that disqualify applicants from driving. Other statutes focus more generally on fitness standards and the management of ill health and disability in the workplace.

Specific categories of workers, such as chemical and mine workers, may have unique requirements for fitness, depending on the occupational risk exposure associated with their occupations. These requirements are outlined in the Hazardous Substances Act 15 of 1973 and the Mine Health and Safety Act 29 of 1996 respectively.

We will now explore the Road Traffic Act in greater detail.

Road Traffic Act 93 of 1996 Chapter IV Sections 15 and 16

■ SECTION 15

The relevant part of this section reads as follows:

15(1) A person shall be disqualified from obtaining or holding a learner's or driving licence if he or she is suffering from one of the following disabilities:

   (i) uncontrolled epilepsy;

  (ii) sudden attacks of disabling giddiness or fainting due to hypertension or any other cause;

  (iii) any form of mental illness to such an extent that it is necessary that he or she be detained, supervised, controlled and treated as a patient in terms of the Mental Health Act, 1973 (Act No.18 of 1973);*

  (iv) any condition causing muscular inco-ordination;

  (v) uncontrolled diabetes mellitus;

  (vi) defective vision ascertained in accordance with prescribed standards;

  (vii) any other disease or physical defect which is likely to render him or her incapable of effectively driving and controlling a motor vehicle of the class to which such licence relates without endangering the safety of the public, provided that deafness shall not of itself be deemed to be such a defect.

  (viii) is addicted to the use of any drug having a narcotic effect or the excessive use of intoxicating liquor.

  (ix) in such other circumstances as may be prescribed, either generally or in respect of a particular class of learner's or driving licence.

■ SECTION 16

This section gives a legal responsibility to the holder of a driving licence to disclose any disqualification on health grounds when applying for a new licence or if a new problem occurs, within 21 days, to the licensing authority.

Categories of drivers

In terms of the Road Traffic Act the employer is required to categorise all drivers according to the relative risks involved specific to the industry, and according to the requirements for the issuing of the professional driving permit (PRDP). Table 74.1 summarises this categorisation. Drivers responsible for transporting people and hazardous goods pose

* The new Mental Health Act 2002 does not alter these rules.

Table 74.1 Categories of driver in terms of the Road Traffic Act 93 of 1996

SASOM category	RTA categorisation
I	Category "D" (PRDP) authorises the driving of a motor vehicle carrying hazardous/dangerous goods Category "P" (PRDP) authorises the carrying of passengers, or passengers and goods
II	Category "G" (PRDP) authorises the driving of a motor vehicle carrying goods
III	Special vehicle drivers in control of specialised vehicles which are used for specific purposes where skill, method of operation and place of operation require attention, e.g. forklift truck operators, crane drivers, etc.
IV	Standard vehicle drivers operating light vehicles in standard transport in circumstances where no special requirements exist over and above the required licence and personal skills to operate the vehicle; this includes category "B" (PRDP), which authorises the driving of a breakdown vehicle

Source: SASOM Guideline No. 6, Medical requirements for fitness to drive, p. 5. SASOM 1999. Reproduced with permission from the South African Society of Occupational Medicine

the greatest potential risk to the public – it is imperative that they meet the minimum standards of fitness.

Health evaluation

The **goals** of health evaluation are as follows:

- To determine whether the driver meets the minimum fitness standards to enable him to perform his duties as a driver safely and effectively

- To determine whether the driving duties are impacting negatively on his health and make recommendations on how best to address this

- To ascertain whether the driver is suffering from any health condition which is likely to impact on his driving ability in the future, such as epilepsy or diabetes, or which may disqualify him from holding a licence in terms of the RTA

- To ascertain his continued fitness to drive following major illness and surgery which may cause impairment, affecting his ability to drive

Table 74.2 provides the recommended health evaluation interval schedule.

With regard to health evaluation action, it is important that the medical officer or occupational health practitioner has a clear understanding of the inherent requirements of the person's job which could impact on his driving ability. A full history must be taken and an examination needs to be performed on all new drivers to provide information for baseline measurements. An efficient record-keeping system is imperative to document baseline clinical status and the progression of disease.

In the absence of an established occupational health service, the person applying for a driving licence should consult his usual health practitioner for continuity of care and early detection of illness.

Table 74.3 gives the recommended health evaluation action protocol.

Declaring a vehicle driver fit/unfit for driving duties

A list of criteria has been developed by the South African Society of Occupational Medicine (SASOM) to assist you as the medical officer in deciding on endorsement or rejection of a driver on health grounds. You can make some decisions only after special investigations have been performed or a specialist opinion has been obtained. You are guided

Table 74.2 Health evaluation interval schedule

Type of health evaluation	RTA categorisation			
	I (D/P)	II (G)	III special	IV (B)
Pre-employment	Yes	Yes	Yes	Yes
PRDP (time interval in months)	24	24		24
Periodic (time interval in months)	12	12	12	On request
Return to work after significant ill health absence (longer than 10 days)	Yes	Yes	Yes	On request
Post-incident (evaluation immediately or soon after a significant health event)	Yes	Yes	Yes	Yes

Source: SASOM Guideline No. 6, Medical requirements for fitness to drive, p. 6. SASOM 1999. Reproduced with permission from the South African Society of Occupational Medicine

Table 74.3 Health evaluation action protocol

Type of health evaluation	Required or optional			
	Pre-employment	**Periodic/PRDP**	**Return to work**	**Post-incident**
Medical past history Current history	Required Required	Required	Required	Required
Occupational past history Current history	Required Required	Required	Required	Required
Physical examination	Required	Required	Required	Required
Sensory vision (and fields) Hearing	Required Required	Required Required	Optional Optional	Optional Optional
Special investigations	Required	Optional	Optional	Optional

Source: SASOM Guideline No. 6, Medical requirements for fitness to drive, SASOM; 1999. p. 6. Adapted with permission from the South African Society of Occupational Medicine

in this by your clinical experience, your understanding of the patient's illness, the nature of his workplace and the occupational requirements of his job, as well as the safety risk that he may pose.

Table 74.4 lists the minimum requirements for fitness to drive for some of the important and commonly encountered medical conditions. The SASOM Guideline (1999) and the Driver and Vehicle Licensing Booklet (2003) list the necessary fitness standards and provide clear management strategies for most conditions that could impair driving ability.

Epilepsy poses a particular problem with regard to the certification of drivers. The South African Society of Occupational Medicine (SASOM) (2004) has compiled an epilepsy guide to address this complex issue, part of which is quoted as follows:

(a) A person who has suffered an epileptic attack whilst awake must refrain from driving for one year from the date of the attack before a driving licence may be issued;

OR

(b) A person who has suffered an attack whilst asleep must also refrain from driving for one year from the date of the attack, unless the seizure was more than three years ago and there have been no attacks whilst awake since then.

AND

(c) The person makes all practical attempts to comply with advised treatment and follow up and the driving of a vehicle by such a person should not be likely to cause danger to the public.

For first-time applicants during the period of 10 years immediately preceding the date when the licence is granted, the applicant/licence holder should be:

1. free from any epileptic attack

AND

2. have not required medication to treat epilepsy

AND

3. not otherwise a source of danger whilst driving.

In addition the liability to seizures arising from a cause other than epilepsy is a prescribed disability. An individual suffering a solitary seizure must satisfy the examiner as to requirements for fitness to drive, but someone with a structural intracranial lesion who has an increased risk of seizures will not be able to drive vehicles until the epilepsy risk has fallen to 2% (no fits in preceding 10 years).

Guidance for withdrawal of anti-epileptic medication on specific medical advice: From a medico-legal point of view, your attention is drawn to the potential risk of further epileptic seizures, which may occur during this therapeutic procedure. If an epileptic seizure does occur, the law will not permit your patient to continue to hold a licence until the driver or applicant is able to satisfy the regulations in regard to epilepsy and driving. These currently require a period of one year free of any manifestation of epileptic seizure or attacks occurring whilst awake, but special consideration is given where sleep-only attacks have occurred. It is also important to remember that if medication is omitted, e.g. on admission to hospital for non-epileptic conditions, and epileptic seizures occur, then the person will be required to meet the epilepsy regulations.

Provoked seizures

For Groups I, II and III drivers with provoked seizures, apart from those caused or precipitated by alcohol or illicit drug misuse, can be dealt with

Table 74.4 Minimum requirements for fitness to drive

Condition	Group I, II or III	Group IV
Cerebrovascular disease and transient ischaemic attacks (TIAs) including stroke due to occlusive vascular disease, spontaneous intracerebral haemorrhage	Recommended refusal/revocation for at least 12 months following a stroke or TIA. Can be considered for licensing after this period if there is a full and complete recovery and there are no other significant risk factors. Licensing will also be subject to satisfactory medical reports including exercise ECG testing	At least one month off driving after the event. When clinical recovery is satisfactory, driving may be resumed. License is retained provided there is no significant residual disability. Should residual limb disability require a restriction to certain controls, this will need to be specified on the licence. A driver experiencing multiple TIAs over a short period of time may require three months' freedom of further attacks before resuming driving. Epileptic attacks occurring at the time of a stroke/TIA or in the ensuing 24 hours may be treated as provoked for licensing purposes in the absence of any previous seizure history or previous cerebral pathology. Seizures that occur at the time of a cortical venous infarct require six months off driving
Liability to sudden attacks of unprovoked or unprecipitated disabling giddiness and fainting, e.g. Meniere's disease, labyrinthine or other brain stem disorders	Recommended refusal or revocation if condition is disabling. If condition is stable, must be symptom free and completely controlled for at least one year before re-application	Cease driving on diagnosis. Driving will be permitted when satisfactory control of symptoms is achieved. Review one-, two- or three-year licence. If remains symptom free for four years, licence is restored until 70 years of age
Hypertension (BP > 140/90)	Disqualify from driving if resting BP consistently 180 mmHg systolic or more and/or 110 mmHg diastolic or more	Driving may continue unless treatment causes unacceptable side-effects
Syncope	Disqualify from driving following single or recurrent episodes. Unexplained syncope requires specialist evaluation to include: 1. Provocation testing 2. Investigation for arrhythmia 3. Neurological review, if appropriate. Re-licensing may be permitted three months after the event provided that the results are satisfactory	Driving must cease while symptoms persist, and may recommence once the cause is identified and symptoms are controlled
Myocardial infarction/ coronary artery bypass grafting	Driving must cease for at least four weeks. Re-licensing may be permitted provided that the exercise test requirements can be met and there is no other disqualifying condition	Driving may recommence after four weeks, provided there is no other disqualifying condition
Angina stable/unstable	Refusal or revocation with continuing symptoms (treated and/or untreated). Re-licensing may be permitted when free from angina for at least six weeks, provided that the exercise test requirements can be met and there is no other disqualifying condition	Driving must cease when symptoms occur at rest or at the wheel. Driving may recommence when satisfactory symptom control is achieved

Table 74.4 Continued

Condition	Group I, II or III	Group IV
Arrhythmia **NB:** Transient arrhythmias occurring during the acute phase only of a myocardial infarction or coronary artery bypass grafting (CABG) do not require assessment under this section	Disqualify from driving if the arrhythmia has caused or is likely to cause incapacity (including systemic embolism). Driving may be permitted when the arrhythmia is controlled for at least three months, provided that the LV ejection fraction is > 0.4, the exercise test requirements can be met and there is no other disqualifying condition	Driving must cease following incapacity due to an arrhythmia. Driving may be re-permitted when underlying cause has been identified and controlled for at least four weeks
Dilated cardiomyopathy	Disqualify from driving if symptomatic. Re-licensing may be permitted provided that there is no other disqualifying condition	Driving may continue provided there is no other disqualifying condition
Loss of consciousness in which investigations have not revealed a cause, i.e. there is an open-ended liability for recurrence, and the cause is unexplained	Recommended refusal or revocation. After five years freedom from such episodes, specialist assessment may be undertaken to decide when driving may restart	With a single episode at least one year off driving with freedom from such attacks during this period and subject to ongoing regular medical review
Serious head injury Acute intracerebral haematoma requiring surgery or compound depressed fracture or dural tear with more than 24 hours post-traumatic amnesia	Recommended refusal or revocation. Specialist assessment to determine if and when driving may restart, depending on significant reduction of prospective epilepsy risk, and to ensure driving performance is not likely to be impaired	Six to twelve months off driving where consciousness was lost, but with none of the complications specified and if clinical recovery is full and complete, driving may resume
Insulin-dependent diabetes mellitus	Disqualify new applicants on insulin. Existing drivers to be assessed individually and control to be defined and regularly checked. Drivers on insulin must be subjected to individual annual specialist assessment. Regulation changes in April 2001 allow for exceptional cases to apply for or retain their entitlement to drive class C1 vehicles (3 500–7 500 kg lorries) subject to annual medical examination	Must demonstrate satisfactory control, recognise warning symptoms of hypoglycaemia and meet required visual standards. One-, two- or three-year licence
Temporary insulin treatment, e.g. gestational diabetes, post-myocardial infarction, participants in oral/ inhaled insulin trials	May retain licence but should stop driving if poor diabetic control. Review again six weeks after delivery, if remains on insulin	May retain licence but should stop driving if experiencing disabling hypoglycaemia. Should be reviewed after six weeks
Diabetes mellitus managed by diet and tablets or diet alone	Drivers will be licensed subject to regular medical review, until 70 years old, unless they develop relevant disabilities, e.g. eye problems affecting visual acuity or visual fields, in which case either refusal or revocation or short-period licence is recommended. If becomes insulin treated then refusal or revocation is recommended	Subject to satisfactory medical inquiries, will be able to retain licence, unless they develop relevant disabilities, e.g. diabetic eye problems affecting visual acuity or visual field or if insulin required

Table 74.4 Continued

Condition	Group I, II or III	Group IV
Anxiety or depression without significant memory or concentration problems, agitation, behavioural disturbance or suicidal thoughts	Minor, short-lived illnesses need not be notified	Need not be notified and driving may continue
Anxiety or depression with significant memory or concentration problems, agitation, behavioural disturbances or suicidal thoughts	Driving should cease pending the outcome of medical inquiry/psychiatric evaluation. A period of stability depending upon the circumstances will be required before driving can be resumed. Particularly dangerous are those who may attempt suicide at the wheel **NB:** It is the illness rather than the medication which is of prime importance	Driving may be permitted when well and stable for six months. Medication must not cause side-effects that would interfere with alertness or concentration. Driving is usually permitted if anxiety or depression is longstanding but maintained symptom free on doses of psychotropic medication that do not impair performance
Alcohol misuse, i.e. a state which because of consumption of alcohol, causes disturbance of behaviour, related disease or other consequences, likely to cause the patient, his family or society harm now or in the future and which may or may not be associated with dependency	Persistent alcohol misuse, confirmed by medical inquiry and/or by evidence of otherwise unexplained abnormal blood markers, will lead to revocation or refusal of a vocational licence for at least one year, during which time abstinence or controlled drinking should be attained with normalisation of blood parameters	Persistent alcohol misuse, confirmed by medical inquiry and/or by evidence of otherwise unexplained abnormal blood markers, requires licence revocation or refusal for a minimum six-month period, during which time controlled drinking or abstinence should be attained with normalisation of blood parameters
Alcohol dependency	Licensing will not be granted where there is a history of alcohol dependency within the past three years	Indicators may include a history of detoxification and/or alcohol-related fits. Alcohol dependency, confirmed by medical inquiry, requires a recommended one-year period of revocation or refusal of the driving licence. During this, abstinence or controlled drinking only should be attained, with normalisation of blood parameters, if relevant
Licence restoration in alcohol misuse	On re-application, independent medical examination with satisfactory blood results and medical reports from own doctor. Consultant support/referral may be necessary	Will require satisfactory independent medical examination, with satisfactory blood results and medical reports from own doctor
Visual acuity Includes severe bilateral cataracts, failed bilateral cataract extractions and post-cataract surgery where these are affecting the eyesight	New applicants are barred by law if the visual acuity, using corrective lenses if necessary, is worse than 6/9 in the better eye or 6/12 in the other eye. Also, the uncorrected acuity in each eye **must** be at least 3/60. In the presence of a cataract, glare may prevent the ability to meet the number plate requirement, even with appropriate acuities	Must be able to meet the prescribed eyesight requirement (corresponds usually to between 6/9 and 6/12 on the Snellen chart). In the presence of a cataract, glare may prevent the ability to meet the number plate requirement, even with appropriate acuities

Table 74.4 Continued

Condition	Group I, II or III	Group IV
Monocular vision Includes the use of one eye only for driving	New applicants are barred from holding a licence. Complete loss of vision in one eye or corrected acuity of less than 3/60 in one eye. Applicants are barred by law from holding a Group II licence. There may be "grandfather" rights for Group III, which depend on when the licence was issued for the first time. An application would need to be accompanied in these particular instances by a certificate of experience	Acceptable if able to meet the visual acuity standard and has adapted to the disability. There should be a normal visual field in the remaining eye
Visual field defects, e.g. homonymous hemianopia and homonymous quadrantanopia, severe bilateral glaucoma, severe bilateral retinopathy, diabetes, retinitis pigmentosa, complete bitemporal hemianopia and other serious bilateral eye disorders	Normal binocular field of vision is required	Driving must cease unless confirmed able to meet recommended medical guideline for visual field
Diplopia	Recommended permanent refusal or revocation if suffering insuperable diplopia	Cease driving on diagnosis. Resume driving on confirmation to the Licensing Authority that it is controlled by glasses or a patch which the licence holder undertakes to wear while driving. If patching, note requirements above for monocularity. Exceptionally a stable uncorrected diplopia of six months duration or more may be compatible with driving if there is consultant support indicating satisfactory function
Night blindness	Cease driving if unable to satisfy visual acuity and visual field requirements at all times. Group II acuity and field standards must be met and cases are considered on an individual basis	Cease driving if unable to satisfy visual acuity and visual field requirements at all times
Colour blindness	Driving may continue with no restriction on licence	Driving may continue with no restriction on licence
Blepharospasm	Refuse or revoke licence	Control with botulinum toxin is not acceptable. If mild, driving can be allowed. Subject to satisfactory medical reports able to retain licence but should inform of any change or deterioration in condition

Source: Drivers Medical Group 2003, The South African Society of Occupational Medicine 2004

Van Schaik Publishers

on an individual basis if there is not previous seizure history. Doctors may wish to advise patients that the period of time likely to be recommended off driving will be influenced inter alia by:

(a) whether a 'liability to epileptic seizures' has been demonstrated, or precipitated specifically as a result of the provoked episode and,

(b) whether the provoking or precipitating factor(s) has been successfully or appropriately treated or removed.

Such cases might include reflex anoxic seizures, seizures with medication, e.g. tricyclic anti-depressants, immediate seizure at time of acute head injury or neurosurgical operation, at onset of acute stroke or TIA or during acute exacerbation of neurological disorders, e.g. with multiple sclerosis. Seizures which occur immediately (within seconds) after a head injury are treated as provoked. For Group I drivers, seizures which occur within the first 24 hours after head injury (other than immediate seizures) require a six-month period off driving.

Similarly, alcohol misuse and dependence are common problems. They account for the vast majority of road accident fatalities on our roads. The RTA provides clear legal guidelines on driving while under the influence of intoxicating liquor or a drug having a narcotic effect, or with excessive amount of alcohol in blood or breath. No person shall on a public road drive a vehicle or occupy the driver's seat with the engine running

- while under the influence of intoxicating liquor or a drug having a narcotic effect
- while the concentration of alcohol in any specimen of blood taken from any part of his or her body (within two hours of the alleged contravention) is not less than 0.05 gram per 100 millilitres, or in the case of a professional driver, not less than 0.02 gram per 100 millilitres
- while the concentration of alcohol in any specimen of breath exhaled (within two hours of the alleged contravention) by such person is not less than 0.24 milligrams per 1 000 millilitres, or in the case of a professional driver, not less than 0.10 milligrams per 1 000 millilitres.
- Any person detained for an alleged contravention shall not consume any substance that contains alcohol of any nature, or smoke until the specimen has been taken. No person shall refuse that a specimen of blood, or a specimen of breath, be taken from him or her.

Source: South African Society of Occupational Medicine 2004

75 How to claim compensation for work-related injuries or diseases

SHAHIEDA ADAMS AND MOHAMED JEEBHAY

There are a number of possible connections between work and ill health. Experience suggests, however, that only the minority of workers are diagnosed and reported, and have claims fully processed for compensation. This has major implications for the quality of life of the individuals affected, as well as their continued employment prospects.

As a medical practitioner with an interest in work-related injuries and diseases, you therefore have an important role to play in the diagnosis, treatment, rehabilitation and future prevention of such injuries and diseases.

Legislation relating to workers' compensation and occupational diseases notification

The two laws dealing with the compensation of occupational diseases and injuries are the Compensation for Occupational Injuries and Diseases Act (COIDA) of 1993 and the Occupational Diseases in Mines and Works Act (ODMWA) as amended in 1994 (Jeebhay 2000). The compensation system under these Acts is funded by employer premiums, but administered mainly by the state.

COIDA provides for mandatory reporting of all occupational injuries and diseases, excluding miners with occupational diseases, to the office of the compensation commissioner in the Department of Labour (DoL). The compensation for occupational lung diseases in the mining industry is compensable under ODMWA and administered by the Department of Health.

Aside from these compensation-related laws, the Occupational Health and Safety Act (OHSA) 85 of 1993 requires medical practitioners to notify all cases of suspected occupational disease to the chief inspector at the DoL. A copy of the first medical report – form WCL 22 – completed for a worker's compensation application usually suffices as such notification.

Definitions

■ OCCUPATIONAL INJURY

An occupational injury is legally defined as an occurrence of an event that arises out of and in the course of an employee's employment of which the date, time and place can be determined and which results in personal injury.

Under COIDA, all occupational injuries or alleged occupational injuries that result in medical expenses being incurred by the worker and/or absence from work for more than three days must be reported within seven days in the prescribed manner. This entails the completion of an employer's report of an occupational injury – form WCL2.

■ OCCUPATIONAL DISEASE

An occupational disease is legally defined as a disease arising out of and contracted in the course of an employee's employment and which is listed in Schedule 3 of the Act (see Appendix 1 below).

An employer is required to report an occupational disease within 14 days of gaining knowledge that such a condition exists. This entails the completion of an employer's report of an occupational disease – form WCL1.

Submitting a claim under COIDA

Usually, a private medical practitioner or the public sector health services make the assessment that could lead to the submission of the claim.

Should the claim be accepted, the worker receives the following benefits:

- **Medical expenses** for treatment of the occupational disease, such as asthma, dermatitis or an injury
- **Temporary disablement benefits**, in which case 75% of wages are paid for the period during which the worker is absent from work, provided that this exceeds three days. The employer is

obliged to make this payment for the first three months. Thereafter, the payments are made directly by the compensation commissioner to the worker and the employer is reimbursed for the first three months.

- **Permanent disablement benefits**, once the case is finalised after a period of two years. The compensation payment is based on the percentage of permanent disability and the wages of the worker. The benefit takes the form of a lump sum payment if the percentage disability is 30% or less, and a monthly pension if it is more than 30%.

- **Additional compensation** if the worker develops an occupational disease or injury or dies as a result of negligence of the employer, or if the condition or disability worsens

- **Death benefit** covers funeral expenses, an initial lump sum payment and pension for life to the widow or widower and children under 18 years, if the worker dies from an occupational disease.

In the submission of a case of an occupational disease or injury under COIDA, the following procedure is indicated (Jeebhay 1996):

- Worker informs employer – form WCL14 or WCL3.★

- Employer reports disease or accident – form WCL1 or WCL2.★

- You complete the first medical report – form WCL22 or WCL4★ – at first visit, and send it to the employer.

- You collate all investigations and specialist opinions. If the disease is occupational then you should include a detailed and chronological description of the patient's past and present jobs, exposures and processes (and the recognised causative agent).

- You counsel the patient about the need to avoid exposure and assist if requested (and appropriate) to have him moved to other work.

- The compensation commissioner assigns a claim number, which must be quoted in all reports or correspondence.

- You assess the degree of your patient's impairment and whether it is temporary and/or permanent. Complete the progress (final) medical report – form WCL26 or WCL5★ – at each subsequent (and final) visit, and send these to the employer or the commissioner.

- Employer completes resumption report – form WCL6★ – once the worker returns to work, and sends it to the commissioner.

Common questions regarding the management of COIDA cases

Answers to certain common questions, which you may also have to consider, are as follows:

- **When do I suspect a work-related disease?** When the worker develops symptoms after having had specific workplace exposure; when symptoms deteriorate over the working day or week; when symptoms improve upon removal from work, such as weekend, leave or holiday; or when the disease is known to be associated with high-risk exposures to a known occupational agent, such as asbestos.

- **What do I do once I have diagnosed an occupational disease?** Remove the worker from further exposure so that it does not aggravate his condition, as in the case of occupational asthma; institute appropriate treatment; submit a claim for worker's compensation; notify the chief inspector in the DoL of the case; investigate and "treat" the workplace.

- **How do I know that a disease is compensable?** It is important for you to take an occupational history to find out about harmful exposures in the workplace. Most compensable occupational diseases are listed in Schedule 3 of COIDA (see Appendix 1 below). The absence of a specific condition on the list requires a more detailed motivation for the claim to be accepted.

- **What are "circular instructions" and of what use are these documents?** For the commissioner to arrive at a decision regarding the degree of permanent disablement caused by an occupational disease, it is necessary for the relevant medical information to be submitted and for the correct documentation to be used. Circular instructions have been developed for the reporting and diagnosis of common occupational diseases – they provide a guideline to medical practitioners as to what information to submit, which documentation to use and what criteria are used for a specific occupational disease or group of diseases (see Appendix 2 below). These circular instructions have been promulgated in the Government Gazette and are also available on the website of the compensation commissioner (www.labour.gov.za).

- **Do I use the same document to report all work-related injuries and diseases?** No, you should use a standard set of documentation for reporting injuries (see Appendix 3 below). Similarly, you should report occupational diseases using a standard set of forms, the exception being

★ These forms differ, depending whether the condition is an occupational injury or disease. The forms are obtainable from the DoL.

work-related upper limb disorders (WRULDs) and post-traumatic stress disorder (PTSD), which have their own set of forms. In cases of occupational lung disease, caused by exposure to fibrogenic dust, and noise-induced hearing loss, you need to complete additional documentation, which provides additional information on work-place exposures – forms WCL111 and OD2 respectively. For all other agents where exposure history is available, you must complete an exposure history form, namely the WCL110 (see Appendix 4 below).

- **If the employer does not complete a WCL1 or WCL2, should I still complete the required COIDA medical reports?** If you believe the injury or disease to have arisen in or during the course of employment, you are legally obliged to report it as such. In the event of the employer refusing to complete the WCL1 or 2, advise your patient to complete an affidavit WCL305 detailing his employment history. Then submit this together with supportive documentation proving his employment, such as a payslip or unemployment fund (UIF) card.

- **From where do I obtain the necessary documents to report COIDA claims?** These are obtainable on the website of the Compensation Fund at www.labour.gov.za or from the provincial office of the DoL or from regional labour centres.

- **Where do I obtain information regarding the progress of claims which I have submitted?** The provincial DoL office or regional labour centre will be able to assist in this regard.

- **Where do I refer my patients when I need assistance with the diagnosis or management of an occupational disease?** See Appendix 5 below for a list of clinics and centres with a special interest in occupational diseases.

- **If the employee disagrees with the percentage of disablement awarded, is there recourse to challenging this decision?** The employee is entitled to lodge an objection in terms of Section 91 of COIDA. You may be subpoenaed to provide expert evidence at a formal hearing in support of the employee's claim.

- **To whom or where do we submit claims?** For cases covered by COIDA:

Compensation Commissioner
PO Box 955
Pretoria
0001
Fax: (012) 323 8627
Tel: (012) 319 9111

For cases covered by ODMWA:

Medical Bureau for Occupational Diseases
PO Box 4584
Johannesburg
2000
Fax: (011) 403 1285
Tel: (011) 403 6322

Appendix 1: Compensable occupational diseases under Schedule 3 of COIDA

Table 75.1 summarises the **respiratory** diseases.

Table 75.1 Respiratory diseases

Occupational respiratory diseases
Pneumoconiosis – fibrosis of the parenchyma of the lung caused by fibrogenic dust
Silicotuberculosis
Bronchopulmonary disease caused by hard-metal dust
Bronchopulmonary disease caused by flax, hemp, cotton or sisal dust (byssinosis)
Occupational asthma caused by one of the following recognised sensitising agents or irritants inherent to the work process: – isocyanates – platinum, nickel, cobalt, vanadium or chromium salts – hardening agents, including epoxy resins – acrylic acids or derived acrylates – soldering or welding fumes – substances from animals or insects – fungi or spores – proteolytic enzymes – organic dust – vapours or fumes of formaldehyde, anhydrides, amines or diamines – latex
Extrinsic allergic alveolitis caused by the inhalation of the following organic dusts and chemicals inherent to the work process: moulds, fungal spores or any other allergenic proteinaceous material; 2,4 toluene-diisocyanates
Siderosis
Chronic obstructive pulmonary diseases due to occupational exposure
Diseases of the lung caused by aluminium
Upper airways disorders caused by recognised sensitising agents or irritants inherent to the work process
Diseases caused by chronic or repetitive exposure to products of combustion

Table 75.2 summarises the **skin** diseases.

Table 75.2 Skin diseases

Diseases	Work involving the handling of or exposure to these elements
Allergic or irritant contact dermatitis	Physical, chemical or biological agents
Occupational vitiligo	

Musculoskeletal diseases can be caused by specific work activities or a work environment in which particular risk factors are present. Examples of such activities or environment include

- rapid or repetitive motion
- forceful exertion
- excessive mechanical force concentration
- awkward or non-neutral postures
- vibration.

Occupational cancer can be caused by the following agents:

- Anthracene or its compounds
- Arsenic
- Asbestos
- Benzene and its toxic homologues
- Benzidine and its salts
- Beta-naphthylamine
- Bis chloromethyl ether (BCME)
- Bitumen
- Chromium or chromium compounds
- Coal tar pitches or soots
- Coal tars
- Coke-oven emissions
- Compounds of nickel
- Crystalline silica
- Ionising radiation
- Mineral oil
- Mycotoxins
- Pitch
- Tar
- Toxic nitro- and amino-derivatives of benzene or its homologues
- Vinyl chloride
- Wood dust
- Products or residues of the above substances

Table 75.3 summarises **other diseases** and **pathological manifestations**.

Table 75.3 Other diseases and pathological manifestations

Disease or pathological manifestation caused by these	Work involving the handling of or exposure to these elements
Chemical agents or their toxic compounds	Acrylonitrile, alcohols, antimony, arsenic, asphyxiants such as carbon monoxide, benzene or its homologues, benzoquinone, beryllium, cadmium, carbon disulphide, chlorine, chromium, copper, disease of teeth caused by mineral agents, fluorine, glycols or ketones, halogen derivatives of aliphatic or aromatic hydrocarbons, hexane, hydrogen cyanide or hydrogen sulphide, lead, manganese, mercury, nitro- and amino-derivatives of benzene or its homologues, nitroglycerine or other nitric acid esters, osmium, oxides of nitrogen, oxides of sulphur, ozone, pesticides and/or herbicides, pharmaceutical agents, phosgene, phosphorus, selenium, thallium, tin, vanadium, zinc
Physical agents	Hearing impairment caused by noise Diseases caused by vibration (disorders of muscles, tendons, bones, joints, peripheral blood vessels or peripheral nerves) Diseases caused by work in compressed air/abnormal atmospheric or water pressure Diseases caused by ionising radiations Diseases caused by extreme temperatures (cold and hot) Diseases caused by ultraviolet radiation
Biological agents	Infectious or parasitic diseases contracted in an occupation where there is particular risk of contamination Toxic/inflammatory syndromes, (such as inhalation fever, toxic pneumonitis, organic dust toxic syndrome) associated with exposure to bacterial and fungal contaminants, (such as endotoxins, mycotoxins, 1-3 B-D glucans, volatile organic compounds)
Other disease	Miner's nystagmus

Appendix 2: Circular instructions for specific occupational diseases under COIDA

Table 75.4 provides the instructions.

Table 75.4 Circular instructions

Circular instruction	Disease covered
CI 171 and CI 171 supplement	Noise-induced hearing loss (NIHL)
CI 172	PTSD
CI 173	Mesothelioma
CI 174	Occupational lung cancer
CI 175	Byssinosis
CI 176	Occupational asthma
CI 177	Irritant-induced asthma
CI 178	Pulmonary tuberculosis in health care workers
CI 179	Pulmonary tuberculosis associated with silica dust exposure
CI 180	WRULDs
CI 181	Occupational contact dermatitis
CI 184	Work-aggravated asthma
CI 187	Work-related upper respiratory tract disorders

Appendix 3: Documentation for a worker's compensation claim for an occupational injury

Table 75.5 lists the WCL forms for occupational injury claims.

Table 75.5 WCL forms for occupational injury claims

WCL number	Title of form
WCL2	Employer's report i.r.o. occupational injury
WCL4	First medical report i.r.o. occupational injury
WCL5	Progress/final medical report i.r.o. occupational injury

Appendix 4: Documentation for a worker's compensation claim for an occupational disease

Table 75.6 lists the WCL forms for the occupational disease claims.

Table 75.6 WCL forms for occupational disease claims

WCL number	Title of form
WCL1	Employer's report i.r.o. an occupational disease
WCL14	Notification of an occupational disease
WCL22	First medical report i.r.o. an occupational disease
WCL26	Progress/final report i.r.o. an occupational disease
WCL301	First medical report i.r.o. a WRULD
WCL302	Progress/final report i.r.o. a WRULD
WCL303	First medical report i.r.o. PTSD
WCL304	Progress/final medical report i.r.o. PTSD
WCL110	Exposure history; additional information required in all cases of occupational disease where applicable
WCL111	Medical report; additional information required in cases of silicosis, asbestosis or other fibrosis of lungs caused by mineral dust
OD2	Exposure history in cases of industrial hearing loss

Appendix 5: Referral/advice centres for assistance with occupational diseases

The centres are as follows:

- **Cape Town**

Workhealth Occupational Diseases Clinic, Groote Schuur Hospital
(021) 404 4369

Provincial Occupational Health Clinic,
Reed Street, Bellville
(021) 946 3790/1/2

Provincial Medical Advisory Panel, Western Cape, UCT Lung Institute
(021) 406 6856

Respiratory Clinic, Tygerberg Hospital
(021) 938 5524

- **Johannesburg**

National Institute of Occupational Health, Braamfontein
(011) 712 6400

Medical Bureau for Occupational Diseases, Braamfontein
(011) 403 6322

- **Durban**

Occupational Medicine Clinic,
King Edward Hospital
(031) 360 3161 or
(031) 260 4471

Provincial Medical Advisory Panel Umbilo, KwaZulu-Natal
(031) 205 8613/9012

Section 8

The newborn

76 How to do a well newborn check

HANNES STEINBERG

Every baby born under the supervision of a health facility should be checked to ensure that basic normal anatomy is present. You need to do an Apgar score on the baby at 1, 5 and 10 minutes after birth. Table 76.1 provides the Apgar score system. Should the Apgar be less than 7, you must resuscitate him (see Chapter 78).

Wipe the newborn, or neonate, that is stable at birth and wrap him in a dry, warm towel. Give him to his mother to care for and bond with as soon as possible after birth. Encourage the mother to breast-feed within 30 minutes of birth, before transferring the baby to the nursery.

It is not essential to bath a neonate immediately after birth. A delay of 24 hours is acceptable, especially if there is much vernix present. However, you should remove blood or meconium staining as soon as possible.

You may well find it convenient to do the first examination of the newborn while doing the first bath. But you can make the examination at any time before the newborn is discharged or within 72 hours of birth.

To conduct the examination, ensure that the environment is friendly and warm, as the neonate must be naked. Preferably, the mother should be present so that she can answer the questions that you will ask. Keep notes of your findings – you can use the national maternity case record book for this purpose, or the form that is provided as Figure 76.1.

Confirm the baby's basic demographic data so that the correct baby is identified. Also establish and confirm the biometric data, that is his weight, height and head circumference.

To take the baby's history, you need to ask the mother these questions:

- Has he been drinking/feeding well?
- Has he passed stools and urine?
- Does he breathe rapidly, or become blue or cyanosed during feeding?
- Did he become jaundiced within the first two days of birth?

To perform the examination from top to bottom, you need to follow this procedure and ask these questions:

- **General**
  - Are the vital signs within normal limits? Pulse should be between 120 and 160 per minute, respiratory rate should be between 35 and 60 per minute.
  - Does he have dysmorphic features, such as a third fontanelle, spina bifida, cleft palate, imperforate anus, extra digits, etc.?
  - Does he "look funny"? Remember that for every "funny-looking kid" (FLK), you need to check for a "funny-looking mother" (FLM) or a "funny-looking parent" (FLP).

Table 76.1 Apgar score system

Sign	Score		
	0	1	2
Heart rate	Nil	< 100 per minute	> 100 per minute
Respiratory rate	Absent	Gasping or irregular	Regular and crying
Muscle tone	Flaccid	Some tone	Active
Response to stimulation	None	Grimace	Cry or cough
Colour	Blue	Pink centrally, blue extremities	Pink

 Van Schaik Publishers

NEONATAL DISCHARGE NOTES

Name of neonate			Date and time of birth	

HISTORY:		Type of delivery:		
Apgar:	/10 /10	Duration of gestation	Weeks	
Drinking	Normal	Poor	Nothing	
Urine.	Yes	No		
Meconium:	Yes	No		
Other problems				

EXAMINATION:				
Mass: kg	Length:	cm	Head circumference	cm
Observations:	Pulse: / min	Resp: /min	Temp: °C	
General:	J	C	O	D
	A	C	L	Haematomas
	Dysmorphism:	No	Extra fingers or toes	Pre-auricular skin tags or sinus
		Small eyes	Low ears	Flat nose
Head and neck:	Head size:	N	Big	Small
	Fontanelles:	N	Bulging	Closed
	Swelling:	N	Caput	Moulding
	Nostrils:	Open	Blocked	Closed
	Mouth:		Complete palate	
	Red reflex of the eye:	Present	Absent	
Cardiovascular:	Heart rate:	<100	N	>180
	Cyanosis:	No	Central	Peripheral
	Femoral pulses:	Right	Left	
	Brachial pulses:	Right	Left	
	Capillary refill on chest:	<4 sec	>4 sec	
	Cardiac failure	No	Oedema	Big liver
Respiratory:	Respiratory distress:	No	Tachypnoea > 60/min	
		Nasal flaring	Grunting	Cyanosis
Gastrointestinal:	Abdominal distension:	No	Yes	
	Umbilicus:	N 3 vessels	Bleeding	Septic
	Anus:	N	Abnormal opening	No opening
Central nervous:	Tone:	Flexion	Atonic	
	Primitive reflexes:	Moro	Grasp	Suck
Musculoskeletal:	Arms:	Movement of both	Contractures	Weakness
	Legs:	Movement of both	Contractures	Weakness
	Fingers and toes:	Fingers	Toes	Extra digits
	Hips:	Stable	Unstable (refer immediately)	
	Club feet:	No	Yes (refer immediately to orthopaedics)	
	Back:	Normal	Spina bifida	
Uro-genital:	External genitalia	Normal male	Normal female	Abnormal
	Both testes:	Present	Absent (follow up)	
	Hydrocele:	No	Yes (follow up)	
	Hernia:	No	Yes (appointment at paed. surgery)	
	Hypospadias:	No	Yes (refer to Urology at 1 year)	
Skin lesions:	Fistulas	Hemangiomas	Palms and soles	
Immunisations:	BCG	OPV		
Any problems				

Name of clinic/hospital:	Practitioner's name:	Signature:
	Date:	Time:

Figure 76.1 Neonatal discharge notes form

- **Head and neck**
  - Does the head appear to be normal size, or too big or too small? Is there caput or moulding? Are there signs of trauma, such as abrasions or lacerations from an assisted delivery?
  - Is there a cephalhaematoma? (If there is, he is more likely to develop jaundice.)
  - Are the fontanelles normal or abnormally splayed? Are they bulging? Are they prematurely closed?
  - Are his ears low lying?
  - Has his nose developed well?
  - Is his mouth normal, without teeth and cleft palate? (Sometimes there is only the soft palate, or the posterior third of the palate has a cleft, which must be excluded if the mother volunteers a history that the baby regurgitates milk through his nose during or after the feeds.)
  - Check his eyes for normality. Any opaqueness of the cornea needs immediate attention. Test for the red reflex by shining an ophthalmoscope light (see p. 135) into the eye and observing a red discolouration behind the pupil. If this is absent, serious pathology may be present. Refer immediately.

- **Cardiovascular system**
  - Is his heart rate normal? Normal is between 120 and 160 beats per minute.
  - Is he cyanosed?
  - Are his pulses felt and equal on both sides, especially the femoral and brachial pulses?
  - Is there normal capillary filling? (To test this, press gently on the anterior chest wall until it blanches. Remove your finger and observe the time that the capillaries take to refill. The normal time is within four seconds. If it takes longer, consider cardiac failure. Does he have signs of cardiac failure, such as tachycardia, a large liver, tachypnoea or cyanosis?)
  - Is there a cardiac murmur present?

- **Respiratory system**
  - Is there respiratory distress? Tachypnoea of more than 60 per minute is abnormal.
  - Is there nasal flaring, grunting or cyanosis?
  - Is the shape of his thorax normal?

- **Gastrointestinal system**
  - Is the umbilicus normal? Can you identify three vessels?
  - Is there abdominal distention?
  - Is there an abdominal wall defect, e.g. gastroschisis?
  - Is there hepatomegaly or other organomegaly?
  - Is the anus patent? Has he passed meconium yet?

- **Central nervous system**
  - Is he flexed or atonic/floppy?
  - *Moro reflex:* Elevate his head slightly and then quickly release it to fall into your hand. The "fright" of that manoeuvre should cause the baby initially to extend his upper limbs and then bring them forward to the midline in a symmetrical fashion.
  - *Suck reflex:* Insert your finger, or ask the mother to place her nipple, into his mouth or onto his cheek, and he should attempt to suckle.
  - *Grasp reflex:* With your finger, stimulate the palmar aspect of his hand. He should grasp your finger with sufficient grip to support his own weight on your finger.
  - Does he respond to tactile stimulation?

- **Musculoskeletal system**
  - Is there normal limb development and movement?
  - Are there contractures in his upper or lower limbs?
  - Does he have extra fingers or toes?
  - Do his hips have a click or are they dislocatable/dislocated when examined with the Barlow and Ortolani manoeuvre? (If so, refer him immediately.)
  - Does he have club feet, which are unable to be reduced to the normal anatomical position? (If so, refer him immediately.)
  - Does his back appear normal? Look for spina bifida and an occulta, or dimple.

- **Uro-genital system**
  - Do the genitalia appear normal?
  - If he is a male, are both his testes descended? (If not, follow up at one year.)
  - Is there a hydrocele?
  - Is there a hypospadias?
  - Is there evidence of an inguinal hernia? (If so, refer him immediately.)

- **Skin**
  - Is there a skin lesion? Is his skin peeling? Does he have congenital syphilis?
  - Are there pustules?
  - Are there haemangiomas?

- **Immunisations**
  - Has he received the BCG and polio immunisations?

77 How to assess gestational age at birth

IAN COUPER AND HAROON SALOOJEE

You can best estimate gestational age from obstetric data, especially the date of the mother's last menstrual period, and ultrasound foetal measurements between 6 and 20 weeks of foetal age, using crown–rump length, femur length and biparietal diameter. These estimates depend on the mothers' regular menstrual cycles and good memory in the former instance, and on her early attendance at antenatal care in the latter. As these factors are frequently absent, many babies are born without accurate dating.

You would assess the gestational age whenever there is doubt about it or when a baby is born preterm. It helps you to decide on interventions such as timing of feeds or the need for surfactant. Furthermore, it helps you to classify whether a low birth weight baby is preterm or small for his gestational age, which has management and prognostic implications. For example, a growth-retarded baby may actually be more mature than it appears, and may need different care than that given to a preterm baby. The gestational age score and the birth weight give early warnings about complications that you can expect as well as any prophylactic action that may be needed.

Estimate the gestational age independent of the baby's weight. Through plotting weight versus gestational age, you can classify the baby as small, appropriate or large for his gestational age. You would also plot his head circumference and length against his gestational age. These parameters, which help you to predict his subsequent growth and development, may be influenced by genetic factors and by abnormal intrauterine states that can predispose him to perinatal problems.

Scoring systems

You can use various systems to score gestational age. The Dubowitz and Ballard systems are highly accurate, but time consuming (Dubowitz, Dubowitz & Goldberg 1970; Ballard, Khoury, Wedig, Wang et al. 1991). These systems evaluate a baby's physical maturity using features such as skin texture, lanugo – which is absent in premature and post-mature babies – plantar creases, breasts, eyes, ears and genitalia within the first two hours of birth; and his neuromuscular maturity within 24 hours of delivery, using posture, hand flexion, arm recoil, knee extension, the scarf sign and the heel-to-ear test.

Parkin scoring system

The Parkin scoring system is a simpler scoring system that you can perform even in an ill neonate without manipulation or movement. It enables you to estimate gestational age to within about 15 days at any time in the first two days of life.

While the Ballard score is known as the "gold standard", the Parkin system is useful, practical and sufficiently accurate in most situations.

The system involves scoring the neonate on only four physical features, as set out in Table 77.1.

You add up the four scores to reach a total. Table 77.2 provides the gestational age corresponding to the total score.

As regards *limitations* of the Parkin system, you would need to slightly modify the definition of skin colour in African and Asian babies (see Brueton, Palit & Rosser 1973). Moreover, the system is least accurate in tiny neonates, with a score of less than 2 applying to any baby under 30 weeks. In this case, you should use a more comprehensive scoring system.

Table 77.1 Parkin scoring system

Feature	Score	Characteristics
Skin texture		Test by picking up a fold of abdominal skin between your finger and thumb
	0	Very thin, with gelatinous feel
	1	Thin and smooth
	2	Smooth and medium thickness; irritation rash and superficial peeling may be present
	3	Slight thickening; stiff feeling with superficial cracking and peeling, especially on hands and feet
	4	Thick, parchment-like; superficial or deep cracking
Breast size		Test by picking up the breast tissue between your finger and thumb
	0	No breast tissue palpable
	1	Breast tissue palpable on one or both sides, but not more than 0.5 cm on either side
	2	Breast tissue palpable on both sides, one or both being 0.5-1 cm in diameter
	3	Breast tissue palpable on both sides, one or both being more than 1 cm in diameter
Skin colour		Test by inspecting the baby when he is quiet
	0	Dark red
	1	Uniformly pink
	2	Pale pink; colour may vary over different parts of body, with some parts very pale
	3	Pale; only pink areas on ears, lips, palms and soles
Ear firmness		Test by palpating and folding the upper pinna
	0	Feels soft and is easily folded into any position, without springing back spontaneously
	1	Feels soft along the edge and is easily folded, but slowly returns to the correct position spontaneously
	2	Can feel cartilage to the edge of the pinna, though it is thin in places; pinna springs back after being folded
	3	Definite cartilage extending to the periphery; pinna springs back immediately after being folded

Source: Parkin, Hey & Clowes 1976. p. 259–63

Table 77.2 Conclusion as a result of Parkin score

Total score	Gestational age in days	Gestational age in weeks
1	190	27
2	210	30
3	230	33
4	240	34.5
5	250	36
6	260	37
7	270	38.5
8	276	39.5
9	281	40
10	285	41
11	290	41.5
12	295	42

Source: Parkin, Hey & Clowes 1976. p. 259–63

78 How to resuscitate a newborn

HANNES STEINBERG

Resuscitation is a series of actions taken to establish normal breathing, heart rate, colour, tone and response in a baby with abnormal vital signs. Every baby that does not breathe well within one minute of delivery, or has an Apgar score of less than 7, needs resuscitation (see Chapter 76).

Asphyxia refers to progressive lack of oxygen; it can be defined as the baby's failure to breathe well within one minute of delivery. If asphyxia lasts for longer than 10 minutes, the baby can become permanently brain damaged or he can die. Other organs, such as the kidneys, heart, lungs and gut, are also affected by asphyxia.

In general, to resuscitate a newborn, you need

- a clean, well-lit and warm environment
- a complete set of clean resuscitation equipment, kept in proper working order (see below)
- the relevant drugs.

Equipment

More specifically, you need the following:

- A clock
- An overhead radiant warmer
- A temperature probe
- Clean, sterile towels
- A stethoscope
- Sterile gloves
- Scissors
- Syringes – 1, 2, 5, 10, 20 ml
- Needles – 18-, 21- and 25-gauge
- Drugs – adrenaline, 10% dextrose and naloxone
- Oxygen supply
- Feeding tubes – 5 or 8 F
- Alcohol swabs
- Adhesive tape
- IV solutions – normal saline, that is 0.9% saline as 200 ml
- IV giving sets with 100 ml buretrol
- Infusion pump or "dial a flow"
- A pulse oximeter
- A suction pump and catheters
- A self-inflating resuscitation bag

Evaluation

Traditionally, you would use the Apgar score to assess the baby after birth. Should the score fall below 7 within one minute of birth, you need to resuscitate the baby. After you have begun resuscitation, you must re-evaluate the newborn every 30 seconds. Should the score fail to climb higher than 7, continue resuscitation for as long as you deem it necessary.

Alternatively, you could ask yourself the following questions to help you decide whether resuscitation is needed:

- Is the baby breathing adequately?
- Is his heart rate above 100 beats per minute?
- Is he centrally pink?

If the answers to these questions are "yes", you do not need to resuscitate the newborn. If the answer to one or more of the questions is "no" then resuscitate him and re-evaluate every 30 seconds.

Figure 78.1 shows the process of resuscitation devised by the Resuscitation Council.

Basic resuscitation

We will now explore the initial procedures that you need to follow to resuscitate a newborn.

Prevent heat loss

Newborns lose heat rapidly owing to their high surface area to body ratio. You should prevent such loss in order to avoid cold stress. After it is born, dry the newborn and place him under a warmer. Then remove the wet linen and wrap him in a second dry, and preferably warmed, towel.

Clear the airway

In order for ventilation to take place adequately, you need to ensure that his airways are clear. Over-vigor-

Newly-Born Life Support Algorithm

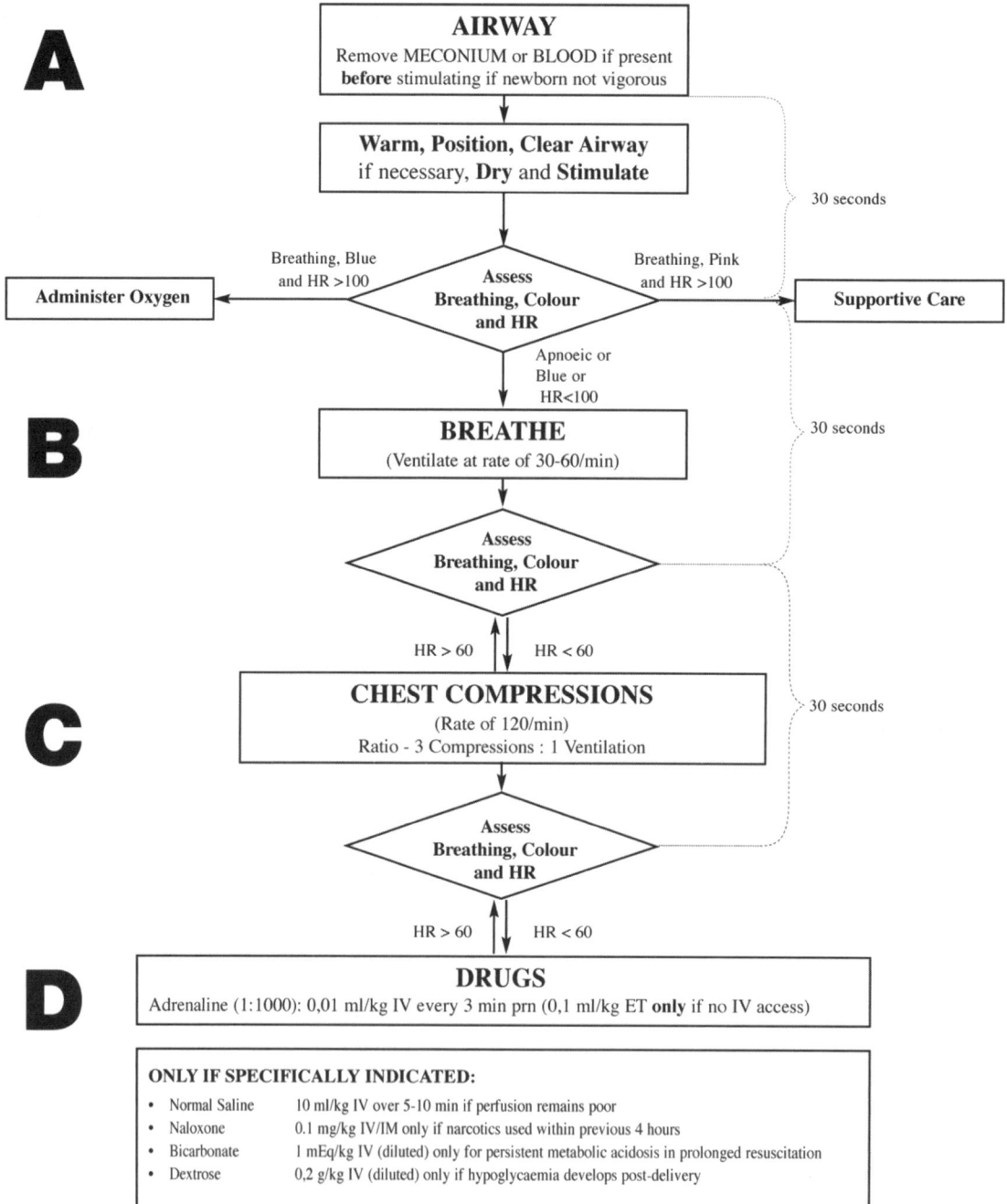

A

AIRWAY
Remove MECONIUM or BLOOD if present
before stimulating if newborn not vigorous

Warm, Position, Clear Airway
if necessary, **Dry** and **Stimulate**

30 seconds

Breathing, Blue
and HR >100

Breathing, Pink
and HR >100

Administer Oxygen

Assess
Breathing, Colour
and HR

Supportive Care

Apnoeic or
Blue or
HR<100

B

BREATHE
(Ventilate at rate of 30-60/min)

30 seconds

Assess
Breathing, Colour
and HR

HR > 60   HR < 60

C

CHEST COMPRESSIONS
(Rate of 120/min)
Ratio - 3 Compressions : 1 Ventilation

30 seconds

Assess
Breathing, Colour
and HR

HR > 60   HR < 60

D

DRUGS
Adrenaline (1:1000): 0,01 ml/kg IV every 3 min prn (0,1 ml/kg ET **only** if no IV access)

ONLY IF SPECIFICALLY INDICATED:
- Normal Saline   10 ml/kg IV over 5-10 min if perfusion remains poor
- Naloxone   0.1 mg/kg IV/IM only if narcotics used within previous 4 hours
- Bicarbonate   1 mEq/kg IV (diluted) only for persistent metabolic acidosis in prolonged resuscitation
- Dextrose   0,2 g/kg IV (diluted) only if hypoglycaemia develops post-delivery

**The algorithm follows the assumption that the previous
step was unsuccessful and the newly-born is deteriorating**

Resuscitation Council of Southern Africa
www.resuscitationcouncil.co.za

Figure 78.1 Algorithm for neonatal resuscitation

ous suctioning can cause vagal bradycardia and apnoea. Suction the airways *only* if they are obstructed, which you can diagnose by listening for the audible sound made by the air passing through secretions in the airways.

Should the neonate be meconium stained and have poor respiration, decreased muscle tone and a heart rate of below 100 beats per minute, do a direct laryngoscopy and suction under vision. You may have to intubate him and suction through the endo-tracheal (ET) tube. Intubation and suctioning of a *vigorous* baby does not improve the outcome; in fact it may cause complications. Check the cords with direct laryngoscopy to see if meconium has passed below them. In this case, consider admitting him to a neonatal unit. He needs to be observed for 12 hours post-delivery.

Do not hold the newborn upside-down by his feet in order to get rid of the secretions; rather turn him on his side or place him on his back or in the knee–chest position for a few minutes.

Give tactile stimulation

Rubbing the newborn with a towel to dry him is usually sufficient tactile stimulation. However, should he not respond to this gentle stimulation, initiate positive pressure ventilation with the bag and mask immediately.

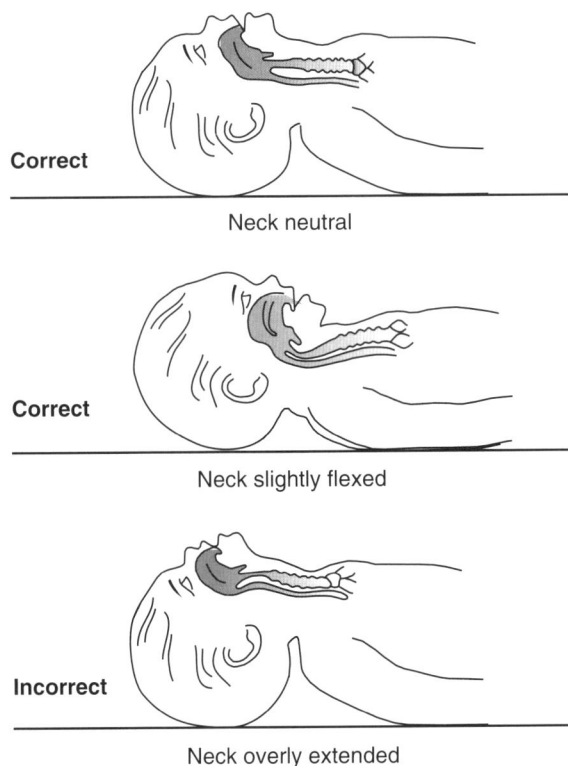

Correct

Neck neutral

Correct

Neck slightly flexed

Incorrect

Neck overly extended

Figure 78.2 Establishing an airway

Give oxygen

It is useful for you to give free-flowing oxygen to the newborn if he is breathing well and his heart rate is good, but he is cyanosed. Flow the oxygen from the tube into your gently cupped hand at the rate of 5 L per minute. Should he remain cyanosed after five minutes, give oxygen via the head box or prongs. Note that the self-inflating bag does not deliver oxygen unless you squeeze it.

Bag and mask ventilation

You can successfully resuscitate the majority of newborns with bag and mask ventilation alone, that is without the need for intubation or cardiac massage. This type of ventilation is the most important step in resuscitating the newborn.

You need to follow this procedure:

* Make sure that the equipment is functional.
* Position the newborn correctly. Refer to Figure 78.2.
* Firmly apply the mask to his face, ensuring an adequate seal.
* Squeeze the bag gently – about 30 ml per breath and not faster than 40–60 per minute.
* If ventilation is effective, you will observe good, equal chest movements and an improvement in the newborn's heart rate and colour.
* Ventilate for 30 seconds then re-assess him.
* There is no need to continue if he is pink and breathing on his own, and if his heart rate is above 100 beats per minute.
* Always resuscitate with 100% oxygen, ensuring that the reservoir bag of the ambubag is filling up. However, ventilation is more important than oxygen at this early stage.

Throughout the procedure, you should

* ensure that there is an adequate seal of the mask
* ensure that the bag is delivering an adequate amount of pressure
* check that the neonate's airways are clear and his head is in the correct position
* check that the oxygen supply has not run out.

Note that prolonged bagging splints the newborn's diaphragm and prevents good chest movements. If he does not respond as expected, you need to exclude the development of a pneumothorax.

Administer naloxone

If the mother received narcotic analgesics within four hours of delivery, you should administer 0.1 mg/kg preferably IV, or IMI (1 ml adult naloxone "Narcan®" contains 0.4 mg) to the neonate. The duration of action of the maternal narcotics may be prolonged, which could mean that you need to administer a second dose to the neonate 20–30 minutes later. If the mother is a drug abuser, her baby may experience withdrawal symptoms.

Note that naloxone is of no use if the mother did not receive opiates.

Apply chest compression

Hypoxia causes poor cardiac output; correcting hypoxia corrects circulatory problems as well. Therefore, few neonates need chest compression and can be adequately resuscitated by bag and mask alone.

Start chest compressions if the newborn's heart rate is below 60 beats per minute after 30 seconds of effective ventilation. Conversely, should his heart rate rise to over 60 beats per minute after chest compression, stop the compressions.

Always have an assistant when starting compressions as part of resuscitation.

We will now explore two techniques: the "two-finger" technique and the "hand-encircling" technique. Figures 78.3 and 78.4 illustrate these. Make the chest compressions about one third of the depth of the newborn's chest. It is recommended that you use three compressions to one breath at a rate of 120 compressions per minute.

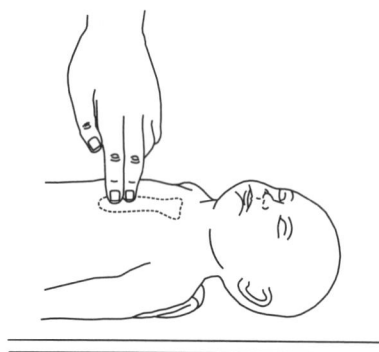

Figure 78.3 Two-finger technique

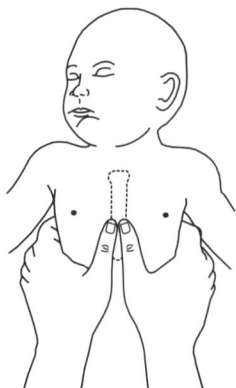

Figure 78.4 Hand-encircling technique

Intubation

Most newborns do not need to be intubated. However, should the neonate need intubation it is recommended that you use the oral rather than the nasal route. There is no need for sedation in this case.

You need a laryngoscope with a straight blade – 1 for a term baby and 0 for a premature baby – and ET tubes, sizes 2.5–4.

To perform the intubation, you need to follow this procedure (see Figure 78.5):

- Place the newborn's head in the neutral or slightly flexed position. See Figure 78.2.
- *Take care* not to hyperextend his neck, as this will obscure your view of the cords.
- Hold the laryngoscope in your left hand and pass the blade into his mouth.
- Always keep the tip of the blade in the midline.
- Gently lift the blade to get his vocal cords in view.
- Occasionally, you may need to apply gentle cricoid pressure.
- Hold the ET tube in your right hand and gently insert the tip through the cords.
- You may need to use the Magill forceps to assist you.

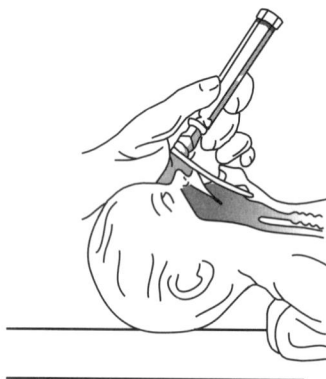

Figure 78.5 Intubation

The formula for calculating the depth of insertion of the tube is as follows:

Insertion depth at lips (cm) = weight (kg) + 6

Table 78.1 shows the calculation scales.

Table 78.1 Calculating depth of insertion

Weight (g)	Tube size	Level of insertion at lip (cm)
< 1 000	2.5	6.5–7
1 000–2 000	3.0	7–8
2 000–3 000	3.5	8–9
3 000–4 500	3.5–4	9–10.5

Indications

You would intubate in the following circumstances:

- Clearing the airways of meconium
- Ineffective or prolonged bag and mask ventilation
- When chest compressions are given, especially if you are the only person doing the resuscitation
- If chest compressions fail to result in an increased heart rate
- To give medication via ET tube

You know that you have performed an intubation successfully if

- the newborn does not cry
- there is good chest movement, with equal air entry bilaterally
- his colour and heart rate improve
- you can see fogging inside the tube with expiration.

Should your attempt be unsuccessful after 20 seconds, restart the bag and mask ventilations, and try intubation again once the neonate has been better oxygenated.

Complications

The following can occur while you are intubating:

- You push the laryngoscope blade too far.
- You do not push the laryngoscope blade far enough.
- You push the laryngoscope blade into one side.
- The newborn's tongue is not sufficiently lifted up.
- Secretions obscure your view.
- His neck is overextended.

Should the neonate not improve after intubation, you should use the following DOPES mnemonic:

- **D**isplaced/dislodged tube
- **O**bstructed tube
- **P**neumothorax
- **E**quipment failure
- **S**tomach distended

Drugs

In the rare cases in which you have intubated and ventilated the newborn correctly, but the response has not been adequate, you need to consider whether to administer drugs or not.

Adrenaline

If the newborn's pulse rate does not rise above 60–80 beats per minute, you can commence administering adrenaline. Note that you *must dilute* the 1:1 000 ampoule of adrenaline to 1:10 000 solution.

Adrenaline causes vasoconstriction and thereby improves circulation and oxygen delivery to the heart and brain. You should administer 0.1 ml/kg of a 1:10 000 solution intravenously (or, if you do not have venous access, through the ET tube). Repeat the dose every three minutes, if needed.

Dextrose

Should resuscitation be prolonged or you note hypoglycaemia, you must administer dextrose intravenously – 2 ml/kg of a 10% solution.

Volume expanders

You must use normal saline as a volume expander in a hypovolaemic neonate post perfusion. Administer 10 ml/kg normal saline intravenously over several minutes. Consider hypovolaemic shock if there is a history of blood loss.

In each of the above situations, to gain rapid access to an intravenous line in the newborn, you may need to insert an umbilical catheter. For the procedure, see Chapter 79.

Post-resuscitation issues

Once you have successfully resuscitated the newborn, you must not forget the following *ongoing care*:

- Check his **glucose levels** for six hours after the procedure.
- It is essential that you **document** the procedure, as birth asphyxia is a medico-legal hazard. Clear and comprehensive notes are imperative.
- Refer the family for **family support**. Explain the events clearly to the parents and warn them of the possibility of subsequent brain damage.

Evidently, you cannot perform resuscitation endlessly. You should stop the procedure when the newborn's heart beat has failed for 15 consecutive minutes, or when there is no spontaneous respiration at 30 minutes.

Should the neonate die, you need to arrange for grief support for the family for the immediate as well as the long-term period.

79 How to insert an umbilical vein catheter

HAROON SALOOJEE AND IAN COUPER

An umbilical vein catheter is used to gain IV access during neonatal resuscitation, when the need for it is urgent but you are unable to establish quickly a peripheral IV line.

Equipment

You need the following:

- Clean examination gloves
- Sterile gloves
- A sterile umbilical catheter or ordinary gastric tube
  - If the baby weighs less than 1.5 kg, use a 3.5 F catheter.
  - If the baby weighs 1.5 kg or more, use a 5 F catheter.
- A sterile infusion set with IV fluid; use a micro-dropper of 60 dpm, if one is available
- A sterile 5- or 10-ml syringe
- Antiseptic swabs or cotton wool balls soaked in antiseptic solution
- Sterile drapes
- A sterile blade
- Cord tie or suture to control bleeding
- Sterile forceps
- Sterile suture or adhesive strapping (to secure the catheter)

Procedure

To insert the catheter, you need to follow this proce-dure:

- Prepare the solution to be infused; use either neonatalyte, normal saline or Ringer's lactate.
- Carefully ensure filling of the infusion set.
- Wash your hands.
- Prepare the umbilicus and surrounding skin by washing in an outward spiral motion with the swab or cotton wool. Repeat two more times, using a new swab or cotton wool ball each time, and allow to dry.

- Put on the sterile gloves.
- Fill the umbilical catheter with IV fluid using a closed 5-ml syringe, that is with the plunger com-pletely inside the barrel of the syringe, attached to the end of the catheter. Ensure that air is not in the catheter and that a closed syringe is attached to the end of the catheter.
- Place sterile drapes over the baby's body so that only the umbilical area is exposed. In the *emer-gency* setting, you cannot or will not have time to do full scrubbing and draping. However, you should perform the rest of the procedure as clean-ly as possible without wasting time.
- Place a cord tie or suture around the base of the umbilical cord to control bleeding after the proce-dure is complete and, using a sterile blade, cut the cord to a length of 1–2 cm. Figure 79.1 illustrates this.

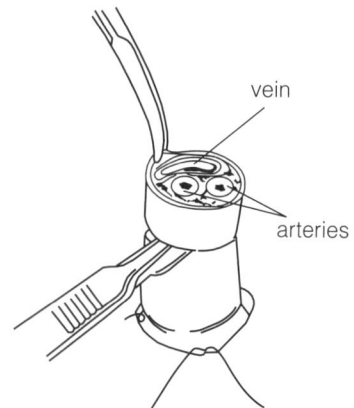

Figure 79.1 Cutting the umbilical cord

- Identify the two umbilical arteries, which are thicker walled and usually contracted, and the single umbilical vein, which usually has a wider opening and is found above the arteries, closer to the baby's head.
- Hold the catheter in one hand, applying gentle traction to the cord with forceps in the other

hand, if necessary, and insert the catheter into the umbilical vein, guiding the catheter towards the baby's head and the baby's right side, as is shown in Figure 79.2.

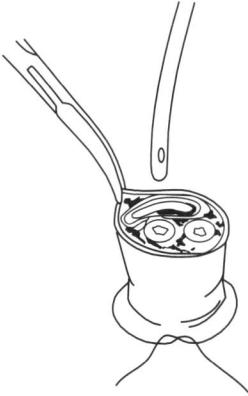

Figure 79.2 Inserting the catheter

- As you advance the catheter, periodically apply gentle suction with the syringe until the blood flows back. Once blood flows back freely through the catheter, which usually happens after the catheter is inserted 5–7 cm, do not advance the catheter any further.
- If you encounter resistance while advancing the catheter, especially in the first 2–3 cm, do not continue. Remove the catheter and try again. Never force the umbilical catheter if you encounter resistance.
- Tie the cord tie or suture around the stump of the umbilicus to hold the catheter in place and to pre-

vent bleeding around the catheter or from one of the arteries.

- Remove the syringe and connect the infusion set to the catheter, ensuring that there are no air bubbles in the set.
- Secure the catheter with suture material or adhesive tape to prevent it from being dislodged, as shown in Figure 79.3.

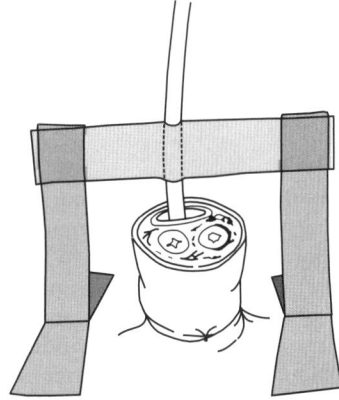

Figure 79.3 Securing the catheter in place

- Inspect the infusion every hour. Look for redness and swelling around the umbilicus, which may indicate infection. If you see redness or swelling at any time, stop the infusion and remove the umbilical vein catheter. Attempt to establish a peripheral IV line, and treat for infection of the umbilicus, that is omphalitis, with broad-spectrum antibiotics.

80 How to establish kangaroo mother care for preterm infants

HAROON SALOOJEE AND IAN COUPER

Kangaroo mother care (KMC) consists of three main components: skin-to-skin contact, breastfeeding and support. It is the best way to keep a premature baby warm, it assists bonding and it also helps to establish breastfeeding. KMC can be started in the hospital as soon as the baby's condition permits, that is the baby does not require special treatment, such as oxygen or IV fluid. However, KMC requires that the mother stay with the baby or spend most of the day at the hospital.

KMC is most appropriate for preterm babies older than 32 weeks gestation. They can be cared for using KMC until they are about 2.5 kg or 38 weeks gestational age.

Preparation

Ensure, firstly, that the mother is fully recovered from any childbirth complications before she begins KMC and, secondly, that she has support from her family to stay at the hospital or to return when the baby is ready for KMC. If possible, discuss with her family the ways in which they can provide support so that she is free to give KMC to the newborn.

Explain to the mother that KMC may be the best way for her to care for her baby once the baby's condition permits, because

- the baby will be warm
- the baby will feed more easily
- the baby will bond with her
- episodes of apnoea will be less frequent.

Separate the baby from the mother only to change napkins, to bath the baby and to assess for clinical findings, as necessary.

Skin-to-skin contact

While the baby is recovering from any illness, the mother can begin to hold him in skin-to-skin contact for one to three hours at a time.

When his condition is stable and he does not require special treatment, the mother can begin continuous KMC.

Follow this procedure:

- Ask the mother to wear light, loose clothing that is comfortable in the ambient temperature, provided the clothing can accommodate the baby.
- Ensure that the room is at least 25 degrees Celsius.
- While the mother is holding the baby, describe to her each step of KMC, demonstrate them, and then have her go through them herself.
- Clothe the baby in a pre-warmed shirt open at the front, a napkin, a hat and socks.
- Place the baby on the mother's chest, *under* her clothes, making sure that he is in an upright position directly against her skin.
- Also ensure that his hips and elbows are flexed into a frog-like position, and that his head and chest are on her chest, with his head in a slightly extended position. This is illustrated in Figure 80.1.
- Fold a soft piece of fabric of about 1 m² diagonally in two and secure it with a knot around mother and baby under her clothes. Make sure that it is tied firmly enough to prevent him from sliding out if she stands, but not so tightly that it obstructs his breathing or movement.
- Special garments are not needed, as long as the mother's clothes keep the baby firmly and comfortably in contact with her skin.
- Cover both of them with a pre-warmed blanket.
- Allow her to rest with the baby, and encourage her to move around when she is ready.

Breastfeeding and support

Have the mother attempt to breastfeed either when the baby is waking from sleep or when he is awake and alert. Ensure that she sits comfortably, and help

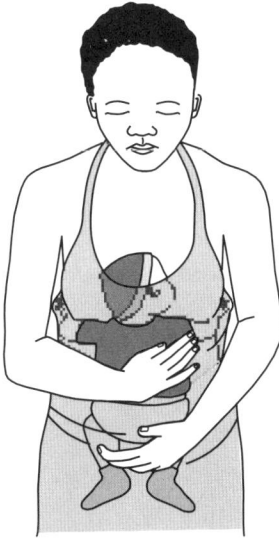

Figure 80.1 Baby in the KMC position under his mother's clothes

her with correct positioning and attachment, if necessary. If she cannot breastfeed, have the mother give expressed breast milk using an alternative feeding method.

Mother and baby's daily life

Ensure that the mother follows these guidelines:

• She must wash her hands frequently.

• During the day, with the baby in the KMC position, she can do whatever she likes – walk, stand, sit or lie down.

• Her best sleeping position is a reclining or semi-recumbent one. If her bed is not adjustable, she can use several pillows to prop herself up. She may also sleep on her side.

• When she needs time away from the baby for hygiene or any other reason, she should either

– have a family member carry the baby in skin-to-skin contact

– or dress the baby, place him in a warm bed, and cover him until she or a family member is available to carry him in skin-to-skin contact.

Monitoring the baby's condition

If the baby is in continuous KMC, measure his temperature twice a day. Teach the mother to observe his breathing pattern, and explain the normal variations. If he stops breathing, have her stimulate him to breathe by rubbing his back for 10 seconds. If he does not begin to breathe immediately, you need to resuscitate him using a bag and mask. Teach her to recognise danger signs, such as apnoea, decreased movement, lethargy or poor feeding. Be available to respond to any concerns that she may have.

Discharge and follow-up

When the baby is feeding well and gaining weight, and has no other problems requiring hospitalisation, you can discharge him. This may be a few days or even some weeks after he is born, depending on his initial size and other problems that he may have had.

Ensure that the mother is confident of her ability to care for him and to continue KMC at home. She must be able to come regularly for follow-up visits.

During the first week following discharge, weigh the baby daily, if possible, and discuss any problems with the mother. Support and encourage her.

After the first week, see the mother and the baby twice weekly until the baby is around 38 weeks gestational age, or when he weighs more than 2.5 kg. Weigh him and advise his mother to begin to wean him off KMC as soon as he becomes less tolerant of the position.

Once he is weaned from KMC, continue to follow up monthly to monitor feeding, growth and development until he is several months old.

The pregnant woman

81 How to use the antenatal growth chart

HANNES STEINBERG

The antenatal growth chart was developed in Brazil by Prof. Belizan. We can thus refer to it as the "Belizan graph". We can also view it as the "Road to Health Chart" of the foetus.

You mainly use the chart to document sufficient growth of the foetus over time. While you need to know the foetus's gestational age – to help your documentation of the growth rate – you should not confuse your measurement of the former with the measurement of the latter (see below).

The use is dependent on your correct and reliable measurement of the symphysis-fundal height, that is the SF measurement. Take the measurement when the mother lies relaxed on her back, having emptied her bladder. Identify the height of the uterine fundus; this need not be in the midline, but is the highest point. Measure the shortest distance between that point and the upper part of the symphysis pubis, laying the tape measure over the uterus with minimal tension. This procedure is illustrated in Figure 81.1.

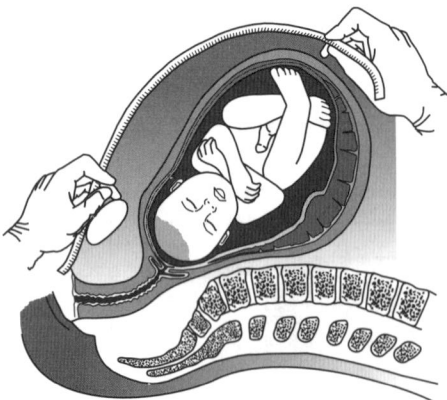

Figure 81.1 Measuring the fundal height of a foetus

This measurement is reliable and useful, provided that

- the foetus is in a longitudinal lie, that is cephalic or breech

- there is no multiple pregnancy
- you have excluded abnormalities in the liquor, such as polyhydramnios and oligohydramnios, by palpation
- the mother is not obese – you can use either the body mass index as a guide, that is BMI greater than 30, or the maternal weight being above 95 kg.

Should you be unable to exclude these conditions, you cannot take the measurement as reliable and therefore cannot make any deductions from it.

Take the SF measurement and chart the distance on the graph accordingly. The measurement should fall between the tenth and ninetieth centiles. If this is not the case, you need to look for possible reasons.

Measure the SF, and document growth, at each follow-up visit that the patient makes. The SF measurement should remain on the original percentile with each subsequent measurement. Should it follow a course outside the abovementioned centiles, you need to consider that the growth of the foetus may be abnormal. If the measurement is above the ninetieth centile, you should consider polyhydramnios, or maternal diabetes in the case of a large baby. Should the tracing of the SF measurement fall below the tenth centile, you should consider oligohydramnios and intrauterine growth restriction (IUGR).

Figure 81.2 provides an example of the form that you need to fill in during these visits.

Criteria for the diagnosis of IUGR are as follows.

The SF measurement

- falls below the tenth centile on any three separate, but not necessarily sequential, occasions
- falls below the tenth centile on two sequential occasions at least two weeks apart
- shows no growth over three measurements at least two weeks apart
- is below the previous measurement.

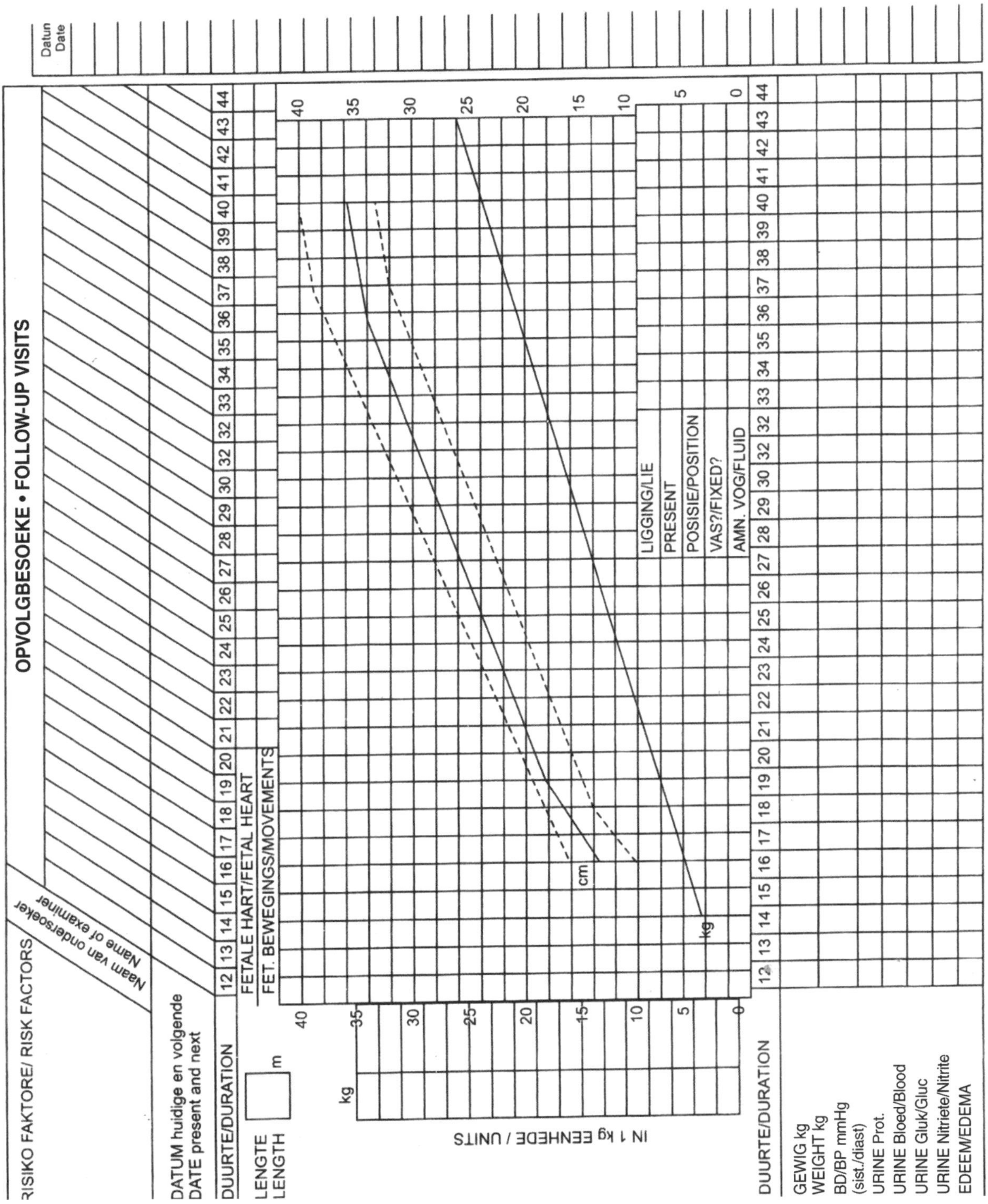

Figure 81.2 Antenatal follow-up visit form

Source: http://www.doh.gov.za/docs/forms/matrec_guide.pdf

As has been touched on above, the SF measurement is sometimes *misused* to determine the **gestation** of the pregnancy. In this case, the distance is charted on the solid middle line of the graph. Then the current gestation can be read off the x-axis. This assumes that the pregnancy is "average" up to that point, that is that no IUGR is present and that the foetus falls into the fiftieth centile. Nevertheless, you still need to accurately monitor for the abovementioned conditions indicated by crossing the centiles.

The three measurements – consisting of the dates, that is the last normal menstrual period (LNMP), the sonar and the SF – should always be used in combination with each other to establish the "final" expected date of delivery (EDD), and thereby gestation. If one of these measurements is missing then your determination becomes less accurate. You need to investigate any incongruity between these parameters.

82 How to examine a pregnant woman

HANNES STEINBERG

Your examination of a pregnant woman, in contrast to an examination of a woman who is not pregnant, differs only with respect to the abdomen. Certain conditions are more frequent with pregnancy, and therefore it is appropriate for you to look for them in this case.

Always ask her to empty her bladder before you examine her abdomen. Moreover, you can use this opportunity to collect a midstream urine specimen.

On the first visit, you should perform a full clinical examination. At follow-up visits for antenatal care, you need check only certain aspects routinely. If your patient complains of a particular symptom, however, you must investigate it fully.

Risk grading is useful and important in antenatal care. Refer to the suggested risk grades that are published in the maternal guidelines for community health centres and district hospitals (Guidelines for maternity care in South Africa. Department of Health: 26–27).

Examination at first visit

Your general examination should include the following:

- Jaundice, anaemia, cyanosis, clubbing, oedema and lymphadenopathy (JACCOL), and vital signs
- Blood pressure (BP), which is also an important focus in antenatal care. If your patient has a diastolic blood pressure of higher than 90 mmHg, you need to treat her actively.
- Weight – monitoring of this should be ongoing.
- Head and neck, checking specifically for lymph nodes, which might indicate TB or HIV, and thyromegaly
- Teeth – owing to progression of dental decay in pregnancy
- Chest – for clear lung sounds
- Heart – to exclude murmurs and valvular lesions
- Breasts – for possible difficulties with breastfeeding, such as inverted nipples

- Spine – as severe scoliosis or kyphosis may limit normal delivery
- Abdominal palpation:
  - SF measurement – see Chapter 81
  - Check the lie of the foetus, if it is older than 34 weeks.
  - Check the presenting part, cephalic or breech, if the foetus is older than 34 weeks.
  - Check for engagement from 36 weeks onwards.
  - Check the foetal heart for rate, variability, and decelerations or accelerations.
  - Check the clinical impression of liquor volume – increased or decreased.
- Vulva – for warts or possible obstructions to the delivery
- Vagina, if suggested by history – to exclude infection and perform a Pap smear
- Special investigations should include the following:
  - Urine dipsticks for protein, blood and sugar – to exclude infection and diabetes
  - Hb determination – to exclude anaemia
  - Blood grouping ABO and Rhesus
  - RPR determination – to exclude syphilis
  - HIV determination with the necessary pre- and post-test counselling – to prevent mother-to-child transmission
  - An anatomical screening sonar at 22 weeks – for screening or for gestational age at 13 weeks (see Chapter 83)
  - Anything else that may be indicated by your patient's history or revealed by the examination

Examination at follow-up visits

Your subsequent examinations should include the following:

- Always check your patient's BP.
- Remember to position her tilted to one side to prevent inferior vena cava syndrome.

- Perform abdominal palpation as described above.

- Always do urine dipsticks to look for infection – leucocytes *and* nitrates – and exclude proteinuria, especially if her BP is raised. You can also use the urine test to screen for gestational diabetes, although it is not that sensitive. If you find glycosuria on more than one occasion, further investigate with a modified glucose tolerance test (GTT).

- Monitor her weight. *Take care* not to over-interpret changes, as the normal range of weight gain in pregnant women is wide.

Examination on admission for labour

Should you need to admit your patient for labour, you also need to perform a basic examination. This examination should include:

- A good history – to assess for signs and symptoms of labour
- The vital signs and JACCOL
- Head and neck

- Chest – for signs of pneumonia
- Heart – to ensure that there are no murmurs or failure
- Abdominal palpation, as for antenatal care. However, in your notes, you would record the engagement of the presenting part and include observation of contractions with regard to frequency and duration.
- Vagina – as described in Chapter 89
- Urine – for protein, blood and glucose
- Hb – to confirm that it is above 10 g/dl
- Anything that follows from her particular history or from an abnormal finding of any of the above

It is essential that you make comprehensive, clear and legible notes after you have completed the examination. You can use the antenatal period effectively in training yourself to keep patient-retained records. Within the state health sector it is common practice to give the patient the record with all the above findings for her to look after and present at further visits.

83 How to do a single screening ultrasound in pregnancy

HANNES STEINBERG

In a normal pregnancy, it is still recommended that the woman has one ultrasound examination during her pregnancy. The timing would depend on the resolution of the equipment. You can do it at 13–14 weeks with high resolution machines, but you should do it at 20–22 weeks for maximum anatomical screening benefit.

Figure 83.1 shows an example of an ultrasound in a normal pregnancy.

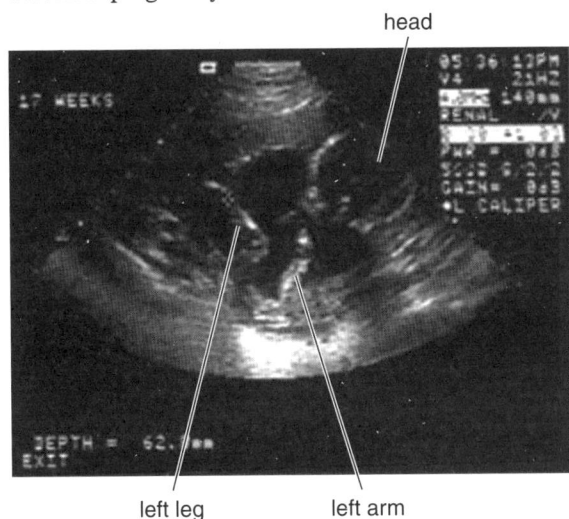

Figure 83.1 Normal pregnancy ultrasound

We will now discuss the main reasons, and their related procedures, for performing an ultrasound during pregnancy.

To confirm the gestational age of the foetus

You take measurements of the different foetal body parts, that is, you perform biometry, and combine them in various ways to produce tables of estimation of the gestational age. Most sonar machines have the biometry tables in their memory banks, to which you can refer once you have taken the measurements.

Follow these procedures:

- In the first trimester, you measure the crown to rump (CRL) length – this is accurate for gestational age. You obtain this by measuring the distance from the caudal pole to the head, that is the entire length of the foetus.

- From about 11 weeks pregnancy onwards, you need to measure the bi-parietal diameter (BPD), the femur length (FL) and the abdominal circumference (AC). Figures 83.2 to 83.4 respectively illustrate these ultrasounds. In order to do so correctly, you need to visualise the anatomical structure in the correct plane and measure from standardised landmarks.

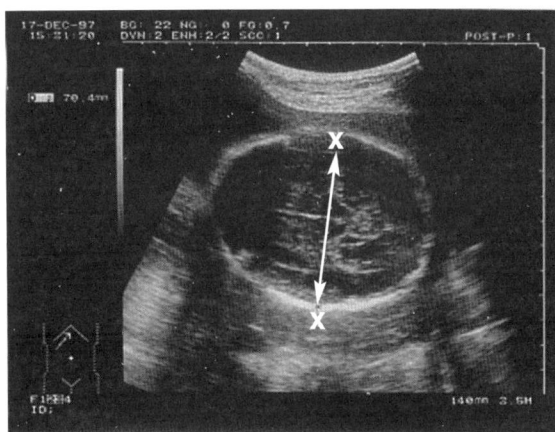

Figure 83.2 BPD ultrasound

- Measure the BPD at the broadest section on the coronal plane, at the level of the lateral ventricles. The picture needs to show symmetry on each side of the falx. Take the greatest distance between the parietal bones, perpendicular to the falx, and measure from the inside of the bone on one side to the outside of the bone on the other side.

- Measure the femur length on a lateral view depicting the entire length of the long bone. *Take*

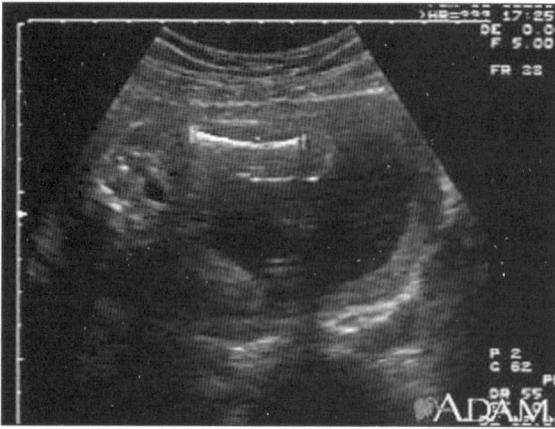

Figure 83.3 FL ultrasound

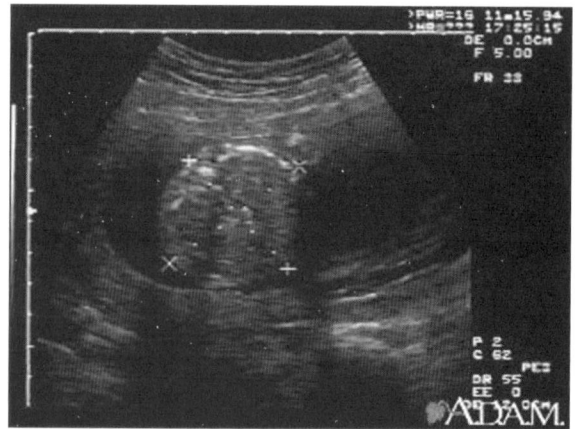

Figure 83.4 AC ultrasound

care to identify the femur correctly, as it can easily be confused with either the tibia and fibula or even the humerus. If the femur is depicted in its entire length it throws a sonographic shadow below.

- Measure the abdominal circumference at the level of the stomach bubble and the liver, below the diaphragm. The circumference should not be squashed, that is it should be a relatively round shape. Also measure the outer circumference of the skin.

- The software program takes these three measurements (BPD, femur length and abdominal circumference) into account. It then calculates an estimated gestational age and foetal weight.

The gestational age estimated in this manner becomes less accurate as the pregnancy progresses. Generally, during the first trimester this method is accurate within one week either side, in the second trimester within two weeks either side and in the third trimester only within three weeks either side. You must be aware of these limits, and note that the sonar is evidently not a suitable tool to measure gestational age in the third trimester.

To locate the placenta

The location of the placenta is significant. You need to review a low-lying placenta at 22 weeks and again at 30 weeks. It is possible that the placenta is initially low lying but that it "migrates up" the uterine wall as the lower segment develops.

Figure 83.5 is an example of a placental ultrasound.

Once you have confirmed the placenta to be praevia in the third trimester, warn your patient about the condition and its presenting symptoms, and manage it appropriately. Should you be able to con-

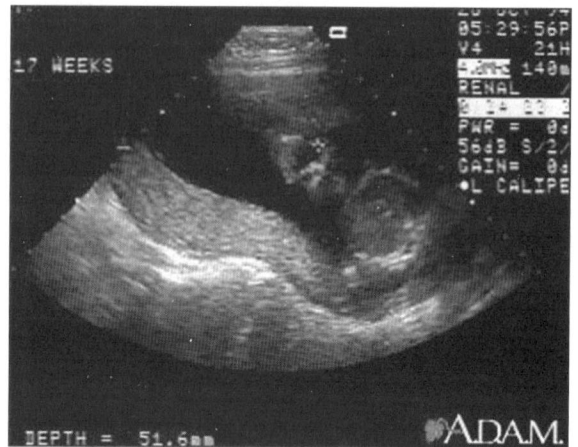

Figure 83.5 Placental ultrasound

firm no praevia in the third trimester follow-up, do not consider a diagnosis of placenta praevia if your patient presents with a vaginal bleed later on in pregnancy.

To do an anatomical screening

It is best for the anatomical screening to be done at 20–22 weeks' gestation by a person trained in the procedure. Screen the foetus from head to toe to establish normality of most major organs.

Follow these procedures:

- Check the brain on various planes, looking for symmetry and the different structures within the skull.

- Screen the back for abnormalities such as spina bifida. Trace the entire spinal column in the coronal as well as sagittal planes to look for widening and symmetry.

- Confirm the four-chamber structure of the heart, and note its size within the thorax. The heart should cover about a third of the thoracic surface area in the coronal plane.

- Confirm the size and normality of the liver, kidneys and bowel, as well as identify the stomach bubble. Should the bubble be absent it may indicate atresia of the gastrointestinal tract.

- Screen the limbs and umbilical cord for normality.

- Comment on the liquor volume, which you determine by establishing the amniotic fluid index (AFI). Calculate the AFI by adding up the length of the deepest pools of liquor measured in each of the four quadrants of the maternal abdomen. Measure the pools in the perpendicular and in centimetres, and do not include the umbilical cord. A normal measurement would be between 5 and 25 cm; less than 5 cm would indicate oligohydramnios and greater than 25 cm constitutes polyhydramnios.

- Many women are interested in knowing the gender of the foetus, which in most cases is of little medical importance. You need a lot of experience to be able to identify the gender correctly.

To exclude multiple pregnancies

You may find it difficult to exclude multiple pregnancies as you can see a single foetus's head from different angles. However, at 22 weeks the foetus should still be sufficiently small for you to be able to distinguish more than one gestation on the ultrasound, for example seeing two heads on one view.

Once you have indeed diagnosed a multiple pregnancy you need to check and measure the foetuses individually. Try to distinguish between twins that are di-amniotic, that is two separate amniotic sacs, or di-chorionic, that is two distinct chorions. This situation will affect your antenatal follow-up plan for this patient. Figure 83.6 is an example of an ultrasound of twin foetuses.

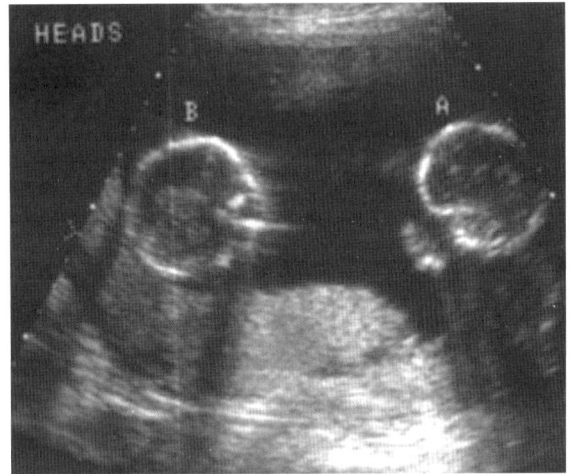

Figure 83.6 Ultrasound of twin foetuses

How to assess foetal well-being through its movements

HANNES STEINBERG

In the audit of unexplained stillbirths published in the "Saving Babies 2003: Fourth Perinatal Care Survey of South Africa", inappropriate response to poor foetal movement, has been cited as the most frequent patient-related avoidable factor (28% of cases).

When a foetus grows as it should, you tend to assume that all is well. You monitor such growth either by the serial SF measurements (see Chapter 81) or by serial sonar measurements, if conditions predisposing to intrauterine growth restriction exist, such as hypertensive proteinuria. It is important that you investigate insufficient growth.

Foetal movements

Another indicator that you can use to assess well-being is the movements of the foetus. Regular movements are a positive sign. Therefore, it is recommended that you make a habit of asking the mother about foetal movements at each antenatal visit after 28 weeks. She should normally feel these movements at about 16 weeks in a **multigravida** and at about 20 weeks in a **primigravida**.

There are two explanations for the possibility that she does not feel movement: she could be too active to feel them, or there are none to feel. In the former case, advise her to stop all activity, to sit or to lie down on her side, to read a book or drink a cup of tea, and to concentrate on feeling the movements for an hour a day, for example after breakfast. In the latter instance, there could be some abnormality, in which case you will need to investigate further.

Managing decreased foetal movements at home

If the mother does feel movement, you need to assess the possibility that those movements are decreasing. In this case, the number of movements that she notices in one hour is less important than a decrease in the number when compared to previous observation periods. If the number decreases to less than half of the "normal" count, the foetus may be at increased risk of foetal distress. Even if the foetus normally moves infrequently, a count of three or fewer movements per hour indicates that the foetus may be in danger.

In the case of reduced foetal movements, advise the mother to lie down for another hour and do a recount. If the number of movements increases, there is little need for concern. However, if the number does not increase, advise her to report to the clinic or hospital immediately. Figure 84.1 illustrates this process step by step.

Managing decreased foetal movements in hospital

- WITHOUT THE AID OF ANTENATAL FOETAL MONITORING

When the mother is in hospital, you need to listen to the foetal heart in order to exclude an intrauterine death (IUD). If you can hear the foetal heart beating, and if antenatal foetal monitoring (AFM) equipment is not available, advise the mother to count the foetal movements over a period of six hours of rest. Having felt four or more movements, she must repeat the count the following day. However, if she feels fewer than four movements, you need to plan the appropriate method of delivery for her baby as a matter of urgency.

Figure 84.2 illustrates this process step by step.

- WITH THE AID OF ANTENATAL FOETAL MONITORING

If the AFM equipment *is* available, you can obtain an AFM strip from a cardiotocograph. Consider the strip "reactive" only if you find these three criteria:

1. Normal baseline heart rate of between 115 and 160 beats per minute.

2. Good beat-to-beat variability on the heart's tracing, that is variation of more than five beats per minute.

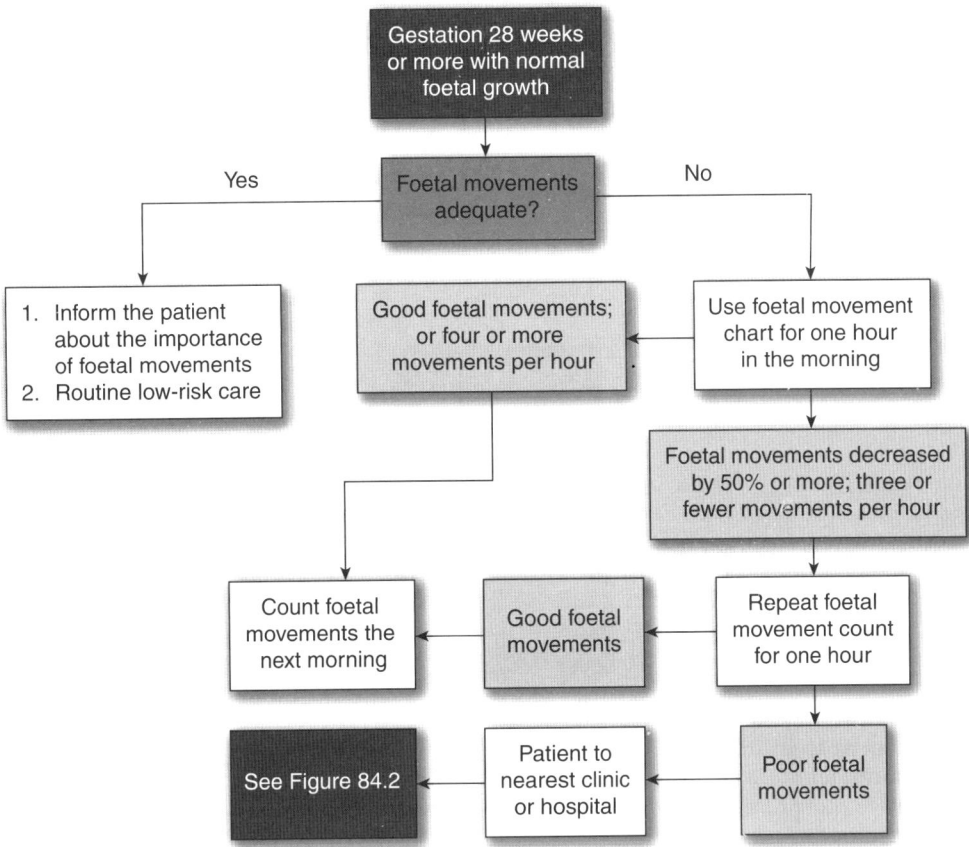

Figure 84.1 Managing decreased foetal movements at home

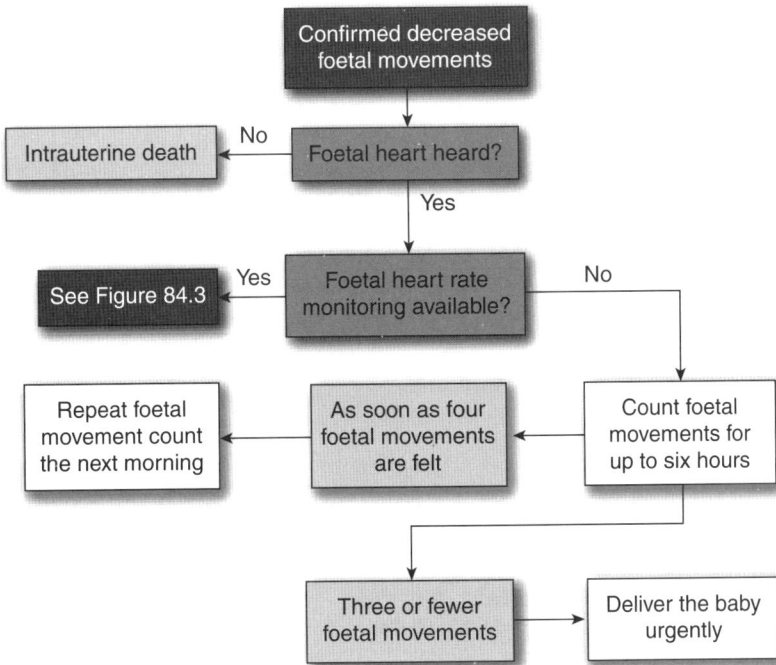

Figure 84.2 Managing confirmed decreased foetal movements in hospital

3. Two accelerations in 10 minutes. (An **acceleration** is an increase of the foetal heartbeat by 15 beats per minute for a period of at least 15 seconds and no deceleration.)

Bear in mind that the foetus has a "sleep–wake" cycle of 20 minutes. A reactive AFM is reassuring as it strongly suggests foetal well-being. However, if you cannot deduct that the strip is reactive, then again you need to plan the appropriate method of delivery for her baby as a matter of urgency.

In this case, you need to consider whether

- the foetus is viable, that is above 26 weeks gestation
- there are facilities to look after a foetus this size
- the mother's cervix is favourable for induction.

Figure 84.3 illustrates this process step by step.

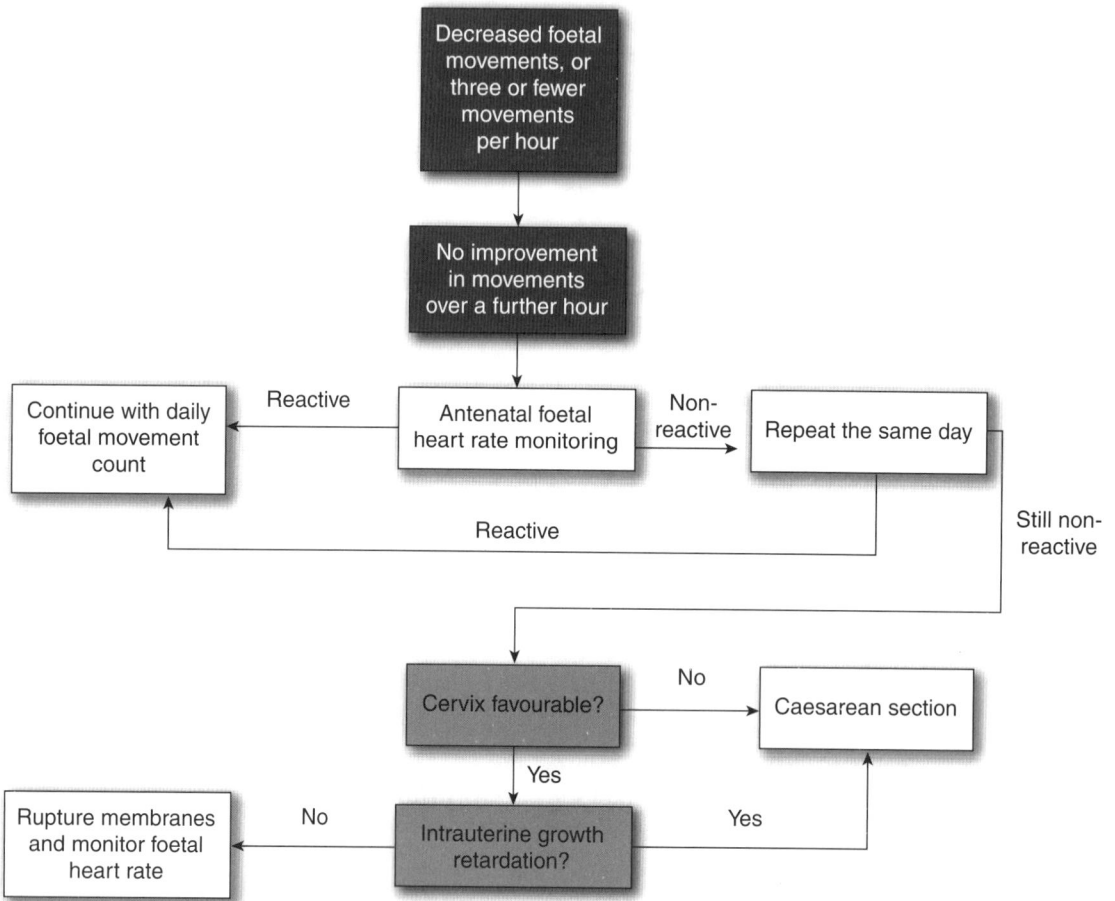

Figure 84.3 Using the antenatal foetal heart rate monitor to consider emergency delivery

85 How to conduct an external cephalic version

HANNES STEINBERG

The external cephalic version has been known to reduce the rate of breech deliveries and Caesarean sections.

Indications

You would attempt the version in a breech presentation beyond 37 weeks' gestation with no contraindication to performing the procedure. You can perform it in a patient in the latent phase of labour or in early labour.

Contraindications

You would not perform the version under the following circumstances:

- Multiple pregnancy
- Ante-partum haemorrhage
- Pregnancy of less than 37 weeks – because this baby still has a good chance of turning on his own
- Rupture of membranes – the liquor is necessary as a medium in which to turn the baby; it becomes too difficult to turn him in the absence of liquor.
- Patient who is scheduled to have an elective Caesarean section for another indication
- Patient has had a Caesarean section previously (a relative contraindication) – the uterine scar can be ruptured if too much force is exerted, and these patients often have elective Caesarean sections
- Hypertensive disease in pregnancy (a relative contraindication) – as the baby may be growth-retarded and the liquor severely reduced
- Suspicion of placental insufficiency
- Mother is HIV positive with a high viral load.

Procedure

You need to confirm the foetal position and well-being before beginning an external cephalic version. Also, if the mother's blood group is Rh negative, you need to administer 100 µg (500 IU) anti-D.

The post-partum dose of 300 µg is still recommended for this patient once she has delivered.

To perform the version, you need to follow this procedure:

- Have the mother lying in a semi-lateral position.
- Administer 10 µg of hexoprenaline to her intravenously to relax the uterus.
- Do not sedate her.
- Use external manual pressure abdominally to lift the presenting part out of the pelvis and then turning, or somersaulting, the foetus around to a cephalic position. Exert pressure with hands placed at either end, that is head and breech, of the foetus, slowly facilitating the turning and taking care not to hurt the mother.
- Do not use excessive force.
- Immediately after the procedure, ensure foetal well-being. You can monitor the foetal heart for up to 20 minutes.

Complications

During the procedure, these complications could occur:

- Abruptio placenta, which you need to manage and deliver by Caesarean section as an emergency
- You may precipitate labour (1% incidence) – then proceed with vaginal delivery and manage as normal labour.
- Spontaneous rupture of membranes. Manage this on merit.
- Foeto-maternal haemorrhage, which is why you need to give the anti-D prophylactically to the Rh-negative mother and why it is not advised for you to do versions in HIV-positive patients with high viral loads
- Tightening of a loop of the umbilical cord with possible foetal demise has been described in the literature, but it occurs rarely.

Should the version be *successful*, you need to verify the position at further follow-up of the patient, and she may await labour. Should the version be *unsuccessful*, you need to work out a delivery plan for your patient. It should be clear to you whether to proceed with a Caesarean section or to attempt a vaginal breech delivery.

However, you would *not* attempt a vaginal delivery of a breech in these circumstances:

- Estimated foetal mass over 3.5 kg
- Estimated foetal mass between 1 000 g and 1 500 g
- Extended foetal head
- Footling breech
- Kneeling breech

86 How to perform amniocentesis

HANNES STEINBERG

Amniocentesis is an invasive procedure that has significant risk, and therefore also has highly specific indications. A 1% foetal loss is frequently cited for this procedure (Nel 1995).

Indications

You will perform amniocentesis if you are

- determining foetal maturity
- diagnosing chromosomal or inherited biochemical abnormalities
- assessing blood group incompatibility.

You may need to perform an amniocentesis in the first abovementioned instance when the foetus is to be delivered electively – for example by elective Caesarean section, or at the mother's request for labour induction for social reasons – but when some doubt exists as to its gestation or maturity and therefore the appropriate time for delivery. Should the foetus be immature, it would be unwise for you to proceed with the elective delivery unless it is obstetrically indicated.

To aid the abovementioned diagnosis and assessment, you need to request specialised laboratory tests, which can only be done in specialised centres.

Procedure

You need to obtain your patient's informed consent for the amniocentesis.

You need to follow this procedure:

- If possible, perform the procedure with ultrasonographic guidance.
- Have your patient empty her bladder.
- Clean her lower abdomen with antiseptic solution and drape it.
- Using external manual pressure, hold the presenting part out of the pelvis.
- Gently insert a 20- or 22-gauge needle attached to a syringe in the suprapubic area and direct it

towards a level just above her kidneys in the midline.
- *Take care* not to damage the foetus, and avoid any resistance to introducing the needle, as this may cause injury.
- As you advance the needle, maintain slight negative pressure in order to aspirate fluid when you encounter the amniotic pool. Figure 86.1 illustrates this part of the procedure.

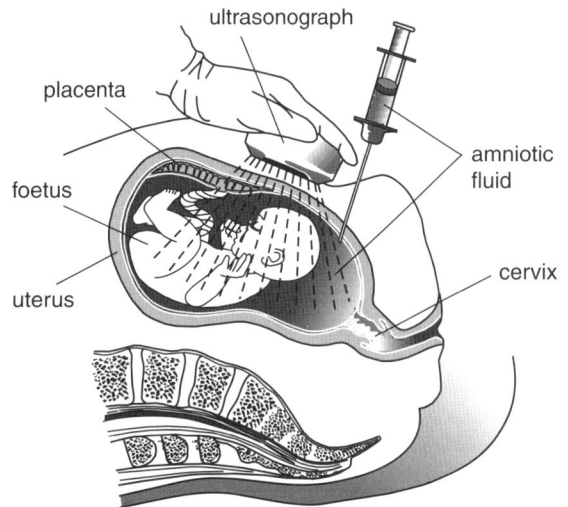

Figure 86.1 Aspirating amniotic fluid

- Ensure that the specimen is not blood-stained.
- Aspirate 4–5 ml amniotic fluid and withdraw the needle.
- Apply a sterile dressing over the skin where the aspiration took place.
- Either send the fluid to the laboratory in the appropriate tube for the determination of the lecithin–sphingomyelin (L–S) ratio, or perform the "shake test" (see below).
- After the procedure check foetal well-being.

Mother and foetus need no further after-care.

The shake test

In this test, mix 1 ml amniotic fluid with an equal amount of alcohol (95%) in a test tube. Shake the tube for 30 seconds and read it after a minute.

If an uninterrupted foam ring has formed on the surface of the fluid for the circumference of the tube, you can regard the test as positive. This result indicates sufficient lung maturity for delivery. The incidence of false negative test results is higher with the shake test than with the laboratory determination of the L–S ratio.

You can also perform this test in a newborn within 30 minutes of delivery, having obtained the amniotic fluid from a gastric aspirate using a nasogastric tube. This could help you to distinguish a hyaline membrane disease from congenital pneumonia in a low birth weight infant.

87 How to assess foetal well-being during labour

HANNES STEINBERG

It is important that you observe the foetus during labour so that you can ensure that it is able to withstand the strains and pressures of the mother's contractions. The stress of normal labour should have no ill effect on a healthy foetus. But at times the foetus does not have sufficient reserves to withstand the stress and it then develops foetal distress (FD). You need to identify this and react to it quickly.

Factors that *reduce* the supply of oxygen to the foetus include:

- Uterine contractions
- Reduced blood flow through the placenta, e.g. maternal hypotension
- Abruptio placenta – if indicated clinically or if you find FD (reduces oxygenation of baby's blood)
- Cord prolapse (causes cord to collapse)

Normally, uterine contractions should not reduce the foetal oxygen supply, as placental blood has sufficient reserves. However, in the situation of placental insufficiency, prolonged and frequent contractions, and cord compression, the foetal oxygen supply may well be compromised. A reduction of oxygen supply to the foetus leads to foetal hypoxia. Severe foetal hypoxia will result in FD and, if prolonged, will result in foetal death.

To assess the condition of the foetus during labour, you need to use these parameters:

- The foetal heart rate, that is the baseline rate and the presence of decelerations
- The presence or absence of meconium in the liquor

The foetal heart rate

It is suggested that in every woman in labour you should observe the foetal heart every 30 minutes. You can listen to and confirm it during and just after a contraction. Do this with a foetal stethoscope, a Doppler machine or electronic foetal heart monitoring strip, otherwise known as a cardiotocograph (CTG). Figure 87.1 is an example of such a graph.

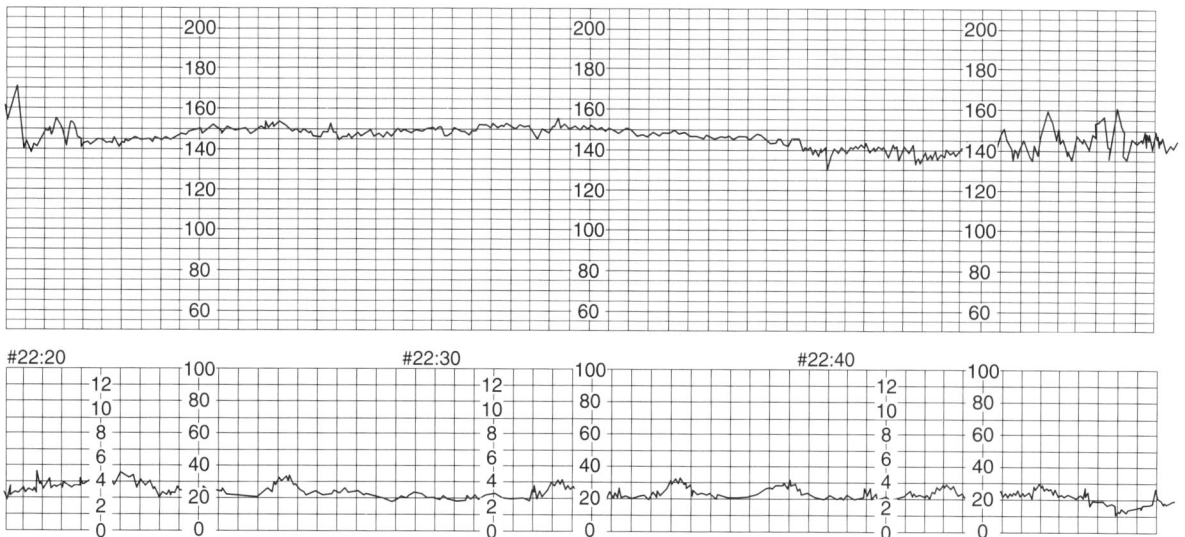

Figure 87.1 A foetal cardiotocograph with the foetal heart rate above and uterine pressure below

You should be able to recognise one of these foetal heart rate patterns:

- **Normal** – baseline of 120–160 beats per minute and no decelerations during or after the contractions
- **Early decelerations** – slowing of the foetal heart rate starting at the beginning of the contraction and returning to normal by the end of the contraction; rapid recovery
- **Variable decelerations** – these have no fixed relationship to contractions
- **Baseline tachycardia** – a baseline rate of above 160 beats per minute
- **Late decelerations** – slowing of the foetal heart rate after the peak of the contraction and returning to the baseline within 45–60 seconds of the contraction having ended; slow recovery (see Figure 87.2)
- **Baseline bradycardia** – baseline rate of below 100 beats per minute

Early decelerations, variable decelerations and a baseline tachycardia indicate an increased risk for FD during labour. Late decelerations and foetal bradycardia indicate FD during labour. If you find FD, you need to initiate intrauterine resuscitation and deliver the foetus as soon as possible.

To perform **intrauterine resuscitation**, you need to do the following:

- Lie the mother on her side.
- Administer intravenous fluids, that is Ringer's lactate at ± 200 ml/hr, to ensure better placental flow.
- Administer oxygen to the mother by mask or nasal prongs.
- Give tocolytics to reduce the burden of the contraction causing the hypoxia – 12.5 µg hexoprenaline (otherwise known as Ipradol®) IVI over three minutes.
- Deliver the foetus as soon as possible.

Meconium in the liquor

Meconium in the liquor indicates that the foetus has passed stools *in utero*. This is not a normal phenomenon unless the foetus is post-date. Moreover, the presence should warn you that either there is or was FD, or there is a high risk of FD. You need to monitor the foetal heart carefully for decelerations. If you find them, you need to manage delivery quickly.

The thickness of the meconium is not necessarily an indicator of the severity of the present distress. However, the thicker the meconium, the greater the damage caused if the infant aspirates the meconium during the birth process.

You need to thoroughly suction the infant's mouth and pharynx *after* the delivery of his head but *before* the delivery of his shoulders and chest, that is before he breathes, irrespective of the method of delivery. Should he need resuscitation, it is imperative that you suction the airways via the endotracheal tube before you start ventilation (see Chapter 78).

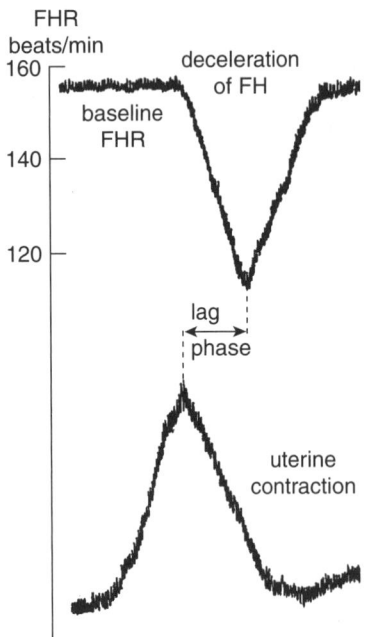

Figure 87.2 Late deceleration

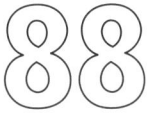

88 How to use a partogram and assess progress of labour

HANNES STEINBERG

The partogram

The partogram was developed in southern Africa by Prof. Hugh Philpott and Barbara Kwast. Through the WHO, it has become a well-known instrument and its use is mandatory during observation of a woman in labour. In its guidelines for maternity care for community health centres and district hospitals (2003), the South African Department of Health describes the failure to use a partogram while observing a patient during labour as substandard care.

The partogram is a document that is designed and standardised for all maternity admissions throughout South Africa, and thus it must be included in each maternity case that is recorded. The partogram includes a graphic representation of the observations that you take during labour. It records the state of affairs of the foetus and the mother, and it clearly captures the progress of labour.

Progress of labour

You should make and record observations every 30 minutes. The following parameters are clearly recorded on the partogram, which as a whole gives a rapid appraisal of the progress of labour:

- You should record the **descent of the presenting part**, which is the head in most cases, on the same graph as the cervical dilatation. Palpate and chart the measure of the proportion of the head, which is expressed in fifths of the head, above the pelvic brim. Record this opposite the appropriate number in the "level of head" section.

- Measure the **contractions** in terms of frequency and duration, and depict them on the partogram. There are five blocks for the contractions. The number of blocks that you colour in on the partogram should correspond to the number of contractions that the mother has had in the 10 minutes that you used for the measuring. The way

that the block is filled in denotes the duration of the contraction. If the contraction lasts less than 20 seconds, fill in the block as a checked flag. If the contraction lasts longer than 20 seconds, but less than 40 seconds, colour in the block with shading. If the contraction lasts longer than 40 seconds, colour in the block solidly. This clearly gives the health professional a graphical indication of the quality of contractions you have measured during the observed labour. The desired frequency is 3–4 contractions in 10 minutes, lasting for 45 seconds each.

- Plot the **cervical dilatation** on the same graph. You measure it in centimetres, with each block on the y-axis representing 1 cm. The lines on the x-axis of the graph represent one-hour intervals. The dilatation of the cervix is expected to be at least 1 cm per hour in the active phase of labour. Should the dilatation not progress at that rate, you can easily diagnose a delay in the progress of labour, which should be followed by the appropriate management. Recorded this as an "X" against the appropriate number in the "cervical dilatation and effacement" section.

These three parameters dictate whether or not the labour is progressing adequately.

Conditions of the foetus and mother

You also need to note the condition of the foetus and the mother throughout the process as a measure of their well-being. You should note the foetus's condition at the top of the partogram, and note the mother's condition at the bottom of the page.

With regard to the **foetus**, you must record its heart rate, its baseline rate, the variability, whether decelerations have occurred and, if so, of what type they were. Should the membranes have ruptured, after each vaginal examination you need to note further what colour the liquor was, as well as the degree of caput and of moulding, (that is whether it is on the sagittal suture – parieto-parieto (PP) – or the lambdoid suture – occipito-parieto (OP)).

Caput denotes the swelling of the foetal scalp due to pressure. **Moulding** refers to the overlapping of the skull bones as the foetus passes through the birth canal so that the diameter of the foetal head is minimised. If the sutures are obliterated this would denote Grade 1 moulding. If the bone plates overlap but are reducible, this denotes Grade 2. If the bone plates are not reducible, this denotes Grade 3, or severe moulding.

With regard to the **mother**, you must note her vital signs and her urine output. Use dipstick tests, such as for glucose, ketones or proteins, to ensure that you identify possible dehydration and exhaustion in good time and manage these conditions appropriately. Although there is no space on most partograms for you to note the psychological state of the mother during labour, you must always assess this state and take it into account as part of her management.

The bottom of the partogram provides a space for you to record the management of the labour. There you should note the results of the reassessment of management that you need to conduct every four hours: the problems or risks that you have identified, and the management that you have planned.

Use of the partogram

In general, you can put your patient on the partogram when she is in *established* labour. This is not always easy to judge, but if she has painful contractions *with* cervical changes, you can regard her as being in labour.

Figure 88.1 is an example of a partogram

If she does not progress in labour as you have expected, that is if she falls below the alert line, then you need to apply the "rule of Ps". The rule comprises the patient, the power, the passage and the passenger. In order for you to establish and then correct any abnormalities, you need to ask the following questions:

- **Patient:**
  - Is the psychological support sufficient?

  - Is the mother exhausted and/or dehydrated?
  - Is she developing ketonuria? If so, you need to correct this.

- **Power:**
  - Are the contractions sufficient, that is 3–4 in 10 minutes lasting for longer than 45 seconds each?
  - If not, is there a contraindication to augmenting the contractions with oxytocin?

- **Passage:**
  - Are there signs of cephalo-pelvic disproportion, that is caput, moulding and no descent of the presenting part? If so, consider Caesarean section.
  - Is there outlet obstruction, that is small contracted pelvis, inlet or outlet? If so, consider Caesarean section.
  - Is the bladder full and obstructing the passage? If so, empty the bladder.
  - Is the rectum loaded and obstructing the passage? If so, empty the rectum.

- **Passenger:**
  - Is the position of the foetal head such that it could obstruct labour, that is occipito-posterior positions, of face, or brow?
  - Are there signs of cephalo-pelvic disproportion (CPD) on the foetus's head, that is caput and moulding?
  - Does the foetus have sufficient reserves, that is will it withstand the pressure of ongoing or stronger contractions, that is heart rate variability and deceleration? If not, you need to proceed to a Caesarean section delivery.

If you find any of the abovementioned abnormalities, you need to correct them. Following a further two hours of labour, you should reassess progress. If she then follows the action line and progresses satisfactorily, you can expect vaginal delivery. However, if she does not respond and progress of her labour continues to be unsatisfactory, you need to plan a Caesarean section delivery.

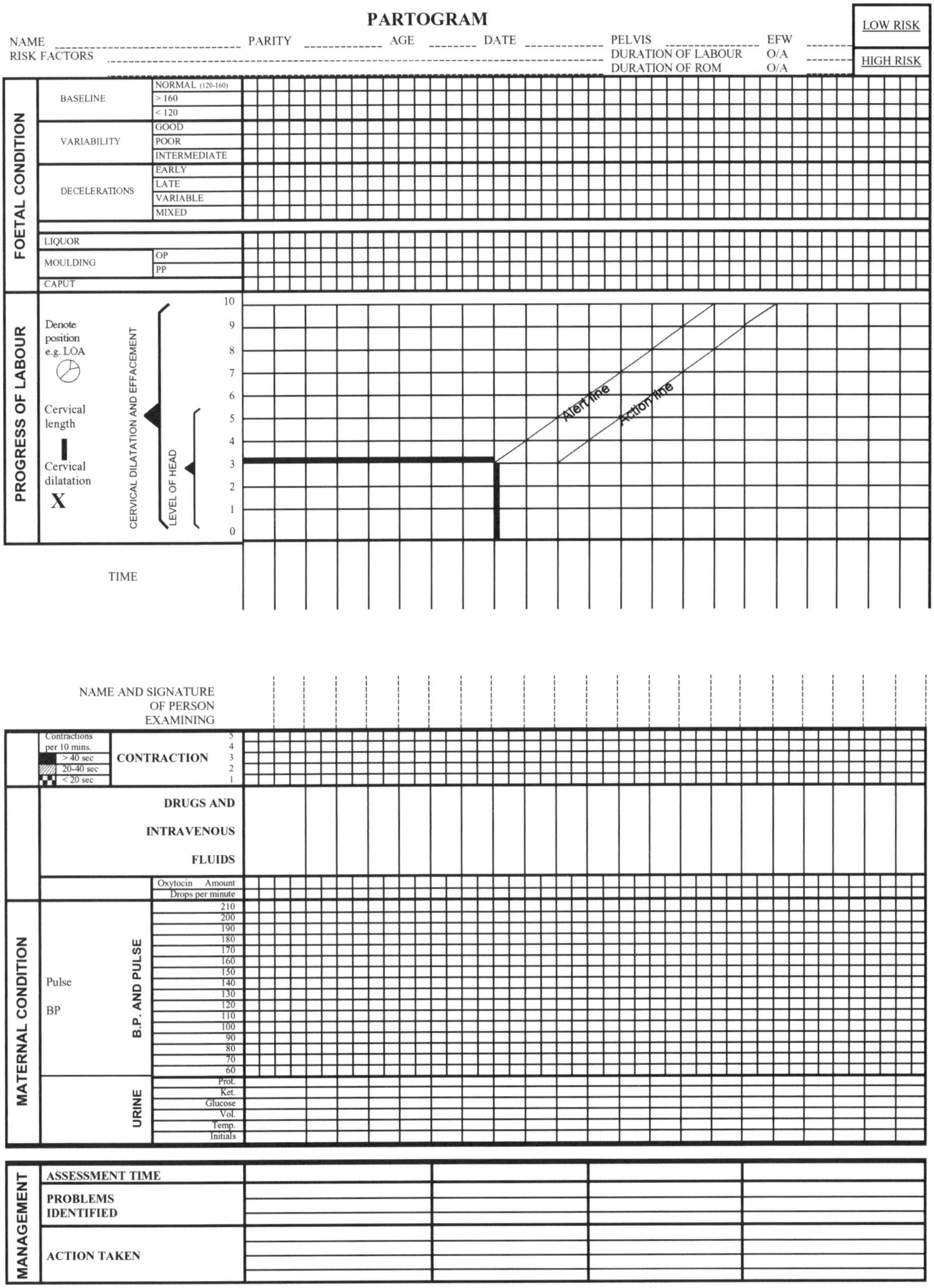

PARTOGRAM

Figure 88.1 A partogram

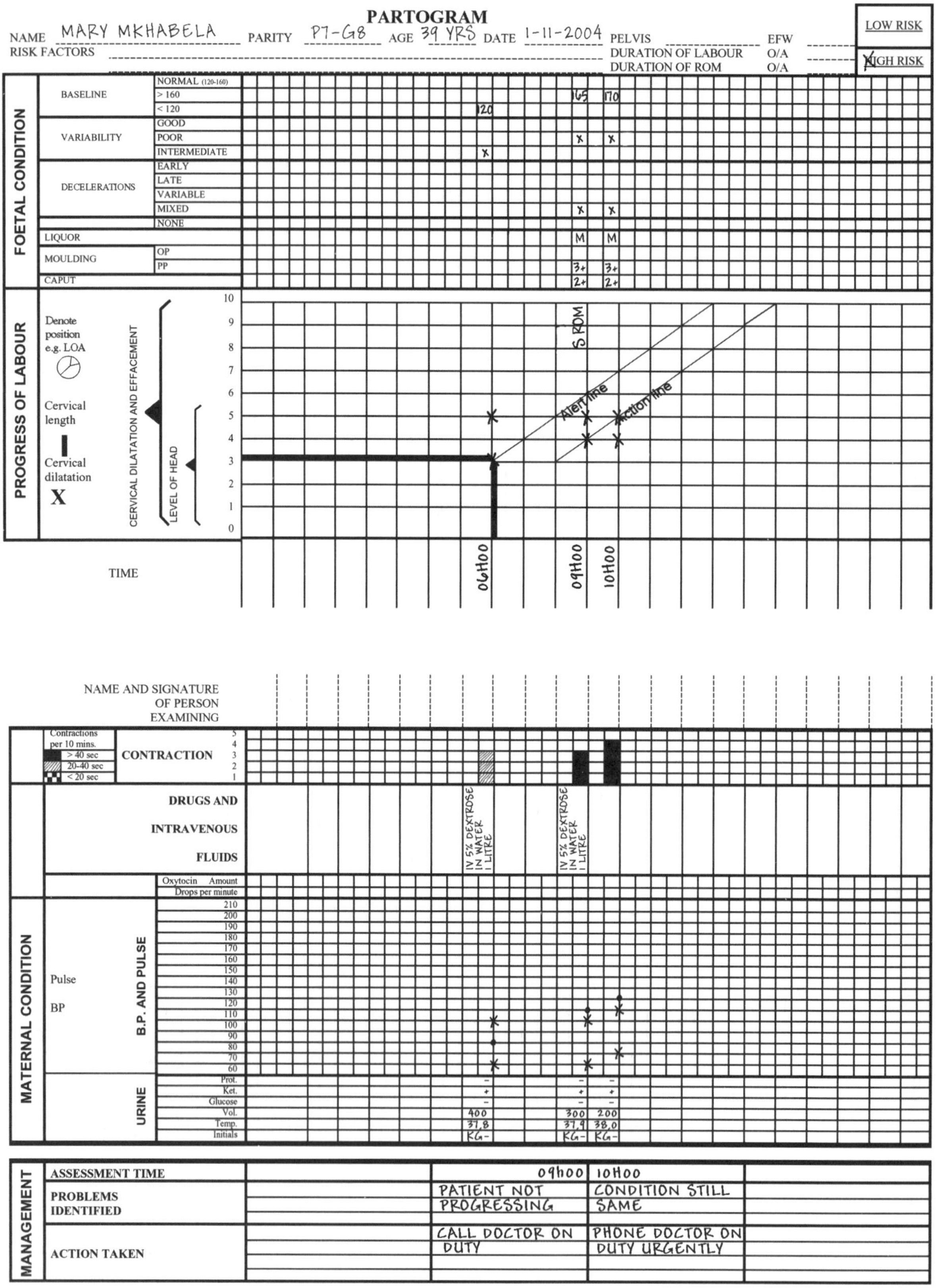

PARTOGRAM

NAME MARY MKHABELA   PARITY P7-G8   AGE 39 YRS   DATE 1-11-2004

RISK FACTORS _____

PELVIS _____   EFW _____

DURATION OF LABOUR O/A _____

DURATION OF ROM O/A _____

LOW RISK

HIGH RISK

FOETAL CONDITION

BASELINE	NORMAL (120-160)							
	> 160					165	170	
	< 120				120			
VARIABILITY	GOOD							
	POOR					X	X	
	INTERMEDIATE				X			
DECELERATIONS	EARLY							
	LATE							
	VARIABLE							
	MIXED					X	X	
	NONE							
LIQUOR						M	M	
MOULDING	OP							
	PP					3+	3+	
CAPUT						2+	2+	

PROGRESS OF LABOUR

Denote position e.g. LOA

Cervical length

Cervical dilatation X

CERVICAL DILATATION AND EFFACEMENT

LEVEL OF HEAD

TIME

(graph with Alert line and Action line, S ROM marked, X plots)

TIME: 06H00, 09H00, 10H00

NAME AND SIGNATURE OF PERSON EXAMINING

MATERNAL CONDITION

CONTRACTION	Contractions per 10 mins.				
> 40 sec					
20-40 sec					
< 20 sec					

DRUGS AND INTRAVENOUS FLUIDS: IV 5% DEXTROSE IN WATER 1 LITRE; IV 5% DEXTROSE IN WATER 1 LITRE

Oxytocin Amount / Drops per minute

B.P. AND PULSE (scale 210–60) Pulse, BP

URINE		400	300	200
Prot.				
Ket.				
Glucose				
Vol.		400	300	200
Temp.		37,8	37,9	38,0
Initials		KG-	KG-	KG-

MANAGEMENT

ASSESSMENT TIME		09h00	10H00	
PROBLEMS IDENTIFIED		PATIENT NOT PROGRESSING	CONDITION STILL SAME	
ACTION TAKEN		CALL DOCTOR ON DUTY	PHONE DOCTOR ON DUTY URGENTLY	

Figure 88.2 Example of a partially completed partogram

How to conduct a normal vaginal delivery

JULIA BLITZ-LINDEQUE

Preparation

Evidently, a normal vaginal delivery will follow a step-by-step process. Before actual delivery begins, try to ensure that your patient empties her bladder, or do it for her. Suggest to her that an empathic and supportive companion be present during the delivery.

Process

Labour consists of three stages. The first stage entails the onset of active labour to full cervical dilatation. The second stage lasts from full dilatation to actual delivery of the newborn baby. The third stage entails the delivery of the placenta.

Without describing the first stage of labour, we will now discuss each step of the delivery process in detail.

Cervical dilatation and appearance of the foetal head

Once the cervix is fully dilated and the foetal head has descended entirely into the pelvis, you can begin the delivery. Encourage the mother to bear down during the contractions. Have her sit in a semi-upright position, as this aids the descent of the foetus.

Check the foetal heart after each contraction. Record the maternal blood pressure and pulse every 15 minutes. The second stage usually lasts less than 30 minutes in a multigravida and 45 up to 60 minutes in a primigravida. Note that the administration of an epidural block can prolong the second stage somewhat.

It is not necessary for you to adhere rigidly to these time limits if the foetal head is descending and both mother and foetus are tolerating labour well, as demonstrated by a reassuring foetal heart rate pattern on cardiotocograph (CTG) or foetal heart sounds on auscultation.

Descent with further flexion

At this stage, the vertex is engaged in the brim of the pelvis, with the sagittal suture lying in the transverse diameter. The suture may be equidistant from the symphysis and the sacral promontory – this is **synclitism**. **Asynclitism**, in which the sagittal suture lies closer to one or other of the landmarks, may indicate reduction in the diameters of the pelvic inlet.

Internal rotation

Once the cervix is fully dilated and the membranes have ruptured, the presenting part descends to the level of the ischial spines, where rotation begins as the foetus's head meets the muscles of the mother's pelvic floor. Further flexion of the head occurs with rotation of the occipit towards an anterior position (occipito-anterior).

Disengagement by extension

With further contractions and maternal pushing efforts, the head continues to descend and the vertex appears, stretching the vulval orifice. At this point, you can assist flexion of the head by applying gentle downward pressure on the occiput, taking care to protect the perineum. These manoeuvres allow you to control the speed of the birth of the head.

The head should extend. Once it has crowned, advise the mother to stop pushing – she should only pant during contractions at this stage in order to help you control the speed of head delivery and allow the perineal muscles and skin to stretch slowly. In the uncommon situation where an episiotomy is required, you should perform it at the height of a contraction. The foetus's head then extends further and the mother's perineum sweeps over the forehead and face to release the head.

Restitution

The foetus's shoulders have now reached the muscles of the mother's pelvic floor, which again causes a rotation so that the bis-acromial diameter becomes antero-posterior in the pelvis. You see this movement as the foetal head returning to the position in which it was at the onset of labour, with the occipit moving from anterior to the right or the left.

Delivery of the shoulders

The shoulders deliver by lateral flexion, first posteriorly to disengage the anterior shoulder from behind the symphysis. You can aid this birth by applying downward and backward traction on the head. If the umbilical cord is looped around the baby's neck, disengage it now by slipping it over his head or cutting it.

Then lateral flexion anteriorly disengages the posterior shoulder. Lift the head gently upwards in an arc towards the mother's abdomen, while maintaining traction. This can help you to avoid damage to the perineum.

Inject 10 IU oxytocin intramuscularly to promote delivery of the placenta (see below).

Delivery of the rest of the foetus

Note that the remainder of the baby is then rapidly expelled. Clamp the umbilical cord in two places and cut between the clamps.

Assess the newborn for obvious congenital abnormalities. Determine a one-, a five- and a ten-minute Apgar score. Dry and wrap the newborn, and place him in his mother's arms. Promote early skin-to-skin contact and breastfeeding. If you need to perform resuscitation of the newborn, remember that warmth and oxygen are valuable adjuncts. See Chapter 78.

Active delivery of the placenta

This stage should take less than 20 minutes. When the mother has a contraction after delivering her baby, you can prevent uterine descent by pushing the uterus upwards towards the umbilicus with your left hand, while grasping the umbilical cord with your right hand and exerting extremely gentle traction in order to pull the placenta from the uterus. Known as the "Brandt Andrews manoeuvre", this is illustrated in Figure 89.1. Twist the membranes into a rope as you exert traction in order to strip them gently off the uterine wall.

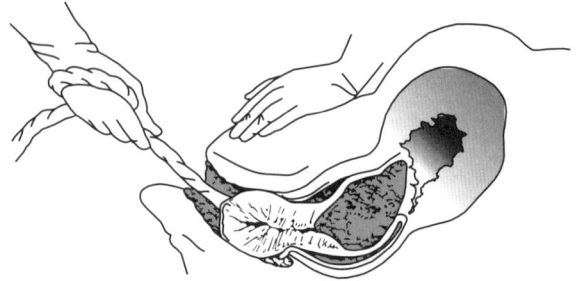

Figure 89.1 Exerting controlled cord traction (the Brandt Andrews manoeuvre)

Post-delivery

Inspect the mother's genital tract for any injuries. Repair any lacerations or the episiotomy, if you performed it (see Chapter 92). Examine the cervix for tears.

Assess completeness of the placenta and membranes. The defect in the membranes from the rupture should be round, not jagged. Ensure that no cotyledons are missing from the placenta. If there is any indication of missing tissue, you should explore the uterus immediately.

Ensure that there are no signs of excessive bleeding. Monitor the mother's pulse rate, her blood pressure, the state of uterine contraction and the amount of bleeding from the vagina.

Comprehensively and clearly record all details of the labour and delivery.

How to conduct an assisted vaginal delivery

HANNES STEINBERG

You would perform an assisted delivery during the second stage of labour to expedite the delivery. This is a common form of obstetric intervention. You can assist the delivery by performing a vacuum extraction or forceps delivery. However, note that both techniques have potential dangers – to perform them successfully, you must understand how to use the instruments.

Vacuum extraction

This is a safe procedure if you execute it correctly. It is the preferred procedure when rotation of the foetal head is necessary.

The instrument consists of a suction cup that is attached to a vacuum source via a vacuum gauge. A chain is attached to the cup through which you can apply traction once you have established the correct vacuum.

Indications

You need to perform this type of delivery in these instances:

- Delay in the second stage of labour, especially when the sagittal suture is in the transverse or oblique diameter
- The foetal head is deflexed during labour.

Contraindications

You should not perform this type of delivery under these circumstances:

- Prematurity, that is the foetus is younger than 34 weeks
- Foetal distress (FD) (a relative contraindication) – as a vacuum takes much longer to perform than a forceps delivery
- Uterine atony – because contractions are required for a vacuum extraction
- Foetal head is two fifths or more above the pelvic brim – as cephalic pelvic disproportion (CPD) is the likely diagnosis.

- A bleeding tendency of the foetus – as this may increase the risk of intracranial bleeding
- Breech or face presentations
- Further attempt after the vacuum cup has slipped off twice
- Cervix not fully dilated

Prerequisites

The following conditions must exist for the vacuum extraction to be safe:

- Vertex presentation, and the foetus must not be preterm
- Head not more than one fifth above the pelvic brim
- Cervix fully dilated
- You feel certain about the position of the presenting part and your ability to apply the suction cup over the occipital area.
- Membranes ruptured
- Maternal bladder and rectum empty
- Mother fully informed, conscious and cooperative
- Presence of strong uterine contractions

Sometimes an episiotomy is suggested but often only performed if the perineum is overstretched.

Procedure

The technique of vacuum extraction is well described by Cronjé, Grobler (2003). To perform the vacuum extraction, you need to follow this procedure:

- When your patient's cervix is fully dilated, you need to apply the largest possible vacuum cup to the occipit of the foetus.
- Apply antiseptic cream to the outside of the cup only.
- *Take care* that *at no stage* is any part of the cervix or vaginal wall sucked into the cup.

- Having correctly placed the cup, increase the vacuum gradually – by –0.2 kg/cm² every two minutes until –0.8 kg/cm² is reached – to allow the chignon to form.
- Apply traction only during contractions, during which you have also asked the mother to bear down. There should be progressive descent of the foetus with each pull.
- Ensure good flexion of the foetal head by initially pulling the occipit in the direction of the anterior fontanelle. Figure 90.1 illustrates this. As soon as you have achieved good flexion, apply traction in such a way that the chain (and tube) remain perpendicular to the dome of the cup. This ensures traction in the direction of the birth canal.

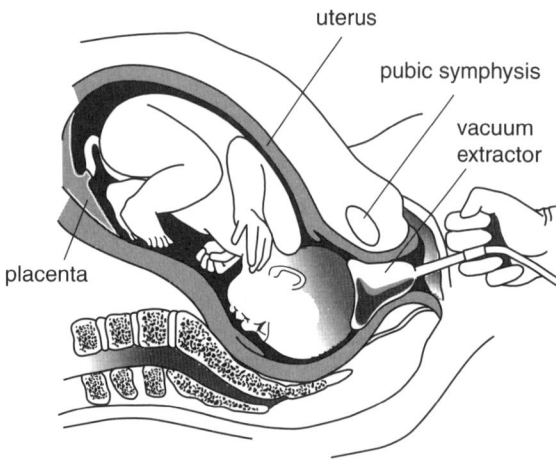

Figure 90.1 Foetus in occipito-anterior presentation

- You may well find it helpful to place your middle or index finger at the junction between the foetal scalp and the suction cup in order to monitor the movement of the cup and thereby prevent excessive traction and slipping off of the cup.
- If you hear air leaking out, it could be from a poor seal or too much traction.
- Should the cup slip off, you can reapply it over the same chignon, but *take care* once again *not* to suck maternal tissue into the cup. You should abandon the procedure after two cup detachments.
- Continuously monitor contractions and foetal heart rate.
- When the head crowns, you may perform an episiotomy.
- As soon as you deliver the foetal head, release the vacuum, remove the cup and deliver the baby as for a normal delivery (see Chapter 89).

In most cases of failed vacuum extraction, you need to perform an emergency Caesarean section. Occasionally, the foetal head may have been turned to a position that is favourable for a forceps delivery.

Complications

These foetal complications can occur:

- Scalp abrasions and contusions, which may later become septic and are theoretically conducive to mother-to-child transmission of HIV
- Cephalhaematoma, which is bleeding under the periosteum, and subcutaneous haematomas, which may lead to anaemia and/or jaundice within the first week of life
- Intracranial injuries, such as tears and haemorrhage of the tentorium cerebelli

The mother could suffer cervical and lower genital tract tears, but these are rare.

Table 90.1 summarises the advantages and disadvantages of this type of delivery.

Table 90.1 Advantages and disadvantages of vacuum extraction

Advantages	Disadvantages
Rotation of the head is allowed in an atraumatic way during delivery	Delivery takes longer owing to the approx. 10 minutes needed to establish the vacuum, therefore it is not suited in the case of FD
Vacuum cup occupies no additional space between the foetal head and the maternal pelvic wall	Risk of foetal injuries is slightly higher than with forceps delivery
Facilitates flexion of the foetal head during delivery	Does not protect the foetal head of the preterm
Vacuum allows a specific degree of traction force – 10 kg as compared to 25 kg in forceps delivery	
Less maternal trauma than with forceps delivery	
Allows the foetal head to find its own way through the birth canal	

Forceps delivery

A forceps delivery has the function of traction as well as the advantage of protection of the foetal head. This is especially important in the preterm infant.

The only situation in which forceps should be used is the so-called outlet forceps delivery where the foetal head is not palpable above the pelvic brim and the sagittal suture is in the antero-posterior (AP) diameter.

Indications

You need to perform this type of delivery in these instances:

- FD – when you need to effect rapid delivery
- Prematurity – the small head of the foetus is protected by the blades of the forceps.
- Deflexed aftercoming head in the case of a breech delivery
- Prolonged second stage with fully dilated cervix
- Any maternal condition that may be aggravated by the bearing down efforts, for example cardiac disease, hypertension or exhaustion

Contraindications

You should not perform this type of delivery under these circumstances:

- Obstructed labour manifested by the head being more than two fifths above the brim and/or parieto-parieto (PP) moulding
- You are inexperienced in performing the procedure.
- Incompletely dilated cervix
- Unknown position and station of the foetal head
- Uterine atony

Prerequisites

The following conditions must exist for the forceps delivery to be safe:

- Foetal head not palpable above the pelvic brim
- Cervix fully dilated
- Membranes ruptured
- Sagittal suture in an antero-posterior position
- Uterine contractions present and normal
- Bladder and rectum empty, as an empty viscus is less prone to damage

Procedure

To perform the forceps delivery, you need to follow this procedure:

- Because this type of delivery is a surgical intervention, you must conduct the procedure in sterile conditions.
- Position your patient in the lithotomy position, having cleaned her with antiseptic solution and draped her.
- Make preparations for an episiotomy with local anaesthetic infiltration of the perineum.

- Assemble the Wrigley's forceps and place them in front of her vulva for correct orientation.
- Cover your right hand with Hibitane cream and insert it into the vagina posterior to the foetal head. Take the left blade of the forceps for the left side of the maternal vagina in your left hand and introduce it into the vagina, with the blade resting on your right hand.
- With the index finger of your right hand feed the apex of the blade around the foetal head. Then slide the blade anti-clockwise until it is situated on the left side of the foetal head.
- Check that you have not trapped vaginal or cervical tissue with the forceps.
- Insert the right blade in the same way, with your hands swapped around and rotating clockwise. Lock the forceps blades, but without force. Should you feel force to be necessary, remove the forceps and redo the insertion of the blades.
- Once you have locked the blades, apply traction in a posterior (downwards) direction. Push the shaft of the forceps posteriorly (downwards) with your left hand while applying traction with your right hand on the handles of the forceps. This is known as the Pajot's manoeuvre. Make sure that the perineum is supported.
- Apply traction only during contractions, with the mother bearing down at the same time.
- As the foetus's hairline becomes visible, move the forceps anteriorly (upwards) while maintaining traction.
- This is the stage at which you should perform the episiotomy, if one is necessary.
- Once you have delivered the foetal head, remove the forceps and deliver the foetus as for a normal delivery (see Chapter 89).
- Once you have delivered the baby, you need to screen the perineum and lower genital tract for possible lacerations or injury. Always cut and suture an episiotomy as usual.

Complications

These foetal complications could occur:

- Death
- Skull fracture
- Neurological injuries including brain tissue injuries, intracranial haemorrhages, facial nerve paralysis and injuries to the brachial plexus
- Contusion and tears on the face or scalp. Figure 90.2 illustrates this, as well as the correct application (which avoids this).
- Umbilical compression

These maternal complications could occur:

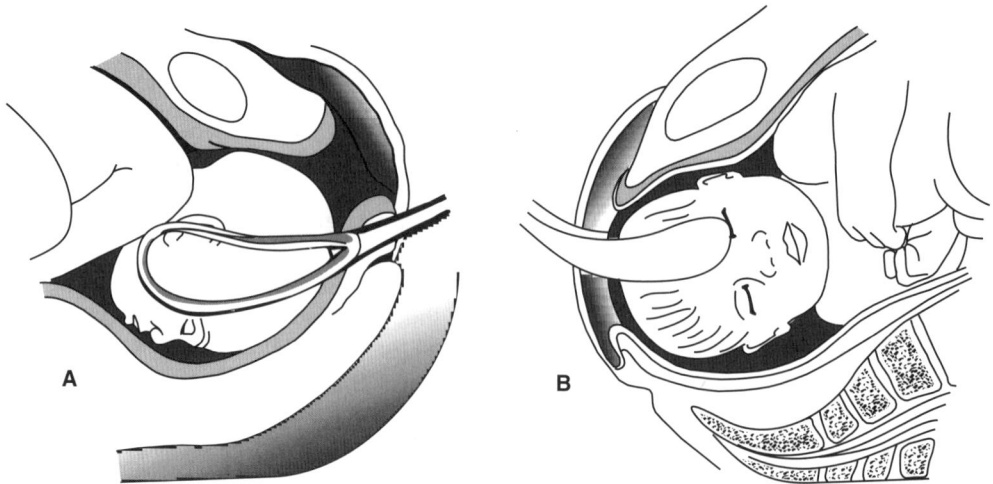

Figure 90.2 Correct (A) and incorrect (B) application of the forceps

- Tears and lacerations in the lower genital tract, cervix, vagina or perineum
- Ruptured uterus – if you apply the blades incorrectly.
- Bladder or urethral injuries
- Fracture of the coccyx
- Rectal injuries and tears

- Haemorrhage from lacerated tissue
- Infection of genital or urinary tract

However, you can avoid most of these complications if you apply the forceps correctly and apply the traction in the correct direction, without too much force.

Table 90.2 summarises the two types of delivery.

Table 90.2 Differences between forceps delivery and vacuum extraction delivery

Condition	Forceps	Vacuum extraction/Ventouse
Foetal distress	Commonly indicated	Mostly contraindicated
Uterine contractions	Preferably strong	Must be strong
Foetal head above pelvis	Contraindicated	Contraindicated
Cervix	Fully dilated	Fully dilated
Position of sagittal suture	Antero-posterior	Any
Maturity	Any	Only mature foetuses
Face, breech	May be used	Contraindicated
Episiotomy	Essential	Suggested
Facilitates flexion	No	Yes
Force of traction	Much	Little
Speed of delivery	Quick	Slow
Risk	Maternal risk higher	Foetal risk higher

Source: Cronjé & Grobler, 2003. p. 320

91 How to do a Caesarean section

JULIA BLITZ-LINDEQUE

In deciding whether or not to perform a Caesarean section, you must consider the indications for operative delivery as well as the risks involved for both the mother and the baby. If you decide to go ahead, you need to obtain the mother's fully informed consent before beginning the procedure.

The preferred form of anaesthesia is regional – either spinal or epidural – except when this is contraindicated by *severe* pre-eclampsia, antepartum haemorrhage or foetal distress.

Indications

You could perform a Caesarean section in these instances:

- Foetal distress (FD)
- Cephalo-pelvic disproportion
- Malpresentation, including breech
- Placenta praevia
- Previous uterine surgery (including Caesarean)
- Failure to progress despite optimal management
- Failed induction of labour
- Cord prolapse with a live viable foetus
- Arm prolapse with a more than 1000 g foetus
- Multiple pregnancy
- Cervical cancer
- Previous surgery for incontinence
- HIV-positive mother without ruptured membranes and who will be able to bottle-feed

Procedure

To perform a Caesarean, you need to follow this procedure:

- Insert an in-dwelling Foley's catheter into your patient's bladder.
- Put a pillow under her right buttock to prevent inferior vena cava syndrome.
- Note that the skin and subcutaneous tissue incision of choice is a Pfannenstiel, that is lower transverse, incision.

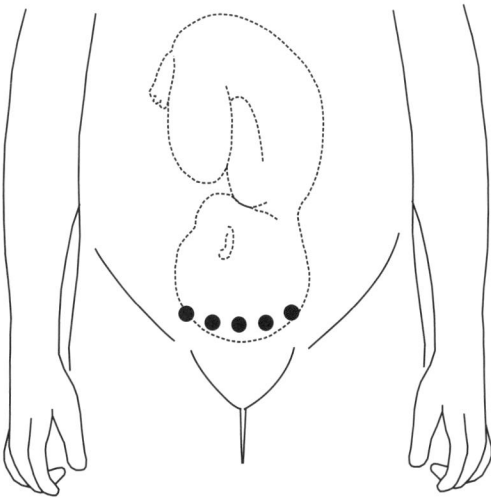

Figure 91.1 Pfannenstiel incision

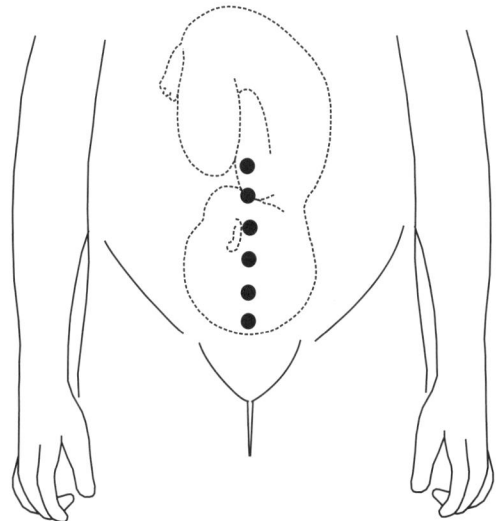

Figure 91.2 Vertical incision

- Open the sheath of the rectus muscle with a transverse incision, undermining the sheath laterally and then incising to either side of the midline with scissors. Do not damage the muscle itself.

- Part the rectus muscles from each other in the midline.

- Isolate and elevate the parietal peritoneum at the upper end of the incision and divide the peritoneum with a small scalpel incision. Enlarge the incision vertically under vision, excluding adhesions in the proposed line of incision. Note that the lower end of the incision should end well short of the bladder dome.

- Insert a Doyen retractor into the lower abdomen to retract the bladder and the lower margin of the wound.

- Correct any uterine rotation.

- Identify the lower uterine segment beneath the loosely attached layer of visceral peritoneum of the uterovesical pouch.

- Elevate and incise this peritoneum (see Figure 91.3).

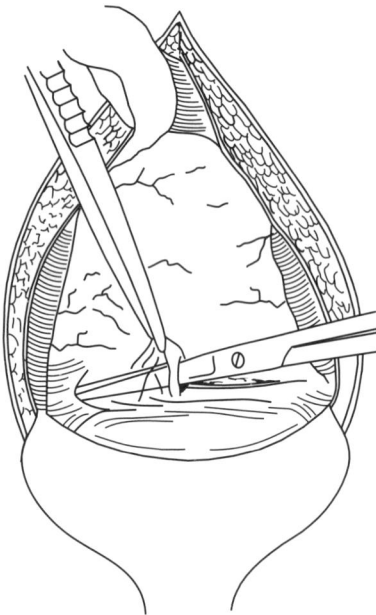

Figure 91.4 Reflecting the peritoneum and bladder off the anterior wall of the uterus

Beware of the uterine arteries at the lateral margins of the incision. Figure 91.5 shows the uterine incision.

- Nick the bulging membranes with a scalpel.

- Insert your right hand into the pelvis to pull the presenting part towards the fundus and out of the lower segment, and to lift it out through the wound as you remove the Doyen retractor. *Under no circumstances* should your hand be wedged against the distal part of the lower segment, as massive tears can result from such a movement.

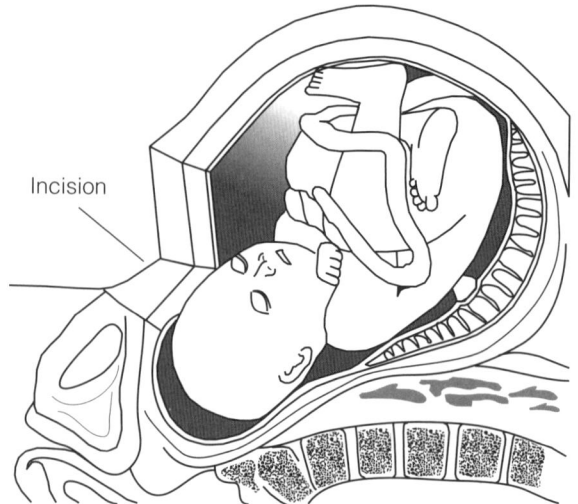

Figure 91.3 Elevating the peritoneum

- Extend the incision transversely with scissors. Beware of the lateral venous plexuses. Use blunt digital dissection to reflect the lower aspect of the peritoneum and the bladder base off the anterior wall of the uterus (see Figure 91.4).

- Lightly score the lower uterine segment with a "smile-shaped" incision using a scalpel. Enlarge the uterine incision laterally by manual stretching.

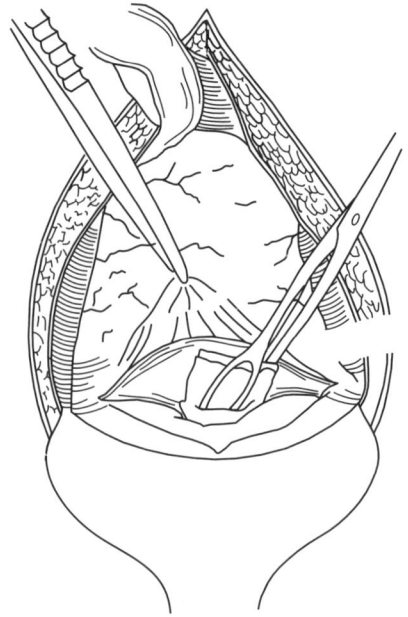

Incision

Figure 91.5 Uterine incision

• Complete the delivery by exerting a combination of fundal pressure (by the assistant) and traction (by the surgeon) on the presenting part. This is illustrated in Figure 91.6.

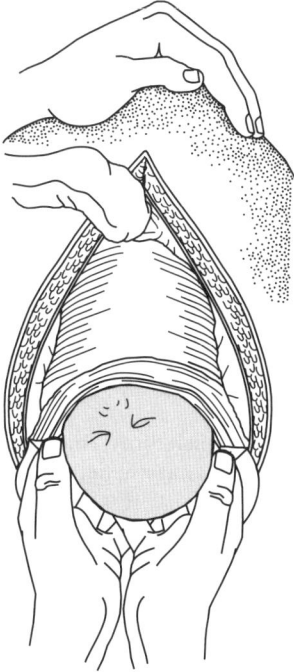

Figure 91.6 Exerting fundal pressure and traction

• Clamp and cut the umbilical cord, and hand the baby to the nurse or attendant for after-care.
• Administer 10 IU oxytocin to the mother.
• Deliver the placenta by applying gentle traction on the cord.
• Re-insert the Doyen retractor into the lower margin of the abdominal wound outside of the uterus.
• Use a Green-Armitage clamp to pick up the lower lip of the anterior uterine wall. Place further clamps on each apex of the uterine incision.
• Secure each apex using 762 chromic catgut or polyglycolic acid suture material on a round-bodied needle. *Take care* to ensure that you insert the suture beyond the apex of the incision in order to secure haemostasis. Use the tied end of the suture

for traction while using the rest of the suture to oppose the margins of the uterus (excluding the decidual layer) in a continuous suture towards the other apex. Do not use unnecessary tension. At this point, you can tie this suture to the haemostatic suture you already placed at the second apex. You can then cut the second apex's suture. There is evidence that single-layer suturing of the uterus is as effective, and faster, than multilayered suturing. Figure 91.7 illustrates this part of the process.

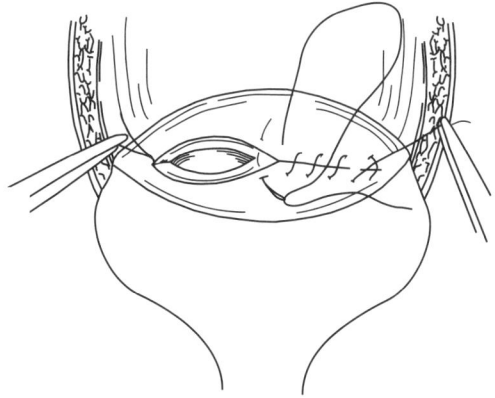

Figure 91.7 Suturing the uterus

• Do not suture the uterine visceral peritoneum, as this increases the risk of formation of adhesions.
• Inspect the wound for any signs of active bleeding and use a figure-of-eight stitch to provide haemostasis.
• Remove the Doyen retractor and remove any clots from the peritoneal cavity.
• Inspect the uterus and its adnexal structures for abnormalities.
• Do not suture the parietal peritoneum. Reconstitute the divided rectus sheath using polyglycolic suture material.
• Close the skin with a subcuticular suture or interrupted skin sutures.
• Rub up the uterus to expel any clots, and dress the wound.
• Do a vaginal examination to exclude active uterine haemorrhage.

92 How to do and suture an episiotomy

HANNES STEINBERG

You would perform an episiotomy in order to enlarge the introitus so that you can prevent a tear. An episiotomy is an incision through the perineal muscles that you would perform just before delivering a baby.

Episiotomy

Indications

You should perform an episiotomy *only* if there is a valid indication, as follows:

- The infant needs to be delivered without delay, as in these instances:
  - Foetal distress (FD) during the second stage of labour
  - Maternal exhaustion
  - Maternal cardiac disease
- The delivery of a preterm infant – to reduce pressure on the foetal head
- There is a high risk of a third degree tear, or when such a tear has occurred previously
- A thick or tight perineum
- You need to perform a breech or assisted delivery.

Note, however, that the mere case of a primigravida is *not* an indication for an episiotomy.

Procedure

If you anticipate an episiotomy, inject your patient's perineum with local anaesthetic, that is 10–15 ml 1% lignocaine.

To perform an episiotomy, follow this procedure:

- Make the incision just before the delivery and during a contraction, when the presenting part is stretching the perineum.
- Start the incision in the midline with the scissors pointed 45 degrees away from the anus. Figure 92.1 shows this step of the process.
- Direct the incision towards the patient's right, although you could also do it towards the left.
- Slip two fingers of your left hand between the perineum and the presenting part in order to prevent injury to the foetus.

If you perform the procedure too soon, excessive bleeding can result. Extension of the episiotomy by tearing may occur.

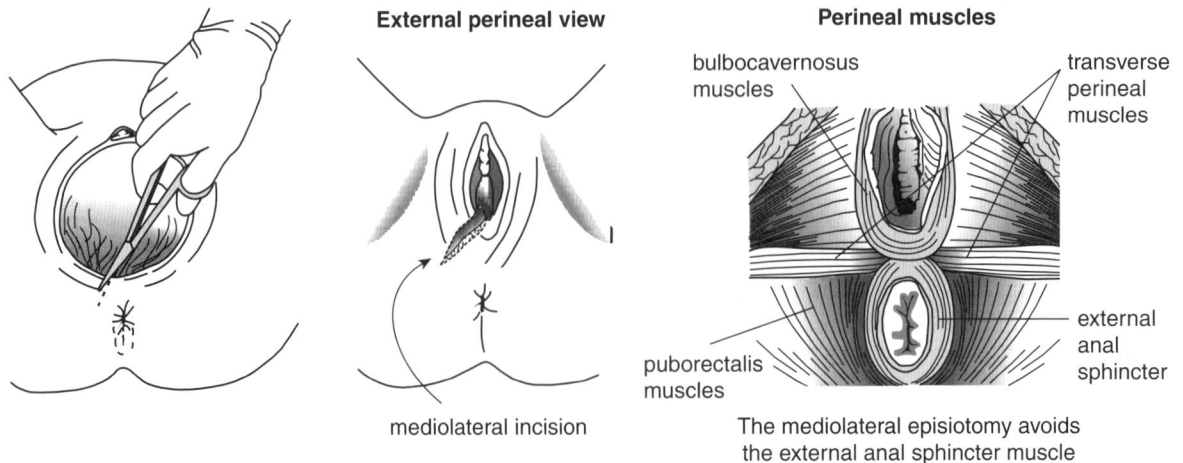

External perineal view

mediolateral incision

Perineal muscles

bulbocavernosus muscles

transverse perineal muscles

puborectalis muscles

external anal sphincter

The mediolateral episiotomy avoids the external anal sphincter muscle

Figure 92.1 Mediolateral episiotomy

Suturing the incision

Before attempting to repair the episiotomy incision and/or tear, you *must* ensure that

- you have explained to your patient what you are going to do and obtained her consent
- she is positioned comfortably, preferably in lithotomy position
- good over-the-shoulder lighting is available – a normal ceiling light is often insufficient
- you provide sufficient local anaesthesia (the pre-procedure dose may be adequate if you are suturing within 30 minutes)
- sufficient absorbable suturing material is present.

Moreover, you need to adhere to these important principles:

- Visualise the vaginal apex and put in a suture there.
- Close any dead space.
- Obtain haemostasis.
- Do not strangulate tissues by excessive pressure.
- Note that you must suture three layers – the muscles, the vaginal mucosa and the perineal skin.
- *Take care* not to injure your fingers; preferably work with instruments.

Procedure

To suture the episiotomy incision, you need to follow this procedure:

- Place a swab high in your patient's vagina to prevent uterine blood descending into the field of work.
- Place a suture at the apex of the incision of the vaginal mucosa using a 2/0 polyglycolic suture.
- Join the deeper muscle layers anatomically with a polyglycolic acid suture. *Take care* not to go too deep or through the rectum.
- Obliterate any dead space.
- Ensure that the vaginal mucosa and perineal skin are correctly/anatomically aligned.
- Suture the vaginal mucosa with continuous absorbable suture.
- Repair the skin with the same absorbable suture on a cutting needle using interrupted sutures. *Take care* not to pull the sutures too tight. Figure 92.2 shows this step of the process.
- Remove the swabs from the vagina and do a rectal examination to ensure that you have not inadvertently placed a suture through the rectum

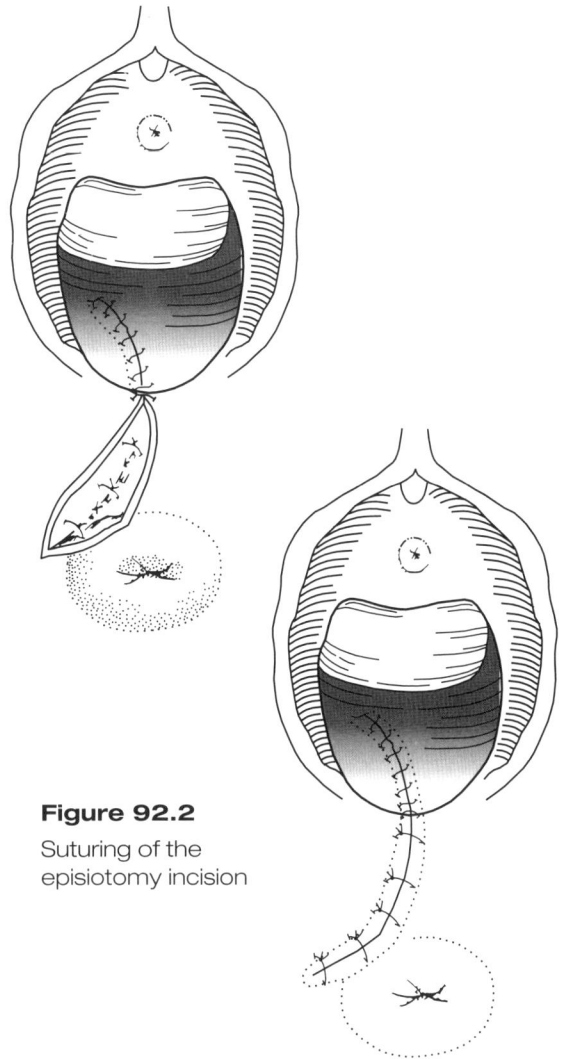

Figure 92.2

Suturing of the episiotomy incision

After-care

Give your patient the following after-care:

- Administer non-steroidal anti-inflammatory drugs for pain relief.
- Advise her to keep the wound clean using saline or Savlon sitz baths three times a day as well as after each bowel motion.
- You can use an infrared lamp cautiously on the perineum to promote healing.
- You do not need to prescribe routine prophylactic antibiotics. However, at times antibiotics may be indicated. Excessive pain may indicate haematoma formation, infection or wound dehiscence.
- Occasionally you may need to perform secondary repair if the wound dehisces.

93 How to repair a third-degree tear

JULIA BLITZ-LINDEQUE

You should perform this repair only if you have the experience and are familiar with the anatomy.

Procedure

To perform the repair, you need to follow this procedure:

- Place interrupted sutures firstly in the rectal submucosa (muscularis only) and then in the fascial layer, using a polyglycolic acid suture.

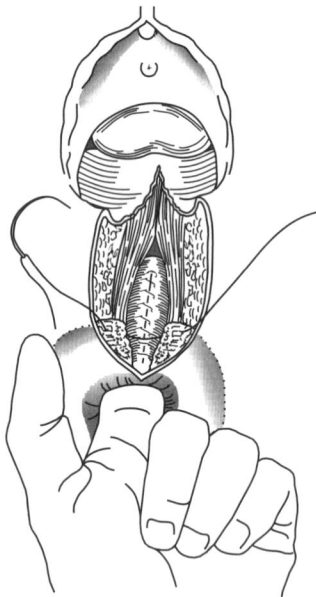

Figure 93.1 Repaired rectal mucosa and suture in external anal sphincter

- It is *essential* that you close the vaginal apex of the tear.
- Seek, identify and unite the anal sphincter, which always retracts, with two interrupted sutures.
- Follow the remainder of the repair as described for an episiotomy (see Chapter 92).

Figure 93.2 illustrates the anatomy.

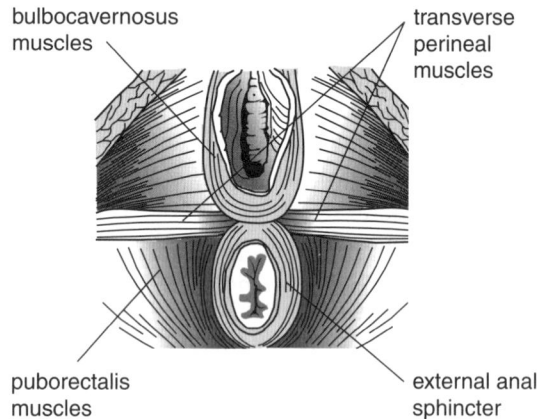

Figure 93.2 Perineal muscle anatomy

After-care

Provide your patient with this after-care:

- Ensure that she follows a low-residue diet.
- Advise her to use a stool softener orally for one week.
- Prescribe anti-inflammatory medication.

94 How to manually remove the placenta

HANNES STEINBERG

If the placenta is not delivered 20–30 minutes after you have delivered the newborn, you should regard it as a "retained" placenta.

Management

To manage a retained placenta, you should initially

- check that the placenta is not already lying in the vagina
- put up an intravenous line with 20 units/litre oxytocin running at 30–60 drops per minute.

Further management of the condition depends on whether or not the mother is actively bleeding.

In the case of little or no bleeding, follow this procedure:

- Allow an hour for separation of the placenta to occur.
- During this time monitor the maternal vital signs, as there may be concealed bleeding.
- If the placenta is not delivered after the hour has elapsed, maintain steady cord traction with uterine counter-pressure for about 10–15 minutes.
- Failing delivery, inject a further 10 units oxytocin bolus intravenously.
- If there is still no change, give glyceryl trinitrate sublingually. This relaxes the uterus temporarily and may encourage the placenta to be delivered.
- Failing all of the above, you need to manually remove the placenta in the operating theatre.

In the case of bleeding, follow this procedure:

- Give oxytocin 10 units IVI stat and then start an infusion of oxytocin with 20–40 units/litre at 250 ml/hr.
- Prepare your patient for manual removal in theatre.

Procedure

You need to remove the placenta manually in the operating theatre with the patient under adequate general anaesthesia.

Follow this procedure:

- Place your patient in the lithotomy position.
- Insert a Foley's catheter and empty her bladder.
- Ensure a sterile operating environment.
- With one hand on the abdominal wall, stabilise the uterine fundus.
- Insert your other hand into the uterus and identify the placental attachment.
- Separate the placenta from the uterine wall using cutting movements of the side of your hand, cleaving between the placenta and the uterus.
- Once you have achieved separation, remove the placenta and check for completeness.
- Re-insert your hand into the uterus and feel for additional products and for integrity of the uterine wall.
- If the placenta is incomplete or there are products still *in situ*, curettage the uterus gently with the largest available blunt curette.
- Observe for, and monitor, blood loss and check the maternal vital signs – pulse, BP and oxygen saturation – throughout the procedure. The patient may bleed profusely, especially if halothane is used as the anaesthetic gas.
- Administer broad-spectrum antibiotics, such as amoxicillin and metronidazole, intravenously and provide an oxytocin infusion for at least eight hours after completing the procedure.

In the event that you can remove the placenta only incompletely or not at all, consider a diagnosis of placenta accreta or increta. Resuscitate your patient and transfer her in a stable condition to a centre which can give her the necessary further management.

While being transported, she should be accompanied by a nurse. Moreover, she should have a bladder catheter and two drips – one grey Jelco with fluid running for resuscitation, and the other with at least 10–20 units oxytocin added to the litre to promote uterine contraction.

The nurse can administer 1 000 mg (five 200 mg tablets) misoprostol rectally if the patient continues to bleed despite the above measures. Currently off-label use of misoprostol is accepted internationally (by WHO) as the appropriate emergency management.

At the referral hospital, conservative treatment can be attempted by performing curettage with a Bums' curette. If the patient's bleeding persists and becomes life threatening, a hysterectomy should be performed.

95 How to run a perinatal mortality meeting

HANNES STEINBERG

A perinatal mortality meeting should be held in every unit that has maternity cases. The meeting should serve as a forum in which members of the perinatal team can talk about issues of concern with regard to patient care.

Monitoring the quality of our work on a regular basis creates the opportunity for us to learn relevant lessons and make necessary adjustments to our practice.

When things go wrong with patient care, blame can seldom be attributed to only one person in the team. The entire team and its system needs to be analysed and brought together in a way that will allow more effective functioning.

Scheduling

Hold the meeting as frequently as is necessary, depending on the number of deliveries and any deaths that occur per week. In the bigger centres it could be held every week or second week, whereas in a district hospital every month may be sufficient.

Hold it at a regular time, so that it creates a fixed routine.

Attendees

Ideally, every person involved in the perinatal care programme should attend the meeting. It should be compulsory for the midwives and doctors from the maternity section and the nursery, as well as the "session" staff in the public sector. Personnel from referring clinics, as well as the Emergency Medical Services (EMS) should attend, if possible.

Do not accept the excuse of insufficient staff as an explanation for non-attendance. The meeting should be part of the **routine work** of a maternity section.

Agenda

Start the meeting with some basic data regarding the work that has been achieved by the service during the period under review, for example the number of admissions, deliveries, Caesarean sections, assisted deliveries, "born before arrivals" (BBAs), perinatal deaths in total, neonatal deaths, and stillbirths, and the rate of low birth weight, teenage pregnancy and perinatal mortality, and the perinatal care index. See Table 95.1 for definitions of these terms.

Table 95.1 Definitions of data terms

Term	Definition
Teenage pregnancy	Percentage of women aged 15–19 who are mothers or who have ever been pregnant
Neonatal death rate (NNDR)	Number of deaths within the first 28 days of life, in a year, per 1000 live births during that year
Stillbirth rate	Percentage of total births that are stillbirths
Perinatal mortality rate	The number or perinatal deaths per 1000 births. The perinatal period starts at the beginning of foetal viability (28 weeks' gestation or 1000 g) and ends at the end of the 7th day after delivery. Perinatal deaths are the sum of stillbirths plus early neonatal deaths.
Low birth weight rate	Percentage of live births under 2500 g
Perinatal care index	Perinatal mortality rate divided by the low birth weight rate

At this point it can be helpful to the team to give positive feedback on things that are improving, before proceeding to discuss areas where things are going less well.

You should openly discuss each relevant perinatal death in order to establish the cause. Identify and list possible avoidable factors, which you can classify into patient-related, administrative and health care worker-related factors. A list of primary obstetrical causes of death, final neonatal cause of death and possible avoidable factors is available from the Perinatal Education Programme Manual and the Perinatal Problem Identification Program (PPIP). You can obtain information about the latter from the MRC Research Unit for Maternal and Infant Care Strategies at the University of Pretoria.

Table 95.2 summarises the avoidable factors.

Table 95.2 Avoidable factors in perinatal deaths

Source of problem	Type of problem
Medical personnel problems	Labour management, e.g. foetal distress not detected, partogram not used, etc.
	Antenatal management, e.g. incomplete examination, multiple pregnancy not diagnosed, etc.
	Neonatal management, e.g. inadequate resuscitation
Patient problems	Inappropriate response to decreased foetal movements/rupture of membranes (ROM)/antepartum haemorrhage (APH)
	Delay in seeking medical attention during labour
	Unbooked
	Booked late and/or infrequent antenatal clinic visits
Administrative problems	Staff insufficiently trained to manage the patient or low staffing levels
	Inadequate facilities
	Lack of transport (patient/clinic/hospital)

Source: www.ppip.co.za

You need to discuss and decide upon any required changes in management protocols. It is important that the different components of the service agree on protocols which will enable the more efficient running of the service.

At times, it is useful to discuss cases with severe morbidity too, or cases that narrowly missed disaster. We can all learn from our mistakes (see also Chapter 155).

The meeting chair

As the person chairing the mortality meeting, you should be a senior staff member with good experience in obstetrics and neonatology. You must also be able to maintain neutrality, and prevent the meeting from escaping the bounds of the discussion.

In the case of a discussion about a death in the section, you need to give each member of the team an opportunity to state his or her case and point of view regarding the sequence of events. You must prevent the meeting from becoming a "blame session" of staff who are not present, or a battlefield in which staff voice personal grievances.

While the discussion should be frank, the meeting's primary function is educational rather than disciplinary. Any change in management practice that is decided upon must be based on evidence and should not be guided by the staff members' opinions of each other.

Remember that a discussion pertaining *only* to the mortalities experienced in the section will provide an incorrect, insufficient picture of the services achieved within the period in question.

Preparations

In preparation for the meeting, you need to have all the files of the perinatal deaths occurring within the given time period available for scrutiny. Each staff member involved in the care of the patient should be prepared to answer any questions during the meeting.

Furthermore, put a system in place to ensure that the basic dataset is available at the time of the meeting so that the relevant numbers and rates can be discussed.

Intention

As touched on above, the primary intention of the meeting is to facilitate learning, and to modify behaviour in order to improve the quality of service rendered.

Minutes

The minute-taker should record the following at the meeting:

- All minutes, especially the decisions that are made
- The lessons that were learned from the relevant cases

This meeting provides the environment for the collection of the data to be entered into the PPIP. With the help of this program the data can be captured in a form that calculates the perinatal rates and give a useful picture of the service rendered as a whole.

The minute-taker should *not* record the following at the meeting:

- Any personal grievances that have been aired
- The names of individuals who have been identified as being in need of correction. Any suggestion of disciplinary action should be taken to the disciplinary committee of the facility, and should not be dealt with in this meeting.

Women's health

How to take a Papanicolaou smear

CLAIRE VAN DEVENTER AND MUSTAPHA MAKINDE

The Papanicolaou smear is more commonly known as the "Pap smear". It is recommended by the Department of Health (DoH) that women undergo three smears in their lives, with a 10-year interval between each one, commencing at 30 years of age.

In terms of WHO guidelines on screening, cervical cancer generally develops slowly from precursor lesions. Therefore, screening can take place relatively infrequently and still have a significant impact on reducing cervical cancer morbidity and mortality. Based on the Alliance for Cervical Cancer Preventions' (ACCP) mathematical modelling studies using observed data (prospective cohort studies, databases and published literature), if resources permit only once-per-lifetime screening, then the focus should be to screen women in their 30s and 40s, especially women between 35 and 40 years. If resources allow screening two or three times per lifetime (rescreening), the optimal interval should be every five years (not every ten years); for example, screening at ages 35, 40 and 45 is better than screening at ages 30, 40 and 50 (Goldie & ACCP 2004, personal communication with S. Goldie, May 2004). If resources permit more frequent screening, however, then screening can be once every three years from age 25 to 49 and then every five years to the age of 64 (International Agency for Research on Cancer, forthcoming).

We recommend that you take your patient's first Pap smear within 10 years of her becoming sexually active, followed by another two smears taken every three years if each previous one was normal. Thereafter, if the previous smear was normal, every five years. Check every patient's status at each visit.

Note that high-risk groups, such as patients with recurrent sexually transmitted illnesses and HIV, require annual smears. Moreover, you need to take a smear in a patient who presents with any of these clinical indications: post-coital bleeding, postmenopausal bleeding, vaginal discharge resistant to treatment, irregular cervix on examination and first trimester of pregnancy.

Procedure

To take a Pap smear, you need to follow this procedure:

- Have all the following equipment ready within reach or with an assistant:
  - The correct size Cusco, or bivalve, speculum
  - Ayres or other spatula
  - Cotton wool swabs
  - Fixative spray
  - Two glass slides, which you have labelled with your patient's name
  - A cotton wool swab for cleaning the cervix.
- Have your patient lie in the lithotomy position.
- If necessary, warm the speculum in warm water.
- Insert the speculum, using little or no K-Y jelly. If you do use the jelly, do not apply it to the tip of the speculum, as it may contaminate the cervical smear, which causes destruction of the cells.
- Gently clean discharge or blood from the cervix, if present, with a cotton wool swab.
- Visualise the cervix clearly and inspect for tumours, ulcers or signs of cervicitis.
- Insert the Pap smear spatula with the endocervical tip, that is the longer part, or brush, into the endocervical canal and turn it 360 degrees. If there is a wide ectropion, apply the other, flat end of the spatula to it and smear onto the slide.
- The Craigbrush, which is currently available in South Africa, is superior to the Pap smear spatula if the transition zone is high and you cannot see it. Turn it gently in five complete circles and apply the smear to the slide in strokes. Figure 96.1 shows the brush. (To obtain this brush, contact Pharmaceutical Enterprises: Tel. (021) 531 1341, fax (021) 531 2692.)
- Within 20 seconds of taking it, apply the smear onto the glass slide with a few light sweeping motions (in order to get a one-cell thickness specimen where possible). Spray immediately with

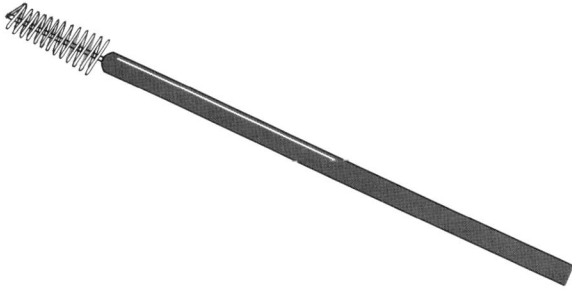

Figure 96.1 The Craigbrush

one spray of fixative, holding the spray bottle upright at about 30 cm from the slide, to prevent drying and decay of the cells.

- Remove the speculum, clean the vulva if necessary, and help your patient to sit up.
- Warn her that she might experience some slight vaginal bleeding.

When you send the smear for laboratory testing, you also need to complete the pathology request form with any findings on the appearance of your patient's cervix and any relevant hormonal influences, such as contraceptives, on the appearance of the cells.

It is crucial that you are able to contact your patient with the results. Therefore, ensure that the address and contact telephone numbers that you have for her are complete and correct.

97 How to insert an intrauterine contraceptive device

CLAIRE VAN DEVENTER AND MUSTAPHA MAKINDE

This device is also known as the "IUCD". Figure 97.1 illustrates the various types.

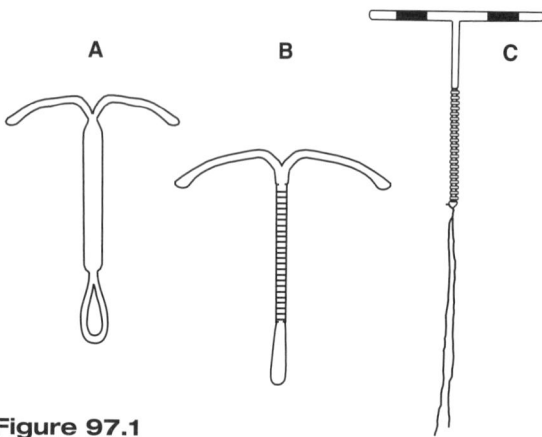

Figure 97.1

IUCDs: Mirena (A), Nova T (B) and copper T (C)

Indications

You would insert an IUCD in the following circumstances:

- For emergency contraception – within five days of your patient having had unprotected sexual intercourse
- Postpartum or post-miscarriage – within 48 hours of delivery or miscarriage. Otherwise, wait until six weeks postpartum or post-miscarriage (interval insertion).

You would *not* perform this procedure if your patient is pregnant, or if you found any pelvic pathology on pelvic examination.

Procedure

Interval insertion

To insert the device using the interval method, you need to follow this procedure:

- Have your patient lie in the lithotomy position.

- Cleanse the vulva with an antiseptic solution, stroking from the urethral opening towards the fourchette. Do not reverse the stroke.
- Gently part the labia and clean the vagina and the cervix. If there is evidence of severe vaginitis or cervicitis, delay the procedure until you have treated the condition.
- Pass a bivalve, or Cusco, vaginal speculum to expose the cervix.
- Grasp the anterior lip of the cervix with a single-tooth tenaculum forceps and maintain steady traction to straighten the uterine-cervical axis.
- Depending on the pain threshold of your patient, you may need to do a paracervical block, as described in Chapter 107. The pain is usually caused by reflex spasm from grasping the cervix and from stretching the cervix during the procedure.
- Carefully determine the length of the uterine cavity by using a uterine sound.
- Preload the side arms of the copper T device into the introducer tube, so that they will be released in a transverse plane. With the Multiload (not shown in Figure 97.1 above), there is no need to preload the side arms into the introducer tube.
- Adjust the cervical stop such that the distance between the stop and the tip of the loaded device is the same as the previously determined length of the uterine cavity. Orientate the stop so that its broader aspect is in the transverse plane.
- Gently insert the introducer until the cervical stop gently rests on the external os. Do not force insertion. Maintain traction on the cervix throughout insertion.
- Next, follow either of these techniques:
  - **Push-in technique – Multiload:** The plunger pushes the device out of the introducer into the cavity. This has a higher risk of perforation.
  - **Withdrawal technique – Nova T:** Using the plunger to maintain the device *in utero*, carefully

withdraw the introducer tube out of the uterine cavity and cervical canal.

- **No push rod – Mirena:** The device is automatically released into the uterine cavity when you withdraw the introducer tube.

- Trim the string to at least 2–3 cm from the external os.

Postpartum and post-miscarriage insertion

This procedure is the same as above, except that because the cervix is fragile you need to hold it with ring forceps and take great care to avoid uterine perforation.

After-care

You need to give your patient the following after-care:

- Inform her about the common side-effects, especially that of mild bleeding within three days post-insertion.
- Give her a mild analgesic such as a non-steroidal anti-inflammatory (NSAID) for uterine cramps.
- Instruct her to feel for the strings regularly after each menstruation, and in particular after the first menstruation.

- See her within 1–3 months to check if the IUCD is still *in situ*, and to discuss any problems or concerns that she may have. An annual check, although not necessary, could be a forum for health promotion.
- If she experiences persistent pain in the first 48 hours despite analgesia, you may need to remove the device and possibly replace it with a device of a smaller size.

Removal

To remove the device, follow this procedure:

- Prepare the vulva and vagina, and insert the speculum as described above.
- Grasp the cervix with a tenaculum and maintain traction to straighten the uterine-cervical axis.
- Grasp the two strings from the device with forceps and gently pull the device out of the uterine cavity.
- If you cannot see the strings, do an ultrasound to locate the device.
- If it is translocated within the uterine cavity, you can retrieve it with minimal dilatation and a gentle curettage. *Take care*, however, to exclude pregnancy first.

98 How to do a mini-laparotomy tubal ligation

CLAIRE VAN DEVENTER AND MUSTAPHA MAKINDE

You would perform a **subumbilical** mini-laparotomy in immediately postpartum patients, while you can consider a **suprapubic** mini-laparotomy for patients with the possibility of intra-abdominal adhesions from previous abdominal surgical procedures.

Laparoscopy is the preferred method for interval tubal ligation (see Chapter 99).

Preoperative investigations

Before going ahead with the procedure, you must do the following investigations:

- A pregnancy test to exclude unsuspected pregnancy
- A Pap smear to exclude infection and cervical intra-epithelial neoplasia (CIN) lesions or early malignancy
- A pelvic examination for assessment of uterine size and exclusion of adnexal pathology, abnormal discharges and other genital abnormalities
- An ultrasound, if indicated following pelvic examination or inadequate pelvic examination, for example in the case of an obese patient
- The haemoglobin level must be above 10 g/dl.

Furthermore, you need to obtain your patient's standard preoperative consent. Her partner's consent is not part of the consent procedure and not legally required; however, if a couple presents for this consultation, it is best for you to discuss the procedure with both people.

Procedure

To perform the laparotomy, you need to follow this procedure:

- Make an incision in the skin of less than 5 cm.
- If you are doing this within 48 hours of delivering your patient's baby, you can use the subumbilical, semilunar incision.

- If you are doing this as an interval procedure, six weeks or later postpartum, then you can use the suprapubic incision. You should aim to place the incision as close to the uterine fundus as possible for easy access to the tube.
- To enter the peritoneal cavity, you can use one of these two approaches:
  - **The subumbilical approach:** Incise the fascia transversely, thus exposing the peritoneum. Enter the peritoneum gently, either bluntly using the finger or by lifting a fold between two pairs of artery forceps. Before you incise it, check the peritoneal fold to ensure that the bowel is not included.
  - **The suprapubic approach:** Open the rectus fascia transversely and part the rectus muscles sideways from the midline. The peritoneum is thus exposed, and you can enter the cavity, gently and with care.
- With manipulation and retraction you can visualise the tube and grasp it with a Babcock clamp. If you are unable to visualise the tube, introduce a finger and run it sideways along the uterine fundus. In this way, you can hook the tube out and apply the Babcock clamp. Identify the fimbrial end of the tube to confirm that it is the Fallopian tube.
- Occlude the tube using either of the following techniques.

Parkland technique

Follow this procedure:

- Grasp the mid segment of the tube in a Babcock clamp.
- Perforate the avascular area in the mesosalpynx directly under the tube with a haemostat forceps, and open the jaws to spread the mesosalpynx, thereby freeing approximately 2.5 cm of tube.
- Then ligate the freed tube proximally and distally with a 0 or 00 chromic or polyglycolic suture.

- Excise a 1–2 cm segment of the tube. This is illustrated in Figure 98.1.
- Repeat this with the other tube.
- Submit the excised tube specimens for histology, carefully and correctly labelled as left and right.

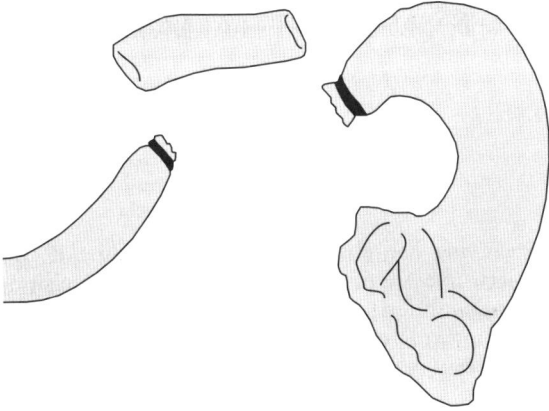

Figure 98.1 The Parkland technique

Failure rates are reported to be in the order of one case in four hundred patients (http://www.emedicine.com/med/topic3313).

Pomeroy technique

This is the simplest and most commonly performed postpartum tubal sterilisation technique.

Follow this procedure:

- Grasp the mid portion of the Fallopian tube with a Babcock clamp, creating a loop.
- Tie the loop with a 2.0 or 0 plain catgut suture, and cut each limb of the tubal knuckle separately. See Figures 98.2 and 98.3.

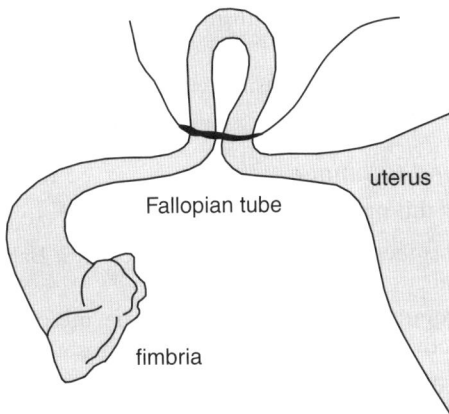

Figure 98.2 Tying the loop

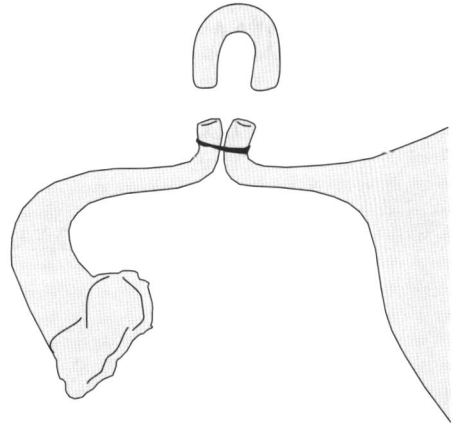

Figure 98.3 Cutting the tubal knuckle

- Hold the ligation sutures while you cut the tube to prevent retraction of the cut tubal stumps into the peritoneal cavity before you can examine them properly for haemostasis. You can apply a second ligature using 1–0 chromic catgut suture.
- You can cauterise the cut ends of the tubes. Figure 98.4 shows the final result.
- Submit the excised tube specimens for histology, having carefully and correctly labelled them as left and right.
- You can close the abdomen as per the routine explained in Chapter 91.

Figure 98.4 illustrates the Pomeroy technique.

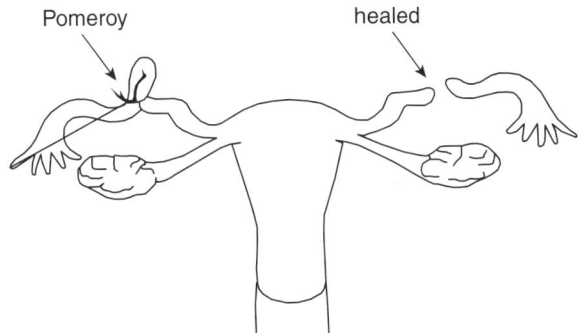

Figure 98.4 The Pomeroy technique

The failure rate is reported as similar to that of the Parkland technique (http://www.emedicine.com/med/topic3313).

After-care

You can give routine after-care. Your patient's discharge depends on adequate vital signs. Give her clear instructions regarding reasons which would necessitate her return, such as severe abdominal pain, vomiting and signs of wound sepsis.

99 How to do a laparoscopic tubal ligation

CLAIRE VAN DEVENTER AND MUSTAPHA MAKINDE

Laparoscopy is the preferred route for interval tubal ligation. In order to be able to perform this procedure, you must undergo specific training.

As with the mini-laparotomy, before beginning the procedure, you need to obtain your patient's informed consent and you need to do certain investigations (see Chapter 98).

Procedure

You would usually perform this procedure under general anaesthesia in theatre. However, some surgeons are capable of performing it in theatre using local infiltration of the skin after giving premedication to the patient.

To perform a laparoscopic tubal ligation, you should follow this procedure:

- Have your patient lie in the lithotomy position.
- Clean her abdomen up to the xiphisternum area with antiseptic solution, and drape her.
- Empty the urinary bladder.
- Pass a Sims vaginal speculum and apply the uterine manipulator, which is usually a cervical cannula supported on vulsellum forceps.
- Place the patient in the Trendelenburg position to displace the small bowel out of the pelvis.
- Make a skin incision of 5–10 mm with a scalpel blade just below the umbilicus across the midline. Figure 99.1 shows both incision sites.

- Steadying the abdominal wall by pulling it up, insert the Veress needle through the incision, pointing inferiorly, and insufflate the peritoneal cavity with carbon dioxide (CO_2), until an intraperitoneal pressure of 12–18 mmHg is attained.
- Remove the Veress needle and replace it with a 10-mm trocar through which you insert the laparoscope.
- Connect the CO_2 supply and the light source to the laparoscope. If available, a video camera can be attached to the lens of the laparoscope for projection of the images on screen.
- Inspect the peritoneal cavity to identify any injury caused by the Veress needle and the 10 mm trocar.
- Make another 5–10 mm suprapubic incision across the midline (see Figure 99.1) and insert the trocar, through which you pass the operating instrument. Do this under direct visualisation.
- With the laparoscope and the manipulator in place, manipulate the uterus to bring the Fallopian tubes into view. Identify the fimbrial end of each tube before performing tubal occlusion of the isthmus. Figure 99.2 illustrates this part of the process.

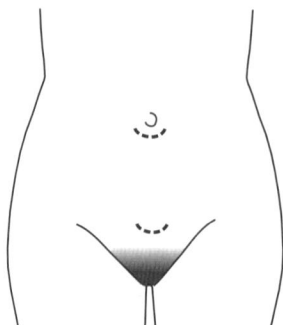

Figure 99.1
Incision sites

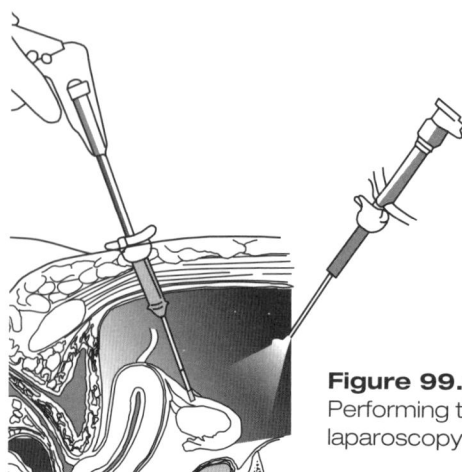

Figure 99.2
Performing the laparoscopy

© Van Schaik Publishers

- You can use one of the following three main techniques of laparoscopic tubal occlusion.

Diathermy coagulation

This can be unipolar or bipolar, although the bipolar diathermy is safer.

Use the cutting mode and set the instrument at 25–30 W. Desiccate the isthmus – at least 2–3 cm of contiguous tissue – and avoid the cornua (see Figure 99.3A).

Clip technique

Follow this procedure (see Figure 99.3B):

- Use either the Hulka (plastic) or the Filschie (titanium) clip applicator.
- Place a clip 3 cm from the cornua at a 90-degree angle across the tube.
- If you are applying the Hulka clip, ensure that the grasped area of the tube looks flattened. This is known as "the envelope sign".
- If you are applying the Filschie clip, expose the lower jaw of the clip through the mesosalpynx before closing the clip on the tube. This ensures that the entire tube diameter is occluded.

Band or ring technique

You need the Fallope ring applicator to perform this technique.

Follow this procedure (see Figure 99.3C):

- Apply the silastic rubber band to the applicator *just before* you begin the procedure – if the rubber band is stretched over the applicator for more than 15 minutes it might lose its elasticity.
- Grasp the isthmus 3–4 cm from the cornua.

- Squeeze the applicator handle slowly while applying the band. This reduces the risk of tubal transection.
- Deflate the abdomen after completing the ligation. Remove the large trocar with the laparoscope *in situ* to ensure that bowel is not accidentally trapped in the port site owing to the high intra-abdominal pressure.
- Close the wounds routinely.

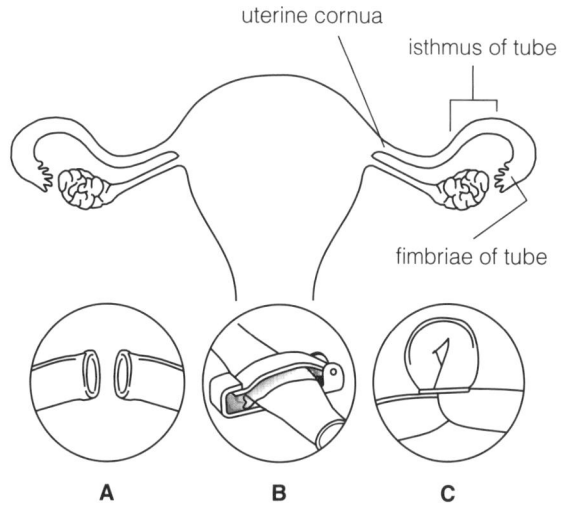

Figure 99.3 (A) Diathermy coagulation; (B) Clip technique; (C) Band technique

After-care

You can discharge your patient after ensuring normal vital signs. Give her clear directions for reasons that would necessitate her return, for example continued and severe abdominal pain and/or distention, vomiting, wound sepsis and fainting.

100 How to do a termination of pregnancy

MUSTAPHA MAKINDE

Termination of pregnancy is more commonly known as "TOP".

Knowledge of the Choice on Termination of Pregnancy Act 92 of 1996 is essential for all health workers in South Africa. Such knowledge allows you to provide counselling to your patient, and to determine the correct management plan within the limits set out in the Act.

Prerequisites

You can perform a TOP once you have ensured the following:

- If you select a medical TOP, your patient must also consent to a surgical TOP in the event of failure of the former. All methods of first-trimester abortion carry a small risk of failure to terminate the pregnancy, thus necessitating a further procedure. The risk for surgical abortion is around 2.3 in 1000 and for medical abortion between 1 and 14 in 1000. (RCOG national evidence-based clinical guidelines: the care of women requesting induced abortion; September 2004.)

- You need to confirm the presence of an intrauterine pregnancy by ultrasound. You can determine and document the gestational age of the foetus.

- You should confirm that there is no intrauterine contraceptive device *in utero*.

- You need to administer anti-D immunoglobulin to your patient if she is Rhesus-negative.

You must *not* perform a TOP under these circumstances:

- Chronic renal failure
- Current long-term systemic corticosteroid therapy
- A history of allergy to mifepristone or misoprostol, or other prostaglandins

- A haemorrhagic disorder, or current anti-coagulation therapy

Medical method of first-trimester TOP

Off-label use of misoprostol is commonly advocated for very early first-trimester TOP.

Follow this procedure:

- **Day 1:** Administer mifepristone orally – 600 mg.

- **Day 3:** Clinically or by ultrasound, assess whether the pregnancy has been terminated. If abortion has not occurred, your patient is likely to experience cramping and bleeding. In this case, give 400 µg misoprostol orally in a health care facility where intravenous plasma expanders can be administered. Check for expulsion of the pregnancy to consider referral for surgical TOP.

- **Days 14–20:** Clinically or by ultrasound, assess whether the pregnancy has been terminated. If you suspect ongoing pregnancy, you may need to perform a surgical TOP.

Medical method of mid-trimester TOP

Follow this procedure:

- **Immediately:** Administer mifepristone orally – 200 mg.

- **3 hours later:** Administer 400 µg misoprostol orally at three-hourly intervals to a maximum of four doses. In the vast majority of the cases, abortion occurs within 15 hours of the first misoprostol insertion. If it has not, consider a surgical TOP.

- **36–48 hours later:** Insert 800 µg misoprostol into the posterior vaginal fornix.

Surgical methods of TOP

See Chapter 101.

101 How to do a manual vacuum aspiration

CLAIRE VAN DEVENTER AND MUSTAPHA MAKINDE

Manual vacuum aspiration, or MVA, is designed to deal with uncomplicated, incomplete miscarriage and uncomplicated, first-trimester termination of pregnancy. Any complicated miscarriage should be managed in theatre.

When performing MVA on the awake patient you need to provide emotional support and encouragement. Your explanation of exactly what the procedure entails and your support during the procedure can help your patient to manage the pain more effectively.

Indications and contraindications

You would perform the procedure in these instances:

- Termination of pregnancy
- Incomplete abortion
- Missed abortion (with dilatation of the cervix)

You would not perform the procedure under the following circumstances:

- Your patient is more than 14 weeks pregnant.
- Septic abortion
- Other complications of abortion
- Your patient has a miscarriage requiring haemo-dynamic resuscitation.

Procedure

You can use the Karman gynaecology aspiration kit, which makes the procedure feasible in the office. Figure 101.1 shows the instruments in the kit. You could also use an electric vacuum unit connected to a plastic suction curette or metal suction curette. This is commonly available in theatres. When used with appropriate suction curettes this procedure is called "suction evacuation".

Three to five hours before the procedure, insert 800 µg misoprostol per vagina. This helps to soften the cervix, thus preventing perforation. Thirty minutes before the procedure, give your patient

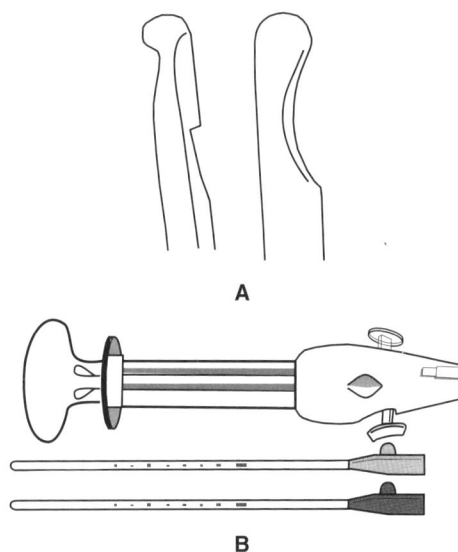

Figure 101.1 (A) Tip of Karman curette;
(B) Complete Karman aspiration kit

diclofenac 75 mg im or ibuprofen 400 mg po. Even if bleeding is slight, also give her oxytocin 10 IU im or ergometrine 0.2 mg im to make the myometrium firmer and reduce the risk of perforation.

To manually perform vacuum aspiration, you need to follow this procedure:

- Put your patient in the lithotomy position.
- Cleanse the vulva and vagina with an antiseptic solution.
- Ensure that all instruments entering the uterus are sterile.
- Prepare the MVA syringe:
  - Assemble the syringe.
  - Close the pinch valve.
  - Pull back on the plunger until the plunger arms lock.
- Perform a bimanual pelvic examination to assess the size and position of the uterus and the adnexa.

- Insert the speculum and clean the cervix.
- Gently grasp the anterior lip of the cervix with a swab-holding forceps, and straighten the uterine-cervical axis and stabilise the cervix.
- You can now do a paracervical block, if necessary (see Chapter 107).
- If your patient has had an uncomplicated, incomplete miscarriage, you do not need to dilate the cervix. For TOP, you can dilate the cervix to Hegar 8. Use graduated Hegar's dilators only if the cannula will not pass through the cervix. You can avoid this by choosing a cannula size one less than the number of weeks of gestation. Begin with the smallest dilator and end with the largest dilator that ensures adequate dilatation – usually 8 mm. *Take care* not to tear the cervix or to create a false opening. Figure 101.2 shows this step of the process.

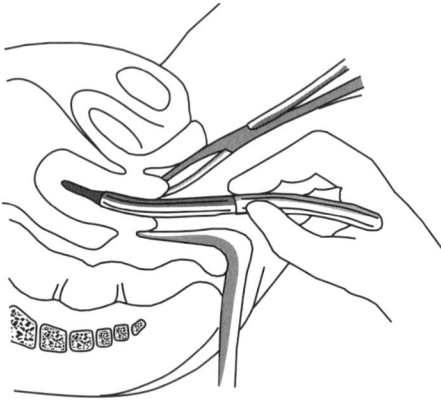

Figure 101.2 Dilatation of the cervix

- While gently applying traction to the cervix, insert the widest gauge suction cannula through the cervix into the uterine cavity just past the internal os. Rotating the cannula while gently applying pressure often helps the tip of the cannula to pass through the cervical canal. Figure 101.3 shows this step of the process.

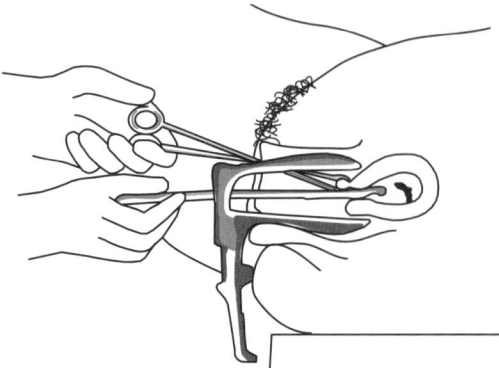

Figure 101.3 Inserting the cannula

- Slowly push the cannula into the uterine cavity until it touches the fundus, but make sure that this is not further than 10 cm. Measure the depth of the uterus by dots visible on the cannula and then withdraw the cannula slightly.
- Attach the prepared 60-ml MVA syringe to the cannula by holding the forceps and the end of the cannula in one hand and the syringe in the other.
- Release the pinch valve(s) on the syringe to transfer the vacuum through the cannula to the uterine cavity.
- Evacuate uterine contents by gently rotating the syringe from side to side while moving the cannula gently and slowly back and forth within the uterine cavity. Figure 101.4 illustrates this step.

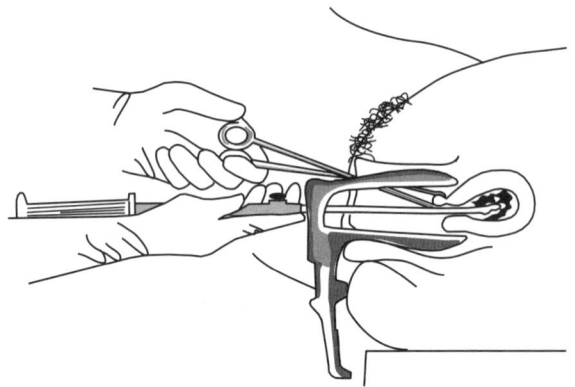

Figure 101.4 Evacuating the contents of the uterus

- Check for signs of completeness:
  - There is red or pink foam but no more tissue in the cannula.
  - You feel a grating sensation as the cannula passes over the surface of the evacuated uterus.
  - The uterus contracts around, or grips, the cannula.
- Withdraw the cannula. Detach the syringe and place the cannula in decontamination solution.
- With the valve open, empty the contents of the MVA syringe into a strainer by pushing on the plunger.
- Perform a bimanual examination to check the size and firmness of the uterus.
- Inspect the tissue removed from the uterus
  - for quantity and presence of products of conception
  - to assure complete evacuation
  - to check for a molar pregnancy which you can diagnose if you see grape-like structures. This is rare.

 © Van Schaik Publishers

- If necessary, strain and rinse the tissue to remove excess blood clots, then place it in a container of clean water, saline or weak acetic acid (vinegar) for examination.
- You can also send tissue specimens in formalin for histology, if indicated.

After-care

Give your patient this after-care:

- Observe her for at least one hour for a drop in blood pressure, increase in pulse rate, the occurrence of vaginal bleeding and her ability to pass urine.
- Give 500 mg paracetamol by mouth as needed.
- For gestation age of 12 weeks or more in a Rhesus-negative woman, give 50 mg anti-D immunoglobulin.

- Give prophylaxis for chlamydia in high-risk cases.
- Encourage her to eat and drink, and walk about as she wishes.
- Offer other health services, if possible, including tetanus prophylaxis and counselling about contraception.
- If her case is uncomplicated, you can discharge her in 1–2 hours.
- Before discharging her, advise her to watch for the following symptoms and signs, which require immediate attention:
  - Prolonged cramping for more than a few days
  - Prolonged bleeding for more than two weeks
  - Bleeding more than normal menstrual bleeding
  - Severe or increased pain
  - Fever, chills or malaise
  - Fainting

102 How to do a laparotomy for ectopic pregnancy

CLAIRE VAN DEVENTER AND MUSTAPHA MAKINDE

Laparotomy, which was the "gold standard" for surgical treatment of ectopic pregnancy in the past, has now been largely replaced by the laparoscopic approach in cases of unruptured ectopic pregnancy. However, laparotomy is still the preferred technique in cases of ruptured ectopic pregnancy where the patient is haemodynamically unstable. Laparotomy is also indicated if the surgeon lacks the necessary skills in laparoscopy, if the ectopic pregnancy is not in a Fallopian tube, if a laparoscopy facility is not available and when laparoscopy is contraindicated due to technical barriers.

Figure 102.1 illustrates an ectopic pregnancy.

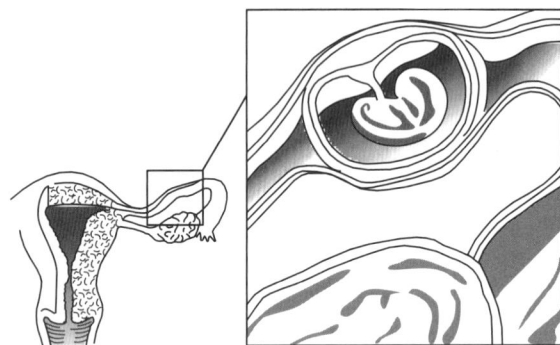

Figure 102.1 Ectopic pregnancy

Preparation

To prepare for the procedure, you need to do the following:

- Organise a full blood count, urea and electrolytes, as well as cross-matched blood.
- Insert a urinary catheter to measure your patient's urine output.
- If she is in shock, you need to correct this with crystalloids, for example normal saline or Ringer's lactate, using two 16-gauge cannulae if possible, as well as colloids, for example Haemaccel®, if

needed. Monitor the clinical signs of shock for improvement.

- Consider the necessity of a rapid-sequence induction.
- Use ketamine as the anaesthesia if she remains hypotensive.
- Obtain her consent, which should show her grasp of the implications of this procedure for future fertility.

Procedure

The incision of choice is the Pfannenstiel incision (see Chapter 91). However, you can also use a sub-umbilical vertical midline incision.

To perform the laparotomy, you need to follow this procedure:

- Prepare your patient's abdomen routinely and drape her.
- Make the incision.
- Pack the bowel into the upper abdomen, and retain it with one or two abdominal swabs.
- Reach into the pelvic cavity and deliver the uterus into the abdominal wound. This naturally brings the Fallopian tubes into view.
- Now identify the pathology and establish its extent. You should remove blood clots but leave free-flowing blood in the peritoneal cavity as the cells are absorbed and the iron is re-used. If the volume of blood makes visualisation of the ruptured tube a problem then you can suction it off.
- Manage the ectopic – see below.
- Inspect the other ovary and tube.
- Remove the packs and close the abdomen.

To treat a ruptured ectopic pregnancy, you need to perform a salpingectomy to stop the bleeding. You need not remove the ovary unless it is bleeding or is part of the pregnancy sac.

If you find the pregnancy to be unruptured, you must take the following considerations into account.

Ampullary ectopic pregnancy

In the vast majority of cases the ectopic pregnancy is in the ampullary region. (http://www.emedicine.com/med/topic3212.htm)

If the ectopic pregnancy is in the ampullary region, perform a linear salpingostomy by making a linear incision over the anti-mesenteric border of the tube. Carefully remove the product of conception (POC), avoiding damage to the lumen of the tube. This is illustrated in Figure 102.2. Cauterise active bleeding points and leave the wound to heal by secondary intention.

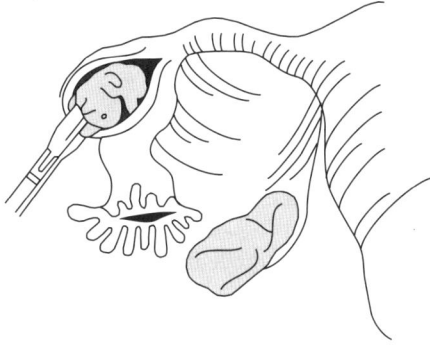

Figure 102.2 Ectopic mass removed from the Fallopian tube

Isthmic ectopic pregnancy

You can treat an isthmic ectopic pregnancy similarly or by resection of the involved segment of the tube. You may do interval re-anastamosis at a later stage under microscopic guidance if your patient's ongoing fertility is of major concern.

Fimbrial ectopic pregnancy

A fimbrial (infundibular) ectopic represents a "tubal abortion" in most cases. The POCs are already being expelled from the tube into the abdomen – all you need to do is remove the POCs at the end of the tube. Do not milk the tube, as this can damage the tubal lumen and cause unnecessary bleeding.

Cornual ectopic pregnancy

This happens very rarely. A cornual (interstitial) ectopic pregnancy presents a challenge because of the vascularity of surrounding myometrium. You need to resect the tube and close the uterine cornu with mattress haemostatic sutures.

Abdominal pregnancy

This happens in about 1–2% of the cases.

Here, the POC has been expelled into the abdomen, usually implanting on vascular tissue like the mesenteric vessels of the bowel. The abundant blood supply may allow the ectopic pregnancy to grow to term. During surgical removal of the POC, leave the placental site *in situ* to avoid fatal bleeding.

This case is not suitable for management at primary care level. You should refer your patient to a large centre. If you make the diagnosis at laparotomy and your patient is not bleeding, consider closing the abdomen and sending her to a referral centre. If bleeding occurs then you can remove the foetus, tie the cord, pack and close the abdomen, and then refer her.

This is a potentially *lethal* condition. It is important to consider this diagnosis in patients with unexplained foetal death with unsuccessful induction of labour.

Ovarian ectopic pregnancy

This happens in less than 1% of the cases.

You would treat ovarian pregnancy by partial or total oophorectomy, that is removal of the ovary, and excising POC with the destroyed ovarian tissue. Usually, you can easily control the resultant bleeding by ligating the vascular pedicles to the ovary, that is the infundibulo-pelvic ligaments.

Cervical ectopic pregnancy

This happens in less than 1% of the cases.

A non-surgical approach should be used in cervical ectopic gestation to avoid the tremendous bleeding that may occur when surgical removal is attempted. Urgently refer your patient.

After-care

Inform your patient of what you found and did. Explain the possibility of future ectopic pregnancy and the need for early diagnosis of pregnancy with confirmation of its intrauterine status by vaginal ultrasound examination at 6–8 weeks.

103 How to do a fine-needle aspiration of a breast cyst or nodule

CLAIRE VAN DEVENTER AND MUSTAPHA MAKINDE

Fine-needle aspiration (FNA) of a painful breast cyst or nodule is a procedure that requires the use of a 22- or 25-gauge needle and a syringe in order for aspirate to be collected.

See also Chapter 57 on wide-needle aspiration biopsy.

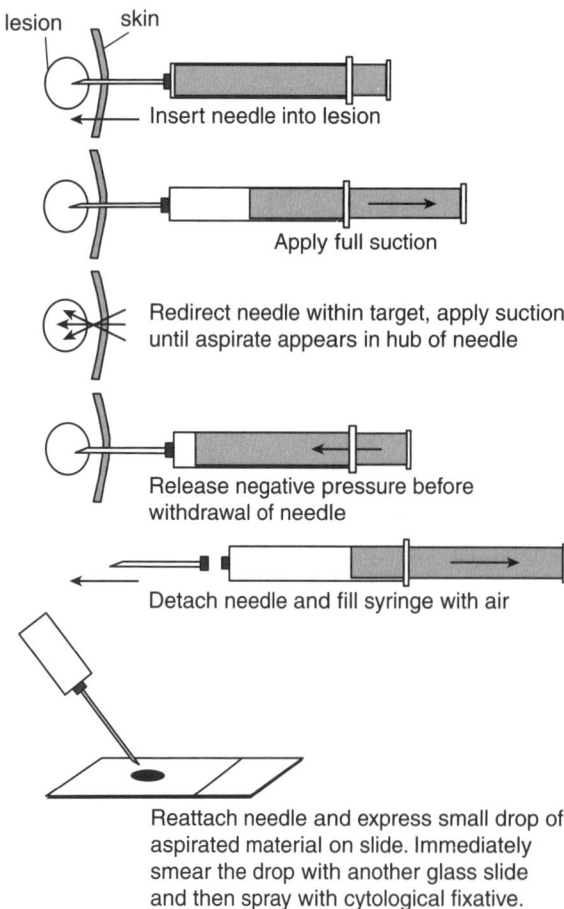

lesion skin

Insert needle into lesion

Apply full suction

Redirect needle within target, apply suction until aspirate appears in hub of needle

Release negative pressure before withdrawal of needle

Detach needle and fill syringe with air

Reattach needle and express small drop of aspirated material on slide. Immediately smear the drop with another glass slide and then spray with cytological fixative.

Figure 103.1 Fine-needle aspiration technique

Procedure

To collect the aspirate, you need to follow this procedure:

- Have your patient sit comfortably or lie down.
- Clean the skin over the cyst or nodule.
- Attach a syringe to the needle.
- You may give local anaesthesia, though this is often as painful as the procedure itself.
- Feel for the cyst or nodule, isolate it and anchor it between two fingers of one hand, while using the other to guide the needle through the skin (Figure 103.2).
- Follow the steps as illustrated in Figure 103.1
- Put a small dressing over the puncture site, and advise your patient that she can usually resume normal activities on the same day.
- In the case of a cyst:
  - Try to empty the cyst of all fluid, which you should then send to the laboratory for cytological examination.
  - After emptying a cyst any residual mass can also be biopsied using FNAB.

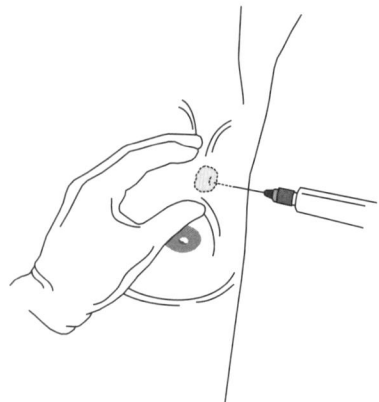

Figure 103.2 Aspirating a breast cyst

104 How to do culdocentesis

CLAIRE VAN DEVENTER AND MUSTAPHA MAKINDE

Culdocentesis was performed for diagnosing fluid in the pouch of Douglas. Today, the diagnosis can be made, less intrusively, by ultrasound examination.

On ultrasound, if you find that the uterus is empty and there is fluid in the pouch of Douglas, consider an ectopic pregnancy and do a beta human chorionic gonadotropin (βHCG).

Once you have confirmed that fluid is in the pouch of Douglas, at some point you should do a laparotomy or laparoscopy for therapeutic purposes.

If you do not have access to ultrasound investigations, this is how you would perform a culdocentesis:

- Insert a speculum into the vagina.
- Gently grasp the posterior lip of the cervix with a tenaculum and gently elevate the cervix to expose the posterior vaginal fornix.
- Place a long needle (e.g. a spinal needle) on a syringe and insert it through the posterior vaginal fornix, just below the posterior lip of the cervix.
- Pull back on the syringe to aspirate the recto-uterine pouch (of Douglas).
- If non-clotting blood is obtained, suspect an ectopic pregnancy.
- If clotting blood is obtained, a vein or artery may have been aspirated. Remove the needle, re-insert it and aspirate again.

- If clear or yellow fluid is obtained, there is no blood in the peritoneum. The woman may, however, still have an unruptured ectopic pregnancy and further observations and tests may be needed.
- If no fluid is obtained, remove the needle, re-insert it and aspirate again. If no fluid is obtained, the woman could still have an unruptured ectopic pregnancy.
- If pus is obtained, the patient will need surgery.

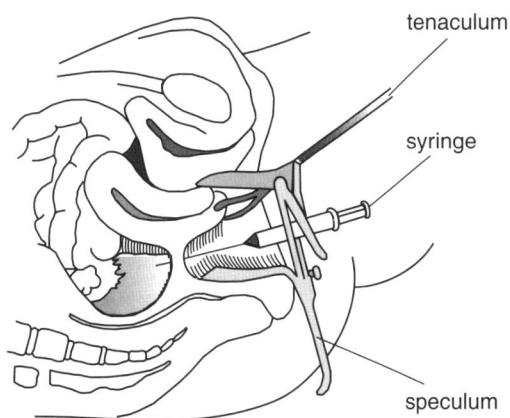

Figure 104.1 Diagnostic puncture of the cul-de-sac

105 How to treat a Bartholin's cyst or abscess

JULIA BLITZ-LINDEQUE

Bartholin's glands are located at the base of the labia minora with the ducts that drain the glands opening on the mucosa near the entrance to the vagina.

Obstruction of the duct due to non-specific inflammation or trauma can result in the glands enlarging and becoming cystic. They can also be infected by *E. coli*, streptococci or staphylococci, or result from an STI (sexually transmitted infection), commonly chlamydia or gonorrhoea.

You can treat a symptomatic cyst or abscess in one of these four ways:

1. Aspirate the contents with a thick needle. However, do *not* consider this in an infected cyst.
2. Perform marsupialisation by removing the roof of the gland with eversion and suturing the gland walls to the surrounding skin. This requires anaesthesia.
3. With simple incision and drainage. This is most commonly used.
4. Completely excising the gland. This is reserved for chronically infected glands, or a peri- or post-menopausal patient, as in these cases there is a small risk of malignancy.

Marsupialisation used to be the treatment of choice because of perceived reduced recurrence rates, but excessive scarring can result from it. You may need to apply electrocautery during the procedure to control bleeding. The initial steps are the same as for incision and drainage (see below). The process then involves the suturing of the abscess wall to the skin (Figure 105.2). You would use interrupted absorbable sutures to approximate the edges of the cyst wall to the adjacent skin or mucosa to hold the cavity open, and you would pack the cavity with topical antibiotic cream or iodine-soaked gauze.

Simple incision and drainage has recently been shown to have no greater recurrence rate in South Africa than marsupialisation (Omole, Simmons & Hacker 2003). As it is a more easily performed procedure, you should consider this the first line of treatment in all cases. Although general anaesthesia is preferred, you can perform the procedure under ethyl chloride spray analgesia.

To treat the cyst or abscess, follow this procedure:

- Place your patient in the lithotomy position.
- Retract the labia majora laterally.
- Stabilise and move the cyst towards the introitus by placing a finger above the cyst in the vagina.
- Make a vertical incision 2–3 cm long at the muco-cutaneous junction over the top of the cyst using a 15 blade. Figure 105.1 shows this step of the process. Then extend the incision deeper into the cyst. Beware of splash of contents.
- Remove the cyst contents and irrigate the cavity.

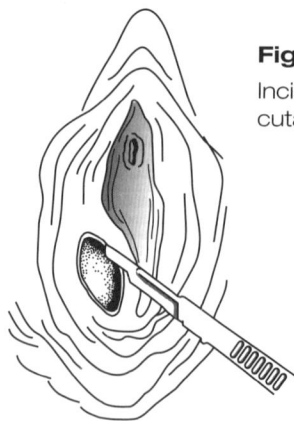

Figure 105.1

Incision at the muco-cutaneous junction

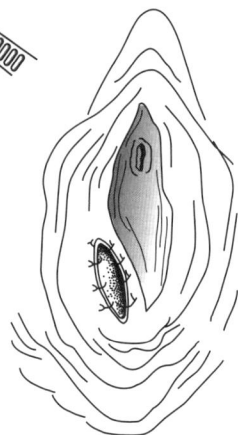

Figure 105.2

The cyst wall is sutured to the overlying skin in marsupialisation

106 How to do an endometrial biopsy

JULIA BLITZ-LINDEQUE

Endometrial biopsy is the accepted initial method of evaluating abnormal perimenopausal bleeding and, in particular, post-menopausal bleeding. You would use it in conjunction with transvaginal ultrasound measurement of endometrial thickness.

Remember that while a histology result that does not find a malignancy is reassuring, you *must* investigate the patient further if abnormal bleeding continues.

You would *not* perform the biopsy under these circumstances:

- Pregnancy
- Acute pelvic inflammatory disease
- Clotting disorders
- Acute cervical or vaginal infections
- Cervical cancer
- Severe cervical stenosis

Procedure

Before beginning the procedure you need to

- exclude pregnancy in a pre-menopausal patient
- consider pre-procedure ibuprofen to prevent prostaglandin-induced uterine cramping.

To perform the biopsy, you need to follow this procedure:

- Place your patient in the lithotomy position.
- Determine the size and position of her uterus by bimanual examination.
- Pass a vaginal speculum, centre the cervix in the speculum and clean the cervix with povidone-iodine.
- If the cervix is stenotic, consider anaesthetising it with a paracervical block.
- If you think that dilatation of the cervix is necessary then you need to perform the procedure under general anaesthesia or a well-functioning paracervical block (see chapter 107).

- Place a tenaculum, its teeth horizontal holding a small bite of tissue, on the anterior cervical lip in order to stabilise the cervix. The tenaculum need not be locked.
- Pull gently outward on the tenaculum in order to straighten the utero-cervical angle. This decreases the chance of posterior uterine wall perforation.
- Insert the endometrial biopsy catheter (Pipelle® or Endopap®) through the cervical os up to the uterine fundus.
- Pull back the internal piston of the catheter to create a vacuum inside the biopsy catheter.
- Move the catheter tip up and down in the endometrial cavity, while simultaneously twirling the catheter to rotate the tip within the cavity.
- Make at least four of these excursions within the uterine cavity in order to sample as wide a field as possible.
- Once the catheter is filled with tissue, remove it from the uterus.
- With the internal piston, push the sample out of the catheter into a formalin-filled histology bottle.
- It is recommended that you make a total of three passes of the catheter. Remember to maintain sterility of the catheter between passes.
- Remove the tenaculum from the cervix.
- Clean the cervix and vagina and remove the speculum.

Follow-up

Check the histology, and manage your patient accordingly.

107 How to do a paracervical block

You would perform this procedure to anaesthetise the cervix when it needs to be dilated for an outpatient procedure such as TOP or an endometrial biopsy.

It is recommended that you do the block with 1% lignocaine, without adrenalin. Usually, an injection of 5 ml on each side is sufficient.

To do the block, insert a thin needle lateral to the cervix on each side: 1 cm lateral to the cervix, 1 cm posterior from the midline and 1 cm deep. You can exclude vascular penetration by aspiration.

Figure 107.1 shows the specific sites of the block.

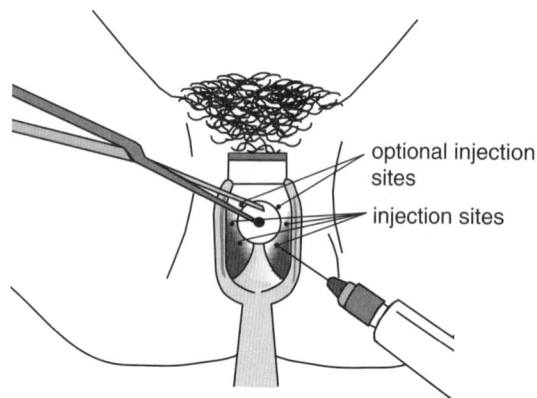

optional injection sites

injection sites

Figure 107.1 Sites for a paracervical block

Emergencies

2006

Basic Life Support for Healthcare Providers

(Adult and Child)

Hazards?

Ensure scene is safe

Hello?

Check Responsiveness

Responsive →

If safe to do so:

Treat illnesses or injuries as necessary

(?Aspirin / Inhaler / Auto-injector)

Get assistance if needed

Reassess continuously

Help!

Call for assistance and Defibrillator/AED

A

Open Airway

Remove visible foreign material

Look for adequate breathing

Breathing adequately →

Place in recovery position

Check for continued breathing

Reassess continuously

Not breathing adequately

B

Breathe

Give 2 effectve (chest rising) breaths at 1 breath/second

(with 0₂ if available).

Feel for pulse for up to 10 seconds.

Is a definite pulse present?

Yes →

Continue Rescue breaths:

- Adult:10/min

- Child: 12-20/min

Reassess continuously

No or Don't Know

C

Compressions

Compress chest at a rate of 100/min (almost 2 compressions/second)

Push hard / Push fast / Ensure full chest recoil / Minimize interruptions

CPR Ratios: 1-Rescuer = 30:2 and 2–Rescuers (Child) = 15:2

Continue until **Defibrillator/AED** available and ready

D

If time from collapse > 5 minutes without CPR,

first do 2 minutes of CPR before analysing

Analyse Rhythm

Shockable

(VF/Pulseless VT)

Non-Shockable

(PEA/Asystole)

After 2 min of CPR, if organized electrical activity returns, check pulse:

- If present – provide post- resuscitation care

- If absent, continue CPR

Give 1 Shock

Biphasic: 120-360J (4 J/Kg)

Monophasic - 360 J (4 J/Kg)

Immediately resume CPR
for 2 minutes

Immediately resume CPR
for 2 minutes

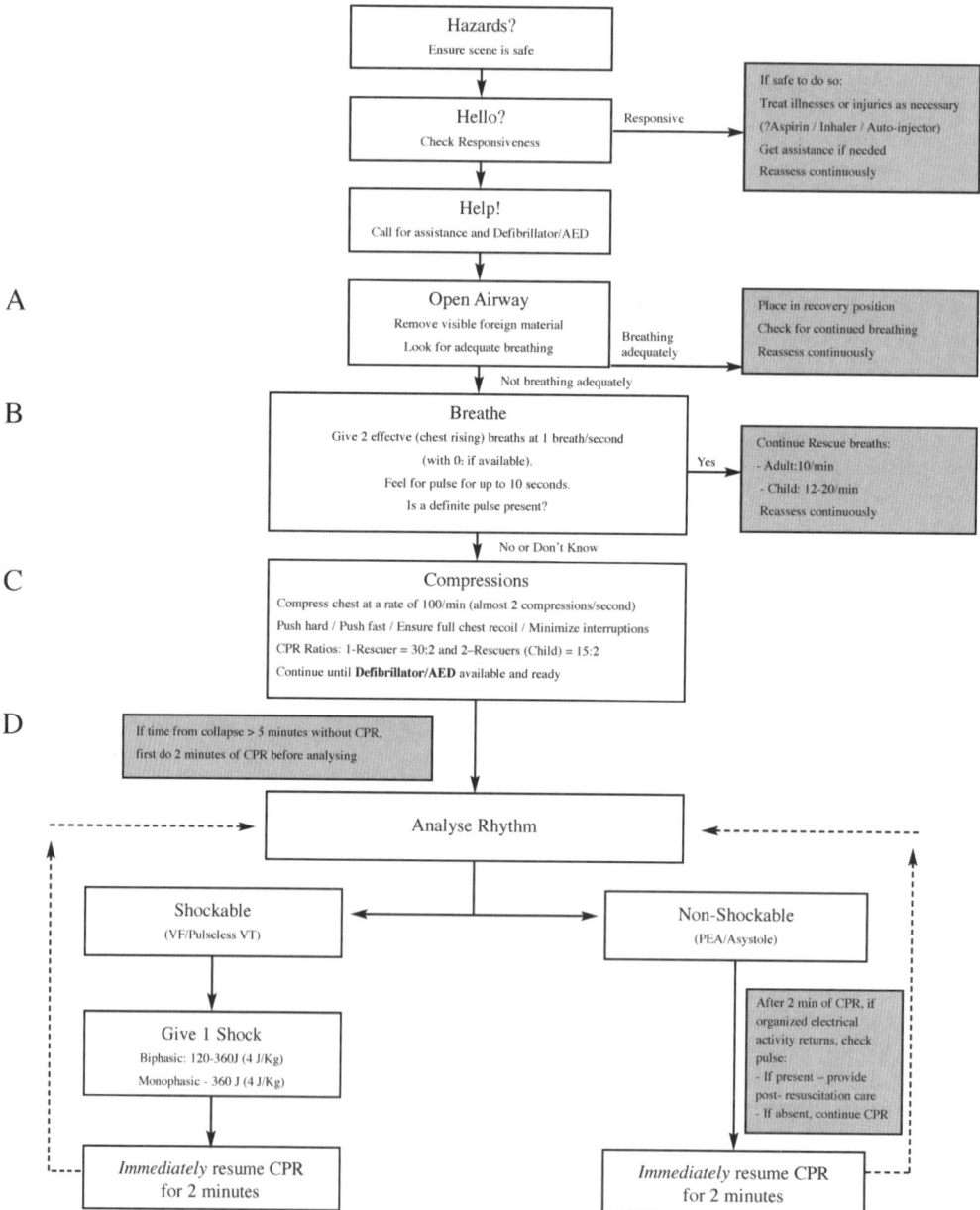

Do not interrupt chest compressions unless absolutely necessary

Resuscitation Council of Southern Africa
www.resuscitationcouncil.co.za

Van Schaik Publishers

Advanced Airway Management Algorithm
(Adult and Child)

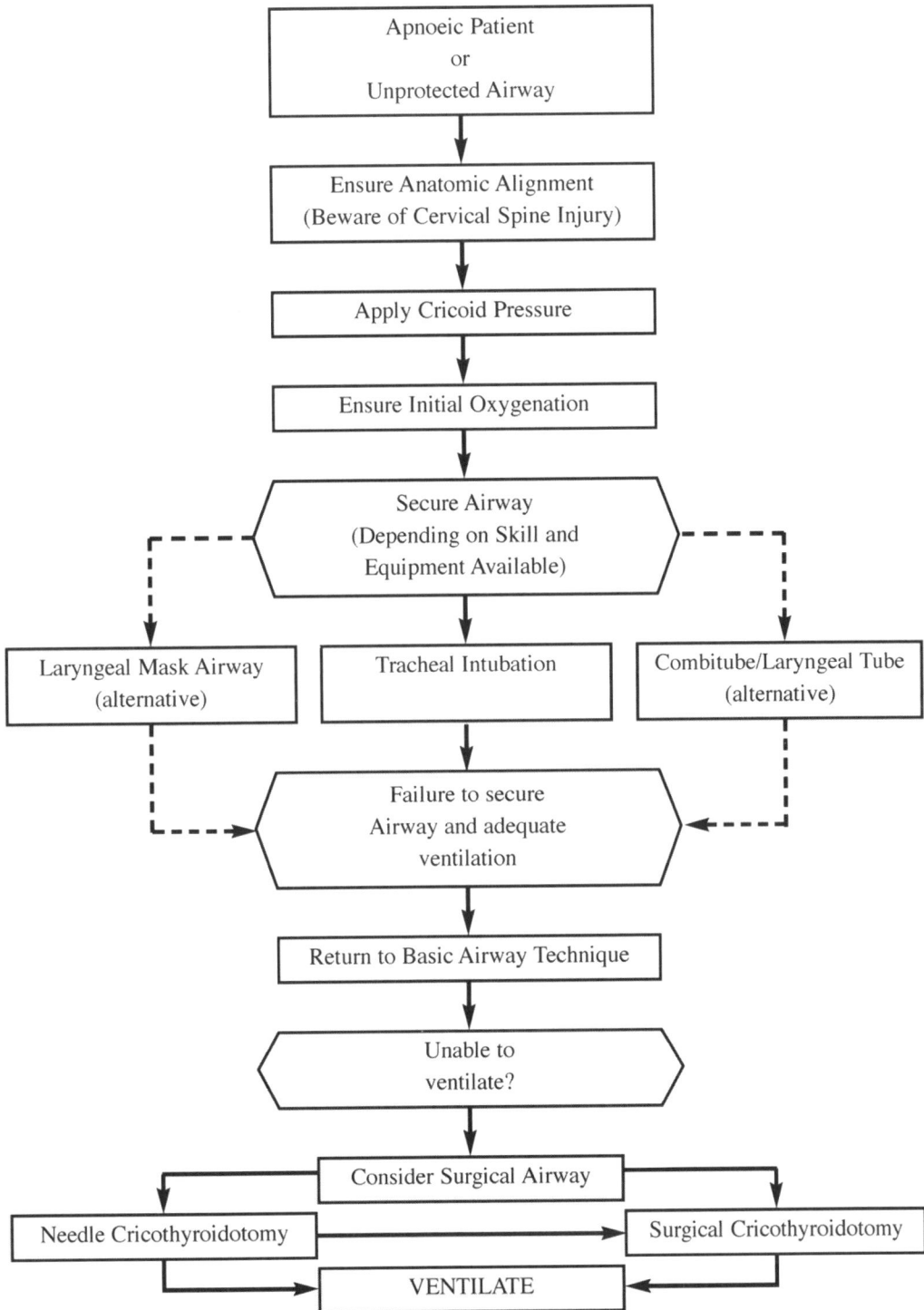

Apnoeic Patient
or
Unprotected Airway

↓

Ensure Anatomic Alignment
(Beware of Cervical Spine Injury)

↓

Apply Cricoid Pressure

↓

Ensure Initial Oxygenation

↓

Secure Airway
(Depending on Skill and
Equipment Available)

Laryngeal Mask Airway
(alternative)

Tracheal Intubation

Combitube/Laryngeal Tube
(alternative)

Failure to secure
Airway and adequate
ventilation

↓

Return to Basic Airway Technique

↓

Unable to
ventilate?

↓

Consider Surgical Airway

Needle Cricothyroidotomy

Surgical Cricothyroidotomy

VENTILATE

Resuscitation Council of Southern Africa
www.resuscitationcouncil.co.za

Advanced Life Support for Healthcare Providers

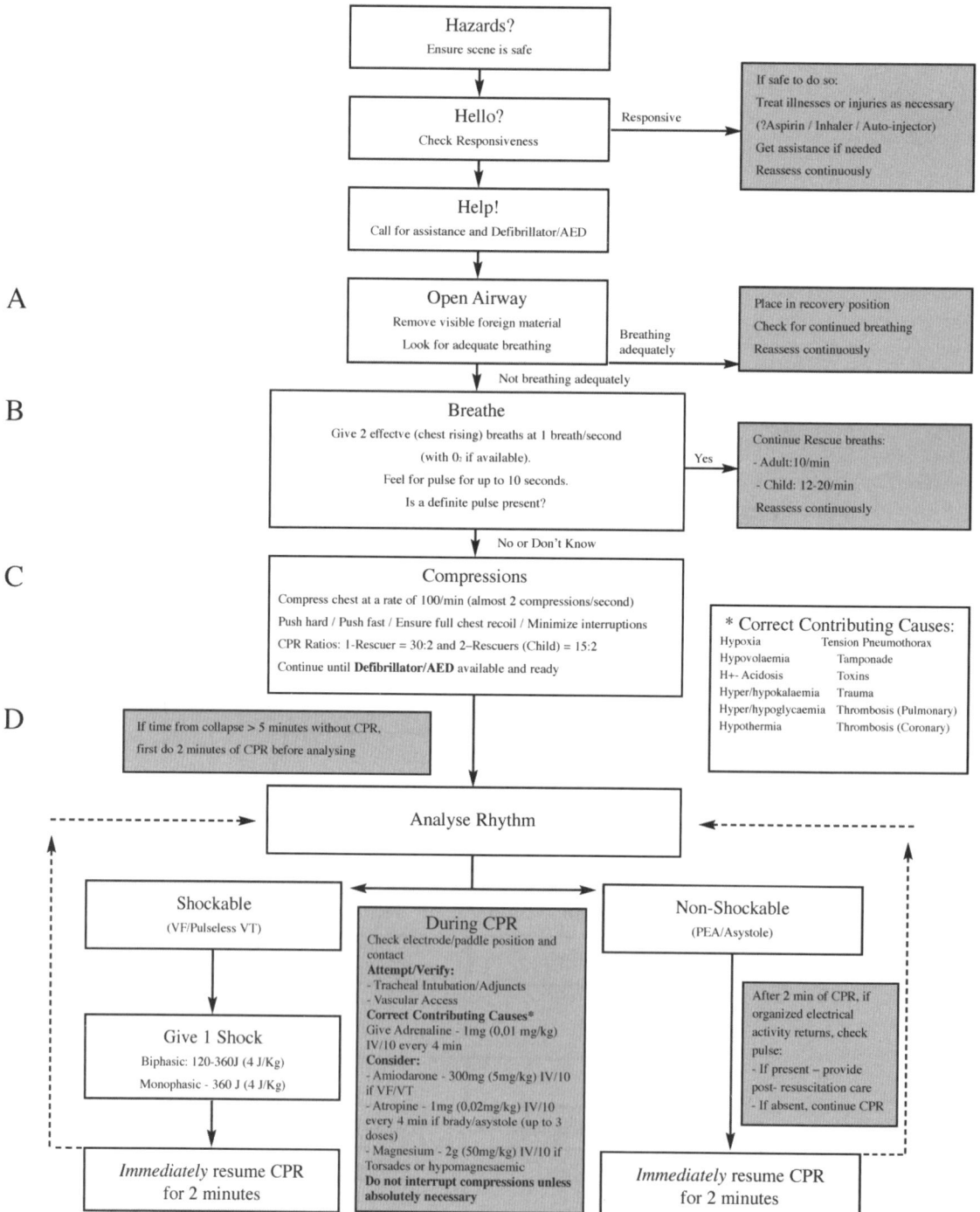

(Adult and Child)

EMSSA

Hazards?

Ensure scene is safe

Hello?

Check Responsiveness

Responsive →

If safe to do so:

Treat illnesses or injuries as necessary

(?Aspirin / Inhaler / Auto-injector)

Get assistance if needed

Reassess continuously

Help!

Call for assistance and Defibrillator/AED

A

Open Airway

Remove visible foreign material

Look for adequate breathing

Breathing adequately →

Place in recovery position

Check for continued breathing

Reassess continuously

Not breathing adequately

B

Breathe

Give 2 effectve (chest rising) breaths at 1 breath/second

(with O₂ if available).

Feel for pulse for up to 10 seconds.

Is a definite pulse present?

Yes →

Continue Rescue breaths:

- Adult:10/min

- Child: 12-20/min

Reassess continuously

No or Don't Know

C

Compressions

Compress chest at a rate of 100/min (almost 2 compressions/second)

Push hard / Push fast / Ensure full chest recoil / Minimize interruptions

CPR Ratios: 1-Rescuer = 30:2 and 2–Rescuers (Child) = 15:2

Continue until **Defibrillator/AED** available and ready

* Correct Contributing Causes:

Hypoxia	Tension Pneumothorax
Hypovolaemia	Tamponade
H+- Acidosis	Toxins
Hyper/hypokalaemia	Trauma
Hyper/hypoglycaemia	Thrombosis (Pulmonary)
Hypothermia	Thrombosis (Coronary)

D

If time from collapse > 5 minutes without CPR, first do 2 minutes of CPR before analysing

Analyse Rhythm

Shockable

(VF/Pulseless VT)

During CPR

Check electrode/paddle position and contact

Attempt/Verify:

- Tracheal Intubation/Adjuncts

- Vascular Access

Correct Contributing Causes*

Give Adrenaline - 1mg (0,01 mg/kg) IV/10 every 4 min

Consider:

- Amiodarone - 300mg (5mg/kg) IV/10 if VF/VT

- Atropine - 1mg (0,02mg/kg) IV/10 every 4 min if brady/asystole (up to 3 doses)

- Magnesium - 2g (50mg/kg) IV/10 if Torsades or hypomagnesaemic

Do not interrupt compressions unless absolutely necessary

Non-Shockable

(PEA/Asystole)

Give 1 Shock

Biphasic: 120-360J (4 J/Kg)

Monophasic - 360 J (4 J/Kg)

After 2 min of CPR, if organized electrical activity returns, check pulse:

- If present – provide post- resuscitation care

- If absent, continue CPR

Immediately resume CPR for 2 minutes

Immediately resume CPR for 2 minutes

Do not interrupt chest compressions unless absolutely necessary

Resuscitation Council of Southern Africa

www.resuscitationcouncil.co.za

Choking Algorithm
(Adult and Child)

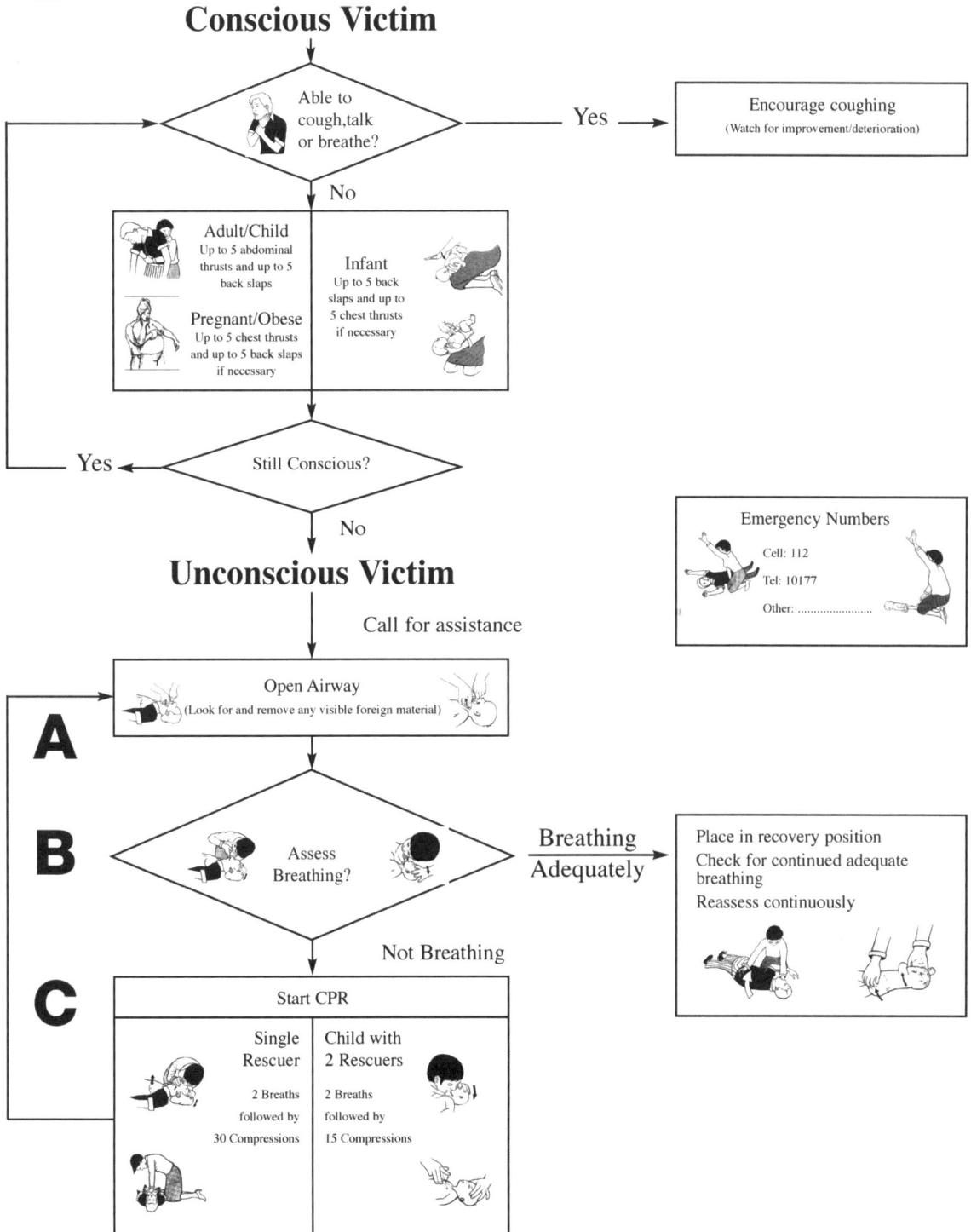

2006

Conscious Victim

Able to cough, talk or breathe?

Yes → Encourage coughing
(Watch for improvement/deterioration)

No

Adult/Child
Up to 5 abdominal thrusts and up to 5 back slaps

Pregnant/Obese
Up to 5 chest thrusts and up to 5 back slaps if necessary

Infant
Up to 5 back slaps and up to 5 chest thrusts if necessary

Still Conscious? → **Yes**

No

Unconscious Victim

Call for assistance

Emergency Numbers
Cell: 112
Tel: 10177
Other: ....

A Open Airway
(Look for and remove any visible foreign material)

B Assess Breathing?

Breathing Adequately → Place in recovery position
Check for continued adequate breathing
Reassess continuously

Not Breathing

C Start CPR

Single Rescuer	Child with 2 Rescuers
2 Breaths followed by 30 Compressions	2 Breaths followed by 15 Compressions

Resuscitation Council of Southern Africa
www.resuscitationcouncil.co.za

109 How to do a primary survey

DRIES ENGELBRECHT AND ISABEL PIENAAR

When you follow this procedure, you follow a step-by-step ABCDE process.

A – Airway and C-spine protection

This step involves the following:

- Assess the patient by looking for signs of respiratory distress, cyanosis and chest expansion, listening for audible stridor/wheeze and good air entry into the lungs, and feeling for movement of air against the cheek. If he can speak normally, this indicates an open airway and unobstructed movement of air from the airways to his lungs.

- Check for direct injury to an airway, such as unstable fractures of the jaw, blunt or penetrating injury to the larynx, oedema of the glottis, foreign bodies in his mouth or pharynx, or a depressed level of consciousness, suggested by a lack of response to verbal or pain stimuli.

- You *must* perform endotracheal intubation if
  - his airway is compromised
  - oxygenation or ventilation is inadequate
  - his airway is unprotected
  - his level of consciousness is decreased, that is his GCS (Glasgow Coma Scale, see Chapter 122) result is less than 9
  - he is combative and at risk for self-injury
  - there is risk of airway loss in the immediate future
  - you need to control the airway for therapeutic or diagnostic procedures.

- Throughout, maintain strict C-spine protection by manual immobilisation or a rigid neck collar.

B – Breathing and ventilation

This step involves your **examination** of the following:

- Inspect his chest for
  - signs of distress, such as tachypnoea, use of accessory muscles, grunting or wheezing
  - any signs of disruption to the chest wall
  - paradoxical movement associated with flail chest.

- Palpate his chest for
  - trachea in the midline
  - surgical emphysema
  - tenderness or crepitus.

- Percuss and auscultate his chest for signs consistent with pneumothorax or haemothorax, that is decreased air entry and changed resonance on the side of the injury.

This step also involves your management of the following:

- Give 40–60% supplemental oxygen with an oxygen mask (see Chapter 112).

- In the case of a tension pneumothorax, immediately insert a 14- to 16-gauge needle into the second intercostal space mid-clavicular line on the side of the injury. Follow-up with an intercostal drain in the fifth intercostal space anterior to the mid-axillary line (see Chapter 114).

- In the case of an open pneumothorax, close the wound with sterile dressings and occlude on three sides. Follow up with an intercostal drain as described above.

- In the case of a massive haemothorax, insert two large-bore IV lines. Obtain blood for transfusion. Insert an intercostal drain as described above. You can make use of an autotransfusion set, if one is available.

- In the case of flail chest and lung contusion, provide adequate pain control with opiate analgesia. You can easily perform rib blocks by injecting 2–3 ml lignocaine 20% directly into the fractured areas of the ribs. *Never* exceed 4 mg/kg as the total dosage of lignocaine. If saturation and bloodgas findings remain poor then you need to intubate and ventilate.

C – Circulation with haemorrhage control

This step involves the following:

- Evaluate the patient's haemodynamic status, that is the level of consciousness, pulse rate and character, skin colour, BP and capillary filling.
- Try to detect the source of hypovolaemic shock by considering these sources:
  - External – check for bleeding into loose bandages, etc.
  - Pleural space – listen for decreased air entry, percuss for dullness.
  - Peritoneum – repeatedly examine the abdomen, do a sonar to test for free fluid, do a diagnostic peritoneal lavage.
  - Pelvis and/or retroperitoneum – check for pelvic stability.
  - Long bone fracture
- Insert two large-bore peripheral lines in a patient with severe trauma.
- Obtain blood for cross matching and haematocrit.
- Do a pregnancy test on every female patient.
- Control external bleeding by proper pressure bandage.

D – Disability (neurological evaluation)

This step involves the following:

- Check the patient by AVPU (used as quick mental ability assessment):
  - A = Alert – answers the following questions correctly: name, date, location, what happened

- V = Responds to verbal stimuli
- P = Responds to painful stimuli
- U = Unresponsive to all stimuli
  A corresponds to GCS 15.
  U corresponds to GCS 3.
  Division between V and P occurs at GCS 9.
(See Chapter 122 The Glasgow Coma Scale.)

- Check his posture – normal, symmetrical limb movement; abnormal flexion or extension response on stimuli.
- Check his pupils – size and reaction; look for slow pupil reflex, or unilateral pupil dilatation indicating intracranial space-occupying lesion.

E – Exposure and environmental control

This step involves the following:

- The patient must be completely undressed for a thorough physical examination.
- Prevent him from suffering hypothermia by covering him and controlling the room temperature.

Essentials

During the survey, you also need to make sure of the following with regard to the patient:

- ECG monitoring
- Urinary catheter and nasogastric tube
- Continued monitoring of vital signs, which includes pulse rate, BP and respiratory rate
- Pulse oximetry and blood gas monitoring
- Pelvis, chest and C-spine lateral, or "Swimmer's view", X-rays

110 How to immobilise the spine

ANRIËTTE HOFFELDT

You should ensure adequate and continuous spinal immobilisation of every patient who is subjected to trauma, and whom you suspect of having a spinal cord injury, until you can declare him free from injury. You can do this after conducting a full medical examination and an appropriate X-ray examination. Note that the absence of neurological deficits does not rule out significant spinal injury.

Spinal immobilisation is a *priority* in a multiple-trauma patient. Excluding a spinal injury should not take precedence over patient stabilisation. To stabilise a fracture, you should splint the joint above and below. In a patient with possible neck injury or fracture, the "joints" above and below are the head and the shoulders.

Procedures

The ideal position of immobilisation is with the whole spine immobilised in a neutral position on a firm surface. You can achieve this manually or with a combination of a semi-rigid cervical collar, side head supports and strapping.

We will now discuss manual immobilisation with and without the aid of a backboard.

Manual in-line immobilisation with a backboard

Follow this procedure:

- The basic principle is that you must maintain the patient's head and neck in line with the long axis of his body.

- One person should hold the patient's head steady in the neutral position, applying only enough traction to relieve the weight of the head from the cervical spine.

- Once the process has begun, it must continue without interruption until his head and spine are immobilised on an appropriate mechanical device, such as a short spine board or vest, or a long spine board. The long spine board is the *only* device which provides complete spinal immobilisation once the patient is properly secured to it.

- The **log-roll** is the standard manoeuvre that allows you to examine his back and transfer him on and off the backboard. You need four people – one holding his head and coordinating the roll, and the other three to each roll his chest, pelvis and limbs. You can minimise lateral motion of the spine by positioning him with his arms extended at the side of his body with his palms against the lateral aspect of the thigh (see Figure 110.1).

Rescuers' positions

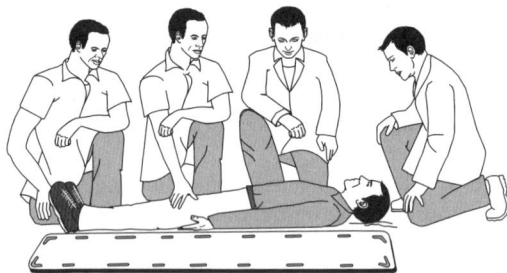

Preparing to roll patient

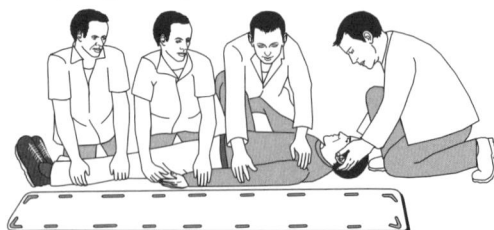

Rolled patient

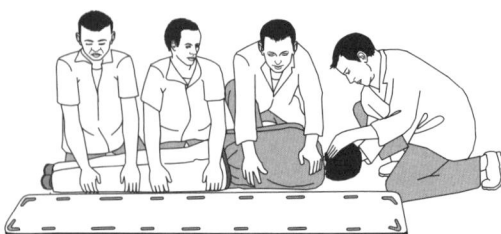

Figure 110.1 Technique of placing a patient onto a long spine board

- Further secure the patient using head blocks or rolled towels and taping his head, torso, arms and legs to the board or trolley.

- After placing most adults on a long or short spine board, there is a significant gap between the back of the head and the spine board. Therefore, add non-compressible padding such as folded towels before securing the head. The amount of padding that you need varies – evaluate it on an individual basis. Children have proportionately larger heads than adults and may require padding under the torso to allow the head to lie in a neutral position.

- If the patient's neck is not in the neutral position, try to achieve alignment. If he is awake and cooperative, he should actively move his neck into line. If he is unconscious or unable to cooperate, this is done passively.

- If there is any compromise of the airway or ventilation, pain, neurological deterioration, neck muscle spasm or resistance to movement you must abandon the procedure and splint the neck in the position in which it was found.

- Apply the semi-rigid cervical collar. It helps to prevent flexion and extension of the neck; it does *not* provide complete stabilisation of the cervical spine. Therefore, you should continue with this immobilisation until you can fully secure the patient's torso and head on a backboard or firm trolley.

- Remember that an improperly fitting collar will do more harm than good. If the proper size is not available, rather place a rolled towel around his neck, and tape it to the backboard.

Manual in-line immobilisation without a backboard

Follow this procedure:

- Use any flat, hard surface or object to prevent movement of the patient's head in relation to his spinal cord.
- Facilitate this by strapping the flat objects to his head with rolled towels alongside his head.
- Maintain in-line immobilisation of his head and spinal cord for as long as is necessary.

A patient who is agitated or restless owing to shock, hypoxia, head injury or intoxication may be impossible to immobilise adequately. Do not use forced restraints or manual fixation of the head, as these may cause further injury to his spine. You may even have to remove any immobilisation devices and allow him to move unhindered.

Figure 110.2 Patient secured on a long spine board

111 How to intubate a patient and manage the airway

DRIES ENGELBRECHT

In giving emergency medical care, you must begin with the patient's airway. The most important process is rapid sequence intubation, or RSI. This technique has emerged as the airway management method of choice when your patient evaluation does not anticipate a difficult intubation (Reid, Chan & Tweeddale 2004).

Indications

You would perform the procedure in these alphabetically arranged instances:

- **Airway obstruction:** GCS (Glasgow Coma Scale, see Chapter 122) is less than 8, and the tongue and soft tissues are obstructing the airway; or the airway is threatened, for example by inhalation burns
- **Breathing problems:** Apnoea, hypoventilation, flail chest with lung contusion
- **Circulatory problem:** All forms of severe shock
- **Drugs:** Adrenaline, atropine, lignocaine and naloxone can be given through the endotracheal (ET) tube.
- **Evacuation:** Get rid of secretions like meconium, vomit or mucous plugs.
- **Flail chest**
- **Gastric distension:** High risk of vomiting and aspiration
- **Hyperventilation** of head injuries

Preparation

Equipment

You should always have the following available:

- Suctioning equipment
- Laryngoscope – connect the blade to the handle and check the bulb for brightness.
- ET tubes. For an adult male you need size 7.5–8.5, for an adult female you need size 7–8. Always make sure that the cuff does not leak. For children, use their little finger as a rough guide to the size of the tube or use the following formula in children up to the age of 12 years: size of tube = (age ÷ 4) + 4. Use a non-cuffed tube for children. Have one smaller and one larger tube ready.
- Introducer
- Magill's forceps
- Oxygen source – an ambubag or ventilator connected to oxygen source
- Strapping

Patient

With regard to the patient, you need to do the following:

- Connect him to monitors for oxygen saturation, BP and ECG trace.
- If you do not suspect a neck injury, place him with his head in the "sniffing" position, that is with his neck flexed and head extended. You may need the support of a pillow. This provides you with the best line of vision during laryngoscopy. Figure 111.1 illustrates this position.
- If you suspect a neck injury, have an assistant immobilise his head and neck for the duration of the procedure.

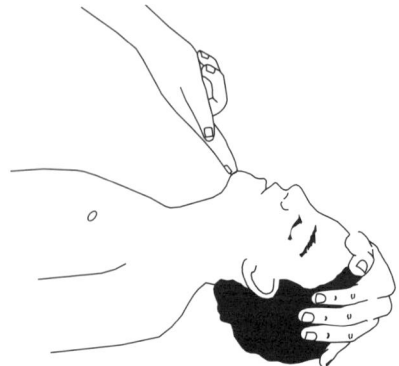

Figure 111.1 "Sniffing" position

Pre-oxygenation

You need to use pre-oxygenation in the following ways before intubating a patient:

- Patient with effective spontaneous breathing. Pre-oxygenate him with a partial rebreathing or non-rebreathing oxygen mask connected to an oxygen source.
- Patient with apnoea or poor spontaneous breathing. Use a bag-valve-mask device connected to an oxygen source to ventilate him.
- Patient with normal cardio-respiratory function. One to two minutes of pre-oxygenation may be adequate.
- Patient with poor cardio-respiratory function. At least five minutes of pre-oxygenation is recommended.
- See Chapter 112 on how to administer oxygen.

Medication

You can usually intubate a patient who is deeply comatose, that is with a GCS of 3, without the use of any medication. In most other cases, the use of an induction agent and short-acting muscle relaxant will help to provide you with optimal conditions for intubation.

You can administer these medicines rapidly and in sequence as follows:

- **Induction:** Etomidate 0.2–0.3 mg/kg IV is used because of its cardiovascular stability, immediately followed by:
- **Muscle relaxant:** Suxamethonium (scoline) 1–1.5 mg/kg IV has an extremely short onset and duration of action, and provides optimal conditions for intubation (Morgan & Mikhail 1996). Avoid it in cases of hyperkaleamia, such as renal failure, burn injuries that are more than 24 hours old and severe muscle injury.

Cricoid pressure, or Sellick's manoeuvre

Have an assistant apply firm pressure to the patient's cricoid cartilage in an upward and backward direction, starting just prior to induction, to occlude the oesophagus against the vertebral column. The process is illustrated in Figure 111.2. This prevents passive regurgitation of gastric fluid. Only after you have inflated the cuff of the ET tube and confirmed correct placement may the assistant release the pressure.

Procedure

To perform intubation, you need to follow this procedure once fasciculations have stopped:

- Hold the laryngoscope in your left hand.

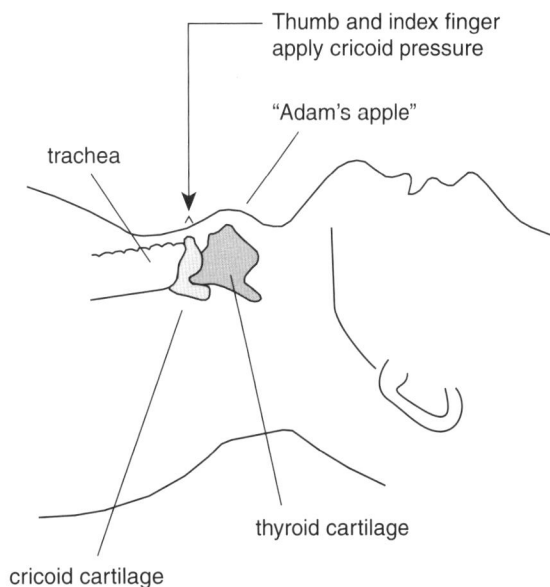

Figure 111.2 Applying Sellick's manoeuvre

- Insert it into the right side of the patient's mouth to displace the tongue to the left.
- Move the tip of the laryngoscope blade into the vallecula between the tongue base and the epiglottis.
- Displace the epiglottis upward by lifting the laryngoscope at a 45-degree angle. Do not use the teeth as a fulcrum.
- You should now see the vocal cords. If not, carefully suction the oropharynx until you do. Figure 111.3 illustrates the laryngoscope's view.
- Gently insert the ET tube through the cords into the trachea.
- In order to avoid intubating the right main bronchus, you must ensure that the cuff is only just past the vocal cords (0.5–1 cm beyond)
- Remove the laryngoscope, while carefully maintaining the position of the ET tube.
- Inflate the cuff with the minimum amount of air to provide an adequate seal – usually 4–6 ml for a 7.5 cuff.
- Confirm correct placement of the tube:
  - Good bilateral air entry on auscultation in the axillae
  - Equal chest expansion on ventilation
  - No bubbling sounds over the epigastrium with ventilation
  - Chest X-ray
  - Capnography and pulse oximetry
  - Oesophageal detector device

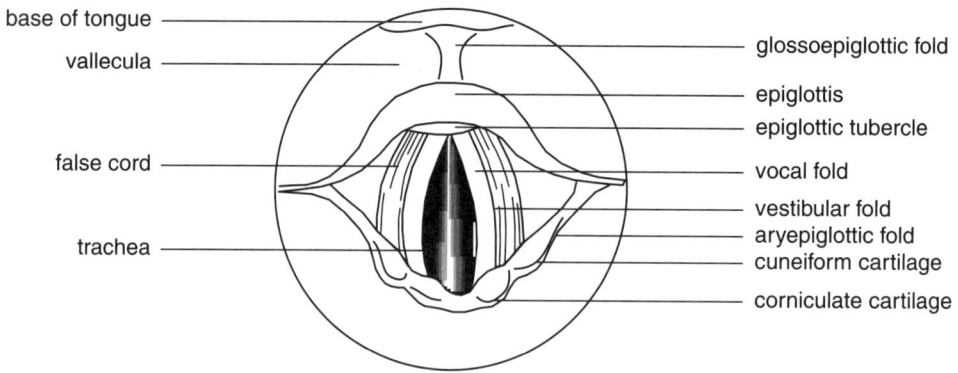

Figure 111.3 View through the laryngoscope

- Insert an appropriately sized oropharyngeal airway alongside the ET tube to ensure that the patient cannot obstruct the ET tube by biting.
- Secure the ET tube in place with strapping.
- Connect the tube to the oxygen supply and ventilation device.

If your first attempt at intubation is unsuccessful:

- You can re-attempt it, but note that repeated unsuccessful attempts without ventilating the patient in between leads to hypoxia and brain damage. As a rough guide, attempts at endotracheal intubation should not take longer than the average length of time that people can hold their breath before exhaling (ATLS Student Course Manual 1997).
- When repeating an intubation attempt, always try to improve the chances of success. The following may help to achieve this:
  - Repositioning the patient
  - Cricoid pressure, if not previously in place
  - Using the Magill's forceps and/or an introducer

  - Drugs such as midazolam or suxamethonium, if you have not already given them
  - Proper suctioning

After-care

Following successful intubation, you should admit the patient to a facility where continuous monitoring of his vital signs, ECG, saturation and ventilation can take place. This is often accomplished in an ICU setting.

If an intubated patient suddenly deteriorates, always consider correction of DOPES:

- **D**isplaced ET tube
- **O**bstructed tube
- **P**neumothorax
- **E**quipment failure
- **S**tomach distension

You should extubate your patient only when the original indication for intubation no longer exists and he is fully awake. He may well make purposeful attempts to remove the tube himself.

112 How to administer oxygen

SOPHIE MATHIJS

Supplemental oxygen is beneficial to every patient who presents to the emergency department. However, because high concentrations of oxygen are damaging to the lungs, you need to keep the amount and duration of oxygen therapy to the minimum.

The amount of oxygen that the patient needs in addition to that present in room air depends on the mechanism of hypoxia. The type of device that delivers the oxygen depends on the amount of oxygen needed. For example, a patient with anaemic hypoxia will require less oxygen than a patient with hypoxic hypoxia.

We will now explore supplemental oxygen devices, which are divided into low-flow and high-flow systems.

Low-flow devices

Low-flow oxygen devices (nasal cannula, simple masks, and masks with a reservoir bag) deliver oxygen at less than the peak inspiratory flow rate. They therefore deliver a variable concentration of oxygen, depending on how the patient is breathing.

1. **Nasal cannula:** It can provide 24–40% oxygen at flow rates from 1 to 6 ℓ/min in adults depending on the patient's minute ventilation. At flow rates of > 4 ℓ/min humidification should be considered.

2. **Simple facemask:** It can provide 35–50% oxygen at flow rates between 5–10 ℓ/min depending on the patient's inspiratory flow and mask fit. Flow rates of 5 ℓ/min minimum should be used to prevent the patient from rebreathing exhaled CO_2 from inside the mask. Caution should be taken when using a simple facemask system in patients who require accurately determined low concentrations of oxygen.

3. **Partial rebreathing mask:** It can provide 40–70% oxygen at flow rates between 6–10 ℓ/min depending on the patient's inspiratory flow. This mask is a combination of a simple

Figure 112.1
Simple facemask

facemask with an additional reservoir bag attached. Sufficient flow rates should ensure that the reservoir bag is always at least ⅓ to ½ full on patient inspiration. You can use a partial rebreathing mask in the following instances:

- A patient who is seriously ill but spontaneously breathing, and who requires a higher oxygen concentration, such as those with myocardial infarction

- A patient who can avoid intubation if acute interventions produce a rapid clinical response such as in chronic obstructive pulmonary disease, asthma or pulmonary oedema

- A patient who has indications for tracheal intubation but who maintains an active gag reflex, or one with clenched teeth or physical barriers for immediate intubation such as head injury, carbon monoxide poisoning or near-drowning

4. **Non-rebreathing mask:** It can provide 80–100% oxygen at a minimum flow rate of 10 ℓ/min. This mask is similar to the partial rebreathing mask except for a series of one-way valves, one of which is placed between the reser-

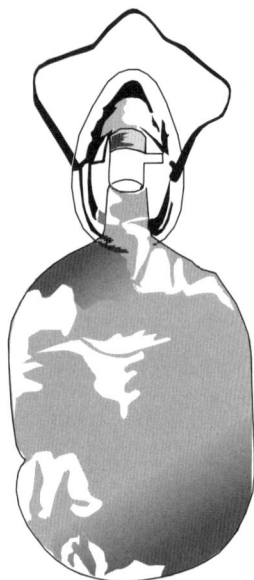

Figure 112.2
Partial rebreathing mask

voir bag and mask to prevent any exhaled air from entering the bag, with another placed on the mask to prevent inhalation of room air into the mask.

High-flow devices

These systems deliver a prescribed gas mixture at flow rates that exceed patient demand and are called Venturi masks. Venturi masks direct oxygen through a constricted tube that increases gas velocity. The jet of oxygen exiting from the constriction generates sufficient negative pressure to draw a much higher volume of air into the breathing circuit. Venturi masks can be used in patients with chronic hypercarbia and moderate to severe hypoxaemia, for example patients with COPD. High oxygen concentrations in these patients may produce respiratory depression because the increase in P_aO_2 blocks the stimulant effect of hypoxaemia on respiratory centers. Currently available air-entrainment Venturi-type masks can accurately deliver predetermined oxygen concentrations of up to 40%.

Patients needing oxygen

A **paediatric** patient has a high oxygen demand per kilogram of body weight because the child's metabolic rate is high. Oxygen consumption in infants is 6–8 ml/kg/min compared to 3–4 ml/kg/min in adults. Therefore, in the presence of apnoea or inadequate alveolar ventilation, hypoxaemia develops more rapidly in the child than in the adult. You should administer oxygen in the highest possible concentration to every seriously ill or injured child with respiratory insufficiency, shock or trauma. Add humidification as soon as possible to prevent obstruction of the small airways by dried secretions.

Allow an **alert child** experiencing respiratory difficulty to remain in a position of comfort since he usually assumes a position that promotes optimal airway patency and minimises respiratory effort. Anxiety increases oxygen consumption and possibly respiratory distress. If he is upset by the method of oxygen support, such as a mask, use an alternative method, for example a face tent or a "blow-by" stream of humidified oxygen which the parent holds toward the child's mouth and nose.

If you need oxygen during the resuscitation of a **newborn**, use 100% oxygen without concern for its potential hazards. Try to warm and humidify the oxygen, although this may not be possible in an emergency. You can deliver free-flow oxygen by a head hood, or by a simple mask held firmly to the neonate's face with at least 5 ℓ per minute oxygen flow (see Chapter 78).

You can provide devices for intermittent positive pressure breathing, continuous positive airway pressure (CPAP) masks, nasal CPAP, nebulisers for inhaled medication and others with supplemental oxygen as needed. Titrate the oxygen according to the P_aO_2 and the oxygen saturation. In serious cases of respiratory distress, you need to place an advanced airway – ET tube or laryngeal mask – and provide 100% oxygen.

You can use Table 112.1 to calculate which device, and at what flow rate, to use if you do not have access to a pulse oximeter or arterial blood gas.

Table 112.1 Oxygen delivery

Oxygen delivery device	Oxygen flow rate ℓ/min	Inspired oxygen concentration range
Nasal cannula	1–6	24–40%
Simple mask	5–10	35–50%
Partial rebreathing mask	6–10	40–70%
Non-rebreathing mask	10	80–100%
Venturi mask	4–12	28–40%

113 How to do a cricothyroidotomy

DRIES ENGELBRECHT

Indications

A clear indication for emergency cricothyroidotomy exists when you cannot intubate and you cannot ventilate a patient who needs a secure airway (ATLS Student Course Manual 1997).

This situation may be caused by trauma such as bilateral jaw fractures, laryngeal fractures, severe bleeding, haematoma or swelling of the upper airway. Non-traumatic causes include infections such as acute epiglottitis, retropharyngeal abscess, or diphtheritic membrane or other causes of severe upper airway swelling like allergic oedema or inhalational burns (King & Bewes 1993).

Procedure

There are two kinds of procedure – needle cricothyroidotomy and surgical cricothyroidotomy. In both, you need to do the following:

- Lie your patient in the supine position.
- If you suspect neck injury immobilise the neck at all times.
- If you have excluded neck injury, a slight extension of the neck may help to make the larynx more prominent.
- Clean his neck with an antiseptic.
- Palpate the cricothyroid membrane between the thyroid and cricoid cartilage. Use your non-dominant hand to stabilise the trachea during the procedure.

We will now explore the two types of procedure in greater detail.

Needle cricothyroidotomy

Follow this procedure:

- Connect an empty 10-ml syringe to a thick intravenous catheter – 14- or 16-gauge Jelco.
- Puncture the skin in the midline over the cricothyroid membrane.

- Aspirate while advancing the needle in a 45-degree caudal direction.
- When air is aspirated the needle should be in the lumen of the trachea, as illustrated in Figure 113.1.
- Gently advance the catheter in the same caudal direction, while pulling out the needle.
- You can place more than one needle in this way for a patient who is breathing spontaneously.
- Ventilate your apnoeic patient by connecting the adaptor of a no. 3 ET tube to the catheter. You can then connect this to a self-inflating bag system.

Surgical cricothyroidotomy

Follow this procedure:

- Make a transverse incision in your patient's skin over the cricothyroid membrane.

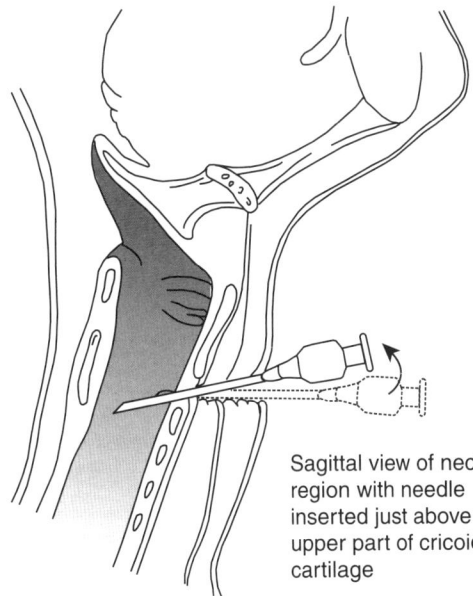

Sagittal view of neck region with needle inserted just above upper part of cricoid cartilage

Figure 113.1 Needle cricothyroidotomy

- Incise through the membrane, as illustrated in Figure 113.2A.

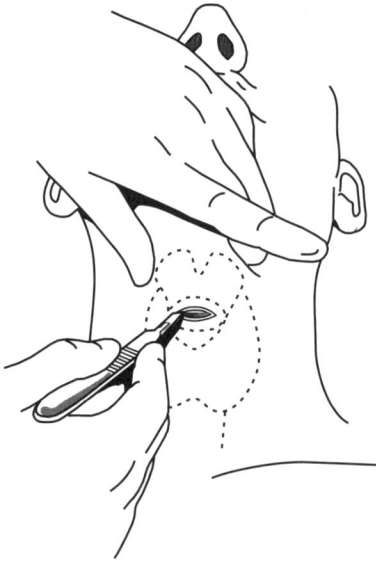

Figure 113.2A Surgical cricothyroidotomy

- Be prepared for droplets of blood and secretions as he coughs through the wound.
- Use the handle of the blade to twist open the hiatus in the membrane.
- Insert a tracheotomy tube or the smallest, cuffed ET tube available, (preferably a 5) as illustrated in Figure 113.2B.
- The handle of the blade can be used to assist with insertion of the ET tube.

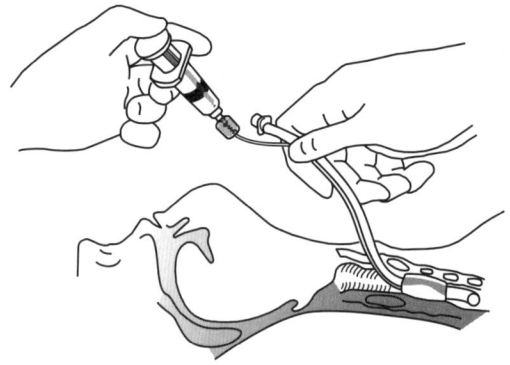

Figure 113.2B ET tube placed through the cricothyroidotomy incision

In an extreme emergency outside the hospital setting, a pocket-knife can be used to cut through the cricothyroid membrane and the plastic tube of a pen, without the nib and ink, can be used as an ET tube.

Complications

These complications can occur during the procedures:

- Inadequate ventilation leading to hypoxia and death
- Aspiration
- You could injure the adjacent structures, for example oesophagus, thyroid, larynx.
- Haematoma
- You could create a false passage into the tissues.

114 How to insert an intercostal drain

Indications

You would insert such a drain in these instances:

- Air in the pleural cavity, that is a pneumothorax.
- Fluid in the pleural cavity:
  - Haemothorax
  - Empyema
  - Pleural effusion causing tension
  - Chylothorax

Refer also to Chapter 34.

Preparation

Before beginning the procedure, you need to make these preparations:

- Obtain your patient's informed consent if his condition allows for it.
- Encourage good cooperation from him, as this will facilitate the procedure.
- Put saline or water in the underwater seal bottle and open the surgical pack.
- Open the following onto the surgical pack:
  - A no. 10 or 15 surgical blade
  - Suturing material – 1 or 0 nylon on a Colts needle and 3-0 nylon
  - Two needles and a syringe for drawing up local anaesthetic
  - The intercostal tube – size 34–36 in adults
- Clamp the end of the tube that will attach to the bottle.
- Determine the position of insertion. This is usually the nipple level, or fifth intercostal space, just anterior to the midaxillary line on the affected side (ATLS Student Course Manual 1997). You have identified this side by the decreased breath sounds, and correctly marked it on the chest X-ray. If possible, mark the position on your patient with a pen.

Procedure

To perform the drain, you need to follow this procedure:

- Place your patient in a supine position with the shoulder of the affected side fully extended and abducted with his hand behind his head.
- Surgically prepare the skin with antiseptic and use sterile drapes.
- Anaesthetise the skin with local anaesthetic. Start over the top of the sixth rib and infiltrate the skin and subcutaneous tissues and the fifth intercostal space.
- You can use the needle to aspirate the pleural space in order to confirm the presence of blood or air in the space.
- Use the surgical blade to make a 2–3 cm incision parallel to the top edge of the sixth rib (Knottenbelt 1992). Avoid the neurovascular bundle that runs in the lower margin of the rib above.
- Make use of blunt dissection with an artery forceps to go through the subcutaneous tissue and intercostal muscles.
- Puncture the parietal pleura with the tip of the artery forceps.
- Use a gloved finger to open the puncture site in the pleura.
- **Caution:** Do *not* use a trocar when inserting the tube as it may accidentally penetrate internal organs such as the heart.
- Insert the tube into the pleural space.
- Connect to the underwater bottle and remove the clamp.
- Anchor the tube to your patient's chest with suturing material. Do this with a circumferential suture around the tube and through the skin. Tie it just tight enough to indent the tube slightly. Place a purse-string suture around the tube and leave the ends untied for use when removing the tube.

You can **confirm placement** with these signs:

- Air bubbles through the fluid in the underwater bottle in the case of a pneumothorax.
- Blood drains into the bottle in the case of a haemothorax.
- There is fogging in the cannula with respiration.
- The meniscus of the fluid in the lower end of the tubing rises and falls with respirations.
- Air entry improves on the affected side.
- In the case of a large haemo- or pneumothorax with significant respiratory distress the patient feels immediate relief.
- In the case of an empyema, foul-smelling pus drains into the bottle.

You can do a chest X-ray immediately after the procedure to confirm correct placement of the tube. Do another within 12–24 hours to confirm expansion of the lung.

Removal

Ensure that your patient's lungs are fully expanded when you remove the drain. This prevents air from entering the pleural space at this point. The best way to achieve this is to ask him to perform a Valsalva manoeuvre by taking a full breath and blowing against a closed mouth and blocked nose. Have an assistant cut the anchoring stitch and withdraw the tube while you tie the purse-string suture.

Complications

You can avoid the following complications by performing the procedure carefully:

- Injury or laceration to intrathoracic and/or abdominal organs, especially when using a trocar
- Infection
- Damaging the neurovascular bundle or the long thoracic nerve
- Incorrect tube position
- Cannula disconnection and kinking
- Persistent pneumothorax
- Subcutaneous emphysema
- Recurrence of pneumothorax upon removal of the chest tube

115 How to relieve a tension pneumothorax

DRIES ENGELBRECHT

A tension pneumothorax develops when air leaks into the pleural space with no means of escape. This can be due to puncturing of the lung or a "one-way valve" developing in a penetrating chest injury. More air is trapped with every inspiratory breath and the negative pleural pressure becomes increasingly positive. The lung on the injured side collapses, the mediastinum is shifted to the opposite side, kinking the large veins and decreasing venous return, which in turn leads to decreased cardiac output. The lung on the opposite side is also compressed, which results in decreased ventilation.

The most common cause of tension pneumothorax is mechanical ventilation in a patient with a visceral pleural injury (ATLS Student Course Manual 1997). Other causes include injury to the lung during insertion of central lines, and penetrating and blunt chest trauma.

Unless air is rapidly let out of the pleural space the patient dies (King & Bewes 1993).

Procedure

To relieve the tension pneumothorax, you need to follow this procedure:

- Do a rapid assessment of your patient, paying special attention to the chest. The patient is usually extremely anxious, possibly hypoxic and short of breath. His neck veins are distended and the trachea is displaced away from the side of the tension pneumothorax (Mieny 1992). Breath sounds are absent on the injured side with hyper-resonance to percussion.
- Give high-flow oxygen while preparing to insert the needle.
- Locate the second intercostal space in the midclavicular line on the side of the injury.
- Clean the area with antiseptic.
- Insert a 16-gauge IV needle just above the second rib in the midclavicular line.

- A gush of air should escape as soon as you puncture the parietal pleura.
- If there is no possibility of inserting an intercostal drain, leave the needle *in situ* and secure the finger of a glove with its tip cut off to the hub of the needle. This acts as a one-way valve for release of air from the pleural space.

You can insert an intercostal drain as soon as possible for definitive management.

Complications

These complications can occur during the procedure:

- Local haematoma
- Lung injury

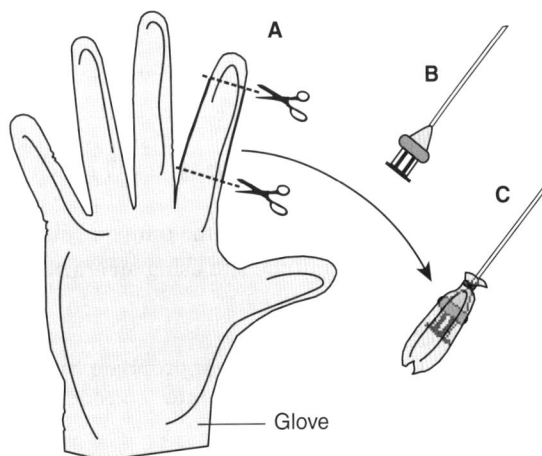

Figure 115.1 Securing the finger of a glove to the hub of the needle: (A) Excising a section of the finger of an examination glove; (B) Needle; (C) Section of glove secured to hub of needle

116 How to insert a peripheral line

CLAUDINE FIRMIN

Procedure

To insert a peripheral line, you need to follow this procedure:

- Select an appropriate site. Note that the large veins of the antecubital fossa and the forearm are ideal.
- Select the appropriate infusion set:
  - High-flow sets for a shocked patient
  - Blood administration sets for transfusion
  - Fifteen or twenty dropper sets for general use
  - Sixty-dropper sets for children and for adults at risk of fluid overload, for example congestive cardiac failure or renal failure
- Select the appropriate fluid:
  - **Medical emergencies:** 0.9% normal saline
  - **Trauma cases:** Ringer's lactate solution
  - **Blood loss or severe anaemia:** Blood products
  - **Hypoglycaemia:** 5% or 10% dextrose
- Attach the intravenous infusion set to the appropriate choice of fluid and fill the set. Maintain sterility of the tip of the set that you will attach to the intravenous catheter.
- Apply a tourniquet just above the puncture site.
- Clean the area around the site using an antiseptic solution or an alcohol swab.
- Put your gloves on.
- Puncture the site using the appropriate size of intravenous catheter, taking into consideration the diameter of the selected vein and the indication for cannulation.
- For haemorrhagic shock use the thickest, shortest cannula available.
  - **14G (orange):** 330 ml per minute = 1 ℓ in three minutes
  - **16G (grey):** 210 ml per minute = 1 ℓ in five minutes
  - **18G (green):** 90 ml per minute = 1 ℓ in eleven minutes
- Thread the catheter into the vein. When you get a back flow of blood, advance the catheter over the stabilised needle.
- Remove the needle and be cautious when disposing of it – use the "sharps container".
- Take blood samples.
- Remove the tourniquet and connect the intravenous infusion set to the catheter.
- Observe for any infiltration caused by the fluid into the tissues. If there is any, remove the catheter and repeat the procedure at another site. If there is none, secure the catheter and tubing to the skin, using OpSite or Elastoplast. Prevent the elbow from flexing if you used the antecubital vein.

Complications

Phlebitis and infection can result from the procedure. Manage these complications by removing the cannula and giving antibiotics.

117 How to do a venous cutdown

CLAUDINE FIRMIN

Indications

You would do a venous cutdown when you cannot get the usual venous access because of collapsed peripheral veins (e.g. hypovolaemic shock).

Procedure

To perform the cutdown, you need to follow this procedure:

- Prepare the skin of the medial aspect of the ankle with an antiseptic solution and drape the area (A).
- Use 0.5% lignocaine to anaesthetise the area over the great saphenous vein (B) (2 cm anterior and 2 cm superior to the medial malleolus).
- Make a 2.5 cm full thickness transverse skin incision through the anaesthetised area (C).
- Use blunt dissection to identify and free the vein from the surrounding connective tissue.
- Elevate and dissect the vein from its bed for a length of about 2 cm (D).
- Ligate the distal aspect of the mobilised vein, leaving a length of the suture material in place for exerting traction on the vein.
- Pass a tie around the proximal aspect of the dissected vein (E).

- Make a small transverse venotomy and gently dilate it with the tip of a closed haemostat forceps (F).
- Introduce a plastic cannula cephalad through the venotomy (G) and secure it in place by tying the proximal ligature around the vein and cannula (H).
- Insert the cannula to an adequate distance, that is at least three quarters of its length, to prevent it from dislodging.
- Attach the intravenous tubing to the cannula and close the incision with interrupted sutures (I).
- Apply a sterile dressing with a topical antibiotic ointment such as Betadine or Bactroban.

Figure 117.1A–I illustrates this process.

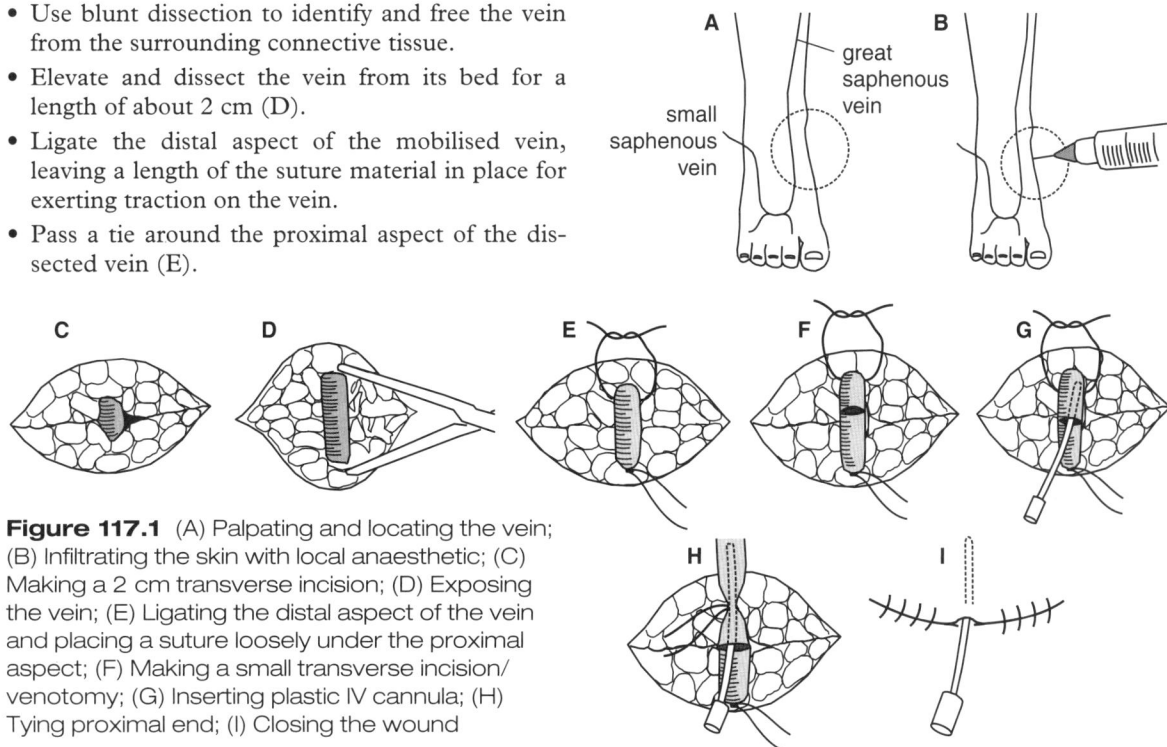

Figure 117.1 (A) Palpating and locating the vein; (B) Infiltrating the skin with local anaesthetic; (C) Making a 2 cm transverse incision; (D) Exposing the vein; (E) Ligating the distal aspect of the vein and placing a suture loosely under the proximal aspect; (F) Making a small transverse incision/venotomy; (G) Inserting plastic IV cannula; (H) Tying proximal end; (I) Closing the wound

Complications

You can avoid the following complications by using careful technique:

- Cellulitis
- Haematoma
- Phlebitis
- Perforation of the posterior wall of the vein
- Venous thrombosis
- Nerve transection
- Arterial transection

118 How to relieve a cardiac tamponade

EDWIN WARAMBWA

Cardiac tamponade is a medical emergency caused by accumulation of fluid, such as blood, effusion, pus, etc., in the finite pericardial space, resulting in reduced ventricular filling and subsequent haemodynamic compromise. Pending drainage, you can take appropriate resuscitative measures such as intubation, intravascular fluid expansion, blood pressure support and so on.

This is potentially a ***highly dangerous procedure*** – do it only as a last resort, such as when thoracotomy is not immediately available. In unskilled hands the pericardiocentesis needle can do significant damage to the moving myocardium.

Pericardiocentesis is only a temporary measure to relieve haemodynamic compromise. Once you have relieved the tamponade, you should refer your patient for further diagnosis and management.

Subxiphoid pericardiocentesis

The safest life-saving temporising measure before thoracotomy is an extra-pleural approach. ECG and/or sonographic guidance increases the success rate and reduces complications. You can use an alligator clamp to connect the needle to the precordial leads V1 or V2.

To relieve the tamponade, you need to perform this procedure:

- Seat patient 45 degrees head up.
- Monitor your patient's vital signs and ECG (see below) throughout the procedure. Insert an IV line.
- Prepare the skin with Betadine, and ascertain mediastinal position by auscultation of the lung fields and the precordium.
- Attach a 16- or 18-gauge over-the-needle catheter, such as that used for central venous catheterisation, that is longer than 15 cm to a 20 ml-syringe using a three-way stopcock.
- Insert the needle 1–2 cm inferior and to the left of the xiphochondral junction at a 45-degree angle

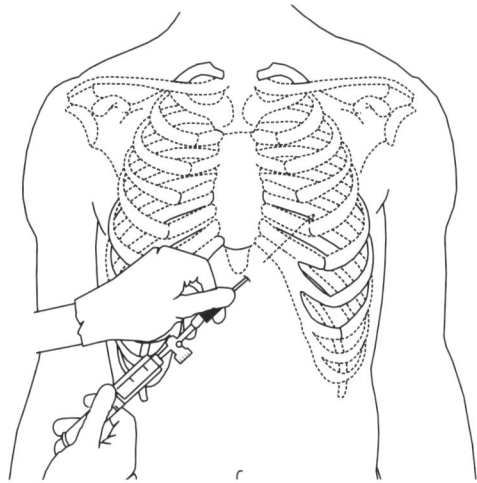

Figure 118.1 Inserting the needle for subxiphoid pericardiocentesis

towards the tip of the left scapula, as illustrated in Figure 118.1

- Gently advance the needle, applying continuous suction until you reach the pericardial sac and withdraw fluid/blood or until a "current of injury", such as premature ventricular ectopic beats, appears on the ECG monitor. These changes imply contact with the myocardium. Withdraw the needle until baseline ECG pattern returns.
- Aspirate as much blood/fluid as possible before closing the stopcock, detaching the syringe, removing the needle and securing the catheter.
- You can then use the catheter to re-aspirate if the tamponade recurs prior to thoracotomy.

Alternatively, you can use the Seldinger technique, which entails

- passing a guide wire through the needle into the pericardial sac
- withdrawing the needle and sliding a 14-gauge catheter over the guide wire

• removing the guide wire and attaching the stop-cock.

You could also use either of the following techniques:

• Use a 16-gauge spinal needle for once-off drainage.
• Insert a short 16- or 18-gauge needle into the left xiphochondral junction perpendicular to skin, 5 mm below the left costal margin, and advance it to inner aspect of the rib cage then direct and advance it to the left shoulder until you reach the fluid. Then place a soft multi-hole pigtail catheter – 6 or 8 – via a guide wire.

Echocardiographically guided pericardiocentesis

You would perform this type of procedure on the left chest wall 3–5 cm from the left parasternal border.

Follow this procedure:

• Assess the size of the fluid collection, distribution and ideal entry site over the area of maximal pericardial fluid collection.

• Measure the distance from skin to pericardial sac and determine the trajectory.
• Insert an over-the-needle catheter in the predetermined direction, angle and depth.
• Remove the needle, advance 2 mm further and secure the catheter.
• **Caution:** Avoid the inferior rib margin to prevent neurovascular damage.

Complications

You can avoid the following complications by paying careful attention to the correct technique:

• Lacerations of other organs
• Lung – pneumothorax
• Oesophagus – mediastinitis
• Stomach – peritonitis
• Spleen/kidney
• Epicardial/myocardial damage
• Aspiration of ventricular blood
• Coronary artery/great vessel damage
• Atrial fibrillation – needle induced due to failure to aspirate because blood is clotted. This is common.

119 How to do a secondary survey

DRIES ENGELBRECHT AND ISABEL PIENAAR

A secondary survey entails a complete history and physical examination.

History

You can obtain your patient's history from your patient, ideally, or from his family and/or paramedics. Use the AMPLE mnemonic, as follows:

- **A**llergies
- **M**edication, including chronic
- **P**ast illnesses or **P**regnancy
- **L**ast meal
- **E**vents/**E**nvironment related to the injury. It is important to enquire about deaths at the scene of an accident, which indicate severe force of injury. This, as well as a history of the patient's position, for example whether he was the driver or whether he was thrown out of the vehicle, may help you to consider serious underlying injuries.

Physical examination

You need to break down the physical examination in order to pay sufficient attention to the various parts of the patient's body. We will now discuss each part.

Head and face, and neurology

Make the following assessments:

- Inspect the patient for signs of injury such as bleeding, fractures (including skull base fracture signs i.e. bruising behind one ear, bruising around both eyes, clear fluid leak from nostril or ear), signs of increased intracranial pressure (persistent headache and/or vomiting), decreased consciousness, and localising neurological signs.
- Conduct a full neurological examination using the Glasgow Coma Scale (GCS) that is presented as Table 119.1 (see also Chapter 122).
- Examine the cranial nerves, peripheral motor and sensory function, coordination and reflexes.

Table 119.1 The Glasgow Coma Scale (GCS)

Response	Specific test	Score
E – Eyes	Open spontaneously	4
	Open on verbal command	3
	Open on painful stimuli	2
	Do not open	1
V – Verbal	Oriented	5
	Confused	4
	Inappropriate words	3
	Incomprehensible sounds	2
	None	1
M – Motor	Obeys verbal commands	6
	Localises pain stimulus	5
	Withdraws on pain stimulus	4
	Abnormal flexion to pain	3
	Abnormal extension to pain	2
	No movement	1
Total		**15***

Source: Teasdale (1974) Lancet 2:81–4

* Minimum = 3, maximum = 15.

- Examine pupils – check pupil size and pupillary reflexes.

Manage the following:

- Intubate and ventilate a patient with signs of increased intracranial pressure.
- Intubate a patient with severe facial injuries because severe swelling will lead to a compromised airway.
- Intubate a head injury patient with a GCS of 9 or less.
- Control bleeding.
- Prevent hypoxia and hypovolaemia to limit secondary brain injury.

• Remember to remove contact lenses.

Cervical spine

Make the following assessment:

• Inspect for signs of injury – blunt or penetrating, deviation of the trachea and use of accessory breathing muscles.
• Palpate for tenderness, deformity, surgical emphysema or tracheal deviation.
• Auscultate for bruits over the carotid arteries.
• Obtain X-rays of complete C-spine (down to C7 – T1 junction).
• Obtain cervical spine CT scan if the patient is unconscious or confused.

Manage by maintaining immobilisation of the cervical spine until you confirm no injury.

Chest

Make the following assessment:

• Do a full clinical re-evaluation of chest, looking for
  – tension pneumothorax
  – open chest wound
  – flail chest
  – cardiac tamponade
  – aortic rupture.
• Obtain a chest X-ray if one has not yet been done.

Manage the following:

• Insert a chest tube, if indicated.
• Perform pericardiocentesis, if indicated.

Abdomen

Make the following assessment:

• Perform a full clinical evaluation. Look for occult intra-abdominal injuries in a patient with unexplained hypotension or neurological injury, who is intoxicated or with unclear abdominal findings.
• Occult injuries include
  – liver or splenic rupture
  – hollow viscus or spinal injuries
  – vascular injuries
  – renal injuries
  – pelvic fractures.

Manage the following:

• Perform peritoneal lavage or abdominal sonar, if indicated.
• Apply a pneumatic anti-shock garment, if indicated.

Pelvis, rectum and vagina

Make the following assessment:

• Look for contusion, haematomas, lacerations and urethral bleeding.
• When examining the rectum look for blood, anal sphincter tone, wall lacerations, bony fragments and prostate position.
• When examining the vagina, look for blood and lacerations, and signs of pregnancy.

Manage the following:

• Perform a pregnancy test in a female patient.
• Apply the pelvic part of the pneumatic anti-shock garment in case of unstable pelvic fracture to splint the fracture. Also, firmly tie the legs together to stabilise a pelvic fracture.
• Do not insert a urethral catheter when the prostate is high riding or not palpable, or when blood is present at the urethral meatus.

Musculoskeletal

Make the following assessment:

• Examine all limbs as well as hands, feet and joints for swelling, tenderness, crepitus or deformity.
• Palpate all pulses for presence.
• Exclude any neurological deficit distal to fractures.
• Do a log-roll and always examine the patient's back to exclude hidden injuries.
• Obtain X-rays of areas with suspected fractures.

Manage the following:

• Splint fractures and reduce dislocations.

Throughout the survey

While you are performing the procedures described above, you also need to pay attention to the following:

• Regularly evaluate the patient's ABCDE (see Chapter 109) and act immediately if it deteriorates.
• A urinary output of 50 ml/hour in adults and 1 ml/kg/hour in children should be maintained.
• Ensure complete spinal immobilisation, especially during transfer, until you have excluded spinal fractures.
• You can use intravenous opiates such as morphine as analgesia titrated to the patient's pain. Look for side-effects of these drugs, such as respiratory depression, depressed consciousness and fall in BP. Always also exclude other causes of these signs. Be aware that opiates may mask certain clinical signs – do further work-up such as peritoneal lavage, sonar or scans to exclude occult injuries.

KAT MYNHARDT

Indications

You would insert a nasogastric (NG) tube in patients requiring stomach decompression, gastric lavage, feeding, and to facilitate clinical diagnosis.

In the presence of head trauma, maxillofacial injury or anterior fossa skull fracture, you should preferably insert an orogastric tube because of the danger of intracranial migration of an NG tube through a base of skull fracture.

Equipment

To perform the procedure, you need the following:

- Lubricating jelly
- A catheter tip syringe – 60 ml
- A bite-block or oral airway
- A stethoscope
- An emesis basin
- An orogastric or an NG tube
- Adhesive tape
- Gloves
- A protective apron or gown
- Goggles and mask
- pH paper – optional
- A specimen container – optional

The type and size of the tube is dictated by the indication for the tube placement. You need a large-bore tube for rapid removal of gastric contents, a smaller-bore tube for diagnostic needs and removal of air and gastric secretions. The size of the patient also makes a difference. You should use these tubes:

- 5–6FG for neonates
- 8FG for infants
- 10FG for small children
- 12FG for larger children
- Up to 18FG for adults

Measure the tube either from the tip of your patient's nose to the tip of the earlobe and down to the xiphoid process, or from the tip of the nose to the umbilicus, and mark the length.

Procedure

We will now explore the two abovementioned procedures.

Nasogastric placement

Prior to inserting an NG tube, manually immobilise your patient's head if he potentially has cervical spine injury (see Chapter 110). *Take particular care with the insertion in a patient whom you know to have oesophageal varices, as it could cause rupture and bleeding.*

Follow this procedure:

- Position the alert patient in an upright or high Fowler's position, and the obtunded patient head down in the Trendelenburg position, preferably lying on his left side.
- Lubricate the tip of the tube, choose the larger nostril and thread the tube through the nostril aiming downwards and backwards.
- When the tube reaches the pharynx, flex the patient's head forward. Encourage the alert patient to swallow.
- Advance the tube until the previously noted level, or mark, is reached.
- Centre and secure the tube in place with adhesive tape or with a gastric tube holder.

Orogastric placement

Use only an orogastric tube in infants, as they are obligate nose breathers. Take into account the anatomical differences, such as a disproportionately large tongue for the oral cavity, smaller nasopharynx and so on.

Follow this procedure:

- Position the patient as described above.
- Place an oral airway or bite-block in the mouth of the uncooperative patient.

- Lubricate the tip of the tube and pass it through the lips and over the tongue, aiming downwards and backwards towards the pharynx, with the patient's head flexed forward.
- Advance the tube until the previously noted mark is reached.
- Centre and secure the tube in place with adhesive tape or with a gastric tube holder.

There are numerous novel suggestions in the literature for easier ways to insert the tube, which include storing it in a refrigerator to keep it rigid with a "memory" of its coiled shape, warming up the tip with hot water, and using small amounts of water to assist the alert patient to swallow.

To verify the position of the tube, you need to use at least two of the following methods:

- Aspirating the gastric contents
- Obtaining a chest X-ray
- Measuring the pH of the gastric contents – pH should be below 5.5

When the NG tube has to stay in for a period of time, for example in the case of intestinal obstruction, secure it to the nose with strapping and connect it to a drainage bag.

After you have performed NG lavage and insertion of activated charcoal for poisonings, you should remove the tube.

Complications

You can avoid the following complications by paying careful attention to proper technique:

- Hypoxia
- Cyanosis or respiratory arrest requiring tracheal intubation
- Cardiac compromise owing to a vagal response secondary to gagging
- Spinal cord injuries if the patient is not completely immobilised
- Intracranial placement in a patient with head or facial injuries
- Vomiting and aspiration secondary to gagging response
- Nasal irritation
- Rhinorrhoea or epistaxis due to nasopharynx trauma
- Skin erosion
- Sinusitis
- Oesophagitis
- Oesophagotracheal fistula
- Gastric ulceration
- Pulmonary and oral infections from prolonged tube placement
- Pharyngeal paralysis
- Vocal cord paralysis
- Rupture of oesophageal varices

121 How to give a blood transfusion

DRIES ENGELBRECHT

Transfusion of blood products involves your evaluation of the risk–benefit ratio to the patient. All blood products carry a risk of adverse effects, ranging from sensitisation (to donor cells or proteins) to transmission of disease, including HIV infection.

You would give a blood transfusion to restore and maintain your patient's normal blood volume and to correct severe anaemia, for example in a case where Hb is less than 8 g/dl.

Legal aspects

You need to take into account the following factors, which affect your patient's safety:

- Correct identity
- Blood compatibility
- Correct handling of the blood prior to and during transfusion
- Informed consent
- Reporting of untoward reactions and death
- Retention of samples
- Determining whether you are allowed to transfuse the patient

Ordering and administration of blood

We will now explore further the factors to which you need to pay special attention in order to ensure the safety of transfusion.

Correct identification and verification of the patient and the unit of blood

When you draw a blood sample for compatibility testing, you need to positively identify your patient. Complete the requisition form that outlines the necessary information in addition to the details of previous medical, obstetric and transfusion history, the diagnosis, the reason for transfusion, the type of component required, the number of units required, and the date and time when the blood or blood components must be available.

You can carry out the identification process by questioning the conscious patient, or suitable other person in the case of an unconscious patient, and by matching the name on the patient's record and name band with that on the unit of blood.

Correct aseptic technique

Follow this procedure:

- You can choose almost any peripheral vein for transfusion; however, those in the forearm are best, as your patient's movement will not be restricted.
- You *must* ensure meticulous skin care and aseptic technique, as blood acts as the ideal culture medium for bacterial growth.
- Clean the proposed site for venepuncture with the recommended antiseptic starting from the area to be cleaned and working towards the "dirty" area.

Careful observation of the patient during transfusion

One of your major tasks in transfusion therapy is monitoring your patient. By accurately and quickly interpreting adverse effects you can prevent a fatal reaction from occurring.

Follow this procedure:

- Record baseline observations of your patient's vital signs prior to commencing the transfusion.
- Observe the patient closely for the first 30 minutes of the transfusion, looking for any untoward events such as haemolytic, anaphylactic or allergic reactions.
- Ensure the desired rate of transfusion.
- In case of major blood loss, ideally you should monitor the central venous pressure (CVP), pulse, BP, respiratory rate and urinary output every 15 minutes throughout the transfusion. In a less acute case, check your patient's vital signs

every half hour after the initial 30-minute observation. Observe a patient with cardiac or renal disease, who is at risk of circulatory overload, for 12–24 hours after the transfusion.

You should **decrease** the rate of transfusion when

- the CVP is greater than 10 cmH_2O
- the BP is greater than 140/100 mmHg in a previously normotensive patient.

You should **increase** the rate of transfusion when

- the CVP is less than 5 cmH_2O
- the BP is less than 90/60 mmHg in a previously normotensive patient.

Special precautions

You need to take the following special precautions.

■ RATE OF TRANSFUSION

The rate depends on your patient's clinical condition. You need to give a patient in acute shock from massive blood loss rapid transfusion of 90–330 ml per minute, whereas you should not give a patient with chronic anaemia more than 2 ml per minute.

In general, it is recommended that you set a relatively slow infusion rate of 5 ml per minute for the first 30 minutes. If there are no signs of untoward reaction, you can increase the rate.

■ FILTERS

You should administer red blood cells, whole blood and fresh frozen plasma (FFP) through a standard blood recipient set, or Y-type administration set.

Preferably use a special platelet administration set for platelets, although you can use the standard 170 μm set in an emergency.

Cover the filter with blood to ensure that the full filtering area is used during transfusion.

■ TEMPERATURE OF THE BLOOD

If you administer cold blood at a slow rate, the temperature does not appear to affect the patient's circulatory system. However, when you need to transfuse blood rapidly, you can avoid complications such as cardiac arrhythmia by warming the blood in a water bath or by using a heating coil. Note, however, that you should never heat blood products to a temperature of higher than 37 degrees Celsius.

You would warm the blood in these cases:

- A massive transfusion of more than 10 units of blood
- An infant in need of a transfusion at a rate greater than 15 ml/kg/h
- A neonate receiving an exchange transfusion or a large-volume transfusion

Available products

Whole blood

Whole blood is considered to be a complex tissue from which numerous components are processed for use in different clinical settings. You would use whole blood only in these two clinical situations:

1. Massive haemorrhage with the possibility of recurrence or continuation
2. Exchange transfusion in a neonate

Standard red cell concentrate

Red cell concentrate, or packed red blood cells, is prepared from a unit of whole blood from which the plasma has been removed. You need this product to improve a patient's tissue oxygenation where this is impaired either by anaemia or by haemorrhage.

You would use the product in these cases:

- Normovolaemic anaemia
- Ongoing haemorrhage, where you have carried out initial volume resuscitation with crystalloid solutions
- Elective or emergency surgical operations to replace whole blood

Fresh frozen plasma

FFP is separated from anticoagulated whole blood within 18 hours of donation. It contains all the clotting factors at normal physiological levels.

You would use FFP in these instances:

- As an adjunct to massive transfusions where clotting factors become depleted
- In a patient in whom you need to reverse the effects of warfarin
- In severe liver disease
- In a patient requiring replacement of specific factors such as antithrombin 3, or factors 11 or 13

Transfusion reactions

A transfusion reaction may be defined as any potentially adverse sign or symptom that occurs after the start of a transfusion of blood or blood products.

You need to look out for the following possible reactions:

- Rigors
- Chills
- Pyrexia
- Pain
- Respiratory distress
- Hypotension
- Haemoglobinuria
- Oliguria

- Anuria
- Jaundice
- Skin rash
- Pruritis
- Anaphylaxis

In any of these cases, you need to

- stop the transfusion immediately
- keep the vein open with normal saline in a new drip set
- contact the transfusion service for advice.

122 How to measure the Glasgow Coma Scale

JULIA BLITZ-LINDEQUE

A coma is a state in which the patient is unrousable and unresponsive.

There are various terms that we can apply to the levels of consciousness between "alert" and "coma". The Glasgow Coma Scale (GCS) objectively assesses these by looking at three markers of consciousness – eye opening, and verbal and motor responses. You can use the GCS most usefully to monitor *trends* in your patient's level of consciousness rather than as a once-off measurement.

First give your comatose patient cardiorespiratory resuscitation. Then take steps to minimise further neurological damage while you evaluate him. Your examination should include an assessment of his level of coma using the GCS, as provided in Table 122.1.

Note that tracheotomy, the presence of an ET tube and facial injuries invalidate the verbal response.

You can record the results in this form:

$$Ex + Vx + Mx = y$$

Consider a GCS result of less than or equal to E2 + M4 + V2 as coma.

Table 122.1 The Glasgow Coma Scale (GCS)

Response	Specific test	Score
E – Eyes	Open spontaneously	4
	Open on verbal command	3
	Open on painful stimuli	2
	Do not open	1
V – Verbal	Oriented	5
	Confused	4
	Inappropriate words	3
	Incomprehensible sounds	2
	None	1
M – Motor	Obeys verbal commands	6
	Localises pain stimulus	5
	Withdraws on pain stimulus	4
	Abnormal flexion to pain	3
	Abnormal extension to pain	2
	No movement	1
Total		**15***

Source: Teasdale (1974) Lancet 2:81–4

* Minimum = 3, maximum = 15.

123 How to insert a central line

A N N A M A R I E   S T E Y N

The insertion of a central line allows secure and prolonged venous access, monitoring of central venous pressure and the introduction of a variety of diagnostic, therapeutic and monitoring devices.

Procedure

You need to reach the superior vena cava percutaneously via the cephalic, subclavian, internal or external jugular vein. The method most commonly used for this is internal jugular or subclavian vein catheterisation.

To insert a central line, it is recommended that you use the Seldinger technique, as follows:

- Place the patient in a 30-degree head down position, that is the Trendelenburg position. This prevents air embolism and distends the neck veins. If you do not suspect a C-spine injury, turn his head away from the side of cannulation.

- You can place a rolled towel or IV bag longitudinally between his shoulder blades to enlarge the costoclavicular space.

- Put on a gown and sterile gloves as part of the necessary aseptic procedure. If this procedure is being done as emergency vascular access for resuscitation you should omit some of the steps for the sake of speed.

- Cleanse the skin and drape.

- Infiltrate 1% lignocaine into the skin, subcutaneous tissue and costoclavicular fascia, at the required area of the insertion.

- Introduce an 18-gauge needle attached to a 10-ml syringe containing 1 ml saline.

- Apply gentle negative pressure on the syringe while slowly advancing the needle into the vein. Use the anterior, central or posterior approach for the internal jugular vein, or the subclavian approach for the subclavian vein.

- A free flow of blood – dark red and lacking pulsatile flow – in the syringe will indicate that you have been successful in cannulating the vein.

- Rotate the bevel to face caudally, remove the syringe and occlude the needle to prevent air embolism.

- Advance the guide wire through the needle while monitoring the ECG for abnormalities.

- Remove the needle but do *not* let go of the wire or it may disappear into the vein, making removal difficult.

- Feed the dilator over the wire. Often, twisting it slightly will facilitate its insertion through the skin.

- Remove the dilator.

- Feed the catheter over the guide wire. The catheter tip should be at the junction of the superior vena cava and right atrium.

- Remove the guide wire.

- Aspirate through each lumen.

- Flush each lumen.

- Auscultate to ensure that your patient's breath sounds are still equal bilaterally.

- Secure the catheter to the skin with a suture and apply a sterile dressing.

- Do a chest X-ray to check the catheter position and exclude pneumo- or haemothorax.

- If the catheter is found on X-ray to be in the right atrium or ventricle, pull it back slightly to prevent arrhythmia.

We will now explore each of these approaches in further detail.

Internal jugular venepuncture

■ ANTERIOR ROUTE

As shown in Figure 123.1, you need to follow this procedure:

- Palpate the carotid artery opposite the thyroid cartilage with your index and third fingers. The internal jugular vein is lateral to the carotid artery.

- Introduce the needle lateral to your fingers at a 30-degree angle to the skin.

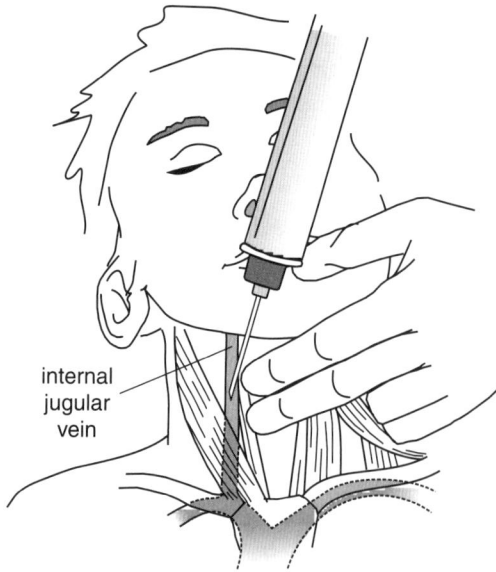

Figure 123.1 Using the anterior route to the internal jugular vein

- Direct the needle in a caudal direction towards the ipsilateral nipple.

■ CENTRAL ROUTE

As shown in Figure 123.2, you need to follow this procedure:

- Identify the triangle formed by the two portions of the sternocleidomastoid muscle with the clavicle at its base.
- Introduce the needle at the apex of the triangle at 30-degree angle to the coronal plane.
- Direct the needle in a caudal direction towards the ipsilateral nipple.

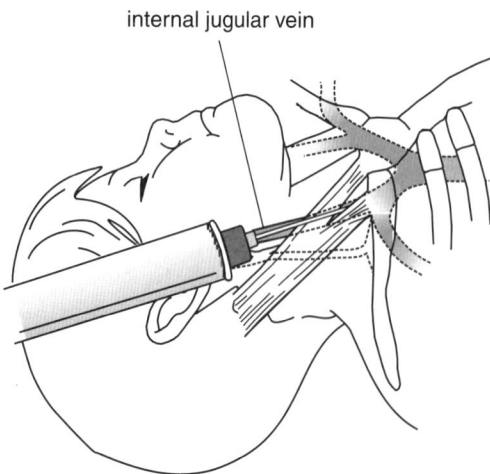

Figure 123.2 Using the central route to the internal jugular vein

■ POSTERIOR ROUTE

As shown in Figure 123.3, you need to follow this procedure:

- Introduce the needle deep to the posterior margin of the sternocleidomastoid muscle at the junction of the middle and lower thirds.
- Direct the needle towards suprasternal notch.

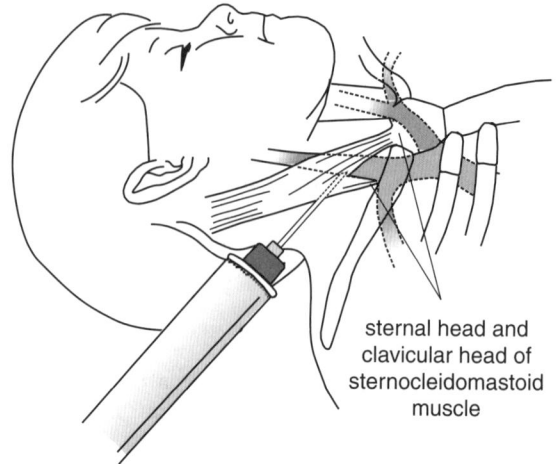

Figure 123.3 Using the posterior route to the internal jugular vein

Subclavian venepuncture

As shown in Figure 123.4, you need to follow this procedure:

- Insert the needle 1 cm below the junction of the medial and middle thirds of the clavicle.
- Move the needle under the clavicle and aim for the suprasternal notch.

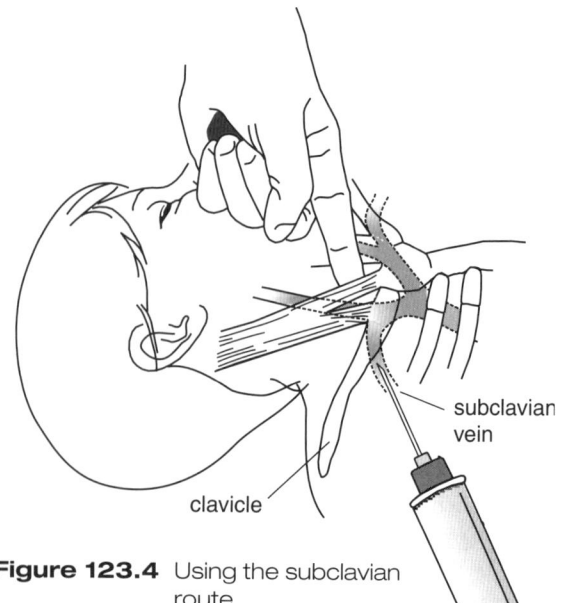

Figure 123.4 Using the subclavian route

Van Schaik Publishers

Complications

- Pneumothorax
- Haemothorax
- Catheter embolisation (shorn off by needle bevel)

- Infection
- Dysrhythmia
- Air embolism

ANDRIES VISSER

The policy in the case of a multi-trauma patient is that you should obtain an X-ray of "everything that hurts". While X-rays are expensive, in this circumstance, the concept of cost control should apply only to your malpractice rates. The only caution is that X-rays of lesser significance or urgency should not take precedence over the treatment of life-threatening problems. For example, do not delay operating on an epidural haematoma to take a hand X-ray of the patient.

If you need to defer an X-ray, note the reason for the delay on your patient's chart, along with a clear list of the X-rays that are necessary. You can obtain the films later. Remember to splint any extremity with a possible fracture if you need to delay the X-ray for the time being.

For almost every patient with severe trauma, you need to obtain a cross-table C-spine X-ray, chest X-ray and pelvis X-ray for the following reasons. You may miss neck pain in a seriously injured patient, and the cost of this, if it is caused by a cervical fracture, is great. The chest may have significant internal injury without external tenderness. Pelvic fractures are often present in patients with trunk trauma, and are often missed. You need to order these important X-rays before your patient leaves the emergency department for other care.

Interpretation procedure

When you look at any X-ray, these are the first things you need to do:

- Check the name of the patient and the date.
- Consider whether the X-ray is of adequate quality. For example, in a C-spine X-ray you should be able to see C1 to T1; in a chest X-ray, you must be able to see the apex of the lungs and the diaphragm.
- Also assess whether the view is rotated.

Once you are satisfied with the quality of the X-ray, you can turn to the interpretation, which we will now discuss by X-ray type.

Cervical spine

The first thing that you should note on a C-spine X-ray is the alignment of the vertebrae on the lateral film. Moreover, the anterior margin and the posterior margin of the vertebral bodies, the spinolaminar line and the tips of the spinous processes, that is C2–C7, should all be aligned. Consider any malalignment as evidence of ligamentous injury or occult fracture. Maintain cervical spine immobilisation until you can make a definitive diagnosis.

Figure 124.1 illustrates this type of X-ray. On it, note the odontoid (dens), the predental space and the spinal canal.

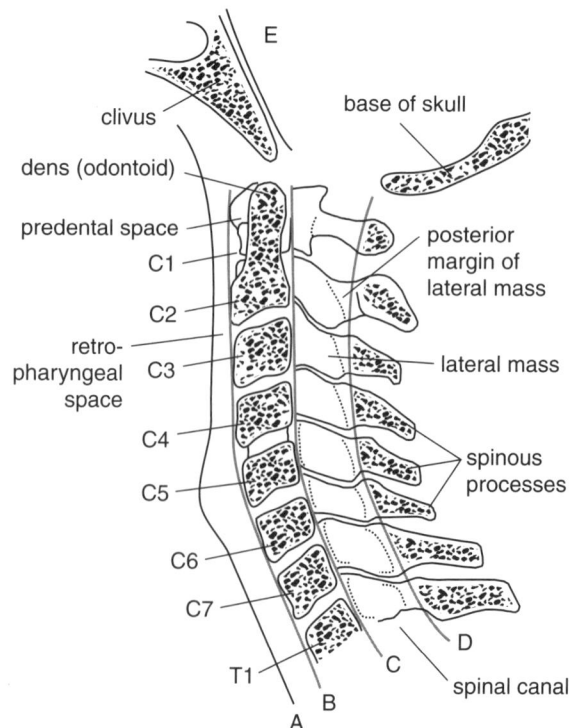

Figure 124.1 Schematic lateral view of the cervical spine: (A) Pre-vertebral soft-tissue line; (B) Anterior spinal line; (C) Posterior spinal line; (D) Spinolaminar line; (E) Clivus base line

Check the following:

- That C1–T1 can all be visualised
- Alignment – trace out the five lines
- Pre-vertebral soft-tissue shadow
- Atlanto-dens interval of 3 mm
- "Open-mouth view" for C1 and C2 fractures
- AP view for facet dislocations

Table 124.1 summarises the parameters that you can measure on a normal C-spine X-ray.

Figure 124.2 shows a spinal fracture called a "Jefferson fracture", which demonstrates lateral mass of C1 lying lateral to the lateral masses of C2 on both the left and right sides as a result of the spread of the ring of C1.

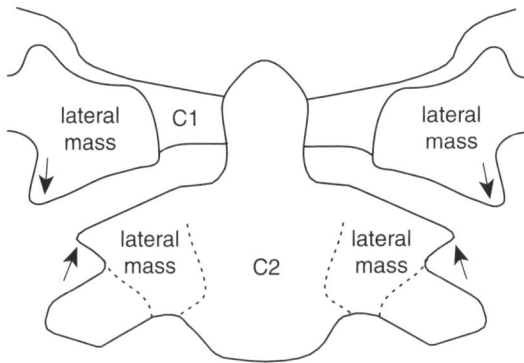

Figure 124.2 Jefferson fracture

Chest

Taking the "ABC approach" to blunt chest trauma, you need to consider the following:

- **A**ortic transection
- **B**ronchial fractures
- **C**ord injury
- **D**iaphragm rupture
- **E**sophageal tear (Remember that this term is also often spelled "oesophageal".)
- **F**lail chest
- **G**as – pneumothorax
- **H**eart – cardiac injury
- **I**atrogenic misplaced tubes and catheters

Check the following:

- Soft tissue for subcutaneous emphysema
- Bones for fractures
- Pleura
- Mediastinum
- Trachea
- Diaphragm

Figure 124.3 is an example of a chest X-ray showing subcutaneous emphysema.

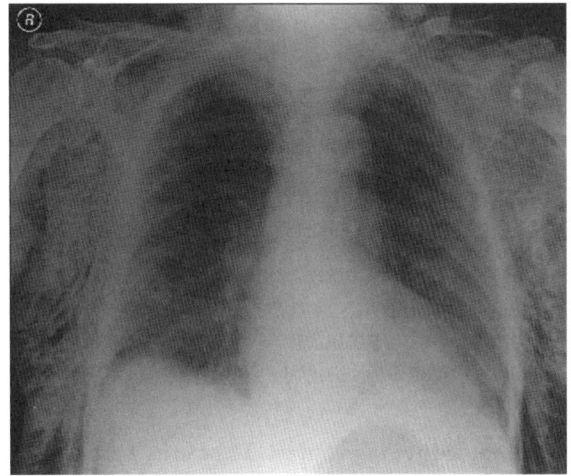

Figure 124.3 Subcutaneous emphysema

Source: http://www.trauma.org/imagebank/chest/images – photo submitted by Harry Voesten, the Netherlands

Pelvis

Figure 124.4 is an example of a pelvic X-ray showing a broken Shenton's line.

In polytrauma, it is essential that you check the following:

- Disruption of the pelvic ring
- Sacroiliac joints

Table 124.1 Measurable parameters of a normal cervical spine

Parameter	Adults	Children
Predental space	3 mm or less	4–5 mm or less
C2–C3 pseudosubluxation	3 mm or less	4–5 mm or less
Retropharyngeal space	Less than 6 mm at C2, less than 22 mm at C6	1/2 to 2/3 vertebral body distance antero-posteriorly
Angulation of spinal column at any single interspace level	Less than 11 degrees	Less than 11 degrees
Cord dimension	10–13 mm	Adult size by six years of age

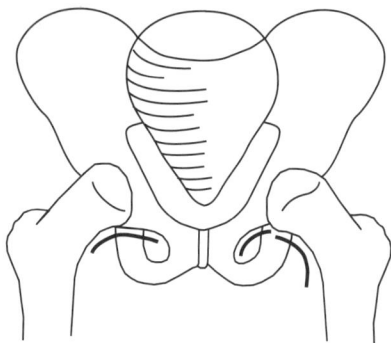

Figure 124.4 Broken Shenton's line

- Shenton's line – the line formed by the top of the obturator foramen and the inner side of the neck of the femur, to determine the position of the femoral head relative to the acetabulum
- Sacral fractures

Ask for further views, if indicated.

Thoracic and lumbar spine

Check the following:

- Loss of vertebral body height
- Displacement of posterior body
- Angulation of spinous processes
- Widening of the inter-pedicular distance on an AP film

A computed tomography (CT) scan is best for the upper thoracic spine.

Figure 124.5 is an example of a thoracic X-ray showing loss of vertebral height.

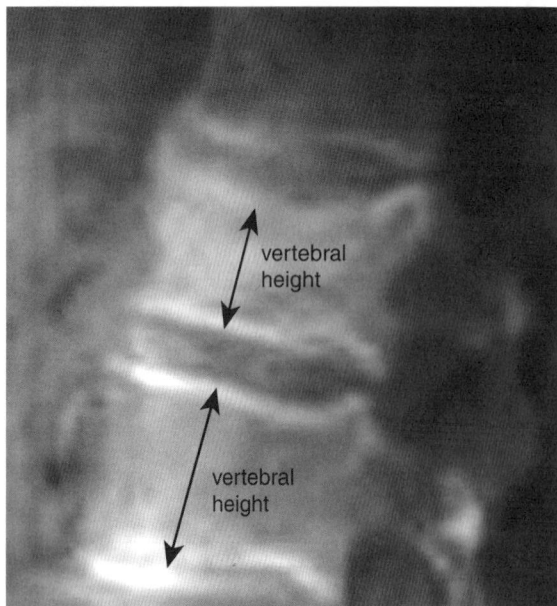

Figure 124.5 Loss of vertebral height

Long bone fracture

In the case of a splinted fracture of a long bone, you need to take account of the following:

- Stabilise the patient haemodynamically before the X-ray is taken.
- Splint the fracture before the X-ray is taken.
- Do not forget that the mechanism of injury that causes a fracture usually also causes soft-tissue damage – this also needs to be assessed and managed. You must be able to see the joint above and below the fracture on the X-ray.
- Always insist on two views – AP and lateral.

Colles fracture

Figure 124.6 is an example of an X-ray showing a Colles fracture of the distal radius and ulna.

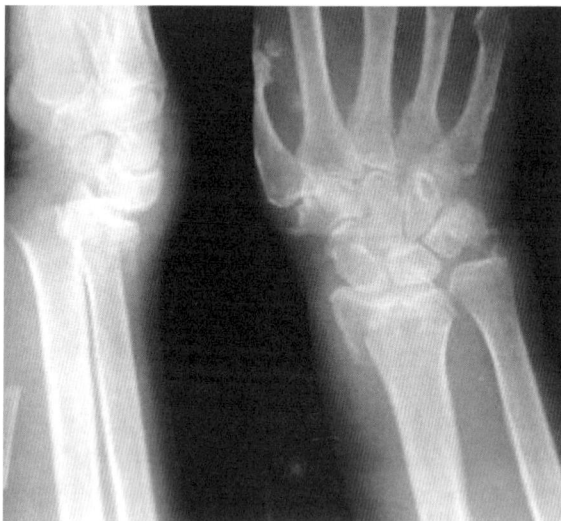

Figure 124.6 Colles fracture

Source: http://www.learningradiology.com

Check the following:

- Displacement
- Angulation
- Shortening
- Radial deviation

Exclude intra-articular fracture.

Shoulder dislocation

Figure 124.7 shows examples of an X-ray of a normal shoulder, an anterior shoulder dislocation and a posterior shoulder dislocation.

Check that the head of the humerus lies below the coracoid. Do not mistake inferior subluxation for dislocation. If you are in doubt, obtain a lateral or trans-scapular view.

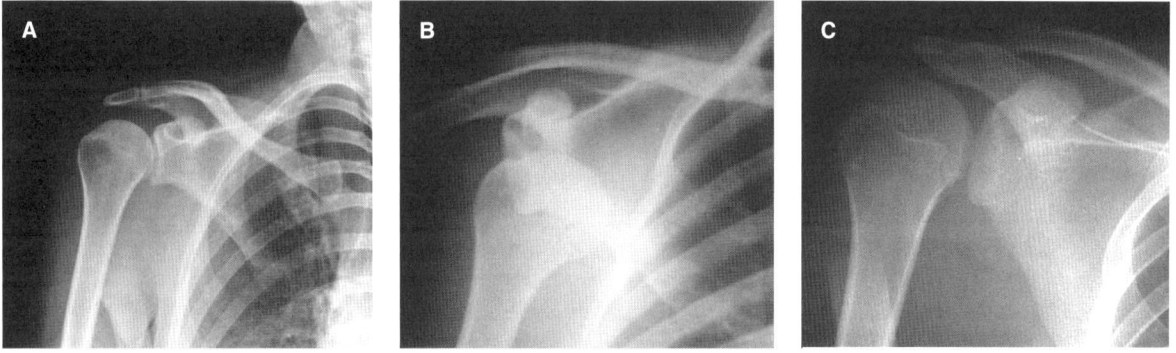

Figure 124.7 (A) Normal shoulder; (B) Anterior shoulder dislocation; (C) Posterior shoulder dislocation

Source of (C): http://www.radiology.co.uk/srs-x/cases/

Malleolar (ankle) fracture

Figure 124.8 is an example of an X-ray showing an ankle fracture.

Reduce dislocation before the X-ray is taken. Check for medial and/or lateral malleolus fractures. Obtain a mortise AP view for talar shift. Consider whether the proximal fibula is fractured. Remember epiphyseal injuries in children.

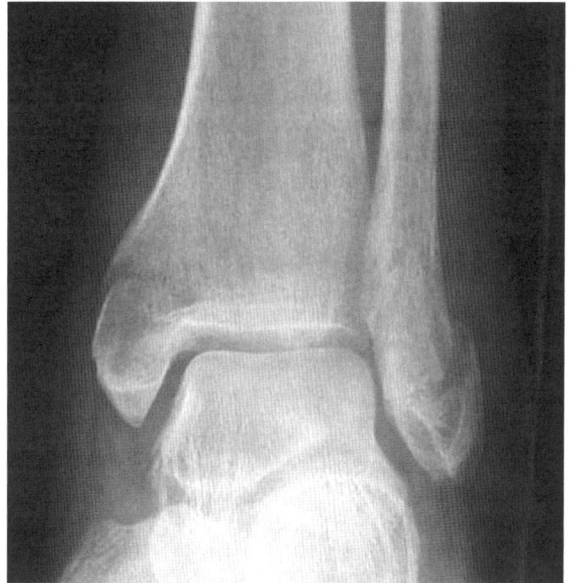

Figure 124.8

Bimalleolar fracture of the ankle

125 How to calculate the percentage of burn

JULIA BLITZ-LINDEQUE

The percentage of body area that is burnt is one of the criteria used for determining appropriate treatment and referral.

The adult body is divided into regions, each representing 9% of the total body surface. These regions are the head and neck, each upper limb, the chest, the abdomen, the upper back, the lower back and buttocks, the front of each lower limb, and the back of each lower limb. This makes up 99% of the human body. The remaining 1% is made up by the genital area.

With an infant or small child, more emphasis is placed on the head and trunk. As a rough guide, the patient's hand represents 1% of his body area.

When more than 10% of a child's body area is burnt and when more than 15% of an adult's body is burnt, they should be admitted to hospital for care. Burns to the face, hands, feet, perineum, inner joint surfaces or concomitant other injury (or disease) as well as electrical and chemical burns should be referred to a burns unit.

The following is relevant when treating a burns patient:

- If you see the patient within an hour of the burn, cool tap water sponged over the burnt area may help to limit the damage.
- Decide on the need for tetanus immunoglobulin or tetanus toxoid.
- Aggressive pain management is required.
- Ensure adequate fluid resuscitation.
- Dress the wound to aid moist wound healing.
- Elevate the burnt area to minimise oedema.

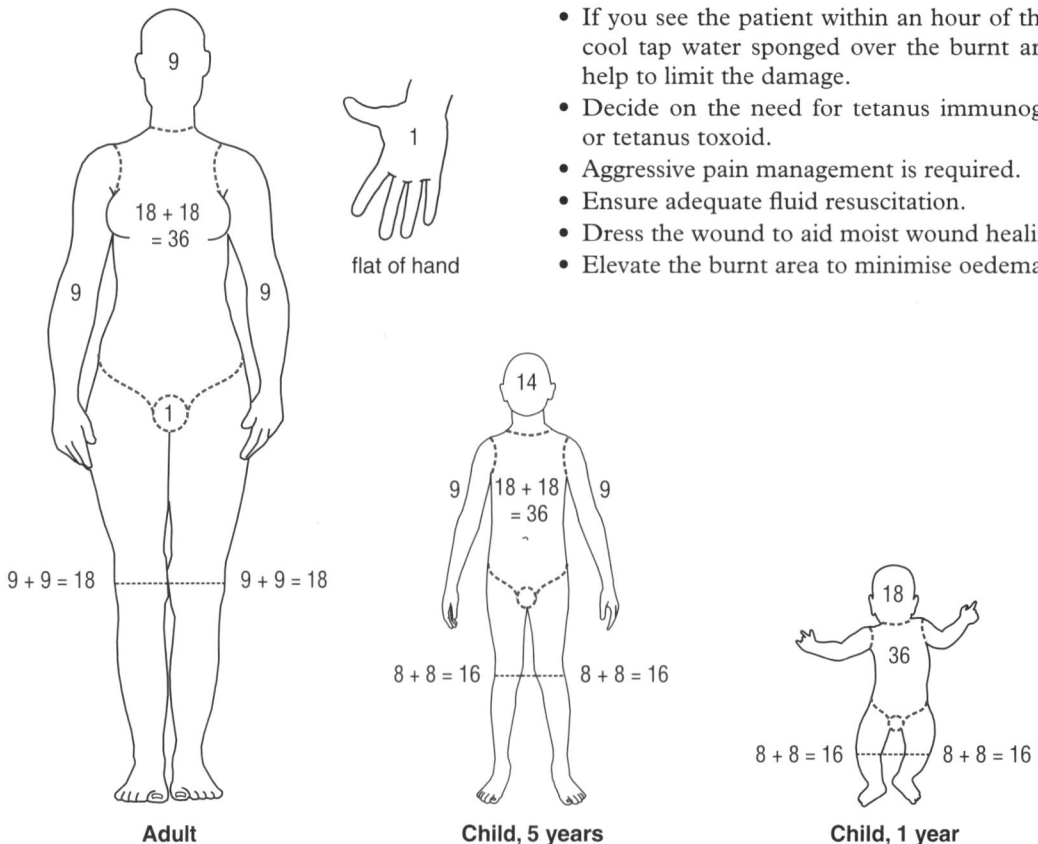

Figure 125.1 How to calculate the percentage of burn in an adult, a child of 5 years and a child of 1 year

126 How to do gastric lavage

KAT MYNHARDT

Indications and contraindications

You would perform gastric lavage to

- remove a potentially toxic, orally ingested substance from a patient who has ingested a life-threatening amount less than an hour before
- remove irritating gastric secretions and prevent nausea and vomiting through gastric decompression
- obtain information on the rate and site of bleeding and to help evacuate clots.

You would *not* perform the procedure in the case of caustic ingestion, such as of acidic or alkaline substances, paraffin, kerosene and other hydrocarbons, or in a patient who has ingested a large or sharp foreign body (FB) or packets of recreational drugs.

Most clinical toxicologists agree that lavage *should* be performed when a patient has ingested a large amount of a potentially dangerous drug, for example calcium channel blocker, tricyclic antidepressant or β-blocker, and presents to the emergency department within an hour of ingestion.

You need to take the following risks into account:

- You can push tablets into the duodenum instead of removing them.
- You can induce bleeding by knocking a clot off a bleeding vessel.
- There is always a risk of aspiration if the patient vomits.

Equipment

To perform the procedure, you need the following:

- An irrigation tray
- A stethoscope
- Adhesive tape
- Gloves
- Protective apron or gown, goggles and mask
- Lubricating jelly
- A catheter tip syringe – 60 ml
- A bite-block

- Pharyngeal suction equipment
- A pulse oximeter
- A large-bore gastric tube
- Irrigation solution such as warm tap water or a normal saline solution
- Endotracheal intubation equipment, if indicated
- Restraints, if indicated
- Lavage tubing setup, including drainage bag
- Tubing clamps
- Activated charcoal

You should use the largest gastric tube that you can safely insert – usually 16–22FG in infants, 24–28FG in children and 36–40FG in adolescents and adults.

Procedure

Before going ahead with the procedure, you need to prepare the patient as follows:

- Set up the pharyngeal suction equipment.
- Initiate pulse oximetry monitoring.
- Restrain him, if necessary.
- Intubate him, if indicated.
- Place him on his left side in the Trendelenburg position to promote the return of the lavage fluid, to help prevent aspiration and to decrease movement of the gastric contents into the duodenum.
- Assemble the lavage tubing and prime it with fluid.
- Place a bite-block in his mouth.
- Insert a large-bore orogastric tube (the same method as the insertion of a nasogastric tube – see Chapter 120).

To perform the lavage, you need to follow this procedure:

- Aspirate the stomach contents and save the initial sample for a toxic screen.
- Unclamp the tubing between the drainage bag and the patient, and instil normal saline warmed to about 38 degrees Celsius: 150–200 ml in adults and 10ml/kg in children.

- Allow the fluid to drain into the bucket using gravity. Use the syringe to pull the fluid and particles gently through the tube if no fluid returns. Massaging or gently rocking the patient's abdomen may also enhance fluid return.
- Repeat the procedure of instilling and removing fluid until the fluid return is clear of stomach contents.
- Keep a running tally of the fluid input and output.
- Instil activated charcoal – 1 mg/kg for infants younger than a year, 1–2 mg/kg for children of 1–12 years and 50–100 mg for adults.
- Remove the lavage tube with the patient in a lateral recumbent position, while observing for vomiting. Suction should be available.

Complications

Make preparations to counter any of the following complications that can occur during the procedure:

- Laryngospasm
- Decreased S_aO_2
- Aspiration pneumonia
- Sinus bradycardia
- ST elevation on ECG
- Diarrhoea
- Ileus
- Oesophageal or gastric perforation or laceration
- Hypothermia – especially in children
- Electrolyte imbalance – if large amounts of non-isotonic solutions are used
- Haemorrhage in a bleeding patient

127 How to apply a plaster cast

SLADE VERMAAK

Before you apply a plaster cast, you need to protect your patient's skin. You can do this in the following two ways:

1. **Stockinette:** You would usually apply this next to the skin. It is particularly useful in long-term plasters as it prevents limb hairs from being caught in the plaster, helps to absorb sweat, protects the skin from the plaster's rough edges and helps in the removal of the plaster.

2. **Orthopaedic wool:** You can apply a layer of wool to protect bony prominences. You need to apply it evenly, overlapping by one half on the previous turn. Where you anticipate swelling, apply it in several layers. You can omit the initial layer of the stockinette.

Types of plaster casts

Plaster slabs

These consist of several layers of plaster bandage the thickness of which depends on the size of the patient and the site of the application. Usually six layers will suffice for a child, but up to 30 may be required for an adult's above-knee plaster, for example.

You would use plaster slabs when potentially serious swelling may occur, or when you are treating a minor injury.

To use this type of cast, you need to follow this procedure:

- **Tailoring:** You should tailor the slab according to the site of application. Cut it to size rather than folding the edges once you have applied it. For example, you should extend a forearm back slab from the metacarpal heads to the olecranon, while you should measure an anterior slab from just distal to the elbow crease (with the forearm at 90 degrees' flexion) to the proximal palmar crease.

- **Wetting:** Use tepid water (plaster setting time is sped up by hot water) which allows more time for you to mould the plaster before it hardens. After

immersing the plaster in water, momentarily bunch it up and express excess water, then smooth it out again, consolidating the layers by holding one side and pulling the layers through two adducted fingers.

- **Applying:** After protecting the skin as described above, carefully position the slab on the limb and smooth it out with your hands without forming ridges on the body contact surface.

- **Reinforcing:** At this stage you need to reinforce any weak spots, for example where the elbow is at 90 degrees in an above-elbow slab, you can apply two small slabs about 10 cm long on either side of the bend.

- **Securing:** Use open-weave bandages, such as those made of cotton, to secure the slabs. Always wet them before application as this avoids tightening after contact with the wet plaster.

- **Checking:** Always check your patient's circulation after you have applied the slab.

Complete plaster casts

When using this type of cast, you need to first protect your patient's skin as described above.

It is recommended that you use the following sizes for the following areas:

- Upper arm and forearm – 150 mm
- Wrist – 100 mm
- Thumb and fingers – 75 mm
- Trunk, hip, thigh and leg – 200 mm
- Ankle and foot – 150 mm

To use this type of cast, you need to follow this procedure:

- **Wetting:** Use tepid water. Secure the end of the plaster roll in one hand, dip the roll into the water at an angle of 45 degrees and hold until the bubbles stop. Remove the excess water with a light squeeze and twist.

• **Applying:** Apply the plaster starting from a proximal point, as this will give you more time to mould it at the fracture site before it sets. Roll it without stretching if you anticipate swelling or if you have not used orthopaedic wool. If you do not anticipate swelling, you can stretch the plaster to compress half the thickness of the ortho-wool. Apply the plaster covering half the thickness of the previous turn, smoothing out the layers as you go, ensuring that no trapped air is left behind.

Once you have applied the cast, advise your patient on the potential of impaired circulation and on what signs to look out for, such as pain or paraesthesia. He should seek immediate medical attention if he has any concerns.

The following figure illustrates various cast types:

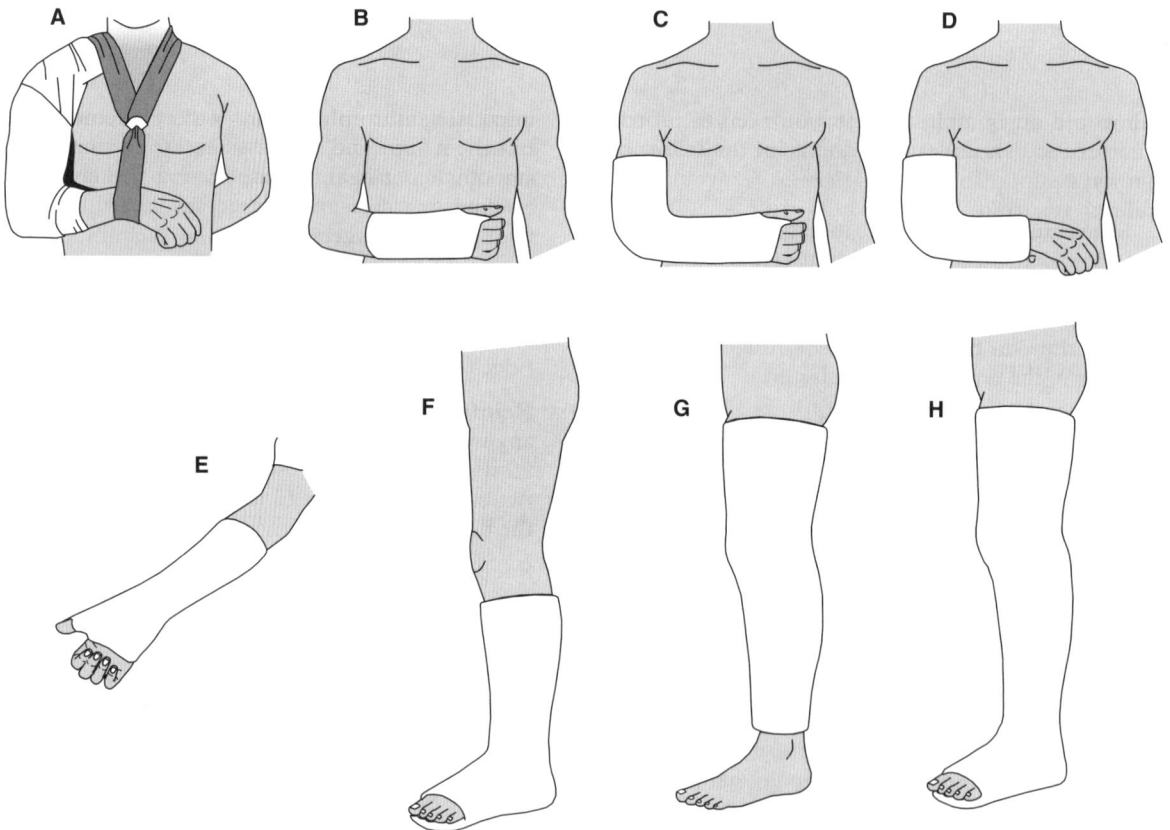

Figure 127.1 Various cast types: (A) U-slab used for shaft of humerus fractures. Apply orthopaedic wool from the shoulder to a third of the way down the forearm. Apply a 15 cm slab from the axillary fold, around the elbow, to above the point of the shoulder in a "U" shape. Smooth down and secure with a wet open-weave cotton bandage; (B) Short arm cast used for distal forearm fractures; (C) Long arm cast used for proximal forearm, elbow and upper arm fractures; (D) Arm cylinder cast used for soft-tissue injury around the elbow; (note: for all these casts, the metacarpo-phalangeal points are left freely mobile); (E) Cast used for scaphoid fractures – note that it includes the thumb MP joint, but leaves the fingers free to move; (F) Short leg cast used for distal lower-leg fractures; (G) Leg cylinder cast used for soft-tissue injury around the knee; (H) Long leg cast used for proximal leg and knee fractures

128

How to set up traction

ROLAND PETER GRÄBE

You would set up **skin traction** in fractures of the femur in children under 12 years of age, as well as in children's supracondylar fractures. You would use **skeletal traction** only in adults with fractures of the femur where you cannot use open reduction and surgery, or closed reduction and intramedullary nails.

Skin traction

We will now explore the three kinds of skin traction.

Femur fracture in a child weighing more than 13 kg

You would apply skin traction to treat a fracture in the shaft of the femur of a child who weighs more than 13 kg and who is less than 12 years of age.

To perform the traction, you need to follow this procedure:

- Clean the child's leg thoroughly with water and soap.

- Apply Tinct Benz Co, otherwise known as friar's balsam, to the skin. It is sticky and helps the Elastoplast to stick to the skin.

- Apply the Elastoplast which cannot stretch lengthwise (usually red) to the medial and lateral aspects of his leg. This is ready-made with two strips and a small wooden block at the end, which you should place 8 cm distal to his foot. On the medial side, ensure that the Elastoplast starts in the groin and on the lateral side at the greater trochanter. Apply it without wrinkles.

- From 5 cm proximal to the medial and lateral malleoli, apply sponge or orthopaedic felt inside the Elastoplast distally. This is to protect the malleoli from getting pressure sores.

- Now use a roll of Elastoplast that *can* stretch lengthwise – it is usually white. Unroll it so that it stretches longitudinally, and then roll it up again, after which you can apply it to the lower leg in a

spiral fashion from 8 cm *above* the malleoli to the groin. The reason for this essential precaution is that if you start too close to the malleoli, the Elastoplast will slowly move distally, which can result in a pressure sore on the dorsum of the ankle (see Figure 128.1).

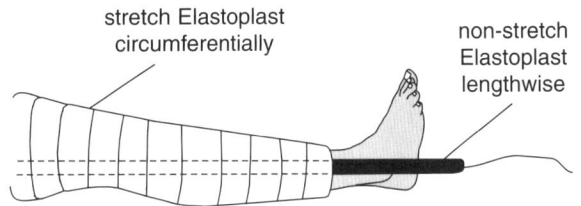

Figure 128.1 Application of Elastoplast for skin traction

- A child younger than four or five years can rest his leg on flat pillows. Do not apply more than 4 kg weight to the string coming from the red Elastoplast and hang it over the end of the bed (see Figure 128.2).

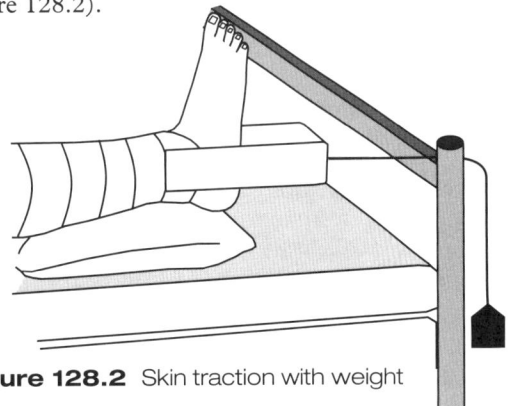

Figure 128.2 Skin traction with weight

- In an older child, you must use a Thomas splint. Measure the splint to fit the child's leg both around the uppermost thigh and lengthwise. In the groin, give an extra 5 cm of the inner circumference of the splint to allow for swelling of the thigh. Tie the string coming from the red Elastoplast to the end of the Thomas splint distal to the foot. Figure 128.3 shows the Thomas splint.

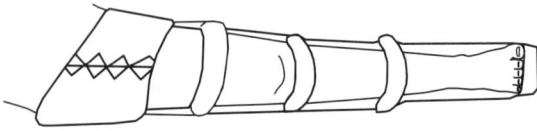

Figure 128.3 Thomas splint

- At the distal end of the splint, apply a weight. It can be slightly heavier in a patient who is slightly older. This distracts the Thomas splint from the child's groin.

Femur fracture in a child weighing less than 13 kg

This method is known as Gallow's traction (see Figure 128.4).

You would apply the red and white Elastoplast as described above, but in this case to *both* legs. Suspend both legs at 90 degrees to the horizontal and tie them to a crossbar that is fitted over the child's

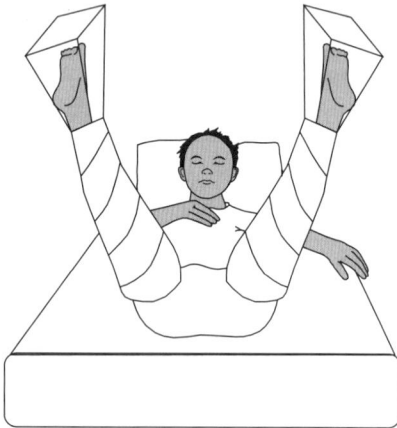

Figure 128.4 Gallow's traction

cot. The tension should be such that you can just get your hand in between the buttocks of the child and the mattress.

You must not use weights when applying this method.

Humerus fracture

Also known as Dunlop traction, this method is used specifically to prevent compartment syndrome in a child with supracondylar fracture of the humerus.

The method is similar to the Gallow's traction. In this case, you would apply the traction from just distal to the elbow as far as the wrist. Apply the white, circular Elastoplast 5 cm proximal to the wrist to just distal to the elbow joint.

If a proper Dunlop apparatus is not available, you can still use this method. Hang the piece of string that is attached to the distal ends of the red Elastoplast over an ordinary drip stand. You can attach

about 2–4 kg weights to the end of the string, depending on the child's age or weight (see Figure 128.5).

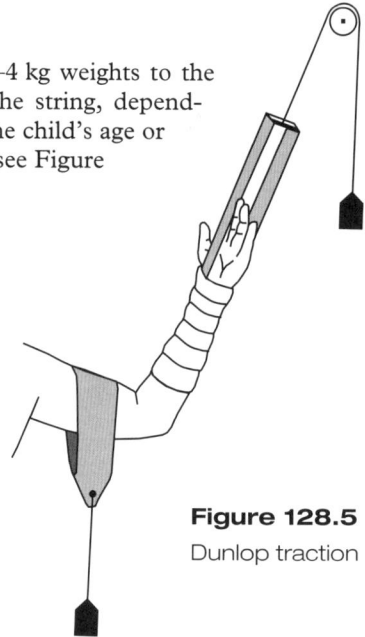

Figure 128.5 Dunlop traction

Skeletal traction

You should use this type of traction *only* with the aid of a Thomas splint and *only* for adults. The most important part of this method is the landmarks for the Steinmann or Denham pin, that is the tibial tuberosity, which is at the insertion of the patellar ligament.

Follow this procedure:

- Put your patient under local or general anaesthetic.
- Insert the nail – always from lateral to medial – 2.5 cm posterior to the tuberosity (see Figure 128.6).
- *Avoid* the common peroneal nerve, which runs directly posterior to the neck of the fibula, at all costs.

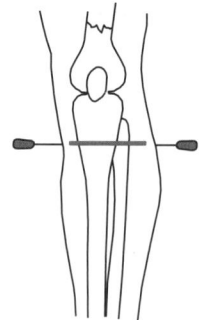

Figure 128.6

The application of skeletal traction – pin transects the tibia

- Fix a stirrup to the nail anterior to the lower leg.
- Tie a string from the end of the stirrup over the pulley and attach the weight (see Figure 128.7).

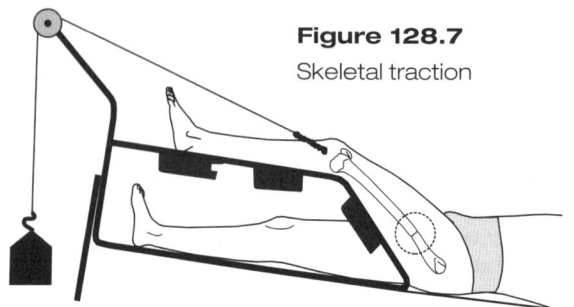

Figure 128.7 Skeletal traction

129

How to reduce a Colles fracture

SILAS MOTSITSI

The clinical deformity arising from this fracture, also known as the "dinner fork deformity", was first described by Abraham Colles in 1814, long before we used X-rays.

The fracture usually occurs in osteoporotic, post-menopausal females. It is a type of pathological fracture because it occurs in pathological bone. The injury that Colles described is a transverse fracture that occurs just proximal to the wrist with dorsal displacement of the distal fragment. A common injury, it affects 17% of women over the age of 50 years. If the fragments are allowed to unite in poor anatomical alignment, a poor functional outcome is more likely. Common practice is to attempt closed reduction to restore bony alignment.

Diagnosis

You would suspect a Colles fracture in these instances:

- The patient gives a history of falling on the extended hand.
- The bone fractures at the cortico-cancellous junction.
- The distal fragment has the following displacements:
  - Proximal displacement leading to impaction
  - Dorsal tilt
  - Volar angulation
  - Radial deviation
- The sum of these displacements gives rise to the typical clinical appearance of the dinner fork deformity.
- There may be an associated ulnar styloid fracture.

Investigations

You must obtain AP and lateral X-rays of the injury to confirm your diagnosis of a Colles fracture (see Figure 124.6):

- **AP view:** This view shows the degree of impaction of the distal fragment, the degree of radius shortening, the radial deviation of the distal fragment and the absence or presence of ulnar styloid process fracture.
- **Lateral view:** This view shows the dorsal tilt of the distal radius fragment and the degree of volar angulation.

Careful analysis of these views helps you to decide how to reduce the fracture.

Indications for reduction

As mentioned above, severely displaced Colles fractures lead to poor functional outcome. You need to assess whether the fracture in question falls within the parameters of the commonly accepted position, in which the dorsal tilt is less than 10 degrees and the radial shortening is less than 5 mm.

You can measure these parameters on AP and lateral X-rays. You do not need a closed reduction of a fracture that falls below these parameters. However, you should use closed reduction with below-elbow plaster of Paris (POP) to treat most Colles fractures.

Procedure

- You can do the reduction under local anaesthetic infiltration of the haematoma, Bier's block, brachial block or general anaesthesia.
- Do this by hyper-extending the distal fragment, then translating it distally (while in the extended position) until it can be "hooked over" the proximal shaft fragment. Then flex the distal fragment over the proximal shaft fragment.
- Avoid placing the wrist in too much flexion – 20 degrees of wrist flexion is adequate.
- Ensure that the POP ends at the level of the metacarpal necks to avoid stiffening of the MP (metacarpo-phalangeal) joints.
- Confirm the position of reduction by X-ray, if possible.
- Leave your patient's thumb and fingers free for early mobilisation, otherwise she will have extremely stiff fingers. Figure 129.1 shows this part of the process.

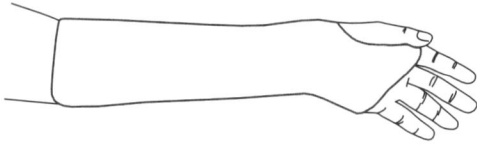

Figure 129.1 Position of reduction and POP for a Colles fracture

- Once you have done the reduction, advise her to elevate the limb as much as possible to decrease swelling, and to start finger mobilisation as soon as possible.
- Just before discharging her, check the position of the reduction.

Remember that

- 50% of these fractures will have displaced within a week. Do the first outpatient review within this period.
- 68–73% will have displaced in five weeks. Do another review during this period.
- you might find it impossible to maintain a comminuted fracture with POP. Therefore, it may need other modalities of treatment, such as
  - external fixators
  - fixation with percutaneous K-wires
  - a combination of the above
  - open reduction and internal fixation with or without bone grafting.

Complications

You need to be aware of and look out for the complications that can result from the procedure, which we will now explore according to the time at which they can occur.

Early complications

These are as follows:

- **Circulatory embarrassment:** This can be caused by tight POP or bandages. If the swelling is severe, you need to split the POP or all constricting bandages. Do not worry about fracture re-displacement – this complication threatens the sur-

vival of the limb, which is more important. You can always redo the reduction of the fracture.

- **Nerve injury:** If the wrist is in too much flexion, compression of the median nerve can occur, leading to carpal tunnel syndrome. This complication is uncommon if you follow the above guidelines. If the compression is severe, carpal tunnel release is advisable.
- **Reflex sympathetic dystrophy, or regional pain syndrome:** This complication is fairly uncommon (the Reflex Sympathetic Dystrophy Syndrome Association of America (RSDSA) reports that the condition appears after 1% to 2% of bone fractures), especially following treatment with an external fixator. The treatment is difficult, and most patients will have stiff fingers and pain.

Late complications

These are as follows:

- **Delayed union and non-union:** This occurs commonly in fractures involving a large part of the metaphysis and in fractures treated with external fixators. If the problem is asymptomatic and there is no function difficulty, you should give conservative treatment. However, symptomatic non-union requires surgical intervention.
- **Shoulder, wrist or hand stiffness:** This is owing to neglect. Encourage early rehabilitation or physiotherapy.
- **Tendon rupture:** This commonly involves extensor pollicis longus and may occur in trivial distal radius fractures. Warn your patient about this.
- **Malunion:** This can occur as a result of poor reduction or loss of reduction. Your management depends on when the malunion is noticed, as follows:
  - **Nascent malunion (less than four weeks):** You can correct either by re-manipulation or open reduction and internal fixation. If necessary, you can use the callus as a bone graft.
  - **Mature malunion (fully united):** You need to perform an osteotomy and fill the gap with bone graft.

130

How to reduce an elbow dislocation

SILAS MOTSITSI

Elbow dislocation is the second most common type of dislocation in adults, and it is more common in adults than in children.

You can usually treat simple dislocation with closed reduction, and conservative management is usually successful. Complex dislocations may be more difficult because of their inherent instability or associated fractures.

You can classify this type of dislocation according to the direction of dislocation, which you see on radiography, into the anterior, posterior, postero-lateral (PL), postero-medial (PM) positions, or according to the degree of complexity of the dislocation – either simple or complex.

A person's elbow dislocates easily if it is flexed 10–30 degrees and is in varus stress, and the forearm is in external rotation. This results in posterior dislocation.

Diagnosis

You would diagnose an elbow dislocation in these instances:

- The patient has a history of falling on the extended elbow.
- He supports his forearm with his elbow in slight flexion.
- He has elbow deformity.
- The normal relationship between the epicondyles and olecranon is lost.
- There is potential involvement of *all* three major nerves and vasculature.

Investigations

You must obtain AP and lateral X-rays of the injury to confirm your diagnosis of a dislocated elbow. A line drawn along the centre of the long axis of the radius shaft must bisect the capitellum in *any* view (see Figure 130.1). Using this simple principle, you can pick up even subtle features such as subluxation, particularly in children.

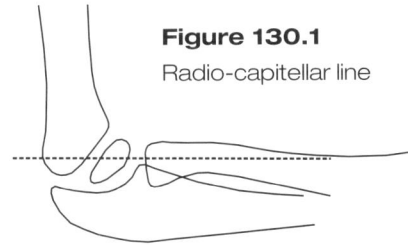

Figure 130.1

Radio-capitellar line

Analyse each bone that forms part of the elbow joint for associated fractures such as fracture of the coronoid process, medial or lateral epicondyle, head of radius and olecranon process. If you find one or more of these fractures, the dislocation is a complex one. Check for the fat pad sign.

Procedure

In order to treat simple posterior dislocation, you need to follow this procedure:

- Perform closed reduction under sedation and brachial block or general anaesthesia.
- The method involves placing the patient in the prone position with the humerus resting on the table and the forearm hanging perpendicular to the plane of the table (see Figure 130.2). The humerus should be supported by the table, with padding, just proximal to the elbow joint. Apply 2

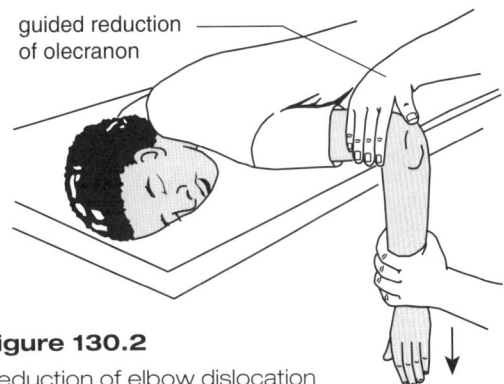

guided reduction of olecranon

Figure 130.2

Reduction of elbow dislocation

to 5 kg of traction to the wrist. Reduction should occur over a period of minutes as the muscles relax.

- Apply short-term immobilisation with collar and cuff and elbow at 90 degrees.
- Advise your patient to initiate motion within two weeks, as this can provide a stable joint with good functional outcome.

Complications

You need to be aware of and look out for the complications that can result from the procedure, which we will now explore according to the time at which they can occur.

Early complications

These are as follows:

- **Vascular:** The brachial artery may be injured, which you should treat as an emergency.
- **Nerve injuries:** The median and ulnar nerves may be injured. Spontaneous recovery occurs in 6–8 weeks.

- **Associated fractures**

Late complications

These are as follows:

- **Myositis ossificans:** Usually occurring 6–8 weeks after trauma, this is fairly common following elbow injury. The degree of involvement differs. If it interferes with elbow function, do an excision when the bone is mature.
- **Calcification of capsule and ligament:** This occurs later than myositis ossificans and is a painless condition, although it may restrict movement to some extent.
- **Unreduced dislocation:** This can occur if a dislocation was missed. You can attempt closed reduction within six weeks of the injury. After this period, you would need to reduce the elbow surgically or by open means.
- **Recurrent dislocation:** If this takes place, look for intra-articular loose bodies. You need to perform elbow reconstruction in these cases to restore joint congruity and stability.

131 How to reduce a forearm fracture in a child

SILAS MOTSITSI

You can effectively treat the majority of fractures in children conservatively. In children, the potential for remodelling is excellent; exact anatomical reduction is not essential. Their fractured limbs tend to overgrow, usually by about 2 cm, so you can allow some shortening.

Certain fractures are unique to children, namely torus fracture, greenstick fracture, plastic deformation and Salter-Harris fractures. Such injuries usually result from a fall on the outstretched hand. You can classify the fracture as either open or closed. Moreover, you can classify it according to the area of the bone involved, that is proximal, middle or distal third.

Diagnosis

You would diagnose a forearm fracture in these instances:

- The history suggests a fall on the outstretched hand.
- There is swelling, pain, deformity and crepitus.

The main objective of your preliminary examination is to pick up or exclude limb-threatening complications.

Investigations

You must obtain AP and lateral X-rays of the injury to confirm your diagnosis of a fractured forearm. Request that each view includes the joint above and the joint below the fracture (in the same X-ray plate). Take the normal side for comparison by requesting and evaluating control X-rays. Request additional X-rays or other investigations only if necessary. Classify the fracture accordingly.

Remember, dislocations hardly ever occur in isolation – always look for an associated fracture (which may be difficult to see).

Procedure

The method of choice for stable forearm fractures is in most cases closed reduction under general anaesthetic, that is manipulation into acceptable alignment.

The position in which the forearm is immobilised depends on the site of the fracture. In order to immobilise the forearm, you need to follow this procedure:

- If the fractures of both forearm bones are proximal to the insertion of the pronator teres (middle of the radial shaft), hold the forearms in supination.
- If the fracture is in the middle third, the neutral position is advisable.
- If the fracture is in the distal third, pronation is the better position.
- Observe the child for possible complications, particularly for the limb-threatening compartment syndrome (increasing pain, especially on passive stretching of involved muscles under the cast despite elevation and analgesia; paraesthesiae) at frequent intervals.
- Bear in mind that these fractures easily re-displace. Do the first follow-up X-rays within a week of the procedure. If the fracture has re-displaced and it is detected during this period, you can do re-manipulation. Note that it is practically impossible for you to successfully re-manipulate fractures after a week.

Remodelling

With regard to remodelling, you must bear in mind these factors:

- Younger children have a greater potential for remodelling compared to older ones. A 25-degree angulation in a one-year-old can be accepted but not in a 17-year-old.

- Fractures nearer the joints have a better chance of remodelling than do those that are further from the joints.
- Fractures that are angulated in the direction of joint motion remodel better than those orientated in other directions.
- Malrotation does not remodel. You can accept angulation, but not malrotation.

Complications

The following complications can occur as a result of the fracture or of the treatment:

- Compartment syndrome
- Malunion
- Non-union
- Nerve injury
- Vascular injury
- Synostosis

132 How to use ketamine

DRIES ENGELBRECHT

You would use ketamine for the induction of general anaesthesia in patients with hypovolaemic shock. It is also highly effective in the emergency setting, where it can be used in sub-anaesthetic dosages for the management of painful procedures in children (Balfour 2004). You would use it less commonly in adults because of unpleasant psychiatric side-effects (such as hallucination) and because adults tolerate local anaesthetic much better than children do.

Indications and contraindications

You can use ketamine in these instances:

- Single agent for short procedures
- Induction of general anaesthesia in hypovolaemic shock patients
- Augmentation of incomplete regional and local blocks
- In disasters, where several patients may have to be anaesthetised simultaneously
- Sub-anaesthetic analgesic dosages for painful procedures in children of between 1 and 10 years of age – suturing lacerations, changing bandages, reducing fractures, incising and draining abscesses, and conducting rape examinations

You would *not* use ketamine under these circumstances:

- History of airway instability, tracheal surgery or tracheostenosis – because of transient airway complications such as laryngospasm and emesis (Brown, Lovato & Parker 2005)
- Psychiatric disorders such as schizophrenia and manic depressive disorder
- Raised intracranial pressure, for example hydrocephalus or head injury
- History of myocardial infarction or angina, or suspicion of ischaemic heart disease, active pulmonary infections other than resolved old TB, or TB on treatment

You *must* obtain consent from parents or guardians for the relevant procedure, and for the use of the anaesthetic agent.

Dosage

To administer the drug, you need to follow these procedures:

- **As an induction agent (IV route recommended):**
  - IV 1–2 mg/kg
  - IM 10 mg/kg
  - Oral and rectal 7–10 mg/kg

- **Sub-anaesthetic analgesic dosages (IM route recommended):**
  - 0.5–2 mg/kg IM. You can add 0.01 mg/kg atropine in order to decrease upper airway secretions associated with ketamine use.
  - If ineffective in 15 minutes or if the procedure takes longer than expected give a second dose of ketamine as follows: 2 mg/kg IM. Do *not* give atropine with the second dose.

Concomitant use of benzodiazepines is often recommended, but it has not been demonstrated to be useful in preventing the patient from growing agitated upon recovery (Brown et al. 2005).

Environment

Administer ketamine *only* in a room where there is suction, oxygen and equipment for advanced airway management. Follow this procedure:

- A nurse *must* closely observe the patient's airway and respiration, that is saturation, respiratory rate and other routine observations, until his recovery is well established.

- The patient must have a drip up.
- Pulse oximetry must be continuous until his recovery is well established.
- Ensure that he is *never* left alone.

Discharge

Once you have determined that you can discharge the patient (returned to pre-treatment level of consciousness)

- warn his parents that the child may have vivid dreams for the next 24–48 hours
- administer post-procedure pain relief.

© Van Schaik Publishers

133 How to administer a spinal anaesthetic

DRIES ENGELBRECHT

Indications and contraindications

You would give the anaesthetic for procedures on the

- lower extremities and hips
- perineum
- lumbar spine
- lower abdomen.

You would *not* administer the anaesthetic in these circumstances:

- Local sepsis at the puncture site
- Systemic sepsis
- Shock or severe hypotension
- Clotting deficiency
- Raised intracranial pressure
- Patient refusal

Nor should you administer the drug in these instances:

- Neurological deficit of the lower limbs
- Severe back pain
- Pre-operative use of aspirin or heparin
- Uncooperative patient or surgeon

Procedure

Preparation

Before beginning the procedure you must make these preparations:

- Obtain your patient's informed consent.
- Obtain a clotting profile and platelet count if there is any suspicion of a coagulopathy.
- Administer premedication with oral benzodiazepine to ensure that the patient is calm before the procedure. Do not do this if the procedure is a Caesarean section.
- You can provide spinal anaesthesia only in a well-equipped theatre, where full resuscitation and general anaesthesia can be also provided if necessary (Morgan & Mikhail 1996).

- Ensure that these monitors are connected: ECG, BP and pulse oximetry.
- Always secure a proper intravenous line before making any attempt to give spinal anaesthesia.
- Give a bolus of approximately 500 ml of isotonic solution to avoid a sudden fall in BP.
- Select the appropriate size spinal needle (preferably pencil-point).
- Decide which position is the best for the patient:
  - **Sitting position:** The patient sits forward on the edge of the bed with his legs on a stool, leaning forward. His arms should be crossed over a pillow. Ask him to flex his lower back. The line between the posterior iliac spines should be parallel to the bed.
  - **Lateral position:** The patient lies on his side with his hips and knees in maximal flexion. His head and neck are flexed towards his knees. The line between the posterior iliac spines should be vertical and at right angles to the bed.

To administer the spinal anaesthetic, you need to follow this procedure (see Figure 12.4 for the relevant anatomy):

- Identify the interspace between L4 and L5 – on the level of the posterior iliac crests.
- Mark the interspace with a fingernail imprint or a marker pen.
- Scrub up and wear full surgical sterile clothing and sterile gloves.
- Use povidone iodine to clean in a widening circle from the marked point.
- Apply a sterile drape and wipe the povidone from the site to avoid introducing it into the subarachnoidal space, which can cause chemical meningitis.
- Use a local anaesthetic to infiltrate the skin and deeper structures.

- Because of the downward angle of the spinous processes, you need to raise the skin weal just below the upper spinous process.
- Introduce the needle with the bevel facing laterally to pass just under and parallel to this spinous process in the midline.
- Contact with bone superficially suggests contact with the spinous process; contact with bone more deeply suggests contact with a lamina or pedicle.
- Smooth passage suggests correct placement.
- You would feel an increase in resistance when the needle enters the interspinous ligaments from the subcutaneous tissues.
- You would feel a drop in resistance when you have penetrated the ligamentum flavum.
- You will feel a final decrease in resistance when you have punctured the dura.
- Withdraw the stylet to confirm the free flow of cerebrospinal fluid.
- Connect a syringe and aspirate a minimal amount of cerebrospinal fluid to finally confirm the position of the needle before you slowly inject the local anaesthetic.
- Once you have injected the local anaesthetic, remove the spinal needle and place a sterile bandage over the puncture wound.
- Position the patient in order to place the local anaesthetic in the correct area of the subdural space.

Dosage and commonly used anaesthetics and mixtures

- Bupivicaine 0.5% plain 8–12 mg (1.5–2.5 ml)
- Bupivicaine 0.5% hyperbaric (contains dextrose) 8–12 mg (1.5–2.5 ml)

Table 133.1 Dosages of hyperbaric bupivicaine

Surgery	Level of block	Dosage
Perineum	S2	1–1.5 ml
Lower limbs	L1	3–3.5 ml
Caesarean section	T6	2–2.5 ml

- Lignocaine 2% plain 20–25 mg (1–1.2 ml)

Positioning the patient after the spinal injection

You need to know the anatomical level of the required anaesthesia in order to determine how to position the patient:

- Isobaric, that is without dextrose, local anaesthetic should stay at the level of injection irrespective of the position of the patient.
- Hyperbaric local anaesthetic mixtures will migrate caudad in the head-up patient and cephalad in the head-down patient, influencing the level of the block.
- Check the level of anaesthesia achieved by testing dermatomes for cold sensation with an alcohol swab.

Post-spinal anaesthetic monitoring

After a spinal anaesthesia the patient should be observed until the effect of the local anaesthetic has worn off. The following should be documented:

- Pulse rate: every 15 minutes
- Blood pressure: every 15 minutes
- Saturation: continuously

Complications

These complications could occur:

- Hypotension owing to high spinal anaesthesia. With extremely high levels bradycardia and respiratory arrest may also occur. Avoid injecting the local anaesthetic too quickly.
- If pulse drops below 50/min give 0.6 mg atropine IV. Hypotension should be treated with oxygen (2–4 ℓ/min via face mask) and fluid therapy. If there is no response, use ephedrine.
- Post-spinal headache due to persistent leak through the dura
- Bacterial meningitis resulting from poor aseptic technique
- Aseptic meningitis due to introduction of caustic substances
- Pain on injection

Please also see Chapter 12.

How does it relate to the situation in the consultation

Section 12

The consultation

134 How to communicate effectively in the consultation

BOB MASH

The consultation is the backbone of family practice. It is essential to the following roles that you as a family physician play (WONCA 2002):

- **Care provider**, who considers the patient holistically as an individual and as an integral part of a family and the community, and provides high-quality, comprehensive, continuous and personalised care within a long-term, trusting relationship.

- **Decision maker**, who makes scientifically sound judgements about investigations and treatments, and uses technologies that take into account the patient's wishes, ethical values, cost-effective considerations and the best possible care for the patient.

- **Communicator**, who is able to promote a healthy lifestyle by effective explanation and advocacy, thereby empowering individuals and groups to enhance and protect their health.

Table 134.1, which is adapted from the Calgary-Cambridge Observation Guide (Silverman, Kurtz & Draper 1998), summarises the necessary communication skills. You can use it as a tool for observing and reflecting on consultations.

Table 134.1 Skills necessary for effective communication

Phase of the consultation	Specific tasks for that phase	Specific skills for that task
Initiating the session	Make appropriate greeting/ introduction and demonstrate interest and respect	Greet the patient, obtain his name, introduce yourself, attend to physical comfort of patient, show interest and respect, establish initial rapport
	Identify and confirm the patient's problem list or issues	Give an opportunity for the patient to list all his issues or problems before exploring the initial problem. For example: "You have a headache and fever. Is there anything else you'd like to talk about?" Summarise and confirm the list with the patient. Patients usually have more than one problem, but the order in which these are presented is not necessarily related to their importance. The tendency is to interrupt the patient after the first problem is mentioned and thus create a dysfunctional consultation in which the other problems are either hidden or introduced only at the end – so-called "door knob" complaints. If necessary, you can also introduce topics at this point that are on your agenda or negotiate with the patient an agenda of what can be covered in the time available
Gathering information	Explore the patient's problems	Use open as well as closed questions, attentive listening, facilitation skills and summarisation, and respond to cues, as opposed to cutting off the patient or using only closed questions in an interrogatory style. Facilitation skills include verbal and non-verbal cues that encourage the patient, such as "uh huh" or nodding, silence, repetition or echoing of the last phrase and paraphrasing. Summarising your understanding of the patient's story shows the patient what you have understood, it allows him to correct or add to the story, gives structure to the consultation and requires you to process the information in a systematic manner.

Van Schaik Publishers

Table 134.1 Continued

Phase of the consultation	Specific tasks for that phase	Specific skills for that task
Gathering information	Make an attempt to understand the patient's perspective	The patient's perspective is often elicited spontaneously in a patient-centred consultation but you should then acknowledge it. You can also elicit his perspective by using specific questions to understand his beliefs, concerns, expectations and feelings. For example: "What did you think might be causing your problem?"; "What was the worst thing you were thinking it might be?"; "What were you hoping we would do today?"; "How did that leave you feeling?"
	Understand the patient's context	Elicit relevant information about the patient's • past medical history, medications and allergies • lifestyle (smoking, alcohol, exercise) • family history, structure and function • occupation • physical environment
	Obtain sufficient information to ensure that no serious condition is likely to be missed	Elicit enough clinical information to establish a working diagnosis and ensure no serious condition is likely to be missed
Explaining and planning	Make a clinically appropriate working diagnosis	Make a diagnosis that is clinically appropriate according to the subjective and objective evidence, and demonstrate sound diagnostic reasoning
	Clearly explain the diagnosis and management plan	Provide an explanation that is well organised and in small chunks, avoid jargon, where appropriate make use of visual methods, leaflets, repetition or signposting
	Give the patient an opportunity to ask for other information and/or seek to confirm patient's understanding	Ask the patient if he would like other information and/or check his understanding by reverse summarising or giving him an opportunity to clarify his understanding
	Ensure that the explanation takes account of and relates to the patient's perspective	Ensure that the explanation connects, responds to or takes into account the patient's beliefs, concerns and expectations
	Involve the patient where appropriate in decision-making	Offer the patient insight into your thought processes and invite him to participate in decision making through use of suggestions, options, choices and the expression of preferences or ideas. Do not simply give orders, directives or instructions of what must be done
	Choose an appropriate management plan	Base the management plan on scientifically sound evidence and ensure that it is appropriate for the diagnosis
Closing	Close the consultation successfully in the time available	Bring the consultation to a conclusion rather than allow it to run out of time. Deal with any remaining issues from the patient
	Provide appropriate safety netting for the patient	Show evidence of having considered how certain you are of the diagnosis, what might go wrong with the treatment, how the patient will know if things do not go well, side-effects that occur or more serious sequelae that develop. Show this in an appropriate plan of safety netting with the patient
Overall	Establish a good doctor–patient relationship	Show sensitivity and empathy when dealing with difficult or emotional issues; develop good rapport and be non-judgemental. Consistently demonstrate respect, interest and concern through both verbal and non-verbal communication. Involve the patient in the consultation by sharing your thought processes and providing a rationale for what you are doing
	Show a well-organised approach	Ensure structure and logical flow in the consultation; do not allow it to become disjointed and confusing

135 How to do a paediatric consultation

BRUCE SPARKS

Paediatric versus adult consultation

The consultation that involves children, from new-born infants to adolescents, usually differs considerably from that with the adult alone. Most studies and models of the consultation in family practice regard the patient as an independent adult. The studies that attempt to describe consultative behaviour, utilisation of health services, reasons for the encounter, help-seeking behaviour, episode-orientated epidemiology, and the role of the doctor in the consultation have considered mainly the behaviour and practice of adults therein (White, Williams & Greenberg 1961; Green, Fryer, Yawn, Lanier et al. 2001; Stewart et al. 2000; Stott 1983; Okkes, Polderman, Fryer, Yamada et al. 2002).

While many stages and processes of the paediatric consultation may be similar to those in the adult interaction, the dynamics of the doctor–patient relationship are significantly changed when the patient is a child. Early in the process, you need to define the "real" patient. In such encounters, it could be the presenting child, the accompanying parent, an accompanying guardian or helper, or indeed the family in its entirety.

The history of the child's problem is often given by the adult who has to interpret the child's possible symptoms and feelings for your benefit, so that you can define the elements of the patient-centred consultation. Often, the child who is able to provide an excellent description of his symptoms and thoughts is neglected here. In this case, you are missing a unique opportunity to understand the child's meaning, motivation and thoughts regarding the illness, family dynamics and relationships. Unfortunately, the consultation could be even more complicated when an interpreter is used.

Context

In all consultations, it is essential to take into account the context of the patient, which perhaps takes on additional significance when you are consulting with a child. The significance derives from the two crucial ways in which children differ from adults: their rapid growth and development, and their dependence on others for protection and sustenance (Okkes et al. 2002). Those factors give rise to a host of contextual factors that are often overlooked or disregarded in the paediatric consultation. One way of reminding yourself about the significance of context is to consider what we call "the child in the doorway". Just as, sociologically, problems are said to be contextually "framed", so the child framed in the doorway of the consulting room is also "framed" by many contextual possibilities.

Who is the child in your doorway? He could be one of any of these examples:

- **The constitutional child:** Children's rights are now enshrined in the Constitution. What are those rights and how can you as a family practitioner uphold them?

- **The signal child:** This is the child whose presenting problem or behaviour is a signal or pointer to problems experienced by other family members.

- **The child of a child:** This is the at-risk child of a teenage mother.

- **The old child:** This is the child who has never been a child, who is serious beyond his years, who has missed out on fun and knows only worry.

- **The frozen child:** This is the still, ever watchful child, too frightened to show emotion, fearful of the ever-present danger of abuse.

- **The chess-board child:** This is the pawn in conflictual parental and other family relationships.

- **The artistic child:** This is the child who can best express fears, anxieties and happiness in drawing, music or painting.

- **The doctor's child:** This is the rather neglected, possibly too independent, attention-needing child.

- **A host of others:** The home-alone child, the controlling child, the "deviant" child, the chaotic child, the transitional child.

You will not find descriptions of these types of children in the DSM-IV, but you will find them in your rooms and in your consultations.

In attempting to contextualise the child-patient you should consider the relationships, roles and functioning within his family itself. For example, a cross-sectional study of 210 families in the Netherlands (Huygen 1990) demonstrated that there was a higher illness rate in children where

- one or both parents were emotionally unstable, and where there was marital discord
- their parents tended to avoid conflict
- their parents were prone to somatic complaints
- their mother was involved in minimal social networks outside the family
- their parents had a less than average sense of well-being
- their mother was strongly inclined to accept the sick role
- there was a discrepancy in their parents' knowledge of the complaints of the spouse.

Consultation enhancement

In order to enhance your paediatric consultation skills, *do* the following:

- Ask yourself early in the consultation: "Is this child ill?" The answer directs your further exploration and management of the child's problem.
- Ask yourself: "What age is he?" followed by: "Does the developmental age correlate with the chronological age and, if not, why not?"
- Ask yourself: "Why is *this* child here with *this* disorder at *this* time?"
- Involve the parents and involve the child. Listen to the parents and the child (Kai 1996). They know their problems best. Wherever possible, consult with the child.
- Use genograms or ecomaps to define relationships, conflicts and health risks.
- Consider the stages of the family life cycle and development, as well as what tasks are facing this child and family at this time.
- Remember that any accident or illness in a child is

perceived by the parents as a crisis – half of the mothers feel guilt.

- Praise the parents where they have done well.
- Support the teenage mother; she is a "child with a child". She may well lack the maturity to deal with the stress of mothering a child.
- Remember, "If the child cries, it is probably your fault".

In order to enhance your paediatric consultation skills, *do not* do the following:

- Make the parents feel incompetent or trivialise their genuine concerns. It is easy to unintentionally undermine parents' confidence by suggesting that their anxieties are unfounded. Facilitate and empathise with parents' often arduous task, rather than make them feel guilty for consulting (Kai 2004).
- Classify a child's illness only in terms of seriousness. You also need to take into account the impact on the family.
- Blame the child who is difficult to examine. Make sure that you obtain his cooperation.
- Wake a sleeping child if you are able to examine his ears and listen to his chest while he sleeps.
- Lie the child down on an examination couch unless it is absolutely necessary. Sitting with his back against his mother's upright abdomen is the most secure position for a young child. You can examine an older child more easily while he is standing.
- Forget that as you are assessing the mother and child, they are assessing you.
- Neglect the "snowed-under" mother. She may be under tremendous stress and, apart from feeling guilty, may be at risk of becoming an abuser.
- Forget that a history of frequent consultations may reflect the need to address the parent's own health and well-being rather than focus only on that of the child.
- Assume that every child with behavioural problems has psychological problems for which the parents are to blame. There may be pathological reasons for such behaviour.
- Ignore the father in discussions about his child's care. An informed father is a supportive father.

BOB MASH

Brief motivational interviewing

Brief motivational interviewing (BMI) is an approach to motivating behaviour or lifestyle change which provides doctors with a broader range of communication skills that are tailored to the individual patient's readiness to change.

The spirit of BMI

The spirit of BMI refers to the paradigm or way of viewing reality within which the particular principles and specific techniques of BMI are situated.

Collaboration

A practitioner who practises BMI sees his relationship with the patient as a partnership within which both the practitioner and patient collaborate. The practitioner is patient-centred in seeking to understand the patient's perspective or view of reality and creates an atmosphere that is conducive to change. This is in contrast to an approach where patients are confronted with the correct view of reality from the practitioner's perspective and where they are coerced into accepting this viewpoint.

Evocation

A practitioner who practises BMI believes that the patient has the necessary internal resources and motivation to change, although he may need to evoke or enhance these resources by working with the patient's own perceptions, goals and values. Again, this is in contrast to an educational approach that attempts to externally correct the patient's perceptions, goals and values, which are presumed to be deficient.

Autonomy

A BMI practitioner is genuinely respectful of the patient's right to make his own choices regarding change and puts the responsibility for change in the hands of the patient. The practitioner guides the patient in his decision-making process and directs him towards healthy choices, but is also released from carrying the burden of responsibility himself. This is in contrast to the practitioner who tells patients what they must do and, if the advice is not followed, feels hurt, frustrated or even angry.

The principles of BMI

Within the paradigm outlined above the practitioner aligns himself with four key principles.

Express empathy

BMI recognises that change is a process and not an event and that individual patients may be at different stages. The cycle shown in Figure 136.1 is helpful in reminding us that not all patients will be ready to change when we consult them. A successful consultation may entail understanding where the individual is in this cycle as well as facilitating movement around it. The cycle also shows us that a relapse is a predictable aspect of attempting to change and that even patients who successfully change are likely to have setbacks. Most patients will be at the contemplative stage where they experience internal ambivalence about changing – there will be "good things" and "not-so-good things" about staying the same or changing. The practitioner seeks to understand and accept the patient's beliefs and feelings while not necessarily agreeing with them. Skills in reflective listening and open questioning to understand the patient's perspective are vital.

Develop discrepancy

BMI seeks to enhance the importance of change by paying attention to the discrepancy between where the patient is and where he would like to be in terms of his own goals and values. This principle means that BMI is directive in guiding the patient to think about a specific change, but does not impose the practitioner's own goals and values. If done skilfully, the patient – and not the practitioner – should present the arguments for change.

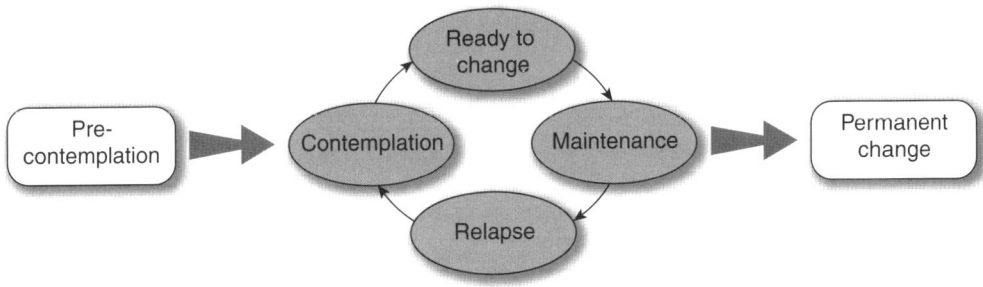

Figure 136.1 Stages of change model

Source: DiClemente & Velasquez 2002. p. 201–16

Support self-efficacy

Whereas developing discrepancy may enhance the importance of change, many patients struggle with confidence in their ability to change. Some may indeed be convinced about the importance of change but do not feel able to do it or have already tried and seemingly "failed". Supporting and building the patient's belief in the possibility of change is therefore essential. At the same time it is important that the practitioner genuinely believes that change is possible, as despondency may be contagious.

Roll with resistance

BMI avoids labelling people as resistant or non-compliant and instead resistance is largely seen as a product of the interaction itself. The skilful practitioner can reduce resistance to change whereas a less skilful practitioner may actually increase it. For example direct persuasion, prescriptive advice and arguing for change may actually have the opposite effect on the patient. Resistance is a sign that a change of direction or approach is needed rather than an indication that more pressure or confrontation is required. Your consultation style should be one of "dancing" rather than "wrestling" with your patient.

Stages of change model

BMI is based on a model of the stages that people go through in deciding whether to change (DiClemente & Velasquez 2002: 201–16). This model is illustrated in Figure 136.1. Doctors tend to assume that all patients are or should be ready to change, and thus often speak about change prematurely.

A menu of specific communication skills can be identified, some of which are more appropriate for different stages of the model. Patients may shift over time, and even within the same consultation, in their readiness to change. Moreover, it goes almost without saying that the categories are not always as clear-cut as the model implies. Nevertheless, the concept that patients can differ in their readiness to change is useful, as is the idea that you should assess and respect the stage at which your patient currently is.

In BMI your initial assessment of your patient attempts to identify at what stage he is. It also implies that a particular consultation may have the more limited goal of shifting the patient's stage of change rather than always having actual change as its goal. You should view change as a process rather than as an event that must occur during *every* consultation.

After briefly discussing the necessity of setting an agenda and understanding the patient's readiness to change, we will explore the required skills in each stage of the model in greater detail.

An agenda

It is important to choose the right time to discuss behaviour change. If your patient is acutely distressed or preoccupied with some other issue, the discussion may be inappropriate. Patient-centred consultations may identify important psychosocial issues that should also be addressed. You should also seek permission to discuss behaviour change and set an agenda of which topics to discuss with your patient.

Readiness to change

Two key factors that are involved in your patient's readiness to change are **importance** and **confidence**, as is illustrated in Figure 136.2. He may feel that stopping smoking is highly important, but may lack confidence in his ability to do so. Alternatively, he may feel confident that he could change his behaviour, but is not convinced that it is important.

Some of the BMI skills should help you to ascertain where the patient is in terms of these dimensions, which in turn will guide the kind of interaction that you have with him (Rollnick, Mason & Butler 1999).

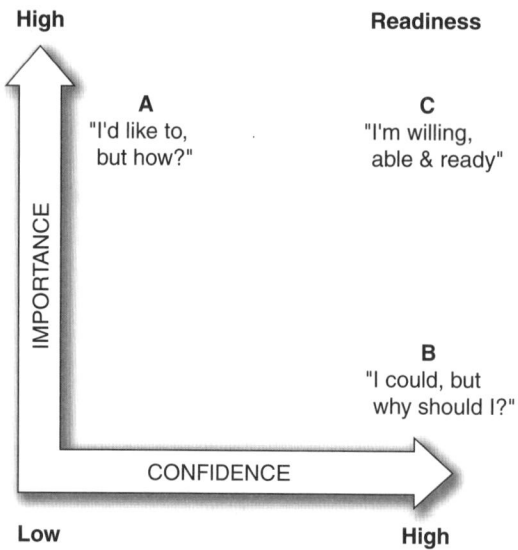

Figure 136.2 Dimensions of readiness to change

You can use **scaling questions** to assess these dimensions. Ask your patient: "If 0 were 'not important' and 10 was 'very important', what number would you give yourself?" Alternatively, you could use the **readiness to change ruler** (Stott, Rollnick, Rees, Pill 1995), which is shown as Figure 136.3. Say to your patient: "Some people find it easier to demonstrate their feelings on the 'readiness to change ruler'. Where on the ruler would you place yourself?"

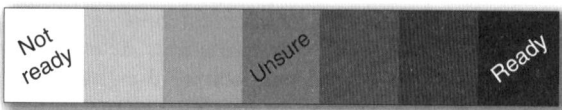

Figure 136.3 Readiness to change ruler

Pre-contemplation

Pre-contemplative patients often appear to be difficult patients, and may be labelled as "non-compliant" because they are not even *considering* the idea of change. They have virtually no motivation to change.

The aim of BMI in such a patient is to help him shift in readiness to change without undermining your relationship with him. This involves exchanging information carefully, and without increasing his resistance through prescribing solutions or imposing derogatory labels on him.

A technique for doing this is the "elicit-provide-elicit" model (Rollnick, Butler & Allison 2001), which you can implement as follows:

- **Elicit** the potential relevance of the information, for example

- "Would you like to know more about exercise and diabetes?"
- "How much do you know about your cholesterol level?"

- **Provide** the information in a neutral way, for example
  - "What happens to some people is ..."
  - "Other people find that ..."

- **Elicit** the possible impact of the information, for example
  - "What do you make of this/these results?"
  - "How have you been affected by ...?"

The final elicit is important in getting your patient to process and personalise the information for himself. This approach may also enable him to obtain more relevant information, rather than the standard "lecture" on losing weight or stopping smoking.

Contemplation

The contemplative patient is pulled in two directions. On the one hand he enjoys, or benefits from, his behaviour, but on the other hand he has some concerns about the negative consequences of not changing. He has *mixed* motivation to change.

In BMI your aim is to help your patient to examine and evaluate his ambivalence and for him to make a more conscious decision about change. The purpose of the skills is to develop awareness of the discrepancy between the patient's current behaviour and his goals and values, to explore the importance of change and to enhance his self-efficacy, and not to manipulate him into agreeing with an agenda that only you have devised.

Your questions at this stage should be designed to help him describe and become conscious of his ambivalence (Rollnick et al. 2001). For example, further to your scaling questions, you can ask him: "You said that it was fairly important to you personally to change. Why have you scored 6 and not 1?" or "What would have to happen for your score to move from 6 to 9? What stops you moving from 6 to 9?"

Alternatively, you could ask more general questions on pros and cons, such as: "What are the good things about your smoking?" and "What are the 'less good' things about your smoking?"

Being ready to change

At this stage, your patient has a high motivation and is ready to plan and implement change. Your BMI aim here is to help him to set concrete and specific goals or targets for change. The focus is on the *practical* aspects of how to change.

You also need to discuss difficult situations that may tempt the patient to slip backwards. Suggest that he identify one supportive relationship with which he can engage to help him implement the change. Your effective communication skills here will help you to build his confidence.

Brainstorm with him in a collaborative process of deciding on possible actions and then identifying a few specific actions that are realistic and feasible. This recognises that there are usually several possible actions, and while you can advise what has worked for other people, ultimately it is the patient who must commit to a course of action that he has chosen for himself. Try to set a concrete target for the agreed action, for example he may want to lose weight by eating less fatty foods – the specific target could be not to buy full-fat milk.

Do not push him into agreeing to change if he is not ready. Remember that it may be sufficient to shift the person's readiness to change and that the counselling session itself may enable the patient to take action after the consultation.

Maintenance and relapse

Even after the patient has made a change successfully, ongoing supportive relationships and attention to potentially difficult situations that could induce a relapse are helpful to maintain the change. Relapse is common and should not be framed as being a permanent or total failure by you or a reason to wallow in guilt, blame and shame by the patient. Relapse is more constructively framed as being temporary, a normal part of changing behaviour and an opportunity to learn how change can be more successful the next time. Start by reassessing the patient's readiness to change. Eventually a permanent change is possible although it may take more than one attempt.

137 How to break bad news

BOB MASH

Family physicians often have to break bad news regarding HIV status, cancer, pregnancy complications, and chronic or life-threatening illness. Sometimes, what is everyday news to you is devastatingly bad news for your patient. Your ability to break bad news in a supportive way builds on the generic consultation skills for explanation and planning discussed in Chapter 134. In addition, you should have a conscious and carefully structured approach to this specific task.

Table 137.1 outlines the key elements involved in the process of breaking bad news (Silverman, Kurtz & Draper 1998: 136–141).

Table 137.1 Skills necessary for breaking bad news

General action	Specific actions
Preparing	If possible, you should prepare for the consultation by ensuring that you have all the relevant information, that you have considered who else should be there to support the patient, and that you have ensured that there will be no interruptions and sufficient time.
Setting the scene	Summarise the chain of events leading to this consultation and ensure that you and your patient have the same understanding of this, as well as of the purpose of the consultation. Assess your patient's prior understanding, in other words, what he already knows, is thinking or has been told. Enquire what has happened since his last visit. Gauge how he is feeling.
Sharing the information	Give a warning that difficult information is coming. For example: "I'm afraid that it looks more serious than we had hoped …" Share the basic information simply, directly and honestly. Do not allude to the bad news in a vague manner but come to the point in good time. Relate the explanation to the patient's perspective. Do not overwhelm him with too much information. Check his understanding. Use language carefully. For example, he may interpret "a positive HIV test result" as a good result, which is the opposite of what is intended.
Being sensitive to the patient	Allow time for him to "shut down" after receiving the bad news – he may be temporarily unable to listen to anything else you may have to say because he is shocked and emotional. Watch for the non-verbal responses of silence, loss of eye contact and anger. Encourage him to express his feelings by asking him: "How does that news make you feel?" Demonstrate empathy and acceptance. If he can ask questions and voice concerns, specifically elicit and respond to these. Try to gauge how much he wishes to know as you proceed. Check for his understanding and interpretation of the information. For example, he may see HIV infection as an immediate death sentence. Do not be afraid to show emotion. Even if he has a family member or friend present, do not let your focus stray from him.
Planning and supporting	Help the patient to break down overwhelming feelings into manageable concerns that he can address now or in the future. Identify a plan and a way forward within a broad timeframe. If possible, give hope that is not unrealistic. Show your willingness to ally yourself with him by saying: "We will work on this together."
Following up and closing	Do not rush the patient to make decisions. Set up an early follow-up appointment. Identify a supportive relationship. Offer to see his spouse or relatives as well.

138 How to develop a counselling style

BOB MASH

In family practice consultations there may be many times when you can appropriately adopt a counselling style, for example when understanding psychosocial problems. Being able to briefly adopt the style is part of the flexibility in your communication skills that you need as a family physician. However, some physicians have a particular interest in becoming counsellors and may engage in special training as well as setting aside times for these sessions that are separate from their normal consultations.

Principles

There are many principles that characterise a counselling style and act as the foundation of specific skills (Gibson, Swartz & Sandenbergh 2002). We will now explore them in more detail.

Knowing yourself

Your personal experience can be a source of useful knowledge, compassion and motivation to help. But it can also create personal distress and an overly sympathetic response when your patient evokes painful memories of your own. Self-awareness and the ability to reflect on your responses are therefore highly important.

Empathic responses demonstrate your understanding of your patient's thoughts and feelings, and are an important aspect of counselling. By contrast, **sympathetic** responses may involve your immersion in the same thoughts and feelings as your patient and can erode your ability to help.

Listening

Your ability to hear is essential to the counselling process, but your ability to listen deeply and attentively is often difficult to achieve and sustain. You can enable listening by creating a safe and supportive setting that is private and confidential, has comfortable seating and is without interruption.

The process of attentive listening communicates respect and it values the patient's narrative,

thoughts and feelings. Your attentive listening can provide a space in which he can make sense of his thoughts and feelings, and resolve his problems.

Specific skills that will assist you here are as follows:

- Being comfortable with silence
- Using open-ended questions
- Using verbal and non-verbal facilitative responses, for example nodding, making eye contact, saying "Go on"
- Summarising your understanding
- Asking for clarification when appropriate
- Listening reflectively, that is, offering reflective listening statements based on your understanding, which may help the patient to make sense of his situation

Coping with feelings

Patients who need counselling are often beset by emotions that they can no longer contain or manage alone. You may need to contain these emotions by reflecting them back in a more manageable way, or "holding" them until the patient is more able to cope.

Furthermore, counselling inevitably evokes emotions in you that *also* need recognition, understanding and self-awareness. At times, your feelings are useful clues to what is happening with your patient. And sometimes it is necessary for us all to live with uncertainty and the "messiness" of feelings that are difficult to understand. If you are involved in counselling you may need to turn to colleagues for help with understanding your reactions and feelings.

Occasionally, you might have to give your patient a sense of security or safety by offering him guidance, or you may even have to confront him, but it is more likely that you will have to fight the temptation to offer advice or solutions to the problem. If you have been trained to fix or cure problems, taking action may feel better to you than having to cope with strong emotion.

Understanding transference and counter-transference

Transference refers to feelings related to a significant person from the past that are attributed to another relationship, usually in the present. Understanding transference enables you to appreciate how your patient sees you and interprets your actions. This means that feelings or reactions the patient has for you as his counsellor may be due to his unconsciously associating you with, say, his mother or father and then following patterns of feelings and reactions from this past relationship in the present doctor–patient relationship.

Counter-transference refers to the feelings that a patient evokes in you, which may be related to your issues or work situation, or could originate from the patient himself. Being aware of this means that you are no longer unconsciously controlled by it and can make choices about how you respond.

Being aware of cultural diversity

You need to be aware of your values and beliefs, and the existence of prejudice. Expect that others will not necessarily see life in the way that you do, and that their perspective is real for them. You should be able to accept the viewpoint of another without necessarily agreeing with it. Try to maintain a spirit of curiosity and appreciation of cultural difference, and do not be afraid to ask for clarification of how others view life.

Specific medical situations

There are several specific medical situations that are associated with the need for counselling. These include the following:

- Pre- and post-test counselling for HIV/AIDS
- Pre- and post-termination of pregnancy (TOP) counselling
- Situations of physical, sexual or emotional abuse
- Traumatic experiences
- Problems of life and relationships

These situations are complex and may necessitate communication skills from other areas, such as informed consent (see Chapter 140), motivating behaviour change (see Chapter 136), breaking bad news (see Chapter 137) and exchanging the correct amount and type of information (see Chapter 134). The principles and skills of communicating in all these areas are complementary, and add to the flexibility and range of responses of which you need to be capable.

We will now pay attention to the first of these situations.

Pre- and post-test counselling for HIV/AIDS

Because these counselling sessions have become common, they have also become highly structured. Be aware of the risk of seeing them as a checklist of issues to be covered, which loses sight of the patient as an individual with his own thoughts, feelings and circumstances.

The following issues are usually seen to be needing discussion or attention (Wilson, Naidoo, Bekker, Cotton et al. 2002).

■ PRE-TEST COUNSELLING

In order to counsel the patient properly, you need to

- assure him of confidentiality
- negotiate explicity for the number of sessions required, depending on the result
- determine his prior knowledge and provide him with relevant information on HIV infection and transmission, and the link to AIDS, sexually transmitted infections (STIs) and TB
- provide information on the technical aspects of the test, that is the window period, how long it will take and how reliable the result is
- explore the implications of a positive or negative result. Discuss how he will cope and the pros and cons of knowing his status.
- consider together who to tell, such as sexual partners, and not to tell, such as employers, and how to do this
- evaluate his risk behaviour and how he might change it to reduce his risk of infection
- identify his support system
- determine if he is ready to consent to the test. If so, document this. Do not apply undue pressure for the test, and respect his decision against it.
- contain his emotional reactions regarding his relationships and situation by acknowledging, holding and reflecting them back in a way that fosters understanding and coping.

■ POST-TEST COUNSELLING IN A POSITIVE RESULT

To provide correct counselling, you should initially do the following:

- Break the bad news appropriately (see Chapter 137).
- Contain the patient's immediate reaction.
- Respond to his immediate concerns and questions.
- Contract with him to attend the next session.
- Discuss how he will cope until then.

Later, you should do the following:

- Contain his emotions.

- Respond to his concerns and questions.
- Remind him about the need to disclose to his partner(s).
- Discuss the need for staging of his infection and the type of treatment that is available or appropriate (including antiretrovirals).
- Consider health promotion in relation to diet, exercise, rest, smoking, alcohol and drugs.

- Consider the need for family planning.
- Discuss safe sex and risk reduction.

■ **POST-TEST COUNSELLING IN A NEGATIVE RESULT**

You need to discuss the window period and motivate behaviour change (see Chapter 136) to reduce risk of infection in the future.

139 How to work with an interpreter

BOB MASH

With 11 official languages in South Africa the need for interpretation in consultations is common. However, it is rare for people to be specifically employed or trained as interpreters and often whoever is available is called upon to help. This may be the cleaner, the student nurse, the clerk, a relative of the patient or even another patient.

This situation can be fraught with problems, as staff members resent being taken away from their work, relatives have their own ideas and perspectives, and the use of other patients breaks confidentiality. Moreover, key parts of the dialogue may be lost in translation. Ideally, therefore, you should do the following:

- At least learn enough of the local language to be able to greet your patient, take a basic history and follow the content of an interpreted consultation (Ellis 1999). This does not necessarily mean consulting without an interpreter.
- Try to work with one interpreter with whom you can form a good working relationship.

Teamwork

If you can work regularly with one person, it is important for the two of you to become an effective team. We will now discuss the four models of teamwork, according to Wood (1993).

Interpreter as interviewer

In this situation the interpreter conducts the interview himself, under your general guidance. For example, you could provide your interpreter with a questionnaire on depression and ask him to interview the patient in another room. Alternatively you may indicate to the interpreter the topic you want addressed and leave it up to him to conduct the mini-inquiry. For example, you might ask: "What social grants are this family receiving?"

Interpreter as your instrument

In this situation you would try to remain in control as much as possible. You need the interpreter to translate word for word what you say and what the patient says. The disadvantage of this model is that it leaves no room for the interpreter to use his knowledge of the patient's or your culture and context. A literal translation may not adequately, or even correctly, convey the meaning of what was said. The interpreter may also resent being used in such a mechanistic manner.

Interpreter as culture broker

In this model the interpreter is given freedom to try to convey the meaning of what is said in a way that is sensitive to the culture and context of both the patient and yourself. Over-identification with either, however, may put pressure on the interpreter. In an example of this model, you could ask the interpreter to explore whether the patient is depressed in whatever way is appropriate, rather than asking him to directly translate the question: "Are you feeling depressed?"

Interpreter as patient advocate

Here the interpreter feels compelled to protect the patient from inappropriate demands or expectations that he perceives you to make.

Ideally, a partnership or teamwork approach is preferable where you and the interpreter recognise and respect each other's complementary skills and expertise.

Presence and use of the interpreter

Interpreters play a "third-person role" in the doctor–patient relationship. The quality of his relationship with you and with the patient may therefore impact significantly on the doctor–patient relationship. For example, if the interpreter knows the patient socially or has a particular attitude towards him or his problems, this may influence what is said or how it is interpreted. Alternatively, if you and the interpreter are in conflict, or the interpreter is distracted by his own issues, the impact will also be negative.

It is important that you try to have an open and honest relationship with your interpreter so that both of you can address any problems that arise.

Bear in mind that misunderstandings in translation do occur and may include omissions, incorrect additions and substitutions, and condensations of what was intended. Emotional, anatomical and technical terms are particularly prone to misunderstanding. However, using an interpreter does not necessarily mean that your patient-centred consultation will be less effective. Indeed, your patient may appreciate the use of an interpreter more than you, and therefore you should not hesitate to use an appropriate interpreter even if this makes you feel less "in control" or breaks the flow of your usual style.

140 How to obtain informed consent

KEYMANTHRI MOODLEY

Ethical basis for consent

Ethically, you need to obtain your patient's informed consent to a procedure or administration of a drug because

- you should **respect his autonomy**, that is his right to decide for himself
- you should **practise beneficence**, that is your duty to "do good".

Legal basis for consent

- The National Health Act 61 of 2003: Chapter 2, Section 6.

  (1) Every health care provider must inform a patient of

  (a) the patient's health status except in circumstances where there is substantial evidence that disclosure of the patient's health status would be contrary to the patient's best interests;

  (b) the range of diagnostic procedures and treatments options generally available;

  (c) benefits, risks, costs and consequences generally associated with each option;

  (d) the patient's right to refuse health services and explain the implications, risks, obligations of such refusal.

  (2) The health care provider must, where possible, inform the patient in a language that the patient understands and in a manner that takes into account the patient's level of literacy.

- Assault – if a procedure or operation is performed without consent, it may result in a charge of battery or assault in keeping with criminal law and based on intent.

- Negligence – a claim of negligence can be made against a health care worker if a procedure/operation is performed without consent.

The process

Obtaining informed consent is not an event that you can complete in a few minutes. Neither is it merely a patient's signature taken by the nurse or medical student just prior to an operation or procedure.

Obtaining informed consent is a process that comprises certain elements, which we will now discuss in detail (adapted from Beauchamp & Childress 1994).

Threshold

The factors include the following:

- **Competence:** The patient should be competent enough to understand and make a decision.

- **Voluntariness:** He should give consent voluntarily and not by being coerced. In the research setting, a patient should not be bribed with money or gifts to participate, as this constitutes an unfair inducement and impairs voluntary participation.

Information

The factors include the following:

- **Disclosure:** The patient needs to know all the potential pros and cons of the procedure.

- **Recommendation:** If asked, tell the patient what you would recommend.

- **Understanding:** Ensure that he understands the information you have given him.

Consent

The factors include the following:

- **Decision:** The patient must decide whether he is against or in favour of your plan of action.

- **Authorisation:** He must authorise the plan.

Timing

Pre-test counselling for HIV testing is an excellent example of the informed consent process. However, such a process should apply to other diseases, tests and procedures as well.

Your examination of a patient, especially a sensitive examination such as vaginal, breast and prostate exams, should be preceded by your obtainment of verbal informed consent from your patient, as should your disclosure of a diagnosis on a medical certificate. As mentioned above, failure to gain this consent may lead to assault or negligence charges being laid against you.

Patient's capacity to consent

The capacity of a patient to give consent is a prerequisite to the consent process. To ascertain this, you need to assess his cognitive ability, as well as his ability to identify information that will be relevant to his decision. Other factors include exclusion of psychiatric illness such as a psychosis that will impair his ability to process information and take a decision. Remember, not every patient with a psychiatric diagnosis lacks the capacity to give consent.

A highly significant issue that relates to capacity is the patient's maturity. Generally, a child lacks the capacity to give consent independently of a parent or adult caregiver. In South Africa, according to the Child Care Act 74 of 1983, children under the age of 14 years cannot give consent without the permission of parents/guardians/caregivers. A child of seven years or older may assent to treatment or research in conjunction with parental consent. Children older than 14 years may consent independently to medical treatment, including HIV testing.

The only exceptions in which HIV testing *may* be conducted *without* consent include the following:

- Testing of an unconscious patient, whose diagnosis is material to his further medical management
- In the event of a needle-stick injury, where a pre-existing sample of blood is available and the patient refuses to consent to a further sample of blood being drawn for HIV testing
- HIV testing that is anonymous and unlinked in the research setting. Testers use left-over blood drawn for other purposes and do not link identifiers to the sample. *Only* HIV testing may be done – no other research may be linked to the test results. Note that linked anonymous HIV testing *does* require consent.

Where contraception is concerned, the consenting patient should be older than 14 years. Prescription of contraception to a girl under the age of 14 years is an ethical decision which depends on the context of the specific case.

Patients over the age of 18 years may consent to surgical treatment independently.

According to the Choice on Termination of Pregnancy Act 92 of 1996, a female of *any age* may consent independently to a termination. Consent of parents, partners or spouses is not required for TOP. If there is surgical intervention and the patient is under the age of 18 years, parental consent is required.

The Human Tissue Act 65 of 1983 indicates that a patient 14 years or older may consent to the donation of blood and organ(s) with the consent of two witnesses. This may be verbal or written. A person of any age may consent to a blood transfusion.

According to the National Health Act 61 of 2003, section 7, if a patient is unable to consent (for example the patient lacks the capacity to consent or is unable to consent for other reasons), such consent may be given by a person who is

(a) mandated by the patient in writing to grant consent on his/her behalf; or

(b) authorised to give consent in terms of any law or court order.

If no person is mandated or authorised to give consent, it may be given by the spouse or partner, a parent, grandparent, adult child, brother or sister – in the order indicated.

Types of consent

Informed consent may be verbal, written or tacit by conduct.

While verbal and written consent are recognised legally as equal, verbal consent is difficult to prove in the event of a dispute. You need to obtain written informed consent in order to be able to perform invasive procedures, including minor and major surgery, as well as in order to be able to conduct research.

It is your primary duty as the patient's doctor to obtain the proper consent.

141 How to consult with the "difficult" patient

CHRIS ELLIS

The so-called "perfect" patient presents with only one, easily solvable complaint, such as the classic features of thyrotoxicosis or diabetes, which you diagnose with appropriate intellectual acumen. The patient is grateful for your efforts and, most importantly, on leaving immediately pays your account in cash.

By contrast, the so-called "difficult" patient is complicated, disorganised, slow, indecisive and, from your point of view, non-compliant. He can be angry, and he can be a hypochondriac.

The case of this type of patient is not only about treating and curing, but also about managing, listening and caring. The consultations that you have with him are frequently repetitive, as the difficult patient tends to gravitate to one or two doctors in the practice or unit.

Here follows this author's personal way of handling a difficult patient:

- I acknowledge to myself that I am dealing with a lifelong relationship that will present many challenges to my sense of worth and to my patience.

- Sometimes only I will find a patient to be difficult, while my colleagues may not. On the whole, however, most difficult patients are difficult to all practitioners in the unit. Nevertheless, if I take a personal dislike to, or have a prejudice against, a patient, I need to recognise and deal with this.

- I remind myself that, phenomenologically, this patient is suffering in a different experiential way to those I normally encounter within the biomedical model. This leads me to the definitions of what it means to be a patient and what are illness, disease and suffering. I try to place myself in the patient's world, otherwise known as the "patient-centred approach". The issue concerns role definition -- I must accept that my role as a physician includes having to deal with a difficult patient.

- I build up a picture of him by writing down everything he says. Some colleagues of mine use computers, others use genograms. The method is less important than the content.

- I examine him and either take the blood pressure, test his urine or do a finger-prick blood glucose test. It is a confirming process for the patient. Normal results expressed to the patient are important. Reassurance that there is no cancer or TB or serious disease is as therapeutic as medication.

- At times, listening and witnessing is sufficient treatment.

- The difficult patient frequently cannot manage his time properly. It is best to arrange for several more follow-up visits than I would for an "easier" patient. I will need most of them, some of which he may not attend or may postpone, in order to collect all his information in preparation for a management plan.

- When I suggest a behaviour change to the patient and he tells me all the reasons why he cannot do it, I resolve to accept his decision but also to try again to a reasonable degree.

- While I do not favour labelling a patient, I find that most difficult patients appear to have a personality disorder or a somatisation disorder. I explore this – it often helps me to know whether I am dealing with intractable psychopathology.

142 How to cope with stress and avoid burnout

IAN COUPER

Stress

Stress is a reaction to external or internal factors that put pressure on or exceed a person's coping abilities and adaptive resources.

Sources of job stress in family practice include the following:

- Heavy workloads
- Fatigue
- Time on call
- The demands on one's time of balancing patients with other responsibilities
- Conflicts between work and personal life
- Dealing with emergencies, death and dying
- Uncertainty and error
- Demands made by patients, and dealing with patient consumerism
- Financial pressures of balancing the caring professional and the sensible business person
- Information explosion; struggling to stay up to date
- Coping with paperwork and administration
- Personality factors

Common results of stress include depression and other mental illness, suicide, alcoholism and drug abuse, physical illness, marital disharmony and social isolation, decreasing satisfaction with work and burnout.

Coping with stress

According to Hilfiker (1987), "the first step is to allow ourselves to know we can't do it all. Recognising our own limitations, we can begin to tailor our work to our own individual gifts. Second, we must recognise that we cannot deal with the stresses of our work alone".

Personal growth is essential to coping with stress. General requirements for this are as follows (Quill & Williamson 1990):

- Self-awareness – personal self-exploration to understand your limitations and develop new strengths
- Sharing of feelings and responsibilities – dealing with powerful emotions and complex conflicts in a safe environment
- Self-care – paying attention to physical and emotional needs
- Developing a personal philosophy – prioritising values and goals

Burnout

Burnout is a state of physical, emotional and mental exhaustion caused by excessive and/or prolonged stress. It is related to unrealistically high personal aspirations and expectations, and impossible goals.

Early warning signs of burnout include:

- Loss of "vision" – no sense of purpose
- Lack of focus – being "all over the place"
- Decreased efficiency – taking longer to do the same amount of work
- Depleted inner resources – difficulty in dealing with emotional issues, conflict, etc
- Irritability – with patients, colleagues, other health workers
- Insecurity – feeling uncertain and unsupported
- Mistakes – increasing rate of error
- Blaming others – not taking responsibility

Preventing burnout

The following "P" activities may help you to prevent burnout:

- **People:** Sharing problems, thoughts, feelings, symptoms, etc. with others:
  - Partners, friends and family
  - Peers, that is trusted colleagues
  - Practitioners, that is your own GP/physician

– Professional help, that is seeing a psychologist or counsellor

- **Physical care:** Ensuring sufficient sleep, a balanced diet, alcohol in moderation, exercise, relaxation, sex
- **Pursuits outside of medicine:** Having a hobby, doing sports, pursuing cultural interests, etc.
- **Private reflection:** Writing in a journal, meditating, etc.
- **Purpose:** Defining your direction, and setting and seeking goals
- **Prayer:** Developing your spiritual dimension

However, if you already suffer from burnout, you need to

- rest completely for a sufficient period of time
- consult your family physician or other medical specialists, a psychiatrist and/or psychologist
- negotiate with your employer regarding time off and future commitments
- notify your impairment (see Chapter 155) to the Committee for Health, Medical and Dental Professional Board, HPCSA
- remember, **self-care is not selfish**.

Family-orientated care

143 How to assess family structure and resources

JULIA BLITZ-LINDEQUE

A genogram

A genogram is a pictorial representation of three generations of a family. It is different from a family tree in that it additionally contains a record of the family structure, organisation, relationship patterns and personal data.

It is a useful tool that allows you to systematically and progressively gather information about your patient's family context and relationships. You can then use it to elicit the patterns of illness throughout your patient's family, to encourage his involvement in the resolution of his problems and to draw attention to the need for preventive care.

Drawing a genogram

There are certain standard methods and symbols that you need to use when drawing a genogram, as are illustrated below. Draw older generations at the top of the page, while drawing younger generations progressing downwards. Show siblings in decreasing age from left to right.

It is important that you include the names of individuals, dates of important events – such as births, marriages, deaths – diagnosis of significant illnesses, occupation, etc. You may find it useful to circumscribe those members who constitute a household. There are also ways for you to depict the relationships between members in terms of closeness, distance or conflict (see Figure 143.1).

Standard symbols

The symbols are as follows:

□	male
○	female
△	pregnancy/foetus
⊤ (filled)	spontaneous abortion
⊤ (x)	induced abortion

▢	index patient (male)
⊠	deceased male
⋀	fraternal twins
△	identical twins
⊤A □	adopted male
⊤F □	fostered male
⎿‾‾⎾	married
⎿‾/‾⎾	separated
⎿‾//‾⎾	divorced
⎿------⎾	not married, living together

Relationship lines

The lines are as follows:

════	close relationship
++++++	conflictual relationship
═══	enmeshed relationship
⟶	dominant relationship
─┤ ├─	estranged relationship
--------	distant relationship

An ecomap

This is a way in which you can visually depict the social environment in which your patient or his family find themselves. It illustrates his and/or his family's "ecology", that is the study of organisms in relation to their environment.

With this map, you can enable your patient to see his part in a system that consists of supports, roles, duties, activities and so on.

Drawing an ecomap

Place your patient/his family/his household inside a

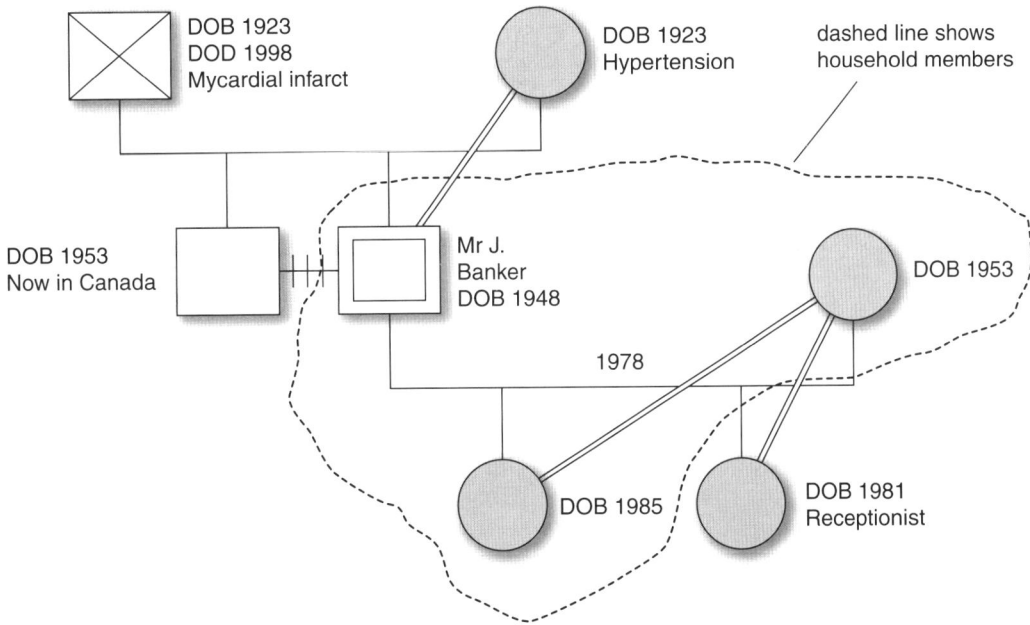

Figure 143.1 A genogram

circle. Surround this circle with a number of smaller circles that represent resources of importance in the patient's or the family's life, which have an impact on his or his family's functioning, for example:

- Extended family
- Social circle
- Cultural and recreational activities
- Religion (rituals, traditions, beliefs)

- Educational activities
- Economic status and occupation
- Medical status

Connect these to the central circle by means of lines showing the degree of support given to or received from each and indicating the direction of the "flow of support".

Figure 143.2 shows an example of an ecomap.

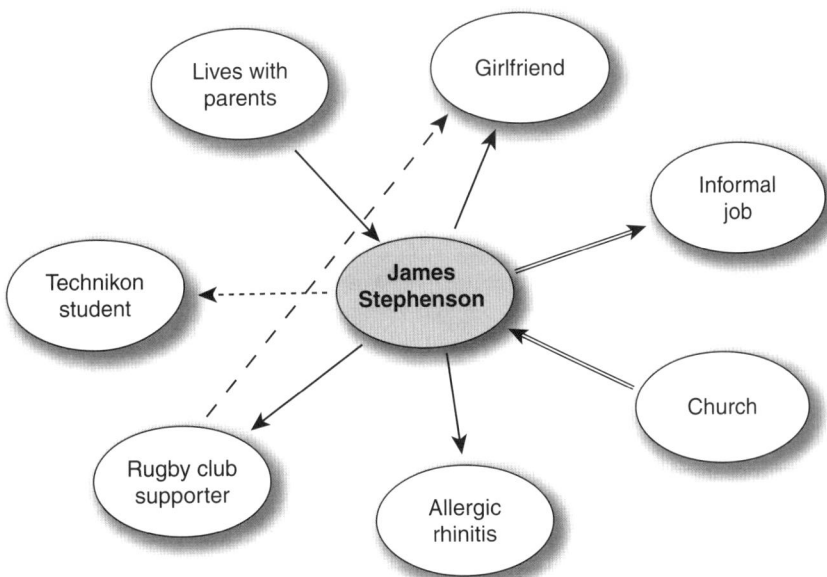

Figure 143.2 An ecomap

144 How to assess family function

JULIA BLITZ-LINDEQUE

You can use the family APGAR questionnaire presented as Table 144.1 to measure your patient's satisfaction with the amount of family support that he receives.

Table 144.1 Family APGAR

APGAR	Situation	Almost always = 2	Some of the time = 1	Hardly ever = 0
Adaptation	How resources are shared; or the patient's satisfaction with the assistance he receives when family resources are needed: "I am satisfied that I can turn to my family for help when something is troubling me."			
Partnership	How decisions are shared; or his satisfaction with mutuality in family communication and problem solving: "I am satisfied with the way my family talks things over with me and shares problems with me."			
Growth	How nurturing is shared; or his satisfaction with the freedom available within the family to change roles and attain physical and emotional growth or maturation: "I am satisfied that my family accepts and supports my wishes to take on new activities or directions."			
Affection	How emotional experiences are shared; or his satisfaction with the intimacy and emotional interaction within the family: "I am satisfied with the way my family expresses affection and responds to my emotions, such as anger, sorrow or love."			
Resolve	How time is shared; or his satisfaction with the time commitment that has been made to the family by its members: "I am satisfied with the way my family and I share time together."			

It has been proposed that an APGAR score of 7 to 10 suggests a highly functional family; a score of 4 to 6 suggests a moderately dysfunctional family; and finally, a score of 0 to 3 suggests a severely dysfunctional family.

Pless and Satterwhite (1973, p. 613–20) designed a self-administered questionnaire by means of which troubled families can be identified. This is presented as Table 144.2.

Table 144.2 Self-administered questionnaire

Aspect of life	Exploratory question	Assessment
Marital satisfaction	Describe how you feel about certain aspects of marriage, for example standard of living, love and affection, companionship	Disappointed, satisfied, enthusiastic
Frequency of disagreement	Would you say disagreements in your household come up more often, about the same, or less often than in other families you know?	More, same, less
Happiness	Would you say that your family is happier than most others you know, about the same, or less happy?	Happier, same, less
Communication	Do you find your spouse an easy person to talk to when something is troubling you?	Yes, sometimes, no
Weekends together	What sort of things do you do as a family at the weekend?	Many things, some things, nothing
Problem solving	Did you discuss with your spouse the most important problem you as a family had to deal with during last year?	Yes, no

As this is a self-administered questionnaire, it is used as a tool to help patients reflect on the aspects of their family life that are important for good family functioning.

145 How to hold a family conference

JULIA BLITZ-LINDEQUE

Indications

It is especially useful for you to call a family conference in the following situations:

- An acute health crisis with a high probability of serious disability
- A slowly evolving health crisis
- When there are treatment choices to be made
- When life-sustaining measures need to be decided upon
- In order to facilitate lifestyle changes in cases of chronic illness
- To improve adherence
- When the family is going through a transitional point in its life cycle, for example pregnancy or adolescence
- In diagnostic problems that are complicated by severe dementia or pain, or depression
- In the case of substance abuse
- In the case of child or adolescent management problems

Pre-conference tasks

You will ensure the success of the conference if you gather the information that you know about the family and build on it in order to develop appropriate goals and strategies for the conference.

Follow this procedure:

- **Set the stage – make contact with the family:**
  - Choose your contact person. This would usually be the patient, unless he is mentally incapable of coping with this, in which case choose another adult family member.
  - Establish the purpose of the meeting and discussion. It should be clear and non-threatening to the patient and his family.
  - Identify the people in his network who will attend, that is who are relevant to the issue at hand.
  - Set the appointment time and duration.

- **Review the genogram – assess what is currently known about the issue at hand:**
  - Prepare or revise the genogram, based on your contact with the patient.
  - Note his life cycle stage.
  - Note his family's life cycle stage.

- **Develop hypotheses – surmise how the family is functioning in terms of the issue at hand:**
  - Set your medical goals for the conference.
  - Develop tentative hypotheses that you will test, which are based on the information available to you in the chart, from speaking to the patient and/or family members, from how the family has coped in the past, and so on. The formulation of a hypothesis is crucial to the conference because it puts you in the active position of having to identify relational patterns. This prevents the family from "scripting" its own conference to designate the "guilty" or "crazy" member.
  - Develop a strategy for conducting the conference. Be aware of specific questions that you want to ask or tasks that you want to accomplish.
  - Remember to be open to the development of *new hypotheses* during the conference, if necessary.

Conference tasks

Follow this procedure:

- **Socialise:**
  - Greet the family. Introduce yourself to and greet each member of the family, including all the children, and invite them to sit wherever they would like. This conveys the fact that you acknowledge the importance of every family member. It allows you to gain some insight into family alliances and disassociations by observing the way in which they seat themselves.

- Orientate the family in the room. Invite the children to play with the toys. Remember to obtain consent if you wish to record the conference.

- Help the family to feel comfortable. Do not introduce problem identification too early, and do not encourage expression of emotions until you have established where and how individual members fit into the system.

- Engage with each family member. Establish demographic details about each person and attempt to convey your respect for him or her by reflecting his or her strengths. Make a particular effort with those who may be distant or uncomfortable. Be aware of non-verbal communication. Be sensitive to any feelings of guilt or blame.

- **Set the goals:**
  - Clarify the reason for the meeting.
  - Elicit each person's ideas of the problems in the family, but do not force anyone to contribute. You could invite each person to describe a relationship or event, as he or she sees it, between two other family members. This is known as the "triadic model". Give this opportunity equally to each member in order to maintain the perception of neutrality in the eyes of the family, and to avoid the perception of building alliances. Allow each member a chance to contribute, if he or she wants to, before encouraging discussion or response from others.
  - If necessary, translate the idea into a clear, concise, realistic goal for the conference.
  - Write the goals up on a board to encourage participation and endorsement.
  - Propose any goals that you feel are important that have not been mentioned, and ensure that the family is ready to deal with these.
  - Set the priority goals for this conference.

- **Discuss the impact of problems or issues:**
  - Remain focused on these priority goals.
  - Solicit each member's view of the issues and their impact on his or her life. Help them to be specific, encourage clarification of thought, do not offer interpretations, do not allow persistent interruptions, be aware of disagreements among family members and affirm the importance of each contribution. During this phase the family demonstrates its style of interaction, its roles and its dynamics.
  - Encourage members to ask questions. Share information with them on the basis of what they want to know.
  - Ask how the family dealt with similar problems in the past.

- **Identify resources:**
  - Ask the members to identify family resources and strengths. This is a supportive exercise for the family and limits the search for resources outside of it. It allows you to understand the family's coping style and their health belief system.
  - Identify medical resources. Enable the family to have realistic expectations of what can be provided.
  - Identify community resources.

- **Establish a plan:**
  - Clarify each person's role.
  - Solicit the family's plan. Each person can suggest one thing that he or she wants to change.
  - Negotiate a "contract" that is acceptable to the family, which consists of what each family member will do and what you will do, if referral is necessary, or if a follow-up appointment is required.
  - Check for any further questions.

- **Conclude:**
  - Reiterate family strengths.
  - Move towards constructive solutions and problem-solving strategies.
  - Reinforce members' feelings of competency and unity.
  - Legitimise the need for expression of differences.
  - Encourage a tolerance for uncomfortable feelings.
  - Accept anger.

Post-conference tasks for the doctor

It is important for you to review the conference to see if the goals devised therein have been met and to record the treatment plan in the patient's notes.

Follow this procedure:

- **Revise the genogram:**
  - Make any corrections or additions that arose from the conference.

- **Revise the pre-conference hypotheses:**
  - Adapt your hypotheses according to the information obtained in order to plan further treatment.

- **Write the conference report:**
  - Note who attended, and who did not (and why not).
  - List the problems that the family expressed as well as those issues still of concern to you.

– Make a global assessment of the family functions, that is family structure, family process
and family life cycle, and its relevant developmental challenges.

– List the family's strengths and resources.

– Formulate the treatment plan, both medical
and family.

Community-orientated care

146 How to assess patient satisfaction

DAVID BUSO

Patient satisfaction tool, or questionnaire

Measuring patient satisfaction has become an integral part of management strategies across the globe. Moreover, the quality assurance and accreditation process in most countries requires that the satisfaction of patients be measured on a regular basis.

Therefore, patient satisfaction tools have been developed, the set of indicators of which is quite comprehensive in that it includes all factors pertaining to the process of health care delivery that are identified as important to patients. An example is provided in Table 146.1. If a health facility performs well on all of these indicators it will almost certainly be satisfying its patients. This has important implications for how to make services more responsive to patients' expectations and improve satisfaction.

There is a step-by-step guide to the process and a checklist which you can use in organising the gathering of the data. The questionnaire should be well designed and administered in a scientific manner. To ensure your patient's full participation, your questionnaire must be easily understood, and it must take cognisance of the patient's ability to complete the survey while it maintains confidentiality.

There are four main components in measuring satisfaction.

Personnel

There are two important aspects that fall under this component. Firstly, the hospital needs to identify a representative from the management team whose duty it will be to manage the whole process. Secondly, a fieldworker needs to be identified who will administer the questionnaire to the patients. Management of this project will entail the following:

The manager should

- be responsible for all activities related to data collection at the hospital, including timing, recruitment of fieldworkers, overseeing fieldwork and the reporting back of the data to the hospital management team
- monitor all trends and report to management
- be available during the week when data is gathered at the hospital
- organise suitable incentives/remuneration for the fieldworker
- ensure that the same person interviews all the patients to avoid inter-fieldworker bias
- provide training for the fieldworker.

The fieldworker should

- not be an employee of the hospital
- have no family who work for the hospital
- be friendly and able to speak the local languages
- have passed matric
- be punctual and available all day long for the whole week
- keep the completed questionnaires until handing them over to the manager.

Timing

It is recommended that the questionnaire be administered

- annually or bi-annually
- from Monday to Friday, that is for one week
- from 8:30 to 16:00.

Fieldwork

There are three important aspects of the fieldwork, namely time keeping, set-up and administering the questionnaire.

■ TIME KEEPING

The fieldworker must be on site from 08:30 to 16:00 every day and cannot be late or leave early, otherwise he may miss clients leaving the hospital early, which will negatively affect the validity of the findings.

■ SET-UP

The fieldworker must try to position himself in a neutral position, that is close to the hospital gate, with tables and chairs that will make it easy for the patient to fill in the questionnaire and allow him to sit down while the fieldworker talks to him. The fieldworker must have sufficient questionnaires (± 30 a day) and pencils. The questionnaires from each day are collated and stored together.

■ ADMINISTERING THE QUESTIONNAIRE

It has been found that for clinics it will be necessary to interview at least 25 patients each day and a minimum of 150 during the week. Try to collect 25–30 patient interviews per day over the week. You may want to consult a statistician to calculate a more accurate sample size. Interview all patients, whether they are inpatients, have been visiting the clinics or are outpatients. If the patient is a child then you need to interview the adult who brought the child in.

Interview the patients as they leave the clinic or hospital, at the gate, *after* they have collected their medications. The fieldworker should

- introduce himself and then ask the client for permission to interview him
- explain that the health services want to try to improve services to all the patients
- emphasise the confidentiality of the study
- take the client through the questionnaire, explaining how it works
- ask the questions clearly as they are written, and let the patient decide his response (remember that it is the client's perception of the service that is being measured)
- thank him for his time
- number the questionnaires in consecutive order each day and date them
- place the completed questionnaires in the marked envelope.

Data analysis and report back

The manager must ensure that the data is analysed and that the trends are reported back to the hospital management.

Table 146.1 An example of a questionnaire

Directions: Based on your experiences as a patient at this hospital, please tell us whether you strongly disagree, disagree, don't know, agree or strongly agree with the following statements. Please mark your answer for each question by circling the number. For example, if you disagree with a statement you would circle 2, if you agree with the statement you would circle 4. You may only choose one answer per question. If you spent at least one night in this hospital, please will you also answer the questions in Part 2. The information on this form will be treated *confidentially*, so please do not place your name on this form. Thank you.

PART 1					
	Strongly disagree	Disagree	Don't know	Agree	Strongly agree
It takes more than 30 minutes to get to the hospital	1	2	3	4	5
It costs more than R7.00 to get to the hospital	1	2	3	4	5
The hospital is in good condition	1	2	3	4	5
The hospital is clean	1	2	3	4	5
The outpatients/casualty department has convenient hours of opening	1	2	3	4	5
The toilets are dirty	1	2	3	4	5
I had to wait a long time to get my folder	1	2	3	4	5
There was a bench for me to sit on while I waited	1	2	3	4	5
The person who gave me my folder was helpful	1	2	3	4	5
The nurse who treated me listened to my problems	1	2	3	4	5
The doctor who treated me was polite	1	2	3	4	5
I was pleased with the way I was treated at the hospital	1	2	3	4	5
The doctor explained to me what was wrong with me	1	2	3	4	5
My privacy was respected by all the staff	1	2	3	4	5
If I received medicines/pills I did not have to wait long for them	1	2	3	4	5
Next time I am ill I will come back here	1	2	3	4	5
PART 2 NB: Please complete the questions below if you have spent at least one night or more in the hospital					
	Strongly disagree	Disagree	Don't know	Agree	Strongly agree
The ward was clean	1	2	3	4	5
The bedding was clean	1	2	3	4	5
The food was good	1	2	3	4	5
Visiting hours were not long enough	1	2	3	4	5
The staff at the hospital answered all my questions about my illness	1	2	3	4	5
I was bored in the hospital	1	2	3	4	5
When I needed help at night, there was always a nurse to help me	1	2	3	4	5
I did not feel safe at night in the hospital	1	2	3	4	5
The hospital made sure I got a lift home	1	2	3	4	5
The hospital will tell my local health clinic about my future care needs	1	2	3	4	5
If my friends are sick I will tell them to come to this hospital	1	2	3	4	5

147 How to do a home visit

STEVE REID

Traditionally, home visits were an important aspect of the work of family physicians in many countries. As McWhinney (2000) comments: "We define family medicine in terms of relationships, and continuity of the patient–doctor relationship is one of our core values. How can we justify breaking our long-term relationships with patients whenever, in sickness or old age, they become housebound?"

However, the frequency of home visiting has declined over the years. The reasons for this are numerous, including rising costs, and the improvement in communications and emergency services. Nevertheless, the home visit is a *crucial* link between clinical practice and comprehensive care, creating the physical and conceptual bridge between facility-based and community-based interventions. So much insight can be gained from a single home visit that not only is the time spent justified, but also the effect on other patients is often significant.

Purpose

A home visit can be either diagnostic or therapeutic, and is often a combination of both. Whereas the ostensible reason may be that the patient cannot travel, or it is felt to be an emergency, as an experienced practitioner you may often take the opportunity to understand your patient's context better, or to demonstrate your commitment to the patient.

Types

There is a distinction between home care and house calls. **Home care** is defined as diagnosis, treatment and ongoing monitoring of your patient in his home, whereas **house calls** refer to your episodic visits for more acute problems, and are a part of home care. There are therefore two types of home visits:

1. Acute care, entailing emergencies and house calls
2. Chronic care, which involves ongoing care of chronic problems, continuing care after dis-

charge from hospital, and palliative or terminal care

Teamwork

In South Africa, home visits are rarely actually done by doctors, and there are various cadres of health and community-based workers and volunteers who visit homes, with whom you need to liaise. The team needs to be focused around the needs of the patient, and your role relates to the development and oversight of a treatment plan that may be carried out by the patient, alone or with the support of the following:

- **Family members.** They often provide the bulk of day-to-day care and also need to be supported. If they suffer from burnout the situation for the patient becomes untenable and you have another patient on your hands!
- **Home-based care workers.** Often, these are volunteers or people employed at minimal rates and supported by non-governmental or faith-based organisations, with varying degrees of expertise.
- **Community health workers.** These people are usually paid and trained by non-governmental organisations or the Department of Health.
- **Enrolled or professional nurses.**

Your functions are as follows:

- Management of medical problems
- Identification of the patient's home care needs
- Establishment and/or approval of a plan of treatment with identification of both short- and long-term goals
- Evaluation of new, acute or emergent medical problems based on information supplied by other team members
- Provision for continuity of care to and from all settings, that is institution, home and community

- Communication with the patient and other team members
- Participation, as needed, in home care/family conferences
- Evaluation of quality of care
- Reassessment of care plan and outcomes of care
- Documentation in appropriate medical records
- Provision of 24-hour on-call coverage for emergencies

Approach

Whether you suggest the visit or your patient requests it, entering a patient's home and dealing with the family is an intimate experience, one which you need to approach with due respect and consideration.

Frequently, in the rural situation in South Africa, you must deal with cross-cultural issues. Even in ethnically homogeneous communities, every interaction between yourself and a patient is, to a certain extent, a cross-cultural event: you have your own "language" and body of knowledge by which you operate, while patients use their own language and norms to understand their illnesses.

It is important that you respect the norms of your patient's culture, for example the simple acts of greeting and sitting down, and eliciting information, all require that you have prior knowledge of them in order to avoid giving offence, however unintentionally. Whereas experienced practitioners have acquired these understandings over the years, students may need to be introduced to cross-cultural issues explicitly by their tutors or local health workers.

An approach to a first-time home visit is as follows:

- **Gather information:**
  - Ask about the illness. What makes it worse? What makes it better? What started it? What could change? Assess the effect of medication or other medical interventions on the illness. What does this family do when someone is ill? Who gets involved in caring and who does not? How could this be different?
  - Explore your patient's role in the family. Explore the family's structure, dynamics and relationships, values, daily activities, educational level, sources of income and stability, support systems (that is extended family, neighbours, church or other groups and community health workers) and other resources.
  - Assess the home environment, its physical infrastructure, hygiene and sanitation, water sources, distance to schools and shops, means of transport, communications, environment, security and stability of tenure.

- **Make a "family diagnosis"**, drawing together all the important findings. It is often useful to draw a genogram or ecomap while at the home in order to elicit and summarise information about the family (see Chapter 143).

- **Make a difference** to the patient, to the family or to any other factor which influences the illness. For example, finding other family members coughing in the home of a TB patient means that you need to make plans to get the whole family screened. In another example, finding carpeted floors or pets in the home of a chronic asthmatic could suggest that specific information and action is needed for that family.

148 How to make a community diagnosis

DAVID BUSO

Definition

Of the many definitions of the term "community" in the literature and practice, we find the following the most useful. A community can be a group of people

- living together and sharing common experiences
- with diverse characteristics who are linked by social ties, share common perspectives, and engage in joint action in geographical locations or settings
- living in the same geographic area, such as a rural village or an urban neighbourhood (that is a geographic community)
- whose members interact but do not live in the same geographic area, such as religious, ethnic and occupational groups (that is a functional community).

Defining community diagnosis

Just as you make a clinical diagnosis, you need to conduct examinations and investigations in a community to make a community diagnosis. You need to select and investigate the appropriate diagnostic indicators that describe and explain the health problems in the community. The appropriate and affordable programmes that you devise as a result should effectively raise the health status of the community. For example, in a particular community in a remote rural area of the Eastern Cape, poverty, malnutrition, respiratory tract infections and diarrhoeal diseases may be important aspects of the community diagnosis, and you would propose primary health care services for this particular community.

Objectives

The objectives of a community diagnosis are as follows:

- To assess the health status of a particular community
- To identify important risk factors affecting the community

- To select effective, efficient, acceptable and affordable intervention programme(s)

Information sources

These are as follows:

- **Interviews:**
  - Members of the community
  - Key stakeholders, that is government departments, NGOs, health workers, etc.
- **Existing records and research:**
  - Annual reports
  - Clinic/hospital registers
  - Death certificates – obtained from the Department of Home Affairs
  - Previous research studies
- **Surveys** conducted for the purpose of the community diagnosis

Important indicators

These are as follows:

- **Geographic:**
  - Size in square kilometres
  - Terrain – roads, rivers, mountains, cities/towns
  - Demarcations – municipalities, health districts
- **Demographic:**
  - Size of the population – total number
  - Age groups – population pyramids
  - Racial distribution
  - Gender distribution
  - Ethnic groups
  - Religious groups
  - Fertility (growth rate)
  - Migration – immigration, emigration
  - Population distribution and density according to the geographic indicators – municipal boundaries, urban or rural
- **Health status – morbidity profile:** What are the commonest causes of morbidity at the differ-

ent levels of care, that is primary, secondary and tertiary levels? Consolidate these into broad categories, such as
- infectious
- chronic conditions
- trauma and injuries.

- **Health status – mortality profile:**
  - Child mortality rates – perinatal, post-neonatal, infant, under five
  - Adult mortality rate
  - Cause of specific mortality rate within different age groups

- **Health status – disability:** What are the causes and rates?

- **Health status – key programme outcomes:**
  - Immunisation coverage
  - Maternal mortality rate
  - Antenatal care attendance
  - Family planning attendance
  - Teenage pregnancy rate
  - Termination of pregnancy rates
  - HIV/AIDS prevalence
  - TB cure rate, multiple-drug-resistant TB (MDR-TB) case rate, etc.

- **Socio-economic:**
  - Poverty level – monthly household income and expenditure
  - Unemployment rate
  - Literacy rate and level of education
  - Housing – formal/informal, size, overcrowding.
  - Access to water and electricity
  - Availability of schools, shops, entertainment areas

- **Environmental health:**
  - Water – clean water access and availability, storage, purification plans
  - Sanitation – access and quality, hand-washing practices
  - Waste disposal – solid, infectious, toxic

- Pollution – water, air, noise
- Insects and rodents – flies, mosquitoes, rats

- **Lifestyle and habits:**
  - Smoking
  - Alcohol
  - Other drug consumption
  - Violence
  - Family instability – divorce rate, single mothers
  - Exercise

- **Health services – clinics, health centres and hospitals:**
  - Availability – number, distribution
  - Access – distance, transport, travelling costs, opening times
  - Affordability
  - Quality – client satisfaction
  - Utilisation
  - Resources – staff, equipment, maintenance, adequacy
  - Community involvement/participation

- **Health promotion and disease prevention programmes:** Are they available, adequate and meaningful?

- **Alternative health services – complementary and traditional healers:**
  - Community beliefs, attitudes, utilisation
  - Relationships with the conventional health services

- **Other community services:**
  - Schools
  - Churches
  - Recreation – sport, theatres, community halls
  - Youth programmes

- **Community structures:**
  - Traditional leaders, structures
  - Political structures – types, power, activities, influence on health services

149 How to work with community structures

MENZELELELI MSAULI

Community participation is important in planning and developing health services and tackling key community health issues. The involvement of community members, however, is often difficult to achieve and may be overlooked by health workers and managers. In order to engage with a community, it is important to firstly identify its leaders, for example through chiefs and headmen in rural areas or civic organisations in urban areas. Do not forget to also include elected officials such as ward councillors. The leadership can then call a community meeting where health issues and services can be discussed. Establish an agenda for the meeting beforehand, emphasising that the main purpose is to strengthen community participation in health and development work. Such a meeting can mandate community representatives to form a clinic health committee or help to select suitable and reliable members who are willing to serve as community health workers. In addition, community members can contribute to making a community diagnosis, as described in Chapter 148, or help to identify and prioritise health needs, as described in Chapter 150.

Community health workers

These workers should be trained in the relevant skills by an organisation which is accredited by the Health and Welfare Sector on Education and Training Authority (HWSETA). Such training leads to a national certificate in Ancillary Health Care (NQF level 1). The purpose of this training is to improve the quality of life of community members by providing improved access to and delivery of primary health care at local level within the context of an intersectoral environment. Ideally, these people should be offered incentives to motivate them in their work. Approach the health and social development departments to assist in this regard.

The key products of this training are health promotion, community development, health care education, basic mother and child care, infection control, counselling, directly observed treatment strategy (DOTS) and improved adherence to antiretrovirals (ARVs), home-based care and referrals. Those who have successfully completed the training will be certified by the South African Qualifications Authority (SAQA) and thus be employable in the health service. This is relevant job creation which promotes the communities' health and development.

Traditional health practitioners

Identify and arrange a meeting with traditional health practitioners in the community. Impress upon them that their work is appreciated and recognised. Up to 80% of black patients consult them (Kale 1995: 1182–5) and Western and traditional systems of healing are not mutually exclusive, hence the need for collaboration at the primary health care level. Mention several examples where their methods are widely used, and examples of their success in some forms of mental illness.

Traditional health practitioners have long waited to be recognised by Western biomedical health systems, which have kept them at a distance. Run workshops with them, especially around issues of sexually transmitted infections, tuberculosis, HIV/AIDS and DOTS.

150 How to prioritise a community-based intervention

STEVE REID

Since communities are complex systems and face a variety of health problems simultaneously, they are forced to compete for limited resources. Decisions regarding what, where, when and how personnel and other resources should be deployed in a given community will depend on the identification of the most important health needs.

You need to identify an appropriate group of people who can carry out the task of prioritisation with you. There may be an existing team, such as a district or sub-district health management team that is responsible for the community in which you are practising, and with whom you will be able to interact.

You must begin identifying the health priorities themselves by listing all the health issues that come to light in the community diagnosis process (see Chapter 148) and revealing the most compelling problems through an open discussion between the members of the primary care team. Brainstorming in response to the question: "What are the most important health issues in this community?" will generate a long list, which you can subsequently whittle down by applying certain criteria.

While you can identify the major causes of morbidity and mortality by analysing health status data, you cannot make these decisions in isolation of the *users* of the health system: the community itself. As Sidney Kark, the pioneer of COPC in the 1950s, suggested, we need to "explore what the community feels, thinks and does about its health needs, since interventions need to be directed towards those aspects about which people can do much themselves" (Kark & Abramson 1981: 65–70).

Thus community involvement in the stages of identification and prioritisation is essential (see Chapter 149). You should invite community representatives from formal representative structures such as local councils, and district or tribal councils to participate, along with key figures in the community, such as the ministers or school principals if appropriate. Without community involvement, any subsequent intervention is unlikely to succeed. Your inclu-

sion in the team of people affected by a high-priority health problem, for example a person living with HIV/AIDS, can greatly enhance the team's efficacy.

Criteria for prioritisation

You need to consider each identified health issue in relation to the following criteria:

1. How common is the problem? Measure this by the prevalence and incidence.
2. How serious is it? Measure this by the case fatality rate.
3. To what extent is the community concerned about it?
4. Is it feasible to intervene?
5. Will an intervention be effective?

Taking the main health issues identified in your community diagnosis, subject each of these to each of the above criteria, and weigh them up relative to one another. Each participant needs to justify their priority ranking of each issue. You could use a scoring system for each issue, and add up the total score.

Method for prioritisation

A method of prioritisation is the **nominal group technique** (Lloyd-Jones, Fowell & Bligh 1999), which entails the following steps:

- **Step 1 – Silent phase:** Give each member of the group a piece of A4 paper on which is written the specific question that you want them to think about. Ask them to write down as many ideas or responses as they can to the question. Each person should work alone and in silence for 15–20 minutes.
- **Step 2 – Item generation, or round-robin phase:** Form people into sub-groups of five or six and have each one elect a scribe. Each person then reads out one idea/response, which the scribe records on a flip chart, until all the ideas

are recorded. This ensures equal participation from everyone. No discussion or comment on the ideas is allowed at this stage.

- **Step 3 – Item clarification phase:** Each sub-group discusses the items recorded to ensure that the meaning is clear and shared by all. They can combine or edit items that duplicate or overlap, but they should not discard any items. At the end of this process they should create a clearer and shorter list of items.

- **Step 4 – Voting phase:** Each person must choose five items from the list that are most important to him or her and rank them in order of priority on a scale of 5 (most important) to 1 (least important). They write down their selection and ranking on a voting paper, all of which are then collected. Then you need to compile all the prioritised items from each sub-group into a master list, though not in rank order.

- **Step 5 – Reassembly of group phase:** The entire group now repeats steps 3 and 4 for the master list. Collect the final voting papers and analyse them to give a final ranking of the items that the group has prioritised.

Management

How to audit or improve the quality of your service

BOB MASH

Quality improvement cycle

You can improve the quality of your service using the **quality improvement (QI) cycle**, which is illustrated in Figure 151.1.

Figure 151.1 The quality improvement cycle

The QI cycle consists of four essential steps, which we will now explore in detail.

Topic

The topic should be interesting, important and amenable to change. You should include your practice team in the QI cycle from the beginning as they will have important contributions to make, they will become familiar with the process and will become allies in improving the area of care.

■ STRUCTURE, PROCESS AND OUTCOME

Consider whether the chosen topic involves the following elements:

• **Structure:** This entails defining what physical equipment, staff, tools and stationery you need to provide a high quality of care to patients.

• **Process:** This involves looking at and recording those things that are done to and with patients during their visit to the clinic in pursuit of optimal medical care of a specific condition.

• **Outcome:** This is a measure of the final effects of care on important clinical endpoints, morbidity or mortality. They can be intermediate outcomes, for example a certain blood pressure or glucose reading; or final outcomes, for example a heart attack or a stroke.

Criteria and target standards

You must create measurable target standards of care, which are a combination of two factors:

1. A criterion of care which is well defined and can be measured
2. A level of performance for that criterion

■ CRITERIA

It is important to match the criteria you create with the particular sophistication and constraints of your own work setting:

• Select criteria from all three areas of structure, process and outcome.

• Choose criteria that explore key areas of concern to the practice team.

• Create a total of five or six measurable criteria. Do not be too ambitious and set too many criteria as you will not have time to collect a massive amount of information.

• Justify why these criteria are important to you and why they are related to quality of care, using available evidence in the medical literature.

Ensure that this step also involves key members of your practice team. You need to guide and lead them to the best choices.

■ PERFORMANCE LEVEL

You can express the level of performance on a sliding scale from ideal, average, minimum to unacceptable, or as a percentage with 100% being the ideal. Note, however, that in criteria involving a negative final outcome, such as death, stroke, myocardial infarction or renal failure, the performance level might be reversed (ideally 0%), in the sense that your ideal standard might be to *avoid* this outcome. Set performance levels with your team for each of your criteria. Again, do not be too ambitious in setting your performance levels. Levels of 100% or 0% are impossible to achieve in real life, and the QI process will not motivate change. Rather set levels that provide an achievable improvement in your performance, such as slightly above the level at which you think your current level of performance is.

Data collection

A proper QI cycle requires careful consideration of bias, confounding factors, chance and sample size – as in a research project. However, you can still obtain useful information and learning even when all these methodological issues are not achieved.

Collect data to measure each criterion that you have defined. You can collect data prospectively as you see patients each day using a simple data collection sheet. You can also use retrospective data from medical records or routinely collected statistics, if they are available.

Data evaluation

You need to analyse the data that you have collected to produce results that you can easily compare to the predefined target standards. You can then compare the actual level of performance to the target level of performance and identify the strengths and weaknesses of current practice identified.

Plan and implement change

You should present your findings to your practice team and discuss the implications. You need to look at, and then implement, the changes that you can make in your practice to improve your performance and the quality of care. Also consider whether you need to modify the target standards for future use.

The QI process is not meant to be a single, isolated event. Rather, it should be a series of events which lead to your progressive improvement of quality of care over time.

Once you have reached your desired level of quality, your aim should shift to maintaining that quality.

152 How to work in a team

RICHARD OSINJOLU

A **team** is a small number of people with complementary skills, values, styles, emotions and culture who are committed to a common purpose, goals and approach for which they hold themselves mutually accountable in a free and nurturing environment (Katzenbach & Smith 1995).

The concept of a primary health care team is frequently promoted as an ideal, but often remains elusive in practice. Nevertheless, you are inevitably part of various teams with differing goals, and you may be called upon to demonstrate skills in team leadership and facilitation.

We will now consider the four stages comprising the formation and functioning of a team.

Forming stage

At this stage the team members are learning to deal with one another, and little actual work is accomplished. People may be unsure of the purpose of the team, and of their role and the roles of others therein. The atmosphere may be one of anxiety and wariness regarding possible prejudices or misconceptions that can lead to disruptive alliances and cliques in the team.

In the South African health care context the team members are often diverse, and may see the world differently owing to differences in culture, gender, age, socio-economic status, and urban or rural background. For example, the "rainbow nation" is made up of at least two mental models: the Western-material-physical or rational model, and the spiritual-soulular model that is primarily practised by African and Asian populations.

It is important for the person entering a team to clarify his values, beliefs and expectations in relation to the team. Building self-awareness enables members to know their strengths and weaknesses, as well as reduces negative interactions based on self-justification, rationalisation, hypersensitivity, blaming, fixation on the past, helplessness, social distancing, relative deprivations and stereotypes.

To help the team progress, you must reassure team members about the reasons for which they were asked to be part of the team, and encourage them to develop a sense of ownership of and responsibility towards the team. You also need to clarify the purpose of the team, as alignment with this purpose will provide cohesion and momentum in the team.

Storming stage

This is the "make or break" stage of team success. Interpersonal conflict is at its highest and it must be resolved before the team can continue to operate.

A certain amount of conflict is a positive sign in the sense that members of a team can present opposing views and ideas that allow the group to take advantage of their collective intelligence. The key to conflict management is to professionalise rather than personalise it, to look for *what* is wrong (rather than *who*) and fix it, and to empathise with each other in an environment of trust.

It is helpful for you to present your problem in an objective, not a judgemental, way by describing how it impacts on you and others and by recognising the benefit that accompanies the solution. Avoid giving ultimatums that force people to take sides. Also, be aware that making amends where appropriate is not a sign of weakness; instead, it is doing what is necessary to set the matter straight. This builds trust. Another relationship builder is giving acknowledgement and praise when it is due.

The most common source of problems in teamwork is ambiguity regarding the purpose of the team and the procedures that the team will follow. In order for people in a team to work effectively, each person must understand what is expected of him and what other members of the team will be doing to ensure that the team achieves its goals.

Norming stage

Following the upheavals of the preceding stage, the team members settle into their roles and a "team feeling" begins to develop. You know you have reached this stage when discussions focus on issues rather than personalities, and when opposing points of view are respected rather than rejected. Team members seek solutions rather than focusing on what is wrong; they work in a synergistic way and the whole becomes greater than the sum of its parts.

Now the team members should jointly create norms that govern their interactions. Using the "TEAM" approach will help you and your team-mates to work together better, to appreciate each other and to accomplish more (Gillespie 2000).

The approach leads to effective teamwork as follows (Gillespie 2000):

- **Teaching** team-mates about one another by identifying each team member's personal strengths, job skills and role on the team, and by clarifying how these roles relate to each other and the contribution to the team.
- **Empathising** with team-mates by reflective listening that attempts to understand their perspective.
- **Asking** a mixture of open, closed, clarifying and "what if?" questions to promote the exchange of ideas.
- **Motivating** team-mates by aligning them with the group's identity, leading by example and looking for ways to praise and affirm team-mates.

Team members often adopt different but important roles in the group, some examples of which are as follows (Parker 1990):

- **Contributors:** These people are task- or result-orientated and are seen as organised and dependable.
- **Collaborators:** These people are interested in the big picture and consider what they do and for whom they do it. They regularly review the team's mission, objectives and goals.
- **Communicators:** These people are process-orientated and positive. They have a "can do" attitude, and they act as the interpersonal "glue" that keeps the team together.
- **Challengers:** These people are innovative and lateral thinkers. They challenge the team's direction and prevent easy consensus and "blind spots".

Performing stage

At this stage the team is united and working on the task at hand. This phase represents a new environment in which each person is willing and able to contribute his best to achieve team objectives, and see each other as unique individuals without characterising anyone by age, gender, race or religion.

Successful participative meetings are essential for the team to communicate, cooperate and achieve objectives. Some tips for the meetings include the following (Nokwe & Mlenzana 2003):

- Select a facilitator to keep the discussion on track, to do pre-meeting planning, and to devise an agenda and time requirements.
- Improve the productivity of the meeting by defining and monitoring meeting behaviour, keeping the meeting on track, improving communications, maintaining maximum energy and increasing participation.
- Encourage creativity by spending time on reflection, learning and dialogue, as well as action. Brainstorming, which allows all ideas to flow forth without judgement, is a useful technique for stimulating creative thinking.
- Gather information in a systematic way that will help the team with the decisions they are facing, for example conducting a strengths-weaknesses-opportunities-threats (SWOT) analysis.
- Consider how the group will make decisions using, for example, the Vroom and Yelton decision-making model; multi-voting; negative voting; three for, three against; and force field analysis (Vroom & Yelton 1974).
- Moving a decision toward action includes setting specific, measurable, appropriate, realistic and time-bound (SMART) goals. Chart actions that include three categories for what should be done, by whom and by when. Break tasks down into specific activities that people can commit to and develop individual action plans.

Evaluate the efficacy of the team meeting, including recognising what went well and assessing opportunities for improvement. There are team efficacy charts that quantifiably measure specific aspects of the meeting, such as levels of communication or satisfaction with results. Decide which components of the interaction the team should measure for efficacy and rate them from 1 (hardly effective) to 5 (highly effective), as is illustrated in Figure 152.1.

You could also use a written questionnaire about the efficacy of the team meeting at the end of the meeting.

Team leadership

There will be a great demand in future for health care professionals, particularly family physicians, to mirror in their practices the changes they seek in teams and the health care industry. These changes primarily concern their power and their principles.

Powerful leadership can be seen as your capacity to mobilise resources and people to achieve objectives rather than your capacity to coerce people into working in a particular direction. If people are not accumulating access to information, resources

PLOT YOUR RESPONSE

5 (high)							
4							
3							
3							
1 (low)							
	A	B	C	D	E	F	G

Team components

A. Communication; B. Satisfaction; C. Conflict resolution;
D. Decisions; etc.

Figure 152.1 Team meeting efficacy chart

and support as they move upward, they are remaining powerless, no matter what their position. This powerlessness corrupts a team.

You should align the principles of family medicine, with their emphasis on relationship building, collaboration and partnership, to the principles of your team participation. In other words, you should seek congruency in your clinical and organisational principles.

Traditional, authentic and bad-mob teams

These types of teams can be defined as follows:

- **Traditional teams:** These are shaped by generations of people born between 1945 and 1962 who believe work is its own reward and who "lived to work", as opposed to the younger generations who tend to "work to live" (Karp, Fuller & Sirias 2002).

- **Authentic teams:** These act as a bridge between the two abovementioned generations. They focus on personal growth, meaning, freedom and a nurturing environment as a means to achieving meaningful and lasting teams, and shaping global citizens.

- **Bad-mob teams:** These are dysfunctional teams. If a problem exists in a team it is usually because there is conflict that has not been resolved, which may be owing to different views of the world of work or personal, local, community, regional, political, racial or gender interests.

Table 152.1 summarises the factors involved in, as well as the attributes of these three types of team.

Table 152.1 Team types and attributes

Team attributes	Traditional	Authentic	Bad-mob
Value	Interdependence is the key value	Individual autonomy is the key value	Independent selfish interest is the key value
Awareness	Give attention to the development of new processes to improve behaviour	Give attention to understanding existing behaviour	Lack awareness of existing behaviour
Working relationship	View good work as a result of a good working relationship	View a good working relationship as a result of doing good work together	View good work as promoting self and sabotaging others
Behaviour	Determine appropriate behaviour by conformance to team norms	Determine appropriate behaviour by individual choice within each situation	Determine appropriate behaviour as that which promotes self-interest
Conflict	Believe that conflicting values must be resolved and integrated	Believe that conflicting values must be expected, understood and managed	Believe that conflicts are personalised and better left unresolved
Decisions	Decide to either use consultative group decision making or allow leadership to make decisions	All participate in decisions and call on leaders only if they do not arrive at one	Leaders makes the decision alone, without inputs from others
Communication	Communicate openly and honestly to reach agreement on shared values	Communicate openly and honestly to understand and accept differences in views and interests	Are cautious of what they say and fear being trapped
Environment	Work in an environment of trust and encourage questions from each other	Are individualistic and work in a personalised work space with growth opportunities	Distrust the motives of colleagues and view disagreement as divisive
Culture	Reflect traditional values	Are dynamic and reflect the global trend in values and substance	Are static and resistant to change
Empowerment	Attempt to empower others	Recognise self-empowerment	Are exploited, with little or no empowerment

153 How to facilitate a small-group learning meeting

MARIETJIE DE VILLIERS

Facilitating a learning or CPD (continuing professional development) small-group meeting is different from chairing a business or management meeting. It is also quite unlike teaching a group of students.

In small-group learning, the participants acquire knowledge through a process of working on a defined problem. As the facilitator, you are likely to be a peer, and you can draw on resource materials or other people providing content expertise in the field under discussion. Remember that the group process in continuing education aims to identify learning needs, to learn through shared experience, to apply knowledge in practice, and ultimately to provide opportunity for reflection.

You need to understand the learning process and your role therein. Learning groups function best if you understand that the learner is more important than you. In a learning meeting you have two roles, namely:

1. **A group maintenance role**

   You must make sure that the group is functioning well by observing and guiding it. Give clear introduction and guidelines at the beginning. Make sure that all the members participate equally. Resolve conflict and handle emotions as they arise. Avoid dominating the group with your own ideas. Make sense of what is happening on a continuous basis. Value each contribution.

2. **A task role**

   You need to make sure that the group focuses on the learning task and achieves the learning goals. Clearly explain the task and make sure that people understand it. Question, clarify and summarise as you go along. Set out and stay with the time limits, but also be careful of forcing the pace. Keep the discussion on track.

Practical steps

To facilitate a learning meeting successfully, you need to follow this procedure:

- Prepare for the meeting. Read background materials, and plan the way you would like to structure the meeting.
- Agree on a contract with the group. Agree on the purpose of the discussion, your role, introductions and expectations, and housekeeping.
- Establish ground rules. Assure confidentiality, and give others a chance to speak.
- Create a positive atmosphere. Respect each viewpoint, discourage negative criticism.
- Keep track of time.
- Be aware of the group's energy level – people tend to lose focus after an hour.
- Use your intuition. If you feel frustrated, the group may be feeling it too.
- Summarise themes as you go along. Use a flip chart, and revisit issues.
- Look out for warning signs, such as side conversations, yawning, signs of agitation, long silences, getting bogged down in detail, and prolonged debates between a few participants.

These are some phrases which you may well find useful:

- That is a very important point you are making.
- I'd like us not to lose that point.
- We seem to be getting bogged down in detail – I wonder if this is helpful?
- I am hearing some mixed messages here.
- That is helpful – can you please expand on it?
- Can I get some reactions to that?
- I am not sure I am expressing this well.

- I can see some yawns – I think it's time for a break.
- Some of you seem to be frustrated – can you help us understand why?
- We seem to have lost direction – let's summarise where we have got up to now.

- This is obviously a difficult issue – I wonder why that may be?
- You have become quiet – would you like to tell us more?
- Is this an important issue for everyone?

154 How to deal with a medical mistake

IAN COUPER

In America medical errors kill 44 000–98 000 people each year and cause 1 000 000 excess injuries (Institute of Medicine 1999). In South Africa, medical errors have not been quantified.

Key issues in the literature

No study in the world has shown that medical care can be provided without error. No setting is free from hazards and no speciality is immune. Patients are at risk no matter what their age, gender or health status.

No large-scale studies have evaluated error in primary care or community hospitals.

Definitions

Definitions of error and related terms are as follows:

- **Error** is the failure of a planned action to be completed as intended, or the use of an incorrect plan to achieve an aim (Institute of Medicine 1999).
- **Negative outcomes** do not equal medical error, as the patient may not be cured of his disease or disability despite receiving the best care.
- **Adverse events** do not equal medical error, as certain of these events result from complications that cannot be prevented, given the current state of knowledge. Adverse events can be seen as bad outcomes caused by medical management.
- **Medical errors** are adverse events that are preventable within the current state of medical knowledge.

Classifications

Medical errors may be classified according to the following:

- Type of health care service provided, such as dispensing of medication and surgical operations

- Severity of the resulting injury – fatal, disabling, minor
- Legal definition, for example errors resulting from negligence
- Type of setting, such as outpatient clinic or intensive care unit
- Type of individual involved – doctor, nurse, patient
- Typologies of error:
  - Errors of omission, that is failure to act, or commission, that is incorrect action.
  - Cognitive errors versus technical errors
  - System errors, that is organisational problems, versus process errors, that is failure to follow the correct process as a practitioner
  - Active errors, that is those of which the effects are felt immediately, versus latent errors, that is those that lie dormant in the system for a long time.

Reactions to mistakes

Having made a mistake, you may well experience the following:

- A wide range of emotions related to the circumstances or connected to the patient, of various degrees of severity
- The typical grieving process, namely shock, denial, negotiation about the meaning of what has happened, acceptance of what has happened and finally re-engagement with life
- Concern regarding your competency
- Emotions and questions in relation to various people:
  - Yourself: How do I see myself?
  - Peers: How do colleagues see me?
  - Patients: How do my patients see me?
  - Statutory bodies: Will I be reported?
  - Lawyers: Will I get sued?

The systems approach

The systems approach to error management attempts to

- limit the incidence of dangerous error
- create systems that limit the effects of the errors that inevitably occur.

At the same time, the developmental and emotional needs of individual practitioners must not be ignored (Reason 2000).

The individual approach

If you have made a mistake, you need to do the following:

- Admit to the mistake and face reality. Do not deny the mistake.
- Examine your motives. Decide whether you were trying to do the right thing at the time.

- Share the burden by talking to colleagues about your mistake.
- Talk to the patient and/or his family.
- Ensure that you know where you went wrong and why, so as to prevent future error.
- Pay attention to self-care.
- Seek professional help when you need it, for example when you are impaired in some way (see Chapter 155).

The group approach

Taking this approach, you should

- learn from your error, and those of others, by evaluating the evidence and circumstances
- talk to trusted peers
- talk to non-medical friends
- establish a forum in which to discuss mistakes.

155 How to manage the impaired doctor or colleague

TUVIAH ZABOW

Mental or physical illness in a doctor can result in impaired judgement and functioning, which may in turn create circumstances that are hazardous to patients and problematic to colleagues. Undetected cases often become the subject of disciplinary action. With ongoing changes in health services and improved education of the patient population, the public seeks assurance that doctors remain competent and safe throughout their practising lives. Some doctors breach standards of professional practice and behaviour, and they must be dealt with in terms of ethical standards and levels of practice. Nevertheless, consideration should be given to those who are ill. Other doctors, who become ill without recognising the consequences for their patients or themselves, require detection, assessment and help to recover their fitness to practice.

The Medical, Dental and Supplementary Health Service Professions Act of 1974 provides for matters connected with impaired health practitioners. In the legislation, the impaired practitioner is differentiated from unprofessional conduct as follows:

- The Act defines **impaired** as "a mental or physical condition, or abuse of or dependence on chemical substances, which affects the competence, attitude, judgement or performance of a student or a person registered in terms of this Act".

- The Act defines **unprofessional conduct** as "improper or disgraceful or dishonourable or unworthy conduct or conduct which, when regard is had to the profession of a person who is registered in terms of this Act, is improper or disgraceful or dishonourable or unworthy".

The relevant Ethical Rules of the Health Professions Council of South Africa (HPCSA) require a practitioner or student to

- *report* impairment in another student or practitioner to the Council if he is convinced that that person is impaired as defined in the Act
- *self-report* his impairment to the Council if he is aware of his impairment, has been publicly informed of being impaired, or has been seriously advised by a colleague to obtain help in view of an alleged or established impairment.

The aims of the reporting process are

- to protect patients from ill doctors impaired in their function
- to provide for continued monitoring and care of sick doctors in their own and patients' interests
- to treat the cases of impaired doctors with the same confidentiality that is owed to all patients.

The Health Committee of the HPCSA subsumes the care of doctors and other health professionals registered therein. The Committee is mandated to look into the interests of registered impaired students and practitioners. It does not perform a disciplinary function; rather, it aims to provide a supportive and preventative function. It must assess and investigate reports of alleged impairment.

Furthermore, the Committee may recommend the suspension of the registration of a student or practitioner conditionally for a specific period pending the outcome of the investigation, and the treatment or rehabilitation, or it may remove the name of the student or practitioner from the relevant register for health impairment reasons.

Section 16

Research

156 How to write an article for publication

GBOYEGA OGUNBANJO

The effort that you put into the challenging process of writing an article for publication is rewarded when the article is published. Grammatical and syntax errors, violation of stipulated maximum word count, poor interpretation of results, unfocused discussions, and conclusions unrelated to the aim and objectives of the study are probably responsible for most of the rejections of submitted articles.

The following format is generic and generally accepted by most scientific journals.

Abstract

Your abstract should state the purpose of your study, the methodology that you used, and your primary findings and conclusions. If it is unstructured (one long paragraph without subheadings), it should not exceed 150 words; if it is structured, 250 words comprise the maximum.

Introduction

You need to clearly state the purpose and rationale of your study. It is mandatory for you to include a short literature review of what is known or has been done in the field. However, do not include data or conclusions of the study in this section.

Methods

Here, a brief description of the study design and sampling frame is required. In addition, you should explain in detail the methods, apparatus, procedures, chemicals and/or drugs (giving generic names) that you used for the study. Clearly state the setting of your study, and your inclusion and exclusion criteria for participants. Finally, describe how you collected and analysed the data. Explain the statistical method (for a quantitative study), or the theoretical model (for a qualitative study), that you used to analyse the data in a clear and concise manner.

Results

Present your results in a logical sequence in the text, in tables and in illustrations. Be cognisant that the emphasis is on the most important findings of your study. Although a table is useful to summarise a large amount of data, a clear graph of key findings is often more easily understood and has a greater impact. In qualitative studies space is often a problem when trying to provide sufficient illustrative quotes from the raw data to validate the themes and conceptual framework proposed. It may be possible to place quotations in a table or in some cases provide them online in a longer version of the article. Avoid discussing the significance of your results in this section.

Discussion

In this section, explain the new and significant aspects of your study, while relating them to observations from relevant existing studies and conclusions that follow from these. It is crucial that you avoid repeating in detail data or other materials that you presented under the introduction and the results. Include the implication(s) of your study findings, their limitations and the need for future research, if applicable.

Conclusions

Your conclusions must be relevant to the aim, objectives and findings of your study. It is imperative that you avoid unqualified statements and conclusions that are not supported by your findings. In addition, you should avoid claiming priority or alluding to studies not yet completed. You may include pertinent recommendations, if necessary.

Acknowledgements

Acknowledge all those who contributed in any meaningful way to the completion of your study, including institutions which gave you a grant. Also state any **conflict of interest,** for example if you are a shareholder in a company that makes the product under investigation.

References

The Vancouver style adopted by the US National Library of Medicine in *Index Medicus* is the accepted referencing style in most scientific journals, unless otherwise stated in the instructions to the authors. Number the references consecutively in the order in which they are mentioned in the text using Arabic numerals in parenthesis or superscript. Abbreviate the titles of journals according to the style used in the "List of Journals" indexed in *Index Medicus*, which you can access at this website: http://www. nlm.nih.gov

Important tips and pitfalls

You should follow these guidelines and try to avoid these pitfalls:

- Ensure that the *topic* of your article is interesting, relevant and applicable to the discipline of the journal to which you have submitted it for publication. Decide whether the information is more beneficial locally or internationally and choose a journal that targets the appropriate local or international audience.
- Identify the appropriate *journal* and know its *requirements*. You can usually find the latter under "Instructions to contributors or authors".
- Answer your research question in the article.

- Tables should have brief descriptions of the content and should be numbered using *Roman numerals*, that is I, II, etc. Number figures and graphs using *Arabic numerals*, that is 1, 2, etc., with brief descriptions of symbols used as footnotes.
- Type the manuscript double-spaced with a font size of 12 point.
- Avoid using an emotional or theatrical tone.
- Base authorship credit on substantial contributions to the conception or design, analysis or interpretation of the data. Acknowledge those who contributed to the seeking of funds or who only collected data, but not as authors.
- Restrict your use of tables and figures to those that explain and support your argument.
- Use the metric system (SI units) to express units of measurement, that is kilograms, centimetres, etc.
- Avoid using abstracts for references. Cite articles accepted for publication but not yet published as "in press" and cite unpublished articles only with the written permission of the author(s).
- Use the citation referred to as "personal communication" only if it provides substantial information not available from a public source.
- Precede abbreviations with the full term before using the abbreviation subsequently in the text.
- At all costs, avoid plagiarism, which is the improper use of and/or failure to acknowledge the source(s) used. It is both a cognitive and non-cognitive failure of the author(s).

157 How to write a research proposal

BOB MASH

As part of your training as a family physician, it is likely that you will be required to perform research. Therefore, you need to develop a research proposal to submit to your university or other educational institution.

Conceptualising your ideas and writing them down in the form of a research proposal is one of the major hurdles to completing the research project. Having a carefully considered plan before embarking on research is critical to successfully completing the research and producing useful results.

The following structure is widely accepted as being suitable for a research proposal.

Project title

Your title should make clear the purpose of the research. It is likely that it will change as your research proposal evolves. Ensure that the final title is not too lengthy or obscure.

Cover page

Provide your name, student number, registered course, supervisors, collaborators, affiliations and contact details, that is address, telephone, fax and email address.

Summary

You may well find this easier to write at the end, once you are clear about the project. It should succinctly summarise the project and stimulate interest in the topic. Ask yourself: "What is my main research question?"; "Why is it important?"; "What methods will I use and what outcomes do I hope to report on?" Usually, 200 words is sufficient.

Background

Set your proposed research in the context of what is already known about the topic, and consider how this project will contribute to that. In addition, your background should show awareness of the current academic debates and conversations that impact on the topic. It is therefore necessary that you do a liter-ature review, in which you focus on a few key studies. In this section, clearly show the importance and relevance of your proposed project.

In the literature review, you may also demonstrate particular evaluation tools, methodological approaches or pitfalls that are relevant to the study design.

If you have performed any preliminary research, such as a pilot study, you need to document this.

Include the expertise of the researchers and how they are able to contribute to this project. The expertise may be particularly methodological, or it may relate to access to the study population or to special interest in the topic. The curriculum vitae of the researchers are often required as an addendum.

Aims and objectives

Your aims are the overall academic and strategic goals of the project. You should define the main research questions that you intend to answer and any hypothesis that will be tested. If necessary, you can break down the broad aims into a number of secondary components or objectives. Be very careful that your choice of words here accurately reflects what you intend to do.

Methodology

In this section, you need to consider the following aspects:

- **Study design:** What type of design is appropriate to achieve your aims and answer your research question? The methodological section will vary according to the type of study design and whether it is in an empirical-analytical paradigm (usually involving quantitative techniques such as ran-domised controlled trials, case-control studies, cohort studies or cross-sectional surveys), an interpretive-hermeneutic paradigm (usually quali-tative techniques) or an emancipatory-critical par-adigm (participatory action research). It should be a clear and well-structured account of what you are going to do, of how you will establish the quality of what you plan to do and of any anticipated problems or limitations.

- **Setting:** Describe the setting of the research study and study population.

- **Assignment:** This refers to the manner in which you select people for the study or assign them to control or intervention groups. Define any inclusion or exclusion criteria. Remember that your calculation of sample size may be relevant.

- **Interventions:** In the case of an experimental-type design, describe the interventions that you will make on different groups.

- **Assessment:** Describe the types of measurements or data collection methods that you will use.

- **Analysis:** Describe the way in which you will analyse this data. You may need to consult a statistician for help. Describe the steps in qualitative data analysis.

- **Interpretation:** What results do you expect to be able to present?

- **Extrapolation:** How generalisable will these results be to other or wider population groups?

Ethical considerations

In this section, deal with any ethical dilemmas or issues as well as how you plan to approach them. For example, informed consent and confidentiality are frequently important. Your proposal should state who will grant ethical approval for the study – it is usually a university ethics committee.

Timetable

Write a simple timetable of how long it will take to complete each part of the research from start to finish. This will include planning and gaining approval, data collection, data analysis and writing up. Be aware that planning and writing up often take longer than you anticipated. Think about how you will set aside time on a regular basis to complete the research project.

Outputs and impact

Consider:

- What are the likely outputs of your research project in terms of reports, articles, presentations or books?

- What is the likely impact of the research on your practice, the health system, the researchers or others?

Funding and budget

Present a budget of the financial support that you need to complete the research and describe the potential sources of funding. Consider whether you should submit formal funding proposals to bodies such as the Medical Research Council.

References

List references to citations given in your proposal in an approved style, such as the Vancouver style, which is used in many journals (see Chapter 156).

158 How to develop clinical guidelines

MICHAEL PATHER

Clinical guidelines may be defined as "systematically developed statements to assist practitioners' decisions and patients' decisions about appropriate health care for specific clinical circumstances" (Sackett 2000, p. 70). Unless clinical guidelines are evidence based, their clinical value and justification may be considerably reduced. Motivations for the development of guidelines include issues such as cost saving, outcomes improvement and reduction of medical error, that is errors of commission and omission.

A clinical guideline is usually developed because the care of a specific condition within a medical community has been shown to exhibit one of the following patterns:

- Wide variation of practice
- Excessive cost
- Substandard outcomes
- New evidence that could have a significant impact on patient management

You must be able to critically appraise guidelines to ensure that they are valid, reliable, useful, relevant and applicable to the context in which you practice. Such guidelines assist you by reducing inappropriate variations in practice and promoting evidence-based health care (Grimshaw & Russell 1993).

Surrounding issues

There are concerns that guidelines may lead to "cookbook medicine", reduce clinical freedom (Rappolt 1997) and stifle innovation. As a practitioner, you may feel that guidelines threaten your sense of competence, and you may be reluctant to implement them if you disagree with the content. Medico-legal implications surround the use of guidelines where they are promoted as "gold standards of practice", as failure to adhere to them may leave you open to accusations of poor practice (Hurwitz 1994; Benech, Wilson & Dowell 1996).

Development

The process of guideline development is time consuming, and therefore the local adaptation of regional or national guidelines should be considered before new guidelines are attempted. This prevents unnecessary duplication and inefficient repetition of the process. Success depends on the process by which guidelines are developed, disseminated, implemented, evaluated and monitored (Anon 1994).

Preparation and dissemination are relatively easier than implementation and monitoring. We will now explore the key elements recommended in the development of a guideline.

Choose a health topic

You should choose a topic that is of local importance and relevance, especially where a wide variation in practice is prevalent, substandard outcomes occur and excessive cost is involved.

Establish a guideline development group

You need to establish an enthusiastic multidisciplinary group to develop the guideline. Identify a leader and roles for each member. Ideally, the guidelines should be developed locally and usually involve a consensus group (Grol 1993). Primary health care professionals should make up the majority of the membership when a guideline is being developed predominantly for management of patients in primary care (Grimshaw & Russell 1995). You can also include patients in the group. You may well find your own involvement in guideline preparation to be a valuable educational experience.

Appraise existing guidelines

It is important that you check whether other guidelines exist before embarking on the development of a new guideline, as it may be easier and cheaper to update or modify the existing one. In this way, you can also avoid inefficient repetition.

Appraise the evidence supporting the recommendations

High-quality and rigorous evidence may not always be available to support the recommendations, and therefore you may choose to produce a guideline with a combination of evidence-linked and consensus recommendations. Your search for the evidence should be as comprehensive and extensive as possible, and you should attempt to grade the quality of the evidence that you do find. Moreover, you need to ensure that the level of evidence is explicitly linked to the recommendations.

However, grading systems such as the one recommended by the US Agency for Healthcare Research and Quality were designed mainly for application to questions of efficacy, where randomised controlled trials (RCTs) are accepted as the most robust study design with the least risk of bias in the results (Harbour & Miller 2001). In many areas of family medicine and primary health care, the undertaking of RCTs may not be practical, feasible, necessary or ethical, and therefore for many topics *other* study designs may provide the best evidence.

Ideally, guidelines are based on the results of systematic reviews. Any existing uncertainty should be clearly stated and can be used as a stimulus for the undertaking of further relevant research. You and your team must make considered judgement about the generalisability, applicability, consistency and clinical impact of the evidence to create a clear link between it and the recommendation (Harbour & Miller 2001).

According to Sackett (2000), the hierarchy of study types in terms of therapeutic recommendations is as follows:

- Systematic review and meta-analysis of randomised controlled trials
- Randomised controlled trial
- Non-randomised controlled trials
- Observational studies – cohort and case control studies
- Cross-sectional studies
- Descriptive research
- Expert opinion

Construct the guideline

Formally construct the guideline and lay it out in an accessible format.

Although thousands of guidelines are available, some are better adhered to than others (Schuster, McGlynn & Brook 1998; Grol 2001). This difference may be owing to the type of health problem addressed, the method of development used, the content of the recommendations, the method of dissemination, the format or layout used or the means of implementation (Davis & Tailor-Vaisey 1997).

Invite external peer review and appraisal

Send a draft copy of the guideline to potential users and independent experts for review. You may find that other guideline development groups send their guideline to *you* for appraisal, in which case you should use the standard appraisal tool, presented as Table 158.1. Other appraisal tools, such as the AGREE instrument, can also be used (AGREE Collaboration 2001).

Once you have obtained the review comments, revisit the preceding step described above.

Disseminate the guideline

Try to disseminate the guideline as widely as possible to ensure that it reaches or is accessible to all practitioners for whom it is intended.

Implement the guideline

In this phase, it is essential that you identify potential barriers to implementation and make attempts to overcome them. The most commonly used methods of publishing the guideline in a medical journal and talking about it in the form of didactic continuing professional development are the least effective methods (Bero et al. 1998). While there is no "magic bullet" to ensure the successful use of the guideline, it appears that multifaceted approaches are more effective and may usefully include aspects such as interactive or participatory workshops, provision of desktop tools or reminders, educational outreach visits to the practice, inclusion in quality improvement activities, local consensus building and adaptation of national guidelines, engagement of local opinion leaders as well as patient-mediated interventions (Bero et al. 1998).

In addition, you need to take account of the "Killer Bs" (Sackett 2000), which include the **burden** of disease, the **beliefs** of the patients' community, whether implementation constitutes a **bargain**, and the potential **barriers** you need to overcome in the implementation process. When considering these aspects, you and your team can ask yourselves the following questions:

- Is the burden of illness too low in our area to warrant implementation of the guideline?
- Are the beliefs of individual patients or communities about the value of the interventions or their consequences incompatible with the guideline?
- Would the cost of implementing this guideline constitute a poor bargain in the use of our energy or our community's resources?

Table 158.1 Evidence-based medicine (EBM) guidelines

Primary question	Specific questions
Are the recommendations in this guideline valid?	Are all the important decision options and outcomes clearly specified?
	Is the evidence relevant to each decision option identified, validated and combined in a sensible and explicit way?
	Are the relative preferences that key stakeholders attach to the outcomes of decisions (including benefits, risks and costs) identified and explicitly considered?
	Is the guideline resistant to clinically sensible variations in practice?
Is this valid guideline or strategy potentially useful?	Does this guideline offer an opportunity for significant improvement in the quality of health care practice?
	Is there a large variation in current practice?
	Does the guideline contain new evidence, or old evidence not yet acted upon, that could have an important impact on management?
	Would the guideline affect the management of so many people, or concern individuals at such high risk, or involve such high costs that even small changes in practice could have a major impact on health outcomes or resources, including opportunity costs?
Should this guideline or strategy be applied in your practice?	What barriers exist to its implementation? Can they be overcome?
	Can you enlist the collaboration of key colleagues?
	Can you meet the following educational, administrative and economic conditions that are likely to determine the success or failure of implementing the strategy?
	• Credible synthesis of the evidence by a respected body
	• Respected, influential local exemplars already implementing the strategy
	• Consistent information from all relevant sources
	• Opportunity for individual discussions about the strategy with an authority
	• User-friendly format for guidelines
	• Implementation is possible within a target group of clinicians, without the need for extensive outside collaboration
	• Freedom from conflict with economic incentives, administrative incentives, patient expectations and community expectations
The Killer Bs	Is the burden of illness – frequency in our community, or our patients' pre-test probability or patients' expected event rate (PEER) – too low to warrant implementation?
	Are the beliefs of individual patients or communities about the value of the interventions or their consequences incompatible with the guideline?
	Would the opportunity cost of implementing this guideline constitute a poor bargain in the use of our energy or our community's resources?
	Are the barriers – geographic, organisational, traditional, authoritarian, legal or behavioural – so high that it is not worth trying to overcome them?

Source: Sackett 2000, p. 176–9

• Are the barriers – geographic, organisational, traditional, authoritarian, legal or behavioural – so high that it is not worth trying to overcome them?

Monitor guideline use

It is important for you and your team to monitor the guideline in practice so that you can ensure its efficacy, effectiveness and efficiency. Although ideally you should use a randomised controlled trial to evaluate the effectiveness of the guideline, you can also use quality improvement cycles in local practices. If the quality improves and the costs are acceptable, the guideline can be used with confidence and be promoted widely.

An effective guideline is a powerful tool, but only in the hands of a great physician (Gross 2001). Changes in evidence, resources available for health care and improvements in currect performance are all possible reasons for updating clinical guidelines. The air of authority surrounding "official" guidelines should not deter you from appraising them carefully.

Teaching and learning

159 How to plan a teaching activity

MARIETJIE DE VILLIERS

The teaching activity

In addition to your clinical duties, as a family doctor you frequently act as teacher, mentor or supervisor in the health district. Every day you provide information to many patients and are often called upon to address the community on health issues. Furthermore, you may become involved in supporting or training undergraduate students, junior colleagues, health workers or giving presentations at continuing professional development (CPD) meetings.

You need to carefully plan any teaching activity in order to achieve its aims and objectives. Even if you have spoken on a topic many times, you must take time to reflect on the particular training activity at hand. Your teaching activities should follow a cyclical planning process with design, development, evaluation and revision stages (Mash 2004), each of which we will now discuss.

Design stage

Follow these steps:

- Think about the identity and circumstances of your audience and at what level you should pitch the activity.
- Identify learning needs for the activity, if possible in collaboration with representative people from the potential audience.
- Write down the learning outcomes that should be achieved by this activity.

Development stage

Follow these steps:

- Clarify the topic in your mind and, ideally with participants, make sure of what it is that needs to be addressed.
- Create a detailed content outline.
- Assess the resources that are easily available to you. If you have none, think about what needs to be developed or obtained in order for you to cover the proposed content.

- Decide which teaching method will be the most appropriate for the audience and for the topic, such as small group discussions, role play, a lecture or a demonstration of skill.
- Prepare the actual content, for example a Power-Point presentation or role play.

Evaluation stage

Follow these steps:

- It is important for you to evaluate the teaching activity in order to ascertain whether the learning outcomes have been met and how you can improve it for future use.
- Think about how you will obtain feedback from the participants on the value and efficacy of the activity from their perspective.
- Prepare a simple evaluation sheet in advance for the participants to complete at the end of the session. Ask a few basic questions such as: What was the most useful element of the activity?; What was least useful, and how would you like to improve it?
- Use this feedback to improve the activity.
- If relevant, for instance if you are doing formal undergraduate or postgraduate teaching, plan how you will assess the participants' learning, that is in the form of reflection, a portfolio or more official examinations such as objective structured clinical examinations (OSCE).

Revision stage

Follow this procedure:

- In this phase you should reflect on the teaching activity, using the following questions to help you:
  - What went well, and why?
  - What did not work well, and why?
  - Did we meet the learning outcomes?
  - How can I improve on the activity in future?

- Study the feedback forms from the participants to see what they enjoyed and what they felt needed improvement.

- Reflect on your own experience with regard to the activity.
- Revise the activity for use in the future.

160 How to use a learning journal or portfolio

MARIETJIE DE VILLIERS

A learning journal or portfolio is a reflective learning tool that you can use highly productively in your continuing professional development (CPD).

Internationally, portfolios or learning journals have become a popular tool in undergraduate and postgraduate education, as well as in CPD. They are described as highly effective in promoting significant adult learning by stimulating experiential learning, encouraging reflection, and supporting autonomy and self-direction by self-identification of learning needs and the intention of meeting outcomes. Furthermore, they are widely used for assessment, including revalidation for continuing licensure. Here, we will focus on the use of portfolios in CPD.

The portfolio

Your portfolio itself could be an ordinary notebook, or an A4 folder or a collection of files on computer. Your portfolio should contain your personal learning plan, evidence of implementation of that plan, and a description of the support received in developing the learning plan.

The contents

As touched on above, the most important part of your portfolio is your **personal learning plan**. In it, you should document the things that you feel you should, or want to, learn about. Having identified these needs, you should work out a plan for fulfilling them, such as discussing them with a colleague, reading the relevant journal, or attending a course on the need.

You must also document your actions towards achieving your learning outcomes. Record what you have done so far, and record your reflection on what happened and what you have learnt. Questions that can guide your reflection are as follows:

- What happened?
- What did you notice and/or find interesting?
- What did you learn from this?
- How will this change your future practice?

Your portfolio should also include some evidence of the support and input you had in developing the portfolio, such as discussion with a colleague, a peer group or a mentor.

While this can be informal, it is nevertheless an important aspect in the optimisation of your learning. The mentor, for example, is seen as valuable in facilitating the development of your ideas, resolving difficulties and supporting the learning progress.

Constraints and advantages

The primary constraint of using a portfolio is that it can be time consuming. However, if you work in a busy practice, portfolio learning is more useful and relevant than taking time to attend a lecture.

The combination of recording information in response to setting your learning outcomes, and active reflection is a highly effective learning process. Research on portfolio use has shown that it enables the achievement of individual learning objectives, and also provides flexibility in both learning methods and timing for an individual's CPD.

161 How to organise continuing professional development

MARIETJIE DE VILLIERS

The objectives of continuing professional development (CPD) is to ensure the maintenance of the professional competence of practitioners in order to impact on the continual improvement of quality patient care, as well as the promotion of high ethical standards in the profession.

When planning a CPD activity, you need to address two components, namely educational issues and organisational issues.

Educational issues

Evidence from educational research underscores the need for you to develop interventions that focus on the learning needs and practice problems of the individual learner. When you plan a CPD activity, it is extremely important that you identify the learning needs of your audience: What do the people attending the activity want to learn about? It is always better to do this in *collaboration* with your audience.

When you plan the method to use, it is important that you realise that didactic lectures are not effective in changing individual doctors' behaviour and have little impact on professional practice as a whole. *Interactive* techniques, such as small-group discussions and practice-based activities, are more effective in facilitating learning.

Make sure that your CPD activity involves more than mere esoteric knowledge acquisition – link the discussion to your participants' practice. You can do this by making sure that your level of presentation is relevant to the practice level of the participants. Providing opportunities for reflection on how the CPD activity will affect their practice, and ultimately influence their patient care, are also highly useful.

Remember that attendance at a CPD activity does not ensure maintenance of competence. The knowledge you provide during the activity is but one part of the cycle of learning that can change practitioners' behaviour. Figure 161.1 provides a practical model for maintenance of competence with the use of various CPD activities as a "menu" from which to choose according to the learning needs of your audience. It is also useful in assisting you to set up a CPD programme in your practice, hospital, clinic or district.

Make sure that you obtain structured feedback after the activity. Prepare a short feedback form consisting of questions such as: What was useful?; What could be improved?; Do you have any comments?; and ask each participant to complete it and return it to you. Using the feedback to inform your CPD programme will greatly assist you in planning your future CPD activities.

Organisational issues

Use the following checklist when planning to facilitate a CPD activity:

- Identify the topic, taking into account the needs of the audience. If possible, consult members of the audience.
- Identify the most suitable format, for example interactive, problem-based and so on.
- Make sure that the programme supports opportunities for reflection.
- Identify a suitable content expert if one is needed to contribute to the activity as a speaker or participant in discussions.
- Select a suitable date, and check the date and venue availability with the the visiting expert.
- Ascertain audiovisual requirements.
- Book the venue and audiovisual equipment.
- Arrange appropriate catering.
- Apply for CPD accreditation timeously.
- Make sure that your CPD complies with HPCSA regulations.
- Send out invitations.
- Prepare the official attendance register with columns for name, MP number and signature of each participant. These are needed as proof of attendance for CPD points.
- Remember to hand out feedback sheets and collect them at the end of the activity.

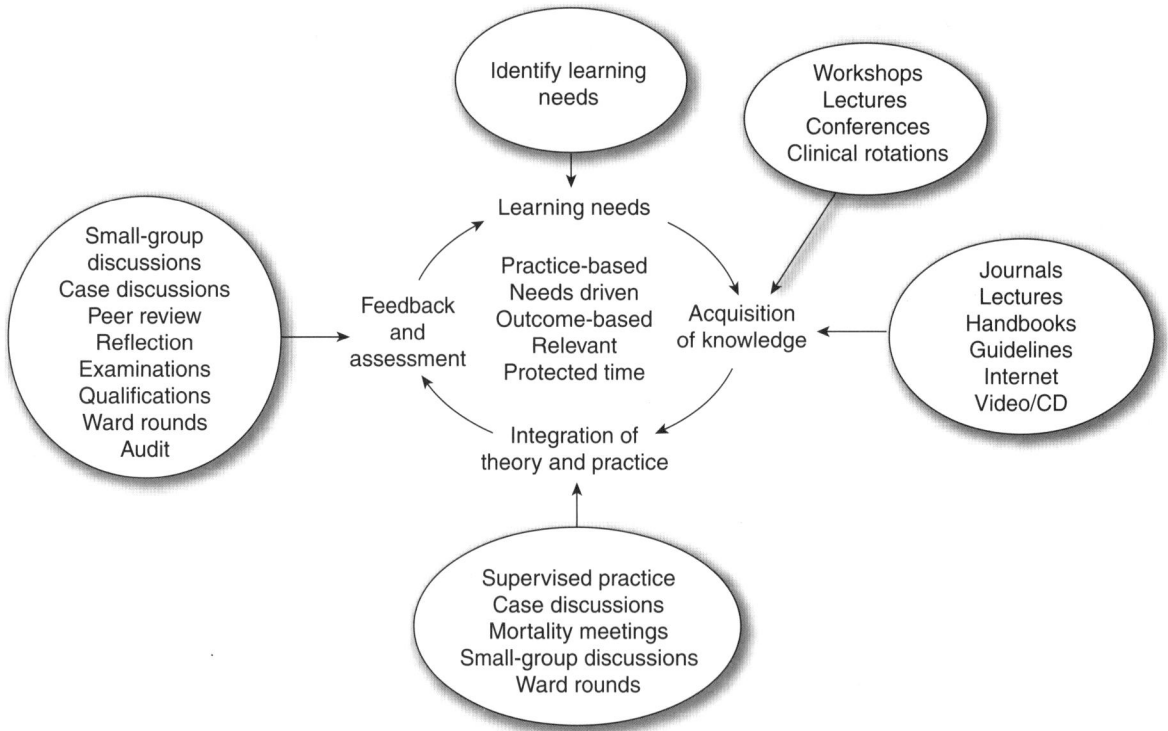

Figure 161.1 Ideal learning cycle for the maintenance of competence

Abbott J, Emmans LS, Lowenstein SR. Ectopic pregnancy: ten common pitfalls in diagnosis. American Journal of Emergency Medicine 1990;8(6):515–22.

Adult Sexual Evidence Collection Kit User Guide. Available from: URL: http://www.sexualassaultkits.co.za Accessed August 2005.

Advanced Trauma Life Support. Student course manual. USA: American College of Surgeons; 1997.

AGREE Collaboration. Appraisal of guidelines for research and evaluation (AGREE) instrument; 2001. Available at: URL: http://www.agreecollaboration.org

American Heart Association. American Academy of Paediatrics. Paediatric advanced life support; 1997.

Annals of Thoracic Surgery, 50:442–5.

Anon. Implementing clinical practice guidelines: can guidelines be used to improve clinical practice? Effective Health Care Bulletin 1994:8.

Aronson J, Puskarich CL. Deformity and disability from treated clubfoot. J Ped Ortho 1990;10:109.

Arredondo R, Garland LM, Googins JC, Haberstroh S, Humphrey JL, Jackson JS et al. Regional Education Team of the TMA. Committee of Physician Health and Rehabilitation. Coping with stress in the practice of medicine. 2005 Nov. Available at: URL: http://www.texmed.org/Template.aspx?id=4460

Bak N. Putting the research proposal together. In: Bak N. Completing your thesis: a practical guide. Pretoria: Van Schaik; 2004. p. 14–36.

Balfour CH. Analgesia and sedation in the emergency environment. Continuing Medical Education (CME) 2004;22(6):315–20.

Ballard JL, Khoury JC, Wedig K, Wang L, Eilers-Walsman BL, Lipp R. New Ballard score, expanded to include extremely premature infants. J Pediatr 1991;119:417–23.

Barners Jewish Hospital Patient care: patient satisfaction survey AKU-AKUH: Patient satisfaction survey; 1997–2000.

Bartlett D. The ABCs of gastric decontamination. Journal Emergency Nursing 2003;29(6):576–7.

Basic Conditions of Employment (BCEA) of 1997. Available at: URL: http://www.acts.co.za/bcoe97/index.htm

Beauchamp TL, Childress JF. Principles of biomedical ethics. New York: Oxford University Press; 1994.

Benech I, Wilson AE, Dowell AC. Evidence-based primary care: past, present and future. Journal of Evaluation in Clinical Practice 1996;2:249–263.

Bercow R, Fletcher AJ, Beers HM. The Merck manual.16th ed. Rahway, NY: Merck Research Laboratories; 1997. p. 393.

Bero L, Grilli R, Grimshaw J, Harvey E, Oxman A, Thomson, M. Getting research findings into practice: closing the gap between research and practice: an overview of systematic reviews of interventions to promote the implementation of research findings. BMJ 1998; 317: 465–8.

Bhaskaran BVP. Chief Executive Officer, Manipal Hospital. Bangalore; HR Solutions (1994–2003): Patient satisfaction survey; 2001.

Blair S, Wright D, Backhouse C, Riddle E, McCollum C. Sustained compression and healing of chronic venous ulcers. BMJ 1988;297:1159–61.

Blamey RW, Wilson ARM. ABC of breast diseases: screening for breast cancer. BMJ Oct 1994;309:1076–9.

Bongard FS, Sue DY. Current critical care diagnosis and treatment. 2nd ed. New York: McGraw-Hill; 2002.

Bradshaw D, Dorrington RE, Sitas F. The level of mortality in South Africa in 1985 – what does it tell us about health? S Afr Med J 1992;82:237–40.

Brawley M. The client perspective: what is quality health care service? USAID Cooperative Agreement 617-00-0000-00; 2000.

Briscoe M. Planning for health care; health in America 1776–1976. Washington D.C.: DHEW. Pub No (HRA) 76–6161; 1976.

Brohi K. Spinal stabilization and management. http://www.trauma.org; 2002 April;7:4.

Brown TB, Lovato LM, Parker D. Procedural sedation in the acute care setting. American Family Physician 2005;71(1):85–90.

Brueton MJ, Palit A, Rosser R. Gestational age assessment in Nigerian infants. Arch Dis Child 1973;48:318.

Buchmann EJ. Breech presentation. In Cronjé HS, Grober CJF: Obstetrics in southern Africa. Pretoria: Van Schaik; 2003:352–63.

Burch V, Keeton G, editors. Guidelines for primary care evaluation and management of common medical problems in adults. 2nd ed. Cape Town: Provincial Administration Western Cape, Metropole Region; 2000.

Caroline NL. Emergency care in the streets. 4th ed. 1991;326–7.

Carter Y. Writing a research proposal and getting funded. In: Carter Y, Thomas C. Research methods in primary care. New York: Radcliffe Medical Press; 1997:19–29.

Cates CJ, Bara A, Crilly JA, Rowe BH. Holding chambers versus nebulisers for beta-agonist treatment of acute asthma. Cochrane review. The Cochrane Library. Chichester, UK: John Wiley & Sons; 2004.

Chadwick HD. The diseases of the inhabitants of the Commonwealth. N Engl J Med 1937;216:8.

Challis M, Mathers NJ, Howe AC, Field NJ. Portfolio-based learning: continuing medical education for general practitioners – a mid-point evaluation. Med Educ 1997; 31:22–6.

Chameides L, Hazinsky MF, editors. Pediatric advanced life support. Dallas: American Heart Association; 1997.

Cilliers JBF. Management of normal labour. In Cronjé HS, Grobler CJF: Obstetrics in southern Africa. Pretoria: Van Schaik; 2003:74–83.

Clinical guidelines for the use of blood and blood products in South Africa. Adcock Ingram; 1999.

Compensation for Occupational Injuries and Diseases Act 130 of 1993, as amended. Schedule 3. Government Gazette No. 26302; 30 April 2004.

Cook J, Sankaran B, Ambrose E, Wasuma O. General surgery at the district hospital. World Health Organization; 1998.

Craig CJT. The taking of adequate Papanicolaou smears. Letter. S Afr Med J 1994;84:636.

Cronjé HS, Grobler CJF. Obstetrics in southern Africa. Pretoria: Van Schaik; 2003.

Crosby JR, Hesketh EA. Developing the teaching instinct 11. Small group learning. Medical Teacher 2004;26(1): 16–9.

Crum R, Anthony J, Bassett S, Folstein M. Population-based norms for the mini-mental examination by age and educational level. JAMA 1993;269:2386–91.

Cummins RO, editor. ACLS provider manual. Dallas: American Heart Association; 2001.

Dada MA, McQuoid-Mason DJ. Introduction to medico-legal practice. Durban: Butterworths; 2001.

Daponte A. Postpartum haemorrhage. In Cronjé HS, Grobler CJF. Obstetrics in southern Africa. Pretoria: Van Schaik; 2003:210–0.

Davis D, Tailor-Vaisey A. Translating guidelines into practice: a systematic review of theoretical concepts, practical experience and research evidence in the adoptions in clinical practice. CMAJ 1997;157:408–16.

Davis DA, Thomson MA, Oxman AD, Haynes RB. Changing physician performance: a systematic review of the effect of continuing medical education strategies. JAMA 1995;274:700–5.

Davis DA, Thomson O'Brien MA, Freemantle N, Wolf FM, Mazmanian P, Taylor-Vaisey A. Impact of formal continuing medical education: do conferences, workshops, rounds, and other traditional continuing education activities change physician behaviour or health care outcomes? JAMA 1999;282(9):867–74.

DeLisa JA, Gans BM. Rehabilitation medicine. 2nd ed. 1993;1151–64.

Demeter SL, Anderson GBL, Smith GM. Disability evaluation; 1996.

Department of Health. Uniform national health guidelines for dealing with survivors of rape and other sexual offences. Available at: URL: http://www.doj.gov.za/2004dojsite/policy/guide_sexoff/sex-guide01.html

Department of National Health. Cervical cancer screening programme. http://www.doh.gov.za/docs/factsheets/guidelines/cancer.pdf Accessed August 2005.

Department of Provincial Administration. Working documents. Western Cape; 1998.

DiClemente C, Velasquez M. Motivational interviewing and the stages of change. In: Miller W, Rollnick S, editors. Motivational interviewing. New York: Guilford Press; 2002; p. 201–16.

Doherty M, Dacre J, Dieppe P, Snaith M. The "GALS" locomotor screen. Ann Rheum Dis 1992 Oct;51(10): 1165–9.

Dries DJ. Initial evaluation of the trauma patient. Available at: URL: http://www.emedicine.com/med/topic3221.htm Accessed August 2005.

Driver and Vehicle Licensing Agency. For medical practitioners: at a glance guide to the current medical standards of fitness to drive. Swansea: Drivers' Medical Group; 2003 January.

Dubowitz LM, Dubowitz V, Goldberg C. Clinical assessment of gestational age in the newborn infant. J Pediatr 1970;77:1–10.

Ellis C. Learning language and culture in the medical consultation. Parktown North: Sue McGuinness Publications; 1999.

Emmons KM, Rollnick S. Motivational interviewing in health care settings: opportunities and limitations. Am J Prev Med 2001;20(1):68–74.

Employment Equity Act of 1998. Government Gazette No. 23702 and amendments in No. 23718.

Epeldegui T. Conceptos y controversias sobre el pie zambo. Madrid: Vincente ed; 1993.

Flegar M, Ball A. Easier nasogastric tube insertion. Anaesthesia 2004;59(2):197.

Florey CV, Weddell JM, Leeder SR. The epidemiologist's contribution to medical care planning and evaluation. Aust NZ J Med 1976;74–8.

Galler D. Critical care considerations in trauma. Available at: URL: http://www.emedicine.com/med/topic3218.htm Accessed August 2005.

Gear J, Hammond M. Measuring community health. 1986.

Gibson K, Swartz L, Sandenbergh R. Counselling and coping. Cape Town: Oxford University Press; 2002.

Gillespie J. Communication briefing. USA: Briefings Publishing Group; 2000.

Godfrey et al. Nomogram. Br J Dis Chest, 1970; 64:15.

Graber MA, Kathol M. Cervical spine radiography in the trauma patient. American Fam Physician 1999 January 15;331–48.

Gray HA. Making sense of the ECG. 2nd ed. Arnold Publishers; 2003.

Green A. An introduction to health planning in developing countries. 1994.

Green LA, Fryer GE, Yawn BP, Lanier D, Dovey SM. The ecology of medical care revisited. N Engl J Med 2001;344:2021–5.

Grimshaw J, Eccles M, Russell I. Developing clinically valid practice guidelines. J Evaluation Clinical Practice 1995;1:37–48.

Grimshaw JM, Russell IT. Achieving health gain through clinical guidelines. Developing scientifically valid guidelines. Quality in Health Care 1993;2:243–8.

Grol R. Development of guidelines for general practice care. Br J Gen Pract 1993;43:143–51.

Grol R. Successes and failures in the implementation of evidence-based guidelines for clinical practice. Med Care 2001;39(suppl. 2):46–54.

Gross R. Guidelines and pathways. Decisions and evidence in medical practice. Applying evidence-based medicine to clinical decision making. St Louis: Mosby Inc.; 2001.

Guidelines for maternity care in South Africa: a manual for clinics, community health centres and district hospitals. Last print March 2002. Department of Health: 26–7.

Guidelines for the completion of the J88 form. Available at: URL: http://www.kznhealth.gov.za/j88guidelines.pdf Accessed August 2005.

Gullapalli N, Rao N. How can we improve patient care? Community Eye Health. 2002;41(15).

Gundling E. Working globesmart: 12 people skills for doing business across borders. Davies-Black Publishing; 2003.

Gurney JW. Department of Radiology; Nebraska Medical Center. Available at: URL: http://www.chestx-ray.com/lectures/ABCweblecture/NavigationABC.html Accessed August 2005.

Hampton J. The ECG in practice. 3rd ed. Saunders Company; 1998.

Harbour R, Miller J. A new system for grading recommendations in evidence-based guidelines. BMJ 2001;323:334–6.

Hilfiker D. Healing the wounds: a physician looks at his work. New York: Penguin; 1987.

Hoek BB. Management of the newborn baby. In Cronjé HS, Grobler CJF. Obstetrics in southern Africa. Pretoria: Van Schaik; 2003:99–106.

Houghton AR, Gray D. Making sense of the ECG. A hands-on guide. 2nd ed. London: Hodder Arnold; 2003.

http://www.trauma.org Accessed August 2005.

Hurwitz B. Clinical guidelines proliferation and medico-legal significance. Qual Health Care 1994;3:3744.

Huygen FJA. Family medicine. The medical life history of families. London: Royal College of General Practitioners; 1990.

ICD-10. International statistical classification of diseases and related health problems. Manual for use by and guidance of the medical profession in the Republic of South Africa. Report No. 09 90 04. Central Statistical Service; 1996 January.

Institute of Medicine. To err is human: building a safer health system. Washington, D.C.: National Academy Press; 1999.

International Committee of Medical Journal Editors. Uniform requirements for manuscripts submitted to biomedical journals. N Engl J Med 1997;336(4):309–15.

Jeebhay MF. Health and safety legislation and worker's compensation for allergic diseases of occupational aetiology. Current Allergy and Clinical Immunology 2000; 13(3):4–8.

Jeebhay MF. Setting up an occupational health service: legal provisions and practical considerations. CME 1996;14(9):1321–7.

Jones R, Britten N, Culpepper L, Gass DA, Grol R, Mant D, Silagy C, editors. Oxford textbook of primary medical care. New York: Oxford University Press; 2004.

Kai J. Approach to the sick infant. In Jones R, Britten N, Culpepper L, Gass DA et al.: Oxford textbook of primary medical care. New York: Oxford University Press; 2004:1001–3.

Kai J. Parents' difficulties and information needs. Coping with acute illness in preschool children: a qualitative study. BMJ 1996;313:987–90.

Kale R. Traditonal healers in South Africa: a parallel health care system. BMJ 1995; 310:1182–5.

Kaplan BC, Dart RG, Moskos M. Ectopic pregnancy: prospective study with improved diagnostic accuracy. Ann Emerg Med 1996 July;28(1):10–7.

Kark SL, Abramson JH. Community-focused health care: introduction. Isr J Med Sci 1981 Feb–Mar;17(2–3): 65–70.

Karp H, Fuller C, Sirias D. Bridging the Boomer-Xer (generation) gap. Davies-Black Publishing; 2002.

Katzenbanch JR, Smith DR. The wisdom of teams. Boston: MacKinfey Company; 1995.

Kibel MA, Wagstaff LA. Child health for all: a manual for southern Africa. Cape Town: Oxford University Press; 2001:2.

Kielkowski D, Steinberg M, Barron PM. Life after death – mortality statistics and public health. S Afr Med J 1989;76:672–5.

King J. Effective facilitation. BMJ 2002;324:S36.

King M, editor. Primary anaesthesia. Oxford Medical Publications; 1996.

King M, Bewes P. Primary surgery. Volume 2. Oxford University Press;1993. p. 161.

Knottenbelt JD. Trauma handbook. Cape Town: University of Cape Town; 1992. p. 58–61.

Knox EG. Epidemiology in health care planning; 1979. p. 111–4.

Kogevinas M, Becher H, Benn T, Bertrazzi PA, Boffetta P, Bueno-de-Mesquita B et al. Cancer mortality in workers exposed to phenoxy herbicides, chlorophenols and dioxins: an expanded and updated international cohort study. Am J Epidemiol 1997;147:1061–75.

Kousa M. Conservative treatment of leg sores in EBM. Guidelines. Duodecim Med Pub [serial on CD-ROM]. 2003.

Laaveg SJ, Ponseti IV. Long-term results of treatment of congenital clubfoot. J Bone Joint Surg [Am] 1980;62:23.

Lalloo UG, Bateman ED, Feldman C, Bardin PG, Plit M, Irusen EM, O'Brien J. Guidelines for the management of chronic asthma in adults – 2000 update. S Afr Med J 2000 May,90(5):540–52.

Lawrence M. What is medical audit? Medical audit in primary health care. Oxford: Oxford University Press; 1993.

Leach RE, Ory SJ. Modern management of ectopic pregnancy. J Reprod Med 1989 May;34(5):324–38.

Lloyd-Jones G, Fowell S, Bligh JG. The use of the nominal group technique as an evaluative tool in medical undergraduate education. Med Educ 1999 Jan;33(1): 8–13.

London L. An evaluation of a Pap smear service in a rural general practice. SA Fam Pract 1993;14:196–202.

MacRae HM, McLeod RS. Comparison of hemorrhoidal treatment modalities: a meta-analysis. Diseases of the colon and rectum 1995;38(7):687–94.

Marsden CD, Fowler T, editors. Clinical neurology. London: Edward Arnold; 1989.

Mash RJ. Instructional design cycle in MFamMed teaching and learning module study guide. Department of Family Medicine and Primary Care, Stellenbosch University; 2004.

Mash RJ. The development of distance education for general practitioners on common mental disorders through participatory action research. Doctoral thesis. Stellenbosch University; 2002.

Mathers NJ, Challis MC, Howe AC, Field NJ. Portfolios in continuing medical education – effective and efficient? Med Educ 1999;33:521–30.

Mayo Clinic and Mayo Foundation. Clinical examination in neurology. London: WB Saunders; 1981.

McDaniel S, Campbell TL, Seaburn DB. Family-oriented primary care: a manual for medical providers. New York, United States of America: Springer-Verlag 1990.

McLatchie GR, Leaper DJ, editors. Oxford handbook of clinical surgery. p. 604–5; 2002.

McRae R. Pocketbook of orthopaedics and fractures. Edinburgh, Scotland: Churchill Livingstone; 2001.

McWhinney IR. The doctor, the patient, and the house: returning to our roots. In: The role of the family physician in home care. The College of Family Physicians of Canada. Missisauga: Ontario; 2000.

Medical and Dental Professions Board. Guidelines for good practice in medicine, dentistry and the medical sciences: ethical and professional rules of the medical and dental professions board: Booklet 3. Pretoria: HPCSA; 2002, Rule 15:5.

Medical Research Council. Aids to the investigation of peripheral nerve injuries. London: Her Majesty's Stationery Office; 1943, reprinted 1967.

Mieny CJ. Algemene chirurgie. Pretoria: Academica; 1992. p. 261.

Mollentze WF. Screening for microvascular complications of diabetes mellitus: missed opportunities. CME 2003;21(10):583–91.

Morgan GE Jr, Mikhail MS, Murray MJ, Larson P Jr. Clinical anaesthesiology. 3rd ed. New York: McGraw-Hill; 2002.

Morgan GE, Mikhail MS. Clinical anaesthesiology. 2nd ed. 1996.

Motala C, Kling S, Gie R, Potter PC, Manjra A, Vermeulen J, Weinberg EG, Green R. Guidelines for the management of chronic asthma in children – 2000 update. S Afr Med J 2000 May;90(5 Pt 2):524–8.

Mouton J. The research proposal. In: Mouton J. How to succeed in your master's and doctoral studies: a South African guide and resource book. Pretoria: Van Schaik; 2001. p. 44–61.

Muralikrishnan R, Sivakumar AK. Patients' perspective: an important factor in assessing patient satisfaction. Community Eye Health 2002;15(41):5–7.

Musick JL. How close are you to burnout? Learn how to control stress before it controls you. Family Practice Management 1997 April.

National Department of Health. Guidelines for maternity care in southern Africa: a manual for clinics, community health centres and district hospitals. National Department of Health; 2002 March.

National Department of Health. South African tuberculosis control programme practical guidelines. Pretoria; 2000. Available at: URL: http://www.doh.gov.za/tb/docs/ ntcpguidelines01.pdf and http://www.doh.gov.za/tb/docs/ ntcpguidelines02.pdf Accessed August 2005.

Nel, JT. Core obstetrics and gynecology. Johannesburg: Heinemann; 1995.

Nkado RN, Mbachu JIC. Causes of, and solutions to client's dissatisfaction in the South African building industry: the client perspectives. Witwatersrand, South Africa; 2001. Available at: URL: http://buildnet.csir.co.za/ cdcproc/docs/3rd/nkado_ mbachu_2.pdf

Nisar PJ, Scholefield JH. Managing haemorrhoids. BMJ 2003;327:847–51.

Nokwe D, Mlenzana S. Team's notes on integrated development plan implementation. Mhlontlo District Health Service 2000–2003. Eastern Cape: Provincial Administration; 2003.

Nokwe D, Mlenzana S. Team's notes on team building and journey into quality assurance with council for health service accreditation of South Africa (Cohsasa). Mhlontlo District Health Service 2000–2003. Eastern Cape: Provincial Administration; 2003.

Odendaal HJ. Acute intrapartum foetal distress. In Cronjé HS, Grobler CJF: Obstetrics in southern Africa. Pretoria: Van Schaik; 2003:275–88.

Okkes IM, Polderman GO, Fryer GE, Yamada T, Bujak M, Oskam SK, Green LA, Lamberts H. The role of family practice in different health care systems. A comparison of reasons for encounter, diagnoses, and interventions in primary care populations in the Netherlands, Japan, Poland, and the United States. J Fam Prac 2002;51:72–3. Available at: URL: http://www.jfponline.com

Omole F, Simmons BJ, Hacker Y. Management of Bartholin's duct cyst and gland abscess. Am Fam Physician 2003;68(1):135–40. Available at: URL: http://www.aafp.org/afp/20030701/135.html

Parker GM. Cross-functional teams. San Francisco: Jossey-Bass; 1999.

Parker GM. Team players and teamwork. San Francisco: Jossey-Bass; 1990.

Parkin JM, Hey EN, Clowes JS. Rapid assessment of gestational age at birth. Arch Dis Child 1976;51:259–63.

Pathology Laboratories of Arkansas, PA. FNA technique. Available at: URL: http://www.pathlabsofark.com/fna Accessed August 2005.

Pattinson RC. Perinatal care surveys 2000–2002. An overview of the challenges. In: Saving babies 2002. Third perinatal care survey of South Africa. MRC (Medical Research Council): Department of Health; 2002. p. 20–6.

Pearson DJ, Heywood P. Portfolio use in general practice vocational training: a survey of GP registrars. Med Ed 2004;38:87–95.

Philpott H, Kwast B. Developers of partogram in southern Africa. Available at: URL: http://www.doh.gov.za/docs/forms/matrec_guide.pdf

Planning and implementing cervical cancer prevention and control programs: a manual for managers 2004. Available at: URL: http://www.who.int/reproductive-health/cancers/prevention_control_cervical_cancer.html

Pless IB, Satterwhite B. A measure of family functioning and its application. Soc Sci Med, 7, 1973; 613–620.

Quill TE, Williamson PR. Healthy approaches to physician stress. Arch Intern Med 1990;150:1857–61.

Rappolt SG. Clinical guidelines and the fate of medical autonomy in Ontario. Soc Sci Med 1997;44:977–87.

RCOG national evidence-based clinical guidelines: the care of women requesting induced abortion; September 2004.

Reason J. Human error: models and management. BMJ 2000;320:768–70.

Reid C, Chan L, Tweeddale M. The who, where, and what of rapid sequence intubation: prospective observational study of emergency RSI outside the operating theatre. Emerg Med J 2004;21:296–301.

Roberston B, Allwood C, Gagiano C. Textbook of psychiatry for southern Africa. Cape Town: Oxford University Press; 2001. p. 49–50, 338–9.

Robums H, Firsley M. Why teams don't work. Princeton: Petersen-Pacesetter Books; 1998.

Rollnick S, Butler C, Allison JA. New videotape for trainers: health behaviour change: a selection of strategies. University of Wales: College of Medicine; 2001.

Rollnick SR, Mason P, Butler C. Health behaviour change: a guide for practitioners. Edinburgh: Churchill Livingstone; 1999.

Ross RT. How to examine the nervous system. Springfield, USA: Charles C Thomas; 1978.

Royal College of General Practitioners. Clinical guidelines for the management of acute low back pain. London: Royal College of General Practitioners. 1999 [cited 2005 Aug 26]. Available at: URL: http://www.nice.org.uk/page.aspx?o=lowbackpain

SA Pulmonology Society. Guidelines for the management of asthma in adults in South Africa. Part II. Acute asthma. S Afr Med J 1994 Jun;84(6):332–8.

Sackett DL. Evidence-based medicine. How to teach and practice EBM. 2nd ed. Edinburgh: Churchill Livingstone; 2000.

Sanders MJ, Lewis LM, Quick G. Mosby's paramedic textbook; 1995. p. 448–57.

SASOM (South African Society of Occupational Medicine). Guideline no. 6. Medical requirements for fitness to drive. SASOM; 1999.

Saxe N, Jessop S, Todd G. Handbook of dermatology for primary care. Cape Town: Oxford University Press SA; 1997. p. 96–100.

Scarisbrick G. The WHO lecture series on radiology and ultrasound. Geneva: World Health Organization; 2002.

Schuster M, McGlynn E, Brook R. How good is the quality of health care in the United States? Milbank Q 1998;76:517–63.

Screening for problem drinking. In: US Preventative Services Taskforce guide to clinical preventive services. 2nd ed. International Medical Publishing; 2002. p.567–82.

Sepilian V. Ectopic pregnancy. http://www.emedicine.com/med/topic3212.htm Accessed August 2005.

Sexually Transmitted Diseases (STD) Protocol. Standard treatment guidelines and essential drugs list for South Africa. Primary Health Care. South African National Department of Health; 2003.

Shanmugam V, Thaha MA, Rabindranath KS, Campbell KL, Steele RJC, Loudon MA. Rubber band ligation versus excisional haemorrhoidectomy for haemorrhoids. The Cochrane Database of Systematic Reviews 2005; 1(CD005034. DOI: 10.1002/14651858.CD005034. pub2).

Shannon S. Facilitating learning groups in CME. The Lancet 2004;363:826.

Silverman J, Kurtz S, Draper J. Skills for communicating with patients. Abingdon: Radcliffe Medical Press; 1998.

Sitas F, Zwarenstein M, Yach D, Bradshaw D. A national sentinel surveillance network for the measurement of ill-health in South Africa. S Afr Med J 1994;84:91–4.

Snadden D, Thomas M. The use of portfolio learning in medical education. Medical Teacher 1998;20(3):192–9.

Souter MC, Farquhar CM. Ectopic pregnancy: an update. Curr Opin Obstet Gynecol 2004 Aug;16(4): 289–93.

South African Family Practice, incorporating Genees-kunde. Information for authors and readers. Available at: URL: http://www.medpharm.co.za/safp/authors.html Accessed 6 September 2005.

South African handbook of resuscitation of the newborn. South African Paediatric Association; 2004.

South African Society of Occupational Medicine. Medical requirements for fitness to drive. 1st rev; 2004 August.

Spillane J, editor. Bickerstaff's neurological examination in clinical practice. 6th ed. Oxford: Blackwell Science; 1996.

Spinal column/cord injuries. Available at: URL: http://www. moondragon.org/ems/spinaltrauma.html. Accessed August 2005.

Statement by the working group of the Allergy Society of South Africa. Endorsed by the South African Pulmonology Society.

Stewart M, Brown BJ, Donner A, McWhinney IR, Oates J, Weston WW, et al. The impact of patient-centered care on outcomes. J Fam Prac 2000;49:796–804.

Steyn DW. Diagnostic procedures. In Cronjé HS, Grobler CJF. Obstetrics in southern Africa. Pretoria: Van Schaik; 2003:620–6.

Stiell IG, McKnight RD, Greenberg GM et al. Implementation of the Ottawa ankle rules. JAMA 1994;271:827–32.

Stiell IG, Wells G, Laupacis A et al. Multicentre trial to introduce the Ottowa ankle rules for use of radiography in acute ankle injuries. BMJ 1995;311:594–7.

Stott NCH. Primary health care: bridging the gap between theory and practice. Berlin: Springer-Verlag; 1983.

Stott NCH, Rollnick S, Rees MR, Pill RM. Innovation in clinical method: diabetes care and negotiating skills. Family Practice 1995;12:413–8.

Strategy and Tactics. Guide to measuring client satisfaction: a collaborative project between the National Department of Health and the initiative for sub-district support, as part of the Health System Trust; 2000.

Swimm DM. Insertion of orogastric and nasogastric tubes. In: Proehl JA, editor. Emergency nursing procedures. 2nd ed. Philadelphia: WB Saunders Company; 1999. p. 333–6.

Teichler M, editor. South African family practice manual. Bryanston: SA Academy of Family Practice and Primary Care; 1995.

Teichler M. Quality assurance in family practice. S Afr Fam Pract 1997;18:18–20.

Toerien A, Potter PC, Buys C. Appendix ix. The skin prick test. In: The Allsa handbook of practical allergy; p.201–204. Cape Town: The Allergy Society of South Africa; 1994.

Treat a casualty with a spine injury. Available at: URL: http://www.medtmg.com/blackboard/spine _injury.htm Accessed August 2005.

Tucker JR. Indications for, techniques of, and efficacy of gastric lavage in the treatment of the poisoned child. Curr Opin Pediatr 2000;12(2):163–5.

Ustun T, Sartorius N. Mental illness in general health care: an international study. Chichester: Wiley & Sons; 1995.

Van der Spuy Z, Anthony J. Handbook of obstetrics and gynaecology. Cape Town: Oxford University Press; 2002.

Vroom VH, Yelton PW. Leadership and decision making. New York: Wiley; 1974.

White KL, Williams TF, Greenberg B. The ecology of medical care. N Engl J Med 1961;265:885–92.

Williams T, Schutt-Aine, Cuca. Measuring family planning service quality through satisfaction exit interviews. In: Department of Health, quality assurance, September 1999. 2000;26(2):63–71.

Wilson D, Naidoo S, Bekker L, Cotton M, Martens G. Handbook of HIV medicine. Cape Town: Oxford University Press; 2002. p. 70–80.

WONCA (World Organisation of National Congresses and Associations of Family Medicine). Improving health systems: the contribution of family medicine. World Organisation of Family Doctors; 2002. p. 47.

Wood B. Interpreters in the medical consultation – a literature review. S Afr Fam Pract 1993;14:347–53.

Word-Medex. How to compose good medical/bioscientific research manuscripts. Available at: URL: http://www. word-medex.com.au/formatting/manuscript.htm Accessed 6 September 2005.

Woods DL, editor. Perinatal education programme manual 2. Newborn care. South Africa: Perinatal Education Trust; 1996.

Woods DL, editor. Perinatal education programme manual 5. The mother and baby friendly care manual. South Africa: Perinatal Education Trust; 2004.

World Bank. World development report. Issues in health. Washington D.C.; 1993.

World Health Organization. International statistical classification of diseases and related health problems. 10th rev. Geneva: World Health Organisation

World Health Organization. Pharmaceutical Newsletter. No. 3; 2002. p.5.

World Health Organization. Reproductive health library No. 5; 2002. Global action for skilled attendants for pregnant women. Available at: URL: http://www.who.int/reproductive-health/publications/global_action_for_skilled_attendants/rhr_02_17_8.html.

Zuber TJ. Office procedures. Baltimore: Lippincott, Williams & Wilkins; 1999.

INDEX

The Day the Mermaid Wept

Keith M. Lloyd

AuthorHouse™
1663 Liberty Drive
Bloomington, IN 47403
www.authorhouse.com
Phone: 1-800-839-8640

First published by AuthorHouse   6/23/2010

ISBN: 978-1-4520-3174-3 (sc)

Printed in the United States of America
Bloomington, Indiana

This book is printed on acid-free paper.

authorHOUSE®

Contents

LORD FEARN OF SOUTHPORT

Councillor for Norwood Ward

Tel: 01704 228577
Fax: 01704 508635

Norcliffe,
56 Norwood Avenue,
Southport,
PR9 7EQ

FORWARD.

What a joy to read Keith Lloyd's book which takes a close look at Southport's most famous cinema, The **Palladium**, later to be called The Gaumont and then the Odeon.

As a person whose first hand knowledge came from the fact that he lived there for many years, Keith was able to view and hear all that went on from his position within the "pent house" flat at the front of the cinema.

The insight and detail are a delight and certainly when I read and then graphically saw so many characters, including Keith's father Ken, the manager, along with stars who had appeared there over the years, I was transmitted into times which I had known.

How great it is to have someone who has such an intimate knowledge about one of Southports most famous buildings, visited by thousands over the years.

Sincerely

Ronnie Fearn

INTRODUCTION

Is it 30 years since the greatest icon of Southport's entertainment life disappeared?

I cannot believe that it is so long and also the number of people that have spoken to me in great affection of their memories of the wonderful time they had.

Because of this and the memories it holds for me personally, I have decided that time has come for the history to be put down for all who hold such similar feelings and for those who have heard tell, but did not have the opportunity to experience what past generations enjoyed.

I do hope that I bring a little joy in this book; my first attempt at the noble art of recording what was and will always remain a part of Southport's history.

There are so many I would like to thank for their contributions, but I must say that without the journalistic expertise of The Southport Visiter staff and photographers whose press cuttings gave me an insight or filled in the gaps, or my father Kenneth B. Lloyd, who was passionate about the subject and hoarded most of the historical, material I would not have been able to start.

So settle back and wallow in the nostalgia of what was
THE PALLADIUM / GAUMONT / ODEON, LORD STREET, SOUTHPORT.

Keith M. Lloyd
2009

Thank you to those who helped

Cedric Greenwood – Author and Journalist for his many column inches
Andrew Brown. Executive Editor. Southport Visiter, for his permission to reproduce and use of past contents.
Phil King - Former Head of Publicity and Attractions for his friendship, memories and informative insight.
The Staff - at the Atkinson Reference Library and Southport Town Planning Office, for letting me delve into their records.
Lord Ronnie Fearn. For his kind words and support.

And to all those nameless people who stood in the queues, worked whilst the public played or just simply loved going to the 'flicks' and became part of mine and Southport's history.

And finally I have to thank my wife Ann who convinced me to sit down and put pen to paper, and her support when it all went pear shaped!

CHAPTER 1.
WELCOME TO SOUTHPORT

Some say that the first sentence of any book is the most important as it either grabs the reader or puts them off instantly. The same can also be said for your new home, first impressions can be either great or down right horrible.

So it was for me at the tender age of 8, when my mother and my 3 year old brother Ian arrived at the Cheshire Lines Railway Station at the south of Lord Street. As one can imagine this was the big adventure. I had been born in Liverpool in 1946 and after a short time moved with my parents to Waterloo where my brother was born. We had followed my father's promotion in the cinema business. He had returned from active service in the war and returned to his pre war occupation as a cinema manager for the Rank Organisation. He had been running the Rivoli Cinema, Aigburth, and for his successes he had been promoted to the Odeon in Crosby Road, Waterloo. In effect he was the local boy made good, as he was from Crosby and had spent his education at Merchant Taylors
It was not long before he had made his mark and in 1955 his endeavours got him the promotion all north western managers dreamt of, The Gaumont Theatre in Southport.

So one day in the summer holidays of that year we boarded the train and travelled to this mysterious land north of Liverpool where we were to live in a home that was unique to any other.

My memories of the train ride are somewhat blurred, but on our arrival at Southport, we were met by my father, a dapper, moustachioed man who always stood ramrod straight, his brylcreamed hair cut to military short back and sides and had a serious problem wearing casual clothes, even in hot weather. It was not until his very senior years, did he discard his tie. This was always a matter of humour for his offspring, who pulled his leg mercilessly, but not then, woe be tide us if we didn't appear in public scrubbed and neat. His reasoning was that if his staff could be well turned out and look professional, then we should. After all we represented what was the best of Southport and as he was its guardian we must at all times be cognisant of this.

Suffice it to say, on occasions this was to be, for one of that age, to fall from grace. In fact I have wry memories of Mr.Tom Smith, the Chief of Staff, a man of Sergeant Major stature, who would pace the foyer in a fearful manner, catching me on my return from school in normal 'Just William' mode. From the lopsided cap on my unkempt hair, past the smudged facial features down to my socks at half mast and shoes, grey from playing footie in the playground.
My appearance must have been scary for Mr. Smith, for he would stride across the foyer, grab this urchin and bundle me into a nearby gents, where he would instruct me on sartorial elegance and ensure that my reappearance into the foyer was a dazzling little cherub. God forbid my father had seen me first, I dread to think what poor old Mr Smith would have been told, and therefore he and I came to an arrangement. I would arrive home and catch his eye, he would give me the all clear [this was also fixed up with other staff members],

I would then do a fast sprint across the front of house and up the back stairs and onwards to the Manager's Flat situated at the top of the building where we now lived.

As we walked from the station, still in awe of the new sights, the smell of steam drifting behind us as we were escorted to the kerb where a big shiny black and gold landau stood with a majestic black horse between its shafts. The wheels were bigger than me and we had to be assisted into the carriage. My father had hired this mode of transport as a welcome to Southport
Off down Lord Street the main road we went, with my father and the driver pointing out all the sights that would become second nature to me as the years rolled by.
The Prince of Wales Hotel, Eastbank St. where a policeman stood in the middle of the junction in a wooden box directing traffic, he waved us through and greeted us with a smile and a ' hello boys' as we passed. Things were very different in those days.

Then onwards passed the Town Hall, Christ Church, were I would later become a choirboy, my father was pointing out more than a few landmarks that we just couldn't take in at once. Then as we clip clopped past the Monument, he announced that we should look towards the right hand side and through the huge elm trees that bordered this big wide road called Lord Street we would see our new home.

For a young lad a home was a house with windows, a front door and a roof with chimneys, what I saw was a huge white palace set back from the road with many windows and doors, a flight of steps leading up to them and with towers on either side, surely this was not our house?. My mother was equally enthralled and could not believe her eyes either. Now as you can imagine, when your father collects you in a horse drawn carriage and after driving you to a wondrous palace that stood out from all the other buildings in the town, you could be forgiven to thinking he had won the national lottery, of course that concept had not been invented yet, and I was unaware of such matters as football pools just yet. Simply in modern vernacular, I was Gob smacked.

In 1955 we arrived at our new home

Southport from the air in 1954. In the foreground is Neville Street with the Colliseum Cinema at the bottom left. To the right of the Monument is the Trocedero Cinema formerly the Palais De Dance. But the building that stands out in all its glory is the Gaumont

This aerial photograph shows the extent of the vast theatre complex, the auditorium roof and the massive stage area with the car park to the rear where the artistes and their equipment were unloaded through the roller shuttered doors

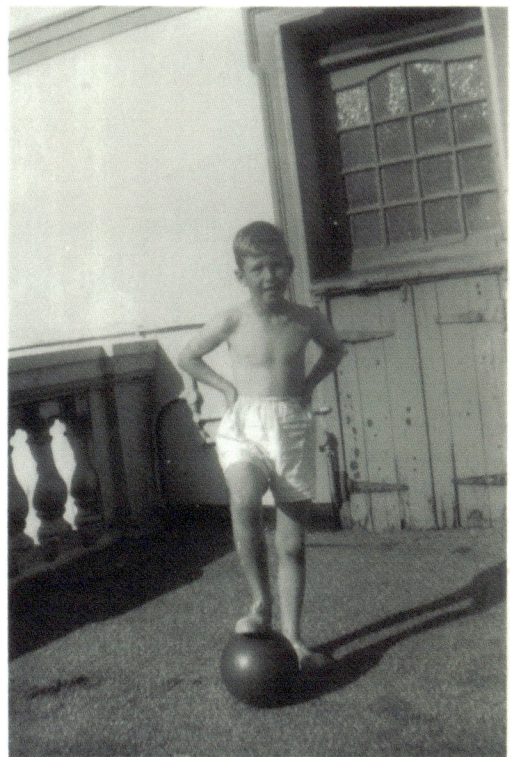

CHAPTER 2.
LIFE AT THE TOP

When someone tells you that they live in the penthouse, be kind, it is not all that it is cracked- up to be. For example, there is the time it takes to get through the front door and up to your residence. Alright, I know there are lifts and so on, but what if they are out of order? I know, some people live at the top of high rise flats and when their lifts are out of action, they suffer the ignominy of climbing all of those stairs to get to their floor. God forbid you live at the top.

Having set the scene, you may have guessed that is where we lived, right at the top of this amazing building.

To get there was a matter of physical endurance, particularly if like my Mother, you may have to lug bags of shopping or pram with howling sibling therein.

But for our first time it was an awesome experience.

Allow me to take you on a guided tour of this elevating experience. As you stood on the pavement outside the theatre [It was in essence a Cinema but it was called a theatre because of its immense theatrical background as you will come to see later] and looking up, it was like standing before a castle with its two great keeps on either side of the main entrance, before you was a flight of steps leading to an outside foyer, or portico, there were pillars on the top step through which you walked to get to the glass doors. There were 3 sets of double doors and 2 sets of revolving doors
It was like entering a very posh London Hotel.
As you passed through these doors, you found yourself in the grand foyer. This was a huge room that would today easily house a couple of bungalows plus gardens. In front of you were two sets of staircases in white marble leading up and away and in between them the main entrance to the stalls or ground floor areas. At each end of the foyer were additional entrances. Our tour now takes us up the right hand side staircase, past the Cashiers' box, where pleasant ladies dispensed your ticket and to their right was the gaily lit and decorated Kiosk where you could obtain your confectionary, soft drinks and tobacco products, of course in those days there was no ban on smoking.

Opposite the stalls entrance was the Manager's Office and the booking office. The Manager's Office was relatively small, it was where my father would meet and greet, dispense wisdom and generally rule his kingdom. This was to become a place of many emotions for me, and a place not to be taken lightly. I will come back later to this throne room.

We climb the stairs away from the foyer and turn right, ahead is a very long staircase approximately 10 feet wide and illuminated with ceiling down lights which cast shadows between the large photographs on either side, of film stars past and present.

After what seemed like an eternity we reached the landing. Off to the left was the entrance area to the Circle with signs for the toilets and waiting areas and to the right was the entrance to the restaurant. Oh yes this was a magnificent building with all mod - cons. but we must keep going.

As you entered the restaurant there was a carpeted staircase to your left and up these we now climb. After about 12 of these steps it turns sharp left and continues to go higher. At this point dear reader, I suggest you stop and take a breather. I used to, onward and upwards to the top. 'Great! Now-What?' I hear you gasp. Well if you had stepped to your right, through a set of double doors you would be in the standing room area of the back circle looking down across the auditorium towards the stage.

For our tour we turn left, through a simple wooden door marked – 'Private Authorised Personnel Only'

Welcome to the balcony area of the theatre. For those who remember the theatre, this was where the Theatre's name was sighted, against a row of carved stone balustrades. For those who don't, have a look at the various photographs and you will understand where we are. For me and my family it was a great vantage point and the flat roof as we called it was many things to us. For me and my brother it was a tennis court, a cricket pitch, it was where we played football it was where we spied on the townsfolk passing lawfully by and where we dropped the odd water bomb on the unsuspecting public. Of course it had its down sides as well. Consider this, you are in the middle of a game of cricket, an easy ball is delivered and you smack it for six, where does it land? Well usually after bouncing off St Georges Church spire, it ended up in the gardens in front of the property. Or if you were unlucky it bounced onto Lord Street.

Now if at some stage dear reader you recall driving along the famous red asphalt in an open top bus enjoying the sights and a tennis ball landed in your lap – could I please have it back?. Just be thankful we didn't use a real cricket ball. We did lose a few strays over the years.

Another reason for not living in a penthouse, chasing after your tennis ball is not recommended.

The flat roof was in fact above the restaurant ceiling, so it was a problem not thumping about disturbing the customers below. We were constantly warned about it. Oh come on we were kids having fun. It had an asphalt surface and was covered in light gravel and when the sun shone it got a bit sticky underfoot, but it was a great place to sun bathe

Finally on the other side of our play-area, was our new home. This was designated the residence of the General Manager.

It was a little unimposing, to the left as you looked at it, was the balcony and then a single level bungalow style building ran to the right until it reached the back wall of the theatre. There was a brick wall about 4 feet high topped off by a number of stained glass window set side by side and above them was a pitched roof. At the right hand side, in the corner was a door with stained glass windows.

As we stepped into our new home I immediately realised how compact it was. In Waterloo we used to live in a converted house with large Victorian rooms.

This was tiny in comparison. The lounge at the balcony end was in fact the left hand turret as you looked at the premises. It was a strange shape, similar to having a square with two sides cut off at 45 degrees. The saving grace was the view. From there we could look all the way down Lord Street towards the monument and beyond.

We could watch the people queuing for the shows and marvel at the numbers and sometimes wonder if the queue would ever end.

Next to the Lounge was a kitchen, basic in content and this was where our mother would cook up various delights. Food rationing was still a memory following the end of the war. We did not have the modern concepts of microwaves yet, and food was still bought fresh. Bread was baked in the oven and Sunday was the family day of roast. Standards were different in those days, we would gather at the table and my father would carve and serve, we would say grace, and then chat about our week past, and what was to come.
We did not have the luxury of a television, in fact my father hated the concept, it would ruin the film industry he would predict. We did enjoy listening to the wireless however, whilst tucking into our meal. At that time the majority of the country listened to comedy shows during the mid Sunday afternoon such as 'The Navy Lark' or 'Educating Archie' and then there was 'Ray's a Laugh' in which top comedian Ted Ray would have us chuckling heartily at humour that now seems very naïve. Later on I will recount my meeting with this funny man.

As we move down the flat from the kitchen, we come to my and Ian's bedroom, which was opposite the front door. This room was about 8 feet by 12 feet, similar in size to the kitchen next door. You couldn't get a lot in there. We had two single beds and a chest of drawers and everything else went under the beds. There was a single window that had to have a blackout curtain due to the bright floodlights that shone up from the street below, illuminating the entire frontage of the building, and as we lay in bed we could hear the music playing from the silver screen within the cinema. At times this was a distraction from sleeping, but the real stirring stuff would send a chill up your spine and bring back memories, particularly as we did not have far to go to watch the film of the week.

The flat was in fact L shaped, the bathroom which was very large, occupied the corner and later revealed a secret trapdoor, this led down to the store room of the restaurant below next to the manager's office. Finally the master bedroom completed the flat. It was the largest room and had a window that looked out onto the flat roof. This was my parent's private place and we rarely entered, unless invited. This was not unusual in those days, it was just the accepted routine of family life then.

So for those who remember the 'kids' from the cinema, and wondered what it was like to live over the shop, I trust that is the enlightenment you all craved. For us it was a life of simple solitude and unlike the kids who lived next door to each other and popped in and out of each other's lives, we had no such companionship. In fact when we made a friend, it was rare if they would be allowed to enter the private and secure world we lived in.

We were however permitted to have our friends join us for free screenings of the family films or on Saturday morning children's club. The best seats in the house were in the circle, upstairs, they were the most expensive so of course having access to them was awesome, getting them for free was beyond awesome, so in those days making friends with me and my brother was a good idea. My father was cognisant of this and would watch out for the false chums who would latch onto us.

I would spend many hours at the window of the lounge watching the world go past, taking in the changing seasons and observing the amazing sights that can only be seen from that level.
For example, there was the spectacular sight of Lord Street flooding, which seemed to happen every time there was a heavy rain storm at the same time as the tide was coming in. The water in the drains which emptied out onto the beach could not take the flow of the incoming tide and swept back up through the drains and onto the

road. The result was the water rose ever higher. I watched as gallant young men carried young ladies across the road from the theatre steps passing a submerged mermaids pond as they went. To this day I always wondered if these chivalrous gents ever succeeded in their courtship. It must have been a great 'pick-up line' – 'Don't worry Luv I'll carry you over the threshold'. I remember collapsing in hysterics as a group of these gallant souls were halfway across when a bus passed by and completely deluged them with the flood water, which was at least knee deep by this time.

On another occasion we were woken up by the unusual sound of a burglar alarm ringing out across the town centre. In those days it was unusual, and people actually took notice. An alarm on a shop was as unique as teeth on a chicken. We dashed from our beds and excitedly watched as a police car, one of those black Wolsley with a bell on the front raced down the footpath across the road and screeched to a halt outside a jeweller shop, someone had done a smash and grab on the window and had it away with the sparklers. It was just like watching the black and white Saturday morning pictures where a Scotland Yard Flying Squad reacted to the activities of the robbers.
It was headline news in the newspapers. I don't know how it turned out, but in those days the detection rate was much better than today and crime was not as prevalent.

Another vision that caught my eye was the all year round display of fairy lights that adorned the grand elm trees that bordered the pavements For some reason they brought warmth and a sense of cheerfulness with their many colours stretching as far as the eye could see in the darkness. When Dutch Elm disease swept across the country, many of those great timbers had to be cut down leaving huge gaps and of course the fairy lights had to go as well. It was a gloomy period in more ways than one. The street looked and felt miserable at times and it was not for many years later that a semblance returned when replacement saplings had matured and the local businesses had a whip round and put lights up for Christmas.

It was about this time that I came to look upon the gardens in front of the theatre as our personal garden. I was convinced that the council would come around each season to ensure our garden was the best in town, particularly as the main feature was the mermaid, who sat on her tail holding a fish, from which a fountain emerged. She sat in a circle of water surrounded by a flower bed of differing plants dependant of the time of year. She seemed to be standing guard and at the same time welcoming people to our front door. She was a magical sight from above, and for you who only see her at ground level, I can reveal she is more than just a statue, of a Mermaid; she is the most impressive sculpture in Southport. You pass her and don't give her a moments thought. For us who watched her, she seemed to be alive and aware of our presence, it was if she knew she was in front of the town's grandest showpiece and she was proud of her position. I do not know who actually created her, but if I could I would shake their hand and thank them. The Mermaid was for me, sitting in the penthouse, a way of coming down to earth and being part of the normal way of life. She is the constant in an ever changing world and I hope she will remain so for ever.

There was another creature in our lives at that time, who shared our adventures with. This was KINE our beloved cat.
She had come with us from Waterloo in her basket and had set up store at the Gaumont as if it was her own personal domain.
It was not unusual for people standing in front of the Mermaid and looking up at the façade of the theatre, to suddenly see her parading along the balcony, sunning herself and preening like one of those aristocrats from a Disney film.
She was named after the Kinematograph Weekly, a trade magazine.

She was a great mouser, and on the odd occasion enjoyed bringing her trophies home for everyone to gaze in admiration at. Unfortunately the usherettes were not as impressed for some reason and banished her from their staff room.

On one occasion though, she did give us a reason to fall about laughing. She decided to go on the prowl, when the theatre had closed for the night, unbeknown to her, the humans had also decided to put on one of those midnight movie things, publicised as a dare. Are you brave enough to sit through this horror film on your own? Sort of thing, and of course some young lady would be selected to sit and watch Phsycho or The Day of the Triffids having had her photograph taken by the press, who then disappeared in my Dads office for a 'Tea Break !!'.

Halfway through the night, Kine thought nothing of curling up on the young ladies lap with the inevitable result.

Cue screams.

Kine was spotted nipping smartly back home and the incident was put down to over active imagination. From thence onwards whenever such a stunt was hatched, the cat was firmly locked in the flat. Although some years later she did venture out, and came face to face with a lion. But that's another story.

Kine the family cat and fearless mouser, would sunbathe in some of the most perilous parts of the theatre. Here she is perched on the balcony with Lord Street behind her and below a formal picture taken after her encounter with Rajah the Lion.

11

CHAPTER 3
THE GOOD, THE BAD AND THE DOWN RIGHT NASTY

As time passed and we settled into our strange new home, it became evident that other matters would have to be taken into account. My mother became pregnant with who was to become our sister Valerie. Ian and I had to go to that social enigma called school and our father got on with his show business.

Ian was shipped off to Holy Trinity Infants School, which was near enough for him to be taken and collected, whilst I endured a slightly longer trip to Linaker Street School, where I was to be educated in the art of using the bus.

In those days, Southport Corporation had regular transport running in its own livery of crimson and cream with the town crest proudly displayed along with the motto 'Salus Populi' which my father, who had learnt Latin told me, meant 'In the service of the people'.
I would pick up my transport at the Monument and travel to school past the shops and houses until it dropped me off near to the school.
I was introduced to education back in Crosby, so going to a new school was a bit of an adventure, I did not realise how much. I was the kid who lived at the cinema where most of the pupils went on Saturday mornings.

This made me a bit of a celebrity and like them I was singled out for attention. Most wanted to know if I could get them in for free. They also told me about the art of 'bunking in '. I was also introduced to the delightful concept of bullying, which was to follow me onto Meols Cop Secondary School where I learnt of my father's attitude towards their older siblings.

I suppose there is always a down side to life and this was to become mine. When Kenneth B. Lloyd became the General Manager of The Gaumont, the local County Borough Police Force, met with him and warned him there was a serious unruly element in the town that tended to meet there. These were the Teddy Boys, the youth of the day who dressed in the now predominant Rock + Roll garb of drainpipe trousers topped with string ties and wide lapelled jackets and not forgetting the thick soled suede shoes. These 'gentlemen' and their lady friends would run riot around the cinema of choice and spoil the entertainment of the general public.

It was not unknown for them to hurl ice cream tubs or orange drinks about and in todays speak, be completely anti social.

That is until Mr. Lloyd entered the scene. He had been a cinema manager in the tough area of Aigburth and then Waterloo; he had been schooled in the various parts of Liverpool that, so called, hard men from Southport had not been to. He was also a veteran of the recently ended World War in which he had been an instructor in weapons training, and had a few scrapes with unfriendly types from other countries. If you remember earlier, I described his military bearing, and he was not ready to surrender his pride and joy to a section of the community whose aim was to cause as much annoyance to their elders and betters.

Now it would be inappropriate to name anyone involved, suffice it to say, there were a number of families in the town who seemed to be at the forefront of these troubles, my father was fully briefed by the Police and other cinema managers as to who they were and consequently, war was declared.

Operation –' Bar the Bloody Lot of Them' was instigated. The staff was bolstered by pep talks and words of support came from all quarters, and at the front dressed as always in his tuxedo was the manager. Everyone who even looked troublesome was denied access and the lesser types were given strong advice. The doormen and Usherettes stood guard over them and these few teenagers were made to feel under constant threat.
It worked for a while, and then after many weeks of pleading and heart rending promises to behave, certain ones were allowed a probationary period of rehabilitation.

Oh well, good idea, maybe, but one group saw it as an opportunity and one Saturday evening sat themselves on the front row of the stalls and started their antics all over again.

The leader of the pack, egged on by his slightly dimmer followers thought it amusing to call out the manager, who obliged by inviting him to have a look at something near the side exit where he may discover something to his advantage.
Foolishly and full of his own self importance this young man swaggered outside, telling his chums, he would be back in a minute. A short time later, and to the amazement of the audience who had stopped watching the main feature to watch this other form of entertainment, Mr Lloyd re entered the auditorium – alone. He closed the exit doors behind him and still looking neat and tidy, his hair still in place, asked the rest of the gang to leave and escorted them through the auditorium to the foyer and out into the night to the spontaneous applause of the relieved film goers.

Before they left, the inevitable question of their leader's whereabouts arose. He apparently was sitting in the side passage somewhat worse for wear and would not dare venture back into the cinema again. Naturally, the word went round like wildfire, and, as a result, cinema takings in the town started to improve. Top of the list and gaining queues and compliments was of course the Gaumont.

The thing is, Dad had a trophy on the mantelpiece, it was a simple brass cup on a plinth, underneath were the words.
'Royal Army Pay Corps'- [detachment 33] -1941.
Light Weight Championship – Winner – Kenneth B. Lloyd.
I still have that memento and the memories of his advice on how to defend yourself from aggression.

Earlier I remarked about the down side, I was happily sitting in class year in and year out, the eldest son of the bloke who had barred their older brothers etc. and was therefore a target for any form of retribution deemed fit. I became very wary of people wanting to make friends with me and learned the art of speedy retreat in the face of adversity. I also found that if whilst under 6 or 7 bodies trying to thump you in the mid morning break, you burst out laughing, it had an unnerving result. How can you take out your frustrations on someone who laughs? It worked most of the time. On the other occasions, I was not so lucky.
I must mention though that, at Meols Cop where most of my suffering occurred, we had a teacher, well loved and respected, George Bromilow. He was the PE instructor.

He spotted my dilemma and had a chat, after that we arranged for my boxing skills to be honed a little and later on, in the gym, we found out who was up for it. Suffice it to say a bully is a coward, and only a few took us up on the challenges. They also went away like the teddy boys, and peace reigned for my final years at school.

I did have the ultimate power on those who caused me the most suffering however. A quiet word and they found that Saturday Morning Children's Club was a no go. There were the odd occasions which I hinted at earlier that involved water bombs but I suppose I should pass this subject by and move on.

Saturday Morning Children's Club

WE COME ALONG ON SATURDAY MORNINGS………
That's how it started on a Saturday morning. This was for nearly a 1000 kids the highlight of the week. In the 50's and 60's, television was a new concept, unaffordable for most. There was no entertainment to speak of, unless you made it yourself, imagination was the stuff of Kings [and Queens], having a gay time meant something totally different and computers, even Flash Gordon hadn't got one of them.

Excited children aged between 6 years and 15 years would queue up outside, clutching their pocket money waiting patiently to enter the great building where their imagination would run riot. Across the marbled foyer to the nice ladies in the pay box would take their 6 pence entrance fee, issue them with their all important ticket and then it was away to the stalls entrance, guided by tall uniformed doormen who had suddenly become their Uncle somebody or other.
The uniformed ladies who must have been someone's Aunt tore your ticket in half and pointed out which way to go, with a friendly smile that made you feel instantly welcome. Then into the magical kingdom they ran.

At 10am on the dot, a buzz of expectation ran around the young audience, the lights suddenly started to dim and the dark red walls with its gold highlights darkened until the only illumination came from the great domed ceiling like an upturned saucer with a chandelier in the centre. The lights hidden inside its rim went out leaving only the footlights shining onto the huge curtains on the stage, and almost immediately these dimmed and the great crimson and gold curtains swished open to reveal the huge silver screen.
The National Anthem would sound and everyone dutifully stood up and respectfully sang the words as if their life depended on it. After all we were British and our parents had just fought a World War, so we were more patriotic than today's children.

Having got the old vocal chords oiled, we were ready for the big one…..

WE COME ALONG ON SATURDAY MORNING
GREETING EVERYBODY WITH A SMILE
WE COME ALONG ON SATURDAY MORNING
KNOWING IT'S ALL WORTH WHILE

AS MEMBERS OF THE GB CLUB
WE ALL INTEND TO BE
GOOD CITIZENS WHEN WE GROW UP
AND CHAMPIONS OF THE FREE

WE COME ALONG ON SATURDAY MORNING
GREETING EVERYBODY WITH A SMILE – SMILE – SMILE
GREETING EVERYBODY WITH A SMILE

This was followed by a big cheer.

[The song was actually written by a Rank circuit organist called Con Docherty, and a film version was made, complete with bouncing ball over the words]

The programme always started with the cartoons, Mighty Mouse, Woody Woodpecker, Looney Tunes, Bugs Bunny and the inevitable Donald Duck and his friends. You got at least 2 of these before the weekly episode of the current serial came on. Usually a black and white extravaganza of mayhem, Flash Gordon [played by Buster Crabbe] fighting the Dustbin Robots from another galaxy, or Batman and Robin spoiling the fun of some bank robber and driving a 1940 style car, the Bat Mobile of the day. Other subjects included some poor group of souls lost in a jungle in South America. Each of these left you hanging on and with some cliff-hanger situation for the hero, to be continued next week. Phew…

And then the interval, the lights came up and those lovely Aunts had changed their clothes and where now stood in front of the stage where the massive organ sat in the orchestra pit that surrounded the stage. They were dressed in crisp white overalls with an apron and carried a tray in front of them. They dispensed ice cream in tubs with a wooden spoon or drinks with a straw for a few pence, but if your pocket money ran to it, you nipped smartly out into the foyer and joined another lengthy queue for your sweets or for real luxury – a choc ice wrapped in silver foil. Then back to your closely guarded seat for the next part of the programme.

The lights dimmed, but not completely, the stage stayed lit up and as the salesgirls vanished, a man suddenly started playing the organ and as the last refrains petered out, a spotlight landed onto the side of the stage and there was the man dressed in a smart suit and tie, greeting all and sundry.
He would stand in front of a microphone very similar to those seen in old BBC pictures of radio broadcasters and he would get you singing and clapping to some song or other and then he would entertain you with a competition, there were fancy dress competitions, talent competitions, you name it he had one up his sleeve, either this week or in time for you get ready, a few weeks down the line. You knew you would be there because like the serial, you didn't want to miss out.

Sometimes there was a community aspect, such as the Guide Dogs for the Blind, this was a very emotive subject, and everyone brought bags of silver paper or tin foil or milk bottle tops and even a junior committee was formed to oversee the collection, until dozens of bags of the stuff filled all sorts of corners. When enough had been collected it was cashed in and the proceeds would be given to Captain Finney a blind war veteran and North West regional director of the charity, along with his boxer guide dog [Kim]. I got to know Arthur Finney very well, his jovial humour and interest in children was not lost on me and he invited me around to his home in Queens Road and helped me understand to problems of blindness. He had been seriously injured in the war and blinded by an explosion. He and his dogs were firm favourites with the club.
Along with this the children's club supported the Sunshine Home for the Blind which had been bombed in the conflict and still carried on until some decades later.

The annual Christmas tree appeal was a way we would collect presents for those who where worse off than we were, and many a parent was pestered to buy something for the tree. This was always a main attraction because the Mayor would come along and would place the first present under it and along with all the pomp and ceremony we would build on it until Christmas week when senior club members or the club prefects or monitors would go with the staff and hand out the presents [with Father Christmas – of course] to local children's homes.

There are many in the town that later went into show business in one way or the other as a result of the talent competitions. Who can forget the Skiffle Groups, everyone was a Lonny Donegan with T chest and washboard for instruments. Then we had the wannabees of the day, there were the Lulu's, the Johnny [Cry] Rays, the Rock'n Rollers and the ballet dancers. Such talent and what fun, as they paraded their stuff on stage, we were doing our version of the X factor in the audience, some of it had to be toned down by the man in the suit, who occasionally entertained us with his own talent.

Yes my father was also a musician. He played the trumpet. In fact he had played with some of the famous bands in the past. His favourite star was Louis Armstrong whom he had met and played with, along with Jack Payne and other orchestras.

His trumpet 'Pocahontas' [why he called it that I am at a loss to know] still has pride of place at my brother's home, which is appropriate, as he became a musician himself, and is still a force to be reckoned with when he emulates Dire Straits at various venues with his group Raw Deal. My sister Valerie also went into show-business and took up dancing and modelling. Our mother, Eunice, had been on stage, singing and playing the piano, so it does not seem unusual that we all had some form of entertainment in our blood. The nearest I came was singing in the choir at Christ Church, although I did enter the Southport Music Festival and came third [there was a flu epidemic at the time so I suppose I was lucky to get that high] as for the rest, I learnt to be an aficionado on tissue paper and comb.

Local groups or bands were invited to play for the children, which was a fantastic chance for them and also for their fans all in one place.

Who would forget the enthusiasm of the budding Rock 'n Rollers with names such as, The Metronomes, The Interns, The Diplomats, The Jokers or The Casuals? One wonders whatever happened to these talented people. Did they achieve stardom as they hoped or did they like the rest of us, enjoy the moment before moving on to more mundane activities.

As a footnote, Dad got together a group of friends and formed 'The Orbit Jazzmen' and held a miniature Jazz Festival for the club. In fact 2 agents came to see them and booked them for engagements [due to managerial commitments Dad could not accept and they got a replacement trumpeter to stand in for him].The kids screamed the house down and really loved the act.

One thing about the Children's Club, it was a great publicity magnet, and Dad being the showman he was, never let an opportunity pass by for a photo call and an entry in the local newspaper. Many young faces of the day can look back and say that was me when such and such happened.

Going by the many press clippings Dad kept, he had the children doing one thing or other and it was a great marketing tool. That is why many people still remember the old place with such affection. They were part of the history.

As the stage show wound up, Dad would bring people up from the audience in the birthday section, if it was your birthday that week, there was a small gift and a moment of fame, and after singing Happy Birthday the organist [Bill Hopper] would bring it all to a close by playing 'Sing as we Go' and if you had forgotten the words, they appeared on the screen to remind you.

And finally, the Big Picture This was a feature length, well in those days at least an hour long. Of course they had to be 'U' certificate stuff, suitable for all ages but at least they were watch able. Every subject from comedy to cowboys, Pirates to Tarzan, action and adventure, it was there to gaze in wonder at on the great silver screen. There were of course the CFF [Children's Film Foundation] pictures made by British studios usually in black and white and starring young people who would one day become household names. They were the sort of feel good 'Famous Five' type stories that were prevalent in those days.

You could always tell what kind of film had been on, by just watching the kids coming out just after mid-day, re-enacting the scenes as they ran up the street and back to their normal lives. Cowboys shooting Indians, pointing fingers in pretend guns and making strange whooshing noises or with raincoats around their neck like Zorro's cape battling pretend swordfights with the Mexican soldiers.

For me and my brother, we didn't have far to go, we of course had the best seats in the house, in the circle, where only a few other kids [who could afford the extra 6 pence] sat.

It was a bit like being in first class, whilst the remainder flew economy. We even had our own Ice cream Lady. Given that there were only about 100 kids at most, sitting in the 500 odd plush seats, you had loads of room. You can see why we were always being hounded by 'friends' when freebies were being handed out. Another factor was that Dad always arranged for us to get a free choc ice at the interval. Oh happy days!.

Two minutes later we were back home and watching the economy class going home and when it was raining [those water bombs get everywhere] having a chuckle at their misfortune.

Flash Gordon and my own planet Mongo

One of the side effects of living in a building the size of our home, was the silence, it was eerie. When it was closed to the public and the cleaners had gone home, or on Sunday afternoons, or late at night when the shows had finished, there was a period of actual peace and tranquillity. This was when I would venture out and explore.

This was real Flash Gordon stuff. Imagine being in a huge cavern, no light and pitch darkness and some where out there was a lost world. This was my play ground and I got to know every nook and cranny. Always aware that there could be a monster or two, around any corner.

Of course the imagination ran rife; my father had two offices in the building, the front office where he would meet and greet dignities - and the back office, situated off stage and at the rear of the dressing rooms. This was the real hub of the place, and the lair of 'Ming the Merciless' [Dad] to be avoided at all costs.

Like dungeons and dragons there were many levels to this game, the easy peasy bits like the front of house and the harder levels like the projection suite or the back stage areas.

Of course there was the sanctuary area as well. This was where the friendly folk would hide me when Ming came by. Known as the staff rooms, these were in 4 locations. The nearest to home was just across the flat roof and occupied the other tower, this was where the operators hung out.

These were the technical chaps who lived at the top of the mountain and viewed the landscape through small apertures cut into the rock face, they spun magic from great whirring machines called projectors, and could at the turn of a dial or flick of a switch bring music alive and colour to the great cavern below.

The access to this level was through a simple door next to my parents' bedroom window on the flat roof, then up the stairs and onto a gantry which ran into the main projection suite. There were a couple of other rooms off this where the operators or projectionists would edit and rewind the films and others with electrical switches and equipment stored on the walls. In the main room were the main projectors, which would be replaced when a more modern type was invented.

This level of the game was fine provided the grand magician was not around. Mr Harold Gale was the Chief Projectionist and a man to be wary of. He ruled his kingdom fiercely and only he could stand up to Ming. His troops though were more than happy to show me around and I was even instructed on how to lace up and check the gates on the awesome ray guns that spilled moving pictures onto the silver screen below. From up there, the screen looked much smaller and so far away.

As I travelled down the labyrinths to the ground floor level, one was always cognisant of being caught by the Chief of Staff, Tom Smith, he of the frog march to the gents for a post school scrub up. His troops however were a wee bit more understanding and I could slip into the foyer, nip past the pay desk and kiosk and visit them in the cellar below. Now those of you who knew the theatre, may be unaware, but under the foyer area and below the kiosk was a large room, accessible by double doors by the right hand side stalls entrance. Down the flight of stone stairs and into another sanctuary your hero would slip. There he could rest and chat with the doormen, the cleaners or the salesgirls. This was where the large chest freezers and ice cream trays where kept along with the various accoutrements for interval sales would be organised. It was also where the doormen could be found having a quiet ciggie or the cleaners stored their buckets, mops, cartons of Ajax and Vim and various other necessities to keep the premises up to standard.

They were in fear of their leader who would set little traps to see if they did their job correctly, like leaving a matchstick on top of a door post to see if they had dusted. In those days dear reader, things were very different than today. It was the expected thing. It also meant the place was immaculate.

Earlier I mentioned the Manager's Office, The Throne room of Ming the Merciless. One did not wish to be ordered into this domain as it could be serious, it was where Dad would hire and fire staff, dispense justice and would oversee the daily comings and goings, and it was the hub of the front of house operation.

Inside it was a simple room, a desk and chairs, a filing cabinet and the all important safe for the takings and important files. This was a large steel box as tall as me and was built into the wall. On the walls were pictures of the great and famous in the entertainment world and also the many certificates awarded to Dad for his work in promoting the business.

Next door was the booking office where the ticket stubs and seating plans were stored, it was the domain of Miss Doris Moore the head cashier who knew everything there was to know about the forthcoming shows and any booking problems. On the door was a full length mirror for the staff to check their appearance. I avoided these rooms; they were not for a Flash Gordon wannabee.

The next sanctuary was the hardest to reach, one had to negotiate ones way through the stalls, via the side aisle to the front of stalls, and this was like crossing no mans land, because as you stepped down the sloping floor you were under the balcony ceiling until half way and in a darker area, but once clear you were exposed by the light from the silver screen and had to move swiftly to the front where a set of double doors nestled in the corner. If you timed it just right, during a dark section of film you could slip unnoticed from the first row of seats across another exposed area and through the doors. This was where most of the public were caught trying to help their friends bunk in without paying.

For the unenlightened, the art of bunking in was as follows. Friend goes in and properly buys a ticket, usually paid for by 5 or 6 others clubbing together. The friend sits as close to the doors in question and at an appropriate time would slip through the doors to the outside exits and open said doors, then slip back, hopefully unnoticed to his seat. The remainder of group would then like prisoners of war in escape mode, enter one by one and mingle with audience.

Simple.

Well actually no, there were problems, like the lights in the corridor which would shine into the darkened cinema, cue the usherettes and or doormen. Also up in the projection suite, the ever vigilant Mr.Gale would telephone his observations.

For those of you who got caught trying this method of access, it wasn't so much the Doormen or Usherettes you had to be wary of, it was the eyes in the sky and because they were behind that bright stream of light above you, they were invisible to you. So now you know. Of course I had an advantage, I knew where and when to look, and could wear my cloak of invisibility just as well.

The auditorium as it was called was a vast place housing the 1500 plush red faux satin tip up seats of the stalls. There were 5 aisles separating them and carpeted in the corporation red and gold. The aisle sloped form the back stalls where many a romance started down to the orchestra pit which could house a full symphony and where the imposing Compton Organ took central position.
I will expand later about the organist, William Cecil Hopper [Bill] who was my father's assistant manager and had followed him from Crosby.

But we must continue on our journey.

Once through the right hand side double doors [on either side of the stage; the left hand side went out to the car park and the right hand side went to the back stage area] the corridor in front split into two. One way went directly to the exit doors, the other went through another door up some stairs and onto the level we now call 'The Stage'.

On this level, there were many hidden traps to catch our young hero as he would explore, there was the Realm of Ming, the back office to you, where the
administration of the theatre was done and next door was the domain of the female, better known as the usherette's staff room.

This was the other sanctuary available, it was not as good as the others, mainly due to the aromas that emanated from it, a mixture of perfumes, face powders, cigarette smoke and so on. It was however a place where if our hero timed it right could be really friendly, the ladies were always maternal towards me, knowing how solitary my life was, and having to keep an eye on my little brother, and his Mum in the family way and he must be lonely..... aaaaah.

Listen, you've played the same game yourself, my variation was no different. It did get me the tea and sympathy card, and they were all like older sisters and aunts, so what!.

As I have indicated by now, my mother was pregnant with Valerie, who would be born at Easter in 1956, and of course would cause changes in our life style as yet unexpected.

But I digress. The stage level also housing other than the stage itself, also housed the 6 dressing rooms that stars of stage, screen, radio, TV and recording labels would and had occupied. These rooms were basically Spartan, with plain brick walls, painted with numerous coats of cream gloss for easy cleaning. These had false wooden panels which ran around the room. The floors were concrete, painted in red tile paint all of which made it simple to keep tidy. The furniture was also basic, there was a counter along one wall with the obligatory mirror with overhead lighting and if you were lucky there may be an armchair to relax on. Other than that and a couple of stools there wasn't much more. Stars did bring their own accessories and made the place more comfortable if they were staying longer than one night. Most did not even have a window, but they were cosy little rooms.

Below the stage was where the orchestra stayed, they had to store their instruments and costumes in rooms which shared the area with heating pipes and trap door equipment along with scenery and lighting equipment. This was a dark and claustrophobic place and at times very warm. It was accessed via the orchestra pit in front of the stairs and via steps from the back of the stage

Number 2 dressing room was next to the realm of Ming and from there he could watch for intruders. Get the idea. You will later when we get to the Beatles and other big names.
In fact I think it only right that the description of the stage area should be left to the end of my memoirs, where in chapter 8 of this book, is my fathers own words and description of the history of the Palladium, Gaumont, Odeon.

However, before we depart from the stage area, I must mention the Organ Room. This was situated within the walls of the building, accessed from a set of stairs just adjacent to stage it self. In fact there was a similar one on the other side of the proscenium arch. Inside this room were housed the huge pipes of steel that carried the various notes from the bellow below. The organ was a major feature of theatres those days and this one was a magnificent example. One word of advise though, if you were in that room when the organist let rip below in the orchestra pit, it was as if you had stuck your head inside Big Ben as the hour was struck. It left you reeling with shock and deafened you beyond belief. This was not a place to be without serious protection.

I mentioned that there were 4 places of sanctuary in this world of adventure. This was the 'Restaurant Managers' office area and stock rooms. I told you that there was a trap door in the floor of our bathroom, well if you lifted this and slipped down the wooden stairs, it led to a door, through which if entered led you to into the stock room full of goodies. At the far end and underneath our lounge was a small office with a window that also looked out onto Lord Street. This was her office and also a place of refuge.

It was also a slick way of getting from the flat to the restaurant without being spotted. There was however one drawback. The Restaurant Manageress, she was in the pay of
Ming and would tut tut and wag her finger if I used this escape route too often. So this Flash Gordon used it only on very necessary occasions. The kitchens for the Restaurant were in fact at the opposite end of the big room full of tables covered in immaculately starched table cloths and this was definitely out of bounds. Well almost definitely if you know what I mean?.

So there you have it, a young lads tour of his adventure playground, oh, there was a lot more to it but I don't want to bore you with all the technical stuff, and anyway it will come up in other chapters ahead.

You probably want to know about the 'other scary things' on my journey through 'Planet Mongo;'.

Fine, I told you how the place could be very eerie when closed and silent. Well it was also a place where even one who lived there could believe that the ghosts of the films and stars could come out to play with your mind.

When I was old enough, I like many of you, got a paper round. This meant that I had to be trusted with a front door key, a very important responsibility and I was lectured on this in no uncertain ways by Dad.

So may I set the scene for you, it is late into 1958, it is dark, it is cold, it is quiet and not a mouse was moving about, just me. I am dressed and ready to go it is coming up to 7am. I pick up my trusty torch which was usually issued to usherettes, with its sturdy black plastic handle and red plastic screw on top, which was paramount when seeing patrons to their seats in the dark.

I set off through the building and down the stairs, the darkness is almost claustrophobic and the portraits looked down on me with silent disdain, not unlike those oil paintings of old monarchs in castles you saw on gothic movies, and finally into the Foyer.
At this moment, something was not right, there was a sensation I was not alone, a moments hesitation and courage summoned I carried on, crossing towards the far exit doors on the car park side of the building.

And then it happened.

Just past the stalls entrance was another flight of stairs that led to the circle and next to that was an area my father used for promotional exhibits. It was also where I met **DRACULA.**
Believe you me; I was totally unaware of Christopher Lee, his blood lusts and his vampire friends, not until this moment.
As I crossed in front of this area, green lights came on and there in the centre was a COFFIN and rising silently towards me was this man dressed in a cloak and as he pointed towards me I could see blood running from his mouth, and he had fangs, big fangs… I did not stop to read the publicity blurbs or scan the posters surrounding this effigy, I ran… very quickly,

How I got outside fumbling for that all important key I do not know, but I managed to escape the building. Once out side I caught my breath and then took off at full speed to the newsagents in Hill Street, where I recounted my experience in all its gory detail, much to the amusement of my employer.

About an hour later, the sun was up and my job was complete, I had to return to collect my school things and catch the bus.

First though I had to return to the area of my fright. As I climbed the steps outside, I was amazed to find this display for the forthcoming Dracula film had also caught out the ladies who came at about 7.30am to commence cleaning duties, and apparently their screams had been heard halfway down Lord Street, much to the amusement of the local constabulary who had spotted this horror show during the night shift.

What's all the fuss about? I would with bravado, trill as I walked boldly past this fearful display. Did the cleaning ladies see me in a different light, who is this brave young man who is not fazed by such sights, who had experienced what had scared the hell out of them without the bat of an eyelid?

I sauntered back up stairs to the flat and then admitted to my father and mother the truth. This had an immediate effect, Dad was delighted and gave me extra pocket money and chortled all the way downstairs to confront his cleaning staff and their somewhat explosive comments regarding their soiled underwear.

As years past I was to see many of these promotional displays, and come to view them in a different light. They were clever, informative and at all times interesting. I did however check more closely, the foyer whenever I went downstairs to do my paper round, just in case.

For the technically minded, the coffin came from Broadbent's funeral parlour and the Vampire came from Madame Tussards in Coronation Walk where they had a House of Horrors attraction at the time, the cauldron of blood you were dared to drink from - was Ribena cordial in a punch bowl. For some reason no-one did drink the Blood of Dracula…!!

Capt. Arthur Finney and guide dog Kim receive a cheque from G.B. Club members for the silver bottle top collections. The 2 young lads were the winners of a Pogo stick competition held on stage and in the car park also raising money for the guide dogs charity. We tried out the pogo sticks on the flat roof without much success, the asphalt surface was too sticky and the restaurant customers complained about the thumping noise as they tried to eat.

The 1956 Christmas Tree Appeal gets under way with admiring looks from G.B. Club members and Tom Smith, ever vigilante watches from the background.

Every year the appeal got bigger and bigger and so did the crowds of children from the Saturday morning club.

It was to become a calendar entry for every Mayor of Southport and their entourage. The tree appeal was opened by the Mayor and the proceeds went to Deserving children's charities and to the Sunshine Home for Blind babies and Children. Between 2000 and 3000 presents were donated each year by the Patrons and well wishers.

The talent competitions held 2 or 3 times a year were highly popular and produced some extraordinary acts.

1960. The Orbit Jazzmen entertain the Satur5day morning children's club. Formed on the spur of the moment and an instant hit.
:BL. is extreme left [trumpet] with Stan Wright [trombone] Dennis Rimmer [drums] Bill Watson on Piano, Les Fashoni [vocals] and W.C.Hopper on the organ.

CHAPTER 4
SAVED BY THE STAFF -
AND ALL CREATURES GREAT AND SMALL

Throughout this book, I have mentioned members of the staff and the various roles they played, but it would be remiss of me not to dwell a short time on the subject.

These Ladies and Gentlemen, of which there were many, were the hard working and well thought of employees by the management. "They worked "- as Dad would say, "When the public played". They ensured the place ran smoothly and there was literally an army of them.

I understand that there were about 70 in total of Full time and part time staff, ranging from the Manager, his assistant a trainee manager, The Projection and Operating staff, The Doormen and Usherettes, the Cashiers and Sales staff, the restaurant workers, the cleaners, the car park attendants
Just to mention a few.
These days of Multi-Plex Cinemas, they seem to only need a couple of people and a computer.

My father was always complimentary of the hard work his team accomplished, and although he was the man to be feared, who hired and fired you, he was always a gentleman, polite and courteous even when chucking you out on your ear for some misdemeanour.

Some of the staff gained their 25 year service badge whilst he was there, an honour Dad would ensure got full and proper notice, both locally and at Rank Organisation HQ in London. He also acquired this honour and wore his 25 yr Badge with pride.

He also made sure that each year; the annual Christmas staff party was a memorable one. Like in 1963 a couple of years before he was to retire, the film at Christmas was "A Stitch in Time" with Norman Wisdom playing a St John Ambulance Brigade member with the usual mayhem only Norman could muster. Dad was in touch with Norman Wisdom and the next thing; he was joining the staff as if he was one of their number.

Some years later I would be walking up Lord Street and bumped into Norman, we got chatting and he recalled in detail that night and his enjoyment that he had been invited to be part of their life.

On another occasion, in 1964, Rank produced a film called "Ladies Who Do" and this coincided with an award that was due to one of the Cleaners, Dorothy Sutton. Dad gets all the Cleaning Ladies together and in front of the press, presents the award and then treated them and their guests to a night at the pictures - and makes sure they get their names and faces in the newspapers.

It was these people I grew up with. There was Old Mr Twist the attendant in the Car Park. He had a large sentry box in the car park from whence he could monitor all the coming and goings. Park your car there, and nothing would happen to it. That was a fact. I used to house my bicycle in a shed in the car park; it was never locked, and it was always there when I came to use it. I have no idea how old he was but Mr Twist seemed to me as if he had been around when Dickens was a lad. He was always good for a chat, and he seemed to have a tea pot freshly brewed every time I popped by. I also learned that this was where the local constabulary could get warm if necessary, whilst pounding their beat.

There was Mr. Tom Smith who I've mentioned, who saved me from myself on numerous occasions, his wife also ran the kiosk and I also suspect that they were aware of my inclination to visit parts that no children should visit. Another was Mr. [Dick] Wareing who would show me how to paste the signs up on the boards over the entrances and taught me about the sizes of posters, how they should be arranged and which stills from the film were best to use.

In the Cashiers Pay Box, was Miss Doris Moores who retired in 1963 along with Tom Smith. There wasn't anything about tickets or Box Office work, she hadn't experienced, she was a fountain of knowledge and a friendly smile whenever I passed by. She also was my other spotter when Tom wasn't around and a swift wave and I could nip smartly upstairs and if I had any pals with me she would also cover for them as well.

Dad's assistant manager Bill Hopper whom I spoke of earlier, was one of those people who had been around for ever. He had followed Dad from Crosby and was one of those melt into the background types happy to take a back seat. He was however unable to do this when seated at the great Compton Organ. This modest, silver haired Geordie had a quick dry wit and could double you up with laughter with just a knowing look. He had joined Gaumont British Corporation in 1936 and remained in the business until his retirement in 1964. He had started out as a pianist on ocean liners and went all over the world. He then settled down in his North Shields home accompanying silent films becoming the resident musician at the Argyle Theatre, Birkenhead. When 'talkies' came around he swapped from piano to the organ, entertaining the audiences during the intervals.
On a personal note, he was invited to play the organ at my marriage to my wife, Ann at St. Cuthberts Churchtown. He jumped at the opportunity and on the day – forgot.

He had an absent minded professor approach to life and on that day went off to Northumberland to visit his family. Luckily the vicar's wife stepped in and the day was not lost. We had a good laugh about it all later when I met up with him. He had known me all my life and was sorely missed when he passed away in 1978 aged 76.

Then there was my "Auntie" Marie, formally known as Miss Marie Tipping, head of the Usherettes and my best mate. She saved my bacon more times than I can count and I swear she enjoyed every minute getting one over my Dad.

Auntie Marie was one of those jovial people you just love to hug. She could be loud but at the same time as quiet as a mouse. Staff didn't smoke on duty, but Marie did, Marie had radar, better than the RAF. She knew where Dad was at all times and what mood he was in. She could sense trouble a mile off and when danger was imminent, she could hide me in an instant. She would have a signal system with her torch that told others what to do and where to go next. It also warned of manager's in the offing.

I of course would reciprocate with inside information. I could also rely on her to cover my back if inadvertently I was found in the wrong place at the wrong time.

Oh yes she was my eyes, ears and my mouth piece. I can recall only being let down once and that involved Alfred Hitchcock's PSYCHO, maybe it was because she and the others were just as terrified of The Bates Motel and its shower room and would hide their eyes from the horror and missed the Boss or maybe I ran out of luck that day.

I had heard all about this film and the fact that once it had started, no-one would be allowed admittance to the screening. There was only one screening a night and Alfred Hitchcock himself had set the ground rules and the Rank Organisation abided to the letter of the law laid down. This was so no-one in those days could give the secret away.
Nowadays we all know about Norman Bates and his Mum and who was who doing what to whom; but in June 1960 it was new, it was scary and it was a definite had to watch film.
The only problem for me was that it was an 'X' rated, over 18's only, Adult horror film. I was still only 13, and although I had managed to slip in and watch other films of the same genre, this was definitely going to be my own Mission Impossible.
I had to do my own version of the bunking in. This time I must not be spotted by Ming the Merciless or his evil henchmen.

It all went horribly wrong when I slipped unnoticed into the back circle and tucked myself into a dark corner where no-one could make you out in the shadows. The cinema was full, every seat in the nearly 2000 seats were full, so no chance of sneaking into a spare. The staff seemed to be on high alert. Even the St John Ambulance Brigade Nurses that attended every night and sat in selected seats, were standing ready to attend the fainting and frightened.

The usherettes were checking and rechecking for the faint hearted. Too much was happening, and the film had only just got under way.

And then the unimaginable happened, Ming the Merciless swooped like a rampant Dragon from nowhere and took Flash Gordon capture.

I was so stunned when a hand grabbed my left ear in a pincer grip and a snarling voice rasped in my other, that I think I was in more need of the St John Ambulance than the faint hearted ladies in need of the smelling salts.

I had chosen by bad luck, poor choice whatever you want to call it, the exact same alcove that my father had decided to stand and observe the film for himself.
Oh woe was I.
He marched me swiftly to the exit, out onto the flat roof and home. He then in no uncertain terms told me about how he could lose his licence, he then went through the
Cinematograph Act in fine detail and in effect left me in no doubt, that I was grounded.

Anthony Perkins was a scary Master Bates, but Ming was definitely scarier. Lesson learnt.

Later that week I sat through the film from another angle, ever watchful, and vigilant of recapture. I wasn't and the film didn't scare me one bit. Maybe I was becoming immune.

~~~~~~~~~~~~~~~~~~~~~~

A theatre is at the forefront of show business and just because it shows films, does not make it any less a stadium of entertainment.

Dad was never behind in coming forward whenever a creature could be involved. He arranged for the foyer to become an aviary with exotic birds on show for another of Mr Hitchcock's masterpieces, The Birds. He used to wander around with a Tawny owl perched on his shoulder like some reincarnation of Long John Silver.

He was friendly with the owners of the Zoo, Frank Farrar and his wife, and the famous stunt that many remember involved Rajah their lion.

This large pussy cat was as docile as a pet kitten. He was in fact so tame I was able on my visits to the zoo, pop in and feed him, just like any of us giving a tit-bit to our domestic pets.

The public and the staff however were not as informed and when this huge cat yawned and showed off his teeth, knees knocked and Grannies fainted, but then he
was a film star. I always believe he had a sense of humour, because if I had the honour of feeding him when the public were around he would act the part and pretend to menace this child with the large chunk of raw meat. I am sure he was just making me look brave. Other time he would come over all soft and lick you to death.

His claim to fame was the film SAFARI, with Victor Mature. He appeared as a killer on the loose and had to leap about, taking lives and ultimately coming face to face with the hero.

So of course Dad got a special screening up and running before the public had a chance to see it. He rings up Frank and his wife and along they troop with Rajah in pride of place, no pun intended. Down to the front stalls and sit back and watch it all happen on the big screen.
Rajah was appreciative and roared with delight when he appeared.

This coincided just as the cleaners, the visiting fire officer checking the extinguishers and Kine our boldly go where no cat has gone before, were passing through the auditorium including the afternoon staff arriving for work...
Oh it is bad enough trying to do your job, whilst somebody is showing a film to an empty theatre, it is quite something else to come face to face with a lion you have just seen tear someone limb from limb in full Technicolor.

The result was, 1st Kine, who had the advantage of 4 legs and local knowledge and a close 2nd the Fire Fighter still clutching extinguisher. In 3rd place the cleaners who left by a number of exits, threatening not to return. Finally in 4th place and probably still there, Marie Tipping who arrived ahead of her usherettes and ended up barricading the Ladies toilets.

The newspapers were full of the story and the photographer was rumoured to have got his pictures and then did a bunk to The Anchor, the nearest pub to settle his nerves. Perhaps it was not surprising that he had to fight his way to the bar, the remainder of the staff had got there before him.

For me it was just another stunt that Dad arranged, I walked past as they went out, gave them a wave and a pretend roar to Rajah, he reciprocated and then like a true star, trooped into the car and was away before autograph hunters could descend.

Other such animal antics, involved dogs [Walt Disney's 101 Dalmatians] and of course the odd horse wandering about the stalls during the interval. Simply to remind the patrons that the Grand National could be seen the same evening of race day on the News, straight from the race track.

I wonder if anyone recalled the film 'The Incredible Shrinking Man'. When it screened Dad contacted the Land of Little People [or Model Village] which was sited in an acre of land just off Rotten Row. This remarkable attraction was an ideal 'link up' as these stunts were called.

The model maker John Goundrey who was 20 at the time in 1961, very proudly constructed a perfect replica of the theatre at his workshop in Shakespeare Street and before it was sent down to the other model village in Great Yarmouth owned by Tom and Bill Dobbins placed an exhibit of a town in the foyer the centrepiece of course the Gaumont.

Perhaps in some corner in Great Yarmouth, is that model and if so, does it still sit proudly in a town centre, the only reminder for us of what should still be, or has it sadly succumbed and been demolished like its big brother back in Southport.

The staff Christmas party with Norman Wisdom. On his right is Les Houghton who would become the manager of the Palace Cinema and on his left, my other conspirator from the projection suite, Raymond 'Tich' Rimmer.   Note the autograph

One of the many presentations arranged for long service and retirements for staff members arranged by Dad, he ensured they got the thanks they deserved. Here we see Mrs. C. Platt retiring after 25 years. My mother is standing on the extreme right with 'Auntie' Marie Tipping.

Farewell presentation gifts to Mr. and Mrs. Tom Smith [Chief of Staff and Head of Kiosk Sales] and to Miss Doris Moores [Chief Cashier] receiving the silver service from 'Ming the Merciless'. Most of the staff member's shown here were 'Flash Gordons' allies.

We got quite attached to Tawny who in turn became attached to Dad and only left when Alfred Hitchock's 'The Birds' had flown

AND THE LION ROARED

Press pictures and advert
when Rajah's visited the showing of 'Safari'

GAUMONT : SOUTHPORT
TO-MORROW (SUNDAY), MAY 6

FOR THE FIRST TIME

CinemaScope
GOES ON SAFARI

COLUMBIA PICTURES
presents
A WARWICK PRODUCTION

VICTOR   JANET
MATURE LEIGH
JOHN   ROLAND
JUSTIN CULVER

SAFARI

LIAM REDMOND   EARL CAMERON   ORLANDO MARTINS
CinemaScope Colour by TECHNICOLOR
Screenplay by ANTHONY VEILLER Directed by TERENCE YOUNG
Produced by ADRIAN D. WORKER
Executive Producers IRVING ALLEN and ALBERT R. BROCCOLI

RAJAH

This model of Southport's Gaumont Cinema has been made by 20-year-old John Goundrey, who is showing it to the Gaumont manager, Mr. Ken Lloyd. It is being placed in a model village at Great Yarmouth.

CHAPTER 5
DO YOU THINK HE'S FAMOUS?

Have you ever had that foot in mouth experience? Perhaps you are the type of person who removes foot only to put the other one in. It is very similar to having mouth in gear and brain in neutral, very embarrassing.

So it was for me, sometimes I knew the stars or famous faces as they passed through the theatre, other times it was a case of – nudge - nudge – is that so and so?

The famous are just that, they do not have a sign hanging around their necks saying ' look at me I'm famous' However for some, like me, who wasn't looking for a face to ogle at, it could be sooooo embarrassing when introduced to a famous person and say "nice to meet you what do you do?" It didn't stop them giving me an autograph but I did get a few strange looks.

There was the occasion when Frankie Howard came to see a film he was starring in, Dad tipped me off that he was in the stalls and positioned me by the front doors so I could get his autograph, I stood there full of anticipation watching the people coming out, Frankie Howard totally ignored me and almost ran out of the front doors much to the amusement of the staff, perhaps my reputation had preceded me.

Some time earlier, Ted Ray, if you recall, our Sunday lunch radio entertainer, had been in to see Dad, he was appearing in comedy film, and was doing the rounds, he also got roped into judging the local beauty competition at the Floral Hall which is how Dad had met him. They found they had a number of things in common and became very friendly.
It was not surprising that when he came along and sat in the rear circle to watch his film, that I and my brother got to sit with him and keep him company.
The problem was that we were so exited to be in the presence of such a big name and funny man, that we kept him in conversation all the way through the film. This pleasant man was ever so polite, he responded to all of our questions and kept us entertained, before delivering us back to the bosom of our family. He then courteously asked Dad if he could pop in on another day to see what he had missed.

So maybe Frankie Howard had heard about me.

Many will know the name David McCallum, this actor has been ongoing for many years, and recently he has starred in NCIS as the Pathologist, Dr. [Ducky] Mallard.
Prior to that he was the Russian side kick, Ilya Kuriakin, in 'The Man from UNCLE' along with Robert Vaughn.

But long before that, back in 1957, he played a troubled teenager who took a school hostage with a machine gun in Liverpool. He starred alongside Stanley Baker and Anne Haywood and the film was directed by Basil Dearden.

'Violent Playground' was ahead of its time and even today one can see similarities between it and occurrences in schools in the USA.

Because it was a Rank Organisation film, the production team decided they needed to watch the day's rushes [these are when a scene is filmed over and over again to get it right] and then select which was the best one for the editor to use.

After the evening show, the production team, led by Basil Dearden and sometimes a star from the film, came along and scrutinised the scenes. The film was shot at a school on Scotland Road, Liverpool and in the side streets nearby and at Gerard Gardens. It was full of faces and names. I was told about this event and had of course curiosity got the better of me, and I slipped into the back circle and watched in awe as the same scene was played repeatedly followed by numbers and clapper boards sights of behind the scenes as cameras still rolling past by the stars and caught other sights that would be edited out, such as groups of people huddled together reading scripts drinking cups of coffee and doing behind the scenes work.

Of course a small adventurer like me sitting in the back circle in his pyjamas at midnight was going to get caught, and so it came to pass. I was duly escorted home to my mother's surprise by Mr Dearden who rewarded my enterprise with his autograph and with a big smile went back to his work. Unfortunately I did not get to meet David McCallum who was sat with him at the time, but I recognised him when the film came around completed, and I recall his look of surprise and then laughing when I was discovered.

Earlier I spoke of the stage. This mighty area of entertainment where big names became huge and unknowns became household names. The stage was in fact the second largest in the North West, the largest being The Empire in Liverpool. This fact was not lost on the major show business organisers and so it was that throughout the life of the Gaumont and later when it changed its name to The Odeon, it would be picked to stage some of the top shows in the country, nothing since then has been, or can compare with the facilities that Southport's leading theatre / cinema could give.

None of the present day shows of West End standard can be played in Southport, but could if that stage was still available. Even the Trade Union Congress was held in this auditorium, completely filling every seat. This was massive and outshone anything that has been held since. Even the political parties spoke of coming to Southport for their conferences, until they heard the Odeon no longer existed.

You see, the stage was a magical place it was to the audience a simple area where the actors strutted their stuff, but behind the scenery was an even greater expanse of technical expertise. There was a huge arch that carried over 30 different scenes, there were cat walks and spotlights, all the usual theatrical needs but on a massive scale.

Behind all this were the access doors. Huge roller shutters that opened up into the car park, where delivery vehicles could off load their finery. It was where I met Cliff Richard and the Shadows [they were the Drifters then] it was where Hank Marvin and Bruce Welch sat practicing chords, away from the hurly burly of the stage manager and his crew creating the scenery and chatted to me as if I was one of them, sharing sandwiches but not their beer and cigarettes [I was too young then].

Great coaches from various parts of the land with names from far reaching locations would park up and disgorge their stars and supporters.

This was a real place of adventure, it was where I got to meet the real stars of stage, screen. Radio and TV. It was where I rubbed shoulders with the famous and got their autographs. Gone were the days of standing at the front of house hoping the star would stop and speak to me, I was now going to them and they had no choice but to stop and speak to me. They were on my territory and in my home,

When I look back, I am amazed at how many stars I did meet, along with their autographs and the programmes they usually wrote them in. It was a period of change for everyone. The music era was changing from the ballads and big bands through rock and roll to the contemporary pop period.

Ian would leave his autograph book backstage and collect it after a show, one day whilst in the dressing rooms it mysteriously disappeared, we've always wondered given the famous names in it, who had stooped so low as to pinch it. Although he may have lost out there, he can add to his claim to fame that he got to meet the country's sweetheart, Petula Clark and spent some time sat on her lap chatting her up, you have to start somewhere, well he was a kid at the time and could get away with it.

At home, things were getting tight, both financially and physically. We now had a sister, who was growing and taking up space and in a 2 bedroom flat that was becoming a problem. Money was also an issue, because although Dad was the General Manager and living in a company flat, he also had to entertain civic persons and media personnel out of his pocket and that meant mum had to seek a job as well.

This put me in charge of the younger siblings and played havoc with my own social life. It did not however stop me getting back stage and into various dressing rooms,

Soon we will as a family move out to live elsewhere but not before the really big events were to come.

I've mentioned Cliff and the Shadows, who topped the bill way back then, along with some names now forgotten but at the time were big like Wee Willy Harris, Peter Elliot, The Rockets and The Batchelors.
Then came John [Johnny Remember Me] Leyton, who went on after his top ten record breaking career to star in films like 'The Great Escape'

He was supported by Gene Vincent who Be Bop a Lula' d his way to through his show with supports from The Voltairs, Patti Brooks and the Jetblacks, and having just split from the Shadows to go it alone, Jet Harris and Tony Meehan.

Jet Harris did for some time later, live in Southport and played with local groups at the various clubs and pubs but then he and Tony were top of the pops with 'Diamonds'

They returned that year along with Patti Brook and her group with Louise Cordet and Jimmy Justice plus others to support the main stars who had arrived from the USA, namely Paul and Paula. This was widely publicised and of course I had no problem slipping up the stairs on the opposite side to Mings Office and saying Hi to the Yanks.

Incidentally they were actually called Ray Hildebrand and Jill Jackson, but you know show business.
On that show, there were last minute hitches and the programmes had Patti Brooks along with Jet Harris and Tony Meehan in support. This was changed at last minute and another local but popular group were put in, did someone mention Gerry and the Pacemakers. Oh yes fun and games all round, this was 1963

That year also saw huge names coming and going, in fact it did not help that we had now moved, but our first home was still on Lord Street, and so were a lot of our belongings, also Mum was working at the GPO as a telephone switchboard operator, so again we had to be in two places at the same time. The flat was a good place to stash siblings whilst carrying out my other mission, meeting and greeting without being caught by Ming and his henchmen. You may ask about stars and their body guards, well in those days they were minimal to say the least and anyway how are they going to stop me, I lived there Ok..!!

The names came and went, but the shows linger in your memory and so it was when a young lass from nowhere suddenly became the hottest property and everyone but everyone wanted a piece of her, this was Helen Shapiro and her show was huge not least for the fact that one of her supporting acts were a group called the BEATLES.

Fine, here I was trying to get into Helen Shapiro's dressing room when down the hallway in another dressing room, some chap called John had been caught by Ming the Merciless slinging pork pies across at another lad called George. The fact that this had been witnessed by Ming and these young Liverpool lads were messing up one of his spotless dressing rooms resulted in a terrifying roar of disapproval. To say he wiped the floor with them is one way of putting it. In fact after lecturing them about conduct and correct mannerisms in a theatre and so on, including pointing out they couldn't spell their name either, he strode off very managerially to oversee the rest of the show.

I in the meantime had given up my mission and fearing the return, made my escape, but not before witnessing John Paul and George cleaning up the cause of my father's irritation. The lads never did spell their name correctly and for some reason actually came back later to head the bill.

On that occasion, the whole family got to meet them officially. Ringo muttered to me; - "*The last time we was 'ere, you wuz 'iding by [Helen] Shapiros room whilst we wuz getting a rollockin off your old man*" It was then I recalled a long haired bloke who I had thought was part of the stage crew hanging by the back door having a smoke, I recalled he gave me a wink as I scooted past him. The others made no comment, Ian and Valerie were unaware and thank God, Ming never found out.

Did I ever get Helen Shapiro's autograph, well yes but I had to go cap in hand to my father for that one.

~~~~~~~~~~~

Just one little rider to that period, when The Beatles show was playing that whole week, with supporting acts Gerry and the Pacemakers along with another top group, The Fourmost, who like the Beatles was Managed by, Brian Epstein.

Brian came to Dad one day and apologised to him, because The Fourmost would have to be pulled that evening, due to a double booking and they had to be in another town. Of course this had ramifications regarding times, complaints from the audience and so on.

He then ASKED my dad for HIS permission to put another act on to fill the gap. It turned out this was the first appearance on any stage of this magnitude in a supporting role of a young lady we have come to know as CILLA BLACK.

I had always wondered and I asked my father many years later what his reaction was. He told me that he agreed to the arrangement, always willing to give an amateur a leg up the ladder; and later congratulated the breathless young lady on a job well done.

He also predicted she would go far. I wonder if she, looking back over her successful career would remember her first outing and what she remembered of that night. {see chapter 9}

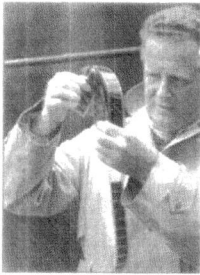

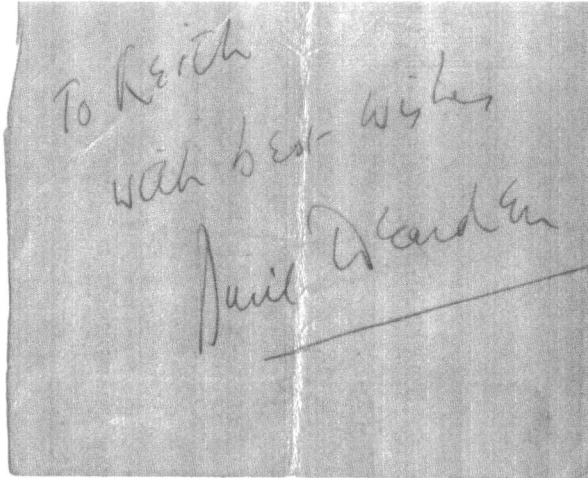

Violent Playground.
Clockwise - Basil Dearden. His Autograph. Publicity still
David McCallum. Stanley Baker taking a rest during filming

ON THE STAGE

GAUMONT
SOUTHPORT

Manager, K. B. LLOYD   *approx 1958*   Phone : 3028

| 1st Performance **6.15** P.M. | **FRIDAY, JULY 10**
TWO PERFORMANCES ONLY | 2nd Performance **8.30** P.M. |

ARTHUR HOWES presents

OH BOY !!
IT'S
CLIFF RICHARD
AND THE DRIFTERS
Hit recorders of " Move It," " High Class Baby " and " Mean Streak "

Sensational Decca Recording Star	"Oh Boy" Ballad Star
WEE WILLIE HARRIS	**PETER ELLIOTT**

Parlophone recording Artistes   The exciting
BACHELORS

The Swinging Beat Music of	Glamorous Young Singer
THE **ROCKETS**	**JACKIE DAY**

Your Compere, ALAN FIELD

PRICES: 7/6,   5/6,   3/6   All Bookable

To the Box Office, GAUMONT THEATRE, SOUTHPORT

Please forward .... TICKETS at 7/6, 5/6, 3/6

for the 6.15/8.30 performance on Friday, 10th July

I enclose stamped addressed envelope and P.O./Cheque value ....

NAME ....

ADDRESS ....

Hastings Printing Company. Portland Place, Hastings.   Phone 2450.

40

ODEON · SOUTHPORT

Manager   K. B. LLOYD   Phone   56816

6.25 — FRIDAY, 1st MARCH, 1963 — 8.40

TWO PERFORMANCES ONLY

FOR ONE
DAY ONLY   **ON THE STAGE**   FOR ONE
DAY ONLY

(INSTEAD OF THE USUAL FILM PROGRAMME)

ARTHUR HOWES PRESENTS
BRITAIN'S INTERNATIONAL TEENAGE STAR

HELEN ♪

SHAPIRO

THE
DYNAMIC   "LOVE ME DO"
BEATLES

THE *BRITAIN'S ACE VOCAL GROUP*
KESTRELS

SPECIAL GUEST STAR
DANNY
WILLIAMS
"MOON RIVER"   "JEANNIE"

THE RED PRICE BAND

THE
HONEYS

YOUR COMPERE
DAVE ALLEN

"UP ON THE ROOF"
KENNY LYNCH

PRICES: 8/6   6/6   4/6

BOX OFFICE
ODEON
SOUTHPORT

POSTAL BOOKING FORM
Friday, 1st March, 1963
Helen Shapiro Show   Date

Please forward   SEATS   8/6 6/6 4/6

for the EVENING 6.25 / 8.40 performance on

I enclose stamped addressed envelope and P.O. / Cheque value
(Please delete words not applicable)

NAME   (Block letters)

ADDRESS

41

ODEON · **SOUTHPORT**

THEATRE · Lord Street

Manager : K. B. LLOYD
Telephone : Southport 56519
BOX OFFICE OPEN DAILY
from 1.30 p.m. (Sunday 5 p.m.)

SUNDAY, JULY 28th at 6 & 8.15
ON THE STAGE
(FOR ONE NIGHT ONLY INSTEAD OF NORMAL FILM PROGRAMME)
THE SUNDAY 'POP' SHOW

AMERICA'S KING OF 'ROCK'
GENE VINCENT

BRITAIN'S
NEW
RECORDING
STAR
HEINZ BURT

DECCA'S HIT RECORDERS
OF 'CHARMAINE'
THE BACHELORS

THE FABULOUS SOUNDS OF
SOUNDS INCORPORATED

THE OUTLAWS   THE SAINTS   PLUS FULL SUPPORTING BILL!

PRICES : FRONT STALLS 8/6   CENTRE STALLS 6/6   REAR STALLS 4/6
FRONT CIRCLE 6/6   REAR CIRCLE 4/6

.... CUT ALONG DOTTED LINE ....

POSTAL BOOKING FORM

BOX OFFICE
ODEON THEATRE
LORD ST., SOUTHPORT, Lancs.

Gene Vincent & Co.   Date.........................

Please forward ....STALLS : 8/6   6/6   4/6   ....CIRCLE : 6/6   4/6

for the EVENING 6.0 / 8.15 performance on Sunday, July 28th, 1963.

I enclose stamped addressed envelope and P.O. / Cheque value £   :   s.   d.
(Please delete words not applicable)

NAME .... (Block letters)

ADDRESS ....
Use this form if inconvenient to call at the Theatre. The best available seats will be allotted to you.

Printed by Electric (Modern) Printing Co. Ltd., Manchester 8.

43

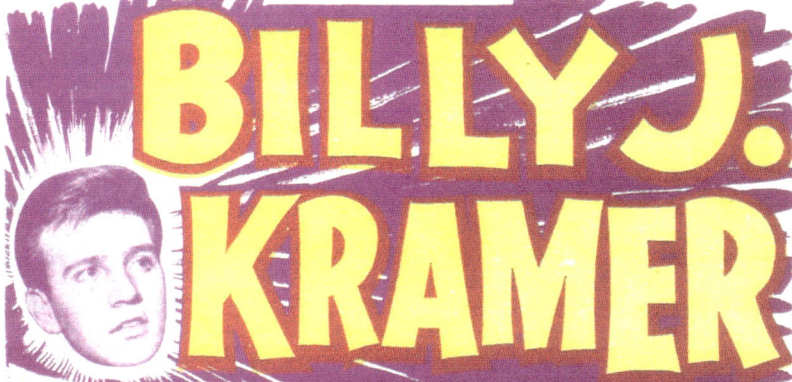

ODEON · SOUTHPORT

Manager : K. B. LLOYD   Phone : 56519

6-25   THURSDAY, 28th NOVEMBER   8-40
TWO PERFORMANCES ONLY

FOR ONE
DAY ONLY
ON THE STAGE
(INSTEAD OF THE USUAL FILM PROGRAMME)
FOR ONE
DAY ONLY

BRIAN EPSTEIN PRESENTS

BILLY J. KRAMER

THE DAKOTAS

JOHNNY KIDD and the PIRATES

THE CARAVELLES

THE FOURMOST

HOUSTON WELLS and the MARKSMEN   TOMMY QUICKLY

THE MARAUDERS   Compere TED KING

PRICES: STALLS 8/6 6/6 4/6   CIRCLE 6/6 4/6

BOX OFFICE   POSTAL BOOKING FORM
ODEON   Thursday, 28th November, 1963
SOUTHPORT   Billy J. Kramer & Co.   Date.................

Please forward ....STALLS 8/6 6/6 4/6 ....CIRCLE : 6/6 4/6

for the EVENING 6.25 / 8.40 performance on ....

I enclose stamped addressed envelope and P.O. / Cheque value £   :   s.   d.
(Please delete words not applicable)

NAME .... (Block letters)

ADDRESS ....

Use this form if inconvenient to call at the Theatre. The best available seats will be allotted to you

Printed by Electric (Modern) Printing Co. Ltd., Manchester.

45

CHAPTER 6
I'LL BE BACK

As I have indicated our time as a family living in the Odeon Cinema passed by and we had to move out to bigger premises. Although for a while my father stayed there as guardian of the place, in fact he did not leave until 1965, by which time we had become somewhat dysfunctional.

For various reasons I would have to visit the Odeon and it was funny, but no matter from which direction I approached, I never failed to be awestruck by the size and grace of its architecture and grandeur. This was something I had not had to experience as I was just coming or going to my home. The queues were still there, but I was at ground level with them. I would feel the excited hubbub that came from the people hoping the 'FULL' sign would not go out, just as they had done when the Beatles 'Hard Days Night' had played and hundreds were turned away.

Of course there would be inevitable glance upwards to the balcony, just in case it was looking like rain, or a water bomb, my old friends the operators still had their staffroom up there, and would have spotted me approaching.

When I started writing this book, I thought it would be a simple task, I would put down some basic memories, some simple facts, a few photographs tidy it up with my father's recollections and then see where it would end up. Since I started, it has .become apparent that you dear reader must be wondering what happened next, did it end there or is there more? Well actually there is.

After I left school and my father retired from the cinema business, I decided to try out this management lark and try and get back to my roots. I went to see my Dad and asked him if he had any advice in getting into the business, he responded, "In one word NO".

When he retired the industry was going through painful times, there were people coming into senior management who were not from show business and were quite frankly ruining everything they touched. Dad had spoken up and for his sins, was slapped down. After you've banged your head against a brick wall a few times you don't feel the pain, that's when to stop and that's when Dad said enough. He left the Odeon whilst it was making money, departing with '**Goldfinger**' and the best wishes of a very emotional staff.
It also meant my links with the planet Mongo where Flash Gordon had enjoyed his adventures was officially terminated.
It also introduces quite nicely my 'Arnie' catch phrase title to this chapter.

When I left school with the satisfaction of knowing that the education system had failed to turn me into an automaton with dozens of certificates to my name, I joyfully entered the real world of wages, income tax and national insurance and became a family breadwinner. My mother was now working for Radio Yellow Top Taxis as a controller at their Lord Street office, Dad was still meeting and greeting the worlds press, local dignitaries the public and my brother and sister were growing up fast.

After starting out as a horticultural nurseryman at a local garden centre as they have now become, I suffered an injury that was to change my life again. As I said earlier, I had asked Dad about the Cinema business and he had given me short thrift, mainly because of his experiences with the new style of management.

He was to be proved right in every respect of his beliefs. The new style leaders came from outside of the industry and with their lack of knowledge and attitudes, caused the steady decline of the industry. Television started to take control and the crowds voted with their feet and started to abandon their favourite haunts.

Cinemas started to close. In Southport back in the 1930's there were about a dozen picture houses / theatres, by the late 60's it had dwindled to less than half that.
When I arrived as an 8 year old full of awe and excitement, there seemed to be one on every block.

So there I was with an injury to my leg that would take a while healing and no prospects of a future in the gardening business. I decided that I should rethink my future and found myself standing in front of my bronze girlfriend on Lord Street. For some reason she seemed to be telling me to come back to the life I had so much
experience in.

I knew that I could not in all honesty walk into the company that had hurt my father's pride, so I wrote off to ABC [Associated British Cinemas] and got an interview. They snatched my hand off and gave me a job as a trainee manager. I do not know to this day whether it was due to my personality, good looks and charming attitude, or whether the District Manager who employed me, was aware of my family history and my father's qualities. I would like to think it was the former but what the heck, if you need a step up sometime, don't be backward in coming up with a little underhand actions.

Dad went ballistic! My ears were ringing with his comments about working for the opposition. Going to work for a second rate company. What did I know about show
business anyway? Ah well what could Flash Gordon expect from Ming the Merciless, a ticker tape parade?

And so it came to pass, I started at the Futurist in Lime Street, Liverpool and swiftly moved onto the Carlton Cinema in Tuebrook as a 2nd assistant Manager, the first assistant was a mild mannered gentleman with a huge knowledge of cinemas which belied his quiet and nervous demeanour.
In later years he would write books about Picture Palaces and Cinemas, this friendly man was Harold Ackroyd who wrote the book 'Southport, Stage and Screen', which dad supplied many historical background and photographic evidence. It is funny how the world revolves. Sadly Harold passed away in 2008 aged 83 and his knowledge was lost to us all

It did not take long before I had climbed the ladder, and like dad finally found myself in Southport at the ABC [Regal] Cinema on Lord Street.

I was back.

Much has been said by others including Harold, about the other pleasure palaces, theatres and cinemas, so I shall brush past and leave it them, my purpose is to enlighten you about my memories about one place.

It was strange though, being on a different planet and negotiating the new landscape. It was not unlike the Odeon but without the stage and behind the scenes attributes, nor was it as big in the seating capacity. It was a modern building with all the concepts of the period. It was definitely not the Odeon we all knew and loved.

I used to meet up with the manager's from the opposition and like my father, would chat about the industry, the films we were playing and the numbers of patrons buying tickets.

One of the managers was Les Houghton, he managed the Palace on Lord Street [this would become the last town centre cinema, it would also be called the ABC] and he was one of my youthful acquaintances at the Odeon. He started out in the operating box / projection room and would be a source of my technical knowledge. Les sadly passed away a few years ago but he and I remained good friends even when I left the business and I miss our nostalgic chats particularly now whilst writing about such times.

Whilst at the Gaumont / Odeon 'Uncle Les' had been one of Harold Gales senior projectionists and along with his colleagues including 'Tich ' Rimmer who was about 4 feet tall they introduced me to the mysteries of that magical stream of light that came from high above.
For the technically minded, or just for fun, I'd like to take you back into that world and tell you about what I learnt. Remember Mr. Gale was chief magician and no young sorcerers apprentice was ever getting behind the scenes, oh no!
He had not counted on his days off though when Les and Tich had charge. So let us enter the realm of the projectionists.

If you recall the entrance was on the flat roof, a simple door that opened outwards and revealed a spiral staircase made of wrought iron that when scaled, brought you onto a gantry and a corridor. Off this was a number of rooms entitled 'switch room' 'arc room' and chief s' office. Then we came to the main suite, a fancy name for a room that was in fact the projection suite.
In here I was to learn the art of putting on a show and these talents are unforgettable and everlasting.
While you sat in the auditorium crunching your popcorn and sucking Kia-Ora through a straw waiting for the lights to dim, the curtains to open and the film to start, up in the operating box as we called it, a flurry of business was going on.
The film came in round tin cans about a foot across and were on 'reels' these 35mm 20 minute long spools of celluloid had been checked for damage and had been spliced and repaired on a work bench to the rear of the two huge Gaumont British Kallee projectors that stood like science fiction ray guns pointing out at the screen through a highly polished window.
These projectors had a large drum at the back with a tiny blue glass window in them so you could see the carbon rods inside. These rods, when joined together made the light source needed. Two copper coated carbon rods about a quarter of an inch thick were positioned tip to tip and when an electric current was passed through them a bright 'spark' would be generated just like an arc welding machine. 'Tich' needed a step ladder to see into the 'lamp-house', and regular checks had to be made to adjust the rods to keep the flame bright.
They burned for just over 20 minutes before being changed. One reason why the reels were only 20 minutes long.
As that reel was playing, we would set up the other 'ray gun'. In front of the lamp house was the gate and above that a round case similar to the cans, the reel was slotted onto a central pivot and the film was fed down a

succession of cogs which would drive the film down to the gate and away to another can below. Correct tension on the film had to be judged and all the sprockets covered. We were now ready for the next stage.

Remember when you watched the film from your plush seats below, a strange mark came up in the top right hand side of the film? It lasted for a second or two, and then about 10 seconds later another one appeared. Well that was when we would do a change-over.

This was completed simply and efficiently and with great timing. When the first marker came up you would switch on the number 2 projector and wait, then when the 2nd marker came up, a lever was pulled and the light from the lamp house would flood out through an aperture onto the film which was now running and at the same time the other projector was shut down.

I could go on but you get the idea. Les taught me all these aspects and more besides, it would come to my aid on a number of times in later life when managing my own show and the operators need additional assistance. It was better than putting on a tuxedo and standing on front of house greeting the public. I believe Dad had a general knowledge, but thanks to Les and his pals, I got my hands dirty.

One up to Flash Gordon

Whilst at the ABC Southport, I was able to fall back on some of the experiences I had, had at the Odeon and improved upon some of the activities. I was unable to do it on the scale of the Odeon due to space. The General Manager, Laurie Hughes was only too happy to let me loose on this aspect having competed with dad for years and to have his son doing publicity and promotions was a sweet revenge.

Let's face it there is no way I could do the promotional displays or put up a Christmas tree, the size I was used to. I was however able to recreate some of the things Dad had done with the Children's Club and with outside promotions with shop window displays and co-operating with the likes of the Crime Prevention Officer.

And here is where things take a strange turn and my life was to alter considerably. I got to know many police officers in the course of my job. There were the regular visits by the Sergeant and his Constable on Saturday mornings to ensure the Cinematograph Act was being adhered to, Ah yes that act, the one I had learnt a great deal about back in the **Psycho** days and then there were the lads who would give you great advice about your street stunts when promoting a film, such as the day when I

persuaded a local haulage company to park up a convoy of army trucks outside to publicise the film The Mercenaries.

That wasn't too bad; it was the jeep racing around the town centre with fully armed, uniformed chaps, hanging off the back that attracted the attention – of the local constabulary - Oh happy days.

Of course there were the unofficial meetings of the local bobby who would pop in and have a cup of tea and watch the pictures whilst plodding around his beat. This was one of their 'brew shops'. In essence it was good public relations and I was quite happy to have an officer of the law on hand, instead of having to tackle any miscreants like my father had in the 1950's.

And so it came to pass that after a few years of following in my father's footsteps and travelling about the North West and ending up at the ABC Preston, my father's words came back to haunt me. His take on the industry was bang on, it was beginning to go down hill due to the increased popularity of television and the poor management and leadership. This was to continue for many years and took almost 20 years before it started to revive.

Realising this I changed occupations. When I had started the there were queues around the cinemas and the courts were empty, now there were queues at the courts and the cinemas were empty, and as Dad used to say, go with the crowds, so I joined the Police Force and became one of those who visited cinemas on Saturday mornings and during rainy evenings, enjoying the odd cup of tea with my old colleagues on the back row of the stalls.

~~~~~~~~~~~~~~~

At this point you may wonder if my memories and experiences of the Odeon had just about dried up and I was just filling up space. Well, not quite, my involvement had one or two twists of fate before ending.

As a local policeman patrolling the beat in the town centre, I would quite naturally pop in and say hello, or stand in the back stalls breathing in the nostalgia. The old staff members had by know retired and the new people did not know me, the managers saw me only as a bobby on the beat, they did not seem to be of the same calibre of their predecessors and did not have the same show business acumen.
I would on my travels pass the Odeon and would take a peek at the façade and the flat area. I would notice the change in curtains, the new paintwork and the ever changing bill boards. The restaurant had long ceased to operate and the windows seemed a little dusty at times and I felt the old place was not being used to its full potential, but that was not my concern anymore I had other priorities to fill my mind. I did however follow a simple routine whenever I passed I would look the Mermaid in the eye and wink knowingly at her. She seemed to understand.

I divulged this little secret to Jack 'Dixon of Dock Green' Warner a few years later and also showed him parts of the old place he did not know existed.

This came about when he came to Southport and specifically the Odeon when filming for television. I was the local bobby at the time and on this day, I was informed by my sergeant that a film crew along with Jack Warner would be at the Odeon and passing attention was required to prevent any inconvenience to the film crew, "bad publicity for the town if they get mobbed – you understand constable?" I understood perfectly and didn't hesitate in getting down there.

Jack Warner was one of the countries best loved actors and his portrayal of the stalwart of Dock Green Police station with his catch phrase "Evening All" made him then and still is the epitome of the traditional bobby on the beat. The show is still quoted world wild and in today's high tech sophisticated, politically correct service, he is still the foundation of what the older age group will call a proper policeman. So when he arrived at the cinema, I was in a good position to shadow him and we had a good old chuckle about the 'Job'.

He was there to film an introduction to a Granada TV programme 'Red Roses Every Night' a programme of World War 2 films. On this occasion a Humphrey Bogart picture entitled 'Sahara' made in 1944.
He was 71 years old at the time [1976] but you would not have known it. This sprightly gentleman, who stood as tall as myself and held himself upright, was on the ball and ready for anything. Even me!.
As soon as he saw me, he strode over and said "I suppose you want a peg in your book young man? " This was a reference to when the Sergeant would meet up with a Constable on the beat and signed in the Constable's notebook to that effect. This was unexpected but delightful, not only was a star coming to me and offering his autograph but this one was one of the truly great stars and a policeman's hero. Oh Joy.

Of course I had to let him get on with his job, but I stuck close turned the radio down, removed helmet and mingled with the crowd. The title of the programme 'Red Roses' was a direct reference to a warning to Cinema Managers at the time of an impending Air Raid, the would sound the alarms and the patrons would get to the shelters nearby.

When the filming was complete, I sidled up to Jack and chatted about this cinema, he was eager to learn about it, after all it was a landmark and he knew it from his earlier days, which surprised me. So I gave him the 'Readers Digest Version' of its history and the 6 penny tour. He was really impressed and wanted to do the Flash Gordon experience but his entourage where champing on the bit and had to move on. They called him Mr Warner, they bowed and scraped they ran around like their job's
depended on it. He smiled a knowing smile and called me Keith and at his insistence called him Jack. Although I must admit, I did call him Sgt. Dixon once or twice.

The press had gathered and saw the opportunity, we had our photo taken together and it appears from the newspapers point of view, I had been pounding my beat and had just came across my childhood hero. As they say, don't believe everything you read. I have to say that back at the station, when the subject came up, I did not deny the quote.

Before he left, having been to places other stars had not been, seen the place through my young eyes and my father's and having shaken my hand yet again for the umpteenth time, we stood by the mermaid and I told him about her, his reaction was thoughtful and kind and he reverted into Sgt Dixon mode, looked me in the eye and told me he thought my taste in women was a bit fishy!. He gave me and Mermaid a wink, and laughing heartily got into his car and was whisked away leaving me alone with my thoughts. What a lovely man, he really did care and was not stuck up like so many other lesser stars I had met.

Funnily enough, this was probably a case of 'what goes around, comes around', when I was living at the flat and sleeping soundly in my bed surrounded by the darkness assisted by the black out curtain in the silence that followed the National Anthem which had signalled the end of the last show of the night, I was awakened by the bedroom door opening and a bright light shining in my face.

There filling the doorframe was the silhouette of a massive person. He was wearing a hat and had a cape around his shoulders. For a second or two I was in my sleepy state unsure as to what or who had come into my room, was it the Phantom of the Opera or some other monster who had escaped from the projection suite, no, it was the local
Policeman who had discovered an unlocked door and had entered the theatre to check if all was well.

In those days the beat patrol would shake hands with door knobs and check everywhere to ensure we slept safely in our beds. Woe betide him if there had been a burglary or damage done and he did not find it. In those days a policeman would be hauled up in front of the Chief Constable and given words of advice and his sergeant would also have words in his ear. So it was to his credit that night that he had found this open door.

Apparently, my father had popped out after the theatre had been closed and was having a quiet game of snooker at the Conservative Club with his friends having overlooked the door. The policeman was impressive and I was left in no doubt that he was someone to look up to and respect. Remember in those days they didn't carry radios to call for backup, they simply walked where angels feared to tread and upheld the law with just their courage and a truncheon.

For this unknown policeman I have to say it must have been daunting to search alone this huge building in the dark. He must have been very surprised to find us sleeping in a flat above the restaurant.

The memory remains to this day and my perception about police officers was scorched into my mind from that day onwards. So perhaps along with Dixon of Dock Green my future was written down that night.

CHAPTER 7
THE DAY THE MERMAID WEPT

In 1975, The Rank Organisation was having financial problems and decided to look at their stock. They considered various options and one was to close a number of Cinemas and Theatres. They looked at Southport and felt this would be one of them that they could sell off to interested parties.

The thought was that another organisation or local authority may benefit from purpose built emporiums of the entertainment genre and at the same time solve their own difficulties.

This was made public and public concern was raised.

This period [September to October 1975] was a low point in my memory and as I patrolled past the Mermaid and looked up at the theatre I was awash with memories, but my metal girlfriend seemed to know that all would be well, and held her fish high and proud, so I was not too worried.

My father also commenced his historical archiving and wrote to various outlets including the Southport Visiter and to the Rank Leisure Services. He received many positive responses and other residents also spoke up and the manager of the time Laurie Hindmarsh was able to report that the November 22nd closure planned, had been reversed by the group's board much to everyone's relief.

Christmas had come early that year and Mermaid and I exchanged knowing looks.

Laurie Hindmarsh had taken over as manager in 1971 and enjoyed playing the organ in the intervals. Dad had saved the organ from being scrapped back in 1964 so he had reasons more than most to see it saved.

Then in May 1979 came the biggest blow of all and the events that signalled the final chapter in the theatres long and magnificent life.

Sainsbury Ltd., the London based grocers stepped in and said they were buying the theatre and would have to demolish the entire façade due to its poor state.

This sparked the most controversial war of words and anger amongst the public, local officials, the press and Civic Societies.
Cedric Greenwood the respected reporter of the Southport Visiter took up the cudgels and reported on a number of times the progression of the situation in the local paper and also wrote to the town planning department.

It was reported by Sainsbury Ltd that they had a report from a firm of stonemasons [The London Stone Cleaning Company] that the façade was in poor condition, this would later be found to be incorrect and that they had reported that in their opinion only the paintwork on the Darley Stone was in need of refurbishment. They also wrote pointing out that the remainder of the fabric was in need of only cosmetic attention and this was not a task they were suited to.

Local artist and campaigner for the theatres retention, Phillip Berrill even visited Sainsbury's HQ in London and confronted their surveyors with the findings and proved they had been less than truthful to the public. Sainsbury Ltd could not refute the allegations.
The Civic Society also wrote complaining that the Lord Street conservation area was in jeopardy if buildings such as the Odeon were to be demolished.
It transpired that many Councillors and other officials had believed that all buildings within a conservation area were listed and could not be pulled down without the permission of the Secretary of State.

This was to be proved wrong insomuch that they were two separate aspects.
[1]. an area can be deemed a Conservation Area, a place of historical and architectural importance but
[2]. buildings have to be separately listed within that area to come under the protection clauses.

It turned out that the Odeon was not one of these buildings. In fact it opened a can of worms that lasts until this day. Many well known landmarks on Lord Street do not have listed building status and can be torn down without any objections, should the town planners so wish.

And so the furore started.

It also transpired that Sainsbury had apparently been given permission by Sefton Council to demolish the shops in Hills Street, in order to make way for a car park. The tenants / owners of these premises had not been made aware and also joined the fight.
Many businesses and commercial outlets that backed onto or were sited in Anchor Street at the rear of the Odeon realised that the road would carry an excessive amount of extra traffic and would cause serious congestion, they also complained.

In fact only Sainsbury Ltd seemed to be for the plan and produced a book with supportive results gained at a viewing of the model of the proposed building at the Arts Centre. This was later proved to be jaundiced when people wrote in to the town planners stating that the way it had been put over was that the Odeon had to be pulled down due to its condition, so would they object to the supermarket being put up in its place? ; Obviously a loaded question.

The local councillor for Tourism and Leisure, Ronnie Fearn, who would become the Member of Parliament and latterly Lord Fearn who has kindly penned the forward to this book, also waded in with a seven point letter which inferred that some aspects of the situation were flawed and the actions being taken by some council officials could be questioned. This was hotly refuted by the Sefton Legal team but many of the questions raised have not been properly answered to this day. One councillor even threatened Mr. Fearn with legal action.

From June of 1979 a steady stream of headlines appeared in the Southport Visiter and letters to the editor were printed. All the writers seemed to be for keeping the theatre and all seemed to agree that the façade of the theatre must stay even if the internal usage was for other aspects. Even my father agreed that there could be alterations to the internal use to reflect the modern needs, such as roller skating and conferences, this was also supported by Phillip Berrill in one of his many missives to the town planners. A large petition was submitted from the public.

On September 19th, the council planning committee met and a heated and lengthy debate took place at Bootle Town Hall.

Records of the minutes which I have reproduced state -

434. Application Nos.S/11532 + S/LBC/11533.
Odeon Cinema Site, Lord St. + 2/14 + 2a Hill St, Southport.

Cllr. Lewis [in chair]
Mrs.Burgomaster, Chapman, Coles, Dawson, Hope, Hunt, Mrs.Jessop, R.E.Jones,
Kenned , Latham, Mahon, Mann, Mitchell ,Mrs .Monk, O'Neill and Rimmer.

' The Committee considered the report of the Borough Planning Officer on an application for the demolition of the Odeon Cinema building and properties nos 2/14 + 2a Hill St. Southport and the erection of a retail supermarket building together with car parking facilities at the site'

Resolved.

That the application be granted, subject to the conditions and reasons stated in the Borough Planning Officers report.

A copy of the report is reproduced later on, obtained from the vast amount of correspondence from all interested parties, in fact all the evidence is held at the Town Planners Office, Eastbank Street on microfiche and includes the newspaper articles, concerns of interested parties and observations by councillors and officials.

One would think that it would end there, not at all. The Press carried on reporting opinions and views and my father wrote to the editor pointing out anomalies and thanked Councillors who had spoken up on behalf of the theatre. He also wrote to the Secretary of State to the Department for the Environment, The Right Honourable Michael Heseltine, M.P. He was not alone; many others also wrote petitioning that the building be saved. He even suggested that a public enquiry be held before the proposed action is ratified.

On Thursday 11th October, 1979 the council passed the proposal at Southport Town Hall.

In May 1980 the demolition contractors, Connell and Finnigan Ltd. of Manchester moved in and commenced work.
Various parts were obtained for preservation, such as the keystone figureheads on the portal arches which were taken by the Southport Civic Society. The thought being to either incorporate them into the new building, or present them to the local museum.
The magnificent Compton organ was believed to have been purchased by enthusiasts, David and Joyce Alldred who installed it at their private residence in Hyde, Cheshire.
Phillip Birrell took the opportunity to sketch the building façade to record its beauty before it was finally torn down.

Dad felt the need to go and see the theatre before it disappeared, something he should not have done, upon seeing the devastation, he burst into tears and had to be led away.
His health was not too good then, this did not help, in fact he never recovered from that day.

When I visited the site, I was now stationed in Liverpool having been promoted and had not seen the start of the demolition. I was devastated at the destruction. Like Dad I walked away feeling empty and alone.

It had had a profound effect and as I stood in front of the site and looked at what had been, and recalled those happy memories which I have just shared with you, I looked into the eyes of the Mermaid, it may have been the water from the fountain that gushed from the fish she held but I really believe - **she was weeping.**

The Mermaid

Was unveiled in 1914, having been commissioned by the Connard family, local jewellers of Lord Street
The family had it designed to stand outside the Palladium. The Connards owned the land at the time and as the Southport Corporation wanted to create gardens along Lord Street they agreed to give the land over, provided the Mermaid was included.
With the co-operation of Southport Corporation it was designed, built and constructed by the Bromsgrove Guild at a cost of £225.

In 2008, as part of the Lord Street refurbishments, The Mermaid Fountain was expertly cleaned and restored to her former glory. The Connard family along with representatives of the Southport Civic Society attended with Sefton Council Technical Staff.

Queuing for 'A Hard Day's Night' - also reminiscent of Saturday morning children's club but with grown ups

1960. Now called the Odeon, the façade was repainted in cream with beige highlights. This was the paintwork that 20 years later was judged to be the 'deterioration of the fabric of the building' and was the major point raised to show the building was allegedly falling apart.

APPENDIX

Item and Application No.	Site and Applicant	Locality	Proposal
S/11532	Odeon Cinema Site, Lord Street, 2-14 & 2A Hill Street, J. Sainsbury Ltd., Stamford Street, London SE1 9LL.	Southport	Erection of a retail Supermarket building (13,400 sq.ft. net of retail floor-space) and layout of car park.
S/LBC/11533	Odeon Cinema Site, Lord Street, 2-14 & 2A Hill Street,	Southport	Demolition of Odeon Cinema building and properties Nos. 2-14 & 2A Hill Street (Within Lord Street conservation area prior to erection of retail Super-market and layout of car park).

1.0 Introduction

1.1 The proposal relates to a site which has been amalgamated from different ownerships. The site is L shaped, being some 1.56 acres in extent with a frontage of 150 feet to St. George Place and Lord Street. The frontage to Hill Street is 130 feet. The site consists of the Odeon Cinema building which fronts onto Lord Street, a public car park operated by N.C.P. with entrance from St. Georges Place at the side of the cinema, a group of garage buildings, a vacant site used for storing of scrapped cars and a row of 8 shops fronting Hill Street with 1st floor accommodation.

1.2 The current application is to redevelop the whole site with a supermarket building on the whole site of the cinema, with the remainder being used as a properly laid out surface car park. The proposed building would consist of the retail unit on the ground floor, a preparation/storage and staff rooms on the first floor, with two self-contained flats on the second floor.

1.3 The existing site is situated within the Lord Street Conservation Area, although none of the buildings contained within have been listed for either special historical or architectural interest. However, despite this, the proposal does require Listed Building Consent, but only insofar as it relates to the demolition of the cinema building and Nos. 2-14 and 2A Hill Street.

2.0 Previous History

There have been previous planning applications relating to that part of the site fronting Hill Street and Anchor Street.

(i) Planning permission was granted in June 1962 for the erection of a car wash building on the site of Nos. 1-11 Anchor Street. This was never implemented. (Reference: DA.5245).

(ii) There were a number of planning applications relating to No. 2A Hill Street between November 1948 and November 1967. The premises consisted of a garage and these applications related to minor details such as petrol pumps and storage tanks.

- 1 -

(iii) In October 1972 outline planning permission was granted for the erection of shops, offices, petrol service station and multi-storey car park. This also included the site of Nos. 39-41 Hoghton Street. (Reference: DA.8593).

(iv) A further outline planning permission was granted in January 1973 for the erection of offices with car parking, on the site of 2-14 and 2A Hill Street only. (Reference: DA.8593A).

(v) A full planning permission was granted in February 1974 for the erection of a retail store and multi-storey car park on the site of Nos. 2-14 and 2A Hill Street. The retail element of this scheme was 12,670 sq. ft. of shopping floorspace.

(vi) The latter scheme was submitted as a renewal of the planning permission in February 1979. The application was considered on 10 April 1979, when planning permission (S/10916) and listed building consent for demolition of 2-14 and 2A Hill Street (S/LBC/10946) were granted.

3.0 Consultations

3.1 Royal Fine Art Commission - Prior to receiving the planning application, the scheme was submitted to the Royal Fine Art Commission for their consideration. The Commission agreed that they would not oppose the demolition of the cinema building, although they felt a greater contribution could have been made to the architectural qualities of Lord Street. Detailed comments related to the archways, pitched roof and good landscaping at the side of the proposed supermarket building.

3.2 Victorian Society

"It is doubtful whether this building will ever be taken seriously by architectural historians, but its showy brand of thirties epic classicism is very appropriate to the architectural character of a seaside resort. The building does make a significant contribution to the Lord Street Conservation Area and would be sorry to see it go if there was any possibility of its being adapted either in whole or in part (the facade is clearly the most important element here) in the new development. Permission should not be granted unless it can be demonstrated that the adaptation cannot be followed".

3.3 Southport Chamber of Trade and Commerce

3.3.1 The Chamber sent out a questionnaire to its members and received 96 replies. 56 indicated they were against the proposed supermarket, 39 in favour and 1 indifferent.

3.3.2 There were alternative suggestions made for the use of the site, the predominant thought being that for a Leisure and Sports Centre development.

3.4 Southport Civic Society

3.4.1 The Society have written four letters concerning various matters relating to the proposal. Their objections to the redevelopments are as follows:-

(i) The facade is typical of theatre architecture of its period and its demolition would be detrimental to the character of Lord Street.

(ii) The proposal is on the east side of Lord Street which is not the main shopping area. Permission on this site would set a precedent.

- 2 -

(iii) Sufficient supermarkets in the town.

(iv) Demolition of shops in Hill Street will be detrimental to the character of Hill Street, which could act as a screen to a three-storey car park.

3.4.2 The Society welcomes the proposed use of the rear as a car park, but would prefer a three-storey car park open to the public. Also consideration should be given to the possibility of retaining the small shops in Hill Street and to retention of cinema building as a Leisure Centre.

3.4.3 The Society after making their general views known wrote further letters concerning the structural state of the Odeon building and alleging that the Royal Fine Art Commission were not aware of the structural soundness of the main auditorium.

3.5 United Reformed Church - no representations received.

3.6 Scarisbrick Estates Office - no representations received.

3.7 Merseyside Police - no observations.

3.8 Merseyside County Engineer - no objection in principle, but suggested detailed amendments to the scheme.

4.0 Publicity

4.1 Both applications were advertised as required by statute in the Southport Visiter. Notices were posted on site in four locations.

4.2 Coverage to the proposed demolition and redevelopment was prominently featured in the Southport Visiter. Articles, letters appeared in 12 different editions of the paper during the months of May, June and July.

4.3 An exhibition with the plans of the proposed supermarket and model took place at the Southport Arts Centre from 30 April to 5 May 1979. There were 253 entries in the Visitor's Book, 175 of which were for the scheme and 78 against.

4.4 As a result of the publicity given, four petitions with 978 signatures and a further 25 letters (including one from Councillor R. Fearn) were received against the proposal. The objections may be summarised as follows:-

(i) Too many supermarkets in the town already.

(ii) Loss of shops in Hill Street.

(iii) Proposed building does not blend with Conservation Area.

(iv) Odeon building should be adapted for another leisure pursuit.

(v) Car parking insufficient (further checks required).

(vi) Anchor Street, too narrow, lead to congestion/conflict.

(vii) Traffic along Anchor Street would cause nuisance to office workers in the area.

- 3 -

(viii) Wrong site for supermarket and will set a precedent.

(ix) Existing Odeon car park is for general use, this will be lost.

(x) Cause blight to business/professional people in area.

(xi) Facade of cinema, typical theatre architecture of 20s. Removal will be detrimental.

(xii) Cause traffic problems at the junction of Hill Street/Lord Street.

(xiii) Will reduce overall employment in other retail food outlets.

5.0 Borough Planning Officer's Observations

5.1 The current application has probably received more publicity and thus created more public reaction than any other application since re-organisation in 1974. With all the representations and comments which have been made, there are three matters which need to be determined:-

(i) The demolition of an unlisted building within a conservation area.

(ii) Whether a retail supermarket should be sited at this particular location in Lord Street and

(iii) Following on from the first two issues any new building in Lord Street should be of the highest possible standard of design, together with satisfactory layout and servicing.

5.2 Demolition of the Odeon Cinema Building

5.2.1 Provision is made within planning legislation for planning authorities to have some form of control relating to demolition of unlisted buildings in Conservation Areas. The purpose is not to protect the individual building as such, but the Conservation Area as a whole. The merits of an unlisted building must therefore not be considered in isolation, but in its relationship with immediate surrounding buildings and its value as an intrinsic part of the physical fabric.

5.2.2 In this particular case, the Odeon stands as an individual building with an Edwardian parade of 4 storeys building immediately adjoining to the south west and St. George's Church on the north east side. The demolition of the cinema and replacement with a building more in character with the quality and setting of the Edwardian Parade, would provide much more sympathetic setting for St. George's Church and this part of the Conservation Area. The character of the Conservation Area would, therefore, not be harmed by the removal of this building, which incidentally, cannot be seen too clearly from Lord Street because of the mature trees.

It is this latter point of the trees together with the spacious layout of the street and buildings which gives this Conservation Area its attractiveness.

5.2.3 The building itself to many, is a symbol of a past era. This is true of the facade, with the neo-classical 'Ben Hur Hollywood' portico and pavilions. Behind this, the main auditorium is a well constructed large building, a mass of common brickwork to the side and rear elevations.

- 4 -

SOUTHPORT VISITER
(second section)

Saturday, November 15, 1975

'The Phantom of the Opera' (Ken Lloyd in disguise) escapes from the theatre as another film publicity stunt

Ken Lloyd led a racehorse through the auditorium and the streets of Southport to publicise the Gaumont British News coverage of the 1957 Grand National

Rajah the lion had the theatre to of Safari in 1956, vainly watching his own performance

Now showing . . . the story behind the pictures

Mr. Kenneth Lloyd, manager 1954-64, the

Mr. Harold Gale wa chief projectionist fro Palladium historian, 1930 to 1980.

THIS might have been the obituary of Southport's Odeon cinema. Twice in its history it has seemed doomed—first with the 1928 fire and then with this year's closure notice. Instead, this is the story of two eras of the history of this theatre as it stands on the threshold of a third era.

Opened in 1914 as the Palladium variety theatre and music hall and rebuilt from the ashes of the old theatre in 1930 as a magnificent moviedrome of the glorious Gaumont thirties, the Odeon (as it was renamed in 1962) is a cathedral of picturegoers which, like cathedrals all over the country, now dwarfs dwindled congregations of the faithful few.

Although not as grand as the Grand, further along Lord Street, the Odeon never succumbed to bingo. It has survived as a 2,020-seat cinema through the age of bowling alleys and the nadir of cinema attendances into the age of twin cinemas and mini cinemas.

Despite an improvement in attendances since the mid 1960s, the Odeon is still running at a loss and the Rank Organisation's Leisure Services subsidiary listed it for closure on November 22, one week from today.

MAKING CONSIDERABLE LOSSES

Now Rank Leisure Services has given it a reprieve. A company spokesman said: "We will keep any cinema open as long as it is not a drag on other theatres. Southport has been making considerable losses and it is still making a loss but we have changed our mind about closing it because by keeping it open we hope to improve the position of the theatre as regards its profitability."

The long term future of the Odeon, Southport, has not been decided yet. For the immediate future it is intended to continue with the restricted operation of the past 12 months with no matinees except on Thursdays, during school holidays and the Saturday afternoon children's show.

The existing oil-fired central heating plant is being

...Lord Street scene as the theatre would be to the resort's entertainment bill. The twin towers, with segmental pediments in the cornice, mark the limits of the original 1,500-seat Palladium theatre built in 1913-14 with Darley Dale stone.

The restaurant behind that colonnaded balcony between the towers is also the original, with Adamesque walls and ceiling and Corinthian pillars. The facade and the restaurant survived the 1928 fire which destroyed the theatre.

The original Palladium was built and operated by Leonard Williamson of Hesketh Park and his reign was succeeded by Southport Palladium Ltd. from 1921 till the fire in 1928.

Films were shown there from the opening day in February, 1914, but this was principally a live theatre and films were confined to Sundays, the artistes' day of rest. Among the artistes who walked its boards were George Formby snr., Hetty King, Marie Lloyd, Ella Shields, Little Tich—and Southport's own male impersonator and dancer, Rosie Walmsley. The theatre also had its own pipe organ and resident orchestra.

Southport Palladium Ltd. in 1921 proposed an extension

with a "palais de dance," palm court lounge and cafe in another neo-classical building with a great cast-iron and glass arched roof. But this scheme never got off the ground. Instead, the General Theatre Corporation and Provincial Cinematograph Theatres jointly bought the burnt ruin of the old Palladium after the mystery fire of 1928 and rebuilt it almost twice the size with an extended frontage in march ing architecture. The 2,120-seat auditorium f a stage 52ft. wide 30ft. high and 30ft. deep with 23 lines for backdrops.

It opened on October 1, 1930, as a cine-variety theatre with combined stage and screen shows and a resident orchestra but from January, 1931, it was a full-time cinema. The resident orchestra proved too expensive to maintain but the new organ, which appeared and disappeared on a lift in a well, continued to play before, between and after the films.

Herbert Steele was the theatre's musical director and resident organist through the 1920s till the fire. He sojourned two years at the Majestic, Leeds, and returned to the Palladium on reopening in 1930 to play the new organ till he retired in 1939. He was succeeded by Cecil Williams (real name William Hopper), one-time pianist at the Argyle Theatre, Birkenhead, who came from the Gaumont, Chester in 1939 and played till 1942—the end of the cinema organ era.

Thanks to Mr. Kenneth Lloyd, manager 1954-64, the organ survived Rank's bid to remove it in 1963, and the present manager, Mr. Laurie Hindmarsh, revived organ recitals at Sunday afternoon family shows in 1971 and '72. The organ was restored by the local branch of the Cinema Organ society, which meets occasionally at the Odeon. The organ, now one of the oldest cinema organs in the country, is a three-manual nine-rank Compton electric pipe organ with 100 stops including church chimes, drums, glockenspiel and xylophone.

Ownership of the theatre passed to the Gaumont British Picture Corporation in the late 1930s, and in 1947 the Gaumont and Odeon Circuits amalgamated under the Rank Organisation.

...he remembers as far back as 1922, when he saw Little Titch on the stage there. At his home, 1a Knob Hall Lane, Marshside, Mr. Lloyd has amassed a room full of files of photographs, press cuttings, posters and other papers about the Palladium/Gaumont/Odeon and it is from Mr. Lloyd that much of the history of the theatre has been compiled for this article.

Previously manager of the Rivoli, Aigburth (1938-40, 1945-50) and the Odeon (now the Classic), Crosby (1950-55), Mr. Lloyd took over management of the Gaumont, Southport in 1955 two weeks before the Trades Union Congress was held there. "The T.U.C. and the Beatles were the rowdiest shows I have ever been connected with as a cinema manager," says Mr. Lloyd.

The Beatles appeared there three times during the heig of Beatlemania in the early 1960s when this magnifice theatre with its spacious stage and dressing rooms was do what the Southport Theatre is doing today—staging one-nig big-name shows. Among others who starred there were Cy Stapleton and his band, Marion Ryan, Ronnie Hilton, C Richard, Helen Shapiro and Gerry and the Pacemakers Cil Black was slotted in unbilled, as part of a programme 1963 when she was an unknown.

During his time as cinema manager, Mr. Lloyd wo dozens of awards from Rank, the film trade press and oth bodies for film promotional publicity. In 1951 he was t Northwest winner of the National Showmanship Conte and he is honorary life member of the Kinematograp Company of Showmen with 11 seals of merit.

Says Mr. Lloyd: "I have always had an affection f the Palladium Theatre. It is a place of substance and chara ter and when the audience had left at night you could sen a tremendous atmosphere which was a most heart-warmin experience.

There was a staff of nearly 70 at the theatre in M Lloyd's time. There were 20 in the restaurant (which close about 1965) and there were doormen, front-of-house me usherettes, salesgirls, projection staff, cashiers, cleaners, ca park attendants, a trainee manager, an assistant manage and the manager himself

Many members of the old Palladium and Gaumont ar still with us in Southport today. Mr. William Hopper, th last resident organist, lives at 1 Mallee Crescent, Marshsid Miss Doris Moores, second cashier 'and' then head cashier from 1930 to 1965, lives at 4 Brook Street, Crossens

Mr. Harold Gale, the chief projectionist and hous engineer who opened the cinema in 1930 and continue until retirement in 1965, lives at 2 Verulam Road, Churcl town. These people have helped to piece together the histor of the Palladium/Gaumont/Odeon...

...When I'd got the theatre in shipshape condition fro engineering point of view, I was supposed to go on to t ford to open the New Victoria. But I liked it here. I notified the company I was ready to move. I left it don So I stayed here and I saw this theatre through three n and ten managers before I retired."

Special feature by Cedric Greenwood

● The cinema's restaurant, which closed about 1965, must be one of the most beautiful rooms in Southport.

● The old 1,500-seat theatre with its small screen, pipe organ and domed boxes.

SOUTHPORT VISITER
(Second section)
Saturday, December 6, 1980

Remembering an old Pal

These were the houses that were demolished in 1913 to make way for the Palladium.

In this photograph of the Gaumont, in May, 1956, the twin towers (or "pavilions") with segmental pediments, mark the limits of the original Palladium of 1913. The extension to the left was added in the rebuilding in 1929-30. Note the latticework and the shrubs. Hanging baskets of flowers festooned the cinema in due season. This photograph is from the collection of Mr. Kenneth Lloyd, of 1st Knob Hall Lane, Marshside, who was the manager from 1954 to 1964.

A steam traction engine and chains were used to pull down the houses.

Life cycle of building that became a toothgap

the previous generation of buildings on the site, the construction of the Palladium picture theatre, later the Odeon, and autographed photographs of artistes who appeared there from 1914 until 1920.

The site was formerly occupied by a large Victorian villa, Haughton House, 144 Lord Street, and a pair of semi-detached houses, 146 and 148, with the characteristic tall, Tudor arched windows of the original houses on Lord Street.

Their front gardens reached down to Lord Street and the loop road known as St. George's Place then began at Brown's, the solicitor's office. The former front gardens were reclaimed as public gardens as St. George's Place was extended in front of the new theatre.

The houses were demolished in the spring of 1913 and the Palladium was opened in February, 1914. The timetable of the redevelopment was a bit quicker than today.

The original Palladium had a 1,300 seat auditorium, a small screen on the stage, a pipe organ and ornate boxes in the circle, framed by columns and domes.

The theatre was built and operated by Leonard Williamson, of 28 Albert Road, Southport, and his reign was succeeded in 1921 by Southport Palladium Ltd.

It was principally a live theatre and among those who walked its boards were George Formby, Snr., Hetty King, Marie Lloyd, Ella Shields and Little Tich. Films were shown on Sundays — the artistes' day of rest.

The stage area and auditorium were destroyed by a mystery fire in 1929. The Darley Dale stone facade and the restaurant (with its Corinthian pillars and Adamesque walls and ceiling) survived to be incorporated in the new Palladium cine-variety theatre opened in October, 1930.

The burnt ruin of the old Palladium was bought jointly by the General Theatre Corporation and Provincial Cinematograph Theatres, which rebuilt the place almost twice the size with an extended frontage in matching architecture, a 2,126

for its first three months; but from January, 1931, it became a full-time cinema. The resident orchestra proved too expensive — but a new organ, which appeared and disappeared on a lift in a well, played before, between, and after the films.

Ownership of the theatre passed to the Gaumont British Picture Corporation in 1938, when it was renamed the Gaumont. In 1947 the Gaumont and Odeon circuits amalgamated under the Rank Organisation, which re-named it the Odeon in 1962.

In the early 1960s the Gaumont/Odeon reverted to cine-variety. This time the film programme was interspersed with one-night big name shows. The Beatles appeared there three times during the height of Beatlemania. Others who starred there were Cyril Stapleton and his band, Marion Ryan, Ronnie Hilton, Cliff Richard, Helen Shapiro and Gerry and the Pacemakers. Cilla Black was slotted-in (unbilled) as part of the programme in 1963, when she was unknown.

Rank owned the Odeon until the end. In 1975 came the threat of closure — and a reprieve. The theatre was given a new coat of paint outside and a supplementary heating system, but there was no appreciable publicity drive nor any effort to capitalise on the beautiful restaurant or the magnificent stage.

The end came in 1979 when the unprofitable theatre was bought by J. Sainsbury Ltd., the London chain grocers, for demolition and redevelopment as a supermarket. The curtain closed on the last show on December 1. The building was demolished in June and July this year. There is still no news from Sainsbury's about the new development.

All the photographs reproduced here of the demolition of the houses and the construction of the Palladium are from the albums produced by the studios of Theo J. Giddm, a commercial photographer, of 491 Lord Street.

As Haughton House disappears into the growing piles of brick and timber, we note the arcading on the ground floor facade that was echoed in George Tonge's design for the Palladium.

• Next week we look at some of the people who brought the old Palladium to life.

The forest of roped-together timber that served as scaffolding inside the theatre.

A once familiar sight takes shape . . .

Construction of the Palladium in 1913. The contractor's name on the jib of the derrick was T. A. Halliwell, a Southport stonemason who built The Monument and many of the town's banks.

Old Mr. Halliwell's son and grandson still run the business from St. Luke's Road, and are now the only stonemasons between Preston and Liverpool.

60

• The Odeon has gone, and with it the echoes of a long roll call of famous artistes from Harry Lauder to The Beatles. Three giant photograph albums, found in a Southport office attic, have provided us with the pictures we saw last week of the houses, their demolition and the construction of the theatre, and these two pages of pictures today portray some of the artistes who appeared at the theatre from 1914 to 1920.

John and Sonia Brettargh remember . . .

Rosie Walmsley, a male impersonator and dancer of the 1920s, lived in Stanley Street, Southport. She was paid £6 to appear nightly at the Palladium for a week, in August, 1923.
Photo: Rose Lloyd collection

This was the original 1,500-seat Palladium theatre, where all the old stagers pictured in this feature appeared. Note the pipe organ, the domed boxes and the small cinema screen. It was a live theatre for six days a week and films were screened on Sunday — the artistes' day of rest.

Requiem for a hall of fame whose ghosts still linger

Report by Cedric Greenwood

Wee Georgie Wood, played at the Palladium in 1917 and returned in 1955 as delegate for the Variety Artistes' Federation, at the T.U.C. conference, in Southport, at the Gaumont, as it then was. He is pictured here with Jimmy Guthrie, of the Football Players Union.

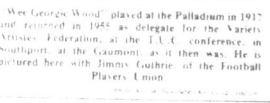

Vesta Tilley was a male impersonator, a sort of female Mike Yarwood.

"Clarice Mayne and That" was the name of this husband-and-wife act. She sang popular songs. "That" was her husband, James Tate. "He was a very good pianist and a good comedian. He also played principal boy in pantomime."

More pictures on page 26.

Coram, who "always appeared in this uniform, was a great ventriloquist with his doll, Jerry."

Wilkie Bard "was a great singer of comic songs. He used to do a famous number called 'I Want to sing in Opera'."

Dorothy Ward, a variety star and comedy actress, appeared at the Palladium in 1918 (as seen here) and the at the Garrick Theatre 40 years later. She is still alive today at 90.

"The Two Bobs", Bob Alden and Bob Adams: "Light and humorous songs at the piano. I remember the words of one that went: 'The body is upstairs — and the seat of his pants was found in France'."

A hall of fame which welcomed the great

Bransby Williams recited classic monologues.

Gertie Gitana, who sang popular songs of the day, lived in Southport during World War II.

• Harry Lauder usually appeared in his kilt, but occasionally in other guises like that of the old sea salt.

Continued from page 25.

• Right: Albert Whelan was the first man to have a signature tune. He whistled it as he came on, took off his topper and gloves and threw his gloves into his topper. He did a light comedy act then whistled his signature tune as he put his topper and gloves on and walked off.

"Little Tich", who played in variety and pantomime, did comic songs and dances: "He used to do a big boot dance, and on one hand he had five fingers and a thumb."

Little big man

"Wee Georgie Wood was a dwarf. He was like Jimmy Clitheroe. He was about 20 in this photograph He used to appear with Dolly Harmer as his mother", says Mr. Brettargh. The inscription reads: "In happy thoughts of a lovely week. Nov. 5th, 1917. Palladium, Southport.

CHAPTER 8

The following chapter is dedicated to my father
KENNETH BERTRAM LLOYD
Who inspired me to carry on his work as the historian and archivist of the theatre.

He was asked to record his life in the theatre and subsequently after retiring, this he did using his extensive knowledge and had he written a book about his life, it would have been quite an eye opener into the history of one man and his accomplishments.

In 1982 he sat down and told of his recollections on tape which was used for the benefit of those who were visually impaired or who relied on talking books and other similar facilities. The body of this chapter are drawn from that recording.

Within this chapter are some of the most interesting illustrations of the theatre its staff and events that shaped the history and memories that are slowly fading into past memory and is now part of the history of Southport.

THE PALLADIUM SHORTLY AFTER THE MERMAID HAD BEEN
INSTALLED AND UNVEILED IN 1914

Leonard Williamson
The original proprietor

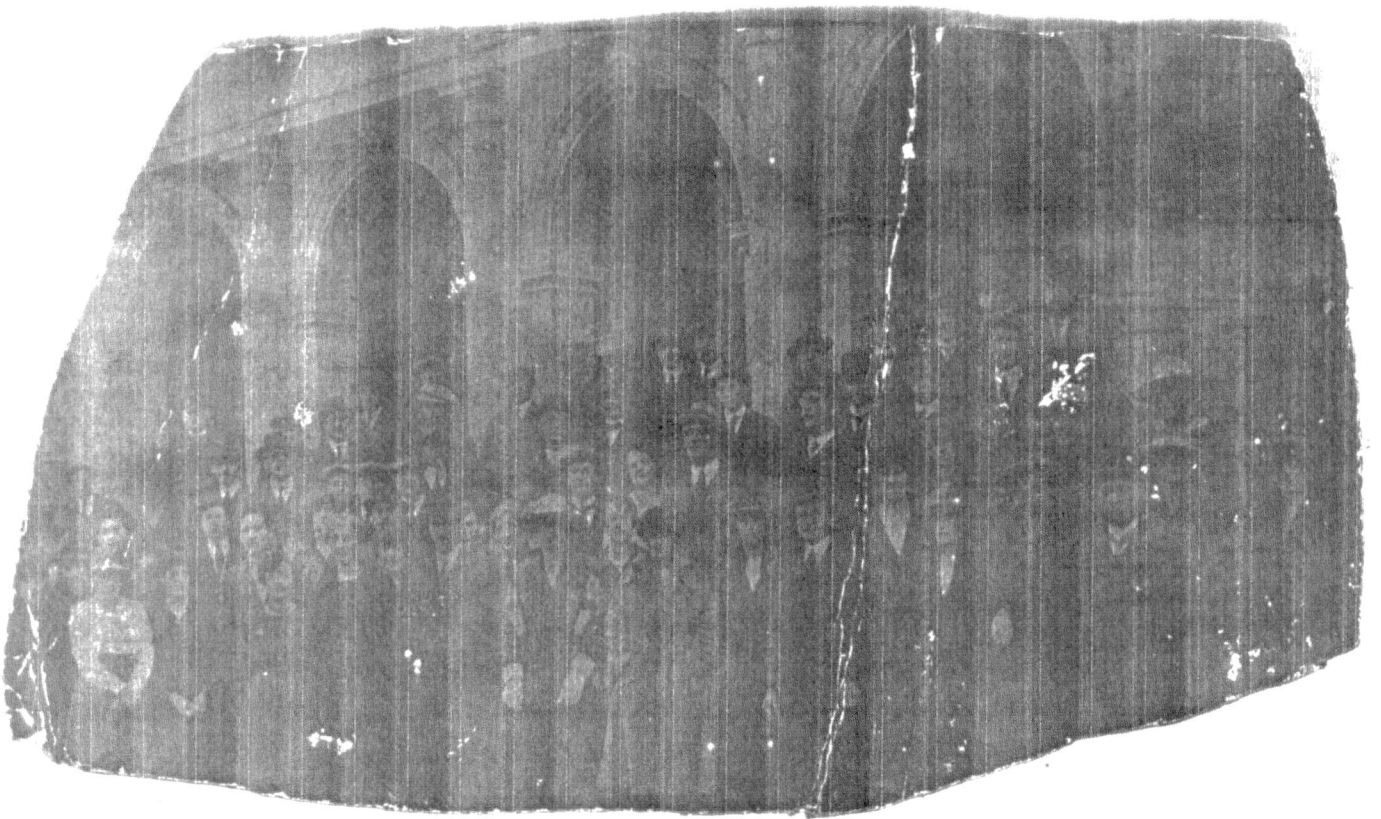

AN EARLY PHOTOGRAPH OF THE PALLADIUM STAFF, THOUGHT TO BE AROUND 1913 WHEN THE PALLADIUM OPENED

THE PALLADIUM,
SOUTHPORT.

HALEY'S JUVENILES.
Saturday, Dec. 14th.

STALLS

[S]

Second House.

This part to be retained.

"Visiter" Printing Works, Southport.

THE PALLADIUM,
SOUTHPORT.

HALEY'S JUVENILES.
Saturday, December 14th, 1918.

Stalls 1/-

Tax Extra.

[S]

SECOND HOUSE.

This part to be given up.

An early stalls ticket for The Palladium.
The Southport Visiter Printing Works produced tickets in those days.

Circa 1920. Staff photograph
Back row – 5th from left. Wilf Manning – projectionist
7th from left. Alfred Wright – stage carpenter
9th from left. John Sumner - projectionist

CHAPTER 9
THE HISTORY BY K.B.LLOYD

The History of the
Palladium / Gaumont / Odeon
Lord Street, Southport
1913 to 1980

By

Kenneth B. Lloyd
General Manager 1955 to 1965

This is the history and the story of the old Palladium Theatre, The new Palladium Theatre, renamed and subsequently called the Gaumont and latterly the Odeon Theatre / restaurant and Cinema, Lord St Southport. [Formerly Lancashire] Merseyside, from 1913 to the summer of 1980.

I fully realise that this old edifice which became an institution in Southport and the North West, may not be known to readers in other parts of the country, but nonetheless I do hope my story may be of interest to all readers and bring back some nostalgic memory as it progresses.

I was the general manager of the Gaumont theatre and restaurant form 1955 until 1965 in which time I was enabled from my research and kindly assistance of my patrons and members of the public, former staff and friends to build up a reasonably reliable and comprehensive story of the old theatres' history throughout its career of almost 7 decades [66 yrs in fact] until it was demolished in May of 1980 to make way for the site of the new supermarket of J Sainsbury Ltd, the London chain grocers. This historical record was made possible by people supplying me with old photographs, press write ups, programmes, letters, posters, and verbal information from residents of the town, combined with my own personal knowledge throughout the theatres existence.

During this period it provided entertainment and happiness for literally millions of Southport residents and visitors to the town from this country and overseas.

Before I go onto the theatre, perhaps it might be appropriate to describe the surroundings and environment of the area before the theatre was built.
The site was formerly occupied by a large Victorian villa called Houghton House which was at 144 Lord Street, and a pair of semi detached houses, 146 + 148 with the characteristic tall Tudor arch windows of the original

houses in Lord St. The front gardens reached down to Lord St as was required by the joint lords of the manor, The Bold-Houghton and Fleetwood-Hesketh families from the 1820s and after the 1840s - especially by Charles Scarisbrick encouraging planned residential development.

The new service road called St Georges Place then began at [Browns] the solicitors offices and the former gardens of the house were reclaimed as public gardens as St Georges Place was extended in front of the then New Palladium Theatre. The houses were demolished in the spring of 1913 the building of the new theatre commenced and the Palladium was opened in February 1914. The theatre was built and operated by Leonard Williamson of 28 Albert Road Southport and his reign was succeeded in 1921 by the Southport Palladium Theatre Varieties Ltd.

The architect of the theatre was Mr. George E. Tonge LRIBA of Manchester Chambers,
371 Lord St. Southport.
The stone mason and contractor was T. A. Halliwell of Southport, who I understand built the monument and several of the town's banks.

It was designed as a super theatre and music hall and comprised of a large auditorium and balcony with extremely comfortable seating for 1,500. The building long had a reputation both at home and abroad of being one of the most beautiful theatres in the British Isles. The elevation of the Palladium was of the free renaissance style of architecture in full sympathy with the purpose for which it was to be used. The beautiful grey Darley Dale Stone gave unique distinction and stability to the elevation. As many may or may not know Darley Dale Stone comes from the Midlands and it is noted for its durability. Because of this the main entrance of the new theatre survived the disastrous fire in March 1929.

The entrance hall and the foyer of the original theatre was 73 feet wide and at each side of the magnificent marble staircase at the centre of the foyer where the entrances to the auditorium stalls and over the entrance hall was the Cafe/Restaurant conceived in the style of the brothers Adam. That character of architecture was generally carried throughout the entire theatre and it created an atmosphere of refinement not always to be found in the most modern theatre.
The stage which competed with the best theatres and music halls in the country was 75 feet wide and 40 feet deep and it was connected on either side with the necessary dressing room accommodation and in front of the stage was a large orchestral well, capable of accommodating over 30 musicians. Hence the best musical accompaniment could be offered to any production that might be staged.
In addition, and in the auditorium was a magnificent orchestral organ. It was of the pipe organ style with the organ pipes on either side of the auditorium and in those days it could not have been installed for a cost of £10,000 and that was going back to the pre 1920 period.
The ventilation system even in those early years was excellent, the air either warmed or cooled, being completely changed every 6 minutes. It was forced into the building by a large fan, through ducts under the floor and thence through ventilating panels in the walls. Before reaching the auditorium, the currents of air were warmed in winter and cooled in summer thus ensuring an equable temperature. In addition to the special ventilation, there was a low pressure hot water system, conveyed through the same ducts to the radiators at various parts of the theatre. To complete the system, a large 6-foot diameter fan in the roof was continually and silently extracting the foul air.
The theatre was equipped as an up to date cinema of that era, silent films of course. The operating room or projection room as it is presently called, was specially built at the back of the theatre and was fitted the latest cinematograph machines or projectors, thus enabling the Palladium to compete favorably with any of the then modern cinemas in the country.

I previously stated that the premises were built primarily as a Theatre and music hall. They showed films on Sundays which was the actors and artistes rest day and there is a lengthy list of bookings for the theatre and there appeared many notable West End variety shows and revues of that era.

Many famous music hall stars including such top line artists as Harry Lauder, Vesta Tilly, Wee Georgie Wood, Coran the Ventriloquist, Dorothy Ward, Clarice Main, Albert Whelan A.F.Sheilds and Little Tich, [whom I recall seeing in 1922. He was an extremely funny, quaint little fellow, who made his entrance through an archway in the backcloth, down some stairs, all on a pair of huge wooden feet].

The booking agents were Messrs Norris and Clayton the then noted London theatrical and variety booking agents who were also the booking agents for Leslie Henson and Tom Walsh Productions and Jack Wallers Productions.

As I previously mentioned, The Palladium opened 5 months before the outbreak of the 1914 / 1918 Great War and this was reflected in the style of the programmes presented during those tragic years, patriotic songs and shows were staged in keeping with those years.

Leonard Williamson under whose control the theatre operated complied some very large and weighty albums of a selection of autographs and photographs of the famous artists who appeared there and many of whom were personal friends of his, and these albums which are still in mint condition also showed the former houses before and after their demolition and the progress of the building of the Palladium. Leonard Williamson also ran charity programmes during the war years and in the programmes showed military personnel , nurses and disabled soldiers.

During my research I looked through considerable correspondence and also received a letter from Mr. Jack Young of 23 Beaconsfield Rd Southport in September 1960. Mr. Young was then an old age pensioner.

Here are some interesting extracts from that letter, which describe the opening and subsequent activities of the theatre, he was apparently employed there for about 12 years from the opening of the theatre up to approx. 1928. He was quite an authority on the theatre.

'I commenced at the Palladium on the back stage staff in the first week of variety and the cast list was Hetty King, R.G.Mills, The Quaint Q's, The Four Londons, Manny and Roberts, a comedy sketch called Won by a Dog, a short film ended the show. As I worked there from the first week of variety until the last day of revues, I saw a great number of staff and also met a great many of the pros who will never be replaced.

The first revue to be staged at the theatre was called Full inside, a good show starring Kenny Benson and Harriet Brown.

The first Stage Manager was a Mr Thomas along with Geoff Pierce and myself. with Teddy Clarkson, Billy Wakeson and Bill Smith the electrician.

In another letter that I received from Mr. Young, he had sketched a detailed and comprehensive plan of the back stage area from memory; there were details of the stage area, the 9 dressing rooms, the stage manager's office, and the band room which was below the stage. As I remarked before the theatre was controlled by Leonard Williamson until 1921 when a new company was formed which was to named, The Palladium Theatre of Varieties, Lord Street Southport, and they took over on January 2nd 1922. [See later]

Just for the record the list of the directorate. It was under the Direction of Mr. Albert Marr, Chairman, Mr. Stanislaus Barron Llb, Mr. John Davies, Mr. J Leslie Green, Sir Charles Thomas Hunt, James Rylands, Mr. Thomas Wood, the Secretary was Mr. Henry Kennedy of 3, Tulketh St, Southport, the Bankers were Manchester and County Bank Ltd, Lord St Southport, the solicitors were Taylor Sons, Bridge and Barron, 26 King St, Wigan, the auditor was Mr. Louis Nicholas, Chartered Accountant of 19 Castle St, Liverpool, and Mr. George Tonge the architect.

At this time silent films were the order of the day and talking films didn't make their debut in this country until 1928/9.

The first cinema in the North West to show 'sound' films, was the Olympia, in West Derby Rd Liverpool and then gradually all the cinemas introduced this new invention. Some of the earlier films were partially silent and partially sound.

It would be remiss of me to omit Mr. Herbert Steele in connection with this History of the Palladium. Mr. Steel was a highly respected resident of this town and a great old friend of mine. He arrived in Southport in 1916. And as organist and musical director was responsible for the music for all of the variety years. In those days you played the organ for the afternoon cinema shows and scored the music for the evening Variety besides doubling with the violins. His work did not end there, at the weekends there were usually orchestral concerts with 25 to 30 members. His career started in music when as a boy soprano he won music festivals up and down the country. Besides being a renowned soprano, Mr. Steele took lessons in organ playing so, that when his voice broke he could continue in the musical field.

Subsequently after his period as the organist he entered into cinema management but in his spare time he was a church organist at St Andrews formally of Eastbank Street.

In a programme dated August 6th 1923 and a contract of employment from that day, there appears an act which was of local interest as it included a young girl called Rosie Walmsley a late resident of Southport who received a princely sum of £6.00 for a twice nightly appearance. She was number 8 on the bill and was described as Southport's own Male impersonator and dancer. In those days the P.A. system [public address] was not as you will find today, with remote microphones and lip sync systems, in those days, to be heard at the back of the theatre you really had to 'belt it out' to succeed.

At that time the prices of admission were from Monday to Fridays, Boxes 18 shillings, " 2/6 , orchestra stalls 2/-,Stalls 1/6, pit stalls 1/- Front Circle 1'6, upper circle 9d . Prices for Saturdays and holidays were upgraded with the Boxes at 21/-, the rest increased by 6d except the upper circle which was 1/- and all the seats were bookable without a fee.

On Sunday there was a film. On this occasion it was 'Two kinds of Women' starring Pauline Frederick who was a big film star of that era.

With the conclusion of the Great War we subsequently arrived at a period known as the 'Roaring 20's' and with the improvement of the silent films of those years, cinemas started to be built all over the country. And therefore, for example the Rialto Cinema and Ballroom, Liverpool was built in, I believe 1924, when the Trocadero Cinema, Camden Street, Liverpool subsequently renamed The Gaumont, was built. Many of these buildings were of a similar architecture with a marble façade.

It was about this time when the Palladium came under new management. The proprietors were the General Theatre Corporation Ltd. which was an associated company of the Gaumont British Picture Corporation Ltd. It might be appropriate to mention at this time that the President of GBPC was Isador Ostrer and the chairman of the directors was Mark Ostrer who was also the chairman of other associated companies. Morris Ostrer was associated with the film production side and was director of many British films which were preceded by 'The Gainsborough Lady' later replaced by Bombardier Billy Wells striking the large gong. This symbolic introduction is still used as a trade mark of the present day Rank Organization.

In 1928 the manager of the Palladium was a Mr. Hughes and during his time cine variety was changing its face, there was more cinema entertainment and less stage activity. They started to screen bi weekly programmes starting on Monday/Tuesday/Wednesday and changing for Thursday, Friday and Saturday. We should of course remember that during that period, talking pictures [or sound films] were imminent and about to be launched in America and then subsequently in this country, about a year later.

As a result the cinema proprietors were attempting to attract more patrons to their matinee shows offering bargain seats for 6d. Patrons were becoming bored with silent pictures with musical accompaniment.

Dancing was the rage by this time and cinemas / theatres were in losing to the competition

About 150 yards down the road from the Palladium was the Southport Palais De Danse [which became The Trocadero Cinema and later Woolworths Store]. Here one could dance to the big band sounds of Billy Cotton who would belt out the 'naughty' music of the Black Bottom and Charleston long. Business was brisk and nightly.

It is difficult when recording ones memories to recapture the atmosphere of Southport over 60 years later and record them for today's audience, but as I remember it some 6 decades ago, Lord Street, Southport [which was a County Borough of Lancashire] was an elegant street with its beautiful stately trees lining the boulevard centre of the town and the little old trams wending their way along simple tracks with loop lines at intervals. The conductors upon reaching these loops would use long bamboo poles to switch the overhead trolleys to an adjacent wire and then start the return journey along this peaceful, serene and luxurious place. In those days, men raised their hats to ladies, etiquette and courtesy prevailed. Rolls Royce motor cars mixed with Daimlers and such distinguished vehicles. Horse drawn landaus were the taxis of the day.

People would flock to the bandstand and listen to the brass bands whilst seated in deck chairs around the Municipal gardens by the Town Hall. Music drifted down the byways and the many visitors would pause and applaud the musicians that entertained them on warm summer's evenings.
One should not forget the many coffee houses which would be packed to capacity in the mornings, such as Thom's, Jolley's, Woodheads, Sissons and The Kardomah. These were the meeting places for residents and visitors alike. Then across the road in London Square where the Monument [obelisk] stands there were bath chairs lined up for hire with their folding hoods and aprons for use in case of a shower of rain. These were the fore runner of today's wheelchairs and were used by the elderly ladies who used to be taken stroll through the town centre shopping areas. I remember that during those days, Pekinese Dogs were very popular and fashionable and sat on the ladies laps.
The other form of transport then was the horse drawn landau with drivers plying for hire with their silk bowler hats taking visitors and residents on sight seeing trips.
But I am drifting away from the subject of the old Palladium and reminiscing too much.

As I indicated earlier, The Palladium had been an institution in Southport. It was famous for its style and comfort and the entertainment which it offered until, on the night of March 26th 1929 and in mysterious circumstances a fire ravaged the building. It left the theatre a mass of burnt out rubbish and twisted metal. Only the beautiful Darley Dale Stone frontage remained.

Now to have rebuilt the theatre on the old lines would have been a comparatively easy matter, but the directors of the G.B.P.C. and the General Theatre Corporation to 'Do It Better' and seized the opportunity with enthusiasm. They succeeded and fine as the old Palladium was, the New Palladium was finer from every point of view; Size, decoration, comfort and with the march of progress, in the film world – future entertainment.

Firstly and most striking, the building was practically doubled in width from the size of the original. With the talking films a new and important point had arisen when designing the picture theatre and that was the question of acoustics and the necessity for hearing the spoken word by every member of the audience. It was a very large theatre and auditorium. To this end a theatre must not be too long, lest the sound be lost in the back seats In the New Palladium the length remained practically the same as the old building but the fortunate possession of the spare land on the side had enabled the capacity to be almost doubled without the patrons' having to strain to hear the entertainment.

In the new elevation, the additional width had been added to the original in a way as to preserve the dignity of the two flanking towers [or Pavilions as the call them in architectural terms] and ensure they were not lost. The same details on the columns and cornices were followed and the open colonnades on the first floor were filled with trellis to display flowers, creepers, shrubs and evergreens in the summer. This was a pleasant feature that worked in conjunction with the gardens on Lord Street. Out side the shops and stores there were hanging baskets and to compliment these, all the archways and entrances were adorned with floral baskets and also within the foyer, floral displays were sited.

Then in keeping with the times and a further development in social history the question of a car park was approved and added to the left of the building. When the old Palladium had been built, car parks were unknown but by this time it was an essential item when considering the new modern super theatre
Up the flight of steps from Lord St. or should I say St.Georges Place was the old main entrance now joined by the new section with complimentary steps which led into the new entrance foyer. This was a hall, 96feet long and 30 feet wide with a marble mosaic floor, an enriched plaster ceiling and beautiful wood lined walls.

From the entrance foyer and box offices or pay boxes, a short flight of stairs led directly to the stalls auditorium and two flights of stairs flanking the centre stalls entrance led to the circle. Before reaching the circle one passes the mezzanine corridor leading up to both sides of the circle and also the café/restaurant and kitchens. In addition to the waiting lounge The Wedgwood decorations of the restaurant had been retained delicate shades of blue and green were a novel feature. The seating capacity had now been increased to 2120 with approximately 1500 in the stalls and 620 in the circle. The old theatre had a total capacity of 1500.

The new Palladium's resident manager was Mr. Reg Halstead, he was appointed on the reopening of the theatre and was a Southport resident. He had extensive experience in the cinema and entertainment business which he had joined in 1908. He had taken part in reviews and shows and had written material for stage productions. He had also been general manager for Messrs. Tate and Lyle Productions and had held a similar position with the famous Fred Karnos.

The reopening ceremony of the now Southport Palladium, was performed by His Worship the Mayor of Southport, Alderman Amos Tomlinson JP on Wednesday 1st October,1930 at 2.30pm.
A 4 page special edition news paper which was published weekly called Picture News [produced later] detailed the programme and prices along with technical details and interesting facts about this new and improved entertainment centre.

The new stage had a 52 foot proscenium arch it was 30 foot high and 30 foot deep, with 23 lines for back drops or scenery. There were facilities for combined stage and film shows and a resident orchestra for the first

3 months. The management dispensed with the orchestra as it proved too expensive. In 1931 it became a full time cinema; however, a new large Compton Organ which rose in front of the stage on a lift was installed along with the pipe work. This was played prior to a show and during the interval, the organist also played as patrons left, all this was called 'link music'.

The Palladium was so called from its opening until about 1943 when it was renamed The Gaumont. Subsequently in 1960/1 I had the duty of renaming it The Odeon which it carried until its demise in 1980.

And so we come to the period when I became the General Manger. In 1955 when I started, there were about 72 members of staff including 20 within the restaurant. Present day standards would perhaps consider this rather high but back then in those years a large was staff was considered essential realizing that with full seating capacity of 2120 one could expect queues from 2000 to 2500 and one needed an efficient front of house staff of men, usherettes and cashiers to ensure the speedy admission and seating of patrons and for the swift house clearances at the conclusion of a show and readmission of the next queue awaiting to gain entrance. During this time one had the salesgirls dispensing ice-cream and soft drinks.

I was very fortunate because I was surrounded by a very efficient and loyal staff most of whom remained with me for years and in my 30 years in the business I had a very low turnover of staff. I always thought as a manager that the theatre was my own and those who worked for me were also friends.

My philosophy was that a 'A successful theatre and cinema manager, in my opinion, should always have had the qualities, or at least the knowledge of being first and foremost' This being the case I was fortunate to be able to adapt to these qualifications and as a result I was fortunate to win many publicity and showmanship awards from this country and also the U.S.A. On one occasion I was invited to the Empire Theatre in Liverpool by Judy Garland to receive 2 showmanship awards from America. She presented them to me in her dressing room surrounded by press journalists and photographers.

It has been very easy for me to chat away now about my years in the entertainment industry- but they were very happy years; and my last ten years at the Palladium / Gaumont / Odeon were perhaps ten of the most notable of my career. Mind you in all the 30 years they were not without their problems as with any business, fortunately I have always had a positive approach to all problems and somehow I was blessed with the ability to overcome them. There were quite a few occasions when irate patrons approached me in what they considered to be a legitimate complaint but after a friendly chat and reasonable explanation they left me with a handshake and very often became firm friends. Very often lengthy queues and inclement weather were the basis for patrons' irritability.

Throughout the years I gained the friendship of many thousands of not only the public themselves but also public figures and stars of stage and screen. I regarded civic and public relations as being most important and an essential backcloth to a theatres atmosphere and popularity in the public eye. I enjoyed an excellent relationship with the Police, the Local Authority and voluntary organizations within the boundaries of the various theatres were under my management. It was always my endeavor to associate the theatre and actively to give assistance to voluntary organizations and to involve myself in addition to my normal duties. I served on committees involving fund raising and public appeals for various charities.
The theatre supported The Guide Dogs for the Blind, The Annual Christmas Tree Appeal, Schools Educational Films in co-operation with the Education Department, Police road safety campaigns, Territorial Army, Junior Service Corps recruitment, Local churches of all denominations, The Boy Scout movement, St John Ambulance Brigade and many others.

The theatre was the hub of activity when it came to promotions. I spent much time organizing the Saturday Morning Children's Club in which I tried to involve the youngsters in communal activities, encouraged musical talent from singing, dancing and instrumental aspects. They raised money for various charities and collected presents for the disadvantaged. I would encourage as much publicity and involved leading figures in the civic, public and entertainment world. This ensured that the theatre was always in the forefront of the public mind and ensured its popularity on a daily basis.

As a result I was visited by various actors and actresses who were only too happy to help. For example Jack Warner was appearing in Hippo Dancing at the Garrick. Frankie Howard dropped by to view his films, Ted Ray was convinced to join me at the Floral Hall and judge a beauty contest, John Gregson the very famous film star of many block buster, would regularly call in to enjoy an evening with his family. He lived in Formby and had his roots in Southport, being descended from William Sutton, the town's founder. I had letters from the likes of Bob Hope, Tommy Handley and Melina Mercouri.

Speaking of visits from stars of the screen, In 1964, I had to premiere The Beauty Jungle, starring Janette Scot and Ian Hendry, a film about a young woman who is plucked from a typing pool to become a beauty queen. I arranged her visit like a military operation, her arrival by helicopter, meeting the civic dignitaries for lunch and judging the Southport Hairdressing Competition and meeting the public. She knew Southport well; as she was a native of Morcambe and endeared herself to everyone she met before being whisked away after having tea with me. It had been a difficult day co coordinating the activities with the Police, Fire Brigade, Air Ministry and Mayor's Office for a one off landing of a helicopter on the beach, unheard of in those days. Organising the civic lunch and hosting her day before returning to the theatre and carrying on with ones normal duties.

Some years earlier in 1958, I played host to a star who had been called Britain's Shirley Temple, this was Violet Plowman. In all cases one was expected to report to head office about any publicity that was favorable to the theatre. This is the report I compiled from that day.

GAUMONT – SOUTHPORT
PUBLICITY CAMPAIGN REPORT

VISIT OF VIOLET PLOWMAN TO SOUTHPORT

This is a report of a story, and our activities through the medium of this theatre, which captured the imagination and interest of local press, Liverpool press and the national weekly magazine 'Blighty'

Nearly twenty years ago, a little curly haired, blonde girl, aged about six, was given V.I.P. treatment at this theatre upon her arrival, and was welcomed by a Mrs. Mae Bamber as she stepped out of a car outside our main front doors on to a red carpeted pavement. She was then appearing as Britain's Shirley Temple, in conjunction with a publicity campaign arranged in connection with the Shirley Temple film 'The Little Princess'. Whilst she was here, she sang to our audiences, to ex-servicemen at Wyborne Gate ex-servicemen's Convalescent Home and also at children's homes. Accompanying the little girl, Violet Plowman, in whose car she arrived, was Sir Arthur [Bob] Keen, who was at that period the publicity manager for Gaumont-British. This story received fine press coverage and created a considerable interest in the town

Twenty years later, Mrs. Bamber, now Councillor Mrs. Mae Bamber and the present Mayor of Southport saw the photograph of the 20 year old story republished in 'Blighty' giving details of Violet Plowman's progress and success in show business and sent her a Mayoral invitation to re-visit Southport as her guest.

The Mayor is perhaps one of the most publicity minded and enterprising Mayor's that the County Borough of Southport has had the good fortune to have as its leading citizen having hit the national headlines on numerous occasions, appearing on radio and is shortly making a lightning visit and tour of America, putting Southport even more prominently on the map.

During her Mayoral year the Mayor, has been an extremely good friend of this theeatre and worked in very close co-operation with us when we then invited Miss Plowman to stay over another 24hrs as the guest of the Gaumont, Southport.

Throughout the advance announcements and arrangements of her visit the press was extremely in the story and gave good coverage.

During the past twenty years, Miss Plowman has never ceased entertaining in various capacities from the age of six and was the youngest principal boy ever to appear in pantomime. She went on from success to success and has toured Europe, appearing on television in Holland, Germany and France, in continental nightclubs, as a pin up on the front of continental magazines and scoring a tremendous success in Vienna. She has also recorded on the continent.

On her arrival in Southport, Miss Plowman was welcomed to the town by Manager K. B. Lloyd, at the request of the Mayor as she was attending a meeting at the time.

In the evening she visited a large ball at the Floral Hall as the guest of the Mayor. The following day history repeated itself, when twenty years later she was re-welcomed outside the theatre, alighting from a car and welcomed by the Mayor and accompanied by – once again – Mr. Arthur [Bob] Keen, now retired after 35 years in the C.M.A.

A happy reunion took place in the theatre restaurant, followed once again by a visit to Wyborne Gate ex servicemen's home, where she entertained and sang to the patients one of whom had been at the home for 40 years and remembered Miss Plowman's original visit.

Following this visit she then proceeded to the Sunshine Home for Blind Children where she sang to and played with the little patients. In the evening at the invitation of local journalists and accompanied by Manager K.B.Lloyd she was guest of honour at the journalists and made a dramatic entry onto the ballroom floor leading a leopard from Southport Zoo.

The following morning Miss Plowman made her last public appearance at our Boys and Girls Club at the Saturday morning performance where she received a tremendous reception after which our members clamoured for her autograph.

Throughout her visit and tour she was accompanied by The Mayor, Mr.A.Brockman [Editor of Blighty] and Gaumont Manager, K.B.Lloyd.

As rehearsals for a stage performance for adult audiences were not possible as we would have required a full orchestra, we substituted her live performance by introducing her through the medium of one of her gramophone records which is shortly to be released on an L.P. disc.

Throughout the visit, considerable interest was displayed by the press who gave excellent editorial and photographic coverage and subsequently in the March 15th edition of the national weekly 'Blighty' a full page article and photographs appeared of the event.

Signed. K.B.Lloyd
Manager

This is just one example of the many reports that were compiled for Head Office, and were designed to explain the events and also to serve as a press release whenever needed.

It was not the first time I had had such a headache but it was more pleasant than the TUC Conference which I found had been booked.

I had taken over the theatre in May 1955 and after arrival had taken over the keys, checked the stock and inventory of this vast pleasure palace which had taken a whole day and then before settling back for a well earned drink, checked the future bookings. It was then I discovered that in September I was to host the Trades Union Congress and all that it would entail.

These days, conferences are held it seems every other week somewhere in the country, but in those days it was a major occasion and given the period in history, it was even more so. We had had a World War which was still in every person's memory and now we were in what was to be called the cold war. Communism was everywhere and we were being told that there were reds under our beds. So you can imagine what effect something like the TUC Conference had on some with national security in mind.

The Conference was to be from 8.30am until 5.30pm Monday to Friday and then the theatre would revert back to being a cinema for the evening.

This meant that after consultation with the Company Engineers and the various agencies, we had just 15 minutes to clear, clean and open up for the public.

To give you an idea what it involved one has to realise that the theatre had hosted the BBC for radio and television, 30 phone lines had to be installed for the press who had been sited in the foyer and included 150 national and international reporters. The stage was full of floral arrangements and there were 2000 delegates to be considered as well and on top of all this, the consideration of national security had to be taken. I had to sneak in observers from the Special Branch without anyone knowing and secrete them in the operating box so they could watch the proceedings, all very cloak and dagger.

[It was also very clear to my father that there were very few places capable of holding such an event other than Blackpool and he felt that Southport was incapable of holding such a large gathering unless premises are built to accommodate them. Hence his distress when his point of view was ignored by certain civic members when he argued against the theatres demolition. He was bemused at the construction of the Southport Theatre, as it could not hold as many delegates and had poor acoustics in comparison he also showed that it was not able to give the staging it needed . "Oh Why?" he would ask "Couldn't Sefton just purchase the theatre and renovate it to their needs it would have been a lot cheaper in the long run and save the rate payers a fortune as well as continue to give pleasure to the paying public"]

A slight aside from this was the question, what does one do with your family whilst all this is going on? Well our mother was stopped at the door and refused admission along with myself and my brother and the family shopping until Dad was summoned and explanations and special passes were issued. When we looked back on this Dad and I would laugh at the security issues but in those days it was taken very seriously.

During my 10 years at the theatre, I was invited to participate in many activities including judging at 3 of the Southport English Rose Beauty Competition, adjudicate at various other competitions and speak at luncheons to various organizations. All this went along way to promoting the public relations aspects. This must have helped when the Lord Mayor Of London accompanied by his official attended and used the premises for a Mayor Making Ceremony.

On another occasion 2000 Boy Scouts held their annual congress in the only place capable of housing them, The Gaumont.

These events led naturally to the theatre becoming the centre of Southport's community and in fact I was told that we were in the news more times than the Mayor. This fact may have caused a ripple or two in civic circles.

In the early 60's Edward Heath was the then Foreign Secretary and was advocating the E.E.C. or Common Market. This gave me an idea to promote Southport and the theatre internationally and therefore I initiated the Overseas Visitors Scheme. I arranged a large display in the theatre foyer with scrolls on the walls in about 20 or 30 languages inviting foreign visitors to sign a visitors book. This was a great success and we had in short time signatures from 41 countries. It was also a cultural success because we gained a great insight into how people saw Southport and their thoughts. Many of the visitors volunteered to assist at Christmas time and deliver presents from the annual Christmas Tree appeal.

After I retired from the industry, I traveled around Europe and reconnected with many of those who had visited Southport. I even taught myself Danish and as a result was visited by TV stations fascinated by this old showman's actions. Whilst abroad, I continued to promote Southport, using the Theatre as an ice breaker and it worked.

But I have digressed a little bit. As I have indicated we were now in the 1960's and the theatre was about to shine even more brightly than ever before. The exterior went through a general refurbishment and the white Darley dale stone was painted a light cream colour with a beige compliment. It was also updated within the technical world and improved stage facilities included. Then they renamed it THE ODEON.

Because of the 1950 period we had become so well known in the entertainment circle that whenever one day stage shows were being put on, Southport was first on the list and so in the late 50's and early 60's we presented many one night stands or package shows instead of films.

We presented the Beatles on 3 occasions. Two one night stands and 1 six day twice nightly show. We dispensed with films that week and over 25,000 attended from all over the North West and coach loads of teenagers descended from just about everywhere.

In addition others who appeared on these shows which we staged quite regularly were Helen Shapiro – Gerry and the Pacemakers – John Leyton – Danny Williams – Kenny Lynch – Gene Vincent – Jet Harris and Tony Meehan – Billy J Kramer – The Fourmost – The Caravelles – Patti Brook – The Dave Clark Five – Elkie Brooks – The Batchelors and many others.

In the mid fifties Ambrose and his Orchestra and also Ted Heath and his Orchestra and Cyril Stapleton and his Showband appeared. At the age of 19 we presented Cliff Richard who was a huge attraction with his group the Drifters [later renamed The Shadows due to the American group also named The Drifters]. I should also mention that the well known Dave Allen compered a show and also Des O'Connor compered another show for me. Both of course went on to greater heights with their own shows on TV.

Amongst the other big names of the day that appeared were, Marion Ryan and Ronnie Hilton, there were visitors from the U.S.A. such as Paul and Paula. One show was a totally different production to these music based extravaganzas, it was presented by the International Brotherhood of Magicians and called 'The Grand International Gala of Magic' featuring magicians from all over the world.

I mentioned Dave Allen and Des O'Connor making their early stage debuts at the Odeon, but I really must recount an interesting incident that happened and I will not forget. Whilst the Beatles were appearing for their 6 day shows, Mr Brian Epstein drew me to one side and remarked " Mr Lloyd I have sent The Fourmost to Blackpool for a one night stand and I'd like you to listen to a young girl singer who I would like to replace them with, I think she has a great future, if that's alright with you?" I agreed and watched from the wings as Cilla Black made her stage debut. She gained tremendous applause and Brian Epstein and I went back stage to congratulate her. I said to her 'Darling – you were great, you'll go right to the top' she replied ' I do hope your right and gave me a kiss, she was ecstatic and when I asked to write something nice in my programme, she modestly replied "But I'm not even on the bill". She was a lovely girl and I was not surprised when Cilla Black was at the top of the hit parade with 'If you ever had a heart' but I didn't expect it be only 3 months after appearing at the Odeon.

From my enquiries I have been able to gather together the names of the managers from its early days. Some of the dates are lost but these were the custodians of the theatre until its closure in 1979.
1916 – Eric Langdon
1923 – Henry Kennedy
- J.B Havesall
1928 – Will Hughes
1930 – Reg Halstead
1936 -Charles E. Brown
? - Mr Kaye
1947 - Norman Lockett
? - T.B.Wilkins
1951 – W.A.Howarth
1955 – Kenneth B. Lloyd
1965 – W.R.Wood
1971 – Laurie Hindmarsh
Finally – Mrs Francis Knowles

I have recorded many of the events and appearances that occurred during my stewardship of the theatre and there were many. Most of them were recorded editorially or photographically by the local and national press and especially the Southport Visiter, with whom I had a wonderful relationship with the editors and staff. Many names I cannot recall but those that stick out are Cedric Greenwood who wrote so passionately about the theatre and the snappers, Phillip Hutchinson, Joe Sadler and Cyril Locker.

We enjoyed some exceptional memories and experiences, from hosting the Kodak Girls who came to Southport and based themselves at the theatre to the Amateur Operatic and Choirs that cut their teeth on our massive stage and to the sports personnel who graced our steps.
One young lady, an usherette of mine, in 1957 was 25 year old Catherine Rimmer of Kensington Road who cycled around the world alone. She worked as a shop assistant as well to raise her funds which was between £30 - £40 enough to get her to Italy where she got another job to help her across Europe to Turkey and India and thence to Mexico and Canada arriving home 1 year later to a huge welcome.

The Theatre wasn't just the centre of the entertainment in Southport, it was the hub of the community and as such will live on for many years to come and I am so grateful I had the opportunity to be part of its history.
Kenneth B. Lloyd [1982]

The preceding narration, recorded by my father in 1982 included details of his visits to the many overseas visitors and his experiences in those lands. I have edited the content to his historical knowledge of the Palladium / Gaumont / Odeon.

Dad always said he would like to write a book about the theatre but although he was a master of the English language, never got around to fulfilling his dream, he believed that no one would be interested. This was the nearest he got along with all the press cuttings, photographs and notes he collected which I am now the custodian of. He loved the theatre and rarely called it a cinema.

To him it was a living thing and as you will have noted from his words, it was the grandest icon in Southport and should have been kept for generations to admire and he was not alone in those thoughts. He always said" You can always tell by the atmosphere, when you walk into a theatre if it's alive and happy or not" and I can from my own experience agree that he was right.

KENNETH BERTRAM LLOYD

Was an only son, born 20th August 1914 in Crosby and grew up in the North West. He was educated at Merchant Taylors School for Boys and studied the classic languages of Latin and Greek.
He joined the 2nd Battalion, The Kings Regiment, Liverpool. He took up boxing and won 19 out of 25 fights including The Army Lightweight Championship.
He bought his discharge and joined the shipping line, United Africa Company and whilst in Lagos, West Africa he nearly died from malaria.
He then returned and worked for the Finance Department and later the Borough Treasurers Office for Crosby

It was then in 1934 he joined the Gaumont British Picture Corporation and then became the youngest Cinema Manager and licensee in the country taking charge of the Rivoli, Aigburth where he remained for the next 5 years until the outbreak of World War 2.
He rejoined his old regiment the 2nd Battalion, Kings Regiment and became a Lance Corporal. He was a weapons trainer to the officers and was an expert on machine guns and carried the crossed rifles of a marksman. Although he was officially attached to the Pay Corp of the Regiment, he found his way to France and Greece in undercover situations; he escorted S.O.E operatives across the channel and transported the gold reserve from the Greek Banks back to Athens from the Bank of England, where it had been in safekeeping.

At the end of the war he married Eunice who he had met during the blitz in London, she was in the A.T.S and hailed from Forest Gate. They had three children, Keith, Ian and Valerie.

He rejoined the Cinema Industry and took over the Rivoli Cinema Aigburth, Liverpool before being promoted to the Odeon Cinema, Waterloo and latterly the Gaumont Theatre,Southport. In 1951 he was area winner of the National Showmanship Contest and was made an honorary life member of Kinematograph Company of Showmen with 10 seals of merit, only 2 others had similar awards.

He retired in 1965. He traveled around Europe meeting old acquaintances and promoting Southport on radio and TV and even taught himself Danish which attracted even more publicity before he returned to his home town and bought a shooting gallery on Pleasureland and became honorary treasurer of the Southport

Amusement Caterers Association. Due to ill health he eventually gave it up after 12 years He was the president of the Southport Entertainment houses Association and also served on the committee of the North Western Branch of the Cinematograph Association.

In 1990, his health now very poor, he and Eunice moved to Lancing on the south coast where his daughter and son Ian lived and there, in May 1996 he passed away aged 82 years.

Many of Southport's residents have been accredited with titles, but the one that surely described **Kenneth B. Lloyd** best, was '**Southport's Mr. Showman**' penned by the Southport Visiter –and who published a trilogy of memories of his, along with archival material and photographs.

On his office wall he had a wooden plaque, the words he said were his inspiration, an insight to his daily approach to his work

I shall pass through this world but once ~ Any good that I can do ~ or any kindness I can show any human being ~ let me do it now and not defer it ~ for I shall not pass this way again.
Chinese sampler AD 420

SOUTHPORT
PALLADIUM

PROPRIETORS .... SOUTHPORT PALLADIUM (1921) LTD.   Managing Director .... JOHN L. DIXON General Manager .... J. B. HOTHERSAL

Week Commencing MONDAY, AUG 6th, 1923.

6-40 — **TWICE NIGHTLY** — **8-50**

FREE LIST SUSPENDED.

TERRY WILSON

ENGLAND'S GREATEST LIGHT COMEDIAN, FROM THE COLISEUM, LONDON.

FISHER & DOROTHY

FRED E. TAYLOR

A Comedian who Acts Daft.

Victor Kelly	Skating Nelson
There is only one Kelly.	Premier Comedy Skating Act.

EDWARD VICTOR

A vendor of Hand-Made Humour, from Maskelyne's Mysterys, LONDON.

Rosie WALMSLEY

Southport's Own Male Impersonator.

THE BOHEMIAN TRIO

IN A DELIGHTFUL OFFERING OF MUSICAL ARTISTRY, VIOLIN—VOICE—PIANO.

PRICES OF ADMISSION FOR MONDAY TO FRIDAY.								PRICES OF ADMISSION FOR SATURDAYS AND HOLIDAYS.							
Boxes	Foetuals	Orch. Stalls	Stalls	Pit Stalls	Stalls	Upp. Circle	Parterre	Boxes	Foetuals	Orch. Stalls	Stalls	Pit Stalls	Stalls	Upp. Circle	Parterre
18/-	2/6	2/-	1/6	1/-	1/6	9d.	9d.	21/-	3/-	2/6	2/-	1/6	2/-	1/-	1/-

Seats Bookable in Advance without extra fee.   TAX EXTRA TO ALL PARTS.
BOOK YOUR SEATS.

THE
SOUTHPORT
PALLADIUM

Programme

SOUTHPORT PALLADIUM (1921) LTD

Rosie Walmsley, Southport's own male impersonator, made her way to the London stage.

The real Rosie Walmsley in a dance dress.

8. Rosie Walmsley

Southport's own Male Impersonator and Dancer.

9. The Bohemian Trio

In a delightful offering of Musical Artistry, Violin Voice-Piano.

SOUTHPORT PALLADIUM (1921) LIMITED.

THE PALLADIUM, SOUTHPORT.

CONTRACT.

An Agreement made the .... day of .... 192....

BETWEEN HENRY KENNEDY, on behalf of SOUTHPORT PALLADIUM (1921) LIMITED, hereinafter called the management, of the one part, and .... hereinafter called the Artiste, of the other part, **Witnesseth** that the management hereby engages the Artiste, and the Artiste accepts an engagement to appear as ....

.... (or in his or her usual entertainment) **at Two Performances Every Evening** at the Theatre and from the dates, for the periods and at the salaries stated in the first Schedule hereto, subject to the said Theatre being in the occupancy and possession of the management, and upon and subject to the undermentioned conditions :—

1. The word "Artiste" shall, when more than one is included in the performance, include the plural.
2. The Artiste agrees to appear at 12 Performances per week, and shall be paid at the rate of one-twelfth of the weekly salary for each performance required by the Management in excess of such number.
3. Where this Contract relates to a partnership, troupe, or sketch, the Artiste shall, at the time when the Contract is signed, furnish the management in writing with such names as the management may require, and shall not substitute a performer for a person so named without the written consent of the management.
4. The Artiste may be transferred during the whole or any part of the engagement (not less than one week) to any other Theatre owned or controlled by or associated with the management, with the consent of the Artiste, such consent not to be unreasonably withheld. All actual expenses reasonably incurred of any transfer shall be allowed and shall be paid within 14 days of the completion of the transferred engagement.
5. **Barring Clause.—The Artiste shall not without the written consent of the management appear at any place of public entertainment within a radius of six miles of the theatres mentioned herein, for fifty-two weeks prior to his appearance, nor for two weeks afterwards, and the Artiste undertakes not to appear at any place of entertainment whatever other than the Palladium Theatre, Southport, during the period of his engagement hereunder.**

   Upon breach of any of the barring clauses the Artiste shall pay to the management as liquidated damages one week's salary for each breach thereof, but nothing in this clause shall affect the right of the management to apply for an injunction to restrain the Artiste from performing in breach of the said clauses, nor the right to determine the Contract.
6. The Artiste shall not infringe any copyright, patent or other proprietary rights of third parties, and in the event of infringement shall be liable for, and on demand pay, the amount of all damages, penalties, and costs incurred by the management.

   The Artiste shall not give, or permit to be given, any colourable imitation or version of his performance within the radius or time prescribed by the barring clauses.

   The Lord Chamberlain's licence, copyright certificate of songs, permits to mimic or impersonate other artistes must be produced at Monday's rehearsal to the Resident Manager.
7. In case the Artiste shall, except through illness certified as hereinafter provided, or accident, proved to the satisfaction of the management, fail to perform at any performance, he shall pay to the management as liquidated damages a sum equal to the sum which the Artiste would have received for such performance, in addition to costs and expenses incurred by the management through the default of the artiste.
8. When the management own or control two Theatres in any provincial town, the Artiste shall act as deputy in cases of emergency upon request, and be paid at a rate to be mutually arranged.
9. The Artiste undertakes that his performance shall not be dangerous to the Artistes, Audience, or Stage Employees. If any accident or injury results from the performance of the Artiste, the Artiste shall pay for any loss, damage, or costs incurred by the management.
10. The management shall not be liable to the Artiste or to the legal personal representative of the Artiste for any loss, damage, or injury to the Artiste's person or property during or in connection with the engagement, unless caused by the negligence of the management.
11. The Artiste shall not assign, mortgage, or charge his salary, nor permit the same to be taken in execution.

    No salary shall be paid for days upon which the Theatre is closed by reason of national mourning, fire, epidemics, strikes, lock-outs, disputes with employees, or order of the licensing or any public authority. No salary shall be payable for any performance at which an Artiste may not appear through illness or his own default, nor provided that eight weeks' previous notice has been given to the Artiste, for the days upon which the Theatre is closed for alterations, decorations, repairs, or any cause which the management may reasonably consider adequate.
12. The Artiste agrees to observe and carry out conditions and regulations imposed by statute, the London County Council, or other public authority, and to comply with the requirements of any public authority that scenery and properties used by the Artiste shall be non-flammable. All flammable material brought into the Theatre by the Artiste may be required to be made non-flammable by him or at his expense by the management.
13. The Artiste declares that at the time of signing this Contract he is under no engagement with any other management that can preclude him from fulfilling the engagements shown herein, and that he has not concealed any change of professional name or description.
14. The rules and regulations endorsed hereon shall be read and construed as forming part of this Contract, and the Artiste agrees to abide by all reasonable rules which may from time to time be made by the management for the good and orderly conduct or special requirements of their Theatres, provided that the rules shall have been served on or brought to the notice of the Artiste.
15. Upon breach by the Artiste of any of the terms and conditions in this Contract, or of Rules 1 to 10, the management, without prejudice to other remedies, and in addition to rights given under the terms and conditions aforesaid or the rules, may forthwith determine this Contract, and the Artiste shall have no claim upon them for salary (other than a proportion for performances played), expenses, costs, or otherwise. The same provision shall apply upon breach by any member of a troupe or company if not remedied after complaint by the management.
16. Any notices under this Contract may be served upon the Artiste by posting the same to his last known address, or to the agent through whom this Contract is made, or while performing at any Theatre, in the manner specified in Rule 11.
17. If the Artiste's performance is contrary to law or is objected to by any licensing or public authority this Contract may be cancelled by the management. If the management be threatened with legal proceedings in respect thereto the Contract may be cancelled unless the Artiste forthwith provides indemnity to the satisfaction of the management.
18. The Artiste shall notify his intention to appear, specifying dates and places, and send matter for billing, programmes, and advertisement, and in the case of a sketch or stage play a copy of the Lord Chamberlain's licence to HENRY KENNEDY, in time to arrive at THE PALLADIUM THEATRE, SOUTHPORT, not later than 21 days before opening.
19. The Artiste is permitted to perform within the barred area of any Theatre referred to herein, not opened for public entertainment, provided that his performance takes place within eight weeks of the making of the Contract for the said performance and that he makes no new Contract for any such performance after receipt of notice from the management that the actual building of any such theatre is then substantially commenced.
20. If any Theatre herein mentioned shall not be in the occupation and possession of the management at the date fixed for performance thereat the engagement shall, provided the best possible notice has been given to the Artiste in writing, be deemed to be cancelled as from the date of such notice.
21. The agreement is subject to written confirmation by the management. If not confirmed within 21 days after receipt by the management of the agreement signed by the Artiste no liability shall attach either to the management or the Artiste.

SCHEDULE

(TWELVE NIGHT PERFORMANCES.)

...... Week	at	commencing .... 19....	at the salary of £	per week
...... Week	at	commencing .... 19....	at the salary of £	per week
...... Week	at	commencing .... 19....	at the salary of £	per week
...... Week	at	commencing .... 19....	at the salary of £	per week
...... Week	at	commencing .... 19....	at the salary of £	per week
...... Week	at	commencing .... 19....	at the salary of £	per week
...... Week	at	commencing .... 19....	at the salary of £	per week
...... Week	at	commencing .... 19....	at the salary of £	per week

RULES & REGULATIONS.

(1) The Artiste shall attend Rehearsals at 11-30 a.m.

(2) The Artiste shall be present in the Theatre and ready for his appearance not less than five minutes before he is due to appear on the stage.

The Artiste may be put on ten minutes later than the specified time, and if required must do the whole of his performance. The management may vary the times specified for appearance at their discretion.

(3) In the event of an Artiste being unable to perform through illness a medical certificate must be sent immediately to the management at the Theatre setting forth the nature of the illness and that the Artiste is unable to appear. If the Artiste is prevented by illness or from any cause whatever from performing on the first night or for three consecutive performances the engagement may either be determined or be treated as postponed to such date as the management decide, subject to engagements entered into by the Artiste.

(4) The Artiste giving expression to any vulgarity or words having a double meaning or using any objectionable gesture when on the stage shall be liable to instant dismissal, and if dismissed shall forfeit the salary for the current week. Any question under this clause to be decided by the management, whose decision shall be final and binding on the Artiste.

(5) Any Artiste being in the Theatre in a state of intoxication may be fined one week's salary or dismissed.

(6) Artistes shall not address the audience except in the regular course of the performance, nor interfere in any manner with other Artistes or employees, nor go in the front of the house without permission.

(7) Singers shall, if required, sing at least three songs at each performance. The management may prohibit the whole or any part of the performance which they consider unsuitable or displeasing to the audience, and in the case of songs may require a copy to be forwarded for approval 21 days before a song is to be sung, and no variations will be permitted from words so approved. The Artiste shall not be required to perform if by the unruly behaviour of the audience his performance would be rendered inaudible.

The Artiste agrees to produce new or revert to any old song, sketch, or business on the reasonable request of the management, and to provide suitable dresses and properties.

(8) Artistes must respond to encores or not as the management shall reasonably direct.

(9) No naked lights shall be carried or matches used, nor any lighting apparatus interfered with by the Artiste. Artistes shall not bring into the Theatre combustible or explosive materials without the written permission of the management.

(10) Smoking is strictly prohibited in dressing-rooms or anywhere in proximity to the stage.

(11) The Artiste must furnish the Hall-keeper with his address, and while performing at any Theatre notice shall be sufficiently served if sent to such address, or, if no address is furnished, by deposit in the place for deposit of letters at the Theatre.

(12) The management shall have the sole right to determine the position of the Artiste's name, the size and nature of the type, and the description of the turn on the bills, programmes, and advertisements.

(13) No person not employed at the Theatre shall go behind the scenes without permission.

PALLADIUM
G.T.C. THEATRE.

THE MOST POPULAR HOUSE IN SOUTHPORT.

ENORMOUS SUCCESS of

HAROLD GEE

AND HIS

ALL BRITISH ORCHESTRA.

Greeted by Thunderous Applause at Every Performance. Acclaimed by Press and Public as the Greatest Combination of Musicians ever presented in any Cinema in Southport.

A Real Delight to Southport Lovers of Music.

AT EVERY PERFORMANCE, *including—*

6d. BARGAIN MATINEES **6d.**

PALLADIUM
G.T.C. THEATRE.

ALL THAT IS BEST IN ENTERTAINMENT.
'Phone 4210.   Proprietors: General Theatres Corporation Ltd.   Manager: Mr. Will Hughes.

PROGRAMME

For WEEK COMMENCING MONDAY, APRIL 16th, 1928.

PRICES OF ADMISSION:

6d. BARGAIN MATINEE Entire Ground Floor 1,000 Seats. Evening—Balcony 1/3. Stalls 9d. **6d.**

| Every Afternoon BARGAIN MATINEES at 2-45. Every Evening CONTINUOUS Non-Stop PROGRAMME From 6-30 to 10-45 Saturdays— Two Distinct Performances at 6-40 and 8-50. | PALLADIUM BOX OFFICE INFORMATION Saturday Evening Performances Every Seat Bookable FOR THIS EVENING ONLY. Box Office Open from 10 a.m. 'Phone 4210. Prices : STALLS, 1/-, BALCONY, 1/6. INCLUDING TAX AND BOOKING FEE. Telephone Seats must be claimed by 6-30 and 8-30 The Right of Refusing Admission Reserved | Sunday Evening Performances at 8-15 p.m. Doors open at 7-45 p.m. Special Selected PROGRAMME of PICTURES and THE FAMOUS WONDER ORGAN. |

PALLADIUM CAFE & LOUNGE
Southport's Select Rendezvous.
OPEN SUNDAYS.

PALLADIUM

A G.T.C. THEATRE.

MANAGER ... ... Mr WILL HUGHES.

NOTE—
SATURDAYS TWO DISTINCT PERFORMANCES
AT 6-40 AND 8-50 P.M.
SEATS MAY BE BOOKED IN ADVANCE.
Balcony 1/6.   Stalls 1/-
Including Tax and Booking Fee.
Box Office Open from 10 a.m.

:: PROGRAMME ::

Week Commencing MONDAY, APRIL 16th, 1928

NEXT WEEK.

ON THE SCREEN.

Monday to Wednesday.

Richard Barthelmess

IN

GLITTER

Every essential ingredient for screen entertainment is contained in First National's Great story of college life.

Much comedy, dramatic situations, the thrills of the great football game, tender romance and a plot that holds interest from start to finish feature this gay story of the football hero who is dethroned through no fault of his own.

ON THE STAGE.

LONDON'S FAVOURITE

RUSSELL CARR

VENTRILOQUIST

Assisted by OLIVE GRAY.

6d. BARGAIN MATINEES **6d.**
EVERY DAY AT 2-45 P.M.
Entire Ground Floor 1,000 Seats.
Wonderful Value.

MONDAY, TUESDAY, WEDNESDAY

1. Pathe Gazette ....All the Latest Topical Events
2. Newlyweds ....Comedy
3. On the Stage
   Victor Bright & Luna Denver *Present* **"NAUTICALITIS"**
4. Musical Interlude by **HAROLD GEE** and his All British Orchestra.
5. The Great Sequel Picture to VAUDEVILLE.

The Phantom of the Circus

In the picture you will find all that is good at the Circus. The prancing white horses that seem almost human in their knowledge are their trick steps, dancing, rearing and jumping; all adding its part to make 'The Phantom of the Circus' the outstanding picture of circus life

THURSDAY, FRIDAY, & SATURDAY

1. Pathe Gazette ....All the Latest Topical Events
2. Screaming ....Comedy
3. On the Stage.
   Victor Bright & Luna Denver *Present* **"NAUTICALITIS"**
4. Eve's Review ....Interesting Tit-Bits
5. Musical Interlude by **HAROLD GEE** and his All British Orchestra.
6. JETTA GOUDAL in

WHITE GOLD

He took her from a pleasant life, to a lonely existence on the burning plains. She gave up all for his love—and when it failed her ...

NEXT WEEK.

ON THE SCREEN

Thursday to Saturday.

The Rival Picture to 'Beau Geste'

CONRAD VEIDT

IN

A Man's Past

Conrad Veidt as the sorrow sodden convict. His acting is the profoundest piece of work ever seen—a masterpiece of screen acting that will never be surpassed.

ON THE STAGE.

LONDON'S FAVOURITE

RUSSELL CARR

VENTRILOQUIST

Assisted by OLIVE GRAY.

WHEN IN LIVERPOOL VISIT
RIALTO BALLROOM
The Acme of Perfection and Refinement.

SHOWING (SUNDAY NEXT) at 8-15 p.m.   Two Super Pictures.
The Stupendous Production : "THE WRATH OF THE GODS."
MR. HERBERT STEELE ON THE FAMOUS WONDER ORGAN.

The following pages reveal the interior of the Palladium as it was and the company's idea of improvements
To include a Palais De Danse extension with a ballroom and restaurant area.

However following the disastrous fire, a new design was formulated
and blue prints were drawn up for the new theatre.

The Foyer and Vestibule.   Decorated and Furnished throughout by Hampton's.

General View Showing Treatment of Proscenium, Organ and Domed Boxes in the Circle.

Side View, Showing Seating, Draperies and General Scheme of Decoration.

Tea Room & Lounge.   Decorated & Furnished by Hampton's in late XVIIIth Century English Manner.

The Palladium Southport

The Palladium Southport

The Palladium Southport

90

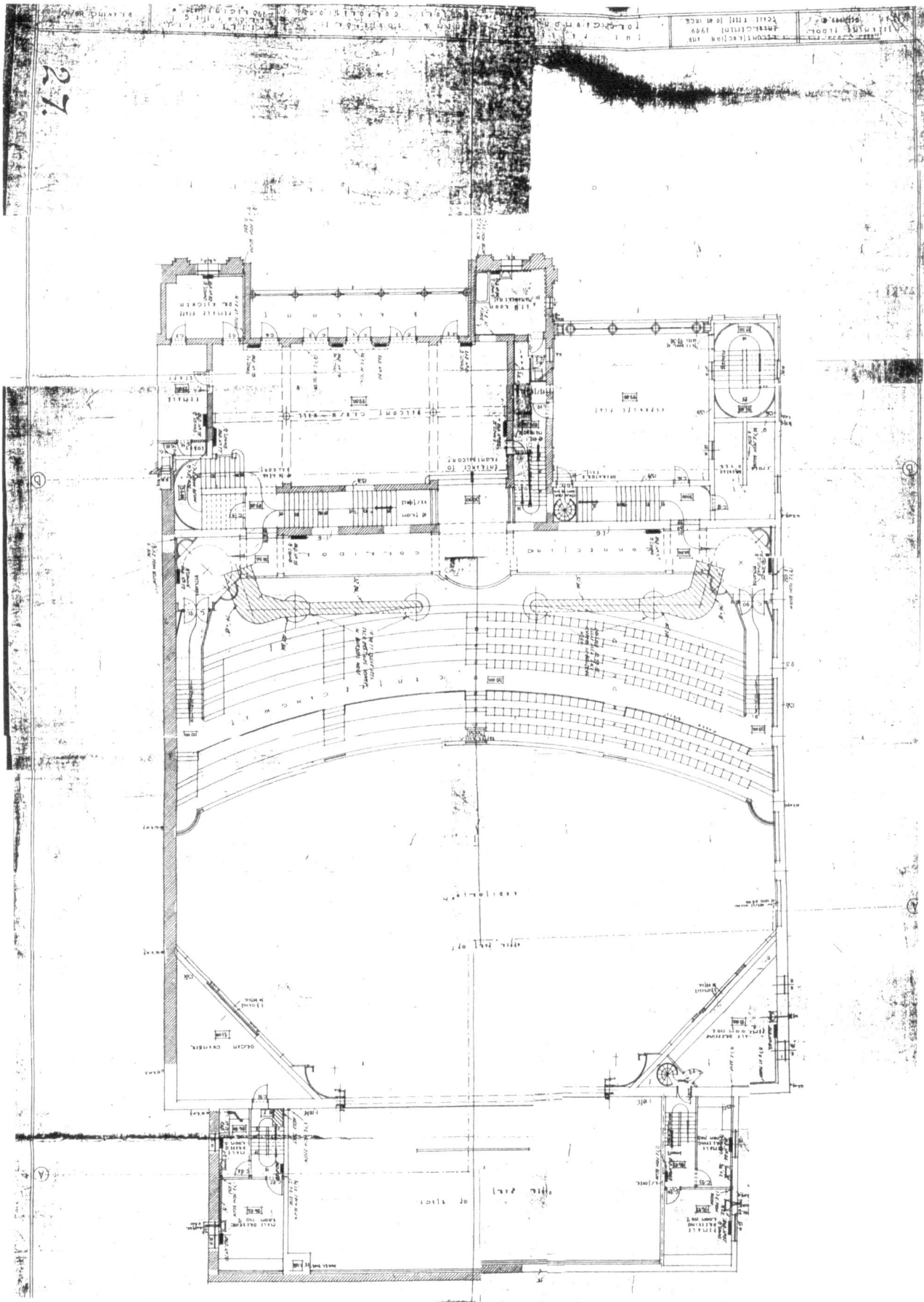

SOUTHPORT PICTURE NEWS

This rare 4 page 'newspaper' documents the
Re-opening ceremony and includes all the
Technical aspects relating to this state of the art
theatre in 1930.

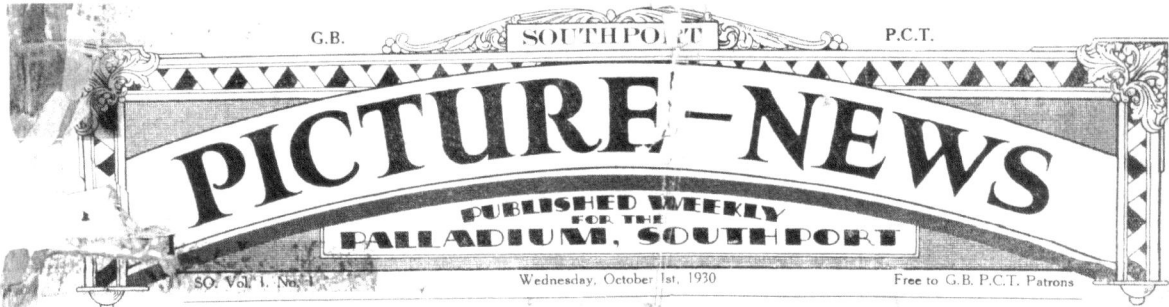

G.B.   SOUTHPORT   P.C.T.

PICTURE-NEWS

PUBLISHED WEEKLY
FOR THE
PALLADIUM, SOUTHPORT

SO. Vol. I, No. 1   Wednesday, October 1st, 1930   Free to G.B. P.C.T. Patrons

SOUTHPORT'S PALLADIUM OPENS TO-DAY

Opening Ceremony to be performed by His Worship the Mayor

ALDERMAN AMOS TOMLINSON, J.P.

WEDNESDAY, OCTOBER 1st at 2.30 p.m.

PROGRESS

To-day sees the re-opening of the Palladium, Southport, a striking example of the progress that is taking place in the cinema world.

The cinema is a tremendous factor in the lives of the world's millions. In an atmosphere of the utmost comfort and at prices within the reach of all, the screen brings before them great dramas, romances, comedies, interest films and news from all over the world. There, in the joys which the motion picture brings, the cares of everyday life are forgotten. Now the advent of sound photography, which has made such rapid strides in the last year, and as reached almost to perfection, gives ... in this respect the Palladium is unrivalled in the possession of a magnificent orchestra and a superb organ. The addition of a specially-produced stage show at every week-day performance completes a programme perfect from every angle of entertainment. What more could one desire as a relaxation from hard work and the day's accumulation of business and household anxieties.

British enterprise and British labour has given Southport through the Palladium a luxurious and comfortable addition to the city's amenities, which should soon become the chief rendezvous of those who wish to pass their leisure hours midst pleasant surroundings created by the skilful blending of comfort and good taste. The entertainment provided at every performance will consist of the very best and latest in talking picture successes, a stage presentation, orchestra and organ music. The opening programme is an indication of the very high standard ... which we have aimed, while a glance ... re programmes will convince that ... to maintain this standard.

PRICES OF ADMISSION
(Including Tax)

Front Stalls	1/-
Back Stalls	1/6
Back Circle	2/-
Front Circle	2/4

Children
(Saturdays, Sunday Evenings and Bank Holidays excepted)

Front Stalls	6d.
Back Stalls	9d.
Back Circle	1/-
Front Circle	1/3

MONDAY TO SATURDAY
Continuous Performance 2 to 10.30. Doors open 1.30.

SUNDAYS
Complete Change of Programme. One Performance at 8.15 p.m. Seats bookable in advance.

PROGRAMME.
(Subject to alteration at the discretion of the Management.)

1. OPENING CEREMONY
   performed by
   HIS WORSHIP THE MAYOR.
   Alderman Amos Tomlinson, J.P.
2. BRITISH MOVIETONE GAZETTE.
3. "ROMAN PUNCH"—
   A "Terry Toon" Sound Cartoon.
4. LESLIE JAMES
   at the
   WONDER ORGAN.
5. LOUIS BAXTER
   and
   SYMPHONY ORCHESTRA.
6. On the Stage:
   THE BLUE SLAVONIC COMPANY.
7. On the Talking Screen:
   "HIGH SOCIETY BLUES,"
   A "Fox" Musical Romance.
   GOD SAVE THE KING.

The PALLADIUM

Your amusement and pleasure will be the first consideration at the Palladium. All that is best in entertainment will be yours at reasonable prices of admission. You may visit the Palladium in the complete confidence that only the most worthy productions obtainable will be presented on our stage and screen.

THE PICTURES

The latest talking picture successes, up-to-the-minute news reels and interest films will be projected by the most perfect system yet discovered. Through the ... famous stars will speak and sing to you, and the hubbub of everyday life in far away lands will be faithfully reproduced.

STAGE PRESENTATIONS.

Every week-day programme will include a specially produced stage presentation chosen from the world's galaxy of talent. Palladium stage shows will play an important part in winning your affections.

MUSIC.

Music lovers will be delighted with the musical programme featured at every performance. Only musicians of the highest talent will perform. The Orchestra, under the direction of Mr. Louis Baxter, and the splendid organ played by Herbert Steele, an old Southport favourite, will soon become a feature of Southport's musical circles.

THE SEATS.

Two thousand two hundred deep, roomy arm-chairs, with room for your knees, your arms, your body—provide that extra comfort which makes the entertainment so much more enjoyable. Beautiful decorations, luxurious carpets and charming lighting effects will add, too, to perfect satisfaction.

VENTILATION.

While your eyes are on the screen your lungs will be breathing clean, fresh air that is changed every minute. Every hour two million cubic feet of air will undergo a washing and disinfecting process, cooling it or warming it to the required temperature. Science will guard your health at the Palladium.

THE NEW PALLADIUM

"Finer from every point of view"

A Modern Luxury Cinema commensurate with the progress in the Film World.

Big Value Programme Regularly to Include Talkies, Stage Shows, Orchestra and Organ.

A Description of The Palladium
by the Architect, Mr. W. E. TRENT, F.S.I.

Many years ago the writer had occasion to visit a building which had just been burnt. The building was a large Technical Institute, with a very fine assembly hall, and around the arch over the stage platform had been written the words "Find out what a man can do, teach him to do it better." The fire had destroyed the greater part of the arch and with it the lettering. All that was left were the words, "Do it better"—an emphatic and striking admonition to the craftsmen who were to rebuild.

Since 1914 the Palladium had been an institution in Southport, famous alike for its style and comfort and the ... of March 26th, came in the ... ous fashion the fire which, whilst leaving the front practically untouched, reduced the theatre to a mass of burnt rubbish and twisted iron.

To have rebuilt the theatre on the old lines would have been a comparatively easy matter, but the Directors of the Gaumont-British Picture Corporation and the associated Company, the General Theatres Corporation, seized the opportunity to do what was so aptly suggested by the incident related above—they resolved to "Do it better." That they have succeeded will be readily granted. Fine as the old Palladium undoubtedly was, the new Palladium is finer from every point of view—size, decoration, comfort and, with the march of progress in the film world, future entertainment.

First and most striking, the building has been practically doubled in width. With the advent of the talking film a new and very important point has arisen in the design of the picture theatre, namely, the question of acoustics and the necessity for the perfect hearing of the spoken word by every member of the audience. To this end a theatre must not be too long, lest the sound be lost in the back seats. In the Palladium the length remains practically the same as that of the old building, but the fortunate possession of spare land on the side has enabled the capacity to be practically doubled without the possibility of any patron being forced to strain his ears to enjoy the entertainment.

In the new elevation the additional width has been made subsidiary to the original front, so that the dignity of the two flanking towers should not be lost. The same detail of arch, column and cornice has been followed, and the open colonnade on the first floor filled in with trellis-work for the display of...

flowers and creepers in the summer will be found a pleasing feature and in harmony with the gardens of Lord Street.

A further sign of the development necessary to keep pace with the rapidly-changing times is found in the spacious car park which has been laid out to the left of the theatre. When the Palladium was first built, a car park was unknown. In a few years it has become almost an essential part of the modern "super cinema."

Up the flight of steps from Lord Street and the patron comes to the Entrance Foyer. This is a hall 96 feet long and 30 feet wide, with a marble mosaic floor, an enriched plaster ceiling and wood-lined walls. Here the note of "modern" decorative treatment is struck immediately, and it is carried consistently throughout the building.

Let it be noted that "modern" decoration is *not* mere eccentricity and a desire to be original at all costs. It is merely an evidence of the desire to break away from the slavish copying of old forms, used so often without the slightest regard for their fitness, which, if persisted in, would render architecture and decoration a lifeless and decadent art. The wall lining of the hall is stained a delicate grey in harmony with the green, grey and silver of the ceiling.

From the Entrance Foyer a short flight of steps leads directly to the Stalls, and two staircases flanking the centre stalls entrance lead to the Balcony. On the first floor is the corridor leading to both sides of the balcony and the waiting lounge and Café. "Wedgwood" decoration of the ... has been retained, although the ...

cate shades of blue and green will be a novel feature. The first thought that comes to the visitor on entering the theatre is the feeling of space and airiness, and the second is probably the unconventionality of the decorative colour scheme. The former is due to the great width of the building (120 ft.) and the wide sweep of the balcony. The latter is characteristically modern and "daring." A dado of narrow bands of dull, polished walnut runs round the base of the walls. Above this, up to the balcony, the walls are coloured a deep blue in bands with narrow vermilion and silver lines. Above the balcony the walls are covered with wide bands of green plush separated by narrow bands of the same material, in red colour, separated by silver lines. The rich ceiling starts ... the wall in deep blue-green grading upwards through neutral grey until the delicate pink and silver of the dome is reached. The organ grilles and brightly-coloured proscenium arch add to the richness and variety of the complete scheme, which is still further enhanced by the varied tints of the concealed lighting, the whole creating a sense of comfort.

The seating, in accordance with the rules of the Southport Corporation, is so spaced that ample "leg-room" is provided. The seats will be found the last word in comfort, being the standard type used by the Gaumont-British Company, and are the result of many years of experience and trial. There are twelve exits, and the theatre can be completely cleared in two minutes. The building is amply protected with fire

hydrants, with a sprinkler installation over the whole of the stage.

The ventilation plant has been designed on the most up-to-date lines to ensure comfortable conditions for the audiences. Before the air is admitted to the auditorium it is passed through a chamber filled with finely atomised water, where it is thoroughly washed and suitably humidified. This fresh, clean air is then warmed to the required degree and admitted to the auditorium, the vitiated air being removed by a powerful exhaust fan.

In addition to films, stage shows and reviews still form a large part of the Palladium entertainment, and the stage is fully equipped with flies, gridiron, scene dock, dressing rooms and chorus rooms.

The electrical equipment of the theatre has been carried ... most up-to-date lines. ... lamps instantly ... colour effects can be obtained as the result of switching on different circuits of lighting, and the seven colours of the spectrum can be obtained and reflected from the ceiling to the theatre. Lamps have been cunningly concealed in the plaster work ... pleasing effect, and the ... chandeliers complete the scheme.

Great thought has been given to the question of illumination and safety of the public in the event of a failure of the ... A large electric battery ... has been installed, which would be automatically switched with ... any human element so that the auditorium, passages, etc., would be adequately illuminated, as all other parts of the house to which the public have access. The batteries are of sufficient capacity to give the whole of the building a sufficient supply of light up to three to four hours in the event of there being a failure of the main supply for that length of time.

The stage lighting comprises ... the very latest and equal to any ... ment in the most ... London or elsewhere. There are over 6,000 electric lamps, and the h.p. of the motors for the ventilation and other machinery installed in this theatre is 150 h.p., and the electrical energy consumed in one hour would supply an ordinary ... dwelling house with lighting, at normal hours of burning, for twelve months.

The installation has been carried out with local labour under the supervision of the Gaumont-British Picture Corporation and Provincial Cinematograph Theatres, Ltd., Engineering Department, and the scheme of planning of the lighting, etc., under the personal supervision of Mr. E. C. Nichols, A.M.I.E.E., Chief Engineer to the companies.

A View of the Interior

British Acoustic Sound System installed at the Palladium

Palladium Patrons ensured of Perfect Reproduction

Entertainment Through the Ages

Amusement has been a *sine qua non* of life from the very earliest times. It was soon universally realised that "the play's the thing," and although the first efforts were necessarily elementary they culminated in the forms with which we are all familiar to-day.

It is a far cry from the bacchanales of Greece to the modern motion picture, but nevertheless these two entirely different arts are related by a series of complicated developments much in the same way as the acorn is related to the oak. From song and dance evolved drama, and it is interesting to note that singing and dancing, though varying to express the needs of each century, have enjoyed an unbroken popularity right through the ages to modern times.

...did not approve ...held in low esteem, and ...there laws in force which insisted that the children of actors had to follow their father's profession. At length they were driven from the Greek cities and compelled to wander all over Europe, giving shows wherever they could receive a favourable hearing. In this way the companies of minstrels, mummers and troubadours were formed which did so much to lighten tedious hours in the Middle Ages. They were well received in the houses of great lords where, on the dais of the great hall, they would act short sketches—a forerunner of the modern stage show. At almost the same period the church was beginning to favour the inclusion of tableaux vivants in festival services. From these arose the miracle and morality plays which performed first in church or the churchyard, later had to be held elsewhere, owing to the large crowds which attended them. Once removed to a secular atmosphere, they soon lost much of their sacred character and gradually

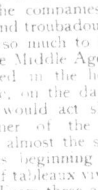

...incorporated many other elements. The ...guilds, in order to save them ...complete decay, each adopted a ...ular play and combined to perform them in cycles at festival times throughout the year. Thus arose the ...pageants or moving stages ...passed through the town. Each ...bore a particular company, who ...their play and then moved on to ...om for the next.

Church history it is but a short secular history and romance,

and soon, with the impetus given by the discovery of classical literature, the drama as we know it began to take shape, and the great dramatists appeared, the chief of whom is our own Shakespeare. But although the drama had travelled far, it still had a long journey to go, and it is instructive to note the difference in presentation of a dramatic entertainment then and now.

Renaissance theatres were little more than platforms erected in the open with no protection from the vagaries of the weather. The audience either stood, or sat on wooden benches, sometimes even on the stage itself, while a trap-door in the floor did double duty as entrance and exit. There was little or no scenery, the indispensable stage properties being a large bed for murders, a throne, various weapons and a certain number of costumes, the chief of which was a "cloak of invisibility." If it was inconvenient to move the bed between scenes it was allowed to remain. The indulgent Elizabethan was not troubled by the incongruity of a four-poster on the sea-shore, or a throne on a battlefield. The audience was very tolerant and imagination supplied what the property-box lacked, and in most cases the only indication of a change of scene was made by a large notice displayed at one side of the stage.

The first plays afforded relaxation only for the poorer classes, but as companies prospered they were patronised by the Court, and were thus gradually able to increase their stock of properties. Then the stage was erected under shelter and the first theatre to have a roof was built in 1600.

By degrees the theatre depended less and less on the imagination of the audience to supply its deficiencies, until it finally had advanced so far that from taxing the imagination it actually came to aid it, so that in modern times we see representations or real things which are far more wonderful than anything ever conceived by fancy.

Gone are the days when two plants in pots, plus a notice, "Thys ys a foreste," were expected to convey to us the great tree-covered areas of the earth. Now the positions are entirely reversed, and the changeling child which has endured so many vicissitudes has been universally adopted and become the fairy godmother of our leisure hours. The theatre, as we know it, has taken nearly three and a half centuries to "grow up," and it is in reality the splendid triumph, the coming of age, as it were, of the theatre which we are celebrating in the opening of the Palladium.

The cinematograph theatre is the home of the twentieth century conception of drama, and the Palladium, the very last word in modern cinema construction, is a striking example of the progress which is taking place in the cinema world. I. L. M.

If enjoyment is to be derived from sound pictures it is obviously important to produce conditions of comfortable hearing. It has long been customary in the majority of cases for architects to design theatres at considerable expense, making special efforts to secure strength, fine architectural lines, beautiful illumination and proper ventilation, but there has always been a doubt as to whether the theatre has the correct acoustic characteristics. To-day this problem no longer can be neglected, and it ranks equally in importance with lighting, heating and ventilation.

The acoustic conditions of a theatre depend on three factors, viz., the size, shape and nature of the surface of the walls and ceiling. The interior of the Palladium has itself received special ...which, after exhaustive tests, proved that its condition acoustically is perfect, and therefore with the best apparatus and ideal acoustic conditions the resulting sound at this theatre is really excellent.

The Palladium is fitted with a

remarkably fine sound system, known as the British Acoustic. The entire installation was designed to meet the very exacting requirements of modern motion picture projection, and is capable of reproducing sound from either disc recording or film recording by means of specially-designed pick-ups. Unlike other forms of sound equipment, the British Acoustic employs a special type of light sensitive cell, known as a selenium cell, and the resulting reproduction is remarkably pure and clear.

The amplifying system is excellently designed and constructed, and has an undistorted output of 90-100 watts. To avoid any possible stoppage in the sound programme, this amplifier system is duplicated so that by ... switching arrangements either an A. or B. amplifier set may be used at will. Moving coil speakers are so arranged behind a specially-constructed porous screen that every part of this vast theatre is adequately filled with sound.

THE BIG SCREEN

The Palladium is equipped with a Big Screen—the latest innovation of the modern cinema. Picturegoers will receive an unprecedented thrill when they see the screen expand before their eyes to huge dimensions. The advantage that this screen has over the ordinary fixed screen is tremendous, as it gives such events as the Derby, Cup Final, Boat Race and other sporting items, in true perspective.

In the making of this screen there are one ton of steel, a woven seamless 50ft. x 30ft. porous screen, which together with its lines and counterweights weighs 2½ tons. All this is operated by a small switch under the control of the operator, and the light used to illuminate this great area is greater than that used in the North Foreland Beacon.

PICTURE-NEWS
PUBLISHED WEEKLY
PALLADIUM, SOUTHPORT

HOW the SOUND NEWS is OBTAINED
MIRACLE OF MODERN SCREEN JOURNALISM
Exclusive to 'The Picture News"

British Movietone Gazette will be a permanent feature in Palladium programmes. This exclusive story of the filming in sound of a big event is therefore particularly interesting.

Here is the story of a sound news-reel at work on a red-hot news story. No one has any idea of the vast organisation required on an important occasion, such as the filming of the Derby by British Movietone news.

The staff work commences months before the actual event takes place. Plans are drawn up, permits obtained, and co-operation is sought with the local police. Each Movietone crew is provided with a map of the course and a detailed instruction sheet as to their own particular part in the proceedings. A dress-rehearsal is gone through, everything is checked up, and every emergency catered for, before the actual day dawns.

The Editors meet and, after viewing the course, decide which are the most advantageous positions from which the crews are to film. This, in itself, is a difficult problem, as each position should have as many different views of the course as possible, in order to provide variety of angle in the presentation of the subject. In some cases special stands have to be erected in order that the camera may have a clear view of the course over the heads of the crowd.

Besides filming every portion of the actual race, arrangements have to be made to film other scenes for cutting in on the big story, and sometimes these are the scenes that make the film. The Royal party entering the Royal box is an ever-popular item, and one that is very difficult to obtain, police regulations being what they are, but with the aid of a telephoto lens all impossibilities can sometimes be overcome.

Crowd shots, bookies calling the odds, gypsies dancing, all the sights that bring Derby Day home to you, combine to make the picture one of the most realistic you have ever witnessed. One of the most difficult shots to obtain is the ground shot of horses' hoofs, but this has to be taken, for it is one of the biggest factors in telling the story of the Derby.

On an occasion such as this, British Movietone News concentrate every one of their recording equipments, it is even necessary to make a duplicate film of the event for America, which is rushed off for shipment directly after the race has finished.

On the course is a specially-selected team of dirt-track riders, their machines ticking over, ready to carry back the precious film to the laboratory, where a staff of experts are waiting to develop it.

On this occasion each crew had, in addition to its complement of cameraman and soundman, a messenger whose business it is to keep in touch with the other crews, and, finally, to carry the exposed negative to the dirt-track riders, who are waiting outside the course to carry the film back to the laboratory.

The laboratory, film editing staff, title-writers and printers are all standing by in readiness for any change in the arrangements.

The result of the great race is received at headquarters, where the title-writers and printers get busy on the job. Out of the numbers of titles that have been shot for the subject they pick those which are required, and write and print any additional ones that may be necessary. These are photographed on to already-scored music and dispatched to the laboratory for development and incorporation in the film itself.

When the film is developed it is run over in the private theatre and cut down from its rough state into the actual subject, after which it is sent back to the laboratory for printing. Out of over 10,000 feet of film the Editor has to select the 1,000 feet that tell the story of Derby Day most graphically most naturally and most realistically.

By the time ordinary race-goers are thinking of returning home the

release of the Derby film will be canned and on its way to the West End cinemas ready for the evening performance.

Not only are prints of the film dispatched to such outlying places as Dublin, Glasgow and Edinburgh, but the Continent is taken care of as well, for a special duping print is despatched by air-mail to Paris, where a negative is taken off it, and copies printed for inclusion in the Continental edition of Fox Movietone News. A special print is also despatched to America for the American issue. All this is done within a few hours of the race taking place. It is incredible to think that sound film journalism has reached this stage of advancement, where you can see and hear an actual event on the screen only a few hours after it has taken place, but for over a year British Movietone News has shown us how it is done.

The Palladium's Resident Manager
Mr. R. Halstead

A Southport Man—Originator of famous "Splinters" Concert Party

Mr. R. Halstead, who has been appointed resident manager of the Palladium, is a Southport man. His first connection with the cinema business was in 1908, when he joined New Century Pictures. Later, he managed and was co-partner of the first cinema in Knaresborough. In 1911 he forsook the screen for the stage, managing concert parties and pantomimes. He joined the army in June, 1915, and received a commission in February, 1918. In view of the fact that the film, "Splinters," has just been shown at a number of cinemas, it is very interesting to note that Mr. Halstead was one of the originators of the famous army show, "Splinters," known in France as "Les Rouges et Noirs," and, in fact, he wrote and produced most of their material. After the war he became general manager for Messrs. Wylie and Tate, which position he held for over four years. Later he held a similar position with Fred Karno. Mr. Halstead has a flair for production and he has written and composed many successful scenes and numbers for revues.

Mr. R. Halstead

Printed by Ernest J. Day & Co., Ltd., Upper Rathbone Place, London, W.1, and Published by The Provincial Cinematograph Theatres in Association with The Gaumont British Corporation Ltd. Edited by H. A. Miller, Section Publicity Manager to the Company.

First birthday photograph in 1931 following the rebuild after the fire in 1930. Reg Halstead, Manager with his staff

In the Foyer. Mid 1930 period

Usherettes from the 1930 period. Ruby Ross and Nellie Smith.

Staff photograph approx. 1938 – Charles Brown, Manager, extreme right.

1947

| W.C. Hopper. Organist. | Harold Gale Chief Projectionist. | Norman Lockett Manager. | Fred Jackson Asst. Manager |

1955 staff party. Held on the stage after the evening show had finished.

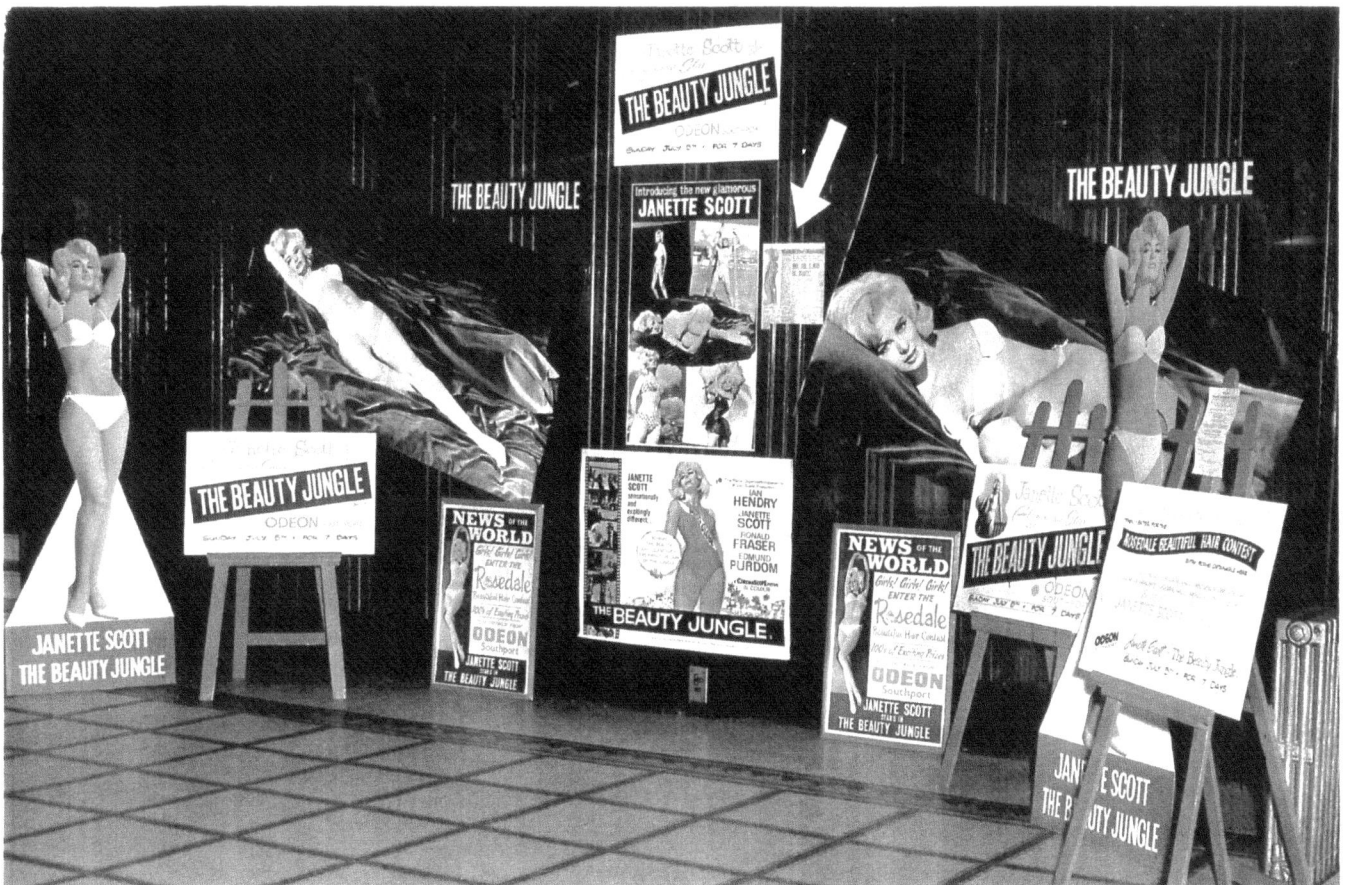

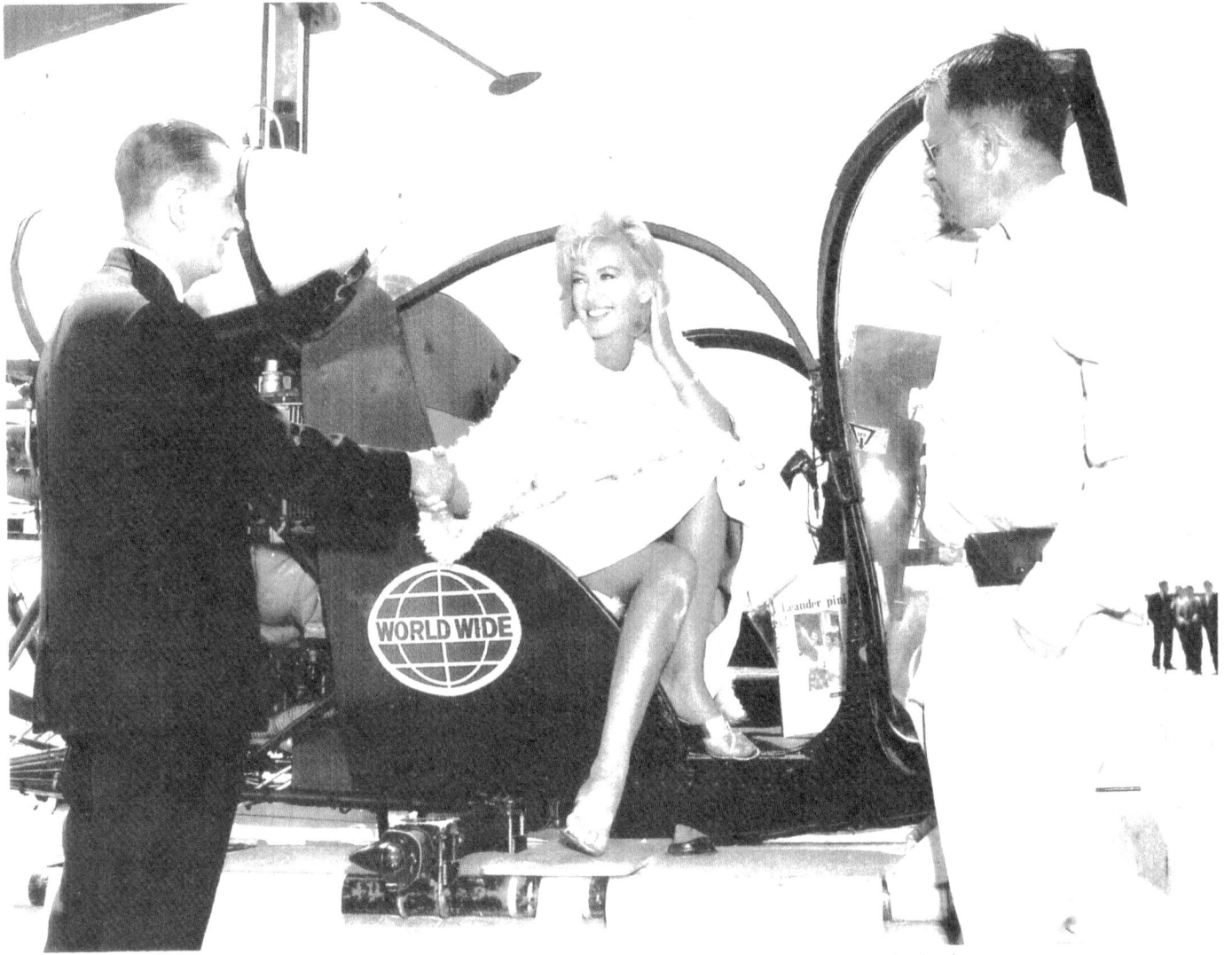

Janette Scott lands on Southport Beach to start her visit and promotional tour for 'The Beauty Jungle'

Janette Scott receives a
Bouquet of carnations from
Miss Anna Stewart-Forshaw
An Odeon Usherette
Prior to judging the
Rosedale Beautiful Hair Contest
in the Floral Hall Gardens.

Looking on is Mr.Eric
of
Andre Bernards Salon.

And the winner
Of the
Rosedale Beautiful
Hair Contest
is
Monica Denmark
of
7 Clinning Road,
Birkdale

1964.   General Manager, Ken Lloyd is presented with the Showman's Gold Star Award, for his promotion of 'The Beauty Jungle' The presentation was made by Rank Organisation's Head of Publicity, Mr.J.D.Payne on behalf of Lord Rank

Cinema Managers
Judge the English Rose
At the Sea Bathing Lake.

L-R
Laurie Hughes [ABC]

Ken Lloyd [Odeon]

Les Houghton [Palace]

T.A.G.Steepes [Garrick]

With

Sylvia Freemantle
Constance Snook
[Winner]
Judith Wannop
Cheryl Driscoll

Violet Plowman

Visit to Southport.

Seen here playing with
Children from the
Home for Blind Children.

Over/

Sharing a quiet moment
With KBL before going
on stage.

'BEFORE + AFTER'
PRESS PHOTOGRAPHS

Before and After. The picture on the left was taken 20 years ago by a Visiter photographer when Mrs. Mae Bamber welcomed Miss Violet Plowman, then known as "Britain's Shirley Temple," to the Palladium (now Gaumont) Cinema. Yesterday Miss Plowman visited the scene again and was once more received by Councillor Mrs. Bamber, this time as Mayor of Southport.

SOUTHPORT VISITER

1955
T.U.C.
Conference.

Senior Officials
On the stage.

Floral displays
Placed into the stage
Lighting canal.

Speakers Podium
On top of the Organ.

Press and Radio.
In the orchestra pit.

The delegates
seated in the stalls

105

1957

There could be no truer comment on the position that Southport Gaumont holds in the community than this panoramic shot of the distinguished guests who attended a 2,000-strong scout and guide service at the theatre to mark the centenary of the birth of their founder, Lord Baden-Powell.

In the centre of the group are the Bishop of Warrington (the Rt Rev C. R. Claxton) and the Mayor and Mayoress (Councillor and Mrs F. E. Thornley).

106

That Grand National stunt.

AT THE CINEMA. Conservative members of the Town Council paid a visit to the Odeon Cinema on Monday evening to see the Civic Trust film "New Face For Britain."

These teams of schoolchildren from Southport and Bebington took part in a road safety quiz the Gaumont Cinema, Lord-street, on Saturday. They are pictured with police and road officials who had charge of the contest.

108

1962. The Overseas Visitors collecting toys for the annual Christmas Tree appeal.

The Kodak Girls get into the pictures.
Miss Pat Williams from Belfast, winner of the Kodak Holiday Competition gets her prize.
Kodak based the event at the Odeon.
L-R. Katie Ward, Jean Fraser, Pat Williams and her Children, KBL and Gillian Adams.

1955. The Christmas Tree Appeal started by the June King Dancing School supported by the Ella Wilson Women's Choir. The audience was entertained before the main feature. Bill Hopper provided the music on the Compton Organ. This was one of the first occasions local entertainers would be given the opportunity to experience the big stage.

The stage was handed over to the Southport Amateur Operatic Society who performed song and dance from the Roaring Twenties.
The Mayor and Mayoress Alderman and Mrs. S.J.Hepworth along with the Chief Constable Mr.J.Pressell, Chief Fire Officer Mr.J.Perkins, Miss J.Snape Borough Childrens officer and Mr.Bircher of the NSPCC all attended and appealed for gifts. The target was 2000 and the Christmas tree appeal far exceeded that number.

ILLUSTRATIVE INDEX

The illustrations, photographs and memorabilia, contained within this book come from the author's private collection and include reproductions of news cuttings or photographs from the Southport Visiter.

CPSIA information can be obtained
at www.ICGtesting.com
Printed in the USA
LVIW011001170412

2787LVUK00005B

9781452031743